Al-Kafi

Volume 5 of 8

English Translation

Al-Kafi

Volume 5 of 8
(Fru' al-Kafi)

English Translation

Second Edition

Compiled by
Thiqatu al-Islam, Abu Ja'far Muhammad
ibn Ya'qub al-Kulayni

Translated by
Muhammad Sarwar

Published by
The Islamic Seminary Inc.
www.theislamicseminary.org

The Islamic Seminary Inc., New York
© 2015 by The Islamic Seminary Inc.
All rights reserved
Second Edition 2015
Printed in the United States of America.

ISBN: 978-0-9914308-7-1

Al-Kafi, Volume 5 of 8. English Translation – 2nd ed.
Jamadi al-Awwal 1436
February 2015

Note to Readers

Dear respected readers, please note the following:

The English translation of this volume from Kitab al-Kafi is now, by the will of Allah, in your hands. It was only because of the beauty of the words of Ahl al-Bayt *'Alayhim al-Salam* that made it all possible. The magnitude of this project had become quite large and complex due to two language texts and it was sometimes difficult to handle.

All comments, suggestions and corrections will be very much appreciated. In fact it will be your participation in the good cause and rewarding in the sight of Allah, most Majestic, most Glorious. Please e-mail your comments, suggestions or corrections to: info@theislamicseminary.org.

With thanks,

The Islamic Seminary
www.theislamicseminary.org

Contents

Part Two: The Book of Commerce

Part Three: The Book of Marriage

An Outline of the Number of Volumes, Sections and Sub-divisions of Kitab al-Kafi

Part 1 - Al-'Usul (Principles)

Volume 1

This part of the book consists of *Ahadith* on the principles of beliefs and it is called 'Usul (principles) in *al-Kafi*.

The sections or chapters in volume 1 are as follows:

1. The Book of Intelligence and Ignorance (*Kitab al-'Aql wa al-Jahl*)
2. The Book of the Excellence of Knowledge (*Kitabu Fad al-'Ilm*)
3. The Book on Oneness of Allah (*Kitab al-Tawhid*)
4. The Book about the people who possess Divine Authority (*Kitab al-Hujja*)

Volume 2

Sections or Chapters in Volume 2:

5. The Book on Belief and Disbelief (*Kitab al-'Iman wa al-Kufr*)
6. The Book on Prayers (*Kitab al-Du'a'*)
7. The Book on the Excellence of the Holy Quran (*Kitabu Fadl al-Quran*)
8. The Book of Social Discipline (*Kitab al-'Ishra*)

PART 2 - Al-*Furu'* (Branches)

Volumes 3-7

This part consists of *Ahadith* on Islamic practical laws such as:

The acts of worship (*'Ibadat*)

Business transactions (*mu'amalat*)

Judicial laws (*al-Qada'*)

Furu' al-Kafi (volume 3 – 7): The rules of conduct, the practical laws of the Islamic system, consists of the following:

9. The Book of Laws of Cleanliness (*Kitab al-Tahara*)
10. The Book of Laws of Menstruation (*Kitab al-Hayd*)
11. The Book of Laws about the dying people and their burials (*Kitab al-Jana'iz*)
12. The Book of Laws of Prayer (*Kitab al-Salat*)
13. The Book of Laws of Charities, Taxes (*Kitab al-Zakat*)
14. The Book of Laws of Fasting (*Kitab al-Siyam*)

15. The Book of Laws of Pilgrimage (*Kitab al- Hajj*)
16. The Book of Laws of Defense (*Kitab al-Jihad*)
17. The Book of Laws of Business (*Kitab al-Ma'ishah*)
18. The Book of Laws of Marriage (*Kitab al-Nikah*)
19. The Book of Laws about New-born (*Kitab al-'Aqiqa*)
20. The Book of Laws of Divorce (*Kitab al-Talaq*)
21. The Book of Laws of Emancipation of Slaves (*Kitab al-'Itq wa al-Tadbir wa al-Mukataba*)
22. The Book of Laws of Hunting (*Kitab al-Sayd*)
23. The Book of Laws of Slaughtering Animals for food (*Kitab al-Dhaba'ih*)
24. The Book of Laws of Foods (*Kitab al-At'imah*)
25. The Book of Laws of Drinks (*Kitab al-Ashriba*)
26. The Book of Laws of Dresses, Beautifying and the Ideal of Manhood (*Kitab al-Zay wa al-Tajammul*)
27. The Book of Laws of Animal Farming and Poultry (*Kitab al-Dawajin*)
28. The Book of Laws of Wills (*Kitab al-Wasaya'*)
29. The Book of Laws of Inheritances (*Kitab al-Mawarith*)
30. The Book of Laws of Penalties (*Kitab al-Hudud*)
31. The Book of Laws of Restitution for Bodily Injuries (*Kitab al-Diyat*)
32. The Book of Laws of Testimony and Witnessing (*Kitab al-Shahadat*)
33. The Book of Judicial Laws (*Kitab al-Qada' wa al-Ahkam*)
34. The Book of Laws of Oaths, Vows and Expiation (*Kitab al-'Ayman wa al-Nudbur wa al-Kaffarat*)

PART 3 - Al-Rawdah (Garden of Flowers (Hadith))

Volume 8

This part consists of miscellaneous *Ahadith* of both the *'Usul* and *Furu'* of *al-Kafi*. The topics are not arranged and organized as in the other volumes. The chapters are not in alphabetical order of *Ahadith* or narrators.

This volume comprises about six hundred *Hadith* on various topics and is a treasure of knowledge of the matters of belief, spiritual discipline, interpretations of many verses of the Holy Quran, accounts of the noble manners of the Holy Prophet and infallible members of his family and information about the system of this and the next life.

In the Name of Allah, the Beneficient, the Merciful

Part One:
The Book of Jihad (Serving in the Army)

Chapter 1 - Virtue and Excellence of Serving in the Army

H 8158, Ch. 1, h 1

A number of our people have narrated from Ahmad ibn Muhammad from Ali ibn al-Hakam from 'Umar ibn Aban from abu 'Abd Allah *'Alayhi al-Salam*, who has said the following:

"The Messenger of Allah has said, 'All good things are with the sword, under the shadow (protection) of sword and people cannot be improved without the sword. Swords are the key to paradise or hellfire.'"

H 8159, Ch. 1, h 2

Ali ibn Ibrahim has narrated from his father, from al-Nawfaliy from al-Sakuniy who has said the following:

"Abu 'Abd Allah, *'Alayhi al-Salam*, has said that the Messenger of Allah has said, 'In paradise there is a door which is called 'the door of people serving in the army'. They walk to it and it is open and they have their swords fixed on them ready and in place. The angels welcome them.' He then said, 'Whoever ignores joining the army, Allah, the Most Majestic, the Most Glorious, dresses him up with humiliation, poverty and his religion is destroyed. Allah, the Most Majestic, the Most Glorious, makes my followers self-sufficient through the hooves of their horses and the points of their spears.'"

H 8160, Ch. 1, h 3

Through the chains of his narrator Ali ibn Ibrahim has narrated the following:

"The Messenger of Allah, *O Allah, grant compensation to Muhammad and his family worthy of their services to Your cause*, has said, 'The horses of the people serving in the army are their horses in paradise, and the gowns of the fighters for the cause of Allah are their swords. The Holy Prophet has said, 'Jibril (Gabriel) has told me something which has made my eyes and heart delightful, "O Muhammad, whoever of your followers fights for the cause of Allah, thereafter even if a drop from the sky falls on him or he experiences a flu, Allah, the Most Majestic, the Most Glorious, lists him as a martyr.'"

H 8161, Ch. 1, h 4

Muhammad ibn Yahya has narrated from Ahmad ibn Muhammad ibn 'Isa from al-Hassan ibn Mahbub from certain individuals of his people who has said the following:

"Abu Ja'far, *'Alayhi al-Salam*, once wrote in a letter to a certain individual of the Amawide rulers the following:

"Of his neglectfulness one example is his disregard of the duty of Jihad (serving in the army) which Allah, the Most Majestic, the Most Glorious, has given preference over all other good deeds. He (Allah) has given preference to those serving in the army over the doers of good deeds a very clear preference in matters of high positions, their receiving forgiveness and mercifulness. This is because by serving in the army religion is supported to become public and it is defended thereby as well. By means of Jihad (a person's serving in the army) Allah has purchased believers' souls and property as their payment for paradise which is a gainful bargain indeed. He (Allah) has set upon them the condition of their abiding by the rules of armed engagement. Of such rules is calling to the obedience of Allah, the Most Majestic, the Most Glorious, instead of obedience to people (servants of Allah), to the worship of Allah instead of worshipping other servants of Allah and to accept guardianship of Allah instead of seeking guardianship of the servants of Allah. Those who are asked to pay taxes but refuse are executed and their families are taken into custody.

"There is no calling of servants of Allah to the obedience of other servants of Allah. Those who agree to pay taxes are not violated, their covenant is safe guarded, and is not burdened beyond what he can afford.

"The properties captured from the enemies belong to all Muslims and not to a particular group. If an armed confrontation takes place and people are captured, the whole issue is dealt with according to his (the Holy Prophet's) dealings and traditions which are of religion's rules in such issues. He (the particular ruler) then placed the burden of serving in the army upon such people as those with disabilities like blind or lame and those who do not have the means to serve in the army, after being excused by Allah, the Most Majestic, the Most Glorious, and those who cannot afford. The residents of a city are required to fight only the nearby enemy with fairness and justice exercised in issues of mobilization. All such laws were disregarded and people are made to live in one of the two conditions: To live like the person who offers a certain service but instead of receiving wages is made to pay, although Allah has already purchased his services; and a person who asks to rent or hire an item but the party of other side of his contract is bankrupt and indebted, although Allah has excused him. He has ignored al-Hajj in disregard and people are left in poverty. Who then is more crooked than this that has made such straightforward laws seem crooked and who is more straightforward than him who properly follows them? Instead he has made people to serve in the army (unduly) and has made such a service an extra burden and this is a great mistake and sin.'"

H 8162, Ch. 1, h 5
A number of our people have narrated from Ahmad ibn Muhammad ibn Khalid from certain individuals of his people from 'Abd Allah ibn 'Abd al-Rahman al-Asamm from Haydarah who has said the following:
"Abu 'Abd Allah, *'Alayhi al-Salam*, has said that Jihad (serving in the army) is the most virtuous task except obligatory (prayers) matters."

H 8163, Ch. 1, h 6
Ahmad ibn Muhammad ibn Sa'id has narrated from Ja'far ibn 'Abd Allah al-'Alawiy and Ahmad ibn Muhammad al-Kufiy from Ali ibn al-'Abbas, from Isma'il ibn Ishaq, all from abu Faraj ibn

Qurrah, who has narrated from Mas'adah ibn Sadaqah. He has said that narrated to him ibn abu Layla' from abu 'Abd al-Rahman al-Sullamiy who has said that Amir al-Mu'minin, *'Alayhi al-Salam*, has said who has said the following:

"Thereafter, (my praising Allah) you must take notice that Jihad (serving in the army) is one of the doors to paradise. Allah has opened it for His special friends whom He has made to deserve it through His generosity toward them and a bounty, which He has stored. Jihad is the garment of piety and it is Allah's invincible gown and strong shield. If one ignores it in disregard Allah dresses him up in humiliation. Misfortune engulfs him, small and worthless issues humiliate him and barriers block his heart. Truth moves away from him due to his disregard of Jihad. Hardship disturbs him and he is denied justice. I certainly have been asking you days and nights, privately and in public to fight those people (supporters of Mu'awiyah), saying, 'Attack them before they do so. By Allah, a people attacked in their own territory are always humiliated.' You kept postponing my calls in betrayal until attacks were launched upon you and territories were captured. It is the brother of Ghamid (Sufyan ibn 'Awf, Mu'awiyah's hit-man) whose troops have entered al-Anbar and have murdered Hassan ibn Hassan al-Bakriy (the governor appointed by Amir al-Mu'minin). Your troops were dislodged from their fortifications. I am informed that their men violate Muslimah women as well as tax-payers' women, took away their bracelets, earrings and their other ornaments and they had no means of defense against them except begging for mercy and saying 'to Allah we return.' They then left with plenty of wealth and none of them suffered any injuries or lost a single drop of blood. If a Muslim would die in sorrow and anguish due to this tragedy he should not be blamed and in my opinion it is worthwhile of him. It indeed is shocking, by Allah, it is shocking. It causes the heart to melt and fills it up with sorrow to see how those people are united around their falsehood and your suffering discord despite your having the truth with you. It is a shame and a disgrace that despite your being their target of attack, you do not counter-attack them. They fight you but you do not fight. Allah is disobeyed and you condone such disobedience. When I command you to march against the enemy during summer you say, 'It is very hot. Give us time until the heat is reduced.' When I command you to march against them during winter, you say, 'It is very cold. Give us time until the cold season is over.' All of such excuses are just to run away from hot and cold elements. If you run away from hot and cold seasons, from swords, by Allah, you will run away much faster. O you, who look like a man, you are not a man of courage. You in wish-fullness are like children and your power of reason is like that of the house-maidens. I wish I had not seen you and had not know you at all. It by Allah has brought only regret and sorrow. I wish Allah fights against you for filling up my heart with sadness as if it is filled with puss and my chest with anguish as if you have made me breathe blows of sorrow with every breath. You have turned my decision to no effect due to your disobedience and betrayal, so much so that Quraysh says, 'The son of abu Talib is a brave man but he does not know how to fight a war.' One should for the sake of Allah, judge what they say. Has anyone among them dealt with wars with greater intensity than the way I have dealt with them or has anyone among them been involved with wars for such a long time as I have been facing wars? I stood firm in wars when I was not yet in my twenties and now I am in my sixties but one who is not obeyed has no opinion."

H 8164, Ch. 1, h 7
Muhammad ibn Yahya has narrated from Ahmad ibn Muhammad ibn 'Isa from Ali ibn al-Hakam from abu Hafs al-Kalbiy who has said the following:
"Abu 'Abd Allah, *'Alayhi al-Salam*, has said that Allah, the Most Majestic, the Most Glorious, sent His Messenger with al-Islam to people. For ten years no one accepted al-Islam. Thereafter He commanded him to fight back. Goodness is with the sword and under the sword. The matter one day will return to how it was in the beginning (Allah's religion will become powerful as it was in the times of the Holy Prophet)."

H 8165, Ch. 1, h 8
A number of our people have narrated from Ahmad ibn Muhammad ibn Khalid from abu al-Bakhtariy who has said the following:
"Abu 'Abd Allah, *'Alayhi al-Salam*, has said that the Messenger of Allah has said, 'Jibril informed me of something and it brought delightfulness to my eyes and happiness to my heart. He said, "O Muhammad, anyone of your followers who fights the enemy for the cause of Allah, even if a drop of rain falls on him from the sky or he experiences a headache, he will, on the Day of Judgment, receive for it a reward equal to that for martyrdom."'"

H 8166, Ch. 1, h 9
Through the same chain of narrators as that of the previous Hadith the following is narrated:
"One for conveying the message of a fighter for the cause of Allah, receives a reward equal to that for setting free a slave and will have a share in the reward for his fighting for the cause of Allah."

H 8167, Ch. 1, h 10
Ali ibn Ibrahim has narrated from his father, from al-Nawfaliy from al-Sakuniy from abu 'Abd Allah, *'Alayhi al-Salam*, who has said the following:
"If one back-bites a believing person who is fighting for the cause of Allah or troubles the fighter's family in his absence by evil manners, he will, on the Day of Judgment, be brought to justice. All of his good deeds will become invalid and he will then be sent into hell, if the fighter has fought in obedience to Allah, the Most Majestic, the Most Glorious.'"

H 8168, Ch. 1, h 11
Ali ibn Ibrahim has narrated from his father from ibn Mahbub in a marfu' the following:
"Amir al-Mu'minin, *'Alayhi al-Salam*, has said, 'Allah, the Most Majestic, the Most Glorious, has made Jihad obligatory, considered it great and has made it His victory (support) and supporter. By Allah, the worldly affairs as well as religious affairs are never enhanced without Jihad."

H 8169, Ch. 1, h 12
Ali ibn Ibrahim has narrated from his father from Harun ibn Muslim from Mas'adah ibn Sadaqah who has said the following:

"Abu 'Abd Allah, *'Alayhi al-Salam*, has said that the Messenger of Allah has said, 'Fight (for the cause of Allah) and leave glory as your legacy for your children.'"

H 8170, Ch. 1, h 13
Through the same chain of narrators the following is narrated:
"On the day of 'Uhud, abu Dujanah al-Ansariy wore his turban and left one end hanging between his shoulders on his back and began walking as if puffed up with pride. The Messenger of Allah said, 'This is a kind of walking that Allah, the Most Majestic, the Most Glorious, dislikes very much except during fighting for the cause of Allah."

H 8171, Ch. 1, h 14
Ali has narrated from father, from al-Nawfaliy from al-Sakuniy who has said the following:
"Abu 'Abd Allah, *'Alayhi al-Salam*, has said that the Messenger of Allah has said, 'You must do Jihad; you will benefit.'"

H 8172, Ch. 1, h 15
"Muhammad ibn Yahya has narrated from Ahmad ibn Muhammad ibn al-Hajjal from Tha'labah from Mu'ammar form abu Ja'far, *'Alayhi al-Salam*, who has said the following:
"All goodness is in the sword, under the sword and under the shadow of the sword."

"I heard him saying, 'Goodness, all of it, is tied to the forehead of the horses (and it remains so) up to the Day of Judgment (horses of the fighters for the cause of Allah).'"

Chapter 2 - Jihad of Man and Woman

H 8173, Ch. 2, h 1
Ali ibn Ibrahim has narrated from his father from abu al-Jawza' from al-Husayn ibn 'Ulwan from Sa'd ibn Tarif from al-Asbagh ibn Nubatah who has said the following:
"Amir al-Mu'minin, *'Alayhi al-Salam*, has said, 'Allah has made Jihad obligatory upon man and woman. Jihad of man is making his wealth and soul available until he is killed in the way of Allah. Jihad of woman is exercising patience when facing hardships caused by her husband and because of his showing strong al-Ghirah (protective feelings) for her. In another Hadith it is said that Jihad of a woman is to maintain good wife and husband relationship."

Chapter 3 - Kinds of Jihad (struggle)

H 8174, Ch. 3, h 1
Ali ibn Ibrahim has narrated from his father and Ali ibn Muhammad al-Qasaniy all from al-Qasim ibn Muhammad from Sulayman ibn Dawud al-Minqariy from Fudayl ibn 'Iyad who has said the following:
"This is concerning my question before abu 'Abd Allah, *'Alayhi al-Salam*, 'Is Jihad Sunnah (optional) or obligatory?' He replied, 'Jihad is of four kinds. Two kinds of Jihad are obligatory and there is an optional Jihad which cannot be established without obligatory Jihad.

'Of the two obligatory Jihad is one's Jihad (struggle) against his soul's desires to disobey Allah, the Most Majestic, the Most Glorious, and this is the greatest form of Jihad. Jihad against the unbeliever (declared) enemies nearby is also obligatory.

'The kind of optional Jihad, which cannot be established without an obligatory Jihad, is when it becomes obligatory upon the whole nation to fight the enemy; and if they disregard such Jihad torment descends upon them. This is the punishment for the nation. Only for the Imam this is optional. He faces the enemy with the support of the nation to fight.

'The optional Jihad is every optional institution for the establishment of which one strives hard to accomplish and revive. Working and the pursuit of such task is of the most excellent deeds; it is reviving of a tradition. The Messenger of Allah has said, 'Whoever establishes a noble tradition he gains the reward therefor and a reward equal to the reward of those who act upon such noble tradition up to the Day of Judgment without any reduction in the rewards of anyone of them.'"

H 8175, Ch. 3, h 2
Through the same chain of narrator he has narrated from al-Minqariy from Hafs ibn Ghiyath who has said the following:
"Abu 'Abd Allah, *'Alayhi al-Salam*, has said that once a man asked my father, *'Alayhi al-Salam*, about the wars in which Amir al-Mu'minin, had taken part. The man asking the question was of our followers. Abu Ja'far, *'Alayhi al-Salam*, replied, 'Allah sent Muhammad, *'Alayhi al-Salam*, with five swords. Three of them are taken out of their sheath and they are not sheathed until war is no more. The day without war will not come until the sun rises from the west. When the sun rises from its westerly direction all people will enjoy peace on that day. On that day a soul's belief will be of no benefit if it did not exist before or has not gained any good thereby. One of those swords is withheld and the other one remains in its sheath and he has uncovered it on people other than us but it is up to us to decide.

'Allah, the Most Majestic, the Most Glorious has said, "Destroy the pagans wherever you find them; capture, detain them and set up surveillance over their activities. If they repent (accept the faith), perform *Salat* (prayer) and pay Zakat, they are your brothers in religion." (9:11) The choice for such people is only acceptance of al-Islam or destruction. Their properties and offspring are held and detained and are dealt with in the way the Messenger of Allah had done. He detained, forgave or released them in exchange for ransom.

'The second sword is in matters of dealing with the taxpayers. Allah, the most Blessed, the most High, has said, "Speak to people good words." (2:83). This verse was revealed about the tax payers. Later it was amended by the following verse, "Fight those, who do not believe in Allah and in the Day of Judgment and do not consider unlawful what Allah and His Messenger have made unlawful. Thus, they do not follow the true religion. However, they are of the followers of the book. (This is the case) until they agree to pay taxes by their own hands with humbleness." (9:30) Those of them who live in the Muslims lands must pay taxes or be destroyed, their offspring detained and no *Fay'* (ransom) is accepted from them. But if they agree to pay taxes it becomes unlawful for us to detain them or touch their properties. It becomes lawful to marry from them. Those of such people who live in the war zones can be detained and their properties withheld. It is not lawful to marry from them and they are given the choices of either moving to the lands of the Muslims, pay taxes or be destroyed.

'The third sword is to deal thereby with non-Arab pagans, such as al-Turk, al-Daylam and al-Khazar. Allah, the Most Majestic, the Most Glorious, in the beginning of the Chapter that speaks of "those who disbelieve" has stated their story and said, "It, then, is to strike their necks until they are subdued and captured, thereafter either freed as a favor or in exchange for ransom until the war is no more." (47:4) His words, "freed as a favor" means after they are detained and His words, "or in exchange for ransom" means in exchange for protection of the interests of the Muslim people. In the case of such people the choice is either destruction or acceptance of al-Islam. It is not lawful for us to marry from them as long as they live in the war zone.

'The withheld sword is to deal thereby with the rebels and people who raise the issue of interpretations of the texts of the law. Allah, the Most Majestic, the Most Glorious, has said, "If two groups of believers fight each other, you must establish reconciliation between them. If one group rebels against the other then you must fight the rebellious one until it submits to the command of Allah." (49:9) When this was revealed the Messenger of Allah said, "Among you there will be those who fight to establish proper interpretation of (the text of law) just as their fighting to establish the revelation of the text of the law." The Holy Prophet then was asked, "Who will be such fighters?" He (the Messenger of Allah) replied, "One who is stitching his shoes", meaning thereby Amir al-Mu'minin, *'Alayhi al-Salam*.

'Ammar ibn Yasar has said, "I have fought under this banner alongside the Messenger of Allah three times and this is the fourth time. I swear by Allah, if they beat us to make us retreat even all the way to the twigs of Bahrain, we will still remain certain of our truthfulness and their following falsehood. Dealings by 'Amir al-Mu'minin *'Alayhi al-Salam*, with them were just like those of the Holy Prophet toward the people of Makkah on the day of its conquest. Their offspring were not detained, and he said, 'Those who keep their doors closed are protected.' Those who put down their arms are protected. So also did Amir al-Mu'minin, *'Alayhi al-Salam*, on the day of Basra. He announced among them, 'You must not detain any of their offspring, you must not attack the wounded, you must not pursue the fleeing and those who close their doors and put down their arms are all protected.'"

'The sword in the sheath is the sword whereby retaliation for a slain person takes place. Allah, the Most Majestic, the Most Glorious, has said, "A soul for a

7

soul and an eye for an eye . . ." (5:45) He has made it ready for the heirs of the slain person but the application of its rule is left upto us to decide. These are the swords that Allah sent to Muhammad, O Allah grant salawat (favors and compensation to Muhammad and his family worthy of their services to your cause). Whoever rejects them or anyone of them or anything of their characteristics or rules has rejected what Allah has revealed to Muhammad, *O Allah, grant compensation to Muhammad and his family worthy of their services to Your cause.*'"

H 8176, Ch. 3, h 3

Ali ibn Ibrahim has narrated from his father from al-Nawfaliy from al-Sakuniy who has said the following:

"Abu 'Abd Allah, *'Alayhi al-Salam*, has said that the Messenger of Allah once mobilized a group of people against the enemy. When they returned back he said, 'I welcome a people who have just come back after completion of the minor Jihad and who yet have to complete the major Jihad.' Someone then asked, 'What is the major Jihad, O Messenger of Allah?' He replied, 'It is Jihad against the desires of one's own soul to disobey Allah.'"

Chapter 4 - To Whom Does the Obligation of Jihad Apply, and to Whom it Does not Apply

H 8177, Ch. 4, h 1

Ali ibn Ibrahim has narrated from his father from Bakr ibn Salih from al-Qasim ibn Burayd from abu 'Amr al-Zubayriy who has said the following:

"This is concerning my question before abu 'Abd Allah, *'Alayhi al-Salam*, 'Instruct me about calling to Allah and Jihad for His cause. Is it only for a certain group besides whom for others it is not permissible or it is permissible for all who believe in Allah, the Most Majestic, the Most Glorious and in the Messenger of Allah? Whoever is as such has permission to call to Allah, the Most Majestic, the Most Glorious, to His obedience and do Jihad for His cause.'

"He (the Imam) replied, 'It is for a certain people only. It is not lawful for others beside them. No one other than one who is of these certain people has the right to do Jihad.' I then asked, 'Who are these people?' He (the Imam) replied, 'They are those who stand by the stipulations of Allah, the Most Majestic, the Most Glorious during the war and Jihad is done by the army. Such people have permission to call to Allah, the Most Majestic, the Most Glorious. Those who do not stand up to the stipulations of Allah, the Most Majestic, the Most Glorious, in war about the soldiers, do not have permission for Jihad and calling to Allah until they make Allah's stipulations about Jihad rule and govern them.' I then said, 'Explain it to me. I pray to Allah to grant you favors.'

"He (the Imam) said, 'Allah, the most Blessed, the most High, informed His prophet in His book how to call people to Him and has described it therein. He has made Jihad of degrees, which can be understood by means of one another and one leads to the other. He, the most Blessed, the most High, has informed that He Himself calls to His own-self and to His obedience and to following His commands. He has begun with Himself saying, "Allah calls to the house of peace and guides whomever He wants to the right path." (10:25) He then has enjoined upon His Messenger and has said, "O Muhammad, call to the path of your Lord with wisdom, good advice and reason with them with that which is good." (16:125) It means that he should reason with them by means of the Holy Quran. One who opposes the commands of Allah, the Most Majestic, the Most Glorious, is not calling to Allah. He only calls to Allah by that which is other than with which He has commanded in His book to call thereby and it is that in which He has commanded not to call by any means other than this (book). About His Holy Prophet He has said, "You certainly guide to the right path." (42:52) It "guide" means you call to the right path. He, the most Blessed, the most High, has joined a third party for this task which is His book saying, "This Quran guides (calls) to that which is upright and gives glad news to the believers." (17:9)

"He then has mentioned those who after His own self, His prophet and His book have permission to call to Him saying, 'Among you there must exist people who call to goodness, command (people) to do what is good and prohibit (people) from committing evil deeds; such are the successful ones.' (3:104) He has given more information about who this 'Ummah (nation) is that it is of the offspring of Ibrahim and Isma'il, of the residents of the sacred land, of the ones who never worshipped anyone besides Allah. They are those on whom it is obligatory to call. It is the call of Ibrahim and Isma'il of the people of al-Masjid about whom Allah has spoken in His book that He has removed from them all *rijs* and has cleansed them thoroughly. They are those whom we have mentioned when speaking of the followers of Ibrahim, *'Alayhi al-Salam* who are meant to be the ones about whom Allah, the most Blessed, the most High, speaks in the following verse, "I call to Allah with awareness on my part as well as those who follow me." (12:108) It is a reference to those who followed him in belief in him and affirmation of his truthfulness about whatever he had brought from Allah, the Most Majestic, the Most Glorious. They are of the 'Ummah in whom he was sent and to whom he belonged and to whom he was sent before the creation of those who never considered anyone as partner of Allah and who never mixed their belief with injustice which is paganism. He then has mentioned the followers of His prophet and the followers of this 'Ummah which He has described in His book as the ones who command people to do good and prohibit them from committing evil and has considered them as the callers to Him and has given them permission to call to Him saying, "O prophet, Allah is sufficient (support for you) and those who follow you of the believers." (8:64) He then has described the followers of His prophet of the believers and He, the Most Majestic, the Most Glorious, has said, "Muhammad is the Messenger of Allah and those who are with him are stern against the unbelievers. They are compassionate to each other. You can see them performing *Ruku's* and *Sajdah*, to seek extra favors from Allah, and pleasure. Their marks are found on their faces because of frequent *Sajdah*. This is how they are described in the Torah and their description in the bible is. . . ." (48:29)

9

'He has also said, "On the day when Allah will not fail the prophet and the believers. They will have their light run in front of them and on their right sides." (66:8) It is a reference to the believers. Allah has said, "Believers are indeed successful." (23:2) He then has praised and described them in a very special way so that no one other than those who are like them can consider themselves as one of them. In their praise and in their description He has said, "They are those who are *khashi'* (very humble) in their *Salat* (prayer), those who stay away from useless matters. . . . they are the ones who inherit, those who inherit paradise wherein they live forever." (23:3-11) He has also said in their praise and in their description, "They are those who do not pray to anyone besides Allah as the Lord and who do not destroy any soul that Allah has prohibited to destroy except for a truthful purpose, who do not commit fornication and those who do so have committed a sin. His punishment, on the Day of Judgment, will double and they live therein forever in humiliation."(24:68-69)

'He then has said that He has purchased from these believers their souls and those who possess likewise of their qualities, "Their souls and properties in exchange for paradise; They fight for the cause of Allah so they destroy the enemy and themselves become martyrs. It is a promise to them in all truth in the Torah, the bible and al-Quran." He then has mentioned their standing by their promise and covenant and their pledging allegiance saying, "Who is more firm in his promise than Allah? Your deal of selling (your souls) is glad news for you and this is the great success." (9:111)

'When this verse (9:111) was revealed a man stood up before the Holy Prophet and said, "O Holy Prophet of Allah, do you think, a man who takes up his sword and fights until he is killed, is considered a martyr?" Allah, the Most Majestic, the Most Glorious, then revealed the following verse to His prophet, "The repenting, those who praise (Allah) who fast, perform *Ruku'* and *Sajdah*, who command people to do good and prohibit them from committing evil, who protect the laws of Allah, (you can) give glad news to the believing people." (9:112) The Holy Prophet, *'Alayhi al-Salam*, then interpreted it as a reference to those of the believers who possess such qualities and praise as martyrs deserving paradise. He said that it means repenting from sins, the worshippers who worship only Allah without considering anything as His partner. Praising (Allah) are those who praise Allah in all conditions; in hardships and in ease. *Sa'ihun* are those who fast. Performing *Ruku'* and *Sajdah* are those who regularly perform their five times' daily *Salat* (prayer), who protect them and safe guard *Ruku'*, *Sajdah* in proper humbleness in their proper times. They thereafter command people to do good and prohibit from committing evil and themselves stay away there-from. He said, "Give glad news of paradise and martyrdom to those who are killed while they stand by these conditions." He, the most Blessed, the most High, then has informed that He has not commanded anyone who does not possess these qualities to do Jihad.

10

'He, the Most Majestic, the Most Glorious, said, "Those who are subjected to injustice are given permission to fight and Allah has the power to help them, those who are expelled from their towns without any good reason, except their saying that Allah is our Lord." (22:39-40)

'This is because everything between the earth and the sky belongs to Allah, the Most Majestic, the Most Glorious, His Messenger and their believing followers who have these qualities. Whatever of the worldly things exist in the hands of the pagans, unbelievers, unjust people and sinful people of those opposing the Messenger of Allah and who turn to disobey them, whatever is found in their hands is because of their doing injustice to the believers who possess those qualities. They have suppressed them (the believers) in matters of what Allah has returned (granted) to His Messenger. Thus, it is of their (believers') rights that Allah has returned to them as *Fay'*. The meaning of *al-Fay'* is whatever goes in the hands of the pagans and then returns whatever, through their suppression of others, they had taken. So whatever of words or deeds returns back to its place is in the condition of *al-Fay'* as it is mentioned in the words of Allah, the Most Majestic, the Most Glorious, "Those who swear to stay away from their women must wait for four months but if they go back Allah is forgiving and merciful." (2:226) The word "fa''u" signifies "to return". He then has said, "If they decide to divorce, Allah is hearing and knowledgeable." (2:227) He has also said, "If two groups of believing people fight each other you must arrange reconciliation between them. If one group rebels against the other you must fight the rebellious ones until they "tafi'u" (go back) to submit themselves to the command of Allah. If they submitted (returned) then arrange reconciliation between them with justice; Allah loves those who practice justice." (49:10) He by his word "tafi'u" has meant "return". This is proof that *al-Fay'* is whatever returns to the place where it was or it belonged. It then is said about the sun when it declines toward the west, "fa''at al-Shams". It is said so when the shadow of an object goes back to increase after decreasing. So also is what returns to the believing people from the unbelievers. It is so because of being of the rights of the believing people, which is returned to them after injustice was done to them by the unbelievers. Of such issues are His words, "Permission is granted to the fighters because of injustice done to them." Believers in general do not qualify for such permission. Such permission is given to those believers who stand by the conditions of their faith and belief, which we already have described. This is because a believer does not have such permission unless injustice is done to him and he cannot be an oppressed one unless he is a believer. He cannot be a believer unless he stands by the stipulations of his belief and faith which Allah, the Most Majestic, the Most Glorious, has set upon the believers and those who do Jihad. When the stipulations of Allah, the Most Majestic, the Most Glorious, are accomplished in him, he becomes a believer. When he is considered a believer he is oppressed and when he becomes oppressed, permission is given to him to do Jihad because of the words of Allah, the Most Majestic, the Most Glorious, "Permission to fight is given to them because of injustice done to them and Allah has the power to help them." If he is not up to the stipulations of belief, he is unjust, and of those against whom doing Jihad is obligatory until he repents. He does not have permission to do Jihad or call to Allah, the Most Majestic, the Most Glorious; he is not of the believers to whom injustice is done and to whom permission to fight is given in the al-Quran. When this verse, "permission to fight . . ." was revealed about Muhajirin (immigrants) who were expelled from Makkah, their homeland and their properties it became lawful, He made it lawful for them to fight.'"

"I then said, 'This was revealed about Muhajirin because of the injustice of the pagans of Makkah. On what basis did they fight Kisra' and Qaysar (Persians and Romans) and others such as pagan Arab tribes?'

"He (the Imam) replied, 'If permission to fight was given only because of the injustice done to them by the pagans of Makkah, they then had no reason to fight such multitudes like Kisra', Qaysar and people other than the people of Makkah of the Arab tribes. This is because those who did injustice to them (al-Muhajirun) were not these people. Instead they were the people of Makkah who had expelled them (al-Muhajirun) from their homeland and had dispossessed them of their properties without good reason. If the verse applied only to al-Muhajirun who were oppressed by the people of Makkah, this verse would remain without any applicable effect to others thereafter al-together; no one of the oppressors and the oppressed would have existed anymore. The obligation mentioned in it would have been lifted entirely after those people; the oppressed and the oppressors would have ceased to exist. In fact, it is not the way you thought it was and not the way I mentioned either. However, al-Muhajirun were oppressed in two ways. People of Makkah oppressed them by expelling them from their homeland and dispossessed them of their properties. Thus, they fought them by the permission of Allah. Kisra' and Qaysar and others besides such people as the Arab and non-Arab tribes who oppressed them by keeping what rightfully belonged to the believing people. They fought them by the permission of Allah, the Most Majestic, the Most Glorious, in this matter. Based on the authority of this verse (22:39), the believing people of all times have the permission to fight. Allah, the Most Majestic, the Most Glorious, however, has given permission to the believing people who stand up to the stipulations which Allah, the Most Majestic, the Most Glorious, has described and fulfill the requirements they need to have in belief and Jihad. Whoever then stands up to such stipulations is a believer, an oppressed and has permission to do Jihad in the sense mentioned. Those otherwise are oppressors and are not oppressed ones. Such ones do not have the permission to fight, to prohibit from committing evil or command people to do good. It is because they are not qualified for such tasks and do not have the permission to call to Allah, the Most Majestic, the Most Glorious. He cannot do Jihad against people like his own-self or call to Allah. One against whom believing people are commanded to do Jihad is not the one who does Jihad; he is prohibited to do Jihad due to lack of qualification. Such people the like of whom is commanded to repent cannot call to Allah, the Most Majestic, the Most Glorious, call to the truth, command others to do good or prohibit others from committing evil. One about whom a command to command him to do good is issued or a command to prohibit him from committing evil is issued cannot prohibit others against evil.

'Only those in whom the stipulations of Allah, the Most Majestic, the Most Glorious, which He has described as the qualified ones among the companions of the Holy Prophet, are complete, are of the oppressed ones. They have the permission to do Jihad just as they (al-Muhajirun) were given permission for Jihad. This is because the commands of Allah, the Most Majestic, the Most Glorious, are the same for the earlier and later generations, unless there is good reason or cause. People of the past generation or those of the coming generations are the same in matters of prohibitions also. People of the earlier generation were held responsible for a duty and so also is true of the people of the later generations who will be held accountable like those before them. One who does not have the qualification of those believing people to whom Allah has given permission to do Jihad is not qualified to do Jihad and does not have permission to do so until his return to the stipulation of Allah, the Most Majestic, the Most Glorious, upon him. When the stipulations of Allah, the Most Majestic, the Most Glorious, upon believing people and those who can do Jihad are found in him in complete form he then is one of those permitted to do Jihad.

'A servant (of Allah) must maintain piety before Allah, the Most Majestic, the Most Glorious, and must not allow himself to be deceived by wishes which Allah, the Most Majestic, the Most Glorious, has prohibited to cherish in the form of the false Ahadith against Allah. It is of the kind of Ahadith, which is falsified by the Holy Quran. It denounces them and the carriers of such Ahadith as well as the narrators. (A servant of Allah) must not act before Allah, the Most Majestic, the Most Glorious, upon a doubtful matter in which he is not excused. In matters of lives involved for the cause of Allah, there is no position that can come in the presence of Allah before such matter. It is the ultimate act in greatness of value. One must have control over his ownself. One must show to himself the book of Allah, the Most Majestic, the Most Glorious, and examine it by means of the book of Allah; no one knows better about a person than his own self. If he finds it up to the stipulations of Allah in matters of Jihad, he then should proceed for Jihad. If he finds shortcomings he must reform them and make himself to stand up to what Allah has made obligatory upon him in the form of Jihad. Thereafter he must take steps for Jihad with a soul clean and cleansed of all filthy matters that come between him and his Jihad. We do not say to those who intend to do Jihad - and he is not up to what we described of the stipulations of Allah, the Most Majestic, the Most Glorious, upon the believing people and those who do Jihad - we do not say to them, "You must not do Jihad." However, we do say to them that we have taught you the stipulations that Allah, the Most Majestic, the Most Glorious, has set upon the people of Jihad with whom He has made a deal and a contract of purchasing their souls and properties in exchange for paradise.

'Therefore, one must reform the shortcomings that he finds in his self in matters of Allah's stipulation. He must examine his soul in matters of the stipulations of

Allah, the Most Majestic, the Most Glorious. If he finds that he is true to the stipulations and has completed them in himself, then he is of those whom Allah, the Most Majestic, the Most Glorious, has given permission to do Jihad. I swear by my life that there is Hadith about one who does not find his soul up to the stipulations of Allah. There is Hadith about one who instead finds his soul persisting in disobedience of Allah and in committing unlawful acts and in involvement in Jihad with confusion and ignorance and in acting against Allah, the Most Majestic, the Most Glorious, ignorantly and on the basis of false Ahadith. Allah, the Most Majestic, the Most Glorious, gives victory to this religion through such people who has no share or interest in it. One must maintain piety before Allah, the Most Majestic, the Most Glorious, and be cautious about becoming as one of them. It is explained to you and now you have no excuse for ignorance after explanation. There is no power without Allah. Allah is sufficient for us. With Him we place our trust and to Him is the destination.'"

H 8178, Ch. 4, h 2

Ali ibn Ibrahim has narrated from his father from ibn abu 'Umayr from al-Hakam ibn Miskin from 'Abd al-Malik ibn 'Amr who has said the following:

"Abu 'Abd Allah, *'Alayhi al-Salam*, said to me, 'O 'Abd al-Malik, how is it that I do not see you go to these places where the people of your town go?' I then asked, 'Which places do you mean?' He (the Imam) said, 'To Juddah, 'Abadan, al-Massisah and Qazwin.' I then said, 'I wait for your cause to materialize and follow you.' He (the Imam) said, 'That by Allah is true. If there was anything good in it they could not arrive there before us.' He (the narrator) has that he then said to him, 'Al-Zaydiyah group says, 'There is no difference between us and Ja'far, except that he does not think Jihad is necessary.' He (the Imam) said, 'Do I not consider it necessary? By Allah, I do consider it necessary but I dislike leaving my knowledge in their ignorance.'"

Chapter 5 - Mobilization Along with People when there is Fear for al-Islam

H 8179, Ch. 5, h 1

Muhammad ibn Yahya has narrated from Ahmad ibn Muhammad ibn 'Isa from Ali ibn al-Hakam from abu 'Amrah al-Sullamiy who has said the following:

"A man once asked abu 'Abd Allah, *'Alayhi al-Salam*, saying, 'I would mobilize (against the enemy) very often, stay away from asking for compensation and remain absent for a long time. This was called impermissible for me and they said, 'There is no mobilization (against the enemy) without the Imam of justice.' May Allah keep you well, what do you say about it?' Abu 'Abd Allah, *'Alayhi al-Salam*, said, 'I can say it for you in general terms and if you want I can say it to you in clear terms.' The man said, 'Say it in general terms.' He (the Imam) said, 'Allah, the Most Majestic, the Most Glorious, will resurrect people on the Day of Judgment according to their intentions.' The narrator has said that it seemed as if he wanted the Imam to say it in clear terms. He said, 'Make it for me in clear terms, may Allah keep you well.' He (the Imam) asked, 'Explain it.'

The man said, 'I mobilized and faced the pagans. Should I fight them before calling them to Allah?' He (the Imam) said, 'If they mobilize and fight, you are drawn in it. If they are a people who have not mobilized and had not fought, you can do nothing but to call them to Allah.' The man said, 'I called them to Allah. One of them accepted the call, affirmed al-Islam in his heart and lived as a Muslim but injustice was done to him in judgment, his honor was violated, his property taken and he was subjected to transgression. What is the solution when I was the one to call him to Allah?' He (the Imam) said, 'Both of you deserve rewards in the matter. He is with you to shield your honor, protect your Qiblah (the sacred location), to defend your book and save your life. This is better for you than his being against you, destroy your Qiblah, violate your honor, shed your blood and burn your book.'"

H 8180, Ch. 5, h 2
Ali ibn Ibrahim and Muhammad ibn 'Isa have narrated from Yunus who has said the following:
"I once asked abu al-Hassan al-Rida', *'Alayhi al-Salam*, 'I pray to Allah to keep my soul in service for your cause, one of followers had heard that a man gives away sword and horse for the cause of Allah. He went to that man and took the two items but he did not know the rules. His companions met him and told him that working in the way (of Allah) with these people is not permissible and they commanded them to return the items.' He (the Imam) said, 'He should do so.' The man said, 'He searched for the man but did not find him. It was said that the man has left.' He (the Imam) said, 'He should serve as a guard but he must not fight.' The man then asked, 'Should he serve as a guard in Qazwin, al-Daylam and 'Asqalan?' He (the Imam) said, 'No, unless there is fear for the (offspring of) other Muslims.' The man then asked, 'Do you say that if Romans entered the lands of the Muslims, they should not stop them?' He (the Imam) said, 'It is to be on their guard but not fighting. However, if the center of al-Islam and Muslims is feared for, then one must fight. In such case his fighting is for his own sake and not for the authority (the king).' The narrator has said that he then asked, 'If the enemy comes to the place where he serves as a guard then what should he do?' He (the Imam) said, 'He fights for the center of al-Islam but not for these people. It is because in the wear and tear of al-Islam is wear and tear of the religion of Muhammad, *O Allah, grant compensation to Muhammad and his family worthy of their services to Your cause.*'"

Ali has narrated from his father from Yahya ibn abu 'Imran from Yunus from al-Rida', *'Alayhi al-Salam*, a similar Hadith.

Chapter 6 - Under Whose Command Obligatory Jihad Takes Place?

H 8181, Ch. 6, h 1
Ali ibn Ibrahim has narrated from his father from 'Uthman from ibn 'Isa from Sama'ah who has said the following:
"'Abu 'Abd Allah, *'Alayhi al-Salam*, has said that 'Abbad al-Basriy met Ali ibn al-Husayn, *'Alayhi al-Salam*, on the way to Makkah and said, 'O Ali ibn al-

Husayn, you have disregarded Jihad because it is difficult but you have inclined toward al-Hajj because of the ease in it. Allah, the Most Majestic, the Most Glorious, says, "Allah has purchased the souls and property of the believers in exchange for Paradise. They fight for the cause of Allah to destroy His enemies and to sacrifice themselves. This is a true promise which He has revealed in the Torah, the Gospel, and the al-Quran. No one is more true to His promise than Allah. Allow this bargain to be glad news for them. This is indeed the supreme triumph.'" (9:111) Ali ibn al-Husayn, *'Alayhi al-Salam*, said, 'Complete the verse.' He then recited: '(The believers) who repent for their sins, worship Allah, praise Him, travel through the land (for pious purposes), kneel down and prostrate themselves in obedience to Allah, make others do good and prevent them from sins and abide by the laws of Allah, will receive a great reward. Allow this to be glad news for the believer.' (9:112) Ali ibn al-Husayn, *'Alayhi al-Salam*, said, 'If we see these kinds of people with these qualities then Jihad along side with them is more virtuous than al-Hajj.'"

H 8182, Ch. 6, h 2

A number of our people have narrated from Sahl ibn Ziyad from Ahmad ibn Muhammad ibn abu Nasr from Muhammad ibn 'Abd Allah and Muhammad ibn Yahya from Ahmad ibn Muhammad from al-'Abbas ibn Ma'ruf from Safwan ibn Yahya from 'Abd Allah ibn al-Mughirah who has said the following:

"Once Muhammad ibn 'Abd Allah said to al-Rida', *'Alayhi al-Salam*, when I was listening, said, 'My father has narrated from the people of his family from their ancestors, *'Alayhim al-Salam*, that he said to a certain one of them (ancestors), "In our location there is a place called Qazwin for keeping guard against the enemy called al-Daylam. Is Jihad or Ribat (guarding) obligatory?" He (the person of our ancestors) said, "You must not miss performing al-Hajj around this House." He repeated the Hadith he had just said and the answer was again, "You must pay attention to this House to perform al-Hajj around it. Do you not agree that one of you stays home to spend on his family of his gains and wait for our cause to materialize? If he finds himself in such a day he is considered like those who were present with the prophet on the day of Badr. If he dies, while waiting for our cause to materialize, he is considered like one standing with the one from us, who will rise with divine authority, in his tent like this" – holding his two index fingers together – saying, "I do not say like this" – holding his index and middle fingers together –"because this one is taller than this."' Abu al-Hassan al-Rida, *'Alayhi al-Salam*, then said, 'He had spoken the truth.'"

H 8183, Ch. 6, h 3

Muhammad ibn al-Hassan al-Tatriy has narrated from those who he has mentioned in his book – from Ali ibn al-Nu'man from Suwayd al-Qalanisiy from Bashir al-Dahhan who has said the following:

"I once said to abu 'Abd Allah, *'Alayhi al-Salam*, 'I saw a dream in which I said to you, "Fighting alongside one who is not an Imam, obedience to whom is obligatory, is unlawful just like consuming dead animals, blood and pork for food. You said to me (in my dream), "That is how it is."' Abu 'Abd Allah, *'Alayhi al-Salam*, then said, 'That is how it is. That is how it is.'"

Chapter 7 - 'Amr ibn 'Ubayd and al-Mu'taziliy Groups' Visiting abu 'Abd Allah, *'Alayhi al-Salam*

H 8184, Ch. 7, h 1

Ali ibn Ibrahim has narrated from his father from ibn abu 'Umayr from 'Umar ibn 'Udhaynah from Zurarah from 'Abd al-Karim ibn 'Utbah al-Hashimiy who has said the following:

"I was sitting in the presence of abu 'Abd Allah, *'Alayhi al-Salam*, in Makkah when a group of people of al-Mu'tazilah among whom 'Amr ibn 'Ubayd was present as well as Wasil ibn 'Ata', Hafs ibn Salim Mawla' ibn Hubayrah and people of their leaders came to visit. This happened during the time when al-Walid was killed and people of al-Sham had differences among them. They spoke (about the situation) a great deal with confusion and made it very lengthy. Abu 'Abd Allah, *'Alayhi al-Salam*, said to them, 'You have spoken a great deal and it is excessive for me. Appoint someone from among yourselves to speak in favor of your arguments and make it short.' They then appointed 'Amr ibn 'Ubayd for this task. He spoke assiduously and made it lengthy. Among other things he said, 'People of al-Sham have killed their Caliph, and Allah, the Most Majestic, the Most Glorious, has struck one group against the other and has scattered their affairs. We have deliberated and found a man who has religion, reason, kindness, position and resource for Caliphate and he is Muhammad ibn 'Abd Allah ibn al-Hassan. We then decided to gather around him to pledge allegiance, then come with him in public. Those who pledge allegiance with us will be of us and we will be for him. Those who stay away from us we will keep away from him. Those who plan against us we will do Jihad and plan against them because of their rebellion and their rejection to return them to the truth and the people of truth. We like to present this plan before you so you will also join us; we need a person like you. It is because of your position and the great number of your followers.' When he finished, abu 'Abd Allah, *'Alayhi al-Salam*, asked, 'Are you all of the same opinion as 'Amr is?' They replied, 'Yes, we are of the same opinion.' He (the Imam) then praised Allah and glorified Him; then asked Him to grant salawat (favors and compensation to Muhammad and his family worthy of their services to His cause). He then said, 'We become angry when Allah is disobeyed but when He is obeyed we become happy.'

'O 'Amr, tell me if the nation will make you the person in charge of their affairs and give you authority without fighting and expenses and said to you, "Whomever you choose to be their ruler with authority is accepted by the nation." Whom then would you choose for the nation?' He replied, 'I will make it Shura' (to be decided by the Muslims). He (the Imam) asked, 'To be decided by all Muslims?' He replied, 'Yes, by all Muslims.' He (the Imam) asked, 'Will it be decided by their scholars of law and good ones?' He replied, 'Yes.' He (the Imam) asked, 'Will such people be of Quraysh and others?' He replied, 'Yes.' He (the Imam) asked, 'Will they be of Arab and non-Arab?' He replied, 'Yes.' He (the Imam) then said, 'O 'Amr tell me, do you love abu Bakr and 'Umar or denounce them?' He replied, 'I love them.' He (the Imam) said, 'But you just opposed them. What do you all say?' They replied, 'We love them.' He (the Imam) then said, 'O 'Amr, were you to be a man who denounced the two of them, then it would have been permissible for him to oppose them. How can you love the two of them when you just opposed them? 'Umar had made a covenant with abu Bakr on the basis of which he pledged allegiance to him and he did not counsel anyone else on the issue. Thereafter abu Bakr returned it to him ('Umar) and did not counsel anyone in the issue. 'Umar then formed a council of six members. He kept all of al-Muhajirun and al-Ansar out of this council except those six people from Quraysh. He made a will about the council to which, I think, neither you nor your friends agree because you make a Shura' of all Muslims.' He asked, 'What did he do?' He (the Imam) replied, 'He commanded Suhayb to lead *Salat* (prayer) for the people for three days and to consult the six people and no one else except the son of 'Umar who consulted them but would have had have no say in their decision. He made a will and advised those of al-Muhajirun and al-Ansar in his presence to do this: "If three days pass before the council finish the task or pledge allegiance to a man, you must cut off the necks of all the members of the council. If four of them agree on a plan before three days pass but two of them oppose, you must cut off the necks of the two opposing members of the council." Do you accept such a plan about the council that you like all Muslims to form?' They replied, 'No.'

"He (the Imam) said, 'O 'Amr, leave this aside. Suppose, I pledged allegiance to your friend to whom you call me and then the nation gathered around you and no two people disagreed with you about your plan. Then you marched against the pagans who reject al-Islam and do not pay taxes. Will there be enough knowledge with your friend or with you with which you can deal according to the traditions of the Messenger of Allah in the matters of the pagans and the war against them?' He replied, 'Yes.' He (the Imam) asked, 'What will you do?' He replied, 'We call them to al-Islam. If they refused we tell them to pay taxes.' He (the Imam) asked, 'What you will do if they will be Majus and not of the people of the book?' He replied, 'They are the same.' He (the Imam) asked, 'Are you telling me from al-Quran?' He replied, 'Yes.' He (the Imam) asked, 'What will you do if they were pagans of Arab people and of idol worshippers?' He replied, 'They are the same.' He (the Imam) asked, 'Are you telling me from al-Quran?' He replied, 'Yes.' He (the Imam) asked read this, 'Fight against those people of the Book who have no faith in Allah or the Day of Judgment, who do not consider unlawful what Allah and His Messenger have made unlawful, and who do not believe in the true religion, until they humbly pay tax with their own hands." (9:29)'

"He (the Imam) asked, 'Is the exception and the stipulation of Allah, the Most Majestic, the Most Glorious, about the people of the book and those not of the people of the book the same?' He replied, 'Yes.' He (the Imam) asked, 'From whom have you learned this answer?' He replied, 'I have heard people say so.' He (the Imam) said, 'Leave this aside. Suppose they refuse to pay taxes and you fight them, and defeat them, then how will you deal with the properties captured from them?' He replied, 'I will deduct one-fifth from it and divide the remainder among those who have fought the war.' He (the Imam) said, 'Tell me about the one-fifth. To whom will you give it?' He replied, 'I will give it to whomever

Allah has told to give.' The narrator has said that 'Amr then recited: 'You must take notice that whatever you gain one-fifth of it belongs to Allah, the Messenger, the relatives, the orphans, the destitute and those who deplete their expenses on a journey.' (8:41) He (the Imam) asked, 'To who will you give that which is for the Messenger?' Who are relatives?' He replied, 'The scholars of the law have different opinions about it. Certain ones among them say, "They are the relatives of the Holy Prophet and his family." Certain others say, "It is the caliph." Still others say, "They are the relatives of those who have taken part in the fighting."' He (the Imam) asked, 'Which one do you think is it?' He replied, 'I do not know.' He (the Imam) said, 'I can see that you do not know. Leave this aside.' He (the Imam) then said, 'Consider the remainder after taking one-fifth. Will you distribute it among all the fighters?' He replied, 'Yes.' He (the Imam) said, 'In doing so you oppose the Messenger of Allah. The decisive factor between you and I is the scholars of the law of al-Madinah and the elders. Ask them. They have no differences on this issue. They do not dispute that the Messenger of Allah made a truce with the Arabs. It said that they can live in their locations and must not migrate. If the enemy will attack him they must rise and fight his enemy but they will have no share in the properties captured from the enemy. You, however, say you will distribute it among all the fighters. In so doing you oppose the Messenger of Allah in his dealings in everything that you have said about the pagans. Despite this what do you say about charity?' He (the Imam) then recited the verse to him. 'Charity is for the poor, the destitute, the charity collectors. . . .' (9:60) He said, 'That is right.' He (the Imam) asked, 'How will you distribute it?' He replied, 'I will divide it into eight portions and give to each category one portion thereof.' He (the Imam) asked, 'Will you do so even if members of one category will be ten thousand and of the members of another category there will be only one or two or three individuals present?' Will you give to one individual an amount equal to what will you give to ten thousand people?' He replied, 'Yes.' He (the Imam) asked, 'Will you collect the charities of the towns and the city in one place and divide among them in equal portions?' He replied, 'Yes.' He (the Imam) said, 'In doing so you oppose the Messenger of Allah in all of his dealings I have mentioned. The Messenger of Allah would give the charities of the people of the towns to the people of the towns and the charities of the people of the city to the people of the city. He would not distribute it among them in equal portions. He distributed it among them according to the number of people present and according to his discretion. He did not set about it a particular time or portion. He, according to the needs of the people present, distributed the charities. If you have doubts about what I said you can meet the scholars of the law of al-Madinah. They have no differences on the issue that the Messenger of Allah would do as I said he did.' He (the Imam) then turned to 'Amr ibn 'Ubayd and said, 'You in this group must maintain piety before Allah. You must maintain piety before Allah. My father was the best of the people on earth. He was more knowledgeable than all of the people on earth about the book of Allah, the Most Majestic, the Most Glorious, and the tradition of the Messenger of Allah. He has said, "The Messenger of Allah has said, 'Whoever strikes people with his sword and calls them to himself while among the Muslims there is someone more knowledgeable than he is, such person is lost and he is a pretender.'"""

H 8185, Ch. 7, h 2
Muhammad ibn Yahya has narrated from Muhammad ibn al-Husayn, from Ali ibn al-Nu'man from Suwayd al-Qalanisiy from Bashir who has said the following:

"I once said to abu 'Abd Allah, *'Alayhi al-Salam*, 'I saw a dream in which I said to you, "Fighting alongside an Imam to whom obedience is not obligatory is unlawful like consuming dead animals, blood and pork for food", and you said to me, "Yes, that is how it is."' Abu 'Abd Allah, *'Alayhi al-Salam*, then said, 'That is how it is. That is how it is.'"

Chapter 8 - The Recommendations of the Messenger of Allah and Amir al-Mu'minin, about Smaller Armed Expeditions

H 8186, Ch. 8, h 1
Ali ibn Ibrahim has narrated from his father from ibn abu 'Umayr from Mu'awiyah ibn 'Ammar – I think – from abu Hamzah al-Thumaliy who has said the following:

"Abu 'Abd Allah, *'Alayhi al-Salam*, has said that when the Messenger of Allah would decide to dispatch a small group of people for an armed expedition he would call them in his presence, make them sit before him and say to them, 'March in the name of Allah, with Allah, in the way of Allah and upon the religion (path) of the Messenger of Allah. You must not be excessive, you must not deform people, you must not betray, you must not kill old people, you must not kill children, you must not kill women and you must not cut down trees unless you are forced to do so. If anyone of the Muslims of the lower or higher position expresses sympathy toward a man of the pagans, he is given protection until he hears the words of Allah. If thereafter he followed you he then is your brother in religion and if he refused you then must send him to his safe place and ask Allah for assistance.'"

H 8187, Ch. 8, h 2
Ali ibn Ibrahim has narrated from his father from al-Nawfaliy from al-Sakuniy who has said the following:

"Abu 'Abd Allah, *'Alayhi al-Salam*, has said that Amir al-Mu'minin, *'Alayhi al-Salam*, has said, 'The Messenger of Allah, *O Allah, grant compensation to Muhammad and his family worthy of their services to Your cause*, prohibited spreading of poison in the lands of the pagans.'"

H 8188, Ch. 8, h 3
Muhammad ibn Yahya from Ahmad ibn Muhammad ibn 'Isa, from ibn Mahbub from 'Abbad ibn Suhayb who has said the following:

"I heard abu 'Abd Allah, *'Alayhi al-Salam*, saying, 'The Messenger of Allah, *O Allah, grant compensation to Muhammad and his family worthy of their services to Your cause*, never launched a surprise attack against the enemy during the night.'"

H 8189, Ch. 8, h 4

Ali ibn Ibrahim has narrated from his father, from al-Nawfaliy from al-Sakuniy who has said the following:

"Abu 'Abd Allah, *'Alayhi al-Salam*, has said that Amir al-Mu'minin, *'Alayhi al-Salam*, has said, 'The Messenger of Allah sent me to Yemen and said to me, "You must not fight anyone before calling him to Allah. I swear by Allah, if Allah guides through you one man it will be more excellent for you than all the things on which the sun shines and sets. You, O Ali, will have his guardianship."'"

H 8190, Ch. 8, h 5

Ali ibn Ibrahim has narrated from his father from ibn abu 'Umayr from Aban ibn 'Uthman from Yahya ibn abu al-'Ala' who has said the following:

"Abu 'Abd Allah, *'Alayhi al-Salam*, has said that Amir al-Mu'minin, *'Alayhi al-Salam*, would not launch attacks against the enemy until after the declining of the sun toward the west. He would say, 'At such time the doors of heaven open up, mercy comes forward and victory descends.' He would also say, 'Such time is closer to the night, prone to reduced killing, pursuers return and fleeing ones disappear.'"

H 8191, Ch. 8, h 6

Ali has narrated from his father, from al-Qasim ibn Muhammad from al-Minqariy from Hafs ibn Ghiyath who has said the following:

"A city of the unbelievers is in the state of war (against Muslims); can it be flooded, set on fire or fired upon with catapults to destroy them even when there are women, children, old people and Muslims taken as prisoners of war and merchants?' He (the Imam) said, 'It can be done and it cannot be stopped because of the people you mentioned. The Muslims do not have to pay any compensation to anyone or ransom.'

"I also asked him, 'Why is it that women do not have to pay taxes?' He (the Imam) said, 'It is because the Messenger of Allah, *O Allah, grant compensation to Muhammad and his family worthy of their services to Your cause*, prohibited fighting women and children in the war zone unless they fight. If women fight, one must cease fire as far as possible and there is no fear of a breach. Since he prohibited fighting in the war zone, in the peace zone (Islamic domain) it certainly is forbidden. If she refuses to pay taxes, destroying her is not possible and when destroying her is not possible there is no tax on her to pay. If men refuse to pay taxes, they will be in breach of the covenant and it is lawful to eliminate them; elimination of men is lawful in pagans' lands. The case of the crippled, ones of the tax payers, blind, old ones, women and children in the war zone is the same and for this reason they are not to pay taxes.'"

H 8192, Ch. 8, h 7

Ali ibn Ibrahim has narrated from his father from al-Nawfaliy from al-Sakuniy who has said the following:

"Abu 'Abd Allah, *'Alayhi al-Salam*, has said that when the Holy Prophet, *O Allah, grant compensation to Muhammad and his family worthy of their services to Your cause*, dispatched a small group of people for an armed expedition, he would pray in their favor."

H 8193, Ch. 8, h 8

Ali ibn Ibrahim has narrated from Harun ibn Muslim Mas'adah ibn Sadaqah who has said the following:

"Abu 'Abd Allah, *'Alayhi al-Salam*, has said that when the Holy Prophet appointed a commander for a small group of people to be dispatched for an armed expedition, he commanded him to maintain piety before Allah in his own affairs, then he commanded him to maintain piety in the affairs of the people under his command. He then said, 'Mobilize in the name of Allah and in the way of Allah. Fight those who reject belief in Allah. You must not betray, or deceive, you must not deform anyone, you must not kill children, you must not kill devoted worshippers who live in desolate places, you must not burn palm trees or flood them in water, you must not cut down fruit-bearing trees, you must not burn down farms because you do not know who will use them for food. When you meet an enemy of the Muslims, give him three choices. If he accepts you also must accept it from him and allow him to live free. Call them to al-Islam. If they accept you must also accept it (their acceptance) and allow them to live free; or ask them to migrate (to the land under the Islamic domain) after their accepting al-Islam. If they accepted you must also accept it from them and allow them to live free. If they refuse migration but choose to remain in their land and refuse to move to migration locations, they are considered as the believing Arabs. Whatever applied to believing Arabs apply to them. They will have no share in *al-Fai'* and any dividend until they move in the way of Allah. If they refuse to accept both of the previous choices, then ask them to pay taxes with their own hands in a humble manner. If they agree to pay taxes then you must accept it from them and allow them to be free. If they refuse all the choices, then ask assistance from Allah and do Jihad against them in the way Jihad must be performed. If the residents of the stronghold are surrounded and they propose that they are ready to accept the laws of Allah in the matter, do not accept their proposal. Ask them to accept your decision in the matter. Thereafter make your decision the way you want. If you leave them according to the laws of Allah, you will not be able to find if you have found Allah's applicable law in the matter or not. When you surround the residents of a stronghold and they ask you to deal with them upon the responsibility of Allah and the responsibility of His Messenger, you must not agree with such a proposal. In fact you must deal with them upon your own responsibility and the responsibility of your fathers and brothers. It is easier for you if you could not keep up with your responsibility and the responsibility of your fathers and brothers, than your failure to keep up with the responsibility of Allah and His Messenger *'Alayhi al-Salam.*'"

H 8194, Ch. 8, h 9

A number of our people have narrated from Ahmad ibn Muhammad from al-Washsha' from Muhammad ibn Humran and Jamil ibn al-Darraj who both have narrated who has said the following:

"Abu 'Abd Allah, *'Alayhi al-Salam*, has said that whenever the Messenger of Allah dispatched a small group for an armed expedition, he called their commander and made him sit on his side. He then called the soldiers and made them sit in front of him and said to them, 'March in the name of Allah, with Allah, in the way of Allah and upon the religion of the Messenger of Allah. You must not betray and you must not act excessively, you must not deform people, you must not cut down trees unless you are forced, you must not kill old people, children and women. If anyone of the Muslims of a higher or lower position looks with sympathy upon any of the pagans, such pagan person is in his protection until he hears the words of Allah. When he, the pagan man, hears the words of Allah, the Most Majestic, the Most Glorious, and if he follows you, he then is considered your brother in religion and if he refused, then ask Allah for assistance against him and send him back to his safe place.'"

Ali ibn Ibrahim has narrated from his father from ibn abu 'Umayr from Jamil from abu 'Abd Allah, *'Alayhi al-Salam*, a similar Hadith. Except that he has said, "If anyone of the Muslims looks on a pagan man with sympathy in the near or far away positions of the army, such pagan man is considered under his protection."

Chapter 9(a) - Granting Immunity

H 8195, Ch. 9a, h 1

Ali ibn Ibrahim has narrated from his father from al-Nawfaliy from al-Sakuniy who has said the following:

"This is concerning my question before abu 'Abd Allah, *'Alayhi al-Salam*, 'What is the meaning of the words of the Holy Prophet, ". . . commitment of a person of the lowest position among them becomes a commitment of all of them (Muslims)?"' He (the Imam) replied, 'It means, if the Muslim army surrounds a stronghold of the pagans and a man comes up saying, "Grant me immunity so I can debate your man." If a man of the lowest position in the Muslim army grants him immunity, it becomes obligatory for all of them to fulfill that commitment.'"

H 8196, Ch. 9a, h 2

Ali has narrated from Harun ibn Muslim from Mas'adah ibn Sadaqah who has said the following:

"Abu 'Abd Allah, *'Alayhi al-Salam*, has said that Amir al-Mu'minin, *'Alayhi al-Salam*, once honored the immunity granted by a Muslim slave to the people of a fortress, saying, 'He is of the believing people.'"

H 8197, Ch. 9a, h 3

Ali ibn Ibrahim has narrated from his father from Yahya ibn 'Imran from Yunus from 'Abd Allah ibn Sulayman who has said the following:

"I heard abu Ja'far, *'Alayhi al-Salam*, saying, 'Whoever provides a commitment of immunity to someone but then kills him, he on the Day of Judgment will come, carrying the banner of betrayal.'"

H 8198, Ch. 9a, h 4

Ali ibn Ibrahim has narrated from his father from ibn abu 'Umayr from Muhammad ibn al-Hakam from abu 'Abd Allah, or abu al-Hassan, recipients of divine supreme covenant, who has said the following:

"If a people surrounds a city and the people of the city ask for immunity and they reply negatively to their request but they think it is a positive response and came out of their fortress, such people are entitled to a binding commitment of immunity."

H 8199, Ch. 9a, h 5
Muhammad ibn Yahya has narrated from Ahmad ibn Muhammad from Muhammad ibn Yahya from Talhah ibn Zayd who has said the following:

"Abu 'Abd Allah, *'Alayhi al-Salam*, has said that he has read in the book of Ali, *'Alayhi al-Salam*, that the Messenger of Allah, *O Allah, grant compensation to Muhammad and his family worthy of their services to Your cause*, wrote the following in a letter for al-Muhajirun, al-Ansar and those who join them from the people of Yathrib: 'Every mobilization that is arranged for an armed confrontation must be continued step by step with legitimacy and justice among the Muslims. It is not permissible to start a war without the permission of the people (who will maintain it). The rights of neighbors are just like one's soul that must be held harmless and sinless. The respect and honor of a neighbor is like the honor and respect of a mother and father. A believing person does not make peace just for himself, ignoring the other believer during a war for the cause of Allah, except on the basis of justice and equality.'"

Chapter 9(b)

H 8200, Ch. 9b, h 1
Muhammad ibn Yahya has narrated from Ahmad ibn Muhammad from Muhammad ibn Yahya from Talhah ibn Zayd who has said the following:

"I heard abu 'Abd Allah, *'Alayhi al-Salam*, saying, 'My father would say, "There are two laws about war: (1) During an ongoing war when the enemy is not defeated about the prisoners of war the Imam has the choice to execute, cut off their hands and legs, one of each of the opposite side, without (doing something to) stopping blood flow so that the victim dies by bleeding. This is stated in words of Allah, the Most Majestic, the Most Glorious: 'The only proper punishment for those who fight against Allah and His Messenger and try to spread evil in the land is to be killed, crucified, or either to have one of their hands and feet cutoff from the opposite sides or to be sent into exile. These are to disgrace them in this life and they will suffer a great torment in the life hereafter.' (5:33)

"Of the choices that Allah has given to the Imam is one and that is execution. There are no different choices.'"

"I then asked abu 'Abd Allah, *'Alayhi al-Salam*, about the words of Allah, the Most Majestic, the Most Glorious, '. . . or that they are exiled. . . .' He (the Imam) said it is up to the search and pursuit of the troops until he flees. If the troops capture him certain of the rules that I just describe will be executed in his case.

"The other law about war (2) is when it is over and the enemy is defeated. About every prisoner of war that is captured, the Imam has the choice to set them free as favor to them or they pay ransom to set themselves free. The Imam may also decide to keep them as slaves.'"

H 8201, Ch. 9b, h 2
Ali ibn Ibrahim has narrated from his father, from al-Qasim ibn Muhammad from Sulayman ibn al-Minqariy from Hafs ibn Ghiyath who has said the following:

"This is concerning my question before abu 'Abd Allah, *'Alayhi al-Salam*, about the two groups of whom one is rebellious and the other deals with justice and the latter group defeats the rebellious group. He (the Imam) replied, 'People of justice must not pursue the fleeing ones, kill the prisoner or hurt the wounded. This is when the rebellious ones do not have a group around to whom then they can return, but if they have such a group, then the prisoners are executed, the fleeing ones are persued and the wounded ones are eliminated.'"

H 8202, Ch. 9b, h 3
Al-Husayn ibn Muhammad al-'Ash'ariy has narrated from Mu'alla' ibn Muhammad from al-Washsha' from Aban ibn 'Uthman from abu Hamzah al-Thumaliy who has said the following:

"I once said to Ali ibn al-Husayn, *'Alayhi al-Salam*, 'The way Ali, *'Alayhi al-Salam*, dealt with people of Qiblah was different from the way the Messenger of Allah, *O Allah, grant compensation to Muhammad and his family worthy of their services to Your cause*, dealt with the pagans.' He the narrator has said, 'He (the Imam) became angry and sat in his place;' then said, 'He by Allah, did deal with them according to the method of the Messenger of Allah on the day of victory. On the day of al-Basra, Ali, *'Alayhi al-Salam*, wrote to Malik who was on the front line, and commanded him, "You must not hit anyone except advancing attackers, you must not kill the fleeing, you must not hurt the wounded and those who close their doors have immunity." Malik received the letter of commandment but he placed it in front of himself on the saddle before reading. He then ordered them to fight and they fought until they were pushed into the alleys of al-Basra. He then opened the letter of commandment and ordered to announce the contents of the letter of commandment.'"

H 8203, Ch. 9b, h 4
Ali ibn Ibrahim has narrated from his father from Isma'il ibn Marrar from Yunus from abu Bakr al-Hadramiy who has said the following:

"I heard abu 'Abd Allah, *'Alayhi al-Salam*, saying, 'In the ways of the dealings of Ali, *'Alayhi al-Salam*, with the people of al-Basra, the benefit for the Shi'ah was greater than all things on which the sun shines. He, *'Alayhi al-Salam*, knew that those people will become dominant. Were he to make them prisoners his followers would have been made prisoners likewise.' I then asked, 'Will al-Qa'im, *'Alayhi al-Salam*, deal with people like his dealings?' He (the Imam) replied, 'No, Ali, *'Alayhi al-Salam*, dealt with them with favors due to his knowledge of their domination. Al-Qa'im will deal with them differently because they will not have any domination.'"

25

H 8204, Ch. 9b, h 5

Ali ibn Ibrahim has narrated from his father from 'Amr ibn 'Uthman from Muhammad ibn 'Adhafir from 'Uqbah ibn Bashir from 'Abd Allah ibn Sharik from his father who has said the following:

"When people on the day of camel were defeated, Amir al-Mu'minin, *'Alayhi al-Salam*, said, 'You must not pursue the fleeing, you must not hurt the wounded, and those who close their door are granted immunity.' On the day of Siffin he eliminated the attackers and the fleeing and gave permission about the wounded. Aban ibn Taghlib said to ''Abd Allah ibn Sharik, 'These are two different ways of dealings.' He (the Imam) said, 'On the day of al-Basra people killed Talhah and al-Zubayr. Mu'awiyah was alive and he was the commander.'"

Chapter 9(c)

H 8205, Ch. 9c, h 1

Muhammad ibn Yahya has narrated from Ahmad ibn Muhammad ibn 'Isa from ibn Mahbub from al-Hassan ibn Salih who has said the following:

"Abu 'Abd Allah, *'Alayhi al-Salam*, would say, 'If one, when advancing against the enemy after facing two men, flees, he is considered fleeing; however one who in such condition on facing three men flees, he is not considered fleeing.'"

H 8206, Ch. 9c, h 2

A number of our people have narrated from Sahl ibn Ziyad from Muhammad ibn al-Hassan ibn Shammun from 'Abd Allah ibn 'Abd al-Rahman al-Asamm from Misma' ibn 'Abd al-Malik who has said the following:

"Abu 'Abd Allah, *'Alayhi al-Salam*, has said that when the Messenger of Allah, *O Allah, grant compensation to Muhammad and his family worthy of their services to Your cause*, sent through Ali, *'Alayhi al-Salam*, the declaration of the abrogation of peace treaty to be announce in Makkah, he sent along with him a group of people. The Messenger of Allah then said (to them), 'Those who turn themselves into captivity without having sustained a disabling wound are not of our people.'"

H 8207, Ch. 9c, h 3

Ali ibn Ibrahim has narrated from his father from al-Nawfaliy, from al-Sakuniy who has said the following:

"Abu 'Abd Allah, *'Alayhi al-Salam*, has said that one who turns himself into captivity without suffering a disabling wound is not ransomed on the expenses of public treasury. He however may be ransomed with payment from his own properties."

Chapter 10 - Challenging the Enemy for a Fight

H 8208, Ch. 10, h 1

Hamid ibn Ziyad has narrated from al-Khashshab from ibn Baqqah from Mu'adh ibn Thabit from 'Amr ibn Jumay' who has said the following:

"Abu 'Abd Allah, *'Alayhi al-Salam*, was asked about challenging (to fight the enemy) while standing between the two confronting armies after the permission

26

of the Imam. He (the Imam) said, 'It is fine but it must not take place without the permission of the Imam.'"

H 8209, Ch. 10, h 2

A number of our people have narrated from Sahl ibn Ziyad from Ja'far ibn Muhammad al-Ash'ariy from ibn al-Qaddah who has said the following:

"Abu 'Abd Allah, *'Alayhi al-Salam*, has said that a man challenged a certain person from banu Hashim to fight. He refused to fight. Amir al-Mu'minin, *'Alayhi al-Salam*, asked, 'What has made you to refuse?' He replied, 'He was a strong man of Arab and I feared that he may defeat me.' Amir al-Mu'minin, *'Alayhi al-Salam*, said to him, 'He has transgressed against you. Were you to fight him, you would have defeated him. If a mountain transgresses against a mountain the transgressor is crushed.' Abu 'Abd Allah, *'Alayhi al-Salam*, said, 'al-Husayn ibn Ali, *'Alayhi al-Salam*, challenged a man to fight and Amir al-Mu'minin noticed it and said, "If you do such a thing again I will reprimand you. If you are challenged and you refuse to fight I will also reprimand you. Have you not noticed that he has transgressed against you?""""

Chapter 11 - Kindness to the Prisoners and Providing Him Food

H 8210, Ch. 11, h 1

Ali ibn Ibrahim has narrated from his father from al-Qasim ibn Muhammad from al-Minqariy from 'Isa ibn Yunus al-Awza'iy from al-Zuhriy from Ali ibn al-Husayn, recipients of divine supreme covenant, who has said the following:

"If you take a prisoner who is not able to walk and you do not have a carriage to carry him, then allow him to go and do not kill him; you do not know what is the command of the Imam about him.' The narrator has said that he (the Imam) then said, 'If a prisoner becomes a Muslim, his life is spared and he is one of us.'"

H 8211, Ch. 11, h 2

Ali ibn Ibrahim has narrated from his father from Hammad from Hariz from Zurarah who has said the following:

"Abu 'Abd Allah, *'Alayhi al-Salam*, has said that feeding the prisoner is upon the one who has captured him even if he wants to eliminate him the next day. He should feed him, quench his thirst, [provide him shadow, shelter] and be kind to him, regardless, he is an unbeliever or not."

H 8212, Ch. 11, h 3

Ahmad ibn Muhammad al-Kufiy has narrated from Hamdan al-Qalanisiy from Muhammad ibn al-Walid from Aban ibn 'Uthman from Mansur ibn Hazim who has said the following:

"Abu 'Abd Allah, *'Alayhi al-Salam*, has said that feeding the prisoner is upon the one who has captured him, even if he is an unbeliever whom he wants to eliminate the next day. He should be kind to him, feed him and quench his thirst."

H 8213, Ch. 11, h 4

Ali ibn Ibrahim has narrated from his father from al-Nadr ibn Suwayd from al-Qasim ibn Sulayman from Jarrah al-Mada'iniy who has said the following:

"Abu 'Abd Allah, *'Alayhi al-Salam*, spoke about feeding the prisoners of war and said, 'Feeding of prisoners of war is on the one who has taken him as a prisoner even if he wants to eliminate him the next day. He must feed him quench his thirst, provide him shadow and be kind to him, regardless, the prisoner is an unbeliever or other.'"

Chapter 12 - Calling to al-Islam before Fighting

H 8214, Ch. 12, h 1

Ali ibn Ibrahim has narrated from his father, from al-Qasim ibn Muhammad from al-Minqariy from Sufyan ibn 'Uyaynah from al-Zuhriy who has said the following:

"Once a group of men of Quraysh came to see Ali ibn al-Husayn, *'Alayhi al-Salam*, and asked him about how to call to religion. He (the Imam) replied, 'You should say, "In the name of Allah, the Beneficent, the Merciful. I call you to Allah, the Most Majestic, the Most Glorious, and to His religion." The main points in it are two issues. (1) It is to acknowledge the existence of Allah, the Most Majestic, the Most Glorious. (2) It is to act according to what pleases Him. Acknowledgement of the existence of Allah, the Most Majestic, the Most Glorious, comes from knowing that He is one, kind, merciful, Majestic, all-Knowing, powerful and that He is high above all things and that He can benefit and cause harm and that He is dominant over all things. No eye is able to see Him but He is aware of all eyes and He is the subtle and aware. Muhammad, *O Allah, grant compensation to Muhammad and his family worthy of their services to Your cause*, is His servant and His Messenger and that what he has brought is truly from Allah, the Most Majestic, the Most Glorious, and all things beside Him are destructible. If they agreed, they then will able to have whatever the Muslims can have and they will be held responsible for whatever Muslims are held responsible.'"

H 8215, Ch. 12, h 2

A number of our people have narrated from Sahl ibn Ziyad from Muhammad ibn al-Hassan from 'Abd Allah ibn 'Abd al-Rahman from Misma' ibn 'Abd al-Malik who has said the following:

"Abu 'Abd Allah, *'Alayhi al-Salam*, has said that Amir al-Mu'minin, *'Alayhi al-Salam*, has said, 'When the Messenger of Allah, *O Allah, grant compensation to Muhammad and his family worthy of their services to Your cause*, instructed me to go to Yemen he said to me, "O Ali, you must not fight anyone before calling him to al-Islam. I swear by Allah, Allah's guiding only one man (to the right path) is better for you than all things on which the sun shines or sets, and to you will belong his guardianship and legacy."'"

Chapter 13(a) - Matters about which Amir al-Mu'minin, *'Alayhi al-Salam*, Recommended at the Time of War

H 8216, Ch. 13a, h 1

Ali ibn Ibrahim has narrated from his father from certain individuals of his people from abu Hamzah from 'Aqil al-Khuza'iy who has said the following:

"Amir al-Mu'minin, *'Alayhi al-Salam*, during a war recommended the Muslims with these words: 'You must perform your *Salat* (prayer) regularly, preserve it, perform it very often and seek thereby nearness to Allah. It was made obligatory for the believing people. The unbelievers found out when they were asked, "What has led to Saqar?" (74:46) They replied, "We were not of those who performed *Salat* (prayer)." The believing people who do not become disturbed because of worldly attractions, delightfulness of their eyes because of wealth and children realize its significance and know its proper time to be performed and think of it as very graceful. Allah, the Most Majestic, the Most Glorious, has said, "There are men who do not become disturbed because of business and trade when they speak of Allah and performing *Salat* (prayer)." The Messenger of Allah after receiving the glad news of paradise had fixed himself in performing *Salat* (prayer). Allah, the Most Majestic, the Most Glorious, has said, "Command your family to perform *Salat* (prayer) and exercise patience during *Salat* (prayer)." (20:132)

'He would command his family to perform *Salat* (prayer) and himself would exercise patience during performing *Salat* (prayer). Thereafter Zakat along with *Salat* (prayer) is made a means of getting nearer to Allah for the people of al-Islam and upon the people of al-Islam. One who does not perform it with his soul delighted and then expects to receive a reward better than *Salat* (prayer) he is ignorant of the Sunnah, suffers loss in matters of his reward and his life ends in confusion. He remains regretful because of disregarding the command of Allah, the Most Majestic, the Most Glorious, and not paying attention to what the virtuous servants of Allah had great inclinations. Allah, the Most Majestic, the Most Glorious, has said, "We turn away whoever follows a path other than that of the believing people, to whatever he loves." (4:115)

'Thereafter is keeping of trust. One who is not a person of trust suffers a great loss and his deeds become confused. It was introduced to the well established heavens, well stretched earth and well fixed mountains. Other things are not taller, wider, higher and greater than them. If tallness, wideness, greatness, power and majesty were needed to refuse they could use them. They feared punishment, thus refused to accept the trust. Thereafter is Jihad. It is the noblest one of the deeds after al-Islam. It is the pillar of religion. The reward for it is great with majesty and highness. It is an opportunity in which there is goodness and glad news of paradise after martyrdom and sustenance with the Lord and honor.

'Allah, the Most Majestic, the Most Glorious, has said, "You must not think of those who are murdered for the cause of Allah as dead. . . ." (3:169) Fear and fright of doing Jihad, when there is demand for Jihad, and supporting to cause confusion is straying in religion, losses in the worldly matters, humiliation and lowliness. In it there is reason to deserve hellfire because of fleeing during advancing against the enemy and fighting. Allah, the Most Majestic, the Most Glorious, has said, "O believers, when you face the unbelievers during and advancing against the enemy you must not turn your backs to them." (8: 15)

29

'You must observe the commandments of Allah, the Most Majestic, the Most Glorious, in such conditions and exercise patience therein. It is honor, salvation and safety in this world and in the next world, which is full of frightening matters and fear. Allah, the Most Majestic, the Most Glorious, is not concerned about what the servant commits during the nights and days although His knowledge of their activities is subtle. All of these are in the book. My Lord does not become confused and forget. You must exercise patience, encourage others to exercise patience and ask Allah for help. You must settle your souls upon fighting. Maintain piety before Allah, the Most Majestic, the Most Glorious. Allah is with those who maintain piety and those who do good deeds.'"

H 8217, Ch. 13a, h 2
In the Hadith of ibn Ishaq the following is narrated from abu Sadiq who has said the following:

"I heard Ali, *'Alayhi al-Salam*, encourage people during three battle places. They were the battle of al-Jamal, Siffin and al-Nahrawan. He spoke to people and said, 'Servants of Allah, you must maintain piety before Allah and cast down your eyes, lower your voices, reduce your speeches, settle your soul on walking in the arena of war to do your best. Face the enemy, make best use of your weapons, strive to win, close up on to the enemy, force your enemy to flee and stay steadfast. Speak of Allah very often, perhaps you succeed. You must not quarrel among yourselves lest you fail and will be humiliated. Exercise patience; Allah is with those who exercise patience.'"

H 8218, Ch. 13a, h 3
In Hadith narrated from 'Abd al-Rahman ibn Jundab from his father who has said the following:

"Amir al-Mu'minin, *'Alayhi al-Salam*, in every battlefield we faced our enemies issued his commandments and said, 'You must not fight the people before they attack you; you by the grace of Allah possess authority and good cause. Your allowing them to attack you first is another valid point in support of the good cause. When you defeat them you must not pursue the fleeing, you must not hurt the wounded and you must not expose anyone's privacy.'"

H 8219, Ch. 13a, h 4
In a Hadith from Malik ibn A'yan the following is narrated:

"In the battle of Siffin, Amir al-Mu'minin, *'Alayhi al-Salam*, encouraging people said, 'Allah, the Most Majestic, the Most Glorious, has shown you a bargain and a deal which will save you from the painful torment. Belief in Allah and Jihad for the cause of Allah bring you very close to goodness. He makes your reward to be forgiveness of your sins and fine dwellings in paradise of Eden. Allah, the Most Majestic, the Most Glorious, has said, "Allah certainly loves those who fight for His cause and stand firm as solid and strong structures." (61:4)

'You must form yourselves in straight lines like solid and strong structures. Allow those with coats of arms to be in front and those without it to be the next. You must fix your back-teeth against each other; it makes the sword strike harder on the head of the enemy. Launch your spears, they move swiftly. Look with a lower angle; it ties down excitement and relaxes the heart. Silence voices; it keeps failure away and it is better for dignity. You must not allow your banners to incline and you must not remove them. You must not allow anyone other than brave people to carry them. The defenders of what is very important, who can exercise patience in difficult conditions, deserve to be the protectors. You must not mutilate those who are killed, and when you reach the men of the enemy you must not expose privacies, you must not enter any house, you must not take anything of their properties except what you find with their army. You must not disturb any woman with mistreatment; and if they use bad words against your honor, men, virtuous ones among you, it is because they suffer from physical, psychological and intellectual weakness. We were ordered to hold our hands back from them and they were pagan women. If a man would take upon women this would remain a flaw in him and in his descendents after him. You must take notice, people capable of protecting important matters deserve to carry the banner to provide it protection and others walk on the sides, behind and in front of them, and they must not lose sight of it (the banner) and must not remain far behind nor must they go far ahead to become separated. I pray to Allah to grant blessings to one who cooperates with his brother (in faith) with his person. One should not leave his peer against his brother so that his peer and his brother fight. This brings regret and humiliation. This inevitably becomes his (enemy's) fight against two people if he holds his hands back and has left his peer alone against his brother and has run away. He just looks to him and this one. If one does it he has angered Allah. You must not expose yourselves to the anger of Allah, the Most Majestic, the Most Glorious. "Running away does not benefit you even if you run away from death, or from being killed, because thereafter you will not benefit more than very little." (33:16) I swear by Allah, if you run away from the swords nearby, you will not escape from the swords later on. You must seek help by exercising patience and truthfulness. Victory comes only after exercising patience. You must do Jihad for the cause of Allah, the way Jihad should be done and there is no power without Allah.'

"He (the Imam), *'Alayhi al-Salam*, passed by the banner of the people of al-Sham and found them holding their position. He said, 'They will not move from their position without a blow which is hard and expels the soul out, and a blow that splits the skull, crushes the bones and makes the arms and the hands to fall off so that their forehead is crushed by the iron bars, their eyebrows scatter over their chest and chin. Where are people of patience and seekers of reward?' A group of the Muslims marched to them. The right flank of this group returned back to the center and exposed those opposite to them. He, *'Alayhi al-Salam*, moved forward until he reached them and said, 'I saw your attack and retreat away from your positioned lines. It was your moving that provided a chance for the unjust and tyrants of al-Sham. You are the top most among Arab and the great peak, the beauty of the nights because of your recitations of the Holy Quran and the callers from among the people of the truth, while the sinners are lost. Were it not for your advance after your retreat and your regrouping after giving way to the enemy, you could have become subject to what those fleeing from the enemy during an advancing operation need to face for turning their backs to the enemy. I would find you of those being destroyed. My concerns are to a small degree reduced and my chest to a small degree is comforted. This happened when I saw you gain the ground over them as they had against you and you were able to remove them from their positions as they had done to you. I saw you strike them with your sword until their first line was toppled over the last line like the camel driven away. You must exercise patience. Comfort has come upon you and Allah has made you steadfast with certainty, so that the defeated notice that he is making his Lord angry. He hates his own self. In fleeing from the battle there is the anger of Allah, the inevitable humiliation, and a remaining stigma and destruction of ways of one's living. There is no increase in the longevity of life of the fleeing person, no barrier between him and his day of death, and his Lord does not become happy with him. One's death with truthfulness before achieving such characteristics is better than remaining with them and dwelling upon them.'

"In another of his speech he, *'Alayhi al-Salam*, has said, 'When you face these people (the enemy) tomorrow do not fight them before they attack you. When they attack you then rise against them. You must remain calm and dignified. You must fix your backside teeth against the teeth of opposite side. It delivers a harder hit on the skulls. Keep your eyes lower and look at the foreheads of the horses and the faces of men. Reduce your speech; it keeps failure and argumentations away. You must settle your souls up facing the enemy openly, to advance and to attack. You must remain steadfast and speak of Allah, the Most Majestic, the Most Glorious, very often. One who protects what is important in difficult times is of the protecting people who keep their banner on the side and others walk on its sides and in front. When you attack do it with such coordination as if it is one man's attack. You must be protective; war is bitter. You must not allow them (enemy) to attack you after retreat or to advance to you after an unpredictable move. If one surrenders, accept it from him. Seek help from exercising patience; victory from Allah, the Most Majestic, the Most Glorious, follows exercising patience. Allah's servants will inherit the earth and the good end belongs to those who maintain piety before Allah.'"

H 8220, Ch. 13a, h 5

Ahmad ibn Muhammad al-Kufiy has narrated from ibn Jumhur from his father from Muhammad ibn Sinan from Mufaddal ibn 'Umar Also 'Abd Allah ibn 'Abd al-Rahman al-Asamm has narrated from Hariz from Muhammad ibn Muslim who has said the following:

"Abu 'Abd Allah, *'Alayhi al-Salam*, has said that Amir al-Mu'minin, *'Alayhi al-Salam*, has said to his companions, 'When you face the enemy during a war you must reduce your speech, remember Allah, the Most Majestic, the Most Glorious, very often. You must not turn your backs to them; Allah, the most Blessed, the most High, becomes angry with you and you will become subject to His anger. If you see one of your brother wounded or one who is captured by the enemy or the enemy is about to harm him, you must protect him with your persons.'"

Chapter 13(b)

H 8221, Ch. 13b, h 1
Muhammad ibn Yahya has narrated from Ahmad ibn Muhammad ibn 'Isa from al-Hassan ibn Mahbub from Hisham ibn Salim from certain individuals of his people who has said the following:

"Abu 'Abd Allah, *'Alayhi al-Salam*, about the Muslim prisoners, their children or servants (slaves), taken by the enemy who were afterwards rescued after a victorious fight, how should they be dealt with, abu 'Abd Allah, *'Alayhi al-Salam*, has said, 'The children of the Muslims do not become the share of the Muslims. They are returned to their parents, or brothers, or their guardian in the presence of witnesses. The slaves however become of the share of the Muslims. They are purchased with money from public treasury and their price is given to their owners.'"

H 8222, Ch. 13b, h 2
Ali ibn Ibrahim has narrated from his father from ibn abu 'Umayr from Hammad from al-Halabiy who has said the following:

"This is concerning my question before abu 'Abd Allah, *'Alayhi al-Salam*, about a man who is captured by the enemy with his properties. Then the Muslims captured him. 'How should they deal with his properties?' He (the Imam) replied, 'If they capture him before the enemies secure for themselves his properties, they should be returned to him. If they capture him after the enemies secure for themselves his properties, such properties become as *Fay'* for the Muslims and he deserves the right of having priority (*al-Shuf'*ah) to purchase them before anyone else does.'"

Chapter 14 - It is not Lawful for a Muslim to Reside in a War Zone

H 8223, Ch. 14, h 1
Ali ibn Ibrahim has narrated from his father, from al-Nawfaliy from al-Sakuniy who has said the following:

"Abu 'Abd Allah, *'Alayhi al-Salam*, has said that once, the Messenger of Allah dispatched an army against the Khath'am. When this army was overpowered by the enemy they sought protection by performing prostration. Certain ones among them were killed. When the news reached the Holy Prophet he said, 'You must pay half of the amount of compensation for their lives because of their prayer.' The Holy Prophet said, 'I certainly denounce one who is a Muslim and yet goes to reside in the war zone with the pagans.'"

Chapter 15(a) - Distribution of the Properties Captured from the Enemy

H 8224, Ch. 15a, h 1
Ali ibn Ibrahim has narrated from his father from ibn Mahbub from Mu'awiyah ibn Wahab who has said the following:

"This is concerning my question before abu 'Abd Allah, *'Alayhi al-Salam*, 'The Imam dispatches a small armed group against the enemy and they capture properties from the enemy. How should they distribute it?' He (the Imam) replied, 'If they fight under the command of a commander appointed by the Imam they should keep aside one-fifth thereof and distribute the rest among themselves. If they have not fought the pagans, then all that they have captured belongs to the Imam who distributes as he finds proper.'"

H 8225, Ch. 15a, h 2
Ali ibn Ibrahim has narrated from his father from and Ali ibn Muhammad all have narrated from al-Qasim ibn Muhammad from Sulayman ibn Dawud from Hafs ibn Ghiyath who has said the following:

"Certain ones of my brothers wrote to me to ask abu 'Abd Allah, *'Alayhi al-Salam*, about certain issue of tradition and I then wrote to the Imam. Of such question one was as follows. 'An army during a war captures certain amount of properties therein. Thereafter another army arrives and joins them before their coming out of the war zone. They do not face any enemy before returning to peaceful zone. Can the second army share in the captured properties?' He (the Imam) replied, 'Yes, they can share.' Another question was about an army in the ship where the horse owners do not use their horses. How do they distribute the properties captured from the enemy?' He (the Imam) replied, 'The share of the owner of horses is twice as much as that of those on foot.' I then asked, 'Even if they have not done any fighting when riding their horses?' He (the Imam) replied, 'Suppose if they are in an army and people on foot move first, fight and capture properties. How would they distribute the properties?' Is not the share of people with horses twice as much as the share of the people on foot who are the ones who had captured the properties and not the people who had horses?'"

H 8226, Ch. 15a, h 3
Abu Ali al-Ash'ariy has narrated from Muhammad ibn Salim from Ahmad ibn al-Al-Nadr ibn al-Suwayd from al-Husayn ibn 'Abd Allah from his father from his grandfather who has said the following:

"If a person had many horses during a war Amir al-Mu'minin, *'Alayhi al-Salam*, would give him the shares for two of his horses only."

H 8227, Ch. 15a, h 4
Ali ibn Ibrahim has narrated from his father from Hammad from certain individuals of his people from abu al-Hassan, *'Alayhi al-Salam*, who has said the following:

"One fifth of the properties captured is first kept aside to distribute as Allah, the Most Majestic, the Most Glorious, has instructed. The remaining properties are distributed among those who have taken part in the war in which the properties were captured and are the authority thereof. He (the Imam) said, 'The Imam has the right to have the best from such properties, the best slave-girls and the best animals, the best cloths and other items which are liked and desired for. Such items are for him (the Imam) before the distribution and before the deduction of the one-fifth. He (the Imam) then said, 'There is nothing for the fighters of the land and not even of that on which they have defeated the enemy except that much which contains the army. The Arabs do not have any share in the properties captured in the war even if they are of the fighters alongside the Imam. It is because the Messenger of Allah had made a treaty with them which said that they can live in their land and do not migrate. In exchange, they must mobilize against those of the enemies who may attack the Messenger of Allah and fight them and will not have any share in the properties captured from the enemy. It is a tradition established in them and others.

"The land which is taken by force and means such as mules and other means are of endowment that is left alone in the hands of those who revive them. They reach a settlement with governing authority on the basis of their abilities to pay back such as half, one-third or two-thirds and so on so that they can benefit and do not suffer losses.'"

H 8228, Ch. 15a, h 5
Muhammad ibn Yahya has narrated from Ahmad ibn Muhammad ibn 'Isa from Muhammad ibn 'Isa from Mansur from Hisham ibn Salim who has said the following:

"This is concerning my question before abu 'Abd Allah, *'Alayhi al-Salam*, 'Is it obligatory for the Arabs to do Jihad?' He (the Imam) replied, 'No, Jihad is not obligatory on them unless al-Islam is feared for.' I then asked, 'Do they have any share in al-Jizyah (taxes)?' He (the Imam) replied, 'No, they do not have any share therein.'"

H 8229, Ch. 15a, h 6
It is narrated from the same narrator (the narrator of the previous Hadith) from Ahmad ibn Muhammad from Muhammad ibn Yahya from Talhah ibn Zayd from abu 'Abd Allah from his ancestors, recipients of divine supreme covenant, who has said the following:

"About a man who joins an army who have captured properties but he has not taken part in fighting Amir al-Mu'minin, *'Alayhi al-Salam*, has said, 'These people are deprived (from reward). He however, commanded to give such people a share.'"

H 8230, Ch. 15a, h 7
Muhammad has narrated from Ahmad ibn Muhammad ibn 'Isa from Mansur ibn Hazim from Hisham ibn Salim who has said the following:

"This is concerning my question before abu 'Abd Allah, *'Alayhi al-Salam*, about properties gained during a war from the enemies. He (the Imam) replied, 'One-fifth is kept aside thereof which is for Allah and the Messenger. The rest is divided among the fighters and the guardian thereof.'"

H 8231, Ch. 15a, h 8
Ali ibn Ibrahim has narrated from his father from and Muhammad ibn Yahya from Muhammad ibn al-Husayn all from 'Uthman from ibn 'Isa from Sama'ah from one of the two Imams, recipients of divine supreme covenant, who has said the following:

"The Messenger of Allah took part in war in company of women so that they could nurse the wounded. He did not give them a share of the captured properties but he did so in an optional manner."

Chapter 15(b)

H 8232, Ch. 15b, h 1
Muhammad ibn Yahya has narrated from Ahmad ibn Muhammad ibn 'Isa from Mehran ibn Muhammad from 'Amr ibn abu Nasr who has said the following:

"I heard abu 'Abd Allah, *'Alayhi al-Salam*, saying, 'The best company is that which has four members. The best group for armed expeditions is that which consists of four hundred people. The best army is that which consists of four thousand soldiers. Any army that consists of ten thousand soldiers does not lose the fight because of its number (is not) small of soldiers."

H 8233, Ch. 15b, h 2
Muhammad ibn Ahmad has narrated from Ali ibn al-Hakam from Fudayl ibn Khaytham who has narrated the following:

Abu Ja'far, *'Alayhi al-Salam*, has said that the Messenger of Allah, *O Allah, grant compensation to Muhammad and his family worthy of their services to Your cause*, has said, 'An army of ten thousand cannot be defeated because of its size.'"

H 8234, Ch. 15b, h 3
Ali ibn Ibrahim has narrated from his father from and Ali ibn Muhammad from al-Qasim ibn Muhammad from Sulayman al-Minqariy who has said that narrated to him al-Nadr ibn Isma'il al-Balkhiy from abu Hamzah al-Thumaliy from Shahr ibn Hawshab who has said the following:

"Al-Hajjaj asked me about the Messenger of Allah's mobilization for the wars in which he, *'Alayhi al-Salam*, took part. I said, 'The Messenger of Allah, *O Allah, grant compensation to Muhammad and his family worthy of their services to Your cause*, mobilized for Badr with three hundred and thirteen people. He mobilized for Uhud with six hundred and for al-Khandaq (Battle of Ditches) with nine hundred people.' He asked, 'Who has said it?' I replied, 'Ja'far ibn Muhammad, *'Alayhi al-Salam*.' He then said, 'By Allah whoever adopts a way other than his way is lost.'"

Chapter 15(c)

H 8235, Ch. 15c, h 1
A number of our people have narrated from Sahl ibn Ziyad from Ja'far ibn Muhammad from ibn al-Qaddah from his father, Maymun who has said the following:

"Abu 'Abd Allah, *'Alayhi al-Salam*, has said that whenever Amir al-Mu'minin wanted to take part in a war he would recite the following supplications:

"O Lord, You have made a way of Your ways public and have placed Your pleasure in it and have called Your friends toward it. You have made it the most noble of Your ways to You in matters of reward, the most honorable before You in matters of endings and of the most beloved ones before You in terms of its direction. In this way You then purchased the souls of the believing people and their properties in exchange for paradise. They are the believers who fight in the way of Allah, they eliminate the enemy and themselves are killed because of the promise of Allah which is the true promise. O Lord, make me one of those from whom You have purchased in this way their souls and then they made their promise and agreement with You to come true. Make me of those who do not flee from the battle and those who do not disregard their promise, and do not replace me with others. Make me of those who do so in response to Your love and to become closer thereby to You. O Lord, make it to be the end of my deed, and turning of my life to its end. O Lord, grant me therein for Your sake with it a battle, which will make me deserve Your pleasure and remove thereby my sins. O Lord, place me among the living (martyrs) who receive sustenance from You because of the acts of the enemy who is disobedient. Make it happen under the banner of truth and the flag of guidance when advancing to support them (the believers) without turning my back to the enemy, or move around with doubts. O Lord, I seek Your protection in the battle against cowardice in frightening conditions and against weakness during the exchanges with champions. I seek Your protection against the sins that turn good deeds invalid, the sins that feed doubts or make me advance without certainty after which my efforts end in destruction and my deeds become unacceptable.'"

Chapter 16 - The Slogan

H 8236, Ch. 16, h 1

Ali ibn Ibrahim has narrated from his father from Ahmad ibn Muhammad ibn abu Nasr from Mu'awiyah ibn 'Ammar who has said the following:

"Abu 'Abd Allah, *'Alayhi al-Salam*, has said that our slogan on the day Badr was, 'O victory of Allah, come close! come close!' The slogan of Muslims on the day of 'Uhud was, 'O victory of Allah, come close!' On the day of banu al-Nadir it was, 'O Holy Spirit, bring comfort!' On the day of banu Qaynaqa' it was, 'O our Lord, no one is able to defeat You!' On the day of Taef it was, 'O Ridwan! (name of a certain angel)' Our slogan on the day of Hunayn was, 'O banu 'Abd Allah! O banu 'Abd Allah!' On the day of al-Ahzab it was, 'Ha Mim, They cannot see!' On the day of banu Quraydah it was, 'O Peace Giver, make them surrender!' On the day of al-Muraysi' which is also called the day of banu al-Mustliq it was, 'Is the matter not in the hands of Allah!' On the day of al-Hudaybiyah it was, 'May Allah condemn the unjust!' On the day of al-Khaybar, also called the day of al-Qamus it was, 'O Ali, come upon them from on high!' On the day of victory it was, 'We are the servants of Allah, indeed, indeed!' On the day of Tabuk it was, 'O the One! O self-sufficient!' On the day of banu al-Maluh it was, 'Higher, higher!' On the day of Siffin it was, 'O Assistance of Allah!' The slogan of al-Husayn, *'Alayhi al-Salam*, was, 'O Muhammad!' Our slogan is, 'O Muhammad!'"

H 8237, Ch. 16, h 2

Ali ibn Ibrahim has narrated from his father from certain persons of his people from al-Sakuniy who has said the following:

"Abu 'Abd Allah, *'Alayhi al-Salam*, has said that certain people from Muzaynah came to the Holy Prophet. He asked, 'What is your slogan?' They replied it is 'unlawful'. He said, 'No, it is 'lawful'."

H 8238, Ch. 16, h 3

It also is narrated that the slogan of the Muslims on the day of Badr was, 'O Victorious, Higher!' The slogan of al-Muhajirun on the day of 'Uhud was, 'O banu 'Abd Allah, (you must strive) O banu 'Abd al-Rahman!' The slogan of al-Aws was, 'O banu 'Abd Allah!'"

Chapter 17 - The Virtue of Maintaining Horses, Racing and Sharp Shooting Contests

H 8239, Ch. 17, h 1
A number of our people have narrated from Ahmad ibn Muhammad from more than one narrator from Aban from Zurarah who has said the following:
"Abu 'Abd Allah, *'Alayhi al-Salam*, has said that horses were wild in Arab lands. Once, Ibrahim and Isma'il *'Alayhima al-Salam*, climbed on Jiyad hills. They then called, 'O horses come home.' He (the Imam) then said, 'Every horse then allowed the two of them to touch their legs and forehead.'"

H 8240, Ch. 17, h 2
It is narrated from the narrator of the previous Hadith from Ali ibn al-Hakam from 'Umar ibn Aban who has said the following:
"Abu 'Abd Allah, *'Alayhi al-Salam*, has said that the Messenger of Allah, *O Allah, grant compensation to Muhammad and his family worthy of their services to Your cause*, has said, 'Goodness is written on the foreheads of the horses to remain up to the Day of Judgment.'"

H 8241, Ch. 17, h 3
It is narrated from the narrator of the previous Hadith from ibn Faddal from Tha'labah from Mu'ammar who has said the following:
"I heard abu Ja'far, *'Alayhi al-Salam*, say the following: 'All of goodness is written on the foreheads of the horses to remain up to the Day of Judgment.'"

H 8242, Ch. 17, h 4
It is narrated from the narrator of the previous Hadith from al-Qasim ibn Muhammad from his grandfather, al-Hassan ibn Rashid from Ya'qub ibn Ja'far ibn Ibrahim al-Ja'fariy who has said the following:
"I heard abu al-Hassan, *'Alayhi al-Salam*, saying, 'If one maintains a horse of pure breed, three of his sins will be deleted every day and ten good deeds will be written in his favor. If one maintains a horse of mixed breed, two of his bad deeds will be deleted every day and seven good deeds will be written in his favor. If one maintains a mule for beauty or for his needs or use in his defense against the enemy, one of his sins will be deleted every day and six good deeds will be written in his favor.'"

H 8243, Ch. 17, h 5
Muhammad ibn Yahya has narrated from Ahmad ibn Muhammad ibn 'Isa from Muhammad ibn Yahya from Talhah ibn Zayd from abu 'Abd Allah, from his father, *'Alayhi al-Salam*, who has said the following:
"The Messenger of Allah, *O Allah, grant compensation to Muhammad and his family worthy of their services to Your cause*, made certain horses that were kept on a special diet to race from al-Hafya' to the Masjid of banu Zurayq and three of the selected ones came ahead of the others. He (the Messenger of Allah) rewarded one palm tree with its fruits to the one that came first, one palm tree with its fruits to al-Musalliy (the racing horse which comes second) and one palm tree with fruits to the one that had come third."

Ali ibn Ibrahim has narrated from his father from Muhammad ibn Yahya from Talhah ibn Zayd from abu 'Abd Allah, *'Alayhi al-Salam*, a similar Hadith."

H 8244, Ch. 17, h 6

Al-Husayn ibn Muhammad al-Ash'ariy has narrated from Mu'alla' ibn Muhammad from al-Washsha' from 'Abd Allah ibn Sinan who has said the following:

"I heard abu 'Abd Allah, *'Alayhi al-Salam*, saying, 'Contest is permissible only in the case of animals with Khuf (feet of camels), Hafir, (feet of horses and the like) and in the case of sharp-shooting.'"

H 8245, Ch. 17, h 7

Muhammad ibn Yahya has narrated from Ghiyath ibn Ibrahim from abu 'Abd Allah, from his father, from Ali ibn Al-Husayn, recipients of divine supreme covenant, who has said the following:

"The Messenger of Allah, *O Allah, grant compensation to Muhammad and his family worthy of their services to Your cause*, made the reward for horse to race for a contest in the form of Awaqiy (a certain weight) of silver."

H 8246, Ch. 17, h 8

Ali ibn Ibrahim has narrated from his father from al-Nawfaliy from al-Sakuniy who has said the following:

"Abu 'Abd Allah, *'Alayhi al-Salam*, has said that the Messenger of Allah, *O Allah, grant compensation to Muhammad and his family worthy of their services to Your cause*, has said, 'If a horse, in enemy's territory, or during Jihad in the way of Allah, refuses to move when led or driven, it should be slaughtered and one must not instead cut off its legs from the knees.'"

H 8247, Ch. 17, h 9

He the narrator of the previous Hadith has narrated from through the chain of his narrators who has said the following:

"Abu 'Abd Allah, *'Alayhi al-Salam*, has said that on the day of Mutah, Ja'far ibn abu Talib had a horse. When they came face to face with the enemy he disembarked from his horse and cut the legs of his horse with his sword, and it was the first such incident in al-Islam."

H 8248, Ch. 17, h 10

Al-Husayn ibn Muhammad has narrated from Ahmad ibn Ishaq from Sa'dan from abu Basir who has said the following:

"Abu 'Abd Allah, *'Alayhi al-Salam*, has said that the angels do not attend anything except (horse racing) contest and man's playing with his wife."

H 8249, Ch. 17, h 11

Muhammad ibn Yahya has narrated from Ahmad ibn Muhammad from Muhammad ibn Yahya from Talhah ibn Zayd from abu 'Abd Allah who has narrated the following from his ancestors:

"Sharp shooting is an arrow of the arrows of al-Islam."

H 8250, Ch. 17, h 12

Muhammad ibn Yahya has narrated from 'Imran ibn Musa' from al-Hassan ibn Tarif from 'Abd Allah ibn al-Mughirah in a marfu' manner the following:

"About the words of Allah, 'Prepare and maintain whatever power and horses you can. . . .' (8:60) the Messenger of Allah, *O Allah, grant compensation to*

Muhammad and his family worthy of their services to Your cause, has said, "It is a reference to sharp-shooting."

H 8251, Ch. 17, h 13

Muhammad has narrated from Muhammad ibn Ahmad from Ali ibn 'Isma'il in a marfu' manner the following:

"He (the Imam), *'Alayhi al-Salam*, has said that the Messenger of Allah, *O Allah, grant compensation to Muhammad and his family worthy of their services to Your cause*, has said, 'You should learn horse riding and sharp-shooting. I like your learning sharp-shooting more than your horse riding.' He then said, 'All playing of believers' is falsehood except three things: horse training, sharp-shooting from his bow and playing with his wife because they are right. However, Allah, the most Majestic, the most Glorious, with the arrow sends three to paradise: one who makes the arrow, one who provides support with it for the cause of Allah and one who shoots it for the cause of Allah.'"

H 8252, Ch. 17, h 14

Ali ibn Ibrahim has narrated from his father from ibn abu 'Umayr from Hafs who has said the following:

"Abu 'Abd Allah, *'Alayhi al-Salam*, has said, 'Contest is permissible only in racing animals with Khuf (feet like camel) or Hafir (with feet like horses and the like) and in sharp-shooting."

H 8253, Ch. 17, h 15

Ali ibn Ibrahim has narrated from his father from ibn abu 'Umayr from Hafs ibn al-Bakhtariy who has said the following:

"Abu 'Abd Allah, *'Alayhi al-Salam*, would take part in horse racing contests and sharp-shooting."

H 8254, Ch. 17, h 16

Ali ibn Ibrahim has narrated from his father from and Muhammad ibn Yahya from Talhah ibn Zayd who has said the following:

"Abu 'Abd Allah, *'Alayhi al-Salam*, has said that the pagans attacked the pasture area of al-Madinah and an announcer announced, 'How bad is this morning!' The Messenger of Allah, *O Allah, grant compensation to Muhammad and his family worthy of their services to Your cause*, heard it when among people with horses. He rode his horse in pursuit of the enemy. The first of his companions who reached him was abu Qatadah on his horse. Both sides of the saddle of the horse of the Messenger of Allah were made of palm tree fibers and it was not fanciful at all. They searched the enemy but did not find anyone and the group of people on horses came one after the other. Abu Qatadah said, 'O Messenger of Allah, the enemy has turned back; if you consider it proper allow us to race our horses for a contest.' He said, 'That is fine.' They raced and the Messenger of Allah became the winner among them. He then turned to them and said, 'I am the descendent of 'Awatik, three women from Quraysh called 'Atikah.' This is al-Jawad al-Bahr (fine horse of the sea that runs in wide manner).'" *

Chapter 18 - Man's Defending Himself Against the Thief

H 8255, Ch. 18, h 1

Ahmad ibn Muhammad al-Kufiy has narrated from Muhammad ibn Ahmad al-Qalanisiy from Ahmad ibn al-Fadl from 'Abd Allah ibn Jabalah from Fazarah from Anas or Haytham ibn al-Bara' who has said the following:

"I asked abu Ja'far, *'Alayhi al-Salam*, about a thief who may enter my house to harm my life or properties.' He (the Imam) said, 'Eliminate him. Allah and those who hear me are my witness; his blood (life) is on my neck (my responsibility).'"

H 8256, Ch. 18, h 2

Ali ibn Ibrahim has narrated from his father from al-Nawfaliy from al-Sakuniy who has said the following:

"Abu 'Abd Allah, *'Alayhi al-Salam*, has said that Amir al-Mu'minin, *'Alayhi al-Salam*, has said, 'Allah, the most Majestic, the most Glorious, hates a man who does not fight back the thief who has entered his house.'"

H 8257, Ch. 18, h 3

The narrator of the previous through his chain of narrators has said the following:

"Once a man came to Amir al-Mu'minin, *'Alayhi al-Salam*, and said, 'O Amir al-Mu'minin, a thief entered in the house of my wife and stole her ornaments. Amir al-Mu'minin, *'Alayhi al-Salam*, said, 'Had he (the thief) entered the house of the son of a clean woman he would not agree with less than overwhelming him (thief) by his sword.'"

H 8258, Ch. 18, h 4

Ali ibn Ibrahim has narrated from his father from ibn abu 'Umayr from Aban ibn 'Uthaman from a man formal-Halabiy who has said the following:

"Abu 'Abd Allah, *'Alayhi al-Salam*, has said that Amir al-Mu'minin, *'Alayhi al-Salam*, has said, 'If a fighting thief enters your house, eliminate him. Whatever responsibility his blood (life) may bring is on my neck (my responsibility).'"

Chapter 19 - The Case of one Murdered over His Stolen Property

H 8259, Ch. 19, h 1

Muhammad ibn Yahya has narrated from Ahmad ibn Muhammad ibn 'Isa from 'Abd al-Rahman ibn abu Najran from 'Abd Allah ibn Sinan who has said the following:

"Abu 'Abd Allah, *'Alayhi al-Salam*, has said that the Messenger of Allah, *O Allah, grant compensation to Muhammad and his family worthy of their services to Your cause*, has said, 'If one is murdered over his stolen property he is a martyr.'"

H 8260, Ch. 19, h 2

It is narrated from the narrator of the previous Hadith from abu Maryam from Abu Ja'far, *'Alayhi al-Salam*, who has said the following:

"The Messenger of Allah, *O Allah, grant compensation to Muhammad and his family worthy of their services to Your cause*, has said, 'If one is murdered over his stolen property he is a martyr.' He (the Imam) then said, 'O abu Maryam, do you know what is 'murdered over his stolen property'? I replied, 'I pray to Allah to keep me in the service of your cause, it is when a man is murdered defending his family, property and similar things.' He (the Imam) said, 'It is of fiqh (proper understanding) to know the truth.'"

H 8261, Ch. 19, h 3

It is narrated from the narrator of the previous Hadith from Ahmad ibn Muhammad from Ali ibn al-Hakam from Al-Husayn ibn abu al-'Ala' who has said the following:

"This is concerning my question before abu 'Abd Allah, *'Alayhi al-Salam*, about a man who fights to defend his property. He (the Imam) said, 'The Messenger of Allah, *O Allah, grant compensation to Muhammad and his family worthy of their services to Your cause*, has said, "If one is murdered when defending his property he is like a martyr."' I then asked, 'Is fighting better or not fighting?' He (the Imam) said, 'Were it to happen to me I would not fight but leave him alone.'"

H 8262, Ch. 19, h 4

It is narrated from the narrator of the previous Hadith from Ahmad from al-Washsha' from Safwan ibn Yahya from Artat ibn Habib al-Asadiy from a man from Ali ibn Al-Husayn, *'Alayhi al-Salam*, , who has said the following:

"If one is subjected to transgression over the charity of his property and he fights back and is murdered he is a martyr."

H 8263, Ch. 19, h 5

A number of our people have narrated from Ahmad ibn Muhammad from ibn Khalid from his father from those whom he has mentioned (in his book) from al-Rida, *'Alayhi al-Salam*:

"If a man is on a journey and with him is his slave-girl. Certain people come and want to take his slave-girl from him. Should he try to stop them even if he fears for losing his life?' He (the Imam) replied, 'Yes, he should try.' I then asked, 'Is it so also if a woman is with him?' He (the Imam) replies, 'Yes, it is.' I then asked, 'Is it so also if it is his mother, daughter of uncle and relatives. Should he stop such people even if he fears for losing his life?' He (the Imam) replied, 'Yes, it is so also.' I then asked, 'Is it so also if it is property which they want to take during one's journey and must stop them even if he fears for his life?' He (the Imam) replied, 'Yes, so also it is.'"

Chapter 20(a) - The Excellence of Martyrdom

H 8264, Ch. 20a, h 1

Muhammad ibn Yahya has narrated from Ahmad ibn Muhammad from Muhammad ibn Khalid from Sa'd ibn Sa'd who has said the following:

"I once asked abu al-Hassan al-Rida, *'Alayhi al-Salam*, about the words of Amir al-Mu'minin, *'Alayhi al-Salam*, 'I swear by Allah, enduring one thousand strikes by the sword is easier than dying on the bed.' He (the Imam) said, 'It means 'for the cause of Allah.'"

H 8265, Ch. 20a, h 2

Ali ibn Ibrahim has narrated from his father from al-Nawfaliy from al-Sakuniy who has said the following:

"Abu 'Abd Allah, *'Alayhi al-Salam*, has said that the Messenger of Allah, *O Allah, grant compensation to Muhammad and his family worthy of their services to Your cause*, has said, 'Over every virtuous deed is a virtuous deed until one is murdered for the cause of Allah; thereafter there is no other virtuous deed which can stand over and before it.'"

H 8266, Ch. 20a, h 3

A number of our people have narrated from Ahmad ibn Muhammad from ibn Khalid from 'Uthaman ibn 'Isa from 'Anbasah from abu Hamzah who has said the following:

"I heard abu Ja'far, *'Alayhi al-Salam*, saying, 'Ali ibn al-Husayn, *'Alayhi al-Salam*, would say, "The Messenger of Allah, *O Allah, grant compensation to Muhammad and his family worthy of their services to Your cause*, has said, 'No drop is more beloved to Allah than the drop of blood spilled in the way of Allah.'"'"

H 8267, Ch. 20a, h 4

Ali ibn Ibrahim has narrated from his father from ibn Mahbub who in a marfu' has said the following:

"On the day of Jamal Amir al-Mu'minin, *'Alayhi al-Salam*, delivered a speech. He praised and glorified Allah; then said, 'O people, I came to these people, called them and presented proof in support of my truthfulness. They then called me for a contest. Their mothers will certainly weep for them; I never was and will not feel threatened by war or intimidated by the pounding of swords. No one is able to defeat experience. They should act thunderously with lightening to frighten people other than me. I am abu al-Hassan. I am the one who turned their sharp edge very blunt and dispersed their large united group. With this kind of heart I am ready to face my enemy. I have firm belief in the promise of my Lord of victory, His support and triumph. I have firm belief in my Lord. I have not even a shred of doubt about the truthfulness of my cause. O people, death does not miss people living at home and those who run away cannot defeat it. There is no escape from death. If one does not die he is killed and the best death is being killed. I swear by the One in whose hand is my soul, enduring a thousand poundings of the sword is easier for me than dying in bed. It is very strange of Talhah who was very close to the son of 'Affan, until the time he was killed soon thereafter he extended his right hand to me to pledge allegiance voluntarily; then he disregarded his pledging allegiance with me. O Allah, clinch him without respite. Zubayr also disregarded his pledge of allegiance with me as well as the good relationship that was his obligation to maintain with me as relatives. He supported my enemies, therefore, O Lord, suffice me against him as You deem proper.'"

H 8268, Ch. 20a, h 5

Ali ibn Ibrahim has narrated from his father from al-Nawfaliy from al-Sakuniy who has said the following:

"Abu 'Abd Allah, *'Alayhi al-Salam*, has said that someone asked the Holy Prophet, *O Allah, grant compensation to Muhammad and his family worthy of their services to Your cause*, 'Why is a martyr not examined and tried in his grave?' The Holy Prophet, replied, 'It is because the sword over his head is a sufficient examinition and trial.'"

H 8269, Ch. 20a, h 6
Al-Husayn ibn Muhammad has narrated from Ahmad ibn Ishaq from Sa'dan from abu Basir who has said the following:
"Abu 'Abd Allah, *'Alayhi al-Salam*, has said, 'If one is killed for the cause of Allah, Allah will not show him any of his sins."

H 8270, Ch. 20a, h 7
Muhammad ibn Yahya has narrated from Muhammad ibn Al-Husayn from Ali ibn al-Nu'man from Suwayd al-Qalanisiy from Sama'ah from abu Basir who has said the following:
"I asked abu 'Abd Allah, *'Alayhi al-Salam*, 'Which kind of Jihad is more virtuous?' He (the Imam) replied, 'It is the one in which the legs of one's horse are cut off and his own blood is spilled for the cause of Allah.'"

Chapter 20(b)

H 8271, Ch. 20b, h 1
A number of our people have narrated from Ahmad ibn Muhammad from ibn Khalid from ibn Faddal from abu Jamilah from Sa'd ibn Tarif from al-Asbagh ibn Nubatah who has said the following:
"'Amir al-Mu'minin, *'Alayhi al-Salam*, has said, 'Allah, the most Majestic, the most Glorious, laughs (loves) at a man in a group of soldiers who are attacked by wild beasts or thieves and he defends them so they can pass by.'"

H 8272, Ch. 20b, h 2
Ali ibn Ibrahim has narrated from his father from al-Nawfaliy from al-Sakuniy who has said the following:
"The Messenger of Allah *O Allah, grant compensation to Muhammad and his family worthy of their services to Your cause*, has said, 'Your helping a weak person is the best charity.'"

H 8273, Ch. 20b, h 3
Muhammad ibn Yahya has narrated from Ahmad ibn Muhammad ibn 'Isa from Ali ibn al-Hakam from Muthanna' from Fitr ibn Khalifah from Muhammad ibn Ali ibn Al-Husayn from his father, recipients of divine supreme covenant, who has said the following:
"'Amir al-Mu'minin, *'Alayhi al-Salam*, has said, 'The Messenger of Allah, *O Allah, grant compensation to Muhammad and his family worthy of their services to Your cause*, has said, "If one defends a community of Muslims in the matters of their water or fire, paradise becomes necessary (allotted) for him.'"

Chapter 20(c)

H 8274, Ch. 20c, h 1
Ali ibn Ibrahim has narrated from his father from ibn abu 'Umayr from Yahya al-Tawil who has said the following:

44

"Abu 'Abd Allah, *'Alayhi al-Salam*, has said, 'Allah, the most Majestic, the most Glorious, has not made the tongue to extend and the hands to withhold but that He has made them to extend and withhold together."

Chapter 21 - Commanding others what is Obligatory and to Prohibit them from doing Evil

H 8275, Ch. 21, h 1

A number of our people have narrated from Ahmad ibn Muhammad from ibn Khalid from certain persons of our people from Bashir ibn 'Abd Allah from abu 'Ismah Qadiy of Marve from Jabir who has said the following:

"Abu Ja'far, *'Alayhi al-Salam*, has said, 'During the last era of time there will be a people who are followed by a certain people who just show off. They worship and perform rituals as youngsters with insufficient understanding and dimwittedness. They do not deem asking others to do good and prohibiting evil as necessary unless doing so is totally harmless for them. They seek for themselves permissions and excuses and follow the mistakes of the scholars and their invalid deeds. They go for *Salat* (prayer) and fasting and things that do not affect them in matters of their lives and properties. If performing *Salat* (prayer) would affect their other activities about their properties and persons, they disregard it just as they disregard highest quality obligations and the noblest ones.

'Asking people to do good and to prohibit them from committing evil is a great obligation by which responsibilities are fulfilled. In such case the anger of Allah, the most Majestic, the most Glorious, becomes complete upon them. His torment encompasses them; thus, even virtuous people are destroyed in the location of the sinful ones and the children along with the grown-up ones. Asking others to do good and prohibiting them from evil is the path of the prophets and the method of the virtuous ones. It is a great responsibility with which obligations are fulfilled and religions are protected, earnings become lawful, usurped properties are retrieved, the land is developed, justice is made available for even the enemies and the matters are kept upright. You must then dislike evil in your hearts, reject it with your tongues, strike it against their faces and do not fear anyone's blames in matters about Allah. If people committing evil accepted your advice and returned to the truth then that is fine. "Blameworthy are those who do injustice to people and rebel in the land without any truthful cause, for them there will be painful punishment." (42: 42) Against such people you must fight with your person and hate them in your hearts without wanting domination, gaining properties or victory through injustice. You must continue until they come to the command of Allah and to obey Him.'

He (the Imam) said, 'Allah, the most Majestic, the most Glorious, sent revelation to prophet Shu'ayb *'Alayhi al-Salam*, "I want to punish one hundred thousand people from your followers, forty thousand of the evil doers and sixty thousand of the good ones." He asked, "O Lord, these are the evil doers but what about the good ones?" Allah, the most Majestic, the most Glorious, sent him revelation that said, "They stopped giving the good advice to the evil doers and did not become angry because of My becoming angry with them.""""

H 8276, Ch. 21, h 2
Ali ibn Ibrahim has narrated from his father from ibn abu 'Umayr from a group of our people who has said the following:
"Abu 'Abd Allah, *'Alayhi al-Salam*, has said, 'A people, who does not take back the rights of the weak ones among them from the stronger ones, without causing any harm, can never become holy.'"

H 8277, Ch. 21, h 3
A number of our people have narrated from Ahmad ibn Muhammad from ibn Khalid from Muhammad ibn 'Isa from Muhammad ibn 'Umar ibn 'Arafah who has said the following:
"I heard abu al-Hassan, *'Alayhi al-Salam*, saying, 'You must ask (command) others to do good and prohibit them to commit evil, otherwise, the evil ones among you will be made your rulers and then the virtuous ones among you pray and their prayers will not be answered.'"

H 8278, Ch. 21, h 4
Muhammad ibn Yahya has narrated from Ahmad ibn Muhammad from Ali ibn al-Nu'man from 'Abd Allah ibn Muskan from Dawud ibn Farqad from abu Sa'id al-Zuhriy from abu Ja'far and abu 'Abd Allah, *'Alayhi al-Salam*, who have said the following:
"Abu 'Abd Allah, *'Alayhi al-Salam*, has said, 'Woe upon a people who do not consider asking others to do good and prohibiting them from evil as part of the religion of Allah.'"

H 8279, Ch. 21, h 5
The narrator of the previous Hadith through his chain of narrators has said the following:
"Abu Ja'far, *'Alayhi al-Salam*, has said, 'A people, who consider asking others to do good and prohibiting them from evil, a blame-worthy act, are a terribly evil people.'"

H 8280, Ch. 21, h 6
A number of our people have narrated from Sahl ibn Ziyad from 'Abd al-Rahman ibn abu Najran from 'Asim ibn Humayd from abu Hamzah from Yahya ibn 'Aqil from Hassan who has said the following:
"Amir al-Mu'minin, *'Alayhi al-Salam*, once delivered a sermon. He first praised and glorified Allah. Thereafter he said, 'People before were destroyed because when they committed sins the Rabbis and Monks did not stop them from committing such deeds. When they continued committing disobedience and the Rabbis and Monks did not prohibit them, torments descended upon them. They then commanded others to do good and prohibited to commit evil, they found this did not make the time of their death closer and nor did it reduce their sustenance. The command comes from the sky to the earth, like the drops of rain, to everyone as Allah measures for it (soul) in matters of increase and reduction. If one of you is affected in matters of family, property or life and finds all such things with his brother in abundance, it should not become matters of trial for him. A Muslim is free of all forms of treachery as long as acts of lowliness do not take place from him (through his hands), about the mention of

which he remains fearful. On the other hand, people of lowly manners remain interested in lowly acts like a gambler who waits for the hit by the first winning arrow which brings him gains and fends off from him the loss. The Muslim who is free of treachery expects from Allah, the most High, one of the two forms of gains. It is either the call from Allah, thus what is with Allah for him is better, or sustenance from Allah. So he has a family, property with religion and valuable status. Wealth and children are worldly plantations but good deeds are plantations for the next life. At certain times Allah places both of them together for certain people. You must remain anxious about your relationship with Allah just as He has told you to be anxious about such relationship. You must worry, without shortcomings and about your status before Him. You must act without showing off and seeking popularity; those who act for something other than Allah, He leaves him to the one for whom he has acted. I pray to Allah to lead us to the destinations of the martyrs, living of those who have gained salvation and the company of the prophets (of Allah).'"

H 8281, Ch. 21, h 7

Ali ibn Ibrahim has narrated from his father from Ali ibn Asbat from abu Ishaq al-Khurasaniy from certain persons of his people who has said the following:

"He (the Imam) has said, 'Allah, the most Majestic, the most Glorious, sent revelation to Dawud (David), *'Alayhi al-Salam*, that said, 'I forgave your sins and placed the blame thereof on the Israelites.' He (Dawud) asked, 'How can that be, O Lord? You do not do injustice. He (the Lord) replied, 'Because they did not express disappointment for what you had done.'"

(This Hadith is addressed to Dawud but it is meant to apply to others. It is one of the cases where the popular expression, 'I address you O slave-girl, but you, the neighbor woman listen.')

H 8282, Ch. 21, h 8

Muhammad ibn Yahya has narrated from al-Husayn ibn Ishaq from Ali ibn Mahziyar from al-Nadr ibn al-Suwayd from Durust ibn abu Mansur from certain individuals of his people who has said the following:

"Abu 'Abd Allah, *'Alayhi al-Salam*, has said that Allah, the Most Majestic, the Most Glorious, once sent two angels to a city to turn it upside down on the people therein. When they came to the city, they found a man praying to Allah with great concern and desperation. One of the angels then asked the other, 'Do you see this person praying?' The other angel replied, 'Yes, I have seen him but I must obey the command which my Lord has issued.' The other angel said, 'No, I will not do anything before asking my Lord about it.' This angel returned to the presence of Allah, the most Blessed, the most High, and said, 'O Lord, I went to the city and found there one of Your servants, so and so praying to You and asking You in desperation and in a helpless condition.' The Lord said, 'You must do as you were commanded to do; he is a man who has never even frowned for My sake as an expression of his anger against evil deeds."

H 8283, Ch. 21, h 9

Humayd ibn Ziyad has narrated from Al-Husayn ibn Muhammad from Sama'ah from more than narrators from Aban ibn 'Uthaman from 'Abd Allah ibn Muhammad who has said the following:

"Abu 'Abd Allah, *'Alayhi al-Salam*, has said that once a man from Khath'am came to the Messenger of Allah, *O Allah, grant compensation to Muhammad and his family worthy of their services to Your cause*, and asked, 'O Messenger of Allah, what is most virtuous in al-Islam?' He (the Messenger of Allah) replied, 'It is belief in Allah.' He then asked, 'What is most virtuous thereafter?' He, the Messenger of Allah, replied, 'It is maintaining good relations with relatives.' He asked, 'What is most important thereafter?' He, the Messenger of Allah, replied, 'It is asking others to do what is good and prohibit them to commit evil.' The narrator has said that the man then asked, 'What is the most hated act in the sight of Allah?' He, the Messenger of Allah, replied, 'It is considering things as partners of Allah.' He then asked, 'What is most hated thereafter?' He, the Messenger of Allah, replied, 'It is cutting off good relations with relatives.' He then asked, 'What is most hated thereafter?' He, the Messenger of Allah, replied, 'It is asking people to commit evil and prohibit them from doing good.'"

H 8284, Ch. 21, h 10

Ali ibn Ibrahim has narrated from his father from al-Nawfaliy from al-Sakuniy who has said the following:

"Abu 'Abd Allah, *'Alayhi al-Salam*, has said that abu 'Abd Allah, *'Alayhi al-Salam*, has said that Amir al-Mu'minin, *'Alayhi al-Salam*, has said, 'The Messenger of Allah, *O Allah, grant compensation to Muhammad and his family worthy of their services to Your cause*, had commanded us to meet sinful people with a frowning face.'"

H 8285, Ch. 21, h 11

A number of our people have narrated from Ahmad ibn 'Abd Allah from Ya'qub ibn Yazid in a Marfu' manner has said the following:

"Abu 'Abd Allah, *'Alayhi al-Salam*, has said, 'Asking people to do good and prohibiting them from committing evil are two creatures of the creatures of Allah. Those who support them, Allah gives them respect and Allah betrays those who betray these two creatures of Him."

H 8286, Ch. 21, h 12

Muhammad ibn Yahya has narrated from Ahmad ibn Muhammad ibn 'Isa from Muhammad ibn Yahya from Ghiyath ibn Ibrahim who has said the following:

"Abu 'Abd Allah, *'Alayhi al-Salam*, when seeing a quarrelling group of people would not pass by without always saying three times loudly, 'You must maintain piety in the presence of Allah.'"

H 8287, Ch. 21, h 13

A number of our people have narrated from Ahmad ibn Muhammad ibn Khalid from Muhammad ibn 'Isa from Muhammad ibn 'Arafah who has said the following:

"I heard abu al-Hassan, al-Rida, *'Alayhi al-Salam*, saying, 'The Messenger of Allah, *O Allah, grant compensation to Muhammad and his family worthy of their services to Your cause*, would say, "When my followers postpone asking others to do good and prohibit them from committing evil they, in so doing, allow affliction to befall upon them from Allah.""""

H 8288, Ch. 21, h 14
Ali ibn Ibrahim has narrated from Harun ibn Muslim from Mas'adah ibn Sadaqah who has said the following:

"Abu 'Abd Allah, *'Alayhi al-Salam,* has said, 'The Holy Prophet, *O Allah, grant compensation to Muhammad and his family worthy of their services to Your cause,* has said, "What will you do when your women will become corrupt, your young people sinful and you will not ask others to do good and prohibit them to commit evil?" They asked, "Will such things happen, O Messenger of Allah?" He, the Messenger of Allah, replied, "Yes, even worse than this will happen. What will you do when you ask others to commit evil and prohibit them from doing good?" It then was asked, "Will such things happen, O Messenger of Allah?" He, the Messenger of Allah, replied, "Yes, even worse than this will happen. What will you do when you see good things as bad and evil things as good?"""""

H 8289, Ch. 21, h 15
The narrator of the previous Hadith through his chain of narrators has said the following:

"The Holy Prophet, *O Allah, grant compensation to Muhammad and his family worthy of their services to Your cause,* has said, 'Allah, the most Majestic, the most Glorious, dislikes a believing, weak person who has no religion.' It then was asked, 'Who is a believing weak person who has no religion?' He, the Holy Prophet, said, 'It is he who does not prohibit committing evil.'"

H 8290, Ch. 21, h 16
Ali ibn Ibrahim has narrated from Harun ibn Muslim from Mas'adah ibn Sadaqah who has said the following:

"I heard abu 'Abd Allah, *'Alayhi al-Salam,* when asked about commanding others to do what is obligatory and prohibiting them from committing what is evil, whether this is obligatory upon the whole nation, saying, 'No, it is not obligatory up on the whole nation.' He (the Imam) was asked, 'Why it is not obligatory upon the whole nation?' He (the Imam) replied, 'It is obligatory only upon the strong ones who are obeyed and who know well what is obligatory and what is evil. It is not obligatory upon the weak ones who are not able to find the way - about what the facts are - to the truth and falsehood. The proof thereof is in the book of Allah, the Most Majestic, the Most Glorious, "Among you there must live a nation who must command to do what is obligatory and prohibit committing evil." (3:104) This verse is of particular sense as opposed to a general sense, just as in the following verse: "Of the people of Moses, there is a nation who guide to the truth and with truth they issue judgments." (7:158) Allah has not said, "It is obligatory upon the nation of Moses or upon his whole nation who in those days formed many nations." Nation is also used to mean one person as well as to mean more than one person. Allah, the Most Majestic, the Most Glorious, has said, "Ibrahim was a nation (person) very obedient to Allah." (16:119) In peace-time when one is not able to enforce such commands it does not apply to his case. . . . .'"

"Mas'adah has said, 'I heard abu 'Abd Allah, *'Alayhi al-Salam*, when asked about a Hadith narrated from the Messenger of Allah, *O Allah, grant compensation to Muhammad and his family worthy of their services to Your cause*, that said, "The best Jihad is saying a word of justice before an unjust Imam." He (the Imam) said, "This is true when commanding to do good, he knows well about what is 'good' as well as knowing that he will accept his command in the matter, otherwise, it (asking to do good) is not obligatory."'"

Chapter 22(a) - Rejecting Evil in one's Heart

H 8291, Ch. 22a, h 1
Ali ibn Ibrahim has narrated from his father from ibn abu 'Umayr from Yahya al-'Attar Sahib al-Minqariy who has said the following:

"Abu 'Abd Allah, *'Alayhi al-Salam*, has said, 'It is enough in terms of honor for a believing person who upon seeing an evil act committed informs (if he finds) Allah, the most Majestic, the most Glorious, that he rejects and denounces such act.'"

H 8292, Ch. 22a, h 2
It is narrated from the narrator of the previous Hadith who has said the following:

"Abu 'Abd Allah, *'Alayhi al-Salam*, has said, 'Only believing people who accept good advice should be asked to do good and prohibit committing evil but not those who have the whip and the sword.'"

H 8293, Ch. 22a, h 3
It is narrated from (Ali ibn Ibrahim) his father from ibn abu 'Umayr from Mufaddal ibn Yazid who has said the following:

"Abu 'Abd Allah, *'Alayhi al-Salam*, once said to me, 'O Mufaddal, if one protests against an unjust ruler and he faces an affliction he will not receive any reward for such suffering nor is he granted any patience to bear in such suffering.'"

H 8294, Ch. 22a, h 4
Ali has narrated from his father from certain persons of his people from Ghiyath ibn Ibrahim who has said the following:

"When seeing a quarrelling group of people abu 'Abd Allah, *'Alayhi al-Salam*, would not pass by without always saying three times loudly, 'You must maintain piety in the presence of Allah.'"

H 8295, Ch. 22a, h 5
Muhammad ibn Yahya has narrated from Ahmad ibn Muhammad from Muhammad ibn Sinan from Mahfuz al-Iskaf who has said the following:

"I saw abu 'Abd Allah, *'Alayhi al-Salam*, who had completed throwing pebbles on Jamarah al-'Aqabah and was moving away. I walked before to clear the path for him. There was a man of yellow complexion from 'Amrak (or a quarrelsome one) who had fixed a peg in the ground and had tied a rope from it to his tent which had blocked people's movement. Abu 'Abd Allah, *'Alayhi al-Salam*, said to him, 'O you, be pious before Allah. This (path) does not belong to you.' He (the narrator) has said that al-'Amraki said to him, 'Why can you not mind your own business instead of imposing on me a burden without knowing who passes by (my tent) and say, "O you, be pious before Allah."' The narrator has said that abu 'Abd Allah, *'Alayhi al-Salam*, then lifted the rope of his camel, bowed his head down and passed by. Al-'Amrakiy, the black person, also left him alone.'"

Chapter 22(b)

H 8296, Ch. 22b, h 1
A number of our people have narrated from Ahmad ibn Muhammad from Muhammad 'Isma'il from Muhammad ibn 'Adhafir from Ishaq ibn 'Ammar from 'Abd al-'A'la', Mawla ale Sam who has said the following:

"Abu 'Abd Allah, *'Alayhi al-Salam*, has said that when the following verse of the Holy Quran was revealed: 'O believers save yourselves and your family from a fire. . . .' (66:6) one man from the Muslims sat straight and began to weep, saying, 'I have failed in saving myself and now I am commanded to save my family also.' The Messenger of Allah, *O Allah, grant compensation to Muhammad and his family worthy of their services to Your cause*, said, 'It is enough for you to ask them to do good as you ask yourself and prohibit them from committing sins as you prohibit yourself.'"

H 8297, Ch. 22b, h 2
It is narrated from the narrator of the previous Hadith from 'Uthaman ibn 'Isa from Sama'ah from abu Basir from who has said the following:

"About the words of Allah, the most Majestic, the most Glorious, '. . . Save yourselves and your family from a fire. . . .' (66:6) I asked him (the Imam), 'How can I save them?' He (the Imam) replied, 'You must order them to do what Allah has commanded to do and prohibit them from what Allah has prohibited them to do. If they obeyed you, you have saved them. If they disobeyed you, you have fulfilled your responsibility.'"

H 8298, Ch. 22b, h 3
Ali ibn Ibrahim has narrated from his father from ibn abu 'Umayr from Hafs ibn 'Uthaman from Sama'ah from abu Basir who has said the following:

"About the words of Allah, '. . . save yourselves and your family. . . .' (66:6) I asked abu 'Abd Allah, *'Alayhi al-Salam*, 'How can we save our families?' He (the Imam) said, 'Command them and prohibit them.'"

Chapter 23 - The Case of those who Displease the Creator to Please the Creatures

H 8299, Ch. 23, h 1
A number of our people have narrated from Ahmad ibn Muhammad ibn Khalid from 'Isma'il ibn Mehran from Sayf ibn 'Amirah from 'Amr ibn Shamir from Jabir from abu Ja'far, *'Alayhi al-Salam*, who has said the following:

"The Messenger of Allah, *O Allah, grant compensation to Muhammad and his family worthy of their services to Your cause*, has said, 'Those who seek to please people by means of things that displease Allah, the most Majestic, the most Glorious, people who praise them turn to blame them. Those who prefer to obey Allah, the most Majestic, the most Glorious, by means of things that displease people, Allah, the most Majestic, the most Glorious, suffices them against the animosity of all enemies, jealousy of all jealous ones, the transgression of all transgressors and Allah is their helper and supporter.'"

H 8300, Ch. 23, h 2
Ali ibn Ibrahim has narrated from his father from al-Nawfaliy from al-Sakuniy who has said the following:
"Abu 'Abd Allah, *'Alayhi al-Salam*, has said that the Messenger of Allah, *O Allah, grant compensation to Muhammad and his family worthy of their services to Your cause*, has said, 'If one pleases a Sultan (king) to displease Allah, he has gone out of al-Islam.'"

H 8301, Ch. 23, h 3
The narrator of the previous Hadith through his chain of narrators has said the following:
"The Messenger of Allah, *O Allah, grant compensation to Muhammad and his family worthy of their services to Your cause*, has said, 'Those who seek to please people by means of things that displease Allah, the most Majestic, the most Glorious, people praising him turn to blame him.'"

Chapter 24 - It is Detestable to Expose One's Self to What He Cannot Endure

H 8302, Ch. 24, h 1
Muhammad in Al-Husayn has narrated from Ibrahim ibn Ishaq al-Ahmar from 'Abd Allah ibn Hammad al-Ansariy from 'Abd Allah ibn Sinan from abu al-Hassan al-Ahmasiy who has said the following:
"Abu 'Abd Allah, *'Alayhi al-Salam*, has said, ' Allah, the most Majestic, the most Glorious, has delegated all affairs of a believer to him but He has not delegated him to humiliate himself. Have you not heard the words of Allah, the most Majestic, the most Glorious, "All honor belongs to Allah, His Messenger and the believers. . . ." (63:7) Thus, believers are honorable but not lowly and humiliated.' He then said, 'All believers are more majestic than mountains. Mountains are reducible by picks and shovels but believers are not reducible, even in small amounts, in matters of their religion.'"

H 8303, Ch. 24, h 2
A number of our people have narrated from Ahmad ibn Muhammad from 'Uthaman ibn 'Isa from Sama'ah who has said the following:
"Abu 'Abd Allah, *'Alayhi al-Salam*, has said, 'Allah, the most Majestic, the most Glorious, has delegated all affairs of believers to them but He has not delegated him to humiliate himself. Have you not heard the words of Allah, the most Majestic, the most Glorious, "All honors belongs to Allah, His Messenger and the believers. . ." (63:7) Believers must stay honorable but not lowly and humiliated. Allah has granted them honor through al-Islam and belief.'"

H 8304, Ch. 24, h 3
Ali ibn Ibrahim has narrated from his father from 'Uthaman ibn 'Isa from 'Abd Allah ibn Muskan from abu Basir who has said the following:

"Abu 'Abd Allah, *'Alayhi al-Salam*, has said that Allah, the most Blessed, the most High, has delegated all affairs of believers to them except their humiliating themselves."

H 8305, Ch. 24, h 4
Muhammad ibn Yahya has narrated from Ahmad ibn Muhammad ibn 'Isa from al-Hassan ibn Mahbub from Dawud al-Riqqiy who has said the following:
"I heard abu 'Abd Allah, *'Alayhi al-Salam*, saying, 'Believers must not humiliate themselves.' It was asked, 'How can one humiliate himself?' He (the Imam) replied, 'This happens when he does things that are not bearable.'"

H 8306, Ch. 24, h 5
A number of our people have narrated from Ahmad ibn Muhammad ibn Khalid from his father from Muhammad ibn Sinan from Mufaddal ibn 'Umar who has said the following:
"Abu 'Abd Allah, *'Alayhi al-Salam*, has said, 'A believer must not humiliate himself.' I then asked, 'In what way can he humiliate himself?' He (the Imam) replied, 'He can do so by involving himself in things that he cannot do.'"

H 8307, Ch. 24, h 6
Muhammad ibn Ahmad has narrated from 'Abd Allah ibn al-Salt from Yunus from Sama'ah who has said the following:
"Abu 'Abd Allah, *'Alayhi al-Salam*, has said that Allah, the most Majestic, the most Glorious, has delegated all affairs of believers to them but He has not delegated him to humiliate himself. Has he not seen the words of Allah, the most Majestic, the most Glorious: 'All honor belongs to Allah, His Messenger and the believers. . . .' (63:7) Believers must stand honorable but not humiliated.'"

The End of the Book of al-Jihad of al-Kafi followed by the Book of Commerce

In the Name of Allah, the Beneficient, the Merciful

Part Two:
The Book of Commerce

Chapter 1 - Al-Sufiy People's Visiting Abu 'Abd Allah, *'Alayhi al-Salam*

H 8308, Ch. 1, h 1

Ali ibn Ibrahim has narrated from his father from Harun ibn Muslim Mas'adah ibn Sadaqah who has said the following:

"Once, Sufyan al-Thawriy visited abu 'Abd Allah, *'Alayhi al-Salam*. He saw the Imam wearing a cloth that was pure white like the membrane between an egg shell and its contents. He then said to the Imam, 'This is not the kind of cloth you should wear.' He (the Imam) said, 'Listen to me and pay proper attention to what I say; it is good for you now and in future if you like to die following the Sunnah and truth and not in heresy. I can tell you that the Messenger of Allah lived at a time when poverty was rampant. When living conditions improve the people most deserving to benefit from the worldly facilities are the virtuous people and not the sinful ones, the believing people and not the hypocrites, the Muslims and not those who reject Islam. What then is it that you, O Thawriy, dislike? When you see me in this condition, you must take notice that, I swear by Allah, from the time I reached the age of maturity, there has never been an evening or morning when Allah had a right in my properties that He had commanded me to payoff and I had not already paid it off.' He (the narrator) has said that then a group of people who showed themselves to people to be abstaining from the worldly matters and called people to become like them in treating their bodies with harshness said to the Imam, 'Our fellow companion has become tonguetied before you and is unable to present his argument properly.' He (the Imam) then asked them, 'What is the argument that you think you have?' They replied, 'It is from the book of Allah.' He (the Imam) then said, 'You then must present it; it is the most rightful fact to follow and upon which one must act.' They said, 'Allah, most Blessed, most High, speaking of a group of people of the companions of the Holy Prophet has said, "They give preference to others over their own-selves even though they particularly are in need of what they give away to the needy. Whoever controls the greed of his soul is of those who find true happiness." (59:10) He has praised their deeds and in another passage He has said, "They offer food for His love to the destitute, the orphan and captives. . . ." (76:8) We think this much from the Holy Quran is enough to support our argument.' A man from among the people present then said, 'We know that you abstain from good food but at the same time ask people to give away from their properties so that you in turn benefit from such properties given away.'

"Abu 'Abd Allah, *'Alayhi al-Salam*, then said, 'You should leave alone the matters that do not benefit you. You however must tell me this. Do you have the knowledge of the abrogating and abrogated matters of the Holy Quran; what are the unequivocal and ambiguous matters in which strayed those who strayed and faced destruction, those who were doomed to face destruction of the members of this nation?' They or certain ones among them replied, 'We do not know all of such matters.' He (the Imam) then said, 'This is where you have difficulties. The same case applies to Ahadith of the Messenger of Allah. However, what you mentioned of the matters that Allah, most Majestic, most Glorious, has spoken to us in His book about a people and their good deeds, you must take notice, such deeds were permissible and lawful. It was not prohibited for them, and their reward for such deeds is with Allah, most Majestic, most Glorious. (It was not obligatory on them) because Allah, most Holy, has commanded to do what is opposite to what they had done. Therefore, His prohibition was abrogating their practice; Allah, most Blessed, most High, out of His mercy toward the believing people, stopped them from harming themselves, their dependents, the weak ones, the small ones like children, the old men and women who are not able to bear hunger. If the loaf of my bread is given away while I have no other loaf of bread, then the lives of such ones (of my dependents) are jeopardized because of hunger. For this reason the Messenger of Allah, *O Allah, grant compensation to Muhammad and his family worthy of their services to Your cause*, has said, "If one has five dates in his possession or five loaves and he wants to give charity, the best charity to give is to spend it on one's parents, then on his own self and dependents, thirdly on his relatives, fourthly on his neighbors, fifthly he should spend it in the way of Allah which is of the lowest degree of rewards." The Messenger of Allah once, when one of the people of al-Ansar at the time of his death had set free five or six of his slaves and had no other possession and had left behind small children, said, "Had you informed me before about what he has done, I would not have given you permission to bury him in the graveyard of the Muslims due to his leaving behind small children with their hands spread before people for help."' He (the Imam) then said, 'My father has narrated to me that the Messenger of Allah has said, "Begin, when giving charity, with your dependents, the nearest ones first and so on." Allah, most Majestic, most Wise, has also said, ". . . those who when giving charity do not exceed proper limits and nor do they act stringently, but give charity in a moderate manner." (25:67) Is it not true that Allah, most Blessed, most High, has said what is other than what I see you call people to do and to give others preference over their own selves, while He has called what you want people to do as exceeding the proper limits in spending? In more than a verse of His book He says, "He does not love those who exceed proper limits in spending." (6:141 and 7:31) He has prohibited from acting as exceeding proper limits in spending and acting very stringently. He has told them to act moderately in between the two manners of spending. One must not give away all of his belongings and then begin to pray to Allah to grant him sustenance. His prayer then is not answered as it is mentioned in a Hadith, narrated from the Holy Prophet, *'Alayhi al-Salam*, that says, "The prayers of certain individuals of my followers are not answered. Of such people is one who prays against his parents, one who prays against his debtor who borrowed money without writing down for the record and appointing two witnesses for what he has borrowed, one who prays against his wife when Allah, most Majestic, most Glorious, in His laws has already authorized him to dissolve the contract of his marriage and one who sits at home without work, then prays to Allah, most Majestic, most Glorious, for sustenance but does not go out to work for a living. Allah, most Majestic, most Glorious, says to him, "My servant, have I not made ways for you to seek means of living and go around in the land by the help of your healthy bodily abilities so that you would not leave any excuse between Me and yourself in matters of your seeking to make a living and in obedience to My command and to avoid becoming a burden on your family? Now you have no excuse. I may grant you sustenance or make you suffer stringent conditions." Another person is a wealthy one who spends all of his wealth and then begins to pray to Allah for his sustenance. Allah, most Majestic, most Glorious, says, "Had I not given you a great wealth? Why did you not act moderately as I had commanded you to do and avoid exceeding the proper limits of spending manners? I had already prohibited you to do so." Yet there is another person who prays against good relationships with his relatives. Allah, most Majestic, most Glorious, then taught his Prophet how to spend in charity. Once there were a few Awqiyyah (certain units of measurement) of gold and he did not like to keep them with him for the night while they are not given away to deserving people. So he gave them away and in the morning there was nothing left with him. A person came to him asking for help but he had nothing to give him. The person asking for help blamed him for his inability to provide any help and he became sad; nothing was left there with him to help and he was a very kindhearted person. Allah most High, disciplined His prophet, by means of commanding him, "You must not keep your hands tied up to your neck and you must not expand them altogether so much so that you then remain blamed and unable to provide any help." (17:31) He says, "People ask you for help and they do not accept your excuses. If you give away all the properties you remain unable to help the needy." These are of the Ahadith of the Messenger of Allah verified by the book which is confirmed by the believing people of the book. Abu Bakr at the time of his death, when asked to make a will, made a will about one-fifth of his legacy saying, "One-fifth is a great deal." Allah, most High, has approved wills about one-fifth. So he made a will about one-fifth. Allah, most Majestic, most Glorious, had given the right to make a will about one-third of one's legacy at the time of one's death. If he knew that one-third is better for him he would have made a will for one-third. People other than abu Bakr, as you know their excellence and restraint from the worldly matters, were Salman and abu Dharr, may Allah be happy with them. Salman's manners were such that whenever he received a gift he would keep aside one year's expenses thereof until receiving his gift of the coming year. It was said to him, "O abu 'Abd Allah, why is it that with all the restraint you exercise in the worldly matters and you do not know whether you will die today or tomorrow, you still keep one year's amount of your expenses aside from the gift you receive?" His answer was as follows, "Why do you not wish for me one more year of living instead of fearing for my death within a year?"' He (the Imam) then said, 'O ignorant people, have you not noticed that one's soul becomes lazy and weak (in worship) when he does not have dependable means of living but when he gains his means of living his soul gains comfort. Abu Dharr owned camels and sheep. He would get milk from them and also use their meat for food whenever he wanted for his family and for his guests or for the people from whom he received water. Whenever he thought they desired he would slaughter for them a camel for food or of the sheep to satisfy their desire for meat. He would distribute the meat among them and himself would get one share without anything more than others. Who is more restraining from the worldly matters than these people? The Messenger of Allah has said about them all that he has said but he has not mentioned anything about their dispossessing themselves altogether of their belongings by giving away everything in charity, just as you command people to give away all of their belongings to give preference to others over themselves and families.

'O people, you must take notice that I heard my father narrating from his ancestors, *'Alayhim al-Salam*, from the Messenger of Allah, *O Allah, grant compensation to Muhammad and his family worthy of their services to Your cause*, who one day said, "No other thing is as astonishing to me as the condition of a believing person. If his body is cut into pieces by scissors, it is because it is for his good and if everything between the east and west is made to become of his belongings is because it is for his good. Everything that Allah, most Majestic, most Glorious, does for him is for his good." I like to know what I have said to you today had any effect on you or I increase my sayings. Have you not noticed that Allah, most Majestic, most Glorious, at the beginning of Islam had made it compulsory on the Muslims to fight each one against ten pagans without turning his back to the enemy and those who did so would have filled his seat with hellfire. He then changed their condition out of mercy and kindness to them and told them to fight each one of them against two men of the pagans. It was a measure of relief in favor of the believers from Allah, most Majestic, most Glorious. This was an abrogation of one Muslims' fighting against ten pagans.

'You should tell me about the judges who rule against one of you to pay the expenses of his wife. Are they unjust judges if the defendant said, "I am a zahid (one who restrains from worldly matters) and I do not possess anything?" If you said such judges are unjust people, Islam will call you unjust, and if you said they are judges of justice, then you have defeated yourselves. By what means will you reject the validity of the will that leaves more than one-third for the poor out of the legacy of a deceased? You must answer to me about this. If all people were Zuhhad (restraining from worldly matters) as you like them to be without needing anything from the worldly matters, then who would receive the charities, expiation for disregard of one's swearing and vows and charities like Zakat of gold, silver, dates, raisin and other items subject to Zakat like camel, cow, sheep and other goods? If it were as you say that no one should keep anything of the worldly things but instead send it as his supplies for the next life even though he may urgently need such items, what you maintain is bad and you have made people to follow what you follow due to ignorance of the book of

Allah, most Majestic, most Glorious, the Sunnah of the Holy Prophet of Allah and his Ahadith (sayings) which are verified by the divinely revealed book, and you have rejected them due to your ignorance and your disregard of the unique passages of the Holy Quran, the explanation of abrogating and abrogated matters, the unequivocal and ambiguous, the command and prohibitions therein. You must tell me if you know about Sulayman (the prophet) son of Dawud *'Alayhi al-Salam*, when he asked Allah to give him a kingdom which no one after him would ever have. Allah, most Majestic, most Glorious, gave him such kingdom. He spoke the truth and acted thereupon. We do not find Allah, most Majestic, most Glorious, blaming him for possessing such kingdom, neither any of the believing people have ever blamed him for possessing such a kingdom. Before him lived Dawud, the prophet with great kingdom and strong control. There is Joseph, the prophet, *'Alayhi al-Salam*, who said to the king of Egypt, "Appoint me a supervisor of the treasures of the land; I am a knowledgeable keeper." (12:56) He became the person in charge of the kingdom of the king up to Yemen. People would come for food supplies to him during food shortages and famine. We do not find any one to blame him for it. Dhul *Qarn*ayn was a servant of Allah who loved Allah and Allah loved him. He prepared for him means and made him to possess the east and west of the land. He spoke the truth and acted thereupon. We do not find any one to blame him for it. You people must discipline yourselves by the disciplines of Allah, most Majestic, most Glorious, for the believing people. Follow the commands and prohibitions of Allah, and leave alone what has become confusing for you and you have no knowledge thereof. Leave issues of knowledge to the people of knowledge; you will be rewarded and excused before Allah, most Blessed, most High. You must seek to learn the knowledge of abrogating and abrogated matters of the Holy Quran, its unequivocal and ambiguous matters thereof. You must learn what Allah has made lawful and what He has made unlawful. This takes you closer to Allah and farther from ignorance. You must leave alone ignorance to its people. People of ignorance are many and people of knowledge are fewer. Allah, most Majestic, most Glorious, has said, "Over every person of knowledge there is one more knowledgeable. " (12: 76)'"

Chapter 2 - The Meaning of *Zuhd* (Restraint from worldly matters)

H 8309, Ch. 2, h 1

Ali ibn Ibrahim has narrated from his father from al-Nawfaliy from al-Sakuniy who has said the following:

"This is concerning my question before abu 'Abd Allah, *'Alayhi al-Salam*, about the meaning of restraint from worldly matters. He (the Imam) said, 'Fie upon you! It is (not difficult to understand) knowing what is unlawful so that you can avoid it.'"

H 8310, Ch. 2, h 2

A number of our people have narrated from Ahmad ibn abu 'Abd Allah from al-Jahm ibn al-Hakam from 'Isma'il ibn Muslim who has said the following:

"Abu 'Abd Allah, *'Alayhi al-Salam,* has said, *'Zuhd* (restraint from worldly matters) is not in wasting one's belongings or making lawful things unlawful.'"

H 8311, Ch. 2, h 3
Muhammad ibn Yahya has narrated from Ahmad ibn 'Isa from Muhammad ibn Sinan from Malik ibn 'Atiyyah from M'aruf ibn Kharbudh from abu al-Tufayl who has said the following:
"I heard 'Amir al-Mu'minin, *'Alayhi al-Salam,* saying, *'Zuhd* (restraint from worldly matters) in the world is to shorten one's hopes, give thanks for every bounty and restrain from everything that Allah, most Majestic, most Glorious, has made unlawful.'"

Chapter 3 - Using the Worldly Resources as Means for Success in the Hereafter

H 8312, Ch. 3, h 1
Ali ibn Ibrahim has narrated from his father from al-Nawfaliy from al-Sakuniy who has said the following:
"Abu 'Abd Allah, *'Alayhi al-Salam,* has said that the Messenger of Allah has said, 'The best helper of piety is (financial) self-sufficiency.'"

H 8313, Ch. 3, h 2
A number of our people have narrated from Ahmad ibn Muhammad from ibn Mahbub from Jamil ibn Salih who has said the following:
"About the words of Allah, most Majestic, most Glorious, 'O Lord, grant us good in this world and in the next world', abu 'Abd Allah, *'Alayhi al-Salam,* has said, 'It is Allah's happiness with one, paradise in the next life, good living and excellent moral manners in this world.'"

H 8314, Ch. 3, h 3
Ali ibn Muhammad Bandar has narrated from Ahmad ibn abu 'Abd Allah from Ibrahim ibn Muhammad al-Thaqafiy from Ali ibn Mu'alla' from al-Qasim ibn Muhammad in a marfu' manner who has said the following:
"Once it was asked of abu 'Abd Allah, *'Alayhi al-Salam,* 'How is it that disciples of Jesus could walk on water and the companions of Muhammad, *O Allah, grant compensation to Muhammad and his family worthy of their services to Your cause,* do not have such ability? Abu 'Abd Allah, *'Alayhi al-Salam,* replied, 'The disciples of Jesus were self-sufficient financially and these people have trouble with their financial matters.'"

H 8315, Ch. 3, h 4
A number of our people have narrated from Sahl ibn Ziyad from ibn Faddal from Tha'labah ibn Maymun from 'Abd al-'Ala' who has said the following:
"Abu 'Abd Allah, *'Alayhi al-Salam,* has said, 'Ask Allah to grant you (financial) self-sufficiency and good health in this world, forgiveness and paradise in the hereafter.'"

H 8316, Ch. 3, h 5
A number of our people have narrated from Ahmad ibn Muhammad ibn 'Isa from abu 'Abd Allah from 'Abd al-Rahman ibn Muhammad from al-Harith ibn Bahram from 'Amr ibn Jami' who has said the following:

"I heard abu 'Abd Allah, *'Alayhi al-Salam*, saying, 'There is not much good in one who does not love to accumulate lawful wealth with which he can safeguard his dignity, pay off his debts and maintain good relations with relatives.'"

H 8317, Ch. 3, h 6

Al-Husayn ibn Muhammad has narrated from Ja'far ibn Muhammad from al-Qasim ibn al-Rabi' in his (Imam's) advice to al-Mufaddal ibn 'Umar who has said the following:

"I heard abu 'Abd Allah, *'Alayhi al-Salam*, saying, 'You should use certain items of these resources to overcome other tasks and do not become a burden on people.'"

H 8318, Ch. 3, h 7

Ali ibn Muhammad ibn Bandar has narrated from Ahmad ibn 'Abd Allah from abu al-Khazraj al-Ansariy from Ali ibn Ghurab who has said the following:

"Abu 'Abd Allah, *'Alayhi al-Salam*, has said that the Messenger of Allah, *O Allah, grant compensation to Muhammad and his family worthy of their services to Your cause*, has said, 'Condemned is one who shifts his burden over on other people.'"

H 8319, Ch. 3, h 8

It is narrated from him (narrator of the previous Hadith) from Ahmad from his father from Safwan ibn Yahya from Darih ibn Yazid al-Muharibiy who has said the following:

"Abu 'Abd Allah, *'Alayhi al-Salam*, has said, 'The worldly resources are best means to overcome the difficulties of the next life.'"

H 8320, Ch. 3, h 9

Ali ibn Ibrahim has narrated from his father from Safwan ibn Yahya from Darih al-Muharibiy who has said the following:

"Abu 'Abd Allah, *'Alayhi al-Salam*, has said that the worldly resources are best means to overcome the difficulties of the next life."

H 8321, Ch. 3, h 10

Ali ibn Ibrahim has narrated from his father from ibn abu 'Umayr from Hisham ibn Salim from 'Abd Allah ibn abu Ya'fur who has said the following:

"A man once said to abu 'Abd Allah, *'Alayhi al-Salam*, 'We, by Allah, ask for the worldly things and we love to receive worldly gains.' He (the Imam) asked, 'What do you want to do with it?' He replied, 'I like to improve my own conditions, the conditions of my family, maintain good relations with others, give charity, perform Hajj and al-'Umrah.' He (the Imam) said, 'This is not asking for worldly things. It is asking for success in the hereafter.'"

H 8322, Ch. 3, h 11

A number of our people have narrated from Ahmad ibn Muhammad from ibn Khalid in a marfu' manner who has said the following:

"Abu 'Abd Allah, *'Alayhi al-Salam*, once said, 'A wealth that keeps you away from injustice is better than poverty which leads you to commit sins.'"

H 8323, Ch. 3, h 12

A number of our people have narrated from Sahl ibn Ziyad from ibn Mahbub from 'Abd Allah ibn Sinan from A number of our people has narrated who has said the following:

"Abu 'Abd Allah, *'Alayhi al-Salam*, has said that the Messenger of Allah, *O Allah, grant compensation to Muhammad and his family worthy of their services to Your cause*, has said, 'A believer's spending days and nights with suffering from the losses of his loved ones is better than his spending days and nights in the state of war. We seek protection with Allah against war.'"

H 8324, Ch. 3, h 13
A number of our people have narrated from Ahmad ibn abu 'Abd Allah from his father from abu al-Bakhtariy in a marfu' manner who has said the following:

"The Messenger of Allah, *O Allah, grant compensation to Muhammad and his family worthy of their services to Your cause*, has said, 'O Allah, grant us blessings with our loaves of bread and do not take them away from us. Without bread we cannot perform *Salat* (prayer) or fast, perform our obligations toward our Lord.'"

H 8325, Ch. 3, h 14
Muhammad ibn Yahya has narrated from Ahmad ibn Muhammad from Ali ibn al-Hakam from Ali al-Ahmasiy from a man who has said the following:

"Abu Ja'far, *'Alayhi al-Salam*, has said, 'The worldly help in one's quest for success in the hereafter is the best help.'"

H 8326, Ch. 3, h 15
A number of our people have narrated from Sahl ibn Ziyad from Ali ibn Asbat from Darih al-Muharibiy who has said the following:

"Abu 'Abd Allah, *'Alayhi al-Salam*, has said, 'The worldly help in one's quest for success in the hereafter is the best help.'"

Chapter 4 - The Degree Of Efforts Which One Must Make In Search For One's Sustenance To Follow In the Footsteps of 'A'immah *'Alayhim al-Salam*

H 8327, Ch. 4, h 1
Ali ibn Ibrahim has narrated from his father and Muhammad ibn 'Isma'il from al-Fadl ibn Shadhan all from ibn abu 'Umayr from 'Abd al-Rahman ibn al-Hajjaj who has said the following:

"Abu 'Abd Allah, *'Alayhi al-Salam*, has said that Muhammad ibn al-Munkadir has said, 'I did not think Ali ibn Al-Husayn, *'Alayhi al-Salam*, might leave behind a successor better than his own-self. Time passed and I one day saw his son, Muhammad ibn Ali, *'Alayhi al-Salam*. I decided to give him certain words of good advice but I, instead, learned a lesson from him.' His people then asked him, 'How did he make you learn a lesson?' He replied, 'One day I went outside the city of al-Madinah when it was very hot and I met Muhammad ibn Ali, *'Alayhi al-Salam*, who was a person of a large body frame and heavy. Two of his black slaves or friends were supporting him. I thought, Allah is free of all defects, here is this old man from Quraysh in this hot time of the day in this condition in search of the worldly gains, thus I must give him certain words of good advice. I went nearer to him and offered him greeting of peace. He responded with somewhat frowning face, and his perspiration drops were falling a great deal. I then said, 'May Allah keep you well. You are a Shaykh of the

Shaykhs of Quraysh. Why should you in such a hot hour of the day in such condition strive for the worldly gains? Suppose if death approached you in this condition what would you do?' He (the Imam) replied, 'If death approaches me in this condition it finds me obeying the commandment of Allah, most Majestic, most Glorious. It finds me safeguarding my dignity, and my family from people like you and others. I should be afraid if death approaches me when I am in a condition of disobeying Allah.' I then said, 'You have spoken the truth. I pray to Allah to keep you well. I wanted to give you good advice; instead I learned a lesson from you.'"

H 8328, Ch. 4, h 2

A number of our people have narrated from Ahmad ibn abu 'Abd Allah from Sharif Sabiq formal-Fadl ibn abu Qurrah who has said the following:

"Abu 'Abd Allah, *'Alayhi al-Salam*, has said that Amir al-Mu'minin, *'Alayhi al-Salam*, would work with a shovel and dig the soil. The Messenger of Allah, *O Allah, grant compensation to Muhammad and his family worthy of their services to Your cause*, placed date stones in his mouth and then planted it and it would sprout in the same hour. Amir al-Mu'minin, *'Alayhi al-Salam*, had set free one thousand slaves for which he paid from his own properties and his own labor."

H 8329, Ch. 4, h 3

A number of our people have narrated from Sahl ibn Ziyad from 'Abd Allah al-Dihqan from Durust from 'Abd al-A'la', Mawla' Ale Sam who has said the following:

"I once came face to face with abu 'Abd Allah, *'Alayhi al-Salam*, in one of the streets of al-Madinah on a very hot summer day. I said, 'I pray to Allah to keep my soul in service for your cause, you have a prominent position before Allah, most Majestic, most Glorious, and you are of very close relatives of the Messenger of Allah and you are (not to be) striving in a day like this.' He (the Imam) said, 'O 'Abd al-'A'la', I came out in search for my sustenance so that I would not need to spread my hands before you (your fellow) humankind for help.'"

H 8330, Ch. 4, h 4

Ali ibn Ibrahim has narrated from his father from ibn abu 'Umayr from Sayf ibn 'Amirah and Salmah Sahib al-Sabiriy from abu 'Usamah Zayd al-Shahham who has said the following:

"Abu 'Abd Allah, *'Alayhi al-Salam*, has said that 'Amir al-Mu'minin, *'Alayhi al-Salam*, had set free one thousand slaves by means of what he had earned with his own hands."

H 8331, Ch. 4, h 5

Ahmad ibn abu 'Abd Allah has narrated from Sharif ibn Sabiq from al-Fadl ibn abu Qurrah who has narrated the following:

"Abu 'Abd Allah, *'Alayhi al-Salam*, has said that 'Amir al-Mu'minin, has said, 'Allah, most Majestic, most Glorious, sent revelations to Dawud, *'Alayhi al-Salam* that said, 'You are a very good servant had you not been spending on yourself from the public treasury while doing no work with your own hands.' He (the Imam) said, 'Dawud *'Alayhi al-Salam* wept for forty mornings. Allah, most Majestic, most Glorious, then inspired Iron, "You must become soft for My servant, Dawud." Allah, most Majestic, most Glorious, softened Iron for him.

Everyday he would make one coat of arms and sell it for one thousand dirham. He made three hundred sixty coats of arm and sold them for three hundred sixty thousand dirham. Thereafter he did not need anything from the public treasury.'"

H 8332, Ch. 4, h 6

Muhammad ibn Yahya has narrated from Ahmad ibn Muhammad from ibn Faddal from ibn Bukayr from Zurarah who has said the following:

"Abu Ja'far, *'Alayhi al-Salam*, has said that a man once visited Amir al-Mu'minin, *'Alayhi al-Salam*, and found him sitting on a camel-load of date stones. He asked, 'What is it on which you are sitting, O abu al-Hassan?' He (the Imam) replied, 'It is a hundred thousand palm trees, by the will of Allah.' He planted them and not one date stone failed sprouting.'"

H 8333, Ch. 4, h 7

Ali ibn Ibrahim has narrated from his father from ibn abu 'Umayr from Abu al-Maghra' from 'Ammar al-Sajistaniy from abu 'Abd Allah, from his father, *'Alayhi al-Salam*, who has said the following:

"Abu 'Abd Allah, *'Alayhi al-Salam*, has said that the Messenger of Allah, *O Allah, grant compensation to Muhammad and his family worthy of their services to Your cause*, once placed a piece of stone on the waterway to prevent it from flowing into his land. By Allah, until this day no human being or camel has moved it away."

H 8334, Ch. 4, h 8

Muhammad ibn Yahya has narrated from Ahmad ibn Muhammad from Ali ibn al-Hakam from Asbat ibn Salim who has said the following:

"I once visited abu 'Abd Allah, *'Alayhi al-Salam*. He (the Imam) asked us about 'Umar ibn Muslim and about what he has done. I replied, 'He is a virtuous man but has given up doing business works.' Abu 'Abd Allah, *'Alayhi al-Salam*, said three times: It is the work of Satan. Did he not know that the Messenger of Allah, *O Allah, grant compensation to Muhammad and his family worthy of their services to Your cause*, once bought a caravan that had come from al-Sham (Syria) in which he saved enough money to pay off his debts and distributed the extra among his relatives? Allah, most Majestic, most Glorious, says, "There are men who are not distracted by selling and buying from speaking of Allah. . . ." (24:36) Story tellers say, "These people (mentioned in this verse) did not involve themselves in trading and in business works." These story tellers speak lies. The fact is that those people did not perform *Salat* (prayer) in (more virtuous) times and such people are more virtuous than those who attend *Salat* (prayer) and ignore trade and business work.'"

H 8335, Ch. 4, h 9

A number of our people have narrated from Sahl ibn Ziyad from Ibn Mahbub from 'Abd Allah ibn Sinan who has said the following:

"Abu 'Abd Allah, *'Alayhi al-Salam*, has said that 'Amir al-Mu'minin, *'Alayhi al-Salam*, would go to work with large quantities of date stones. He was asked, 'What are these, O abu al-Hassan?' He (the Imam) replied, 'They are palm trees, by the will of Allah.' He then planted them and not a single piece failed sprouting."

H 8336, Ch. 4, h 10

Sahl ibn Ziyad has narrated from al-Jamuraniy from al-Hassan ibn Ali ibn abu Hamzah from his father who has said the following:

"I once saw abu al-Hassan, *'Alayhi al-Salam*, working in his land and his feet were drenched in perspiration. I asked, 'I pray to Allah to keep my soul in service for your cause, where are men (workers)?' He (the Imam) replied, 'O Ali, people better than my father and I worked in their land.' I then asked, 'Who were they?' He (the Imam) replied, 'They were the Messenger of Allah, *O Allah, grant compensation to Muhammad and his family worthy of their services to Your cause*, and 'Amir al-Mu'minin, and my ancestors, *'Alayhim al-Salam*, all of them worked with their hands and it is of the practice of the prophets, messengers, the executors of the wills and the virtuous people.'"

H 8337, Ch. 4, h 11

Muhammad ibn Yahya has narrated from Ahmad ibn Muhammad from ibn Sinan from 'Isma'il ibn Jabir who has said the following:

"I once visited abu 'Abd Allah, *'Alayhi al-Salam*, and found him inside his walls with a shovel in his hand. He was opening the waterway. His shirt was of a fabric made of thick cotton threads (karabis) which was of very small size for him."

H 8338, Ch. 4, h 12

A number of our people have narrated from Sahl ibn Ziyad from Ali ibn Asbat from Muhammad ibn 'Adhafir from his father who has said the following:

"Abu 'Abd Allah, *'Alayhi al-Salam*, once gave my father one thousand seven hundred dinars and told him to use them in business. He (the Imam) then said, 'I am not interested in its profits, even though profits are desirable. I love, however, that Allah, most Majestic, most Glorious, see me work to make profits.' He (the narrator) has said, 'I then made one hundred dinar profit for him. I met him and informed him about the one hundred dinar profits.' He (the narrator) has said that abu 'Abd Allah, *'Alayhi al-Salam*, became very happy about it and told me to keep it with his capital. He (the narrator) has said that my father passed away and goods were with him. Abu 'Abd Allah, *'Alayhi al-Salam*, then wrote to me, 'May Allah grant to us and to you good health. There is my one thousand eight hundred dinar with abu Muhammad which I had given him to use in business. You must give this amount to 'Umar ibn Yazid.' He (the narrator) has said, that I then checked the record of my father and found that one thousand seven hundred dinars were due in favor of abu Musa, *'Alayhi al-Salam*, and I had earned one hundred dinars profit, 'Abd Allah ibn Sinan and 'Umar ibn Yazid knew him."

H 8339, Ch. 4, h 13

A number of our people have narrated from Ahmad ibn 'Abd Allah from his father from al-Nadr ibn Suwayd from al-Qasim ibn Muhammad ibn Sulayman who has said that narrated to him Jamil ibn Salih from abu 'Amr al-Shaybaniy who has said the following:

"I once saw abu 'Abd Allah, *'Alayhi al-Salam*, with a shovel in his hand wearing a very thick dress working inside his walls and his back drenched in perspiration. I then asked, I pray to Allah to keep my soul in service for your cause, allow me to help you.' He said to me, 'I Love that man endures hardships in the hot sun to make a living."

H 8340, Ch. 4, h 14
Ali ibn Ibrahim has narrated from his father from ibn abu 'Umayr from 'Umar ibn 'Udhaynah from Zurarah who has said the following:

"Once a man came to abu 'Abd Allah, *'Alayhi al-Salam*, and said, 'I am not good in working with my hands and I am not good in doing business, thus I am deprived and needy.' He (the Imam) said, 'You must work and carry it on your head and set yourself free from asking people for help. The Messenger of Allah, *O Allah, grant compensation to Muhammad and his family worthy of their services to Your cause*, carried a stone on his shoulder to place it in a certain place of his walls. The stone is still in its place, and it is not known how large it is, but it is there [by his miracle]'"

H 8341, Ch. 4, h 15
A number of our people have narrated from Ahmad ibn Muhammad ibn 'Isa from al-Husayn ibn Sa'id from al-Qasim ibn Muhammad from Ali ibn abu Hamzah from abu Basir from who has said the following:

"I once heard abu 'Abd Allah, *'Alayhi al-Salam*, saying, 'I work in a certain site of my work to perspire, even though there are people who can do all the work instead of me but I work so Allah, most Majestic, most Glorious, finds me striving to find lawful sustenance.'"

H 8342, Ch. 4, h 16
Ali ibn Muhammad has narrated from Ahmad ibn abu 'Abd Allah from Muhammad ibn 'Isma'il from Muhammad ibn 'Adha'fir from his father who has said the following:

"Once abu 'Abd Allah, *'Alayhi al-Salam*, gave me seven hundred dinars and said, 'O 'Adha'fir you can spend it; I do not have any desire for it but I loved that Allah, most Majestic, most Glorious, finds me working for its profits.' 'Adha'fir has said, 'I made one hundred dinar profit with it. During al-Tawaf I said to him, "I pray to Allah to keep my soul in service for your cause, Allah, most Majestic, most Glorious, has granted one hundred dinar profit."' He (the Imam) said, 'Add it to my capital money.'"

Chapter 5 - Promoting The Quest For Sustenance And Work To Make A Living

H 8343, Ch. 5, h 1
Muhammad ibn Yahya has narrated from Ahmad ibn Muhammad from ibn Faddal from ibn Bukayr from 'Amr ibn Yazid who has said the following:

"I once said to abu 'Abd Allah, *'Alayhi al-Salam*, that a man says, 'I stay home, perform *Salat* (prayer), fast and worship my Lord. My sustenance will come to me.' Abu 'Abd Allah, *'Alayhi al-Salam*, said, 'This is one of the three (classes of people) whose prayer is not answered.'"

H 8344, Ch. 5, h 2

Ali ibn Ibrahim has narrated from his father from ibn abu 'Umayr from Al-Hassan ibn 'Atiyah from 'Umar ibn Yazid who has said the following:

"Abu 'Abd Allah, *'Alayhi al-Salam*, has said, 'Do you think the sustenance of a man who stays in his home and closes his door, keeps falling on him from the sky?'"

H 8345, Ch. 5, h 3

Muhammad ibn 'Isma'il has narrated from al-Fadl ibn Shadhan from ibn abu 'Umayr from Ibrahim ibn 'Abd al-Hamid from Ayyub, brother of 'Udaym Bayya' al-Harawiy who has said the following:

"Once we were in the presence of abu 'Abd Allah, *'Alayhi al-Salam*, when al-'Ala' ibn Kamil came in and sat in front of abu 'Abd Allah, *'Alayhi al-Salam*, and asked, 'Please pray for me so Allah will make me affluent.' Abu 'Abd Allah, *'Alayhi al-Salam*, said, 'I will not pray for you. Has Allah, most Majestic, most Glorious, not commanded you to seek and find your sustenance?'"

H 8346, Ch. 5, h 4

A number of our people have narrated from Ahmad ibn Muhammad ibn Khalid from his father from abu Talib al-Sha'raniy from Sulayman ibn Mu'alla' ibn Khunays from his father who has said the following:

"Once abu 'Abd Allah, *'Alayhi al-Salam*, asked about a man, when I was present, and it was said to him, 'He has become very needy.' He (the Imam) then asked, 'What is he doing today?' It was said, 'He is in his home worshipping his Lord.' He (the Imam) then asked, 'Wherefrom he receives for his living?' It was said, 'It comes from a certain one of his brothers.' Abu 'Abd Allah, *'Alayhi al-Salam*, then said, 'By Allah, the one who provides him his living does a much more powerful worship than his worship.'"

H 8347, Ch. 5, h 5

A number of our people have narrated from Ahmad ibn Muhammad ibn 'Isa from ibn abu 'Umayr from 'Abd Allah ibn al-Mughirah from Muhammad ibn al-Fudayl from abu Hamzah who has said the following:

"Abu Ja'far, *'Alayhi al-Salam*, has said that one who works to earn his sustenance in this world so he would not need to spread his hands before people for help, to better the living conditions of his family and to show kindness to his neighbors will, on the Judgment Day, go before Allah, most Majestic, most Glorious, with his face as bright as the full moon.'"

H 8348, Ch. 5, h 6

A number of our people have narrated from Sahl ibn Ziyad from Ibn Mahbub from abu Khalid al-Kufiy in a marfu' manner from abu Ja'far who has said the following:

"Abu Ja'far, *'Alayhi al-Salam*, has said that the Messenger of Allah, *O Allah, grant compensation to Muhammad and his family worthy of their services to Your cause*, has said, 'Worship has seventy parts. The most excellent part in it is working to make lawful living.'"

H 8349, Ch. 5, h 7

Ali ibn Ibrahim has narrated from his father from ibn abu 'Umayr from 'Isma'il ibn Muhammad al-Minqariy from Hisham al-Saydalaniy who has said the following:

"Abu 'Abd Allah, *'Alayhi al-Salam*, once said to me, 'O Hisham, even if you find yourself in the two armies facing each other to fight, you must not neglect working for your sustenance on such day.'"

H 8350, Ch. 5, h 8

Ahmad ibn 'Abd Allah Muhammad from Ahmad ibn Muhammad from ibn abu 'Abd Allah from Safwan from Khalid ibn Najih who has said the following:

"Abu 'Abd Allah, *'Alayhi al-Salam*, has said, 'Say Salam (greeting of peace) to whoever of your people you meet and say to them, "So and so son of so and so (the Imam) says Salam (greeting of peace)." Then say to them, "You must maintain piety before Allah, most Majestic, most Glorious. You must observe such issues through which you can receive whatever of the reward is with Allah. By Allah, I do not command you to do such things that we do not command our own souls to do. You must work hard and strive. After performing your morning *Salat* (prayer) you must go out early in the morning to work for your sustenance and seek lawful sustenance. Allah, most Majestic, most Glorious, will grant you sustenance and assists you to find such sustenance.'"

H 8351, Ch. 5, h 9

Ali ibn Ibrahim has narrated from his father from ibn abu 'Umayr from Al-Husayn ibn Ahmad from Shihab ibn 'Abd Rabbihi who has said the following:

"Abu 'Abd Allah, *'Alayhi al-Salam*, once said to me, 'Even if you find enough reason to believe that this task (the rise of al-Qa'im with divine authority) will take place tomorrow, still you must not neglect work for a living. If you cannot complete the work do (what you can)'"

H 8352, Ch. 5, h 10

Humayd ibn Ziyad has narrated from al-Hassan ibn Muhammad ibn Sama'ah from those whom he has mentioned from Aban from al-'Ala' who has said the following:

"I heard abu 'Abd Allah, *'Alayhi al-Salam*, saying, 'Why should anyone among you be weaker than an ant which pulls (food) to its colony?'"

H 8353, Ch. 5, h 11

Sahl ibn Ziyad has narrated from al-Haytham ibn abu Masruq from Muhammad ibn 'Umar ibn Bazi' from Ahmad ibn 'A'idh from Kulayb al-Saydawiy who has said the following:

"This is concerning my question before abu 'Abd Allah, *'Alayhi al-Salam*, to pray for me for sustenance; my affairs are turning to the worse.' He (the Imam) quickly said, 'No, you must go out and work to make a living.'"

Chapter 6 - Al-'Ibla' (Trying) in the Work for Living

H 8354, Ch. 6, h 1

A number of our people have narrated from Ahmad ibn Muhammad ibn Khalid from 'Abd al-Rahman ibn Hammad from Ziyad al-Qandiy from Al-Husayn al-Sahhaf from Sadir who has said the following:

"This is concerning my question before abu 'Abd Allah, *'Alayhi al-Salam*, 'What should a man do for work to make a living?' He (the Imam) replied, 'If you open your door and spread your merchandise, you then have done what should have been doing.'"

H 8355, Ch. 6, h 2

Muhammad ibn Yahya has narrated from Ahmad ibn Muhammad from ibn Faddal from the one whom he has mentioned from al-Tayyar who has said the following:

'Abu Ja'far, *'Alayhi al-Salam*, once asked me, 'What do you manage? What do you make?' I replied, 'I am not in anything.' He (the Imam) said, 'Find a house, (a facility) broom its yards, sprinkle water around, spread the merchandise on it. In doing this you have done what should have been done.' I (the narrator) followed his instruction and found sustenance.'"

Chapter 7 - Meticulous Effort to Make a Living

H 8356, Ch. 7, h 1

Muhammad ibn Yahya has narrated from Ahmad ibn Muhammad and a number of our people have narrated from Sahl ibn Ziyad from ibn Mahbub from abu Hamzah al-Thumaliy who has said the following:

"Abu Ja'far, *'Alayhi al-Salam*, has said, 'The Messenger of Allah during his farewell Hajj said, 'The trustworthy spirit has inspired my understanding that no soul dies before its sustenance is complete (depleted). You must maintain piety before Allah, most Majestic, most Glorious, be meticulous in your work to make a living. You must not allow procrastination to make you fall behind in the work for living. You must not work in disobedience to Allah; Allah, most Blessed, most High, has divided sustenance among His creatures in a lawful way. He has not divided it in unlawful ways. One who maintains piety before Allah, most Majestic, most Glorious, He provides him sustenance from the lawful kind. One who tears the covering curtain in hastiness and takes it by unlawful ways, it is reduced from his lawful sustenance and he is held accountable for it on the Day of Judgment.'"

H 8357, Ch. 7, h 2

A number of our people have narrated from Ahmad ibn 'Isa from al-Husayn ibn Sa'id from Ibrahim ibn abu al-Balad from his father who has said the following:

"Abu Ja'far, *'Alayhi al-Salam*, has said, 'There is not a single soul whose sustenance Allah, most Majestic, most Glorious, has not assigned of the lawful kind and in good health. He has disclosed the unlawful kind also but in another aspect. If the soul achieves a certain amount of the unlawful kind it is reduced from its lawful sustenance which He has assigned for him. Besides these two kinds of sustenance, there is a great deal of extra with Allah as is mentioned in the words of Allah, most Majestic, most Glorious, 'You must ask Allah to grant you (sustenance) from the extra with Him. . . .' (3:37)"

H 8358, Ch. 7, h 3

Ibrahim ibn abu al-Balad has narrated from his father from one of the two Imams, *'Alayhi al-Salam*, who has said the following:

"The Messenger of Allah, *O Allah, grant compensation to Muhammad and his family worthy of their services to Your cause*, has said, 'O people, the trustworthy spirit has inspired my understanding that a soul never dies until it completes (depleting of) its sustenance even if it takes place with a certain degree of delays. You must maintain piety before Allah, most Majestic, most Glorious, and seek your sustenance meticulously. You must not allow certain degrees of delays from Allah, most Majestic, most Glorious, to cause you to indulge in Allah's disobedience. What is with Allah is only achieved through obedience to Him.'"

H 8359, Ch. 7, h 4
Muhammad ibn Yahya has narrated from Muhammad ibn Al-Husayn from 'Abd al-Rahman ibn abu Hashim from abu Khadijah who has said the following:
"Abu 'Abd Allah, *'Alayhi al-Salam*, has said, 'Even if a servant lives in a hole, Allah has his sustenance for him. Thus you must seek your sustenance meticulously.'"

H 8360, Ch. 7, h 5
Ali ibn Ibrahim has narrated from Salih ibn al-Sindiy from Ja'far ibn Bashir from 'Umar ibn abu Ziyad from Ishaq ibn 'Ammar who has said the following:
"Abu 'Abd Allah, *'Alayhi al-Salam*, has said that Allah, most Majestic, most Glorious, has created the creatures and with them He has created their sustenance of the lawful and beautiful kind. If anyone achieves a certain amount of unlawful sustenance it, then is deducted from his lawful sustenance.'"

H 8361, Ch. 7, h 6
Ali ibn Muhammad has narrated from Sahl ibn Ziyad in a marfu' manner the following:
"Amir al-Mu'minin, *'Alayhi al-Salam*, has said, 'There is many a soul who tires itself (by work) and lives stringently. On the other hand there are those who moderately seek their sustenance; and measures favorably assist them.'"

H 8362, Ch. 7, h 7
Ali ibn Muhammad ibn 'Abd Allah al-Qummiy has narrated from Ahmad ibn abu 'Abd Allah from 'Isma'il al-Qasir from those whom he has mentioned from abu Hamzah al-Thumaliy who has said the following:
"The condition of very high prices was mentioned before Ali ibn Al-Husayn, *'Alayhi al-Salam*. He (the Imam) said, 'Very high prices do not affect me; it is only against Him. If it becomes very high, it is against Him, and if it becomes very low, it is against Him.'"

H 8363, Ch. 7, h 8
It is narrated from him (narrator of previous Hadith) from ibn Faddal from the one whom he has mentioned who has said the following:
"Abu 'Abd Allah, *'Alayhi al-Salam*, has said that your effort in work for living must be above the efforts of a losing person and below that of a greedy one who is happy with confidence in the worldly matters. You must keep your soul in the position of the fair and conservatives ones, and lift your soul above the position of neglectful and weak ones. You must earn what is necessary. Those who are granted wealth but do not appreciate it they, in fact, have no wealth at all.'"

H 8364, Ch. 7, h 9
Ali ibn Muhammad has narrated from ibn Jumhur from his father in a marfu' manner who has said the following:
"Abu 'Abd Allah, *'Alayhi al-Salam*, has said that Amir al-Mu'minin, *'Alayhi al-Salam*, very often would say, 'You must take notice with absolute certainty that Allah, most Majestic, most Glorious, does not allow a servant, no matter how

intensely he strives, how great the kind of means he prepares, and no matter how numerously he suffers fatigue, to exceed the limit which He has mentioned in His book of wisdom. It does not change anything for a man, with his weakness and his little means, in reaching what is already assigned for him in the book of wisdom. O people, one's wisdom does not increase a naqir (a certain unit of measurement) for him and one's lack of understanding does not reduce anything against him. One who knows this and acts accordingly is the greatest of people to enjoy comfort in profit, and one who knows it but ignores to act accordingly does the biggest work to cause losses. There are many of those who are led to destruction in the process of receiving favors, and also there are many of those who are thought of among people as being deceived, but in reality receive favors. O you who strive hard, beware of your struggle, hold back your haste and wake up from the slumber of your unawareness. Think about what has come from Allah, most Majestic, most Glorious, through the tongue of His Holy prophet. Preserve these seven letters; they are of the words of the people of reason and of the decisive issues in the book of wisdom. One cannot reach before Allah, most Majestic, most Glorious, with the presence of any single of these habits in him: considering things as partners of Allah in the matters that Allah has made obligatory on him, quenching his anger by destruction of his soul, claiming to have done what in fact others have done, seeking success before a creature by means of a heretic act in his religion, enjoying people's praising him for what he has not done, acting oppressively and conceitedly, and being of honorable position but speaking lies. O people, what is important for beasts is transgression, and what is important for animals is to eat, what is important for women is their men; and believing people are anxious, fearful and afraid. I pray to Allah to make us one of them (such believers).'"

H 8365, Ch. 7, h 10

A number of our people have narrated from Ahmad ibn Muhammad ibn 'Isa from Ali ibn al-Hakam from Rabi' ibn Muhammad al-Musalliy from 'Abd Allah ibn Sulayman who has said the following:

"I heard abu 'Abd Allah, *'Alayhi al-Salam*, saying, 'Allah, most High, has expanded the sustenance of the dimwitted ones so that people of reason learn a lesson and take notice that the worldly things are not achieved by means of work and means only.'"

H 8366, Ch. 7, h 11

Ahmad ibn Muhammad from has narrated from Ali ibn al-Nu'man from 'Amr ibn Shamir from Jabir from abu Ja'far *'Alayhi al-Salam*, who has said the following:

"Abu Ja'far, *'Alayhi al-Salam*, has said that the Messenger of Allah, *O Allah, grant compensation to Muhammad and his family worthy of their services to Your cause*, has said, 'I have not left anything that can take you closer to paradise or keep you away from hellfire but that I have informed you of all such matters. You must take notice that the Holy Spirit has inspired my understanding and has told me that a soul does not die until it completes (depleting) its sustenance. You must maintain piety before Allah, most Majestic, most Glorious, and work for your living meticulously. Certain delays in reaching of sustenance must not take you to find sustenance by means of disobedience to Allah, most Majestic, most Glorious; what is with Allah, most Majestic, most Glorious, can be achieved only by means of obedience to Him."

Chapter 8 - Receiving Sustenance from Unexpected Sources

H 8367, Ch. 8, h 1
Ali ibn Ibrahim has narrated from his father from ibn abu 'Umayr from abu Ayyub al-Khazzaz from Muhammad ibn Muslim who has said the following:

"Abu 'Abd Allah, *'Alayhi al-Salam*, has said that Allah, most Majestic, most Glorious, disdains to provide sustenance for a believing person from any source other than an unexpected source."

H 8368, Ch. 8, h 2
Muhammad ibn Yahya has narrated from Ahmad ibn Muhammad from Ali ibn al-Hakam from abu Jamilah who has said the following:

"I heard abu 'Abd Allah, *'Alayhi al-Salam*, saying, 'Your hope for help from an unexpected source should be greater than an expected source. Musa *'Alayhi al-Salam*, went to find fire for his family and came back as a Prophet commissioned to preach.'"

H 8369, Ch. 8, h 3
A number of our people have narrated from Ahmad ibn abu 'Abd Allah from Ali ibn Muhammad al-Qasaniy from the one whom he has mentioned from 'Abd Allah ibn al-Qasim ibn Muhammad from abu 'Abd Allah from his father, from his grandfather *'Alayhi al-Salam*, who has said the following:

"Abu Ja'far, *'Alayhi al-Salam*, has said that Amir al-Mu'minin, *'Alayhi al-Salam*, has said, 'Your hope for help from an unexpected source should be greater than an expected source. Musa (Moses) *'Alayhi al-Salam* went to find fire for his family, Allah, most Majestic, most Glorious, spoke to him and he came back as a messenger prophet. Queen of Sheba' (Saba') went out and became a Muslim with Sulayman (Solomon). The magician went out to defend Pharaoh's majesty then returned as believing people.'"

H 8370, Ch. 8, h 4
It is narrated from him (narrator of previous Hadith) from Safwan from Muhammad ibn abu al-Haz Haz from Ali ibn al-Sariy who has said the following:

"I heard abu 'Abd Allah, *'Alayhi al-Salam*, saying, 'Allah, most Majestic, most Glorious, has made the sustenance of the believing people to come unexpectedly; when a servant (of Allah) does not know wherefrom his sustenance comes, he prays a great deal.'"

H 8371, Ch. 8, h 5
It is narrated from him (narrator of previous Hadith) from Muhammad ibn Ali from Harun ibn Hamzah from Ali ibn 'Abd al-'Aziz who has said the following:

"Abu 'Abd Allah, *'Alayhi al-Salam*, once asked me, 'What has 'Umar ibn Muslim done?' I replied, 'I pray to Allah to keep my soul in service for your cause, 'he has devoted himself in worship and has given up doing any business.' He (the Imam) said, 'Fie upon him! Does he not know that the prayer of one who neglects work to make a living is not answered? A people of the companions of the Messenger of Allah, when this was revealed, "Those who maintain piety before Allah, He makes a way out for them and provides them sustenance from unexpected sources" (66:7), closed their doors and begun to worship. They said, "We have found what we needed." This was reported to the Holy Prophet who called them in his presence and asked, "What made you do what you had been doing?" They replied, O Messenger of Allah, you guaranteed our sustenance, and thus, we devoted ourselves in worship." He said, "Whoever does this his prayer is not answered. You must work for your living."""

Chapter 9 - The Detestability of Sleeping and Passing Time without Work

H 8372, Ch. 9, h 1

A number of our people have narrated from Sahl ibn Ziyad from ibn Mahbub from Yunus ibn Ya'qub from the one whom he has mentioned who has said the following:

"Abu 'Abd Allah, *'Alayhi al-Salam*, has said, 'Excessive sleeping causes one to lose his religion as well as the worldly matters.'"

H 8373, Ch. 9, h 2

Muhammad ibn Yahya has narrated from Ahmad ibn Muhammad from ibn Faddal from the one whom he has mentioned (in his book) from Bashir al-Dahhan who has said the following:

"I heard abu al-Hassan, Musa, *'Alayhi al-Salam*, saying, 'Allah, most Majestic, most Glorious, dislikes an excessively sleeping servant who passes his time without work.'"

H 8374, Ch. 9, h 3

A number of our people have narrated from Ahmad ibn Muhammad ibn Khalid from his father from ibn Sinan from 'Abd Allah ibn Muskan from Salih al-Niliy who has said the following:

"Abu 'Abd Allah, *'Alayhi al-Salam*, has said, 'Allah, most Majestic, most Glorious, hates one's excessive sleeping and passing time without work.'"

Chapter 10 - Detestability of Laziness

H 8375, Ch. 10, h 1

A number of our people have narrated from Sahl ibn Ziyad from Ja'far ibn Muhammad al-Ash'ariy from ibn al-Qaddah who has said the following:

"Abu 'Abd Allah, *'Alayhi al-Salam*, has said, 'Laziness is an enemy of work.'"

H 8376, Ch. 10, h 2

Sahl ibn Ziyad has narrated from ibn Mahbub from Sa'd ibn abu Khalaf from abu al-Hassan, Musa, *'Alayhi al-Salam*, who has said the following:

"Abu al-Hassan, Musa has said, 'My father, *'Alayhi al-Salam*, once said to a certain one of his sons, "Beware of laziness and impatience; these two can deprive you of your share in this world as well as in the hereafter."""

H 8377, Ch. 10, h 3

Ali ibn Ibrahim has narrated from his father from ibn abu 'Umayr from 'Umar ibn 'Udhaynah from Zurarah who has said the following:

"Abu 'Abd Allah, *'Alayhi al-Salam*, has said, 'If one feels lazy to cleansing himself and to take wudu' for *Salat* (prayer), there is nothing good in him in regards to his affairs in the hereafter. One who feels lazy in organizing his living conditions, there is nothing good in him for his worldly life.'"

H 8378, Ch. 10, h 4

Muhammad ibn Yahya has narrated from Muhammad ibn Al-Husayn from Safwan from 'Ala' from Muhammad ibn Muslim who has said the following:

"Abu Ja'far, *'Alayhi al-Salam*, has said, 'I dislike a man –or dislike for a man– who is lazy in his worldly affairs. One who is lazy in his worldly affairs is lazier in the affairs of his hereafter.'"

H 8379, Ch. 10, h 5

A number of our people have narrated from Ahmad ibn Muhammad from ibn Faddal from Sama'ah ibn Mehran from abu al-Hassan, Musa, *'Alayhi al-Salam*, who has said the following:

"Abu al-Hassan, Musa, *'Alayhi al-Salam*, has said, 'Beware of laziness and impatience; with laziness you do not work and with impatience you do not yield to the truth."

H 8380, Ch. 10, h 6

Ahmad ibn Muhammad from has narrated from certain persons of our people from Salih ibn 'Umar from al-Hassan ibn 'Abd Allah who has said the following:

"Abu 'Abd Allah, *'Alayhi al-Salam*, has said, 'Do not seek help from a lazy person and you must not consult a helpless one.'"

H 8381, Ch. 10, h 7

Ahmad ibn Muhammad from has narrated from al-Haytham al-Nahdiy from 'Abd al-'Aziz ibn 'Amr al-Wasitiy from Ahmad ibn 'Umar al-Halabiy from Zayd al-Qattat from Aban ibn Taghlib who has said the following:

"I heard abu 'Abd Allah, *'Alayhi al-Salam*, saying, 'Avoid wishing (daydreaming); it destroys the beauty of Allah's favors to you and causes to suffer feeling of failure in your daydreaming and what you imagined.'"

H 8382, Ch. 10, h 8

Ali ibn Muhammad has narrated in a marfu' manner the following:

"Amir al-Mu'minin, *'Alayhi al-Salam*, has said, 'When things (works) double, laziness and failure join hands, and they both give birth to poverty.'"

H 8383, Ch. 10, h 9

Ali ibn Ibrahim has narrated from Harun ibn Muslim from Mas'adah ibn Sadaqah who has said the following:

"Abu 'Abd Allah, *'Alayhi al-Salam*, once wrote to one of his companions the following: '. . . thereafter take notice of the following. You must not excessively argue with the scholars, you must not verbally quarrel with the dimwitted ones; the scholars will hate you and the dimwitted ones will abuse you. You must not be lazy in the work for your sustenance; you will become a burden on the others' – or that he (the Imam) said, 'a burden on your family.'"

Chapter 11 - One's Working in His House

H 8384, Ch. 11, h 1

Ali ibn Ibrahim has narrated from his father from ibn abu 'Umayr from Hisham ibn Salim abu 'Abd Allah, *'Alayhi al-Salam*, who has said the following:

"Amir al-Mu'minin, *'Alayhi al-Salam*, would bring firewood, water and sweep the house. Fatimah al-Zahra', *'Alayha al-Salam*, would grind wheat, make dough and bake."

H 8385, Ch. 11, h 2

Ahmad ibn 'Abd Allah has narrated from Ahmad ibn abu 'Abd Allah from 'Abdul ibn Malik from Harun ibn al-Jahm from al-Kahiliy from Mu'adh, Bayya' al-Akyisah who has said the following:

"Abu 'Abd Allah, *'Alayhi al-Salam*, has said, 'The Messenger of Allah, *O Allah, grant compensation to Muhammad and his family worthy of their services to Your cause*, would milk his family's goat."

Chapter 12 - Amending one's Properties and Planning for one's Living

H 8386, Ch. 12, h 1

A number of our people have narrated from Ahmad ibn Muhammad from Ali ibn al-Hakam from Ali ibn al-Hakam from Muhammad ibn Sama'ah from Muhammad ibn Marwan who has said the following:

"Abu 'Abd Allah, *'Alayhi al-Salam*, has said, 'It is in the wisdom of Ale (family) Dawud that a reasonable Muslim should not travel unless it is for three kinds of tasks: amending one's means of living, supplies for the hereafter or enjoyment with lawful matters. A reasonable Muslim should assign certain hours of his time to work on the matters between him and Allah, most Majestic, most Glorious, certain hours to meet his brothers (in belief) with whom he speaks and they speak with him about the issues of the hereafter, and certain hours for himself and matters of enjoyment with lawful matters which are helpful during these two hours."

H 8387, Ch. 12, h 2

Muhammad ibn 'Isma'il has narrated from al-Fadl ibn Shadhan from ibn abu 'Umayr from Rib'iy from a man who has said the following:

"Abu 'Abd Allah, *'Alayhi al-Salam*, has said, 'All of perfection is in three things.' He mentioned in the third of the three things to be planning for one's living."

H 8388, Ch. 12, h 3

A number of our people have narrated from Ahmad ibn Muhammad from ibn Faddal from Tha'labah and others from a man who has said the following:

"Abu 'Abd Allah, *'Alayhi al-Salam*, has said, 'Keeping one's wealth in a proper shape is part of belief.'"

H 8389, Ch. 12, h 4

Ahmad ibn Muhammad has narrated from ibn Faddal from Dawud ibn Sarhan who has said the following:

"I saw abu 'Abd Allah, *'Alayhi al-Salam*, measure dates with his own hands; and I said, 'I pray to Allah to keep my soul in service for your cause, I wish you would have ordered certain persons of your servants or sons to help you.' He (the Imam) said, 'O Dawud, a Muslim cannot achieve a proper condition without three things: proper understanding of religion, exercising patience in hardships, and proper planning for his living and sustenance.'"

H 8390, Ch. 12, h 5

Ali ibn Muhammad ibn 'Abd Allah has narrated from Ahmad ibn abu 'Abd Allah from Muhammad ibn Ali from 'Abd Allah ibn Jabalah from Darih al-Muharibiy who has said the following:

"Abu 'Abd Allah, *'Alayhi al-Salam*, has said, 'When Allah, most Majestic, most Glorious, wills good for a family He grants them ease in their living conditions.'"

H 8391, Ch. 12, h 6

It is narrated from him (narrator of previous Hadith) from certain persons of our people from Salih ibn Hamzah from certain persons of our people Hamzah who have said the following:

"Abu 'Abd Allah, *'Alayhi al-Salam*, has said, 'You must manage your wealth properly; it increases respect for you and freedom of want from envious ones.'"

Chapter 13 - Hard Work for the Family

H 8392, Ch. 13, h 1

Ali ibn Ibrahim has narrated from his father from ibn abu 'Umayr from Hammad ibn 'Uthman from al-Halabiy who has said the following:

"Abu 'Abd Allah, *'Alayhi al-Salam*, has said, 'A person working hard for his family is like Mujahid (fighter) for the cause of Allah.'"

H 8393, Ch. 13, h 2

A number of our people have narrated from Ahmad ibn abu 'Abd Allah from 'Isma'il ibn Mehran from Zakariya' ibn Adam from abu al-Hassan, al-Rida', *'Alayhi al-Salam*, who has said the following:

"Abu al-Hassan, al-Rida', *'Alayhi al-Salam*, has said, 'One who works to find sustenance of the extra-generosity of Allah, most Majestic, most Glorious, to provide for his family is granted a reward greater than a Mujahid (fighter) for the cause of Allah, most Majestic, most Glorious.'"

H 8394, Ch. 13, h 3

Muhammad ibn 'Isma'il has narrated from al-Fadl ibn Shadhan from ibn abu 'Umayr from Rib'iy ibn 'Abd Allah from Fudayl ibn Yasar who has said the following:

"Abu 'Abd Allah, *'Alayhi al-Salam*, has said, 'If one has difficulty in providing for his family and works to meet his own needs and the needs of his family and does not work for unlawful kind of sustenance, he is like a Mujahid (fighter) for the cause of Allah."

Chapter 14 - Earning Lawful kind of Sustenance

H 8395, Ch. 14, h 1

A number of our people have narrated from Ahmad ibn Muhammad from Ahmad ibn abu Nasr who has said the following:

"Once I asked abu al-Hassan, *'Alayhi al-Salam*, saying, 'I pray to Allah to keep my soul in service for your cause, please pray for me to Allah, most Majestic, most Glorious, so He grants me lawful sustenance.' He (the Imam) asked, 'Do you know what lawful sustenance is?' I replied, 'I pray to Allah to keep my soul in service for your cause, according to our information it is clean earning.' He (the Imam) said, 'Ali ibn Al-Husayn, *'Alayhi al-Salam*, would say, 'Lawful sustenance is the sustenance of the chosen ones.' You, however, should say, 'I pray to You to grant me wide-ranging sustenance.'"

H 8396, Ch. 14, h 2

Muhammad ibn Yahya has narrated from Ahmad ibn Muhammad ibn 'Isa from Mu'ammar ibn Khallad and Ali ibn Muhammad ibn Bandar from Ahmad ibn abu 'Abd Allah from Muhammad ibn 'Isa all from Mu'ammar ibn Khallad from abu al-Hassan, al-Thani, who has said the following:

"Once abu Ja'far, *'Alayhi al-Salam*, looked at a man who said, 'O Lord, I pray to You to grant me lawful sustenance.' Abu Ja'far, *'Alayhi al-Salam*, said, 'You have asked of the kind of sustenance of the prophets. Say, "O Lord, grant me of Your extended and clean sustenance.""""

Chapter 15 - Saving for One's Living Expenses

H 8397, Ch. 15, h 1

Muhammad ibn Yahya has narrated from Ahmad ibn Muhammad from ibn Faddal from al-Hassan ibn al-Jahm who has said the following:

"I heard al-Rida', *'Alayhi al-Salam*, saying, 'If one saves food for one year, his burden becomes light and he feels comfortable. Abu Ja'far and abu 'Abd Allah, *'Alayhim al-Salam*, would not buy anything before reserving their food for one year."

H 8398, Ch. 15, h 2

Abu Ali al-Ash'ariy has narrated from abu Muhammad al-Dhuhliy from abu Ayyub al-Mad'iniy from 'Abd Allah ibn 'Abd al-Rahman from ibn Bukayr from abu al-Hassan, *'Alayhi al-Salam*, who has said the following:

"Abu al-Hassan, *'Alayhi al-Salam*, has said that the Messenger of Allah *O Allah, grant compensation to Muhammad and his family worthy of their services to Your cause*, has said, 'When a soul reserves its sustenance it settles down."

H 8399, Ch. 15, h 3

Ali ibn Ibrahim has narrated from Harun ibn Muslim from Mas'adah ibn Sadaqah who has said the following:

"Abu Ja'far, *'Alayhi al-Salam*, has said that Salman, may Allah be pleased with him, has said, 'The soul disturbs its owner when he does not have dependable sustenance; but upon reserving sustenance his soul becomes comfortable and settled."

Chapter 16 - Detestability of Offering Oneself for Hire

H 8400, Ch. 16, h 1

Muhammad ibn Yahya has narrated from Ahmad ibn Muhammad from 'Isma'il ibn Bazi' from Mansur ibn Yunus from al-Mufaddal ibn 'Umar who has said the following:

"I once heard abu 'Abd Allah, *'Alayhi al-Salam*, saying, 'One who offers himself for hire prohibits sustenance to himself.' In another Hadith it is said that how can it be anything other than prohibition when whatever one finds goes to his master?'"

H 8401, Ch. 16, h 2
Ali ibn Muhammad ibn Bandar has narrated from Ahmad ibn abu 'Abd Allah from his father from ibn Sinan who has said the following:
"I once asked abu al-Hassan, *'Alayhi al-Salam*, about the case of a man who places himself for hire. He (the Imam) said, 'It is not harmful if he remains fair within the limits of his abilities. Moses allowed his self to be hired with stipulation that said, 'If you like make it eight or ten' and Allah, most Majestic, most Glorious, sent the statement that said, 'I want that you work for me for eight years; but if you make it ten years, it will be out of your choice.'"

H 8402, Ch. 16, h 3
Ahmad his has narrated from his father from Muhammad ibn 'Amr from al-Sabatiy who has said the following:
"This is concerning my question before abu 'Abd Allah, *'Alayhi al-Salam*, about the case of a man who places himself for hire; if what he achieves he has to give it all. He (the Imam) said, 'He should not place himself for hire; instead ask sustenance from Allah, most Majestic, most Glorious, and himself do business, because if one places himself for hire he prohibits sustenance upon himself.'"

Chapter 17 - Performing Personally one's Business Tasks

H 8403, Ch. 17, h 1
Ali ibn Ibrahim has narrated from Muhammad ibn 'Isa ibn 'Ubayd from Yunus from a man who has said the following:
"Abu 'Abd Allah, *'Alayhi al-Salam*, has said that you must do the greater tasks of your affairs personally and assign others to perform the easier ones. I then asked, 'Like what kinds of tasks are they?' He (the Imam) answered, 'Like real estate deals and similar tasks.'"

H 8404, Ch. 17, h 2
A number of our people have narrated from Ahmad ibn abu 'Abd Allah from his father from 'Amr ibn Ibrahim from Khalaf ibn Hammad from Harun ibn al-Jahm from al-Arqat who has said the following:
"Abu 'Abd Allah, *'Alayhi al-Salam*, once said to me, 'You must not roam around in market places and you must not perform small tasks personally; it is not proper for a Muslim man of good position and religion to buy small things personally, except three kinds of items, in which case a person of good position and religion should personally perform, such as real estate, slaves and camels.'"

Chapter 18 - Buying and Selling Real Estate

H 8405, Ch. 18, h 1
Muhammad ibn Yahya has narrated from Ahmad ibn Muhammad ibn 'Isa from Mu'ammar ibn Khallad who has said the following:

"I heard abu al-Hassan, '*Alayhi al-Salam*, saying, 'Once a man came to Ja'far, '*Alayhi al-Salam*, as if giving him good advice; he said, 'O abu 'Abd Allah, '*Alayhi al-Salam*, why have you made the properties in scattered pieces? Had they been in one piece, more profit with fewer expenses could have been made.' Abu 'Abd Allah, '*Alayhi al-Salam*, replied, 'I have kept them scattered so that if losses affect one piece, others remain unaffected, but a bag keeps all of them together (vulnerable to losses).'"

H 8406, Ch. 18, h 2
Ali ibn Ibrahim has narrated from his father from ibn abu 'Umayr from the one whom he has mentioned (in his book) from Zurarah who has said the following:

"I heard abu 'Abd Allah, '*Alayhi al-Salam*, saying, The most difficult to property to protect is of the silent kind (gold and silver).' I then asked, 'What should one do about it?' He (the Imam) replied, 'One should keep them inside walls, a garden or a house.'"

H 8407, Ch. 18, h 3
Humayd ibn Ziyad has narrated from al-Hassan ibn Muhammad ibn Sama'ah from more than one person from Aban ibn 'Uthman who has said the following:

"Once Ja'far, '*Alayhi al-Salam*, called me and asked, 'Has so and so sold his land?' I replied, 'Yes, he has done so.' He (the Imam) said, 'It is written in the Torah that whoever sells a piece of land or water and does not replace it by another piece of land or water, its price (money received) loses its blessings.'"

H 8408, Ch. 18, h 4
Ali ibn Muhammad ibn Ali has narrated from Salih ibn abu Hammad from al-Hassan ibn Ali from Wahab al-Haririy who has said the following:

"Abu 'Abd Allah, '*Alayhi al-Salam*, has said, 'The buyer of real property receives sustenance and the seller thereof suffers a serious loss.'"

H 8409, Ch. 18, h 5
Al-Hassan ibn Muhammad has narrated from Muhammad ibn Ahmad al-Nahdiy from Ya'qub ibn Yazid from Muhammad ibn Murazim from his father who has said the following:

"Abu 'Abd Allah, '*Alayhi al-Salam*, once said to his Mawla', Musadif, 'Find some real property or goods; when man faces hardship or misfortune, and then finds out that behind him there is something for support of his family, he feels more generous to allow his soul to depart (his body).'"

H 8410, Ch. 18, h 6
Ali ibn Muhammad ibn Bandar has narrated from Ahmad ibn abu 'Abd Allah Muhammad ibn Ali ibn Yusuf from 'Abd al-Salam from Hisham ibn Ahmar who has said the following:

"Abu Ibrahim, '*Alayhi al-Salam*, has said that the price (money) received in exchange for real estate is a loss unless another piece of real estate is purchased therewith."

H 8411, Ch. 18, h 7
Abu Ali al-Ash'ariy has narrated from Muhammad ibn al-Hassan ibn Ali al-Kufiy from 'Ubays ibn Hisham from 'Abd al-Samad ibn Bashir from Mu'awiyah ibn 'Ammar from, who has said the following:

"Abu 'Abd Allah, *'Alayhi al-Salam* has said, that when the Holy Prophet, *O Allah, grant compensation to Muhammad and his family worthy of their services to Your cause*, arrived in al-Madinah he drew a line around its houses and said, 'O Allah, do not make it a blessing for those who sell its houses.'"

H 8412, Ch. 18, h 8
A number of our people have narrated from Sahl ibn Ziyad from Muhammad ibn al-Hassan ibn Shammun from al-Asamm from Misma' who has said the following:
"Once I said to abu 'Abd Allah, *'Alayhi al-Salam*, 'I have a piece of land in which buyers are much interested to purchase.' He (the Imam) said, 'O abu Sayyar, do you know that whoever sells land or water (like a fountain for irrigation and so on), his wealth goes away as a bad loss.' I then said, 'I pray to Allah to keep my soul in service for your cause, I will sell it for a high price and then I can buy a piece of land bigger than this one.' He (the Imam) said, 'Then it is all right.'"

Chapter 19 - Debts and Borrowing

H 8413, Ch. 19, h 1
A number of our people have narrated from Sahl ibn Ziyad from ibn Mahbub from 'Abd al-Rahman ibn Hajjaj from who has said the following:
"Abu 'Abd Allah, *'Alayhi al-Salam*, has said, 'You must seek protection with Allah against over-powering debts, dominating (increasing) number of men and single women.'"

H 8414, Ch. 19, h 2
Muhammad ibn Yahya has narrated from Ahmad ibn Muhammad from al-Husayn ibn Sa'id from al-Nadr ibn Suwayd from Yahya al-Halabiy for Mu'awiyah ibn Wahab who has said the following:
"I once said to abu 'Abd Allah, *'Alayhi al-Salam*, 'We are told that a man from al-Ansar died while he owed two dinar to pay. The Holy Prophet, *O Allah, grant compensation to Muhammad and his family worthy of their services to Your cause*, did not perform *Salat* (prayer) on his dead body and said, "You must perform *Salat* (prayer) on the dead body of your companion." (It was the case) until someone of his relatives guaranteed to pay the two dinars on his behalf.' Abu 'Abd Allah, *'Alayhi al-Salam*, said, 'That is the right.' He (the Imam) said, 'The Messenger of Allah did so to teach people a lesson to pay back the debts they owe to each other and must not take the issue of debts lightly. The Messenger of Allah, *O Allah, grant compensation to Muhammad and his family worthy of their services to Your cause*, passed away while he owed payable debts, al-Hassan, *'Alayhi al-Salam*, died while he owed payable debts and Al-Husayn, *'Alayhi al-Salam*, was murdered while he owed payable debts.'"

H 8415, Ch. 19, h 3
Muhammad ibn Yahya has narrated from Ahmad ibn Muhammad from Ali ibn al-Hakam from Musa ibn Bakr who has said the following:
"Abu al-Hassan, *'Alayhi al-Salam*, said to me, 'Whoever works to provide sustenance for himself and his family is considered a Mujahid (fighter) for the cause of Allah, most Majestic, most Glorious. If poverty over-powers him, he then should borrow upon the responsibility of Allah and His Messenger for his

sustenance and his family. If he dies and cannot pay back, it then becomes the responsibility of the Imam to pay it. If he did not do so, he will be held responsible. Allah, most Majestic, most Glorious, says, 'Charities are for the poor, destitute and the charity (tax) collectors . . . ., and those suffering bankruptcy.' (9:61) He is poor, destitute and bankrupt.'"

H 8416, Ch. 19, h 4

Ahmad ibn Muhammad from has narrated from Hamdan ibn Ibrahim al– Hamadaniy in a in a marfu' manner from the truthful ones who has narrated the following:

"He (the Imam), *'Alayhi al-Salam*, has said, 'I like for a man, who is indebted, to sincerely have the intention of paying it off.'"

H 8417, Ch. 19, h 5

Muhammad ibn Yahya has narrated from Muhammad ibn Al-Husayn from Muhammad ibn Sulayman from a man of the people of al-Jazirah called abu Muhammad who has said the following:

"A man asked al-Rida', *'Alayhi al-Salam*, when I was listening, 'I pray to Allah to keep my soul in service for your cause, Allah, most Majestic, most Glorious, says, "If one has difficulty to pay his debts, he should be given respite until he is able to pay." (2:281) Explain to me the limits of this "respite" of which Allah, most Majestic, most Glorious, has spoken in His book. When a person with such difficulties is required to pay back? He has taken from the properties of the lender to spend on his family. He does not have any farm to wait for the harvest season, has not lent money to anyone to wait for payment time or an amount of lost property that he hopes will be found.' He (the Imam) said, 'He is given respite until the Imam is informed about his condition who will pay on his behalf of the share of the bankrupt people, if he has spent what he has borrowed in obedience to Allah, most Majestic, most Glorious. If he has spent in disobedience to Allah, then the Imam is not responsible for his debts.' I (the narrator) then asked, 'What happens if the lender who trusted him and did not know if he (borrower) spends it in obedience or disobedience to the command of Allah?' He (the Imam) said, 'He can try to get back what he has lent from the properties of the borrowers who must yield."

(Fatwa best explains the last part of the above case.)

H 8418, Ch. 19, h 6

Ali ibn Ibrahim has narrated from his father from [ibn abu 'Umayr] from Hanan ibn Sadir from his father who has said the following:

"Abu Ja'far, *'Alayhi al-Salam*, has said, 'Being killed for the cause of Allah, most Majestic, most Glorious, serves as expiation for all kinds of sins except debts, for which there is no expiation other than paying it back or those liable pay or the owner of the lending right waives it in favor of the borrower.'"

H 8419, Ch. 19, h 7

Muhammad ibn Yahya has narrated from Ahmad ibn Muhammad ibn 'Isa from al-'Abbas the one whom he has mentioned (in his book) who has said the following:

"Abu 'Abd Allah, *'Alayhi al-Salam*, has said, 'The Imam pays off the debts of the believing people except Muhur (dowry) of women.'"

H 8420, Ch. 19, h 8

Ali ibn Ibrahim has narrated from his father from ibn abu 'Umayr from Hammad ibn 'Isa from al-Walid ibn Sabih who has said the following:

"Once a man came to abu 'Abd Allah, *'Alayhi al-Salam*, saying that al-Mu'alla' ibn Khunays owed him a certain amount and said, 'He has destroyed my rights.' Abu 'Abd Allah, *'Alayhi al-Salam*, said, 'Your rights are destroyed by the one who murdered him (al-Mu'alla').' He (the Imam) then told al-Walid to pay back his rights, 'I like to cool down his skin which was cool already.'"

H 8421, Ch. 19, h 9

A number of our people have narrated from Ahmad ibn abu 'Abd Allah from Muhammad ibn 'Isa from 'Uthman ibn Sa'id from 'Abd al-karim, of the people of Hamadan from abu Thumamah who has said the following:

"I once said to abu Ja'far, al-Thaniy, *'Alayhi al-Salam*, 'I like to reside in Makkah or al-Madinah, but there is a certain amount of debt that I must pay. What do you advise me to do?' He (the Imam) said, 'You must return to pay off what you owe, and bear in mind that you must go before Allah, most High, when there is no debts due on you. A believing person does not commit treachery.'"

H 8422, Ch. 19, h 10

Ali ibn Muhammad has narrated from Ishaq ibn Muhammad al-Nakha'iy from Muhammad ibn Jumhur from Fadalah from Musa ibn Bakr who has said the following:

"I heard abu al-Hassan, Musa, *'Alayhi al-Salam*, read the following: 'O mother, if I may become indebted (consider) that Moses son of 'Imran would also borrow.'"

H 8423, Ch. 19, h 11

A number of our people have narrated from Sahl ibn Ziyad from Ja'far ibn Muhammad al-Ash'ariy from ibn al-Qaddah who has said the following:

"Abu 'Abd Allah, from his ancestors from Ali, *'Alayhi al-Salam*, has stated this Hadith. 'Beware of debts; it humiliates during the day and causes sadness during the night and it is payable both in this world and in the hereafter.'"

Chapter 20 - Payment of Debts

H 8424, Ch. 20, h 1

A number of our people have narrated from Ahmad ibn Muhammad from 'Abd al-Rahman ibn abu Najran from al-Hassan ibn Ali ibn Ribat who has said the following:

"I once heard abu 'Abd Allah, *'Alayhi al-Salam*, saying, 'If one is indebted and he intends to pay it back, from the side of Allah, most Majestic, most Glorious, there will be two guards to help him to keep his trust; but if his intention falls short they also fall behind in their help proportionate to the degree of the fall of his intention.'"

H 8425, Ch. 20, h 2

A number of our people have narrated from Sahl ibn Ziyad and Ahmad ibn Muhammad from ibn Mahbub from abu Ayyub from Sama'ah who has said the following:

"I once said to abu 'Abd Allah, *'Alayhi al-Salam*, if one of us has a few things in his possession with which he meets his expenses and he also is indebted. Should he feed his family with that which he owns and wait until Allah, most Majestic, most Glorious, grants him ease then pay his debts, or should he borrow on his back in difficult times for earning, or should he accept charity?' He (the Imam) said, 'He has to pay the debt with what he owns, so he does not consume people's belongings, except if he has something with which he can pay off their rights. Allah, most Majestic, most Glorious, has said, "You must not consume your belongings among yourselves in false manners unless it is a trading by mutual consent among you." (4:29) He must not borrow on his back unless he has something with which he can make payment, he may also go door to door and they may send him back with a morsel or two or one piece of date or two, unless he has a heir (guardian) who pays off after him; no one of us dies for whom Allah, most Majestic, most Glorious, does not make a heir (guardian) who takes charge of his means and his debts to make payments by his means.'"

H 8426, Ch. 20, h 3
Ali ibn Ibrahim has narrated from his father from al-Nadr ibn Suwayd from al-Halabiy who has narrated the following:
"Abu 'Abd Allah, *'Alayhi al-Salam*, has said that a servant and a house must not be sold; it is necessary for a man to have a shelter and a servant."

H 8427, Ch. 20, h 4
Ali ibn Muhammad ibn Bandar has narrated from Ahmad ibn abu 'Abd Allah from 'Abd Allah ibn al-Mughirah from Burayd al-'Ijliy who has said the following:
"I once said to abu 'Abd Allah, *'Alayhi al-Salam*, 'I am indebted' – I think he said, 'to the orphans' and I am afraid if I sell my property I will be left without any assets.' He (the Imam) said, 'You must not sell your property; however, you should pay a certain part and keep certain other parts.'"

(Fatwa best explains this Hadith)

H 8428, Ch. 20, h 5
Ali ibn Muhammad has narrated from Ibrahim ibn Ishaq al-Ahmar from 'Abd Allah ibn Hammad from 'Umar ibn Yazid who has said the following:
"Once, when I was present, a man came to abu 'Abd Allah, *'Alayhi al-Salam*, asking to pay his debts. He (the Imam) said, 'There is nothing with us today; however, tomorrow we will receive Khitr and wasma (henna) which will be sold and Allah willing, we will help you.' The man then said, 'Promise me.' He (the Imam) said, 'How can I promise you if I am more hopeful for what I do not expect than for what I do expect to happen?'"

H 8429, Ch. 20, h 6
Muhammad ibn Yahya has narrated from Muhammad ibn Ahmad from Yusuf ibn al-Sukht from Ali ibn Muhammad ibn Sulayman from al-Fadl ibn Sulayman from al-'Abbas ibn 'Isa who has said the following:
"Once, Ali ibn Al-Husayn, *'Alayhi al-Salam*, was placed under pressure. He went to one of his Mawla' (friend or follower) and asked him to lend him ten thousand dirham up to the time he is able to pay back. He (his friend) said, 'No, because it is not with me; however, I want a promissory note.' He (the narrator) has said, 'He (the Imam) tore a piece from his gown and said this is the

promissory note.' His Mawla' did not like it and became angry. He (the Imam) said, 'Am I more trustworthy or Hajib ibn Zurarah?' He (his Mawla') replied, 'You are more trustworthy than Hajib ibn Zurarah.' He (the Imam) said, 'How is it that Hajib by depositing his bow, only a piece of wood, as a guarantee to bail out one hundred, also being a non-Muslim, kept up to his words and I will not keep up my word despite depositing a piece of my gown?' He (the narrator) said that his Mawla' took the piece of his gown and lent him the dirhams and placed the piece of fabric in a container. Allah, most Majestic, most Glorious, granted him ease and he (the Imam) took the dirhams to return to the man and said, 'Here is the dirhams. Where is the promissory note (the piece of my gown)? He replied, 'I pray to Allah to keep my soul in service for your cause, I have lost it.' He (the Imam) said, 'You then cannot have your dirhams from me. One like me is not treated lightly in matters of trust.' He (the narrator) has said, 'He then brought the container and the piece of fabric was in it. Ali ibn Al-Husayn, *'Alayhi al-Salam*, gave the dirhams to him and took the piece of fabric and threw it away and left.'"

H 8430, Ch. 20, h 7
It is narrated from him (narrator of previous Hadith) from Yusuf ibn al-Sukht from Ali ibn Muhammad ibn Sulayman from his father from 'Isa ibn 'Abd Allah who has said the following:
"'Abd Allah was about to die and his creditors gathered around him demanding payment. He said to them, 'I do not have any property to pay you but you may choose one of the sons of my uncle, Ali ibn Al-Husayn, *'Alayhi al-Salam*, and 'Abd Allah ibn Ja'far who will assume responsibility to pay you.' They said, "'Abd Allah ibn Ja'far is a procrastinator and slow to respond. Ali ibn Al-Husayn, *'Alayhi al-Salam*, does not have any properties but is a truthful person and more beloved one of the two to us.' He then sent someone to inform him of the case, and he said, 'I assume responsibility to pay you by the time of harvest,' although he did not have any harvest but he said so to show kindness. The people said, 'We accept your offer.' He assumed the responsibility and when time for harvest came Allah, most Majestic, most Glorious, made it possible for him to pay and he did so."

H 8431, Ch. 20, h 8
Ali ibn Ibrahim has narrated from his father and Muhammad ibn 'Isma'il from al-Fadl ibn Shadhan all ibn abu 'Umayr from Ibrahim ibn 'Abd al-Hamid from 'Uthman ibn Ziyad who has said the following:
"Once I said to abu 'Abd Allah, *'Alayhi al-Salam*, that a man owes me a certain amount and wants to sell his house to pay me. Abu 'Abd Allah, *'Alayhi al-Salam*, said, 'I seek protection for you with Allah against taking him out of the shadow on his head.'"

H 8432, Ch. 2, h 9
A number of our people have narrated from Ahmad ibn abu 'Abd Allah from his father from Khalaf ibn Hammad from Muhriz from abu Basir who has said the following:
"Abu 'Abd Allah, *'Alayhi al-Salam*, has said that the Messenger of Allah, *O Allah, grant compensation to Muhammad and his family worthy of their services to Your cause*, has said, 'Debts are three. One man is he who when a lender

gives the borrower respite and the borrower pays it off without delay. In his case it is all for him and it is not against him. There also is a man who as lender asks for payment and as a borrower he pays in time. In his case there is nothing for or against him. There is a man who as a lender demands payment and he as a borrower delays payment. In his case it is against him but not for him."

Chapter 21 - To Retaliate and Offset for Debts

H 8433, Ch. 21, h 1
A number of our people have narrated from Sahl ibn Ziyad ibn Mahbub from ibn Ri'ab from Sulayman ibn Khalid who has said the following:
"This is concerning my question before abu 'Abd Allah, *'Alayhi al-Salam*, about the case of a man who had a certain amount of my property with him. He played arrogantly with me about it and swore to deny it. Thereafter a certain amount of his property came in my control. Can I take his property in place of my property with him, deny the existence of his property with me and swear just as he did against me? He (the Imam) said, 'If he betrayed, you must not act like him and must not enter into something for which you blamed him.'"

H 8434, Ch. 21, h 2
Ali ibn Ibrahim has narrated from his father from and Muhammad ibn 'Isma'il has narrated from al-Fadl ibn Shadhan from ibn abu 'Umayr from Ibrahim ibn 'Abd al-Hamid from Mu'awiyah ibn 'Ammar who has said the following:
"This is concerning my question before abu 'Abd Allah, *'Alayhi al-Salam*, about the case of a man who owes to me a right but he denies it and then leaves in my trust a certain amount of his property: if I can offset my rights with him from his property with me. He (the Imam) said, 'No, you cannot do so because it is treachery'"

H 8435, Ch. 21, h 3
A number of our people have narrated from Sahl ibn Ziyad from ibn Mahbub Sayf ibn 'Amirah from abu Bakr al-Hadramiy who has said the following:
"This is concerning my question before abu 'Abd Allah, *'Alayhi al-Salam*, about the case of a man who has a certain amount of property with another person who denies the existence of such thing with him and goes away with it. Later a certain amount of the property of this person comes in the control of the first one; Can he offset his property for what has come in his control? He (the Imam) said, 'Yes, he can do so but he must say the following: "O Lord, I take this property in place of my property which he has taken from me and I do not take it with treacherous intention and injustice.'"

Chapter 22 - When a Man Dies Payment of his Debts becomes Due

H 8436, Ch. 22, h 1
Abu Ali al-Ash'ariy has narrated from Muhammad ibn 'Abd al-Jabbar from certain persons of his people from Khalaf ibn Hammad from 'Isma'il ibn abu Qurrah from abu Basir who has said the following:

"Abu 'Abd Allah, *'Alayhi al-Salam*, has said, 'When a man dies, payment of all of loans for and against him opens up (becomes due).'"

H 8437, Ch. 22, h 2
Muhammad ibn Yahya has narrated from Ahmad ibn Muhammad from al-Hassan ibn Mahbub from 'Abd Allah ibn Sinan who has said the following:
"About the case of a man who dies indebted and someone guarantees the creditors to pay them on behalf of the deceased, abu 'Abd Allah, *'Alayhi al-Salam*, has said, 'If the creditors agree with such guarantees, the deceased becomes free of his responsibility for payment of debts he owed.'"

Chapter 23 - The Case of One Who Borrows But Does Not Intend To Pay Back

H 8438, Ch. 23, h 1
Muhammad ibn Yahya has narrated from Muhammad ibn al-Husayn from al-Nadr ibn Shu'ayb from 'Abd al-Ghaffar al-Jaziy who has said the following:
"This is concerning my question before abu 'Abd Allah, *'Alayhi al-Salam*, about the case of a man who dies owing debts. He (the Imam) said, 'If such debts have become due upon him and it is free of his involvement in corruption, Allah will not hold him responsible if He will find in him the intention to pay back. However, if he did not have the intention to pay back what was in his trust, he then is considered a thief and so also is Zakat and destroying *Mahr* (dowry) of women.'"

H 8439, Ch. 23, h 2
Ali ibn Muhammad has narrated from Salih ibn abu Hammad from ibn Faddal from certain persons of his people who has said the following:
"Abu 'Abd Allah, *'Alayhi al-Salam*, has said, 'One who borrows without the intention to pay back is considered a thief.'"

Chapter 24 - Sell off Debts in Exchange for Debts

H 8440, Ch. 24, h 1
Muhammad ibn Yahya has narrated from Ahmad ibn Muhammad from ibn Mahbub from Ibrahim ibn Mihzam from Talhah ibn Yazid who has said the following:
"Abu 'Abd Allah, *'Alayhi al-Salam*, has said that the Messenger of Allah has said, 'It is not lawful to buy a debt with debt (on credit).'"

H 8441, Ch. 24, h 2
Ahmad ibn Muhammad has narrated from al-Hassan ibn Ali from Muhammad ibn al-Fudayl from abu Hamzah who has said the following:
"I once asked abu Ja'far, *'Alayhi al-Salam*, about the case of a man to whom another person owes a loan and a third person buys the loan from the creditor to collect it from the debtor. The collector demands the debtor for payment; and (what is the Imam's) judgment in this issue. Abu Ja'far, *'Alayhi al-Salam*, made a pronouncement that said, 'The debtor can pay to the collector what he (the collector) has paid to the creditor.'"

H 8442, Ch. 24, h 3

Muhammad ibn Yahya and others have narrated from Muhammad ibn Ahmad from Muhammad ibn 'Isa from Muhammad ibn al-Fudayl who has said the following:

"I once asked al-Rida', *'Alayhi al-Salam*, about the case of a man who buys a loan to collect it from the debtor and demands the debtor for payment. He (the Imam) said, 'The debtor pays what the collector has paid to the creditor and in so doing becomes free of the responsibility of paying all that was due on him.'"

Chapter 25 - Etiquette of Asking for Payment

H 8443, Ch. 25, h 1

Al-Husayn ibn Muhammad has narrated from Mu'alla' ibn Muhammad from al-Hassan ibn Ali from Hammad ibn 'Uthaman who has said the following:

"Once, a man came to abu 'Abd Allah, *'Alayhi al-Salam*, to complain before him (the Imam) against one of his companions. In a little while the defendant came in and abu 'Abd Allah, *'Alayhi al-Salam*, asked, 'Why does so and so complain against you?' He replied, 'It is because I asked him for payment of what he owes to me.' He (the narrator) has said that abu 'Abd Allah, *'Alayhi al-Salam*, then sat straight with anger and said, 'It seems as if when you demand for payment of what others owe, you do not consider it maltreating him. Consider what Allah, most Majestic, most Glorious, has said in His book, 'They fear dreadful accounting.' (13:21) Do you think they fear that Allah will do injustice to them? No, by Allah, that is not the case. They did not fear anything but demand for payment of what is owed to them and Allah, most Majestic, most Glorious, has called it (demand for payment) dreadful accounting, thus one who demands payment has maltreated him (debtor).'"

H 8444, Ch. 25, h 2

Muhammad ibn Yahya in a marfu' manner has narrated the following:

"He (the narrator) has said that a man once said to abu 'Abd Allah, *'Alayhi al-Salam*, 'A man of Al-Husayniy people owes me a certain amount. Asking him for payment has become tiring for me. We had an argument about it and I am afraid something may happen between us that will make me sad.' Abu 'Abd Allah, *'Alayhi al-Salam*, said, 'This is not a proper manner of asking for payment. When you go to him next time sit with him for a long time and remain quiet.' The man has said, 'I followed the instruction and shortly thereafter I received full payment.'"

H 8445, Ch. 25, h 3

Ali ibn Ibrahim has narrated from his father and Muhammad ibn 'Isma'il has narrated from al-Fadl ibn Shadhan all from ibn abu 'Umayr from Ibrahim ibn 'Abd al-Hamid from Khidr ibn 'Amr al-Nakha'iy who has said the following:

"About the case of a man to whom another person owes a certain amount of assets but denies such liability one of the two Imam, (abu Ja'far or abu 'Abd Allah), *'Alayhim al-Salam*, has said, 'If he (creditor) makes him (the debtor) to take an oath, thereafter he (the creditor) is not entitled to take anything from him (the debtor), but if he does not make him to take an oath his right remains enforced upon the debtor.'"

H 8446, Ch. 25, h 4

A number of our people have narrated from Sahl ibn Ziyad from Harun ibn Muslim from Mas'adah ibn Sadaqah who has said the following:

"Abu 'Abd Allah, *'Alayhi al-Salam*, has said that the Messenger of Allah, *O Allah, grant compensation to Muhammad and his family worthy of their services to Your cause*, has said, 'No other ache is a serious ache except an eye ache, and no anxiety is a serious anxiety except the anxiety because of debts.'"

H 8447, Ch. 25, h 5

Through the same chain of narrators as that of the previous Hadith the following is narrated:

"Abu 'Abd Allah, *'Alayhi al-Salam*, has said that the Messenger of Allah, *O Allah, grant compensation to Muhammad and his family worthy of their services to Your cause,* has said, 'Debt is the loop of Allah on earth and when He wants to humiliate a person. He places it on his neck.'"

H 8448, Ch. 25, h 6

Muhammad ibn Yahya has narrated from Ahmad ibn Muhammad from Muhammad ibn Sinan from Hammad ibn abu Talhah Bayya' al-Sabiriy and Muhammad ibn al-Fudayl and Hakam al-Hannat all from abu Hamzah who has said the following:

"I heard abu Ja'far *'Alayhi al-Salam*, saying, 'One who withholds the assets of a Muslim, despite his ability to give it to him, just because of fear of standing in need, Allah, most Majestic, most Glorious, has greater power to impoverish him because of wasting his time and soul for holding back such right.'"

Chapter 26 - The Case of Delaying Due Payment

H 8449, Ch. 26, h 1

Muhammad ibn Yahya has narrated from Ahmad ibn Muhammad from ibn Faddal from 'Ammar who has said the following:

"Abu 'Abd Allah, *'Alayhi al-Salam*, has said that 'Amir al-Mu'minin, *'Alayhi al-Salam*, would keep in custody a procrastinating debtor; then command to distribute his assets among his creditors proportionate to their shares, and if he (the debtor) disagreed, he (the Imam) sold his assets, then distributed it among his creditors.'"

H 8450, Ch. 26, h 2

Ahmad ibn Muhammad has narrated from Ali ibn al-Hassan from Ja'far ibn Muhammad ibn Hakim from Jamil ibn Darraj from Muhammad ibn Muslim who has said the following:

"Abu Ja'far, *'Alayhi al-Salam*, has said, 'The debt of an absent person is paid from his assets when enough proof is presented to prove his indebtedness. His assets are sold to make necessary payments in his absence and he faces the proof against him. One who has presented proofs receives payments upon providing guarantee and security, if he does not want to wait.'"

Chapter 27 - Lodging With a Borrower When Demanding Payment

H 8451, Ch. 27, h 1
Muhammad ibn Yahya has narrated from Ahmad ibn Muhammad from al-Husayn ibn Sa'id from al-Nadr ibn Suwayd from al-Qasim ibn Sulayman from Jarrah al-Mada'iniy who has said the following:

"Abu 'Abd Allah, *'Alayhi al-Salam*, has said, 'It is *Makruh* (undesirable) for a creditor to lodge with his debtor, even if he has already picked the amount he owes and has made it ready to pay, except for three days.'"

H 8452, Ch. 27, h 2
A number of our people have narrated from Ahmad ibn Muhammad from 'Uthman ibn 'Isa from Sama'ah who has said the following:

"This is concerning my question before abu 'Abd Allah, *'Alayhi al-Salam*, about the case of a man who lodges with his debtor; if he can use his food. He (the Imam) said, 'Yes, he can do so for three days but not for more than three days.'"

Chapter 28(a) - The Case of Gift to a Creditor

H 8453, Ch. 28a, h 1
Muhammad ibn Yahya has narrated from Ahmad ibn Muhammad from Muhammad who has said the following:

"Abu 'Abd Allah, *'Alayhi al-Salam*, has said that once a man came to Ali, *'Alayhi al-Salam*, and said, 'Someone who owes to me a certain amount of debts has sent me a gift.' He (the Imam) *'Alayhi al-Salam*, said, 'Count it as part of payment for what he owes you.'"

H 8454, Ch. 28a, h 2
A number of our people have narrated from Ahmad ibn Muhammad from Sahl ibn Ziyad from ibn Mahbub from Hudhayl ibn Hayyan, brother of Ja'far ibn Hayyan al-Sayrafiy who has said the following:

"I once said to abu 'Abd Allah, *'Alayhi al-Salam*, 'I have given a certain amount of assets to my brother Ja'far and he gives me what I pay for my expenses, for performing al-Hajj and giving charity. I asked certain people for both of us and they mentioned that it is invalid and unlawful. I like to take your words as the final ones.' He (the Imam) asked, 'Did he give you such things before you gave him the assets you just mentioned?' I replied, 'Yes, he did so.' He (the Imam) then said, 'You can take what he gives you, use it for food, drink, al-Hajj and charity, and when you go back to Iraq tell him that Ja'far ibn Muhammad has given me this fatwa.'"

H 8455, Ch. 28a, h 3
Muhammad ibn Yahya has narrated from Muhammad ibn al-Husayn from Musa ibn Sa'dan from al-Husayn ibn abu al-'Ala' from Ishaq ibn 'Ammar who has said the following:

"I once asked abu al-Hassan, *'Alayhi al-Salam*, about the case of a man who is a debtor and pays a certain amount out of his profit to his creditor for fear of the creditor's demand for payment, but there is no such condition between them. He (the Imam) said, 'It is not harmful as long as it is not a condition.'"

Chapter 28(b) - Bail out and Assignment or Referral

H 8456, Ch. 28b, h 1

Ali ibn Ibrahim has narrated from his father and Muhammad ibn 'Isma'il has narrated from al-Fadl ibn Shadhan all from ibn abu 'Umayr from Hafs ibn al-Bakhtariy who has said the following:

"I once remained behind from performing al-Hajj and abu 'Abd Allah, *'Alayhi al-Salam*, asked, 'What caused you to remain behind from performing al-Hajj?' I replied, 'I pray to Allah to keep my soul in service for your cause, I bailed out a person but he violated his responsibility.' He (the Imam) said, 'What do you have to do with bailsman-ship? Did you not know that people of the centuries before were destroyed?' He (the Imam) then said, 'A people committed a great many sins. They then became severely afraid. Another people came to them and said, 'Your sins are upon us.' Allah, most Majestic, most Glorious, sent upon them suffering and He most Blessed, most High, said, 'You were afraid of Me, then you defied Me.'"

H 8457, Ch. 28b, h 2

Ali ibn Ibrahim has narrated from his father from ibn abu 'Umayr from Jamil from Zurarah who has said the following:

"About the case of an assignment if the assignee says to the debtor, 'I wave in your favor what you owe me because of the assignment, one of the two Imam', (abu Ja'far or abu 'Abd Allah), *'Alayhim al-Salam*, has said, 'If the assignee waves it in favor of the debtor he (assignee) loses the right to ask the debtor for any payment; but if he (the assignee) does not wave it in favor of the debtor, he (assignee) has the right to ask the assignor for payment.'"

Muhammad ibn Yahya has narrated from Ahmad ibn Muhammad from Ali ibn Hadid from Jamil from Zurarah has narrated from a similar Hadith.

H 8458, Ch. 28b, h 3

Humayd ibn Ziyad has narrated from al-Hassan ibn Muhammad al-Kindiy from Ahmad ibn al-Hassan al-Mithamiy from Aban ibn 'Uthman from abu al-'Abbas who has said the following:

"This is concerning my question before abu 'Abd Allah, *'Alayhi al-Salam*, about the case of a man who bails out a person assigning his own person as security, and the bailee says, 'If you did not bring the bailed out person you must pay five hundred dirham.' He (the Imam) said, 'The guarantor is required only to present himself and there is no dirham due on him. However, if the bailsman says, "I on failing to bring the bailed out person, will pay five hundred dirham," payment of dirham becomes binding upon him if he does not present the bailed out person.'"

H 8459, Ch. 28b, h 4

Humayd has narrated from al-Hassan ibn Muhammad from Ja'far ibn Sama'ah from Aban from Mansur ibn Hazim who has said the following:

"This is concerning my question before abu 'Abd Allah, *'Alayhi al-Salam*, about the case of a man who assigns another man to collect a certain amount of dirham from his debtor; if the assignee can demand payment from the assignor. He (the Imam) said, 'No, he can never do so unless the debtor was bankrupt before assignment.'"

H 8460, Ch. 28b, h 5

Muhammad ibn Yahya has narrated from certain persons of our people from al-Hassan ibn Ali ibn Yaqtin from ibn Khalid who has said the following:

"I once said to abu al-Hassan, *'Alayhi al-Salam*, I pray to Allah to keep my soul in service for your cause, what do you say about people's saying, 'The bailsman suffers loss.' He (the Imam) said, 'The bailsman is not responsible for any loss. The one who has consumed the asset is responsible for the loss.'"

H 8461, Ch. 28b, h 6

Muhammad ibn Yahya has narrated from Ahmad ibn Muhammad from ibn Faddal from 'Ammar who has said the following:

"Abu 'Abd Allah, *'Alayhi al-Salam*, has said that once a man who had presented his person to bail out another man was brought before 'Amir al-Mu'minin who placed him in custody and commanded him to present the man whom he had bailed out.'"

Chapter 29 - Working for al-Sultan and his Rewards

H 8462, Ch. 29, h 1

A number of our people have narrated from Sahl ibn Ziyad from Ali ibn Asbat from Muhammad ibn 'Adha'fir from his father who has said the following:

"Abu 'Abd Allah, *'Alayhi al-Salam*, once said to me, 'O 'Adha'fir, you cooperate with abu Ayyub and al-Rabi', how will your condition be when you will be called along with the helpers of unjust ones? He (the narrator) has said that my father became extremely depressed and abu 'Abd Allah, *'Alayhi al-Salam*, upon seeing the condition of my father said, 'O 'Adha'fir, I alarmed you the way Allah, most Majestic, most Glorious, has alarmed me.' Muhammad has said, 'My father came home and continued to remain depressed until he died.'"

H 8463, Ch. 29, h 2

Ali ibn Ibrahim has narrated from his father from ibn abu 'Umayr from Hisham ibn Salim and Muhammad ibn Humran from al-Walid ibn Sabih who has said the following:

"I once went to visit abu 'Abd Allah, *'Alayhi al-Salam*, and I met Zurarah who received me when he was coming out of the presence of the Imam. He (the Imam) said to me, 'O Walid, is it not strange to you that Zurarah asks me about working for these people? What does he want me to say? Does he want me to say no, so that he can narrate it from me?' He (the Imam) then said, 'O Walid, when did the Shi'ah ask about working for them? The Shi'ah would only say, 'You can eat their food, use their drink and live under their protection.' When did the Shi'ah ask about it (working for them)?'"

H 8464, Ch. 29, h 3

A number of our people have narrated from Sahl ibn Ziyad from ibn Mahbub from Hadid who has said the following:

"I heard abu 'Abd Allah, *'Alayhi al-Salam*, saying, 'You must maintain piety before Allah and protect your religion by means of restraint from sins and strengthen your religion by means of taqiyah (caution), and self-sufficiency with Allah, most Majestic, most Glorious. Whoever is submissive before al-Sultan and those who oppose one's religion seeking thereby the worldly things in their hands, Allah, most Majestic, most Glorious, suppresses his mention and hates him and leaves him to his own self. If he finds something of the worldly things Allah will take away blessings thereof and will not reward him for anything that he may spend thereof for al-Hajj, setting free slaves or for any good cause.'"

H 8465, Ch. 29, h 4

Ali ibn Muhammad ibn Bandar has narrated from Ibrahim ibn Ishaq from 'Abd Allah ibn Hammad from Ali ibn abu Hamzah who has said the following:

"I had a young friend who worked as clerk for Amawide rulers. He asked me to ask permission for a meeting with abu 'Abd Allah, *'Alayhi al-Salam*, I asked for permission and it was granted. He came for the meeting, offered greeting of peace and sat down. He then said, 'I pray to Allah to keep my soul in service for your cause, I worked in the offices of these people (Amawide rules) and I received from their world a large amount of wealth. I did not object to what he demanded.' Abu 'Abd Allah, *'Alayhi al-Salam*, then said, 'If the Amawides did not find people who would work for them as clerks, collect taxes for them, fight for them and join their community, our rights would not have been taken away from us. Had people left them alone with what they have in their hands, they would not find more than what they had.'" He (the narrator) has said, "The young man then asked, 'I pray to Allah to keep my soul in service for your cause, is there a way for me to safety?' He (the Imam) asked, 'If I said, "Yes, there is a way" will you then follow?' He replied, 'Yes, I will follow.' He (the Imam) said, 'Come out of all that you have gained from their offices. Return all the properties of those people whom you can find and give in charity on behalf of those whom you cannot find. I guarantee for you paradise from Allah, most Majestic, most Glorious.'" He (the narrator) has said, "The young man bent down his head for a long time and then said, 'I have done it, I pray to Allah to keep my soul in service for your cause.'" Ibn abu Hamzah has said, "The young man returned with us to al-kufah. He did not leave anything on earth without moving himself away therefrom even clothes that he wore." He (the narrator) has said "I then assigned a share for him. We bought clothes for him and provided him provisions. After a few months he became ill and we would visit him during his illness. After one day when he was about to die, he opened his eyes and then said to me, 'O Ali, by Allah, your friend has kept his promise to me.'" He (the narrator) has said, "He died and we took care of his funeral. I then left to visit abu 'Abd Allah, *'Alayhi al-Salam*. He (the Imam) looked at me and said, 'O Ali, we by Allah fulfilled our commitment to your friend.' He (the narrator) has said, 'I then said, "You have spoken the truth, I pray to Allah to keep my soul in service for your cause. This is what exactly he said at the time of his death."'"

H 8466, Ch. 29, h 5

Ali ibn Ibrahim has narrated from his father from ibn abu 'Umayr from Hisham ibn Salim from abu Basir who has said the following:

"I once asked abu Ja'far, *'Alayhi al-Salam*, about working for them (sultans). He (the Imam) said, 'O abu Muhammad, no, not even for moving a pen. For whatever one finds from them of the worldly things, one's religion is harmed proportionately or that he (the Imam) said that until his religion is harmed; - uncertainty is from ibn abu 'Umayr.'"

H 8467, Ch. 29, h 6

Ibn abu 'Umayr has narrated from Hisham ibn Salim who has said the following:

"I once was sitting in the presence of abu Ja'far, *'Alayhi al-Salam*, near the door of his house and he (the Imam) looked at the people passing in throngs and mobs. He (the Imam) asked someone near him, 'Has anything happened in al-Madinah?' He replied, 'I pray to Allah to keep my soul in service for your cause, a new governor is assigned for al-Madinah and people are served lunch to welcome and congratulate him.' He (the Imam) said, 'The man serves people lunch to receive their congratulation and he is a door of the doors of the fire.'"

H 8468, Ch. 29, h 7

Ibn abu 'Umayr has narrated from Bashir from ibn abu Ya'fur who has said the following:

"Once I was in the presence of abu 'Abd Allah, *'Alayhi al-Salam*, when a certain man of our people came and said, 'I pray to Allah to keep you well, one of us may face hardship and straitened conditions and is called to construct a building, work a canal or a dam. What is your decision in such case? He (the Imam) replied, 'I do not like it. I have knotted for them a knot and tied down the opening end of the bag of 'no'. It is no and not even the moving of a pen. The helpers of the unjust ones on the Day of Judgment will be kept in chambers of fire until Allah will judge all of His servants.'"

H 8469, Ch. 29, h 8

Muhammad ibn Yahya has narrated from Ahmad ibn Muhammad from Muhammad ibn Sinan from Yahya ibn Ibrahim ibn Muhajir who has said the following:

"I once said to abu 'Abd Allah, *'Alayhi al-Salam*, 'So and so has offered you Salam (greeting of peace) and so also is so and so.' He (the Imam) said, 'Greeting of peace is upon them.' I then said, 'They request you to pray for them.' He (the Imam) asked, 'What is the matter with them?' I said, 'Abu Ja'far, (Abbaside ruler) has imprisoned them.' He (the Imam) then asked, 'What they had to do with him and what had he to do with them?' I replied, 'He appointed them as his agents and then imprisoned them.' 'What is the matter with them and what is the matter with him? Had I not prohibited them, had I not prohibited, had I not prohibited them from the fire, from fire, from fire?' He (the Imam) then said, 'O Lord, plan for them against their ruler.' I (the narrator) then left Makkah and asked about them and found out that they were released three days after (my) conversation (with him (the Imam))."

H 8470, Ch. 29, h 9

Ali ibn Ibrahim has narrated from his father from ibn abu 'Umayr from Dawud ibn Zurbiy who has said the following:

"A Mawla' (servant or friend) of Ali ibn al-Husayn, *'Alayhi al-Salam*, told me, 'I was in al-Kufah when abu 'Abd Allah, *'Alayhi al-Salam*, came to al-Hirah and I went to see him. I said to him (the Imam), 'I pray to Allah to keep my soul in service for your cause, can you speak to Dawud ibn Ali or others of these people to admit me in anyone of these states (government)?' He (the Imam) said, 'I will never do so.' I then returned home and thought about it and said to myself that he (the Imam) did not refuse except for fear that I may do injustice and transgress. By Allah I will go to him and provide all kinds of guarantees and swear extremely seriously, like divorce, freeing slaves and so on, not to do injustice and transgression. I then went to him (the Imam) and said, 'I pray to Allah to keep my soul in service for your cause, I thought about your refusal to speak for me and I thought you have refused and disliked it just because of your fear of my doing injustice and transgression against someone instead of acting with justice.' He (the Imam) said, 'Why did you say that?' I then repeated my demand and swearing. He (the Imam) raised his head to the sky and said, 'Your reaching the sky is easier than what you want me to do for you.'"

H 8471, Ch. 29, h 10
Ali ibn Ibrahim has narrated from his father from ibn abu 'Umayr from Hisham ibn Salim from Jahm ibn Humayd who has said the following:

"Abu 'Abd Allah, *'Alayhi al-Salam*, once said to me, 'Do you use the power of these people for cover?' I replied, 'No, I do not do so.' He (the Imam) asked, 'Why do you not do so?' I replied, 'It is because of my running away with my religion.' He (the Imam) asked, 'Are you determined in this issue?' I replied, 'Yes, I am determined.' He (the Imam) said, 'Now your religion is safe for you.'"

H 8472, Ch. 29, h 11
Ali ibn Ibrahim has narrated from his father from and Ali ibn Muhammad al-Qasaniy from al-Qasim ibn Muhammad from Sulayman al-Minqariy from Fudayl ibn 'Iyad who has said the following:

"This is concerning my question before abu 'Abd Allah, *'Alayhi al-Salam*, about several issues of earning. He (the Imam) prohibited and said, 'O Fudayl, the losses these people cause to this nation are more severe than the losses that Turks and Daylam may cause.' He (the narrator) has said, 'I then asked him (the Imam) about abstaining from people.' He (the Imam) said, 'Restraining (to stay away from sin) are those who restrain from committing what Allah, most Majestic, most Glorious, has made unlawful and to stay away from these people. If one does not stay away from doubtful matters, he becomes involved in unlawful matters. These people know it. When one sees an unlawful matter and does not dislike when he is able to do so, he has loved to disobey Allah, most Majestic, most Glorious, and one who loves to disobey Allah, has defied Allah, most Majestic, most Glorious, with animosity, and one who loves to see the unjust survive has loved to disobey Allah. Allah, most Blessed, most High, has praised Himself because of His destroying the unjust, 'He then cut down the end of the people who had committed injustice, all praise belongs to Allah, cherisher of the worlds.'" (6:45)

H 8473, Ch. 29, h 12
A number of our people have narrated from Sahl ibn Ziyad in a marfu' manner the following:

"About the words of Allah, most Majestic, most Glorious, 'You must not take sides with the unjust ones; consequently the fire will touch you,' (11:13) he (the Imam), *'Alayhi al-Salam*, has said, 'This is a man who works with the sultan and loves his remaining in power so that he can have a hand in his achievements and receive grants from him.'"

H 8474, Ch. 29, h 13
Muhammad ibn Yahya has narrated from Ahmad ibn Muhammad from al-Husayn ibn Sa'id from al-Nadr ibn Suwayd from Muhammad ibn Hisham from those whom he has mentioned who has said the following:

"Abu 'Abd Allah, *'Alayhi al-Salam*, has said, 'A people of those who believed in Musa, *'Alayhi al-Salam* decided to join the army of Pharaoh so that they can benefit from their worldly gains and if Musa *'Alayhi al-Salam* succeeded to join him. They did as they had decided to do. When Musa *'Alayhi al-Salam* and his followers went to the sea running away from Pharaoh, those people also rode their stumpers and rushed to join Musa *'Alayhi al-Salam* and his army to remain with them but Allah, most Majestic, most Glorious, sent an angel who turned the faces of their stumpers toward the Pharaoh and his army, as a result, they drowned along with those who drowned.'"

Ibn Faddal has narrated from Ali ibn 'Uqbah from certain persons of our people who has narrated the following:

"Abu 'Abd Allah, *'Alayhi al-Salam*, has said, 'It is a right on Allah, most Majestic, most Glorious, to make you with those whom you loved in the world.'"

H 8475, Ch. 29, h 14
A number of our people have narrated from Sahl ibn Ziyad from Ahmad ibn Muhammad al-Barqiy from Ali ibn abu Rashid from Ibrahim ibn al-Sindiy from Yunus ibn Hammad who has said the following:

"I once spoke to abu 'Abd Allah, *'Alayhi al-Salam*, about certain people who believe in Divine Authority of 'A'immah, *'Alayhim al-Salam*, but work for the Sultan. He (the Imam) said, 'They have achieved authority, therefore, they benefit you and help you.' I (the narrator) then said, 'Certain ones among them do so and certain others do not do so. 'He (the Imam) said, 'You must denounce those of them who do not help and benefit you as Allah has denounced them.'"

H 8476, Ch. 29, h 15
Ali ibn Ibrahim has narrated from Muhammad ibn 'Isa from Yunus from Hammad from Hamid who has said the following:

"This is concerning my question before abu 'Abd Allah, *'Alayhi al-Salam*, about my becoming the in charge person of a certain work (for the sultan), if there is a way for me out of it. He (the Imam) said, 'How many are those who want a way out but it becomes difficult for them.' I then asked, 'What is your decision? He (the Imam) said, 'I say that you must remain pious before Allah, most Majestic, most Glorious, and do not go back to such work.'"

Chapter 30 - The Conditions to Work for al-Sultan

H 8477, Ch. 30, h 1
Al-Husayn ibn al-Hassan al-Hashimiy has narrated from Salih ibn abu Hammad from Muhammad ibn Khalid from Ziyad ibn abu Salmah who has said the following:

"I once went to visit abu al-Hassan Musa, *'Alayhi al-Salam*, and he (the Imam) asked me, 'O Ziyad, do you work for Sultan?' I replied, 'Yes, I do so.' He (the Imam) said to me, 'Why do you do so?' I replied, 'I am a man of fairness and I have a family to feed. I do not have any other means for support.' He (the Imam) said, 'O Ziyad, if I fall from the top of a mountain and I am cut into pieces, it is more beloved to me than working for any of these people, or spread the furnishing of any of them except for what?' I replied, 'I do not know, I pray to Allah to keep my soul in service for your cause.' He (the Imam) said, 'Except for relieving the agony of a believer, freeing him from his shakle, or paying his debts. O Ziyad, the least that Allah will do to those who become agents of these people for a certain work is that He will place them in the chamber of fire until Allah completes His judging all creatures. O Ziyad, if you become the person in charge of a certain work for them, you must do good to your brothers in belief one for one and Allah is behind it (to keep the account). O Ziyad, if anyone of you becomes the person in charge of a certain work for these people, then treats you just as he treats them, you must tell him that he is a pretending liar. O Ziyad, if you find yourself to have power over people, you must also remember the power of Allah over you tomorrow, and that what you give them will soon perish and what you receive remains forever.'"

H 8478, Ch. 30, h 2

Abu Ali al-Ash'ariy has narrated from Muhammad ibn 'Abd al-Jabbar from ibn abu Najran from ibn Sinan from Habib from abu Basir who has said the following:

"In the presence of abu 'Abd Allah, *'Alayhi al-Salam*, a man of this group (followers of 'A'immah) was mentioned and that he had become the in charge person of an official position of the rulers. He (the Imam) asked, 'How is his dealing with his brothers in belief?' I (the narrator) replied, 'There is nothing good in him in this issue.' He (the Imam) said, 'It is awful. They involve themselves in something which they are not supposed to do; then they do not do anything good for their brothers in belief.'"

H 8479, Ch. 30, h 3

Muhammad ibn Yahya has narrated from those whom he has mentioned from Ali ibn Asbat from Ibrahim ibn abu Mahmud from Ali ibn Yaqtin who has said the following:

"I once asked abu al-Hassan, *'Alayhi al-Salam*, 'How is working for these people?' He (the Imam) said, 'If you do not have any choice, you must observe caution about properties of al-Shi'ah.' He (the narrator) has said that Ali told me, 'He would collect funds from al-Shi'ah in public, then return it to them secretly.'"

H 8480, Ch. 30, h 4

Ali ibn Ibrahim has narrated from his father from Ali ibn al-Hakam from al-Hassan ibn al-Husayn al-Anbariy who has said the following:

"I wrote to abu al-Hassan, al-Rida', *'Alayhi al-Salam*, for fourteen years asking his permission to work for Sultan. In the last letter I wrote saying that I fear for my life if I did not work for the Sultan, because he calls me a Rafidiy (rejecter) saying, 'We have no doubt that you have refused to work for the Sultan because of your rejection.' Abu al-Hassan, *'Alayhi al-Salam*, wrote to me, 'I have noted what you have mentioned in your letter and your fear for your life. If you know that on accepting to work for him you will not violate what the Messenger of Allah, *O Allah, grant compensation to Muhammad and his family worthy of their services to Your cause*, has commanded you to do and employ people from your nation to work for you as clerks and helpers, and if you gain anything you will assist the poor believing people until your gains and help is equal, otherwise, it (permission) is negative.'"

H 8481, Ch. 30, h 5

Muhammad ibn Yahya has narrated from Ahmad ibn Muhammad from Ahmad ibn al-Husayn from his father from 'Uthman ibn 'Isa from Mehran ibn Muhammad ibn abu Nasr who has said the following:

"I once heard abu 'Abd Allah, *'Alayhi al-Salam*, saying, 'With every tyrant there is a believing person with whom Allah defends the believing people, and he (such believing person) receives the least of rewards in the next life because of his association with the tyrant.'"

H 8482, Ch. 30, h 6

Muhammad ibn Yahya has narrated from Muhammad ibn Ahmad from al-Sayyariy from Ahmad ibn Zakariya al-Saydalaniy from a man of banu Hanifah from the people of Bust and Sajistan who has said the following:

"I accompanied abu Ja'far, *'Alayhi al-Salam*, in the year that he performed al-Hajj in the beginning of the Khilafat of al-Mu'tasam. I once said to him (the Imam) when I was with him (the Imam) on the table in the presence of a group of the supporters of the Sultan, 'Our governor, I pray to Allah to keep my soul in service for your cause, is a man who supports you, Ahl al-Bayt and loves you. In his office there are taxes due on me. If you consider it proper, please write. I pray to Allah to keep my soul in service for your cause, write to him a letter for me to kindly help me in this matter. He (the Imam) said, 'I do not know him.' I then said, 'I pray to Allah to keep my soul in service for your cause, as I mentioned, he is one who loves you Ahl al-Bayt and your letter will benefit me in his office.' He (the Imam) picked up a piece of paper and wrote, 'In the name of Allah, the Beneficent, the Merciful. Thereafter, the bearer of this letter that I have written has spoken good things about you. You must take notice that of your deeds what is for you is what you do good. Thus, do good to your brothers in belief. You must also take notice that Allah, most Majestic, most Glorious, will question you about things as small as an atom and mustard seeds.' He (the narrator) has said, 'When I arrived in Sajistan the news reached al-Husayn ibn 'Abd Allah al-Naysaburiy, the governor. He came two farsakh from the city (twelve miles) away to meet me. I gave him the letter. He kissed it and placed it on his eyes. He then asked me about the kind of help I needed. I said, 'In your office payable taxes are recorded against me and I need relief.' He commanded to write it off, and said, 'You do not have to pay taxes as long as I will have this work.' He then asked about my family and their condition which I explained to him and he commanded to appropriate a certain amount for them enough for our expenses and with something extra. I did not pay taxes as long as he had that work and lived and he did not discontinue the grant that he had assigned for us.'"

H 8483, Ch. 30, h 7

Ali ibn Ibrahim has narrated from his father from ibn abu 'Umayr from certain persons of our people from Ali ibn Yaqtin who has said the following:

"Abu al-Hassan, *'Alayhi al-Salam*, once said to me, 'Allah, most Majestic, most Glorious, has friends with the Sultan through whom He protects His friends.'"

Chapter 31 - Selling Arms to al-Sultan

H 8484, Ch. 31, h 1

A number of our people have narrated from Ahmad ibn Muhammad from Ali ibn al-Hakam from Sayf ibn 'Amirah from Abu Bakr al-Hadramiy who has said the following:

"Once, we visited abu 'Abd Allah, *'Alayhi al-Salam*, and Hakam ibn al-Sarraj asked him (the Imam), 'What is your decision about carrying saddles and things related to al-Sham (Syria)?' He (the Imam) said, 'It is not harmful. Today you are like the companions of the Messenger of Allah. You live in peace time. When there is hostility, then it is unlawful for you to carry to them saddles and arms to them.'"

H 8485, Ch. 31, h 2

Ahmad ibn Muhammad has narrated from ibn Mahbub from Ali ibn al-Hassan ibn Ribat from abu Sarah from Hind ibn Faddal-Sarraj who has said the following:

"I once asked abu Ja'far, *'Alayhi al-Salam*, saying, 'I pray to Allah to keep you well, I used to carry arms to sell to people of al-Sham. Ever since Allah has helped me to recognize the matter (Divine Authority of 'A'immah) it bothers me, and I think I must not deliver arms to the enemies of Allah.' He (the Imam) said, 'You can do so because Allah repels through them our enemy and your enemy–the Romans - and sell it to them. When there is war among us, then do not carry arms to them. Those who carry arms to our enemies which help them against us, such people are like pagans.'"

H 8486, Ch. 31, h 3

Ahmad ibn Muhammad has narrated from Ali ibn al-Hakam from Hisham ibn Salim from Muhammad ibn Qays who has said the following:

"This is concerning my question before abu 'Abd Allah, *'Alayhi al-Salam*, about the two groups of falsehood who fight each other; if I can sell arms to them. He (the Imam) said, 'You can sell to them protective materials, like shields and shoes and so on.'"

H 8487, Ch. 31, h 4

Ahmad ibn Muhammad from abu 'Abd Allah al-Barqiy from al-Sarrad who has said the following:

"I once said to abu 'Abd Allah, *'Alayhi al-Salam*, that I sell arms. He (the Imam) said, 'You must not sell them in times of mischief.'"

Chapter 32 - The Crafts (Technologies)

H 8488, Ch. 32, h 1

A number of our people have narrated from Ahmad ibn Muhammad from al-Qasim ibn Yahya from his grandfather, al-Hassan ibn Rashid from Muhammad ibn Muslim from abu 'Abd Allah, *'Alayhi al-Salam*, who has said the following:

"Amir al-Mu'minin, *'Alayhi al-Salam*, has said, 'Allah, most Majestic, most Glorious, loves persons who are trustworthy and possess technical skills.'"

In another Hadith it is said, 'Allah, most High, loves the skillful believer.'"

H 8489, Ch. 32, h 2

Ali ibn Ibrahim has narrated from his father from Salih ibn al-Sindiy from Ja'far ibn Bashir from Khalid ibn 'Umarah from Sadir al-Sayrafiy who has said the following:

"I once said to abu Ja'far, *'Alayhi al-Salam*, 'A Hadith has reached me from al-Hassan al-Basriy. If it is a true Hadith then, 'We are for Allah and to Him we return.' He (the Imam) asked, 'What does it say?' 'I am told that al-Hassan al-Basriy would say that even if his brain comes to a boiling point due to the hot sun, he will not seek shelter of the shadow of a wall that belongs to a money changer. Even if his liver cracks down because of thirst he will not use the water that comes from the house of a money changer.' This is my business and profession. With this business my flesh and blood have grown. With this business I have performed Hajj and 'Umrah.' He (the Imam) sat straight and said, 'Al-Hassan has spoken a lie. Take with fairness and give with fairness. When it is time for *Salat* (prayer), stop doing business and rise for *Salat* (prayer). Did you know that people of the cave were *Sayarifah* (money exchangers)?'"

H 8490, Ch. 32, h 3

Muhammad ibn Yahya has narrated from Ahmad ibn Muhammad from ibn Faddal who has said the following:

"I heard a man asking abu al-Hassan, al-Rida, *'Alayhi al-Salam*, saying, 'I prepare (special kind of flour) and sell it but people say that it should not be done.' Al-Rida, *'Alayhi al-Salam*, said to him, 'What is wrong with it? There is no offense in selling things in which a servant maintains piety before Allah.'"

H 8491, Ch. 32, h 4

Muhammad ibn Yahya has narrated from Muhammad ibn Ja'far ibn Yahya al-Khuza'iy from his father, Yahya ibn abu al-'Ala' from Ishaq ibn 'Ammar who has said the following:

"I once visited abu 'Abd Allah, *'Alayhi al-Salam*, and informed him of the birth of my son. He asked, 'Why do you not name him Muhammad?' I replied, 'I have already done so.' He (the Imam) then said, 'You must not beat up a Muhammad and do not abuse him. Allah will make him the delight to your eyes during your life time as well as a truthful successor for you.' I then asked, 'I pray to Allah to keep my soul in service for your cause, in what kind of profession should I involve him?' He (the Imam) said, 'If you keep him away from five kinds of professions then instruct him in whatever you like. You must not train him in money changing business; he will not remain safe from unlawful interest. You must not teach him selling coffins; such people become happy with the coming of plague when such disease is around. You must not teach him in selling foods; they do not remain safe from stockpiling (hoarding) food. Do not instruct him as a butcher; it reduces his kindness. You must not instruct him in how to sell slaves; the Messenger of Allah, *O Allah, grant compensation to Muhammad and his family worthy of their services to Your cause*, has said, "The worst people are people sellers.""""

H 8492, Ch. 32, h 5
Ahmad ibn Muhammad has narrated from Muhammad ibn Yahya from Talhah ibn Zayd who has said the following:
"This is a narration of abu 'Abd Allah, Ja'far ibn Muhammad, *'Alayhi al-Salam*, from the Messenger of Allah, *O Allah, grant compensation to Muhammad and his family worthy of their services to Your cause*. He (the Messenger of Allah) has said, 'I gave a boy to my aunt and prohibited her from making him a butcher, cupping person or a jewelry carver.'"

H 8493, Ch. 32, h 6
Ali ibn Muhammad ibn Bandar has narrated from Ahmad ibn abu 'Abd Allah from al-Qasim ibn Ishaq ibn Ibrahim from Musa ibn Zanjawayh al-Taflisiy from abu 'Amr al-Hannat from 'Isma'il al-Sayqal al-Raziy who has said the following:
"Once I visited abu 'Abd Allah, *'Alayhi al-Salam*. I had two pieces of fabric materials with me. He (the Imam) said, 'O abu 'Isma'il, from your area people bring us many kinds of fabrics but not like these two pieces that you carry.' I said, 'I pray to Allah to keep my soul in service for your cause, the mother of 'Isma'il prepares threads and I weave them.' He (the Imam) asked, 'Are you a weaver?' I replied, 'Yes, I am a weaver.' He (the Imam) said, 'You must not be a weaver.' I then asked, 'What kind of work then I should do?' He (the Imam) said, 'Work as a sword polisher.' I had two hundred dirhams with me with which I purchased swords and sold. I took them to al-Rayy, sold them and made a large profit.'"

H 8494, Ch. 32, h 7
Ali ibn Ibrahim has narrated from his father from who has said that a Shaykh from our people of al-Kufah has said following:
'Once 'Isa ibn Shafaqiy visited abu 'Abd Allah, *'Alayhi al-Salam*. He was a magician. People would come to him and he charged them a certain amount for wages. He said, 'I pray to Allah to keep my soul in service for your cause, I work as a magician and I charge a certain amount as my wages to earn for my living. From such incomes I have performed Hajj and Allah has granted me the opportunity to visit you. I have repented before Allah, most Majestic, most Glorious. Is there a way out to safety for me from this?' He (the Imam) said, 'Open it up (turn it ineffective) but do not tie down (make it effective).'"

(Fatwa best explains this hadith and the following Chapters. Please consult Fatwa.)

Chapter 33 - The Legal Status of Income from Cupping Operation

H 8495, Ch. 33, h 1
A number of our people have narrated from Sahl ibn Ziyad from ibn Mahbub from ibn Ri'ab from abu Basir from who has said the following:

"I once asked Abu Ja'far, *'Alayhi al-Salam*, about the legal status of earning by means of cupping. He (the Imam) replied, 'There is no offense in the earning by such means, if it is not with an established pre-condition.'"

H 8496, Ch. 33, h 2

Sahl ibn Ziyad has narrated from Ahmad ibn Muhammad ibn abu Basir from Hanan ibn Sadir who has said the following:

"Once we visited abu 'Abd Allah, *'Alayhi al-Salam*, when Farqad al-Hajjam was also with us. He (Farqad) asked him (the Imam) saying, 'May Allah keep my soul in the service of your cause, I perform a certain kind of work and I have asked more than one person about the legal status of what I do and they think it is a detestable work. I like to ask you. If it is as they say I will stop performing such works. Instead I will find some other kind of work. I will take your word as the word in the matter.' He (the Imam) asked, 'What kind of work is it?' He (the man) replied, 'It is cupping.' He (the Imam) said, 'You can use the income thereof for living, give charity, pay the expenses of your Hajj and marriage thereof, O brother, (in faith). The Holy Prophet had used cupping services and paid for them. Had it been unlawful he would not pay for it.' He (the man) then asked, saying, 'I pray to Allah to keep my soul in service for your cause, I have a he-goat. People hire it for goat grooming. What do you say about the income thereof?' He (the Imam) replied, 'You can use the income thereof; it is lawful, although people may dislike it.' I (Hanan) then asked, 'Why people dislike it when it is lawful?' He (the Imam) replied, 'It is because people scorn each other about it.'"

H 8497, Ch. 33, h 3

Abu Ali al-Ash'ariy has narrated from Muhammad ibn 'Abd al-Jabbar from Ahmad ibn al-Nadr from 'Amr ibn Shamir who has said the following:

"Abu Ja'far, *'Alayhi al-Salam*, has said that the Messenger of Allah, *O Allah, grant compensation to Muhammad and his family worthy of their services to Your cause*, did use cupping services. A Mawla' (slave) of banu Bayada performed cupping service for the Messenger of Allah and paid for such services. Had it been unlawful he would not pay for it. When cupping was complete the Messenger of Allah asked, 'Where is the blood?' He (the slave) replied, 'I drank it, O Messenger of Allah.' The Messenger of Allah said, 'You should not have done so. Allah, most Majestic, most Glorious, has made it a curtain between you and the fire but do not do it again.'"*

H 8498, Ch. 33, h 4

Muhammad ibn Yahya has narrated from Ahmad ibn Muhammad from ibn Faddal from ibn Bukayr from Zurarah who has said the following:

"I once asked Abu Ja'far, *'Alayhi al-Salam*, about the legal status of income from performing cupping. He (the Imam) replied, 'It is detestable for him to establish stipulations (to receive payment), but there is no offense in establishing stipulations to receive payment and bargaining for the price. It is only detestable but there is no offense for you to receive payment.'"

H 8499, Ch. 33, h 5

Ali ibn Ibrahim has narrated from his father and Muhammad ibn 'Isma'il from al-Fadl ibn Shadhan from ibn abu 'Umayr from Mu'awiyah ibn 'Ammar who has said the following:

"This is concerning my question before abu 'Abd Allah, *'Alayhi al-Salam*, about the legal status of the income from cupping. He (the Imam) replied, 'There is no offense in it.' I then asked about income from he-goat for goat-grooming. He (the Imam) replied, 'Even though Arab people consider it scornful, there is no offense in receiving such income.'"

Chapter 34 - Income from Eulogizing Someone to Make People Mourn

H 8500, Ch. 34, h 1

A number of our people have narrated from Ahmad ibn Muhammad from Ali ibn al-Hakam from Yunus ibn Ya'qub who has said the following:

"Abu 'Abd Allah, *'Alayhi al-Salam*, has said, 'My father said to me, 'O Ja'far, assign a certain amount from my so and so properties as endowment, so payments can be made to people who will eulogize to mourn for me in Mina for ten years.'"

H 8501, Ch. 34, h 2

Ahmad ibn Muhammad has narrated from Ali ibn al-Hakam from Malik ibn 'Atiyah from abu Hamzah who has said the following:

"Abu Ja'far, *'Alayhi al-Salam*, has said, 'When al-Walid ibn al-Mughirah died, 'Umm Salamah asked the Holy Prophet, for permission. She said, "The family of al-Mughirah has organized a gathering to mourn for al-Walid. Can I also attend their gathering?" The Holy Prophet granted her permission. She dressed up. She was beautiful like a fairy. When standing she released her hairs and it covered her body. She tied her khalkhal on both sides. She then eulogized her cousin before the Messenger of Allah saying:

"I announce passing away of al-Walid ibn al-Walid, abu al-Walid, the young man of the family, protector of truth, with glory and rising for good manners. He was a thirst-quenching rain for years, a crystal clear brook and supplies."

He (the narrator) has said that the Holy Prophet did not disapprove her eulogies and did not say anything."

H 8502, Ch. 34, h 3

Ali ibn Ibrahim has narrated from his father Muhammad ibn Yahya has narrated from Ahmad ibn Muhammad ibn 'Isma'il all from Hanan ibn Sadir who has said the following:

"In our neighborhood there was a woman who had a slave-girl who sang eulogies. She came to my father and said, 'O Uncle, you know about my means of living from Allah, most Majestic, most Glorious, and then it is from this slave-girl's singing eulogies. I like if you ask abu 'Abd Allah, *'Alayhi al-Salam*, for me about it if it is lawful; otherwise, I will sell her and use the funds from selling her until Allah opens up a door for me.' My father said to her, 'I consider abu 'Abd Allah, *'Alayhi al-Salam*, greatly exalted and cannot ask such things from him.' He (the narrator) has said that when we visited him (the Imam) I informed him (the Imam) about it and abu 'Abd Allah, *'Alayhi al-Salam*, asked, 'Does she set a condition?' I replied, 'By Allah, I do not know if she does or does not do.' He (the Imam) said, 'Tell her not to set up a condition for payment but accept whatever is given to you.'"

H 8503, Ch. 34, h 4

Ali ibn Ibrahim has narrated from his father from ibn abu 'Umayr from al-Hassan ibn 'Atiyyah from 'Adhafir who has said the following:

"I once heard abu 'Abd Allah, *'Alayhi al-Salam*, saying, when he was asked about the income from eulogies, 'She can make it lawful by tapping one of her hands against the other.'"

Chapter 35 - The Legal Status of Income from Hairdressing and Circumcising

H 8504, Ch. 35, h 1

A number of our people have narrated from Ahmad ibn Muhammad ibn 'Isa from Ahmad ibn Muhammad from ibn abu Nasr from Harun ibn al-Jahm from Muhammad ibn Muslim who has said the following:

"Abu 'Abd Allah, *'Alayhi al-Salam*, has said, 'When women migrated toward the Messenger of Allah, *O Allah, grant compensation to Muhammad and his family worthy of their services to Your cause*, among them there was a woman called 'Umm Habib and she circumcised girls. When the Messenger of Allah, *O Allah, grant compensation to Muhammad and his family worthy of their services to Your cause,* saw her, he asked, 'O 'Umm Habib, do you still do the work you did or have you stopped?' She replied, 'Yes, O Messenger of Allah, I still practice unless it is unlawful and you prohibit. He (the Messenger of Allah) said, 'No, I do not prohibit. It is lawful. Come closer to me so I can teach you.' She has said, 'I went closer to him and he said, "O 'Umm Habib, when you circumcise, you must not make a large cut from the root. You must only do it like a sniff (a little scrape) because it brightens the face and is enjoyable for the husband."' 'Umm Habib had a sister called 'Umm 'Atiyyah. She was a hairdresser. When 'Umm Habib returned to her sister and informed her about what the Messenger of Allah had said 'Umm 'Atiyyah then came to the Messenger of Allah and told him about what her sister had told to her. The Messenger of Allah of said, 'Come closer to me, O 'Umm 'Attiyah, when you work on the hairs of a girl you must not wash her face with rags; it absorbs the water of the face (affects the beauty of the face).'"

H 8505, Ch. 35, h 2

Ahmad ibn Muhammad has narrated from Ahmad ibn 'Ashaym from ibn abu 'Umayr from a man who has said the following:

"Abu 'Abd Allah, *'Alayhi al-Salam*, has said, 'Once a hairdresser came to the Messenger of Allah, *O Allah, grant compensation to Muhammad and his family worthy of their services to Your cause*, and he asked her, 'Have you stopped the work you were doing or not?' She replied, 'O Messenger of Allah, I still do it unless you prohibit. If so I will stop.' He said, 'You can still do it but when doing a hair dressing do not clean the face with al-Khiraq (tatter); it takes away the beauty of the face, and do not connect someone else's hair to another person's hair.'"

H 8506, Ch. 35, h 3
Muhammad ibn Yahya has narrated from Muhammad ibn Al-Husayn from 'Abd al-Rahman ibn abu Hashim from Salim ibn Mukram from Sa'd al-Iskaf who has said the following:

"Abu Ja'far, *'Alayhi al-Salam*, was asked about women's decorating their hairs with silk fibers or hairs and so on. He (the Imam) replied, 'There is no offense in women's beautifying themselves for their husbands.' I (the narrator) said, 'We are told that the Messenger of Allah, *O Allah, grant compensation to Muhammad and his family worthy of their services to Your cause*, had condemned (hairs) connecting and connected women. He (the Imam) said, 'It does not apply in this case. The Messenger of Allah, *O Allah, grant compensation to Muhammad and his family worthy of their services to Your cause*, had condemned only the connectors who commit fornication when they are young and when old lead men and women to commit fornication. This is called connecting and connected.'"

H 8507, Ch. 35, h 4
A number of our people have narrated from Sahl ibn Ziyad from Ali ibn Asbat from Khalaf ibn Hammad from ibn Thabit who has said the following:

"Abu 'Abd Allah, *'Alayhi al-Salam*, has said, 'There was a woman called 'Umm Taybah. She would circumcise girls. The Holy Prophet, *O Allah, grant compensation to Muhammad and his family worthy of their services to Your cause*, called her and said to her, 'O 'Umm Taybah, when you circumcise girls do not allow it to become excessive. It clears the color of the face and is more enjoyable for the husband.'"

Chapter 36 - The Legal Status of the Income of Female Singer from Singing and Selling Singers (Slave-girls)

H 8508, Ch. 36, h 1
A number of our people have narrated from Ahmad ibn Muhammad from al-Husayn ibn Sa'id from Ali ibn abu Hamzah from abu Basir who has said the following:

"I once asked Abu Ja'far, *'Alayhi al-Salam*, about the legal status of the income from female music playing singers. He (the Imam) said, 'Such singing and playing music of females where men are also present is unlawful. There is no offense in inviting female singers on the occasion of a wedding program. It is in the words of Allah, most Majestic, most Glorious, "Among people are those who purchase useless talk to make people lose the path of Allah." (31:6)'"

H 8509, Ch. 36, h 2
It is narrated from him (narrator of the previous Hadith) from Hakam al-Hannat from abu Basir, who has said the following:

"Abu 'Abd Allah, *'Alayhi al-Salam* has said, 'The income of a female singer who attends wedding ceremonies is lawful.'"

H 8510, Ch. 36, h 3

Ahmad ibn Muhammad from has narrated from al-Husayn ibn Sa'id from Al-Nadr ibn Suwayd from Yahya al-Halabiy from Ayyub al-Hurr from abu Basir who has said the following:

"Abu 'Abd Allah, *'Alayhi al-Salam*, has said, 'The payment that a female singer receives from singing in wedding ceremonies is lawful, provided men do not attend her singing program.'"

H 8511, Ch. 36, h 4

A number of our people have narrated from Sahl ibn Ziyad from al-Hassan ibn Ali al-Washsha' who has said the following:

"Abu al-Hassan al-Rida', *'Alayhi al-Salam*, was asked about the legal status of purchasing a female singer. He (the Imam) said, 'Sometimes a slave-girl of a man makes him go astray. What is then paid for such a slave-girl is like payment to purchase a dog. Payment for a dog is Suht (unlawful and filthy) and Suht is in the fire.'"

H 8512, Ch. 36, h 5

A number of our people have narrated from Sahl ibn Ziyad and Ali ibn Ibrahim has narrated from his father from all from ibn Faddal from Sa'id ibn Muhammad al-Tahir from his father who has said the following:

"A man once asked abu 'Abd Allah, *'Alayhi al-Salam*, about selling slave-girl singers. He (the Imam) said, 'Buying and selling them is unlawful, teaching them (singing) is disbelief and listening to them is hypocrisy.'"

H 8513, Ch. 36, h 6

Abu Ali al-Ash'ariy has narrated from al-Hassan ibn Ali from Ishaq ibn Ibrahim from Nasr ibn Qabus who has said the following:

"I once heard abu 'Abd Allah, *'Alayhi al-Salam*, saying, 'A singer female is condemned, and condemned is one who consumes the income from her singing.'"

H 8514, Ch. 36, h 7

Muhammad ibn Yahya has narrated from certain persons of his people from Muhammad ibn 'Isma'il from Ibrahim ibn abu al-Balad who has said the following:

"Ishaq ibn 'Umar made a will about his singer slave-girls at the time when he was about to die that said, 'They must be sold and funds from their sale delivered to abu al-Hassan, *'Alayhi al-Salam*. Ibrahim has said, 'I sold the slave-girls for three hundred thousand dirham and took it to him (the Imam) and said, 'One of your followers, called Ishaq ibn 'Umar has made a will at the time he was about to die to sell his singer slave-girls and take the funds from their sale to you. I have sold them and this is the three hundred thousand dirham from the sale. He (the Imam) said, 'I do not need them. It is Suht (filthy), teaching them is disbelief, listening to them is hypocrisy and funds from their sale are Suht (filthy) unlawful.'"

Chapter 37 - The Legal Status of Income from Teaching

H 8515, Ch. 37, h 1

A number of our people have narrated from Ahmad ibn Muhammad from Muhammad ibn 'Isma'il ibn Bazi' from al-Fadl ibn al-Kathir from Hassan al-Mu'allim who has said the following:

"This is concerning my question before abu 'Abd Allah, *'Alayhi al-Salam*, about teaching on hire like poetry, letter-writing and similar issues on condition of payment. He (the Imam) said, 'Yes, it is permissible if children are treated with equality in teaching without any preference for anyone of them over the others.'"

H 8516, Ch. 37, h 2
Ali ibn Muhammad ibn Bandar has narrated from Ahmad ibn abu 'Abd Allah from Sharif ibn Sabiq from al-Fadl ibn abu Qurrah who has said the following:

"I once said to abu 'Abd Allah, *'Alayhi al-Salam*, 'They say that receiving payment for teaching is Suht (filthy and unlawful). He (the Imam) said, 'They, the enemies of Allah, have spoken a lie. They want to stop teaching of al-Quran. If one gives blood money for his child to a teacher it (payment) is lawful for the teacher.'"

Chapter 38 - The legal Status of Income from Selling Copies of the Holy Quran

H 8517, Ch. 38, h 1
Muhammad ibn Yahya has narrated from 'Abd Allah ibn Muhammad from Ali ibn al-Hakam from Aban from 'Abd al-Rahman ibn Sulayman who has said the following:

"I once heard abu 'Abd Allah, *'Alayhi al-Salam*, saying, 'Pages (of al-Quran) can never be bought; if you buy say, 'I buy from you the sheet and whatever is in it, like skin and decoration and the work of your hand for such and such amount.'"

H 8518, Ch. 38, h 2
A number of our people have narrated from Ahmad ibn Muhammad from 'Uthman ibn 'Isa from Sama'ah who has said the following:

"This is concerning my question before abu 'Abd Allah, *'Alayhi al-Salam*, about buying and selling pages of al-Quran. He (the Imam) said, 'The book of Allah, most Majestic, most Glorious, cannot be purchased but iron sheets and covers can be bought. One can say, 'I buy from you such and such items for such and such amount.'"

H 8519, Ch. 38, h 3
Ahmad ibn Muhammad has narrated from ibn Faddal from Ghalib ibn 'Uthman from Ruh ibn 'Abd al-Rahim who has said the following:

"This is concerning my question before abu 'Abd Allah, *'Alayhi al-Salam*, about buying pages of al-Quran and selling them. He (the Imam) said, 'Only pages (of al-Quran) were placed near the pulpit. The passage between the wall and the pulpit was no bigger than what a sheep could pass through or a man in a sideways manner.' He (the Imam) said, 'A man would come and write down from the pages that were there. Thereafter they bought them.' I then asked, 'What do you say about it (buying).' He (the Imam) replied, 'I like buying more than selling.' I then asked, 'What do you say if I pay for writing al-Quran?' He (the Imam) said, 'It is not harmful but in their time that was their way of dealing.'"

H 8520, Ch. 38, h 4

Ali ibn Muhammad has narrated from Ahmad ibn abu 'Abd Allah from Muhammad ibn Ali from 'Abd al-Rahman ibn abu Hashim from Sabiq al-Sindiy from 'Anbasah al-Warraq who has said the following:

"This is concerning my question before abu 'Abd Allah, *'Alayhi al-Salam*, about the case of my selling al-Quran saying, 'If you prohibit I stop selling.' He (the Imam) asked, 'Is it not the case that you buy pages and write down on them?' I replied, 'Yes, that is true and I put more work in it.' He (the Imam) said, 'It is not harmful.'"

Chapter 39 - Gambling and Looting

H 8521, Ch. 39, h 1

A number of our people have narrated from Ali ibn al-Hakam from Sayf ibn 'Amirah from Ziyad ibn 'Isa and he is abu 'Ubaydah al-Hadhdha' who has said the following:

"This is concerning my question before abu 'Abd Allah, *'Alayhi al-Salam*, about the words of Allah, most Majestic, most Glorious, 'You must not consume your assets in invalid dealings among your selves. . . .' (2:184) He (the Imam) said, 'Among Quraysh a man gambled even his wife and property. Allah, most Majestic, most Glorious, prohibited such dealings.'"

H 8522, Ch. 39, h 2

Abu Ali al-Ash'ariy has narrated from Muhammad ibn 'Abd al-Jabbar from Ahmad ibn al-Nadr from 'Amr ibn Shamir from Jabir who has said the following:

"Abu Ja'far, *'Alayhi al-Salam*, has said that when Allah, most Majestic, most Glorious, sent to His Messenger, *O Allah, grant compensation to Muhammad and his family worthy of their services to Your cause*, the following verse, 'Wine, gambling, idols and gambling arrows are of the filthy deeds of Satan, you must avoid them' (5:93), it was asked, 'O Messenger of Allah, what is al-Maysir?' The Messenger of Allah replied, 'It is everything with which gambling is conducted, like cubes and walnuts and so on.' It then was asked, 'What is al-Ansab?' The Messenger of Allah replied, 'It is what they slaughter for their gods.' It then was asked, 'What is al-Azlam?' The Messenger of Allah replied, 'It is the arrows that they used to distribute certain items.'"

H 8523, Ch. 39, h 3

A number of our people have narrated from Sahl ibn Ziyad Ahmad ibn Muhammad from Ahmad ibn Muhammad from all from ibn Mahbub from Yunus ibn Ya'qub from 'Abd al-Hamid ibn Sa'id who has said the following:

"Once, abu al-Hassan *'Alayhi al-Salam*, sent one of the slaves to buy eggs for him. The slave took one or two eggs and gambled with them. When the slave came back he (the Imam) used the eggs for food. A servant told him (the Imam) about gambling. He (the Imam) asked for a washbowl and threw up."

H 8524, Ch. 39, h 4

Muhammad ibn Yahya has narrated from Muhammad ibn al-Husayn from Muhammad ibn Sinan from abu al-Jarud who has said the following:

"I once heard abu Ja'far, *'Alayhi al-Salam*, saying, 'The Messenger of Allah, *O Allah, grant compensation to Muhammad and his family worthy of their services to Your cause*, has said, 'A fornicator does not fornicate while he is a believing person, a thief does not steal while he is a believing person and an honorable person does not do Nahbah Dhata Sharaf (an honor-loot) while he is a believing person.' Ibn Sinan has said that I then asked abu al-Jarud, 'What is a 'Nahbah Dhata Sharaf'?' He replied, 'It is like what Hatim did when he said, "Whoever takes something it is his.""'

H 8525, Ch. 39, h 5
Muhammad ibn Yahya has narrated from Muhammad ibn al-Husayn from Safwan from al-'Ala' from Muhammad ibn Muslim who has said the following:

"One of the two Imam, (abu Ja'far or abu 'Abd Allah), *'Alayhim al-Salam*, has said, 'Gambling and plundering are not righteous deeds.'"

H 8526, Ch. 39, h 6
Ali ibn Ibrahim has narrated from his father from al-Nawfaliy from al-Sakuniy who has said the following:

"Abu 'Abd Allah, *'Alayhi al-Salam*, would prohibit utilization of walnuts, that children bring after using in gambling, saying that it is Suht (filthy), unlawful.'"

H 8527, Ch. 39, h 7
Muhammad ibn Yahya has narrated from al-'Amrakiy ibn Ali from Ali ibn Ja'far from his brother who has said the following:

"I once asked abu al-Hassan, *'Alayhi al-Salam*, about the case of what is spread of sugar, almond and so on, on happy occasions if is permissible. He (the Imam) said, 'It is detestable to consume what is plundered.'"

H 8528, Ch. 39, h 8
A number of our people have narrated from Ahmad ibn abu 'Abd Allah from Muhammad ibn Ali from 'Abd Allah ibn Jamilah from Ishaq ibn 'Ammar who has said the following:

"This is concerning my question before abu 'Abd Allah, *'Alayhi al-Salam*, about what people scatter on certain people during an entertaining occasion or wedding ceremony. He (the Imam) said, 'It is unlawful but what they give, you can take it.'"

H 8529, Ch. 39, h 9
A number of our people have narrated from Sahl ibn Ziyad from Al-Washsha" who has said the following:

"I once heard abu al-Hassan, *'Alayhi al-Salam*, saying, 'Al-Maysir is gambling.'"

H 8530, Ch. 39, h 10
Al-Husayn from Muhammad has narrated from Muhammad ibn Ahmad al-Nahdiy from Ya'qub ibn Yazid from 'Abd Allah ibn Jabalah from Ishaq ibn 'Ammar who has said the following:

"This is concerning my question before abu 'Abd Allah, *'Alayhi al-Salam*, about the case of children who play with walnuts and eggs and gamble. He (the Imam) said, 'You must not consume them for food; it is unlawful.'"

Chapter 40 - Earning in Unlawful ways

H 8531, Ch. 40, h 1

A number of our people have narrated from Ahmad ibn abu 'Abd Allah from his father from those whom he has mentioned who has said the following:

"Abu 'Abd Allah, *'Alayhi al-Salam*, has said that the Messenger of Allah, *O Allah, grant compensation to Muhammad and his family worthy of their services to Your cause*, has said, 'What I fear most for my followers after me are these unlawful earnings, concealed desire and unlawful interest.'"

H 8532, Ch. 40, h 2

Ali ibn Ibrahim has narrated from Salih ibn al-Sindiy from Ja'far ibn Bashir from 'Isa al-Farra' from Aban ibn 'Uthman who has said the following:

"Abu 'Abd Allah, *'Alayhi al-Salam*, has said, 'Four things are not lawful in four issues: treachery, excessiveness, theft and unlawful interest are not lawful in al-Hajj, al-'Umrah, Jihad and charity.'"

H 8533, Ch. 40, h 3

A number of our people have narrated from has narrated from Ahmad ibn Muhammad from ibn Faddal from ibn Bukayr from those whom he has mentioned who has said the following:

"Abu 'Abd Allah, *'Alayhi al-Salam*, has said, 'If a person earns in unlawful ways, then uses such income for the expenses of al-Hajj and says al-Talbiyah (here I am O Lord, to obey Your command) it is called about him, "You are not welcome and there is no salvation for you." If it (earning) is through lawful ways upon his saying Talbiyah it is called about him, "You are welcome and there is salvation for you."'"

H 8534, Ch. 40, h 4

Ahmad has narrated from ibn Faddal from ibn Bukayr from 'Ubayd ibn Zurarah who has said the following:

"Abu 'Abd Allah, *'Alayhi al-Salam*, has said, 'The effects of unlawful earning shows up in one's offspring.'"

H 8535, Ch. 40, h 5

Ali ibn Ibrahim has narrated from his father from al-Nawfaliy from al-Sakuniy who has said the following:

"Abu 'Abd Allah, *'Alayhi al-Salam*, has said that once a man came to 'Amir al-Mu'minin saying, 'In my earnings I have been neglectful about lawful and unlawful matters, and I want to repent, but I do not know which item in my possession is lawful and which is not.' 'Amir al-Mu'minin, *'Alayhi al-Salam*, said, 'Give one-fifth of your assets in charity. Allah, most Glorious is whose name, accepts one-fifth of things. The rest of your assets are lawful for you.'"

H 8536, Ch. 40, h 6

Ali ibn Ibrahim has narrated from his father from Ali ibn Muhammad al-Qasaniy from a man whom he has mentioned from 'Abd Allah ibn al-Qasim al-Ja'fariy who has said the following:

"Abu 'Abd Allah, *'Alayhi al-Salam*, has said, 'The world tried to attract a people with purely lawful matters but they passed (without paying any attention) away. Then it tried to attract another people with lawful and doubtful matters and they said, "We do not need any doubtful matters." However, they expanded the lawful matters. It then tried to attract another people with unlawful and doubtful matters. They said, "We do not need unlawful matters." However, they expanded the doubtful matters. It then tried to attract another people with unlawful matters only, and they seek to achieve it but they cannot find. The believing people in this world eat like one living through emergencies.'"

H 8537, Ch. 40, h 7

Ali ibn Ibrahim has narrated from Dawud al-Sarmiy who has said the following:

"Abu al-Hassan, *'Alayhi al-Salam*, once said to me, 'O Dawud, unlawful earnings do not grow. Even if anything grows, it does not have any blessings for him: what he spends does not bring any reward for him and what he leaves behind becomes his supplies to the fire.'"

H 8538, Ch. 40, h 8

Muhammad ibn Yahya has said the following:

"Once Muhammad ibn al-Hassan wrote to abu Muhammad, *'Alayhi al-Salam*, and asked about the case of a man who buys goods or a slave-girl in exchange for a certain amount of assets from one who plunders people on the road or from a thief; if it is lawful for him to use the benefits, or fruits thereof or marry the slave-girl which he has bought from a thief or road plunderer. He (the Imam) signed the answer that said, 'Nothing is good in whatever originates from an unlawful source; and using such matters is not lawful.'"

H 8539, Ch. 40, h 9

A number of our people have narrated from Ahmad ibn Muhammad from ibn Mahbub from abu Ayyub from Sama'ah who has said the following:

"This is concerning my question before abu 'Abd Allah, *'Alayhi al-Salam*, about the case of a man who had found a certain amount of property from banu 'Umayyah. He gives charity thereof, helps his relatives, performs al-Hajj therewith, so that Allah may forgive what he has earned and says, 'Good deeds remove bad deeds.' Abu 'Abd Allah, *'Alayhi al-Salam*, said, 'Sins do not expiate sins. Only good deeds remove sins.' He (the Imam) then said, 'If he has mixed lawful with unlawful and is not able to distinguish, then it is not harmful.'"

H 8540, Ch. 40, h 10

Ali ibn Muhammad has narrated from Salih ibn abu Hammad from ibn abu 'Umayr from certain persons of his people who has said the following:

"About the words of Allah, most Majestic, most Glorious, 'We arrived upon what they had done and turned it into scattered dust', (25:25) abu 'Abd Allah, *'Alayhi al-Salam*, has said, 'Even if their deeds are whiter than Coptic fabrics Allah, most Majestic, most Glorious, says, "Become dust." It is because when they come upon unlawful matters they take it.'"

Chapter 41 - Unlawful Earnings in the form of al-Suht such as Buying and Selling of Intoxicating Liquors . . .

H 8541, Ch. 41, h 1
A number of our people have narrated from Sahl ibn Ziyad Ahmad ibn Muhammad from ibn Mahbub from ibn Ri'ab from 'Ammar ibn Marwan who has said the following:
"I once asked abu Ja'far, *'Alayhi al-Salam*, about seizing (other's assets). He (the Imam) said, 'Whatever of the belonging of the Imam seized is Suht (unlawful like filth), consuming the properties of orphans is Suht, involvement in doubtful matters is Suht and there are many forms of Suht. Of such matters is payment for indecent (sexual) relation, payment for wine and intoxicating beer and receiving unlawful interest, after having clear proof, is Suht. A bribe, however, is disbelief in Allah, most Great and His Messenger, *'O Allah, grant compensation to Muhammad and his family worthy of their services to Your cause.'*"

H 8542, Ch. 41, h 2
Ali ibn Ibrahim has narrated from his father from al-Nawfaliy from al-Sakuniy who has said the following:
"Abu 'Abd Allah, *'Alayhi al-Salam*, has said, 'Receiving payment for carcasses, dogs, wine, indecent (sexual) relation and a bribe to issue a judgment and payment for foretelling is Suht (unlawful and filthy).'"

H 8543, Ch. 41, h 3
A number of our people have narrated from Ahmad ibn abu 'Abd Allah from al-Jamuraniy from al-Hassan ibn Ali ibn abu Hamzah from Zur'ah from Sama'ah who has said the following:
"Abu 'Abd Allah, *'Alayhi al-Salam*, has said, 'There are many kinds of Suht (unlawful and filthy). Of such matters is income from cupping on the basis of a condition (for payment), payment for indecent acts of (sexual) relation and payment for wine. Accepting a bribe is however, disbelief in Allah, most Great.'"

H 8544, Ch. 41, h 4
Muhammad ibn Yahya has narrated from Ahmad ibn Muhammad from Muhammad ibn Sinan from ibn Muskan from Yazid ibn Farqad who has said the following:
"This is concerning my question before abu 'Abd Allah, *'Alayhi al-Salam*, about Suht (unlawful and filthy). He (the Imam) said, 'It is accepting a bribe to issue a judgment.'"

H 8545, Ch. 41, h 5
Ali ibn Muhammad ibn Bandar has narrated from Ahmad ibn abu 'Abd Allah from Muhammad ibn Ali from 'Abd al-Rahman ibn abu Hashim from al-Qasim ibn Muhammad ibn al-Walid al-'Ammariy from Ibrahim al-Asamm from Misma' ibn 'Abd al-Malik from abu 'Abd Allah al-'Amiriy who has said the following:
"This is concerning my question before abu 'Abd Allah, *'Alayhi al-Salam*, about payment for dogs that do not hunt. He (the Imam) said, 'It is Suht (unlawful and filthy), however, payment for a hunting dog is not Suht (unlawful and filthy).'"

H 8546, Ch. 41, h 6

Ali ibn Muhammad has narrated from Salih ibn abu Hammad from more than one person from al-Shu'ayriy who has said the following:

"Abu 'Abd Allah, *'Alayhi al-Salam*, has said, 'If one works the whole night without giving the eyes their share of sleep, such earning is unlawful.'"

H 8547, Ch. 41, h 7

A number of our people have narrated from Sahl ibn Ziyad from Muhammad ibn al-Hassan ibn Shammun from 'Abd Allah ibn 'Abd al-Rahman al-Asamm from Misma' ibn 'Abd al-Malik who has said the following:

"Abu 'Abd Allah, *'Alayhi al-Salam*, has said, 'If a technician remains awake the whole night working, his earning becomes Suht (unlawful and filthy).'"

H 8548, Ch. 41, h 8

Ali ibn Ibrahim has narrated from his father from al-Nawfaliy from al-Sakuniy who has said the following:

"Abu 'Abd Allah, *'Alayhi al-Salam*, has said that the Messenger of Allah, *O Allah, grant compensation to Muhammad and his family worthy of their services to Your cause*, prohibited earning of slave-girls because if they cannot find work, they fornicate, except for a slave-girl who knows a skill and she is better than a slave-boy who due to not knowing any skills, when unable to find work steals.'"

Chapter 42 - Consuming the Properties of Orphans

H 8549, Ch. 42, h 1

A number of our people have narrated from Ahmad ibn Muhammad from 'Uthman ibn 'Isa from Sama'ah who has said the following:

"Abu 'Abd Allah, *'Alayhi al-Salam*, has said, 'Allah, most Majestic, most Glorious, has issued two kinds of warnings about consuming properties of orphans. One is the suffering by the fire in the next life. The punishment in this life is mentioned in the words of Allah, most Majestic, most Glorious, "Those who leave behind weak offspring for whom he is afraid. . . ." (4:11) It means that one must be afraid of leaving behind weak offspring who will be treated as he has treated the orphans.'"

H 8550, Ch. 42, h 2

Ali ibn Ibrahim has narrated from his father from ibn abu 'Umayr from Hisham ibn Salim from 'Ajlan abu Salih who has said the following:

"This is concerning my question before abu 'Abd Allah, *'Alayhi al-Salam*, about the case of a man who consumes the properties of orphans. He (the Imam) said, 'It is as Allah, most Majestic, most Glorious, has said, "Those who consume the properties of orphans unjustly, they only consume fire in their bellies and will feel the heat of the fire." (4:12)' He (the Imam), *'Alayhi al-Salam*, then said without my asking, 'Whoever provides an orphan until his condition as an orphan is over and becomes self-sufficient Allah, most Majestic, most Glorious, makes paradise certain for him as He makes the fire definite for those who consume the properties of orphans.'"

H 8551, Ch. 42, h 3

A number of our people have narrated from Sahl ibn Ziyad from Ahmad ibn Muhammad from ibn abu Nasr who has said the following:

"I once asked abu al-Hassan, *'Alayhi al-Salam*, about the case of a man who in his hand has properties of orphans and is needy. He extends his hand to take a certain amount with the intention to return. He (the Imam) said, 'It is not proper for him to consume it, except with moderation and without excess; but if his intention is not to return, he then is like the one about whom Allah, most Majestic, most Glorious, has said, "Those who consume the properties of orphans unjustly. . . ." (4:12)'"

H 8552, Ch. 42, h 4

Muhammad ibn Yahya has narrated from Ahmad ibn Muhammad from Ali ibn al-Hakam from 'Abd Allah ibn Yahya al-Kahily who has said the following:

"Once it was said to abu 'Abd Allah, *'Alayhi al-Salam*, 'We visit a brother in belief in the house of orphans with their servant. We sit on their furnishings, drink from their water and their servant serves us and perhaps eat of the food of our friend in which there is the orphans' food also. What do you say about it? He (the Imam) said, 'If your visit is beneficial for them, it is not harmful and if it is harmful it is not permissible.' He (the Imam), *'Alayhi al-Salam*, said, 'Man is well aware of his own-self. It is not hidden from you that Allah, most Majestic, most Glorious, has said, "If you mix with them they are your brothers in belief and Allah knows who is corrupt and who is improving and a peacemaker."'"

H 8553, Ch. 42, h 5

Muhammad ibn Yahya has narrated from Muhammad ibn al-Husayn from Dhubyan ibn Hakim al-Awdiy from Ali ibn al-Mughirah who has said the following:

"I once said to abu 'Abd Allah, *'Alayhi al-Salam*, 'I have an orphan girl of my brother. At certain times gifts are given to her and I eat a certain amount thereof. Thereafter I feed her a certain amount from my properties and I say, "O Lord, this is for what I have used." He (the Imam), *'Alayhi al-Salam*, said, 'It is not harmful.'"

Chapter 43 - The Amount a Supervisor of the Properties of Orphans Can Lawfully Use

H 8554, Ch. 43, h 1

A number of our people have narrated from Ahmad ibn Muhammad from 'Uthman ibn 'Isa from Sama'ah who has said the following:

"About the words of Allah, most Majestic, most Glorious, 'One who is poor can eat to the proper limit', (4:6) abu 'Abd Allah, *'Alayhi al-Salam*, has said, 'It is one who manages the properties of orphans but is needy and does not have anything to support himself. He collects debts that people owe to them (orphans) and looks after them, he can eat from their assets only what he needs without excess, but if their assets do not take his time to work for his own-self, then he must not use anything of the properties of the orphans.'"

H 8555, Ch. 43, h 2

'Uthman has narrated from Sama'ah who has said the following:

"About the words of Allah, most Majestic, most Glorious, 'If you mix with them then they are your brothers in religion', abu 'Abd Allah, *'Alayhi al-Salam*, has said, 'It is a reference to orphans. If one becomes the person-in-charge of the affairs of orphans, one must take from one's own assets a certain amount, and equal to this amount from every one of the orphan assets take the same amount; then mix them for the use of all of them together. One must not use anything from their property; it is the fire.'"

H 8556, Ch. 43, h 3

A number of our people have narrated from Sahl ibn Ziyad and Ahmad ibn Muhammad from all from ibn Mahbub from 'Abd Allah ibn Sinan who has said the following:

"About the words of Allah, most Majestic, most Glorious, 'He must eat to the proper limit', abu 'Abd Allah, *'Alayhi al-Salam*, has said, 'Al-Ma'ruf (proper limit) is what one needs for sustenance. It applies to the executor of the will or one who is appointed as the custodian of their assets and to work for their welfare.'"

H 8557, Ch. 43, h 4

Muhammad ibn Yahya has narrated from Ahmad ibn Muhammad from Muhammad ibn 'Isma'il from Hanan ibn Sadir who has said the following:

"Abu 'Abd Allah, *'Alayhi al-Salam*, has said that 'Isa ibn Musa asked about guardians of orphans, camels and what is lawful in matters of camels. I said, 'If he repairs their water tank, finds the lost ones, scratches their itch, he then is entitled to use their milk without excessive use of their udder or harming their young.'"

H 8558, Ch. 43, h 5

Ahmad ibn Muhammad has narrated from Muhammad ibn al-Fudayl from abu al-Sabbah al-Kinaniy who has said the following:

"About the words of Allah, most Majestic, most Glorious, 'One who is poor can eat within the proper limits', abu 'Abd Allah, *'Alayhi al-Salam*, has said, 'He is a man who holds himself back from making his living (to help the orphans). It is not harmful if he eats within the proper limits when he looks after their properties. If the properties are of a small amount he must not eat thereof.' I (the narrator) then asked, 'What is the meaning of the words of Allah, most Majestic, most Glorious, "If you mix then they are your brothers in religion"?' He (the Imam) said, 'You must take out from their property an amount that is sufficient for them for a certain time and from your own property a similar amount which is sufficient for you; then you can spend it.' I then asked about the case where certain ones are smaller and others are bigger and of different amount of expenses for food and clothing. He (the Imam) said, 'In matters of clothes each individual pays what is spent for that individual, but in matters of food they all share; a small person perhaps uses as much food as a larger one.'"

H 8559, Ch. 43, h 6

Abu Ali al-Ash'ariy has narrated from Muhammad ibn 'Abd al-Jabbar from certain persons of our people from 'Is ibn al-Qasim who has said the following:

"This is concerning my question before abu 'Abd Allah, *'Alayhi al-Salam*, about an orphan whose income every month is twenty dirham; how I must spend it. He (the Imam) said, 'Spend what the orphan needs of food and dates.' I asked if spending one-third is sufficient. He (the Imam) said, 'Yes, you must spend half of the income.'"

Chapter 44 - Using the Properties of Orphans in Business and Lending

H 8560, Ch. 44, h 1
Muhammad ibn Yahya has narrated from Ahmad ibn Muhammad from Ali ibn al-Hakam from Asbat ibn Salim who has said the following:

"I once said to abu 'Abd Allah, *'Alayhi al-Salam*, 'I had a brother who has died and made a will in which he appointed my brother who is elder to me and myself as executors. He has left behind a small son and has left behind a certain amount of assets. My brother uses that asset in business and gives the extra to the orphan and has taken the responsibility for the assets of the orphan. He (the Imam) said, 'If your brother's own asset is sufficient to cover the assets of the orphan, then it is not harmful; but if he does not have that much asset he must not bother with the assets of the orphan.'"

H 8561, Ch. 44, h 2
Ali ibn Ibrahim has narrated from his father from Hammad ibn 'Isa from Hariz from Muhammad ibn Muslim who has said the following:

"About the case of the assets of orphans, abu 'Abd Allah, *'Alayhi al-Salam*, has said, 'One who uses the assets of the orphan in business is responsible and the profit belongs to the orphan, if the worker does not have anything of his own assets in it.' He (the Imam) said, 'This person is responsible to pay for any damage caused.'"

H 8562, Ch. 44, h 3
Muhammad ibn 'Isma'il has narrated from al-Fadl ibn Shadhan from ibn abu 'Umayr from Rib'iy ibn 'Abd Allah who has said the following:

"About the case of a man who has the assets of an orphan with him, abu 'Abd Allah, *'Alayhi al-Salam*, has said, 'If he is poor and has no assets of his own, he must not touch the assets of the orphan; and if he uses it in business, he is responsible for it and the profit belongs to the orphan.'"

H 8563, Ch. 44, h 4
A number of our people have narrated from Sahl ibn Ziyad from Ali ibn Asbat from Asbat ibn Salim who has said the following:

"I once said to abu 'Abd Allah, *'Alayhi al-Salam*, that my brother has told me to ask you about the assets of an orphan who is under his (my brother's) guardianship and he uses the assets of the orphan in business. He (the Imam) said, 'If your brother's assets are sufficient to cover the assets of the orphan in case it is destroyed, it is permissible; otherwise, it is not permissible and he must not hassle with the assets of the orphan.'"

H 8564, Ch. 44, h 5
Abu Ali al-Ash'ariy has narrated from Muhammad ibn 'Abd al-Jabbar from Safwan ibn Yahya from Mansur ibn Hazim who has said the following:

"This is concerning my question before abu 'Abd Allah, *'Alayhi al-Salam*, about the case of a man who is the person in charge of the assets of an orphan; if he can borrow from such assets. He (the Imam) said, 'Ali ibn al-Husayn, *'Alayhi al-Salam*, would borrow from the assets of orphans under his guardianship, thus, it is not harmful.'"

H 8565, Ch. 44, h 6
Al-Husayn from Muhammad has narrated from Mu'alla' ibn Muhammad from al-Hassan ibn Ali from Aban ibn 'Uthman from Mansur ibn Hazim who has said the following:
"This is concerning my question before abu 'Abd Allah, *'Alayhi al-Salam*, about the case of a man who is the person in charge of the assets of orphans; if he can borrow from such assets. He (the Imam) said, 'Ali ibn al-Husayn, *'Alayhi al-Salam*, would borrow from the assets of orphans under his guardianship.'"

H 8566, Ch. 44, h 7
Ali ibn Ibrahim has narrated from his father and Muhammad ibn 'Isma'il has narrated from al-Fadl ibn Shadhan from ibn abu 'Umayr and Safwan from 'Abd al-Rahman ibn al-Hajjaj who has said the following:
"I once asked abu al-Hassan, *'Alayhi al-Salam*, about the case of a man in whose family someone has the assets of orphans and he gives a certain amount of dirham to him that he needs; and the person with whom there are the assets of orphans does not know if he has taken anything from their assets. He thereafter becomes affluent. Is it better for him to give it back to the one who had given him such assets or to the orphan who has reached maturity? Is it sufficient if he gives it to the one from whom he had received the amount in the form of gifts without informing him about his borrowing anything from him? He (the Imam) said, 'Either way is sufficient. To give it as gift to his friend is sufficient because it is of the secret matters, if he had the intention to return to the orphan who has become mature, and in whatever manners he returns even if he does not inform him about his borrowing or if he wants he can return to the one from whom he had received the amount.' He (the Imam) said, 'If his friend is absent, he then must return it to the one from whom he had received the amount.'"

H 8567, Ch. 44, h 8
Muhammad ibn Yahya has narrated from Ahmad ibn Muhammad from ibn Mahbub from Khalid ibn Jarir from abu al-Rabi' who has said the following:
"Once abu 'Abd Allah, *'Alayhi al-Salam*, was asked about the case of a man who becomes the person in charge of the assets of orphans and borrows a certain amount thereof. He (the Imam) said, 'Ali ibn al-Husayn, would borrow from the assets of orphans under his guardianship.'"

Chapter 45 - Safe Return of Trust

H 8568, Ch. 45, h 1
Ali ibn Ibrahim has narrated from his father from ibn abu 'Umayr from al-Husayn ibn Mus'ab al-Hamadaniy who has said the following:
"I heard abu 'Abd Allah, *'Alayhi al-Salam*, saying, 'There are three issues in which one has no choice: They are safe return of trust of a virtuous or sinful

person, keeping one's promise to a virtuous or sinful person, and kindness to parents, regardless, of their being virtuous or sinful ones.'"

H 8569, Ch. 45, h 2

A number of our people have narrated from Ahmad ibn Muhammad from Ali ibn al-Hakam from ibn Bukayr from al-Hassan al-Shaybaniy who has said the following:

"This is concerning my question before abu 'Abd Allah, *'Alayhi al-Salam*, 'One of your Mawaliy (followers) considers use of the properties of Amawide people lawful as well as their lives. Something that they had left with him for safe-keeping is in his possession.' He (the Imam) said, 'You must return trusts to the rightful people even if they are of Zoroastrian people. Such matters will happen only when the one with Divine Authority from us, Ahl al-Bayt will rise. He will decide what is lawful and what is not lawful.'"

H 8570, Ch. 45, h 3

A number of our people have narrated from Ahmad ibn Muhammad from ibn Khalid from al-Qasim ibn Muhammad ibn Yahya from his grandfather, al-Hassan ibn Rashid from Muhammad ibn Muslim who has said the following:

"Abu 'Abd Allah, *'Alayhi al-Salam*, has said that Amir al-Mu'minin, *'Alayhi al-Salam*, has said, 'You must return a trust even if an assassin of the children of the prophet has left it with you.'"

H 8571, Ch. 45, h 4

Ali ibn Ibrahim has narrated from his father from 'Isma'il ibn Marrar from Yunus from 'Umar ibn abu Hafs who has said the following:

"I heard abu 'Abd Allah, *'Alayhi al-Salam*, saying, 'You must maintain piety before Allah and you must return a trust to the one who has entrusted you with it. Even if the assassin of Ali ibn abu Talib entrusted me with something, I had to return it to him safely.'"

H 8572, Ch. 45, h 5

Muhammad ibn Yahya has narrated from Ahmad ibn Muhammad from Muhammad ibn Sinan from 'Ammar ibn Marwan who has said the following:

"Abu 'Abd Allah, *'Alayhi al-Salam*, has said in one of his advices, 'You must take notice that even if the assassin of Ali, *'Alayhi al-Salam*, who struck him (the Imam) with his sword had entrusted me with something, asked for my opinion and consultation and I had accepted, I most certainly had to return his trust safely.'"

H 8573, Ch. 45, h 6

Abu Ali al-Ash'ariy has narrated from Muhammad ibn 'Abd al-Jabbar from Safwan ibn Yahya from Ishaq ibn 'Ammar from Hafs ibn Qurt who has said the following:

"I once said to abu 'Abd Allah, *'Alayhi al-Salam*, 'There was a woman in al-Madinah and people left their slave-girls with her to train them. We said that there is no one on whom wealth is poured as it is poured before her.' He (the Imam) said, 'It is because she spoke the truth, returned the trust safely and that is what attracts wealth.' Safwan has said, 'I heard this Hadith from Hafs later on.'"

H 8574, Ch. 45, h 7

Ali ibn Ibrahim has narrated from his father from al-Nawfaliy from al-Sakuniy, who has said the following:

"Abu 'Abd Allah, *'Alayhi al-Salam*, has said that the Messenger of Allah, *O Allah, grant compensation to Muhammad and his family worthy of their services to Your cause*, has said, 'One who does not keep a trust safely is not of our people.' The Messenger of Allah has said, 'Trustworthiness attracts wealth and treachery attracts poverty.'"

H 8575, Ch. 45, h 8

Muhammad ibn Yahya has narrated from Ahmad ibn Muhammad ibn 'Isa from Muhammad ibn Khalid from al-Qasim ibn Muhammad from Muhammad ibn al-Qasim who has said the following:

"I once asked abu al-Hassan, Musa, *'Alayhi al-Salam*, about a man who entrusted another man with a certain amount of property. The man with whom goods were left was from Arab people and he was not able to return anything. The other man was not able to do anything against him. The entrusting man was a filthy foreigner and has not asked for anything.' He (the Imam) said to me, 'Tell him to return his trust; he entrusted him with trust of Allah, most Majestic, most Glorious.' I then said, 'Ali ibn al-Nu'man has purchased from an 'Abbaside woman a certain piece of their (land) and he has a document that says she has received payment; but in fact she has not received any payment. Should he pay her or refuse to pay?' He (the Imam) said to me, 'Tell him to deny paying her with strongest denial; she has sold what did not belong to her.'"

H 8576, Ch. 45, h 9

Al-Husayn ibn Muhammad has narrated from Muhammad ibn Ahmad al-Nahdiy from Kathir ibn Yunus from 'Abd al-Rahman ibn Sayabah who has said the following:

"When my father, Sayabah, passed away, one of his brothers came to me and knocked at the door. I went out to meet him. He offered me condolence and asked, 'Has your father left anything?' I replied, 'No, he has not left anything.' He then gave to me a bag with a thousand dirham in it and said, 'Keep it (the capital) safe and use its profits.' I went to my mother while I was very happy and informed her about it. During the night I visited a friend of my father and he purchased for me certain Sabiriy goods. I then opened a shop and Allah, most Majestic, most Glorious, granted me a great deal of good things. The time for Hajj came and I felt in my heart about performing Hajj. I went to my mother and informed her of my feeling about performing Hajj. She then told me to return the dirhams of so and so. I then took the dirhams and gave it to him. He became so happy as if he had received a gift. He said, 'Perhaps, it is not enough. I am ready to give you more dirhams.' I replied, 'No, I thank you. I desire to perform Hajj and I like that your thing is in your own possession.' I left for Hajj and completed the acts of Hajj. I then returned to al-Madinah and along with people went to visit abu 'Abd Allah, *'Alayhi al-Salam*. Appointment was not required for visitation. I sat in the last rows of people; I was young. People asked him questions and he (the Imam) answered them. When many people left and the gathering was reduced he (the Imam) pointed to me and I went closer. He (the Imam) asked, 'Do you need anything?' I replied, 'I pray to Allah to keep my soul in service for your cause, I am 'Abd al-Rahman ibn Sayabah.' He (the

Imam) asked, 'What has your father done?' I replied, 'He has passed away.' He (the narrator) has said, 'He (the Imam) expressed sorrow and sympathy.' He (the narrator) has said, 'He (the Imam) then asked, 'Has he left anything?' I replied, 'No, he has not left any thing.' He (the Imam) then asked, 'By what means then were you able to perform Hajj?' He (the narrator) has said, 'I explained to him the story of the man with dirham. He (the Imam) did not allow me to finish the story and asked,'What did you do with the thousand dirhams?' He (the narrator) has said, 'I said, "I returned it to its owner."' He (the narrator) has said that he (the Imam) said, 'You have done a very good deed' and he said to me, 'Would you like if I give a good advice?' I replied, 'Yes, I pray to Allah to keep my soul in service for your cause.' He (the Imam) said, 'You must speak the truth and return a trust safely; you will share people in their wealth like this' –he joined his fingers side by side. I followed his advice and was able to pay in charity three hundred thousand dirham.'"

Chapter 46 - A Father and Son's Using Each Others Properties

H 8577, Ch. 46, h 1
Ali ibn Ibrahim has narrated from his father from Hammad from Hariz from Muhammad ibn Muslim who has said the following:
"This is concerning my question before abu 'Abd Allah, *'Alayhi al-Salam*, about a man whose son owned a certain amount of wealth and his father was needy. He (the Imam) replied, 'He has permission to use such wealth for food; however, a mother does not have such permission but she can borrow on her own responsibility.'"

H 8578, Ch. 46, h 2
A number of our people have narrated from Sahl ibn Ziyad from Ali ibn Asbat from Ali ibn Ja'far who has said the following:
"I once asked abu Ibrahim, *'Alayhi al-Salam*, about a man who used the properties of his sons for food. He (the Imam) replied, 'No, unless he is compelled by pressing needs, in which case he spends in a fair manner but it is not proper for the sons to spend the properties of their father without the permission of the father.'"

H 8579, Ch. 46, h 3
Sahl ibn Ziyad has narrated from ibn Mahbub from abu Hamzah al-Thumaliy who has said the following:
"Abu Ja'far, *'Alayhi al-Salam*, has said that the Messenger of Allah, *O Allah, grant compensation to Muhammad and his family worthy of their services to Your cause*, once said to a man, 'You and your property belong to your father.' Abu Ja'far, *'Alayhi al-Salam*, then said, 'I do not like his spending from the property of his son more than what he needs for his bare necessities; Allah, most Majestic, most Glorious, does not love destruction.'"

H 8580, Ch. 46, h 4
Abu Ali al-Ash'ariy has narrated from al-Hassan ibn Ali al-Kufiy from 'Ubays ibn Hisham from "Abd al-Karim from ibn abu Ya'fur who has said the following:

"This is concerning my question before abu 'Abd Allah, *'Alayhi al-Salam*, about a man whose son owned a certain amount of wealth and liked to take something from it. He (the Imam) replied, 'He has permission to do so; however, were his mother alive I would not like her taking anything from his property except as a loan on her own responsibility.'"

H 8581, Ch. 46, h 5
Sahl ibn Ziyad has narrated from ibn Mahbub from al-'Ala' ibn Razin from Muhammad ibn Muslim who has said the following:

"I once asked abu Ja'far, *'Alayhi al-Salam*, about a man who needed to spend from the property of his son. He (the Imam) replied, 'He has permission to use the property of his son for food as much as he wants but without excess.' He (the Imam) said, 'It is in the book of Ali, *'Alayhi al-Salam*, that a son does not have permission to spend from the property of his father anything unless his father grants him permission. A father has permission to take from the property of his sons as he wants. He may also have carnal relations with the slave-girl of his son if his son has not yet engaged in carnal relations with her.' He (the Imam) also mentioned that the Messenger of Allah, *O Allah, grant compensation to Muhammad and his family worthy of their services to Your cause*, once said to a man, 'You and your property belong to your father.'"

H 8582, Ch. 46, h 6
Muhammad ibn Yahya has narrated from 'Abd Allah ibn Muhammad from Ali ibn al-Hakam from Al-Husayn ibn al-'Ala' who has said the following:

"This is concerning my question before abu 'Abd Allah, *'Alayhi al-Salam*, 'How much can a father spend from the property of his sons?' He (the Imam) replied, 'He can take for his basic necessities without excess when pressing needs compel him.' I (the narrator) then asked about the words of the Messenger of Allah, *O Allah, grant compensation to Muhammad and his family worthy of their services to Your cause*, to a man who came to him and had brought his father also. The Messenger of Allah said to him, 'You and your property belong to your father' He (the Imam) replied, 'He brought his father before the Holy Prophet saying, "O Messenger of Allah, he has done injustice to me in the matters of the legacy of my mother." The father informed him of his spending her legacy on the son and for his own expenses. Then he (the Messenger of Allah) said, "You and your property belong to your father." The man did not own anything. Should the Messenger of Allah stop the father benefiting from the son?'"

Chapter 47 - A Husband and Wife's Using Each Other's Properties

H 8583, Ch. 47, h 1
A number of our people have narrated from Ahmad ibn Muhammad from al-Husayn ibn Sa'id from 'Uthman ibn 'Isa from Sa'd ibn Yasar who has said the following:

"This is concerning my question before abu 'Abd Allah, *'Alayhi al-Salam*, saying, 'I pray to Allah to keep my soul in service for your cause, a woman gave a certain amount of property to her husband from her own property so he can use in business and she said to him upon the delivery, "You can spend from it and if something happens to you, it is lawful for you and if something happens to me and whatever you may spend is lawfully clean for you.'" He (the Imam) asked, 'Say it again, O Sa'id.' When I wanted to repeat the question the person involved in the case was present so he repeated the same question. When he completed the question, he (the Imam) pointed with his finger to the person involved in the case saying, 'If you know that she has left it up to your decision which you make before Allah, most Majestic, most Glorious, then it is lawfully clean for you'- he said it three times. He (the Imam) then said, 'Allah, most Majestic is whose name, has said in His book, "If they (the wives) agree about something of it (their property) for your spending thereof you may consume it in good health and pleasure." (4:4)'"

H 8584, Ch. 47, h 2
Muhammad ibn Yahya has narrated from Ahmad ibn Muhammad from ibn Faddal from ibn Bukayr who has said the following:

"This is concerning my question before abu 'Abd Allah, *'Alayhi al-Salam*, about how much is lawful for a woman to give as charity from the house of her husband without his permission. He (the Imam) replied, 'It is al-Ma'dum (sauce, curry or gravy).'"

Chapter 48 - Found and Lost Properties

H 8585, Ch. 48, h 1
Al-Husayn ibn Muhammad has narrated from Mu'alla' ibn Muhammad and Ali ibn Muhammad al-Qashaniy from Salih ibn abu Hammad all from al-Washsha' from Ahmad ibn 'A'idh from abu Khadijah, who has said the following:

"Abu 'Abd Allah, *'Alayhi al-Salam*, has said, 'In the beginning of time when people found something and took it this (act) caused them to lose the ability to move even one step until they threw away what they had found. The rightful owner then came to pick it up. People became daring to greater wrong acts but it will in a certain time come back again.'"

H 8586, Ch. 48, h 2
A number of our people have narrated from Sahl ibn Ziyad from Ahmad ibn Muhammad ibn abu Nasr from Dawud ibn Sarhan who has said the following:

"Abu 'Abd Allah, *'Alayhi al-Salam*, has said that one who finds something of value must (continue to) announce his finding for one year. Thereafter it becomes like the rest of his property." (Consult fatwa also)

H 8587, Ch. 48, h 3
A number of our people have narrated from Sahl ibn Ziyad and Ahmad ibn Muhammad from all from ibn Mahbub from Jamil ibn Salih who has said the following:

"This is concerning my question before abu 'Abd Allah, *'Alayhi al-Salam*, about the case of a man who has found a dinar in his house. He (the Imam) asked, 'Does anyone else enter his house?' I (the narrator) replied, 'Yes, many people enter his house.' He (the Imam) said, 'This is a case of lost and found property.' I (the narrator) then asked about the case of a man who has found a dinar in his box. He (the Imam) asked, 'Does anyone besides him enter his hand in his box?'

I (the narrator) replied, 'No, no one else does so.' He (the Imam) said, 'It then is for him.'"

H 8588, Ch. 48, h 4

Ali ibn Ibrahim has narrated from his father from ibn abu 'Umayr from Muhammad ibn abu Hamzah from certain persons of his people who has said the following:

"This is concerning my question before abu 'Abd Allah, *'Alayhi al-Salam*, about lost property found. He (the Imam) said, 'You must (continue to) announce your finding in public for one year, regardless of its quantity - whether small or a large quantity.' He (the Imam) then said, 'If it is less than a dirham one does not need to make any announcements.'"

H 8589, Ch. 48, h 5

Ali has narrated from his father from ibn Mahbub al-'Ala' ibn Razin from Muhammad ibn Muslim who has said the following:

"I once asked abu Ja'far, *'Alayhi al-Salam*, about a house wherein certain leaves (coins of silver) are found. He (the Imam) replied, 'If it is livable and the dwellers live therein, it belongs to them; but if it is not livable, whose inhabitants have abandoned it, then it is for the one who has found it.'"

H 8590, Ch. 48, h 6

A number of our people have narrated from Ahmad ibn Muhammad from 'Abd Allah ibn Muhammad al-Hajjal from Tha'labah ibn Maymun from Sa'id ibn 'Amr al-Ju'fiy who has said the following:

"I once left for Makkah and my financial condition was the worst among people. I mentioned to abu 'Abd Allah, *'Alayhi al-Salam*. When I left his meeting at the door I found a bag with seven hundred dinar in it. I immediately returned to the Imam and informed him about it. He (the Imam) said, 'Sa'id, be pious before Allah, most Majestic, most Glorious. You must announce your finding in all the places (Mashahid) where people perform the acts of Hajj.' I had a degree of hope about Imam's permission for me to use some of that money. I then left and I was sad. I went to Mina and moved far from people, searched around and ended up to the places endowed for the benefit of people. I found a room away from people and then announced, 'I have found a bag. Whoever has lost it must give proper description and collect it from me.' As soon as I made the announcement a man stood over my head saying, 'I am the owner of the bag.' I (the narrator) said to myself I wish you had not said it. I then asked, 'What is the description of the bag?' He gave me the exact description and I gave it to him.' He moved to one side and counted them and found it to be the same amount. He then counted seventy dinars and said, 'Take this lawful money; it is better than seven hundred unlawful dinars.' I took them and visited abu 'Abd Allah, *'Alayhi al-Salam*, and informed him of the story in details. He (the Imam) said, 'When you complained before me about your condition I ordered to keep aside thirty dinars for you. O girl, bring for him those dinars.' I took them and was of the best financial condition in my people.'"

H 8591, Ch. 48, h 7

Muhammad ibn Yahya has narrated from Muhammad ibn Ahmad from Musa ibn 'Umar from al-Hajjal from Dawud ibn abu Yazid who has said the following:

"Once a man said, 'I have found a certain amount of property and because of it I am afraid for myself. I wish to find the owner to free myself of this difficulty. He (the narrator) has said, that abu 'Abd Allah, *'Alayhi al-Salam*, asked him, 'Will you, by Allah, on finding the owner give it to him?' He replied, 'Yes, by Allah, I will do so.' He (the Imam) said, 'I am the one. By Allah, it has no owner besides me.' He (the Imam) made him to take an oath to do with what he has found as he (the Imam) commands him to do. He took an oath and he (the Imam) commanded him to distribute it among his brothers, saying, 'You will be safe from what you are afraid of.' He has said, 'I distributed it among my brothers.'" (Consult fatwa about this Hadith)

H 8592, Ch. 48, h 8

Ali ibn Ibrahim has narrated from his father from certain persons of our people from abu al-'Ala' who has said the following:

"This is concerning my question before abu 'Abd Allah, *'Alayhi al-Salam*, 'A man found a certain amount of goods and he announced about it in public for one year. He then bought a slave-girl. A man then claiming to be the owner came to him and found the slave-girl who was purchased with that money to be his daughter.' He (the Imam) said, 'He is entitled to take the dirhams but not the slave-girl. The money belongs to him but his daughter is the slave-girl of other people.'"

H 8593, Ch. 48, h 9

Muhammad ibn Yahya has narrated from 'Abd Allah ibn Ja'far who has said the following:

"I once wrote to the man, *'Alayhi al-Salam*, and asked him about the case of a man who had bought camels or cows for sacrificial offering. When he slaughtered, he found a bag of dinar or diamond inside the animal. To whom this found property belong?' He (the Imam), *'Alayhi al-Salam*, wrote back to me, 'He must announce it before the seller and if he did not know about it, then whatever is found is what Allah has granted to him.'"

H 8594, Ch. 48, h 10

Ali ibn Muhammad has narrated from Ibrahim ibn Ishaq from 'Abd Allah ibn Hammad from abu Basir who has said the following:

"Abu Ja'far, *'Alayhi al-Salam*, has said, 'Whoever finds something it is for him to benefit thereby until the owner comes. He then must give it to the owner." (Consult Fatwa also.)

H 8595, Ch. 48, h 11

Ali ibn Ibrahim has narrated from his father from Hammad ibn Hariz from Muhammad ibn Muslim who has said the following:

"I asked abu Ja'far, *'Alayhi al-Salam*, about lost property found. He (the Imam) said, 'He must not pick it up, and if he did so, it becomes his responsibility to announce for it up to one year. If the owner did not come forward, it then becomes subject to what his other properties are until someone searching for it comes forward; and if no one came forward he must make a will about it.'"

H 8596, Ch. 48, h 12

Ali ibn Ibrahim has narrated from his father from ibn abu 'Umayr from Hisham ibn Salim , who has said the following:

"Abu 'Abd Allah, *'Alayhi al-Salam,* has said that once someone came to the Holy Prophet, *O Allah, grant compensation to Muhammad and his family worthy of their services to Your cause,* saying, 'I have found a sheep.' The Messenger of Allah said, 'It is for you or your brother or a wolf.' He then said, 'I have found a camel.' The Messenger of Allah asked, 'Does it have its shoes and water container? Nevertheless, take notice, its shoes are its feet and its water container is its hump. You must not bother the camel.'" (Consult fatwa also.)

H 8597, Ch. 48, h 13

A number of our people have narrated from Ahmad ibn Muhammad from and Sahl ibn Ziyad from ibn Mahbub from 'Abd Allah ibn Sinan who has said the following:

"Abu 'Abd Allah, *'Alayhi al-Salam,* has said, 'If one finds a certain amount of goods, or a camel in wilderness which has become tired has stopped walking and its owner has abandoned it; someone other than the owner then takes it, tends to it and incurs expenses to revive it from tiredness and death; it then is for him. He (the owner) has no reason to claim it. It then is like a lawful thing for him (the finder).'"

H 8598, Ch. 48, h 14

Muhammad ibn Yahya has narrated from 'Abd Allah ibn Muhammad from his father from 'Abd Allah ibn Mughirah from al-Sakuniy who has said the following:

"Abu 'Abd Allah, *'Alayhi al-Salam,* has said that Amir al-Mu'minin, *'Alayhi al-Salam,* issued a judgment about the animal of a man who had abandoned it as follows: 'If he has left it near water, and proper and safe pasture it is for him. He takes it wherever he finds it. If he has left it in an unsafe place, without water and pasture, it then is for the one who finds it.'"

H 8599, Ch. 48, h 15

Ali ibn Ibrahim has narrated from his father from Hammad from Hariz who has said the following:

"Abu 'Abd Allah, *'Alayhi al-Salam,* has said, 'There is no offense in picking up a stick, pieces of wood used in the saddle of camels, stage, ropes, and harnesses and similar items. He (the Imam) then said, 'Abu Ja'far, *'Alayhi al-Salam,* has said, "Such things are not wanted items."'" (Consult fatwa also.)

H 8600, Ch. 48, h 16

A number of our people have narrated from Sahl ibn Ziyad from Muhammad ibn al-Hassan al-Shammun from al-Asamm from Misma' who has said the following:

"Abu 'Abd Allah, *'Alayhi al-Salam,* has said that Amir al-Mu'minin, *'Alayhi al-Salam,* has said, 'If a horse is released by its owner or if he is not able to feed it or pay its expenses, it then is for one who revives it.' He (the Imam) has said, 'Amir al-Mu'minin, *'Alayhi al-Salam,* issued a judgment about the case of a man who had left his horse in an unsafe place. The judgment said, "If he has left it in a safe place with water and pasture, it is for him whenever he wants; but if he has left it in an unsafe place without water and pasture then it is for the one who has revived it."'"

H 8601, Ch. 48, h 17

Sahl ibn Ziyad has narrated from ibn Mahbub from Safwan al-Jammal who has said the following:

"I heard abu 'Abd Allah, *'Alayhi al-Salam*, saying, 'One who finds a lost animal but does not announce in public what he has found and then it is found by the owner, it then is for the care-taker (owner) or its kind (current value) from the assets of the one who has kept it in hiding.'"

Chapter 49 - Gifts and Presents

H 8602, Ch. 49, h 1

Ali ibn Ibrahim has narrated from his father from al-Nawfaliy from al-Sakuniy, who has said the following:

"Abu 'Abd Allah, *'Alayhi al-Salam*, has said that the Messenger of Allah, *O Allah, grant compensation to Muhammad and his family worthy of their services to Your cause*, has said, 'Gifts are of three kinds: One is a gift to compensate a favor, another is a gift for understanding (bribing) someone, and another gift is a gift from Allah, most Majestic, most Glorious.'"

H 8603, Ch. 49, h 2

A number of our people have narrated from Sahl ibn Ziyad and Ahmad ibn Muhammad from all from ibn Mahbub from Ibrahim al-Karkhiy who has said the following:

"I asked abu 'Abd Allah, *'Alayhi al-Salam*, about the case of a man who possesses a great deal of goods. On the times of festivities or the day of Nawroz, they give him as gifts which they did not have to give him but they wanted to become nearer to him. He (the Imam) asked, 'Are they not the ones who perform prayers?' I (the narrator) replied, 'Yes, they perform prayer.' He (the Imam) said, 'He must accept their gift and reciprocate. The Messenger of Allah, *O Allah, grant compensation to Muhammad and his family worthy of their services to Your cause*, has said, "Even if a foot of sheep is given to me as a gift I accept it. It is part of the discipline of religion. On the other hand, if an unbeliever or hypocrite gives me as gift, a whole load of goods, I do not accept. It is of the discipline of religion. Allah, most Majestic, most Glorious, disdains my accepting gifts of unbelievers and hypocrites."'"

H 8604, Ch. 49, h 3

Ibn Mahbub has narrated from Sayf ibn 'Amirah from abu Bakr al-Hadramiy who has said the following:

"Abu 'Abd Allah, *'Alayhi al-Salam*, has said, 'Arabs during pre-Islamic age of ignorance were of two groups. One was al-Hull and the other al-Hums. Al-Hums were Quraysh and al-Hull was the rest of Arabs. Everyone of al-Hull group had to have a protector from al-Hums people; otherwise, they could not perform Tawaf except in a naked condition. The Messenger of Allah, *O Allah, grant compensation to Muhammad and his family worthy of their services to Your cause*, was the protector of 'Iyad ibn Himar al-Mujashi'iy. 'Iyad was a person of great importance. He was a judge for the people in 'Ukaz during the age of ignorance. When visiting Makkah 'Iyad removed his dress of sins and filth. He dressed up with the dress of the Messenger of Allah for being clean. He dressed up and performed Tawaf around the house, then returned them to him after completing Tawaf. When the Messenger of Allah declared his mission, 'Iyad brought a gift for him. The Messenger of Allah refused to accept it saying, 'O 'Iyad, if you accept Islam I accept your gift. Allah, most Majestic, most Glorious, disdains my accepting gifts from pagans.' 'Iyad then afterwards accepted Islam and made it to be good. He then gave a gift to the Messenger of Allah, *O Allah, grant compensation to Muhammad and his family worthy of their services to Your cause*, and he accepted his gift.'"

H 8605, Ch. 49, h 4

A number of our people have narrated from Sahl ibn Ziyad from ii; ibn Mehran from abu Jarir al-Qummiy who has said the following:

"I once, about the case of a man who gifts something to a relative who is a sultan but he seeks thawab (reward from Allah), asked abu al-Hassan, *'Alayhi al-Salam*. He (the Imam) replied, 'What is for Allah, most Majestic, most Glorious, and to keep good relations with relatives is permissible. He must accept the gift if it is for thawab.'"

H 8606, Ch. 49, h 5

Sahl ibn Ziyad has narrated from Ahmad ibn Muhammad from 'Abd Allah ibn al-Mughirah who has said the following:

"Muhammad ibn 'Abd Allah al-Qummiy once said to abu al-Hassan, *'Alayhi al-Salam*, 'On our land there are facilities that house firehouses of al-Majus (Zoroastrians) who offer cows and sheep and dirham. Can the owners of these villages receive such things and these facilities have keepers who maintain them?' He (the Imam) said, 'The owners of these villages must take it and there is no offense in it.'" (Consult Fatwa also)

H 8607, Ch. 49, h 6

Muhammad ibn Yahya has narrated from those whom he has mentioned from Yahya al-Mubarak from 'Abd Allah ibn Jabalah from Ishaq ibn 'Ammar who has said the following:

"I once asked him (the Imam) about a poor man who presents to me a gift seeking nearness to me thereby and I accept it and do not give him anything as a gift. Is this lawful for me?' He (the Imam) replied, 'It is lawful for you, however, you must not neglect to give him something.'"

H 8608, Ch. 49, h 7

A number of our people have narrated from Ahmad ibn Muhammad ibn Khalid from 'Isma'il ibn Mehran from Sayf ibn 'Amirah from 'Amr ibn Shamir from Jabir who has said the following:

"Abu Ja'far, *'Alayhi al-Salam*, has said that the Messenger of Allah, *O Allah, grant compensation to Muhammad and his family worthy of their services to Your cause*, would use gifts for food but not charity and he would say, "You must exchange gifts, it gently removes resentment and clears grudges due to animosity and malice.""

H 8609, Ch. 49, h 8

Ali ibn Ibrahim has narrated from his father from al-Nawfaliy from al-Sakuniy, , who has said the following:

"Abu 'Abd Allah, *'Alayhi al-Salam*, has said that the Messenger of Allah, *O Allah, grant compensation to Muhammad and his family worthy of their services*

to Your cause, has said, 'Of a believer's upholding the honor of his Muslim brother is to accept his gifts and present him a gift of whatever is possible for him without over-burdening himself.'"

H 8610, Ch. 49, h 9

Through the same chain of narrators as the previous Hadith he has said the following:

"The Messenger of Allah, *O Allah, grant compensation to Muhammad and his family worthy of their services to Your cause*, has said, 'Even if a gift as small as the foot of a sheep is presented to me I accept it.'"

H 8611, Ch. 49, h 10

Ali ibn Muhammad has narrated from Ahmad ibn Muhammad from certain persons of his people from Aban from Ibrahim ibn 'Umar from Muhammad ibn Muslim in a Maqtu' manner who have said the following:

"He (the Imam), *'Alayhi al-Salam*, has said, 'People in the meeting with the recipient of a gift all have a share in that gift.'"

H 8612, Ch. 49, h 11

Ahmad ibn Muhammad from has narrated from 'Uthman ibn 'Isa in a marfu' manner who has said the following:

"He (the Imam), *'Alayhi al-Salam*, has said, 'If one receives a gift such as food or fruits and so on, during a meeting with people around him they also have a share in such gift.'"

H 8613, Ch. 49, h 12

Ali ibn Ibrahim has narrated from his father from ibn abu 'Umayr from Al-Nawfaliy from al-Sakuniy, who has said the following:

"Abu 'Abd Allah, *'Alayhi al-Salam*, has said that Amir al-Mu'minin, *'Alayhi al-Salam*, has said, 'Presenting a gift to my Muslim brother which can benefit him is more beloved to me than giving charity.'"

H 8614, Ch. 49, h 13

Al-Husayn ibn Muhammad has narrated from Ja'far ibn Muhammad from 'Abd al-Rahman ibn Muhammad from Muhammad ibn Ibrahim al-Kufiy from Al-Husayn ibn Zayd who has said the following:

"Abu 'Abd Allah, *'Alayhi al-Salam*, has said that the Messenger of Allah, *O Allah, grant compensation to Muhammad and his family worthy of their services to Your cause*, has said, 'You should exchange gifts of berries; it revives affection and friendship.'"

H 8615, Ch. 49, h 14

Ali ibn Ibrahim has narrated from his father from al-Nawfaliy from al-Sakuniy, who has said the following:

"Abu 'Abd Allah, *'Alayhi al-Salam*, has said that the Messenger of Allah, *O Allah, grant compensation to Muhammad and his family worthy of their services to Your cause*, has said, 'You should exchange gifts; you will find affection. You should exchange gifts; it removes malice.'"

Chapter 50 - Rule about Unlawful Interest

H 8616, Ch. 50, h 1
A number of our people have narrated from Ahmad ibn Muhammad ibn 'Isa from ibn abu 'Umayr from Hisham ibn Salim, who has said the following:

"Abu 'Abd Allah, *'Alayhi al-Salam*, has said, 'The sin of receiving one dirham of *Riba'* (unlawful interest) is more serious than having carnal relations with one's relatives (with whom marriage is unlawful)."

H 8617, Ch. 50, h 2
Ali ibn Ibrahim has narrated from his father from ibn abu Najran from 'Asim ibn Hamid from m h ibn Qays, who has said the following:

"Abu 'Abd Allah, *'Alayhi al-Salam*, has said that Amir al-Mu'minin, *'Alayhi al-Salam*, has said, 'One who consumes *Riba'*, one who feeds *Riba'* and one who documents it, are all the same (in committing this sins).'"

H 8618, Ch. 50, h 3
Muhammad ibn Yahya has narrated from Ahmad ibn Muhammad from Muhammad ibn 'Isa from Mansur from Hisham ibn Salim who has said the following:

"This is concerning my question before abu 'Abd Allah, *'Alayhi al-Salam*, about the case of a man who consumes *Riba'* and he considers it lawful. He (the Imam) replied, 'It does not harm him as long as he does not consume it knowing that it is unlawful, in which case he will face the condition of one who is mentioned in the words of Allah, most Majestic, most Glorious. "Those who take unlawful interest will stand before Allah (on the Day of Judgment) as those who suffer from a mental imbalance because of Satan's touch; they have said that trade is just like unlawful interest. Allah has made trade lawful and has forbidden unlawful interest. One who has received advice from his Lord and has stopped committing sins will be rewarded for his previous good deeds. His affairs will be in the hands of Allah. But one who turns back to committing sins will be of the dwellers of hell wherein he will live forever." (2:275)'"

H 8619, Ch. 50, h 4
Ahmad ibn Muhammad from has narrated from al-Washsha' from abu al-Mighra' from al-Halabiy, who has said the following:

"Abu 'Abd Allah, *'Alayhi al-Salam*, has said, 'Any kind of *Riba'* people have consumed in ignorance then repented, such repentance is accepted if such repentance is found in them.' He (the Imam) then said, 'If a man inherits goods, from his father and knows that there is *Riba'* in it but is mixed in trade with other lawful goods it is lawful and clean for him and he has permission to consume such properties. If however, he comes to know the *Riba'* item, he then must separate his capital and return the *Riba'* property. If one earns a great deal of property in which there is a great deal of *Riba'* but does not know such property exactly and afterwards comes to know it and wants to remove it, what is passed is for him but he must stay away from *Riba'* in coming times.'"

H 8620, Ch. 50, h 5
Ali ibn Ibrahim has narrated from his father from ibn abu 'Umayr from Hammad from al-Halabiy who has said the following:

"Abu 'Abd Allah, *'Alayhi al-Salam*, has said that once a man came to my father and said, 'I have inherited a certain amount of property and I knew the owner from whom I inherited received Raba' and I know with certainty there is *Riba'* in it and I do not feel happy to consume it because of my knowledge about it. I asked the scholars of law of Iraq about it and they said, 'It is not lawful to consume it.' Abu Ja'far, *'Alayhi al-Salam*, said, 'If you know exactly *Riba'* property in it and you know the owner also, you must separate it and return to the owner. If it is mixed you can consume it in good health and pleasure. It is your property but you must stay away from what the previous owner would do. The Messenger of Allah, *O Allah, grant compensation to Muhammad and his family worthy of their services to Your cause*, granted relief to what is passed and prohibited from *Riba'* in coming times. If one is ignorant he is exempt, until he comes to know of the unlawfulness of *Riba'*. Once a person learns that *Riba'* is unlawful and punishment becomes necessary if one consumes *Riba'* just as it (punishment) is necessary for one who has consumed *Riba'*.'"

H 8621, Ch. 50, h 6

Ali ibn Ibrahim has narrated from his father from Hammad ibn 'Isa from Ibrahim ibn 'Umar al-Yamaniy who has said the following:

"Abu 'Abd Allah, *'Alayhi al-Salam*, has said that *Riba'* is of two kinds: One kind is that which is consumed and the other kind is not consumed. The gift that one presents to someone in order to receive Thawab (rewards from Allah) is better. Of this kind is the *Riba'* which is consumed as it is mentioned in the words of Allah, most Majestic, most Glorious, 'The *Riba'* in which you are involved so it increases in people's property does not increase before Allah.' (30:38) The other kind of *Riba'* is that which Allah, most Majestic, most Glorious, has prohibited and has warned those involved in it with punishment in the fire."

H 8622, Ch. 50, h 7

A number of our people have narrated from Ahmad ibn abu 'Abd Allah from 'Uthman ibn 'Isa from Sama'ah who has said the following:

"I once said to abu 'Abd Allah, *'Alayhi al-Salam*, 'I have noticed that Allah, most High, has mentioned *Riba'* in more than one passages of the Holy Quran. He (the Imam) asked, 'Do you know why He has done so?' I (the narrator) replied, 'No, I do not know.' He (the Imam) said, 'It is because He wants people not to deny performing good and benevolent deeds.'"

H 8623, Ch. 50, h 8

Ali ibn Ibrahim has narrated from his father from ibn abu 'Umayr from Hisham ibn Salim who has said the following:

"Abu 'Abd Allah, *'Alayhi al-Salam*, has said that Allah, most Majestic, most Glorious, has prohibited receiving *Riba'* so that people do not deny acts of benevolence and compassion."

H 8624, Ch. 50, h 9

A number of our people have narrated from Sahl ibn Ziyad and Ahmad ibn Muhammad from all from ibn Mahbub from Khalid ibn Jarir from abu al-Rabi' al-Shamiy who has said the following:

"This is concerning my question before abu 'Abd Allah, *'Alayhi al-Salam*, about the case of a man who received *Riba'* in ignorance, then he wanted to stay away from *Riba'*. He (the Imam) said 'What is passed is for him and he must stay away in the coming times.' He (the Imam) then said, 'Once a man visited abu Ja'far, *'Alayhi al-Salam*, and said, "I have inherited a certain amount of property and noticed that the owner of that property was involved in *Riba'*. I asked the scholars of law of Iraq and Hijaz and they said that consuming it is not lawful." Abu Ja'far, *'Alayhi al-Salam*, said, "If you know the *Riba'* item distinctly and know the owners of such property, you must return it to them, if you know it is *Riba'*, take away your capital and leave the rest. If the property is mixed, you can consume them in good health and with pleasure; the property is your property and stay away from what your companion was involved in. The Messenger of Allah, *O Allah, grant compensation to Muhammad and his family worthy of their services to Your cause*, exempted what had passed of *Riba'*. One who is ignorant is exempt and is allowed to consume such property. Once he comes to know then it becomes unlawful for him to consume. If he consumes after knowing, it becomes necessary on him what has become necessary on one who consumes *Riba'*."""

H 8625, Ch. 50, h 10
A number of our people have narrated from Ahmad ibn Muhammad from ibn Faddal from ibn Bukayr from 'Ubayd ibn Zurarah who has said the following:

"I once heard abu 'Abd Allah, *'Alayhi al-Salam*, saying, '*Riba'* comes in existence only in what is measured or is weighed."

H 8626, Ch. 50, h 11
Ahmad ibn Muhammad from has narrated from ibn Faddal from ibn Bukayr from 'Ubayd ibn Zurarah from who has said the following:

"Abu 'Abd Allah, *'Alayhi al-Salam*, was informed about a man who consumed *Riba'* and called it fresh milk. Abu 'Abd Allah, *'Alayhi al-Salam*, said, 'Had Allah, most Majestic, most Glorious, made it possible for me I most certainly would strike his neck.'"

H 8627, Ch. 50, h 12
Ahmad ibn Muhammad from has narrated from ibn Faddal from abu Jamilah from Sa'd ibn Tarif who has said the following:

"Abu Ja'far, *'Alayhi al-Salam*, has said, 'The filthiest earning is earning by means of *Riba'*."

Chapter 51 - Unlawful Interest Does Not Apply Between a Father and Son

H 8628, Ch. 51, h 1
Hamid ibn Ziyad has narrated from al-Khashshab from ibn Baqqah from Mu'adh ibn Thabit from 'Amr ibn Jumay' who has said the following:

"Abu 'Abd Allah, *'Alayhi al-Salam*, has said that Amir al-Mu'minin, *'Alayhi al-Salam*, has said, 'There is no *Riba'* between a man and his sons as well between a master and his slave.'"

H 8629, Ch. 51, h 2

Through the same chain of narrators as the previous one is the following Hadith:

"The Messenger of Allah, *O Allah, grant compensation to Muhammad and his family worthy of their services to Your cause*, has said, 'There is no *Riba*' between us and those in the state of war with us. We can receive a thousand dirham from them for just one dirham. We have permission to receive from them but we must not give them anything.'"

H 8630, Ch. 51, h 3

Muhammad ibn Yahya has narrated from Ahmad ibn Muhammad from Muhammad ibn 'Isa from Yasin al-Darir from Hariz from Zurarah who has said the following:

"Abu Ja'far, *'Alayhi al-Salam*, has said, '*Riba*' does not apply in the case of a man and his sons, his slave and his wife. *Riba*' applies when you do not own certain goods.' I then asked, 'Does it apply between me and the pagans?' He (the Imam) replied, 'Yes, it applies.' I said, 'They are slaves.' He (the Imam) said, 'You do not own them. You own them along with others. You and people other than you are equal about them. What is between you and them is not of that nature; your slave is not like the slave who is your slave as well as the slave of someone other than you.'"

Chapter 52 - The Excellence of Doing Business and Giving It Proper Attention

H 8631, Ch. 52, h 1

Ali ibn Ibrahim has narrated from his father from ibn abu 'Umayr from Hammad ibn 'Uthman, who has said the following:

"Abu 'Abd Allah, *'Alayhi al-Salam*, has said, 'Quitting business reduces one's power of reason.'"

H 8632, Ch. 52, h 2

A number of our people have narrated from Ahmad ibn Muhammad from ibn Faddal from ibn Bukayr from those who narrated to him who has said the following:

"Abu 'Abd Allah, *'Alayhi al-Salam*, has said, 'Doing business increases one's power of reason.'"

H 8633, Ch. 52, h 3

Ali ibn Ibrahim has narrated from his father from ibn abu 'Umayr from Muhammad al-Za'faraniy from who has said the following:

"Abu 'Abd Allah, *'Alayhi al-Salam*, has said, 'One who seeks business becomes independent of people.' I then asked, 'Even if he has dependents?' He (the Imam) replied, 'Yes, even if he has dependents; nine-tenth of sustenance is in business.'"

H 8634, Ch. 52, h 4

Ahmad ibn 'Abd Allah has narrated from Ahmad ibn Muhammad from his father from ibn abu 'Umayr from abu al-Jahm from Fudayl al-A'war who has said the following:

"I was present when Mu'adh ibn Kathir said to abu 'Abd Allah, *'Alayhi al-Salam*, 'I have become affluent so I want to quit business.' He (the Imam) said, 'If you do so your power of reason will decrease'- or similar expression."

H 8635, Ch. 52, h 5

Ali ibn Ibrahim has narrated from his father from ibn abu 'Umayr from abu 'Isma'il from Fudayl ibn Yasar who has said the following:

"Abu 'Abd Allah, *'Alayhi al-Salam*, once asked, 'What do you do?' I replied, 'I am not doing anything today.' He (the Imam) said, 'This is how your wealth goes away and it becomes difficult for you.'"

H 8636, Ch. 52, h 6

Muhammad ibn Yahya has narrated from Ahmad ibn Muhammad ibn 'Isa from Ali ibn al-Hakam from abu al-Faraj al-Qummiy from Mu'adh, Bayya' al-Akyisah who has said the following:

"Abu 'Abd Allah, *'Alayhi al-Salam*, once asked me, 'O Mu'adh, have you become weak in doing business or have withdrawn thereof?' I replied, 'I have not become weak or withdrawn.' He (the Imam) asked, 'What then is the matter?' I replied, 'We were waiting for a certain issue because when Walid was killed, I had a great deal of goods which was in my possession; and I did not owe anything to anyone and did not think I can finish it before my death.' He (the Imam) said, 'So you have quitted business, but quitting business takes away one's power of reason. Strive for the sake of your dependents and never give them a chance to complain against you.'"

H 8637, Ch. 52, h 7

Muhammad and others have narrated from Ahmad ibn Muhammad ibn 'Isa from ibn abu 'Umayr from Ali ibn 'Atiyyah from Hisham ibn Ahmar who has said the following:

"Abu al-Hassan, *'Alayhi al-Salam*, would say to Musadif, 'Proceed toward your honor, meaning thereby place of business, the market place.'"

H 8638, Ch. 52, h 8

Ali ibn Muhammad ibn Bandar from Ahmad ibn abu 'Abd Allah, from Sharif ibn Sabiq from al-Fudayl ibn abu Qurrah who has said the following:

"Abu 'Abd Allah, *'Alayhi al-Salam*, once asked about a man, when I was present, 'What is holding him back from performing Hajj?' It was said, 'He has quit business and his wealth is reduced.' He (the narrator) has said, that he (the Imam) was leaning and he moved to a straight sitting position, and said, to them, 'You must not quit doing business to become humiliated. Do business, I pray to Allah to grant you blessings.'"

H 8639, Ch. 52, h 9

Ahmad ibn Muhammad from has narrated from al-Qasim ibn Muhammad ibn Yahya from his grandfather, al-Hassan ibn Rashid from Muhammad ibn Muslim who has said the following:

"Abu 'Abd Allah, *'Alayhi al-Salam*, has said that Amir al-Mu'minin, *'Alayhi al-Salam*, has said, 'Engage yourselves in business; it helps you become independent of what is in the hands of people.'"

H 8640, Ch. 52, h 10

Muhammad ibn Yahya has narrated from Ahmad ibn Muhammad ibn 'Isa from Muhammad ibn Sinan from Hudhayfah ibn Mansur from Mu'adh ibn Kathir, Bayya' al-Akyisah who has said the following:

"I once said to abu 'Abd Allah, *'Alayhi al-Salam*, 'I am thinking to quit doing business in market place while there is a certain amount of wealth in my hands.'

He (the Imam) said, 'Then your opinion becomes of no value and no one will seek help from you.'"

H 8641, Ch. 52, h 11

Ali ibn Ibrahim has narrated from his father from ibn abu 'Umayr from 'Umar ibn' Udhaynah from Fudayl ibn Yasar who has said the following:

"I once said to abu 'Abd Allah, *'Alayhi al-Salam*, 'I have quit doing business and have withdrawn thereof.' He (the Imam) said, 'Why is that, are you helpless? This is how your wealth goes away. You must not quit doing business. You must continue to seek favors from Allah, most Majestic, most Glorious.'"

H 8642, Ch. 52, h 12

A number of our people have narrated from Ahmad ibn Muhammad from 'Abd Allah al-Hajjal from Ali ibn 'Uqbah from Muhammad ibn Muslim who has said the following:

"Burayd al-'Ijliy wanted to get married. Burayd said, to Muhammad, 'Ask abu 'Abd Allah, *'Alayhi al-Salam*, about what I am planning to do. I want to return people's properties left with me for safe-keeping and it keeps me involved. Thereafter I like to stay away from the worldly things and return everyone's things that belong to them. He (the narrator) has said, 'Muhammad asked abu 'Abd Allah, *'Alayhi al-Salam*, about it, informed him of the story and asked about his decision.' He (the Imam) said, 'Does he want to start a fight against his own soul? He must not do so. Instead, he must give and take for the sake of Allah, most Majestic, most Glorious.'"

H 8643, Ch. 52, h 13

Muhammad ibn Yahya has narrated from Ahmad ibn Muhammad ibn 'Isa from Ali ibn al-Hakam from Ali ibn 'Atiyyah who has said the following:

"Abu al-Khattab (meaning Muhammad ibn Miqlas al-Asadiy al-Kufiy) before destroying his belief would present the legal questions of the members of the community before the Imam and bring back the answers. He has narrated from abu 'Abd Allah, *'Alayhi al-Salam*, the following: 'You should purchase goods even if prices are high; sustenance comes by means of buying.'"

Chapter 53 - Etiquettes of Doing Business

H 8644, Ch. 53, h 1

A number of our people have narrated from Ahmad ibn Muhammad from ibn 'Uthman ibn 'Isa from abu al-Jarud from al-Asbagh Nubatah who has said the following:

"I heard Amir al-Mu'minin, *'Alayhi al-Salam*, saying from the pulpit, 'O people who do business, you must learn fiqh (laws), then go in business, you must learn fiqh (laws) then go in business, you must learn fiqh (laws) then go in business. I swear by Allah, *Riba'* creeps in this nation more quietly than an ant's moving on a hard and smooth rock. Blend your belief with truthfulness. A sinful business person is a criminal, and a criminal person is in the fire except those who take what is right and give what is right.'"

H 8645, Ch. 53, h 2

Ali ibn Ibrahim has narrated from his father from al-Nawfaliy from al-Sakuniy, who has said the following:

"Abu 'Abd Allah, *'Alayhi al-Salam*, has said that the Messenger of Allah, *O Allah, grant compensation to Muhammad and his family worthy of their services to Your cause*, has said, 'One who buys and sells must not engage in five things; otherwise, one must not engage in business of buying and selling: One must stay away from *Riba'*, swearing, hiding defects in the merchandise, admiring the merchandise when selling and belittling it when buying.'"

H 8646, Ch. 53, h 3

A number of our people have narrated from Sahl ibn Ziyad and Ahmad ibn Muhammad from and Ali ibn Ibrahim has narrated from his father all from ibn Mahbub from 'Amr ibn abu al-Miqdam from Jabir, who has said the following:

"Abu Ja'far, *'Alayhi al-Salam*, has said that 'Amir al-Mu'minin, *'Alayhi al-Salam*, lived among you in al-Kufa. He would have one loaf of bread everyday for his lunch and walk in market-places of al-Kufah one by one with a durrah (whip) on his shoulder. It had two strips and it was called al-Sababiyah. He addressed the people of every market-place and said, 'Those people who do business must maintain piety before Allah, most Majestic, most Glorious.' People on hearing his voice dropped down whatever they had in their hands, their hearts repented and their ears listened. He (the Imam) would say, 'You must seek goodness (from Allah) and conclude a transaction with ease, stay close to buyers, dress up with forbearance, stay away from swearing, lying and injustice. Exercise fairness with the oppressed and do not become close to *Riba'*. Maintain proper measurement and balance. You must not reduce people's things and you must not spread corruption in the land.' He (the Imam) would walk in all of market-places of al-Kufah and then return to meet people."

H 8647, Ch. 53, h 4

Ali ibn Ibrahim has narrated from Ali ibn Muhammad al-Qasaniy from Ali ibn Asbat from 'Abd Allah ibn al-Qasim ibn Muhammad al-Ja'fariy from certain persons of his family who has said the following:

"He (the Imam) has said that the Messenger of Allah, *O Allah, grant compensation to Muhammad and his family worthy of their services to Your cause*, did not give permission to Hakim ibn Hizam for business until the later promised to settle the price with a buyer who is regretful about the transaction, extend the time of payment for one who has difficulty to pay and receive the right complete or not as such."

H 8648, Ch. 53, h 5

A number of our people have narrated from Ahmad ibn abu 'Abd Allah, from his father from Khalaf from Hammad from Al-Husayn ibn Zayd al-Hashimiy who has said the following:

"Abu 'Abd Allah, *'Alayhi al-Salam*, has said, 'Once Zaynab al-'Attarah al-Hawla' visited the wives of the Holy Prophet, and the Holy Prophet, *O Allah, grant compensation to Muhammad and his family worthy of their services to Your cause*, also came home when she was with his wives. The Holy Prophet said, 'When you visit our houses they become full of sweet smelling fragrance.' She then responded saying, 'Your houses with your own fragrance are the best, O the Messenger of Allah.' The Messenger of Allah, *O Allah, grant compensation to Muhammad and his family worthy of their services to Your cause*, then said, 'When you sell perfumes, you must make certain it is not adulterated; maintaining a greater degree of piety before Allah is more protection for wealth.'"

H 8649, Ch. 53, h 6

Ali ibn Ibrahim has narrated from his father from and Muhammad 'Isma'il from al-Fadl ibn Shadhan all from ibn abu 'Umayr from Hisham ibn al-Hakam who has said the following:

"Abu 'Abd Allah, *'Alayhi al-Salam*, once said to me, 'If someone asks you to buy for him a certain merchandise, you must not buy it for him from your own shop even if the merchandise from your shop be better.'"

H 8650, Ch. 53, h 7

Ali ibn Ibrahim has narrated from his father from al-Nawfaliy from al-Sakuniy, who has said the following:

"Abu 'Abd Allah, *'Alayhi al-Salam*, has said that the Messenger of Allah, *O Allah, grant compensation to Muhammad and his family worthy of their services to Your cause*, has said, 'Generosity is of profits.' The Messenger of Allah said it to a man who had asked for good advice and who had certain merchandise that he wanted to sell.'"

H 8651, Ch. 53, h 8

Through the same chain of narrators as the previous one is the following Hadith:

"Amir al-Mu'minin, *'Alayhi al-Salam*, once said to a butcher about a slave-girl who had purchased meat from his shop and who was asking for more, 'You must give her more; it has greater blessings.'"

H 8652, Ch. 53, h 9

Muhammad ibn Yahya has narrated from Ahmad ibn Muhammad ibn 'Isa from 'Abd al-Rahman ibn abu Najran from Ali ibn 'Abd al-Rahim from a man who has said the following:

"I once heard abu 'Abd Allah, *'Alayhi al-Salam*, saying, 'If a man says to another man, 'Come with me, I will offer you a good deal,' it becomes unlawful for him to make any profit in that deal.'"

H 8653, Ch. 53, h 10

Al-Husayn ibn Muhammad has narrated from Mu'alla' ibn Muhammad from certain persons of our people from Aban from 'Amir ibn Juza'ah who has said the following:

"I (the narrator) once asked abu 'Abd Allah, *'Alayhi al-Salam*, about a man who had set a price on a certain item of his merchandise. Thereafter whoever purchased that merchandise without asking for any discount, he sold it to them for the same price; but those who asked for a discount he instead increased the price. He (the Imam) said, 'There is no offense in such increases for two or three men, but if he does so with everyone who asks for a discount then I do not like his selling but for one and the same price.'"

H 8654, Ch. 53, h 11

Ali ibn Ibrahim has narrated from his father from al-Nawfaliy from al-Sakuniy, who has said the following:

"Abu 'Abd Allah, *'Alayhi al-Salam*, has said that the Messenger of Allah, *O Allah, grant compensation to Muhammad and his family worthy of their services*

to Your cause, has said, 'The owner of merchandise is more rightful to set up the price for his merchandise.'"

H 8655, Ch. 53, h 12

A number of our people have narrated from Ahmad ibn Muhammad ibn Khalid from Ali ibn Asbat in a marfu' manner' has the following:

"He (the Imam) has said that the Messenger of Allah, *O Allah, grant compensation to Muhammad and his family worthy of their services to Your cause*, prohibited bargaining between dawn and sunrise."

H 8656, Ch. 53, h 13

Ahmad ibn Muhammad from has narrated from 'Abd al-Rahman ibn Hammad from Muhammad ibn Sinan who has said the following:

"Abu Ja'far, *'Alayhi al-Salam*, has said, 'I dislike two kinds of transactions: To say, "Drop the merchandise and receive payment", and buying something without seeing it.'"

H 8657, Ch. 53, h 14

Ahmad ibn Muhammad ibn Ali has narrated from abu Jamilah from Ishaq ibn 'Ammar who has said the following:

"Abu 'Abd Allah, *'Alayhi al-Salam*, has said, 'Selling above a fair price to one who has left it (pricing) to the seller is Suht (unlawful and filthy).'"

H 8658, Ch. 53, h 15

It is narrated from the narrator of previous Hadith from 'Uthman ibn 'Isa from Muyassir who has said the following:

"Abu 'Abd Allah, *'Alayhi al-Salam*, has said, 'Selling above fair piece to a believing person is unlawful.'"

H 8659, Ch. 53, h 16

Ahmad ibn Muhammad has narrated from Ali from Yazid ibn Ishaq from Harun ibn Hamzah from abu Hamzah who has said the following:

"Abu 'Abd Allah, *'Alayhi al-Salam*, has said, 'If one accepts a Muslim's request to return a merchandise Allah, most High, on the Day of Judgment (returns) reduces his sins.'"

H 8660, Ch. 53, h 17

Ahmad has narrated from Ali from Ahmad ibn Ishaq ibn Sa'd al-Ash'ariy from 'Abd Allah ibn Sa'id al-Daghshiy who has said the following:

"Once I was at the door of Shihab ibn 'Abde Rabbihi when the slave of Shihab came out and said, 'I want to ask Hashim al-Saydananiy about the Hadith on "price and merchandise."' He (the narrator) has said, 'I then visited Hashim and asked him about that Hadith.' He (Hashim) said, "I asked abu 'Abd Allah, *'Alayhi al-Salam*, about this Hadith and he (the Imam) said, 'Yes, whoever has a merchandise or goods with him, Allah, most Majestic, most Glorious, sends someone to profit him. He may accept such profit, otherwise, it is turned away from him to others; it is a rejection of the favor of Allah, most Majestic, most Glorious.'"""

H 8661, Ch. 53, h 18

Muhammad ibn Yahya has narrated from Ahmad ibn Muhammad ibn 'Isa in a marfu' manner' has said the following:

"Abu 'Amamah, a companion of the Messenger of Allah, *O Allah, grant compensation to Muhammad and his family worthy of their services to Your cause*, has said, 'I heard the Messenger of Allah saying, "One who has four things his earning is fine: When buying does not belittle the merchandise, when selling does not admire the merchandise, does not adulterate and in between does not swear."'"

H 8662, Ch. 53, h 19

Ahmad ibn Muhammad has narrated from Salih ibn abu Hammad from Muhammad ibn Sinan from Hudhayfah ibn Mansur from Muyassir who has said the following:

"I once said to abu 'Abd Allah, *'Alayhi al-Salam,* 'Most of my clients are from our brothers (in belief). I request you to set for me a limit, how should I deal with them in a transaction so that I will not go beyond that limit.' He (the Imam) said, 'If you consider your brother (in belief) as the person in charge it is fine, otherwise, deal with him in a transaction as one deals with a well aware hairsplitting person.'"

H 8663, Ch. 53, h 20

A number of our people have narrated from Ahmad ibn Muhammad ibn 'Isa from ibn Sinan from Yunus ibn Ya'qub from 'Abd al-'A'la' ibn 'A'yan who has said the following:

"I was told about abu Ja'far, *'Alayhi al-Salam,* that he disliked two kinds of transactions: 'Drop the merchandise without turning its other side and receive payment', and 'buying merchandise without seeing'."

H 8664, Ch. 53, h 21

A number of our people have narrated from Sahl ibn Ziyad from Al-Husayn ibn Bashshar from a man in a marfu' manner' who has said the following:

"About the words of Allah, most Majestic, most Glorious, 'There are men who do not become distracted from speaking of Allah because of trading and business.' (24:37) He (the Imam) said, 'They are the business people who do not become distracted from speaking of Allah, most Majestic, most Glorious, because of trade and business when it is time for *Salat* (prayer). They yield to the rights of Allah in such times.'"

H 8665, Ch. 53, h 22

Muhammad ibn Yahya has narrated from Muhammad ibn Al-Husayn from Muhammad ibn 'Isma'il ibn Bazi' from Salih ibn 'Uqbah from Sulayman ibn Salih and abu Shibl who has said the following:

"Abu 'Abd Allah, *'Alayhi al-Salam,* has said, 'A believer's making profit on another believer is *Riba'* accept if he buys more than a hundred dirham worth of goods, in which case, he can make a profit equal to the expenses of his day, or if he buys it for business and reselling. You may in this case make a profit but you must deal with kindness.'"

H 8666, Ch. 53, h 23

Muhammad ibn Yahya has narrated from Ahmad ibn Muhammad from Muhammad ibn Yahya from Talhah ibn Zayd who has said the following:

137

"Abu 'Abd Allah, *'Alayhi al-Salam*, has said, 'Amir al-Mu'minin, *'Alayhi al-Salam*, has said, 'If one does business without knowledge, he plunges in *Riba'* again and again.' Amir al-Mu'minin, *'Alayhi al-Salam*, would also say, 'One who does not understand buying and selling must not sit in the market place for doing business.'"

Chapter 54 - Excellence of Keeping Accounts and Books

H 8667, Ch. 54, h 1
Muhammad ibn Yahya has narrated from Ahmad ibn Muhammad from Ahmad ibn abu 'Abd Allah, from a man from Jamil who has said the following:
"I heard abu 'Abd Allah, *'Alayhi al-Salam*, saying, 'It is from Allah, most Majestic, most Glorious, upon people, virtuous and sinful ones to write down and keep proper accounting. Without this they, certainly, suffer confusion and mistakes.'"

Chapter 55 - Entering the Market Before Others

H 8668, Ch. 55, h 1
Muhammad ibn Yahya has narrated from Ahmad ibn Muhammad from Muhammad ibn Yahya from Talhah ibn Zayd who has said the following:
"Abu 'Abd Allah, *'Alayhi al-Salam*, has said that 'Amir al-Mu'minin, *'Alayhi al-Salam*, has said, 'The market-place of Muslims is like their Masjid. Whoever comes first to a place in it is more rightful than others to benefit thereof.' He did not charge any rent for the use of houses of the market-place.'"

H 8669, Ch. 55, h 2
Ali ibn Ibrahim has narrated from his father from ibn abu 'Umayr from certain persons of our people who has said the following:
"Abu 'Abd Allah, *'Alayhi al-Salam*, has said, 'The market-place of Muslims is like their Masjid, that is, whoever comes to a place first is like the Masjid for him (in regards to having more right than others to use it).

Chapter 56 - Speaking of Allah, Most High, in the Market

H 8670, Ch. 56, h 1
Muhammad ibn Yahya has narrated from Ahmad ibn Muhammad from Muhammad ibn 'Isma'il from Hanan from his father who has said the following:
"Abu Ja'far, *'Alayhi al-Salam*, once said to me, 'O abu al-Fadl, do you have a place where you can sit and do business with people?' I replied, 'Yes, I have such a place.' He (the Imam) then said, 'Whoever of believing people during the morning or evening goes to his market-place and says this when setting foot in the market-place, "O Allah, I pray to You to grant me goodness thereby and from its people", Allah, most Majestic, most Glorious, assigns someone to protect him and guard him until he returns to his home; and then says to him, "This day you were protected from the evil of that place and its people by the permission of Allah, most Majestic, most Glorious. This day you were granted goodness thereby and from its people." If one takes his place and says, "I testify

that no one, other than Allah who is one only and has no partner, deserves worship and I testify that Muhammad is His servant and Messenger. O Allah, I pray to You to grant me of your extra favor, in lawful manners and clean. I seek protection with You against my doing injustice or suffer injustice by others. I seek protection with You against losing transactions and false swearing." When he says this the angel assigned with him says, "There is glad news for you about your market place. Today there is no one more fortunate than you in it. You were quick to perform good deeds and delete evil ones. What Allah has made your share will come to you a great deal, lawful, clean and with blessings in it.""""

H 8671, Ch. 56, h 2
A number of our people have narrated from Ahmad ibn Muhammad from ibn Mahbub from Mu'awiyah ibn 'Ammar who has said the following:

"Abu 'Abd Allah, *'Alayhi al-Salam*, has said, 'When you enter your market-place you should say this, 'O Allah, I pray to You to grant me of its (market-place) good things and its good people. I seek protection with You against its evil and the evil of its people. O Allah, I seek protection with You against my own injustice and injustice done to me, against my own transgression and the transgression committed against me, against my own excess and excess acts against me. O Allah, I seek protection with You against the evil of Satan and his armies, against the criminal ones of Arab and none-Arab people. Allah is sufficient for me. No one, except Allah, deserves worship. I entrust Him with my affairs and He is the Lord of the great Throne.'"

Chapter 57 - Words to Say When Buying for Resale Purposes

H 8672, Ch. 57, h 1
Ali ibn Ibrahim has narrated from his father from Hammad ibn Hariz who has said the following:

"Abu 'Abd Allah, *'Alayhi al-Salam*, has said, 'When you buy merchandise or something say *Takbir* (Allah is great beyond description). Then say, 'O Allah, I have purchased this and I seek in it your extra favor, *O Allah, grant compensation to Muhammad and his family worthy of their services to Your cause*. O Allah, place in it of your extra favors. O Allah, I have purchased it and seek in it sustenance from You. O Allah, place sustenance in it.' Thereafter repeat each of the above three times.'"

H 8673, Ch. 57, h 2
A number of our people have narrated from Ahmad ibn Muhammad from ibn Faddal from Tha'labah ibn Maymun from Hudhayl who has said the following:

"Abu 'Abd Allah, *'Alayhi al-Salam*, has said, 'When you want to buy a slave-girl say this, 'O Allah, I consult You and pray to You to grant me what is good.'"

H 8674, Ch. 57, h 3
A number of our people have narrated from Ahmad ibn Muhammad from and Sahl ibn Ziyad from ibn Mahbub from Mu'awiyah ibn 'Ammar who has said the following:

"Abu 'Abd Allah, *'Alayhi al-Salam*, has said, 'When you decide to buy something say this, "O Living, O Guardian, O Eternal, O Compassionate, O Merciful I pray to You through Your majesty, Your power and all that Your knowledge encompasses, grant me of business the greatest share of sustenance, vastest extra favors and the best of consequences; there is no goodness in that which is void of good consequences."' He (the narrator) has said that abu 'Abd Allah, *'Alayhi al-Salam*, then said, 'When you buy an animal or a head (living thing) say this, "O Allah, make it to live the longest, benefit the most and of the best consequences."'"

H 8675, Ch. 57, h 4

Ali ibn Ibrahim has narrated from his father from ibn abu 'Umayr from Mu'awiyah ibn 'Ammar, who has said the following:

"Abu 'Abd Allah, *'Alayhi al-Salam*, has said, 'When you decide to buy an animal, say this, "O Allah, if this is of great blessings, extra benefits and of a fortunate nature, I pray to You to make its purchasing easy for me. If it is otherwise, then turn me to what is better than this; You know and I do not know. You have power over all things but I do not have such power and You know the unseen." You should say this three times'"*

Chapter 58 - People With Whom Doing Business Is Not Recommended

H 8676, Ch. 58, h 1

A number of our people have narrated from Ahmad ibn Muhammad from ibn Mahbub from al-'Abbas ibn al-Walid ibn Sabih from his father who has said the following:

"Abu 'Abd Allah, *'Alayhi al-Salam*, once said to me, 'You must not purchase from a Muharaf (unfortunate) person; making a deal with such people is devoid of blessings.'"

H 8677, Ch. 58, h 2

Muhammad ibn Yahya and others have narrated from Ahmad ibn Muhammad from Ali ibn al-Hakam from those whom he has mentioned from abu Rabi' al-Shamiy who has said the following:

"This is concerning my question before abu 'Abd Allah, *'Alayhi al-Salam*, saying, 'In our area there are Kurdish people who come and sell certain things. Can we intermingle with them and purchase from them?' He (the Imam) said, 'O abu Rabi', you must not intermingle with them; Kurdish people are a tribe of the tribes of Jinn from whom Allah has removed covering, so do not intermingle with them.'"

(Consult Fatwa about this hadith)

H 8678, Ch. 58, h 3

Ahmad ibn 'Abd Allah, has narrated from Ahmad ibn abu 'Abd Allah, from more than one person of his people from Ali ibn Asbat from Husayn ibn Kharijah from Muyassir in 'Abd al-'Aziz who has said the following:

"Abu 'Abd Allah, *'Alayhi al-Salam*, once said to me, 'You must not form contracts with people suffering from crippling diseases; they are of most unjust things (they do not avoid transmitting their diseases to others).'"

H 8679, Ch. 58, h 4

Ali ibn Ibrahim has narrated from his father from ibn abu 'Umayr from Hafs al-Bakhtariy who has said the following:

"Once an agent of abu 'Abd Allah, *'Alayhi al-Salam*, borrowed a certain amount of food (grain) for abu 'Abd Allah, *'Alayhi al-Salam*. The lender insistently demanded replacement. He (the Imam) said to his agent, 'Did I not prohibit you the borrowing from one who did not have anything (who has) just then come to own something?'"

H 8680, Ch. 58, h 5

A number of our people have narrated from Ahmad ibn Muhammad from ibn Faddal from Zarif ibn Nasih who has said the following:

"Abu 'Abd Allah, *'Alayhi al-Salam*, has said, 'You must not form contracts with anyone other than those who are established in goodness."

H 8681, Ch. 58, h 6

Ahmad ibn Muhammad has narrated from in a marfu' manner' the following:

"Abu 'Abd Allah, *'Alayhi al-Salam*, has said, 'Avoid forming contracts with people who suffer from crippling diseases; they do (not avoid transmitting their disease to others) the most unjust things.'"

H 8682, Ch. 58, h 7

Muhammad ibn Yahya has narrated from Ahmad ibn Muhammad from Ahmad ibn Muhammad ibn 'Isa from al-Hassan ibn Ali ibn Yaqtin from Al-Husayn ibn Mayyah from 'Isa who has said the following:

"Abu 'Abd Allah, *'Alayhi al-Salam*, has said, 'You must remain on your guard in intermingling with lowly people; lowly people do not end up in goodness.'"

(Al-Saduq in Ma'ani al-Akhbar has said the following to be of the qualities of lowly people: People indifferent to what they say or what is said against them, those who play tambourine, those who are indifferent to favor and insult or those who falsely claim to be trustworthy.)

H 8683, Ch. 58, h 8

Ali ibn Muhammad ibn Bandar has narrated from Ahmad ibn Muhammad from ibn abu 'Abd Allah, from his father from Fadl al-Nawfaliy from ibn abu Yahya al-Raziy who has said the following:

"Abu 'Abd Allah, *'Alayhi al-Salam*, has said, 'You must not intermingle or form contract with anyone except those who are established in goodness.'"

H 8684, Ch. 58, h 9

A number of our people have narrated from Ahmad ibn Muhammad ibn Khalid from A number of our people have narrated from Ali ibn Asbat from Husayn ibn Kharijah from Muyassir ibn 'Abd al-'Aziz who has said the following:

"Abu 'Abd Allah, *'Alayhi al-Salam*, has said, 'You must not form contracts with people who suffer from crippling diseases; they are most unjust things' (do not avoid transmitting their disease to others)."*

141

Chapter 59 - Using Proper and Improper Measurements in Business

H 8685, Ch. 59, h 1
A number of our people have narrated from Ahmad ibn Muhammad ibn Khalid from ibn Faddal from ibn Bukayr from Hammad ibn Bashir who has said the following:

"Abu 'Abd Allah, *'Alayhi al-Salam*, has said, 'Proper weighing is only when a balance tilts to one side.'"

H 8686, Ch. 59, h 2
Through the same chain of narrators as the previous one from Ya'qub ibn Yazid from Muhammad ibn Murazim from a man from Ishaq ibn 'Ammar who has said the following:

"Abu 'Abd Allah, *'Alayhi al-Salam*, has said, 'If one uses a balance with the intention to weigh for himself properly ends up weighing heavier for himself, and one who intends to weigh equally, ends up weighing less.'"

H 8687, Ch. 59, h 3
Through the same chain of narrators as the previous one from al-Hajjal from 'Ubayd ibn Ishaq who has said the following:

"I once said to abu 'Abd Allah, *'Alayhi al-Salam*, 'I own palm trees. Instruct me how to be proper in my giving and taking.' Abu 'Abd Allah, *'Alayhi al-Salam*, said, 'Keep your intention to maintain it (crop) properly fair; if despite such intention, less proper fairness takes place, you are of those who maintain it properly. On the other hand, if you intended it to be less proper, but maintained it properly, you are of those who maintain it less properly.'"

H 8688, Ch. 59, h 4
Muhammad ibn Yahya has narrated from Ahmad ibn Muhammad ibn 'Isa from Ali ibn al-Hakam from al-Muthanna' al-Hannat from certain persons of our people who has said the following:

"I once said to abu 'Abd Allah, *'Alayhi al-Salam*, 'There is man who has the intention to maintain proper weighing; but when he weighs cannot do it properly.' He (the Imam) asked, 'What do people around say about him?' I (the narrator) replied, 'They say, 'He does not maintain it properly.' He (the Imam) said, 'He should not do weighing.'"

H 8689, Ch. 59, h 5
Ali ibn Ibrahim has narrated from his father from ibn abu 'Umayr from more than one person who has said the following:

"Abu 'Abd Allah, *'Alayhi al-Salam*, has said, 'It is not a proper weighing until a side of balance tilts.'"

Chapter 60 - Cheating in Business

H 8690, Ch. 60, h 1
Ali ibn Ibrahim has narrated from his father from and Muhammad ibn Yahya from Ahmad ibn Muhammad from all from ibn abu 'Umayr from Hisham ibn Salim who has said the following:

"Abu 'Abd Allah, *'Alayhi al-Salam*, has said, 'One who cheats is not of our people.'"

H 8691, Ch. 60, h 2

Through the same chain of narrators as the previous it narrated who has said the following:

"Abu 'Abd Allah, *'Alayhi al-Salam*, has said that the Messenger of Allah, *O Allah, grant compensation to Muhammad and his family worthy of their services to Your cause*, once said to a man who sold dates, 'O master so and so, do you know that one who cheats Muslims is not one of them?'"

H 8692, Ch. 60, h 3

Muhammad ibn Yahya has narrated from certain persons of our people from *Sajdah* from Musa ibn Bukayr who has said the following:

"Once we were in the presence of abu al-Hassan, *'Alayhi al-Salam*, while in front of him there were certain pieces of dinars. He (the Imam) looked at one piece and picked it up and broke it into two pieces. He (the Imam) said to me, 'Throw it in the trash so an adulterated thing is not purchased anymore.'"

H 8693, Ch. 60, h 4

Abu Ali al-Ash'ariy has narrated from al-Hassan ibn Ali ibn 'Abd Allah from 'Ubays ibn Hisham from a man of his people who has said the following:

"Once, a man who sold flour came before abu 'Abd Allah, *'Alayhi al-Salam*. He (the Imam) said to him, 'Beware of cheating; one who cheats in matters of properties, cheating takes place in his properties, if he does not have any property cheating takes place in his family (wife).'"

H 8694, Ch. 60, h 5

Ali ibn Ibrahim has narrated from his father from ibn abu 'Umayr from al-Nawfaliy from al-Sakuniy, who has said the following:

"Abu 'Abd Allah, *'Alayhi al-Salam*, has said that the Messenger of Allah, *O Allah, grant compensation to Muhammad and his family worthy of their services to Your cause*, prohibited mixing of milk with water to sell.'"

H 8695, Ch. 60, h 6

Ali ibn Ibrahim has narrated from his father from ibn abu 'Umayr from Hisham ibn al-Hakam who has said the following:

"Once when I was selling al-Sabiriy (a certain kind of fabric) in the shade, abu al-Hassan, *'Alayhi al-Salam*, passed by and said to me, 'O Hisham, selling in shade is cheating and cheating is not lawful.'"

H 8696, Ch. 60, h 7

Ali ibn Ibrahim has narrated from his father from ibn abu 'Umayr from ibn Mahbub from abu Jamilah from Sa'd al-Iskaf who has said the following:

"Abu Ja'far, *'Alayhi al-Salam*, has said, 'Once, in the market place of al-Madinah, the Holy Prophet, *O Allah, grant compensation to Muhammad and his family worthy of their services to Your cause*, passed by a place where food was sold. The Holy Prophet said, to the owner, "I can see your food is good." He then asked about its price. Allah, most Majestic, most Glorious, sent revelation and told him to check the lower levels of the food for sale. When he checked a bad quality of food came out. He then said to the owner, "Now I can see you have collected betrayal and cheating for the Muslims."'"

Chapter 61 - Swearing at the Time of Buying and Selling

H 8697, Ch. 61, h 1

Abu Ali al-Ash'ariy has narrated from Muhammad ibn 'Abd al-Jabbar from Ahmad ibn abu Nadr from abu Ja'far al-Fazariy who has said the following:

"Once abu Ja'far, *'Alayhi al-Salam*, called one of his servants named Musadif and gave him a thousand dinar. He (the Imam) told him to prepare for traveling to Egypt and added, 'The number of my dependents has increased.' He (the narrator) has said that the servant prepared certain items of merchandise along with the traders to go for trade to Egypt. When they arrived near Egypt they met a caravan coming out of Egypt. They asked the outgoing caravan with regards to the condition of their merchandise, which was of general nature, in the city. The outgoing people informed them that no such merchandise was available in the city. They (people of the incoming caravan) made an agreement among themselves on oath not to sell their merchandise for less than a profit of one dinar for each dinar worth of merchandise. After taking possession of their belongings, they returned to al-Madinah and Musadif came to abu 'Abd Allah, *'Alayhi al-Salam*, with two bagfuls of dinars, each of which had a thousand dinars. He said, 'I pray to Allah to keep my soul in service for your cause, this is the capital and this is the profit.' He (the Imam) said, 'This is a great deal of profit. However, what did you do with the merchandise?' He (Musadif) told the story of their agreement on oath. He (the Imam) said, 'Allah is free of all defects. Why do you make an agreement on oath against a Muslim people not to sell for less than a profit of one dinar for each dinar worth of merchandise?' He (the Imam) then took the two bags and said, 'This is my capital and we do not need this profit.' He (the Imam) said, 'O Musadif, settling with sword is easier than earning by lawful ways.'"

H 8698, Ch. 61, h 2

Through the same chain of narrators as the previous one is the following Hadith from al-Hassan ibn Ali al-Kufiy from 'Ubays ibn Hisham from Aban ibn Taghlib from abu Hamzah in a marfu' manner' has said, the following:

"Amir al-Mu'minin, *'Alayhi al-Salam*, once stood on the house of ibn abu Mu'ayt where camel men stayed, and said, 'O middlemen people, you must reduce swearing; it makes a merchandise easily marketable but destroys the profit.'"

H 8699, Ch. 61, h 3

A number of our people have narrated from Ahmad ibn Muhammad ibn Khalid from Muhammad ibn 'Isa from 'Ubayd Allah al-Dihqan from Durust ibn abu Mansur from Ibrahim ibn 'Abd al-Hamid who has said the following:

"Abu al-Hassan, Musa, *'Alayhi al-Salam*, has said, 'On the Day of Judgment, Allah, most High, will not look to three kinds of people. Of such people one kind is a man who does not buy or sell anything without swearing.'"

H 8700, Ch. 61, h 4

Muhammad ibn Yahya has narrated from Ahmad ibn Muhammad ibn 'Isa from Muhammad ibn al-Hassan Za'lan from abu 'Isma'il; in a marfu' manner' has said, the following:

"Amir al-Mu'minin, *'Alayhi al-Salam*, would say, 'Beware of swearing; it may make a merchandise easily sell, but it destroys the blessings.'"

Chapter 62 - The Case of Prices of Goods

H 8701, Ch. 62, h 1

Muhammad ibn Yahya has narrated from Muhammad ibn Ahmad from Ya'qub Yazid from al-Ghifariy from al-Qasim ibn Muhammad ibn Ishaq from his father from his grandfather who has said the following:

"He (the Imam), *'Alayhi al-Salam*, has said that the Messenger of Allah, *O Allah, grant compensation to Muhammad and his family worthy of their services to Your cause*, has said, 'Of the signs of happiness of Allah, most High, with His creatures is the existence of a just ruler and low prices. Of the signs of unhappiness of Allah, most High with His creatures is the existence of an unjust ruler and high prices.'"

H 8702, Ch. 62, h 2

A number of our people have narrated from Sahl ibn Ziyad from Ya'qub ibn Yazid from Muhammad ibn Aslam from those whom he has mentioned who has said the following:

"Abu 'Abd Allah, *'Alayhi al-Salam*, has said, 'Allah, most Majestic, most Glorious, has assigned an angel on prices. Prices do not go high because of shortages and do not lower because of bounteousness.'"

H 8703, Ch. 62, h 3

Muhammad ibn Yahya has narrated from Ahmad ibn Muhammad from ibn al-'Abbas ibn Ma'ruf from al-Hajjal from certain persons of his people from abu Hamzah al-Thumaliy who has said the following:

"Ali ibn Al-Husayn, *'Alayhi al-Salam*, has said, 'Allah, most Majestic, most Glorious, has assigned an angel who regulates prices by His command.'"

H 8704, Ch. 62, h 4

Sahl ibn Ziyad has narrated from Ya'qub ibn Yazid from those whom he has mentioned who has narrated the following:

"Abu 'Abd Allah, *'Alayhi al-Salam*, has said, 'Allah, most Majestic, most Glorious, has assigned an angel on prices who regulates them (as needed).'"

H 8705, Ch. 62, h 5

A number of our people have narrated from Ahmad ibn Muhammad ibn Khalid from 'Abd al-Rahman ibn Hammad from Yunus ibn Ya'qub from Sa'd from a man who has said the following:

"Abu 'Abd Allah, *'Alayhi al-Salam*, has said, 'When things were given in the control of Joseph ibn Ya'qub, *'Alayhi al-Salam*, he placed the grain in houses (storage) and issued an order to his servants to sell for a price of such and such amount. Prices were fixed. When he learned that prices are high he disliked to speak of high prices and then said, 'Go and sell without mentioning prices.' The agent before going far away returned to him. He said, 'Go and sell.' He disliked speaking of high prices. The agent went back and the first buyer came. The agent measured for him and when it was still less than the amount of the previous day by one measurement the buyer said, 'It is enough; I only wanted this much for this much.' The agent realized that prices are still high. Then another buyer came and asked him to measure for him. He measured for him and it still was one less than the measurement for the previous buyer when this buyer said, 'This much is enough. I only wanted this much (grain) for this much (money).' The agent realized that prices are still high and so on until it came down to one for one.'"

H 8706, Ch. 62, h 6

Muhammad ibn Yahya has narrated from Ahmad ibn Muhammad from Muhammad ibn 'Isma'il al-Sarraj from Hafs ibn 'Umar from a man who has said the following:

"Abu 'Abd Allah, *'Alayhi al-Salam*, has said, 'High prices worsens moral discipline, destroy trust and cause suffering to the Muslims.'"

H 8707, Ch. 62, h 7

Ahmad ibn Muhammad from has narrated from certain persons of his people in a marfu' manner' who have said the following:

"About the words of Allah, most Majestic, most Glorious, 'I see you in goodness . . . .' (11:84) He (the Imam) said, 'It is a reference to their prices.'"

Chapter 63 - The Case of Monopolization (Hoarding) Goods in Public Demand

H 8708, Ch. 63, h 1

Muhammad ibn Yahya has narrated from Ahmad ibn Muhammad from Muhammad ibn Yahya from Ghiyath ibn Ibrahim who has said the following:

"Abu 'Abd Allah, *'Alayhi al-Salam*, has said, 'Monopolization (Hoarding) of goods in public demand applies to wheat, barley, dates, raisins and cooking butter only.'"

H 8709, Ch. 63, h 2

Muhammad ibn Ahmad has narrated from Muhammad ibn Sinan from Hudhayfah ibn Mansur who has said the following:

"Abu 'Abd Allah, *'Alayhi al-Salam*, has said, 'Once during the times of the Messenger of Allah, *O Allah, grant compensation to Muhammad and his family worthy of their services to Your cause*, a severe shortage of food took place and the Muslims came to the Messenger of Allah saying, "O Messenger of Allah, food supplies are exhausted and there is no food left except that which so and so has hoarded; so command him to sell to people." He, the Messenger of Allah praised Allah and glorified Him and then said, "O so and so, the Muslims have informed me that food supplies have become serious. Food is not available except that which is with you. You must bring it in public and sell them as you like, but you must not keep it in hoarding."'"

H 8710, Ch. 63, h 3

Ali ibn Ibrahim has narrated from his father from ibn abu 'Umayr from Hammad from al-Halabiy who has said the following:

"Abu 'Abd Allah, *'Alayhi al-Salam*, has said, 'Hoarding means buying such food supplies of a city beside which no other food supplies are available. If other food supplies are available in a city or someone else sells food, then it is permissible to buy food supplies and keep them hoarded to sell later with higher prices.' He (the narrator) has said, I asked him about oil and he replied, 'If it is available with people other than you then there is no offense in it.'"

H 8711, Ch. 63, h 4

Abu Ali al-Ash'ariy has narrated from Muhammad ibn 'Abd al-Jabbar from Safwan from abu al-Fadl Salim al-Hannat who has said the following:

"Abu 'Abd Allah, *'Alayhi al-Salam*, once asked me, 'What is your business?' I replied, 'It is selling wheat. At times business is good and sometimes it is not good so I hold selling.' He (the Imam) then asked, 'What do people who visit you say about it?' I replied, 'They say, "He is a hoarder."' He (the Imam) asked, 'Does anyone else sell wheat besides you?' I replied, 'I sell only one out of a thousandth of what is sold in the market.' He (the Imam) said, 'Then there is no offense in what you do. The person who hoarded food was Hakim ibn Hizam. He would buy all food supplies that came to al-Madinah. The Holy Prophet, *O Allah, grant compensation to Muhammad and his family worthy of their services to Your cause*, passed by his place and said, "O Hakim ibn Hizam, you must not hoard (food supplies)."'"

H 8712, Ch. 63, h 5

Ali ibn Ibrahim has narrated from his father from ibn abu 'Umayr from Hammad from al-Halabiy who has said the following:

"This is concerning my question before abu 'Abd Allah, *'Alayhi al-Salam*, about a man who hoarded food supplies and waited for higher prices. Is it permissible?' He (the Imam) replied, 'If there is plenty of food available to people to buy, then there is no offense in it; but if there are food shortages and people are not able to buy from other places, then it (such hoarding) is undesirable to leave people without food.'"

H 8713, Ch. 63, h 6

A number of our people have narrated from Sahl ibn Ziyad from Ja'far ibn Muhammad al-Ash'ariy from ibn al-Qaddah who has said the following:

"Abu 'Abd Allah, *'Alayhi al-Salam*, has said that the Messenger of Allah has said, 'One who supplies the market receives his sustenance and a hoarder is condemned.'"

H 8714, Ch. 63, h 7

Ali ibn Ibrahim has narrated from his father from al-Nawfaliy from al-Sakuniy who has said the following:

"Abu 'Abd Allah, *'Alayhi al-Salam*, has said, 'At a time when food is abundantly available, keeping food for forty days is considered hoarding, but at the time of shortages of food holding back food supplies for three days is considered hoarding. After forty days at a time when food is abundant a hoarder is condemned and at the time of scarcity of food after three days the hoarder is condemned.'"

Chapter 64 - Another Chapter

H 8715, Ch. 64, h 1

A number of our people have narrated from Ahmad ibn Muhammad ibn Khalid from 'Isma'il ibn Mehran from Hammad ibn 'Uthman who has said the following:

"Once shortages of food took place in al-Madinah and even affluent people would mix wheat and barley for food and buy only a small amount of food. Abu 'Abd Allah, *'Alayhi al-Salam*, had a good quality of food which he had purchased earlier in the beginning of the year. He (the Imam) then asked one of his agents to buy a certain amount of barely and mix it with their good quality of food or sell this good quality of food; adding, 'I do not like to consume good quality of food when people consume a worse quality of food.'"

H 8716, Ch. 64, h 2

Muhammad ibn Yahya has narrated from Ali ibn 'Isma'il from Ali ibn al-Hakam from Jahm ibn abu Jahm from Mu'attib who has said the following:

"Abu 'Abd Allah, *'Alayhi al-Salam*, once, when food prices were rising, asked me, 'How much food do we have?' I (the narrator) replied, 'There is enough food for several months.' He (the Imam) said, 'Take it out to sell.' I (the narrator) I said, 'There is not enough food in al-Madinah.' He (the Imam) said, 'You must sell it.' When I sold he (the Imam) said, 'You must buy food every day as other people do.' He (the Imam) said, 'O Mu'attib, make half the supplies of food for my family from wheat and the other half barely; Allah knows that I can provide them wheat as it is, but I like that Allah see me planning my finances in a good manner.'"

H 8717, Ch. 64, h 3

Ali ibn Muhammad ibn Bandar has narrated from Ahmad ibn abu 'Abd Allah, from Muhsin ibn Ahmad from Yunus ibn Ya'qub from Mu'attib who has said the following:

"Abu al-Hassan *'Alayhi al-Salam*, would command, at the time of harvest of fruit, to take them out and sell and then buy every day as Muslim people do."

Chapter 65 - Excellence of Buying Wheat and Food

H 8718, Ch. 65, h 1

A number of our people have narrated from Ahmad ibn Muhammad from ibn Mahbub from Nasr ibn Ishaq al-Kufiy from 'Abbad ibn Habib who has said the following:

"I heard abu 'Abd Allah, *'Alayhi al-Salam*, saying, 'Buying wheat removes poverty but buying flour brings poverty and buying bread is destruction.' I (the narrator) then asked, 'I pray to Allah to grant you long life, what about one who is not able to buy wheat?' He (the Imam) replied, 'That is for one who is capable but does not do so.'"

H 8719, Ch. 65, h 2

Muhammad ibn Yahya has narrated from Salmah ibn al-Khattab from Ali ibn al-Mundhir al-Zabbal from Muhammad ibn Fudayl who has said the following:

"Abu 'Abd Allah, *'Alayhi al-Salam*, has said, 'If you have one dirham buy wheat with it; buying flour is destruction.'"

H 8720, Ch. 65, h 3

A number of our people have narrated from Ahmad ibn Muhammad ibn Khalid from Muhammad ibn Ali from 'Abd Allah ibn Jabalah from abu al-Sabbah al-Kinaniy who has said the following:

"Abu 'Abd Allah, *'Alayhi al-Salam*, once said to me, 'O abu al-Sabbah, buying flour is humiliation, buying wheat is honor and buying bread is poverty; we seek protection with Allah against poverty.'"

Chapter 66 - Detestability of Estimating and Preferability of Using Measurements

H 8721, Ch. 66, h 1

A number of our people have narrated from Ahmad ibn Muhammad from ibn Faddal from Yunus ibn Ya'qub, who has said the following:

"Abu 'Abd Allah, *'Alayhi al-Salam*, has said, 'A people complained before the Holy Prophet, *O Allah, grant compensation to Muhammad and his family worthy of their services to Your cause*, against quick depletion of their food supplies. He (the Holy Prophet), asked, 'Do you measure or just dump?' They replied, 'We just dump, O Messenger of Allah, that is, we do not measure.' He (the Holy Prophet) said, 'You must measure, you must not dump, measuring has greater blessings.'"

H 8722, Ch. 66, h 2

Ali ibn Muhammad ibn Bandar has narrated from Ahmad ibn abu 'Abd Allah from his father Harun ibn al-Jahm from Hafs ibn 'Umar who has said the following:

"Abu 'Abd Allah, *'Alayhi al-Salam*, has said that the Messenger of Allah, *O Allah, grant compensation to Muhammad and his family worthy of their services to Your cause*, has said, 'Measure your food; blessings come with measured food.'"

H 8723, Ch. 66, h 3

A number of our people have narrated from Sahl ibn Ziyad from Muhammad ibn al-Hassan Shammun from 'Abd Allah ibn 'Abd al-Rahman from Misma' who has said the following:

"Abu 'Abd Allah, *'Alayhi al-Salam*, once said to me, 'O abu Sayyar, when the female servant prepares food, ask her to measure; blessings come with measurement.'"

Chapter 67 - Continuing Profitable Businesses

H 8724, Ch. 67, h 1

A number of our people have narrated from Ahmad ibn abu 'Abd Allah, from 'Amr ibn 'Uthman from Muhammad ibn' Adhafir from Ishaq ibn 'Ammar who has said the following:

"Abu 'Abd Allah, *'Alayhi al-Salam*, has said, 'A man once complained before the Messenger of Allah, *O Allah, grant compensation to Muhammad and his family worthy of their services to Your cause*, against his deprivation. He (the Holy Prophet) said, 'Consider selling. You must buy then sell. In whatever merchandise you find profit, hold to it.'"

H 8725, Ch. 67, h 2

Ali ibn Ibrahim has narrated from his father from al-Nawfaliy from al-Sakuniy who has said the following:

"Abu 'Abd Allah, *'Alayhi al-Salam*, has said, 'If one starts a certain business, if he does not find any profit in it, he then must change it for another kind of business.'"

H 8726, Ch. 67, h 3

A number of our people have narrated from Ahmad ibn Muhammad from ibn Faddal from Ali ibn Shajarah from Bashir al-Nabbal who has said the following:

"Abu 'Abd Allah, *'Alayhi al-Salam*, has said, 'When you (in a business) find sustenance in a certain item then you must continue with it."

Chapter 68 - Permissibility or Otherwise of Approaching Merchandise Long Before Other Merchants

H 8727, Ch. 68, h 1

Abu Ali al-Ash'ariy has narrated from Muhammad ibn al-Jabbar from Ahmad ibn al-Nadr from 'Amr ibn Shamir from 'Urwah ibn 'Abd Allah who has said the following:

"Abu Ja'far, *'Alayhi al-Salam*, has said that the Messenger of Allah, *O Allah, grant compensation to Muhammad and his family worthy of their services to Your cause*, has said, 'You must not travel to meet the caravan of suppliers out of the city before other buyers. One must not buy for the ones who are not present. Allah grants sustenance to the Muslims through one another.'"

H 8728, Ch. 68, h 2

A number of our people have narrated from Sahl ibn Ziyad and Ahmad ibn Muhammad from ibn Mahbub from Muthanna' al-Hannat from Minhal al-Qassab who has said the following:

"Abu 'Abd Allah, *'Alayhi al-Salam*, once said, 'You must not travel to meet the caravan of suppliers out of the city before other buyers, you must not buy from those you meet in this way and you must not eat from items purchased in this way.'"

H 8729, Ch. 68, h 3

Ibn Mahbub has narrated from 'Abd Allah ibn Yahya al-Kahily from Minhal al-Qassab who has said the following:

"I once asked him (the Imam), *'Alayhi al-Salam*, 'What is the limit of going out to meet a caravan of suppliers?' He (the Imam) replied, 'It is a distance of one Rawhah (four Farasikh which is equal to six miles)'"

H 8730, Ch. 68, h 4

Ali ibn Ibrahim has narrated from his father from ibn abu 'Umayr from 'Abd al-Rahman ibn al-Hajjaj from Minhal al-Qassab who has said the following:

"Abu 'Abd Allah, *'Alayhi al-Salam*, once said, 'You must not travel to meet the caravan of suppliers out of the city before other buyers; the Messenger of Allah, *O Allah, grant compensation to Muhammad and his family worthy of their services to Your cause*, prohibited it.' I then asked, 'What are its limits?' He (the Imam) replied, 'It is less than a morning or evening's journey.' I then asked,

'How much is that?' He (the Imam) replied, 'It is four farasikh (which is equal to six miles).'"

Ibn abu 'Umayr has said, 'Above this distance does not apply to "meeting suppliers."

Chapter 69 - Stipulations and the Choice to Dissolve a Business Deal

H 8731, Ch. 69, h 1

A number of our people have narrated from Sahl ibn Ziyad and Ahmad ibn Muhammad from all from ibn Mahbub from 'Abd Allah ibn Sinan who has said the following:

"I once heard abu 'Abd Allah, *'Alayhi al-Salam*, saying, 'If one forms a stipulation against the book of Allah, it is not permissible for him as well for the other party. However, the Muslims must stand by their stipulations which agree with the book of Allah, most Majestic, most Glorious.'"

H 8732, Ch. 69, h 2

Ibn Mahbub has narrated from Ali ibn Ri'ab who has said the following:

"Abu 'Abd Allah, *'Alayhi al-Salam*, has said, 'A stipulation, the right and choice to return a merchandise, in the case of an animal is applicable only up to three days in favor of the buyer, regardless he has formed any stipulation or not. If the buyer *Ahdatha* (does something to the animal) before the passing of three days, it is his agreement and acceptance of what he has purchased and it is the end of stipulation.' Someone asked, 'What is *Ahdatha*?' He (the Imam) replied, 'It means such as his touching, kissing or looking to what is not lawful for him to look at before buying.'"

H 8733, Ch. 69, h 3

Ibn Mahbub has narrated from ibn Sinan who has said the following:

"This is concerning my question before abu 'Abd Allah, *'Alayhi al-Salam*, about a man who buys an animal or a slave and sets condition good for one or two days; then the slave or animal dies or Ahdatha (does something to it). Who then is responsible for this?' He (the Imam) replied, 'It is on the seller until the time of stipulation of three days expires. Thereafter it belongs to the buyer.'"

H 8734, Ch. 69, h 4

Ali ibn Ibrahim has narrated from his father from ibn abu 'Umayr from Jamil and ibn Bukayr from Zurarah who has said the following:

"I once heard abu Ja'far, *'Alayhi al-Salam*. saying, 'The Messenger of Allah, *O Allah, grant compensation to Muhammad and his family worthy of their services to Your cause*, has said, "The buyer and the seller each has the choice to dismiss a contract before they depart each other. In a deal for animals it is for three days."' I then asked, 'What happens if a man buys something from another man and leaves it with the seller to keep until his return with the purchase price?' He (the Imam) said, 'If he returns within three days the contract is valid, otherwise, there is no deal.'"

H 8735, Ch. 69, h 5

Abu Ali al-Ash'ariy has narrated from Muhammad ibn 'Abd al-Jabbar from Safwan from al-'Ala' from Muhammad ibn Muslim who has said the following:

"Abu 'Abd Allah, *'Alayhi al-Salam*, has said that the Messenger of Allah, *O Allah, grant compensation to Muhammad and his family worthy of their services to Your cause*, has said, 'Both buyer and seller, each one of them, has the choice to dismiss a deal before they depart each other; and in a deal for an animal the choice to return the merchandise remains for three days.'"

H 8736, Ch. 69, h 6

Muhammad ibn Yahya has narrated from Ahmad ibn Muhammad from ibn Mahbub from Jamil from Fudayl who has said the following:

"This is concerning my question before abu 'Abd Allah, *'Alayhi al-Salam*, 'What is a stipulation in a deal for animals?' He (the Imam) replied, 'It is valid for three days in favor of a buyer.' I then asked, 'What is it in a deal for non-animal?' He (the Imam) replied, 'A buyer and a seller have the choice to dismiss a deal until they depart each other. After their departing each other there is no choice after their agreement.'"

H 8737, Ch. 69, h 7

Ali ibn Ibrahim has narrated from his father from ibn abu 'Umayr from Hammad from al-Halabiy who has said the following:

"Abu 'Abd Allah, *'Alayhi al-Salam*, has said, 'If a man buys something from another man, he has the choice to dismiss the deal before they depart each other. When they depart the deal becomes binding.' He (the narrator) has said, 'Abu 'Abd Allah, *'Alayhi al-Salam*, then said, 'My father once purchased a piece of land called "al-'Arid". He purchased it for a few dinars and said to the seller. "I will give you a leaf (silver) for every dinar ten dirhams." He purchased it and moved. I followed him and asked, "O father, why did you move so quickly?" He (the Imam) replied, "I wanted the transaction to become binding."'"

H 8738, Ch. 69, h 8

Ali ibn Ibrahim has narrated from his father from ibn abu 'Umayr from abu Ayyub from Muhammad ibn Muslim who has said the following:

"I heard abu Ja'far, *'Alayhi al-Salam*, saying, 'I once purchased something from someone; then I got up and walked a few steps, then returned to the meeting place so that the deal becomes binding.'"

H 8739, Ch. 69, h 9

Humayd ibn Ziyad has narrated from al-Hassan ibn Muhammad ibn Sama'ah from more than one person from Aban ibn 'Uthman from 'Abd al-Rahman ibn abu 'Abd Allah, who has said the following:

"This is concerning my question before abu 'Abd Allah, *'Alayhi al-Salam*, about a man who purchases a slave-girl from another man with a stipulation for one or two days and she dies with him and the price is paid. Who is responsible?' He (the Imam) replied, 'There is no responsibility on the buyer until the time of stipulation expires.'"

H 8740, Ch. 69, h 10

Muhammad ibn Yahya has narrated from Muhammad ibn Al-Husayn from Safwan from Ishaq ibn 'Ammar who has said the following:

"One who had heard from abu 'Abd Allah, *'Alayhi al-Salam*, informed me saying, 'A man asked the Imam, *'Alayhi al-Salam*, when I was present. A Muslim man needed to sell his house and he went to his brother and said. "I want to sell this house to you because I like it to be with you instead of being with others, with one condition that if within a year I come back with money to pay you, return it back to me."' He replied, 'I agree. If you come back with payment within a year I will give it back to you.' I further said, 'This house had a certain amount of income. Who then can have the income?' He (the Imam) replied, 'Income belongs to the buyer; were it (the house) to burn down it would come from his property.'"

H 8741, Ch. 69, h 11

Muhammad ibn Yahya has narrated from Ahmad ibn Muhammad from Ali ibn Hadid from Jamil from Zurarah who has said the following:

"I once asked abu Ja'far, *'Alayhi al-Salam*, about the case of a man who purchases something from a man and leaves it with him saying, 'I will come back with payment.' He (the Imam) said, 'If he comes back with payment within three days the transaction is valid, otherwise, it is not valid.'"

H 8742, Ch. 69, h 12

Muhammad ibn Yahya has narrated from Muhammad ibn Al-Husayn from Muhammad ibn 'Abd Allah ibn Hilal from 'Uqbah ibn abu Khalid who has said the following:

"This is concerning my question before abu 'Abd Allah, *'Alayhi al-Salam*, about the case of a man who purchases something from a man and makes a binding deal and then leaving the merchandise with him without taking possession saying, 'Tomorrow, by the will of Allah, I will come back.' Someone steals the merchandise. Whose property is it considered? He (the Imam) replied, 'It is the property of the seller until the buyer takes possession and it is taken away from the seller's house. When this happens the buyer is responsible until he returns it back to the seller.'"

H 8743, Ch. 69, h 13

Muhammad ibn Yahya has narrated from Ahmad ibn Muhammad from al-Washsha' from 'Abd Allah ibn Sinan who has said the following:

"Abu 'Abd Allah, *'Alayhi al-Salam*, has said, 'Abu 'Abd Allah, *'Alayhi al-Salam*, has said, 'In the case of slaves the deal becomes binding after three days. If slaves may have certain defects such as mental condition, leprosy and so on. It becomes binding after one year if the defect is insanity. After one year the choice does not remain of any effect.'"

H 8744, Ch. 69, h 14

Abu Ali al-Ash'ariy has narrated from Muhammad ibn 'Abd al-Jabbar from Ali ibn al-Nu'man from Sa'id ibn Yasar who has said the following:

"I once said to abu 'Abd Allah, *'Alayhi al-Salam*, 'We meet people who live in tents far from cities and others. We sell to them certain things and make profit like ten, twelve or thirteen and for a payment after a year and so on. The buyer writes for us to leave his house or land if he did not come with payment. He has taken possession and purchase is finalized. We then wait. If he came with payment within the set time his things are returned to him and if he did not come within the set time with payment we take his things. What do you say about it?' He (the Imam) said, 'I say that if he did not come with payment within the set time his things become yours but if he comes within the set time you must return his things to him.'"

H 8745, Ch. 69, h 15
Muhammad ibn Yahya has narrated from mad from Ya'qub ibn Yazid from Muhammad ibn abu Hamzah or others from those whom he has mentioned who has said the following:
"About the case of a man who buys something which is perishable the same day and leaves it with the seller to bring payment, abu 'Abd Allah, or abu al-Hassan, *'Alayhi al-Salam*, has said, 'If he brings payment from that time until night falls the transaction is valid, otherwise, he has no deal.'"

H 8746, Ch. 69, h 16
Ali ibn Ibrahim has narrated from his father from al-Hassan ibn Al-Husayn from Safwan ibn Yahya from 'Abd al-Rahman ibn al-Hajjaj who has said the following:
"I once purchased a carriage and paid a certain amount of the price, then left it with the seller. I remained engaged for several days then went to the seller to take possession. He said, 'I have sold it.' I laughed and said, 'By Allah, I will not allow you to do this without asking for a judgment.' He said, 'Will you agree to go for judgment before abu Bakr ibn 'Ayyash?' I replied, 'Yes, I agree.' We went to him and told him about our stories. Abu Bakr asked, 'On the basis of whose words you want me to decide?' He (the narrator) has said that I asked him to decide on the basis of the words of my companion (Imam).' He said, 'I heard him (Imam) say, "If one brings payment within three days the deal is valid, otherwise, there is no deal in his favor."'"

H 8747, Ch. 69, h 17
Ali ibn Ibrahim has narrated from his father from al-Nawfaliy from al-Sakuniy who has said the following:
"Abu 'Abd Allah, *'Alayhi al-Salam*, has said that 'Amir al-Mu'minin, *'Alayhi al-Salam*, once issued the following judgment: A man had purchased a dress with a stipulation to pay until midday. The buyer was offered profit and he wanted to sell. He (the Imam) said, 'He must present testimony to prove that the seller agreed and the deal was binding, then he can sell it if he so wants. If he displays it in the market without selling, it makes the transaction binding.'"

Chapter 70 - Buying an Animal Which Produces Milk Which He Uses then Returns It

H 8748, Ch. 70, h 1
A number of our people have narrated from Ahmad ibn Muhammad from those whom he has mentioned from abu al-Mighra' from al-Halabiy who has said the following:
"This is about the case of a man who had purchased a sheep and had kept it for three days; then returned it, abu 'Abd Allah, *'Alayhi al-Salam*, has said, 'If

during those three days he had consumed its milk he returns it with three handful of food. If the sheep did not have any milk he then does not owe anything.'"

Ali ibn Ibrahim has narrated from his father from ibn abu 'Umayr from Hammad from al-Halabiy from abu 'Abd Allah, *'Alayhi al-Salam*, a similar Hadith.

Chapter 71 - Dispute between Buyer and Seller

H 8749, Ch. 71, h 1
A number of our people have narrated from Sahl ibn Ziyad from Ahmad ibn Muhammad ibn abu Nasr who has said the following:
"About the case of a man who sells something and the buyers says, 'I pay so and so' which is less than what the seller wants, abu 'Abd Allah, *'Alayhi al-Salam*, has said, 'The words of seller are accepted on oath if the merchandise still exists.'"

H 8750, Ch. 71, h 2
Muhammad ibn Yahya has narrated from Ahmad ibn Muhammad from Al-Husayn 'Umar ibn Yazid from his father, who has said the following:
"Abu 'Abd Allah, *'Alayhi al-Salam*, has said, 'If the two business people speak the truth the transaction is a blessing for them; but if they speak lies and cheat, it does not become a blessing for them. They have the choice to keep or dismiss the transaction as long as they you must not depart each other. After they depart the words of the owner of merchandise are accepted or they can mutually agree to dismiss the transaction.'"

Chapter 72 - Buying and Selling Fruits

H 8751, Ch. 72, h 1
Muhammad ibn Yahya has narrated from Ahmad ibn Muhammad from al-Hajjal from Tha'labah from Burayd who has said the following:
"I once asked abu Ja'far. *'Alayhi al-Salam*, about al-Ratbah (a grass, cattle feed) which is sold in the form of one, two or three crops. He (the Imam) said, 'There is no offense in it.' I asked many such questions and every time he (the Imam) said, 'There is no offense in it.' I then said, 'May Allah keep you well' - because of feeling shy due to my numerous questions and his words, 'There is no offense in it'- those nearby may spoil for us all of this. He (the Imam) said, 'I think they have heard the Hadith of the Messenger of Allah about palm trees.' At this time someone caused an interruption and I remained quiet. I then asked Muhammad ibn Muslim to ask abu Ja'far, *'Alayhi al-Salam*, about the words of the Messenger of Allah in regard to palm trees. Abu Ja'far, *'Alayhi al-Salam*, said, 'The Messenger of Allah, *O Allah, grant compensation to Muhammad and his family worthy of their services to Your cause*, once came out and heard a great deal of noise. He (the Messenger of Allah) asked about it. It was said to him, "People buy fruits of the coming year of palm trees in exchange for dates." The Messenger of Allah said, "If they do so they must buy the fruits of the coming

year when something of such fruits appears, and they must not make it unlawful.""""

H 8752, Ch. 72, h 2

Ali ibn Ibrahim has narrated from his father from ibn abu 'Umayr from Hammad ibn 'Uthman from al-Halabiy who has said the following:

"Someone once asked abu 'Abd Allah, *'Alayhi al-Salam*, about buying dates, grapes and fruits of three or four years. He (the Imam) said, 'There is no offense in it. He (the buyer) can say, "If fruits will not grow this year they will do so next year." If you buy the fruits of one year only then you must not do so until they are ripe. If you buy them before three years there is no offense in it if the deal takes place before they are ripe.' Someone asked about buying a certain fruit of a certain land but the fruit of all of that land is ruined. He (the Imam) said, 'There was dispute about it and it was brought before the Messenger of Allah, *O Allah, grant compensation to Muhammad and his family worthy of their services to Your cause*, and they kept speaking about it. When he found out that they do not stop disputing, he prohibited them from such transactions until ripening of fruits and did not make it unlawful. However, he did so because of their disputes.'"

H 8753, Ch. 72, h 3

Al-Husayn ibn Muhammad has narrated from Mu'alla' ibn Muhammad from al-Hassan ibn al-Washsha' who has said the following:

"I once asked al-Rida', *'Alayhi al-Salam*, 'Is buying dates permissible when they are formed?' He (the Imam) replied, 'It is permissible when they Yazhu.' I then asked, 'What is Yazhu?' He (the Imam) replied, 'It is when they turn red, yellow and so on.'"

H 8754, Ch. 72, h 4

Muhammad ibn 'Isma'il has narrated from al-Fadl ibn Shadhan from ibn abu 'Umayr from Rib'iy who has said the following:

"I once said to abu 'Abd Allah, *'Alayhi al-Salam*, 'I have palm tree fruits in Basrah. I sell them for a certain price excluding one Kur (a certain measurement) of the dates or more or the cluster of dates.' He (the Imam) said, 'There is no offense in it.' I then said, 'I pray to Allah to keep my soul in service for your cause, what do you say about selling for two years?' He (the Imam) said, 'There is no offense in it.' I then said, 'I pray to Allah to keep my soul in service for your cause, this is great among us.' He (the Imam) said, 'As you mentioned it, the Messenger of Allah, *O Allah, grant compensation to Muhammad and his family worthy of their services to Your cause*, had made it permissible but they wronged each other. He, *'Alayhi al-Salam*, then said, 'You must not buy it until fruits appear and are out of danger.'"

H 8755, Ch. 72, h 5

Muhammad ibn Yahya has narrated from Muhammad ibn Al-Husayn from Safwan from Ya'qub ibn Shu'ayb who has said the following:

"Abu 'Abd Allah, *'Alayhi al-Salam*, has said, 'If inside the walls there are different fruits and certain kinds are ripe, then there is no offense in buying all of it.'"

H 8756, Ch. 72, h 6

Humayd ibn Ziyad has narrated from ibn Sama'ah from more than one person from 'Isma'il ibn al-Fadl who has said the following:

"I once asked him (the Imam) about selling fruits. 'Is it permissible to buy fruits before they are formed?' He (the Imam) replied, 'If in that area such deals are made and they are profitable which is achieved then there is no offense in such transaction.'"

H 8757, Ch. 72, h 7

A number of our people have narrated from Ahmad ibn Muhammad ibn Khalid from 'Uthman ibn 'Isa from Sama'ah who has said the following:

"I once asked him (the Imam) about selling fruits. 'Is it permissible to buy fruits before they are formed?' He (the Imam) replied, 'No, it is not permissible unless something else alongside is also purchased, like animal feed or vegetables when the buyer says, 'I buy this much animal feed and dates from you and this tree in exchange for so and so prices.' In case, if no fruits appeared the buyers' capital remains with animal feed or vegetables.' I then asked him (the Imam) about buying tree leaves. Is it permissible to buy them in three or four kharatat (crops)?' He (the Imam) said, 'If you can see leaves on the tree you can buy it for whatever number of cropping you may like.'"

H 8758, Ch. 72, h 8

Muhammad ibn Yahya has narrated from Ahmad ibn Muhammad from al-Husayn from al-Qasim ibn Muhammad al-Jawhariy from Ali ibn abu Hamzah who has said the following:

"This is concerning my question before abu 'Abd Allah, *'Alayhi al-Salam*, about the case of a man who buys a garden with palm trees and trees in it of which certain ones have become edible and others are not edible yet. He (the Imam) said, 'It is not harmful when there are edible ones.' I then asked him (the Imam) about the case of a man who buys a garden with palm trees in it which does not have anything yet except green dates. He (the Imam) said, 'No, until they Yazhu.' I then asked, 'What is yazhu?' He (the Imam) said, 'It is when their color changes.'"

H 8759, Ch. 72, h 9

Muhammad ibn Yahya has narrated from Muhammad ibn al-Husayn from Safwan ibn Yahya from Ya'qub ibn Shu'ayb who has said the following:

"This is concerning my question before abu 'Abd Allah, *'Alayhi al-Salam*, about the case of a man whom I gave twenty dinar for his fruits saying that when your fruits become fruits these dinars are payments, if then I will like I will take the fruits, and if I will not like I will not take them. He (the Imam) said, 'You cannot give him or stipulate for anything.' I said, 'I pray to Allah to keep my soul in service for your cause, he does not say anything and Allah knows his intention.' He (the Imam) said, 'It is not valid if it is in his intention (the merchandise must exist).'"

H 8760, Ch. 72, h 10

Ali ibn Ibrahim has narrated from his father from ibn abu 'Umayr from Hammad from al-Halabiy who has said the following:

"This is about the case of a man who says to another man, 'Sell to me fruits of your palm tree for two *Qafiz* (a certain measurement) of dates or less or more...' specifying the amount as he likes and he sells it. He (the Imam) said, 'It is not harmful.' He (the Imam) said, 'Dates and half ripe dates of a palm tree are the same and it is not harmful. Mixing old dates and half ripe fresh dates is not valid and so also is true for raisins and grapes.'"

H 8761, Ch. 72, h 11

A number of our people have narrated from Sahl ibn Ziyad from Ahmad ibn Muhammad from ibn abu Nasr from Mu'awiyah ibn Muyassir who has said the following:

"This is concerning my question before abu 'Abd Allah, *'Alayhi al-Salam*, about selling palm trees for two years. He (the Imam) said, 'It is not harmful.' I then asked if fresh dates can be sold in the form of one or several pickings fresh from the trees each time they ripen. He (the Imam) said, 'It is not harmful.' He (the Imam) then said, 'My father would sell the plant of henna in the manner of several harvests.'"

H 8762, Ch. 72, h 12

Humayd ibn Ziyad has narrated from al-Hassan ibn Muhammad ibn Sama'ah from more than one person from Aban ibn 'Uthman from Yahya ibn abu al-'Ala' who has said the following:

"Abu 'Abd Allah, *'Alayhi al-Salam*, has said, 'If one sells palm trees which are pollinated, the fruit then belongs to the seller unless the buyer has stipulated otherwise. This is how the Messenger of Allah, *O Allah, grant compensation to Muhammad and his family worthy of their services to Your cause*, judged a case.'"

H 8763, Ch. 72, h 13

Ali ibn Ibrahim has narrated from his father from ibn abu 'Umayr from Hammad from al-Halabiy who has said the following:

"About the case of buying fruits, abu 'Abd Allah, *'Alayhi al-Salam*, has said, 'When it becomes something buying it is not harmful.'"

H 8764, Ch. 72, h 14

Muhammad ibn Yahya has narrated from Ahmad ibn Muhammad ibn 'Isa from Muhammad ibn Yahya from Ghiyath ibn Ibrahim who has said the following:

"Abu 'Abd Allah, *'Alayhi al-Salam*, has said that 'Amir al-Mu'minin has said, 'If one sells palm trees which he has pollinated, its dates belong to the seller unless the buyer stipulates otherwise. Ali, *'Alayhi al-Salam*, then said that this is how the Messenger of Allah, *O Allah, grant compensation to Muhammad and his family worthy of their services to Your cause*, judged a case.'"

H 8765, Ch. 72, h 15

Ali ibn Ibrahim has narrated from his father from 'Isma'il ibn Marrar from Yunus who has said the following:

"The explanation of the words of the Holy Prophet, 'People of the city must not sell to the people of countryside' is that fruits and all kinds of grains which are transported from countryside to the market place, it (their sale) then is not permissible for the people of the market place to buy such items from them to sell to the people. The transporting ones from the countryside and wilderness must sell them. However, those who transport such items from one city to another city can sell them because it is like trading.'"

H 8766, Ch. 72, h 16
Muhammad ibn Yahya has narrated from Ahmad ibn Muhammad from ibn Mahbub from Ibrahim al-Karkhiy who has said the following:

"This is concerning my question before abu 'Abd Allah, *'Alayhi al-Salam*, that I had sold palm trees each for such and such number of dirham. The palm trees had fruits on them. The buyer then sold them to another man for a certain amount of profit but he had not paid me anything and had not received any delivery from me. He (the Imam) said, 'It is not harmful. Had he not taken responsibility for payment?' I replied, 'Yes, he had done so. He (the Imam) said, 'The profit then belongs to him.'"

H 8767, Ch. 72, h 17
Muhammad ibn Yahya has narrated from Muhammad ibn al-Husayn from Muhammad ibn 'Abd Allah ibn Hilal from 'Uqbah ibn Khalid who has said the following:

"Abu 'Abd Allah, *'Alayhi al-Salam*, has said that the Messenger of Allah, *O Allah, grant compensation to Muhammad and his family worthy of their services to Your cause*, had judged that the fruits of the palm trees pollinated belong to the seller unless the buyer stipulates otherwise.'"

H 8768, Ch. 72, h 18
Muhammad ibn Yahya has narrated from Ahmad ibn Muhammad from Ahmad ibn al-Hassan from 'Amr ibn Sa'id from Musaddiq ibn Sadaqah from 'Ammar ibn Musa who has said the following:

"This is concerning my question before abu 'Abd Allah, *'Alayhi al-Salam*, about vines when it is permissible to sell them. He (the Imam) said, 'It is permissible when they form into vines.'"

Chapter 73 - Buying and Selling Food

H 8769, Ch. 73, h 1
A number of our people have narrated from Ahmad ibn Muhammad from 'Uthman ibn 'Isa from Sama'ah who has said the following:

"I once asked him (the Imam), *'Alayhi al-Salam*, about buying food which is exchanged by means of weighing or measuring, if such items can be bought without weighing or measuring. He (the Imam) said, 'If you find a man with food which he has weighed or measured and it is bought from him with profit for him, it is not harmful if you buy it without weighing and measuring. If the first buyer had bought it by weighing and measurement and you say when buying, "I give you such and such amount of profit and I accept your weighing and measuring then it is not harmful."'"

H 8770, Ch. 73, h 2
Ali ibn Ibrahim has narrated from his father and Muhammad ibn Yahya has narrated from Ahmad ibn Muhammad from ibn abu 'Umayr from Hammad from al-Halabiy who has said the following:

"About the case of a man who buys a certain amount of food then sells it without weighing or measurement, he (the Imam) said, 'It is not a valid deal.'"

H 8771, Ch. 73, h 3
Muhammad ibn Yahya has narrated from Ahmad ibn Muhammad from Ali ibn Hadid from Jamil ibn Darraj who has said the following:

"About the case of a man who buys food then sells it before receiving delivery, he (the Imam) said, 'It is not harmful.' 'Can he appoint the second buyer as his agent to receive delivery?' He (the Imam) said, 'It is not harmful.'"

H 8772, Ch. 73, h 4
Ali ibn Ibrahim has narrated from his father from ibn abu 'Umayr from Hammad from al-Halabiy who has said the following:

"About the case of a man who buys food from another man, a package by means of known measurement then the party asks the buyer to buy from him another similar package without measurement, because it is similar to the other package already bought. He (the Imam) said, 'It is not valid without measurement.' He (the Imam) said, 'Venturous estimation in food items which are exchanged by measurement is not valid and it is of undesirable matters in food items.'"

H 8773, Ch. 73, h 5
Humayd ibn Ziyad has narrated from al-Hassan ibn Muhammad ibn Sama'ah from more than one person from Aban ibn 'Uthman from 'Abd al-Rahman ibn abu 'Abd Allah who has said the following:

"This is concerning my question before abu 'Abd Allah, 'Alayhi al-Salam, about the case of a man who owes one kur (a certain amount) of food. He then buys one kur of food from another man and asks his creditor to come to receive the Kur of food owed to him. He (the Imam) said, 'Such a transaction is not harmful.'"

H 8774, Ch. 73, h 6
Muhammad ibn Yahya has narrated from Muhammad ibn al-Husayn from Safwan ibn Yahya from Ishaq ibn 'Ammar from abu al-'Atarud who has said the following:

"I once said to abu 'Abd Allah, 'Alayhi al-Salam, that I buy food in a deal in the beginning of which I lose and in the end I gain profit. I then ask my friend to reduce a certain amount on each kur. He (the Imam) said, 'There is nothing good in it, however, he can reduce a certain sum.' I then asked, 'Can he reduce more than I have lost?' He (the Imam) said, 'It is not harmful.' I then asked if I can keep aside one or two kur and the man asks me to give him according to my measurement. He (the Imam) said, 'It is not harmful if he can trust you.'"

H 8775, Ch. 73, h 7
Muhammad ibn Yahya has narrated from Muhammad ibn al-Husayn from Safwan ibn Yahya from abu Sa'id al-Mukariy from 'Abd al-Malik ibn 'Amr who has said the following:

"This is concerning my question before abu 'Abd Allah, 'Alayhi al-Salam, about food that I buy and I measure it when someone witnesses my measuring but I measure it for myself. He then says, 'Sell it to me.' I then sell it to him by means of the same measurement that I made for myself. He (the Imam) said, 'It is not harmful.'"

H 8776, Ch. 73, h 8
Ali ibn Ibrahim has narrated from his father from ibn abu 'Umayr from Jamil who has said the following:

"This is concerning my question before abu 'Abd Allah, *'Alayhi al-Salam,* about the case of a man who buys hay which is on the threshing floor, each kur for a certain amount. He receives delivery of hay and sells it before measuring the hay. He (the Imam) said, 'It is not harmful.'"

H 8777, Ch. 73, h 9

Muhammad ibn Yahya has narrated from Muhammad ibn al-Husayn from Safwan from ibn Muskan from Ishaq al-Mad'iniy who has said the following:

"This is concerning my question before abu 'Abd Allah, *'Alayhi al-Salam,* about the case of a people who embark in a ship and buy food and bargain about it. Then one man buys from them. They ask him and he gives them what they ask for of food. So he who collects payment and gives them food becomes the owner of food. He (the Imam) said, 'It is not harmful. I do not see anything else except that they were partners.' I then said, 'The owner of food asks a measuring person who measures for us and we have workers who examine and finds increases and decreases. He (the Imam) said, 'It is not harmful if errors are not many.'"

Chapter 74 - The Case of Change of Prices of Certain Merchandise before Delivery

H 8778, Ch. 74, h 1

Ali ibn Ibrahim has narrated from his father from ibn abu 'Umayr from Hammad from al-Halabiy who has said the following:

"About the case of a man who buys food for a few dirham of which he takes one-half and leaves the other half. Thereafter he comes back when prices have risen or have fallen down, Abu 'Abd Allah, *'Alayhi al-Salam,* has said, 'If on the day of purchase he prices them and determines the amount then such price is what it is, but if he has taken a certain amount and has left the rest without pricing he must pay the price of the day that he takes whatever it is.'"

H 8779, Ch. 74, h 2

Ali ibn Ibrahim has narrated from his father from ibn abu 'Umayr from Jamil who has said the following:

"About the case of a man who buys food, every kur (a certain amount) for a certain price, then prices rise or fall when he has measured only a certain part, and the owner of food refuses to deliver to him the rest, abu 'Abd Allah, *'Alayhi al-Salam,* has said, 'If on the day of purchase he has priced the food and that the food is his, then the remaining food is also his; but if he had only bought without any condition then only what he has paid for is his.'"

H 8780, Ch. 74, h 3

Muhammad ibn Yahya has narrated the following:

"Muhammad ibn al-Hassan once wrote to abu Muhammad, *'Alayhi al-Salam,* asking, 'A man has hired another man to work and build a structure for another person and he gives the worker food, cotton and other things; then the prices of food and cotton rise or fall and change from the day he gave him, if he can count on him with the price of the day of delivery or the price of the day of finalizing the account. He (the Imam) signed the answer, 'He must pay according to the prices of the day he set mutual conditions (prices, work and so on) if Allah so wills.' He (the Imam), *'Alayhi al-Salam*, about the question of goods that one receives and pays food for it without determining prices which then change, signed the answer, 'Prices are that of the day he has given the food.'"

Chapter 65 - Excellence of Using Measuring and Weighing Tools

H 8781, Ch. 75, h 1

Ali ibn Ibrahim has narrated from his father from ibn abu 'Umayr ibn 'Atiyyah who has said the following:

"This is concerning my question before abu 'Abd Allah, *'Alayhi al-Salam*, about the case of our buying food from ships. We then measure and find extra amount. He (the Imam) said, 'Perhaps you find it to be less also.' I replied, 'Yes, that also happens.' He (the Imam) then asked, 'Do they give you the deficit?' I replied, 'No, they do not give the deficit. He (the Imam) said, 'It is not harmful.'"

H 8782, Ch. 75, h 2

Muhammad ibn 'Isma'il has narrated from al-Fadl ibn Shadhan from ibn abu 'Umayr from 'Abd al-Rahman ibn al-Hajjaj who has said the following:

"This is concerning my question before abu 'Abd Allah, *'Alayhi al-Salam*, about the extra in measurement and weighing. He (the Imam) said, 'If it is not excessive, it is not harmful.'"

H 8783, Ch. 75, h 3

Muhammad ibn Yahya has narrated from Muhammad ibn al-Husayn from Ali ibn al-Hakam from al-'Ala' ibn Razin who has said the following:

"I once said to abu 'Abd Allah, *'Alayhi al-Salam*, that I may pass by a man and he speaks to me about food and says, 'You have found the kind of foodstuff that you need.' I then ask him to show me and I will give such and such amount of profit for each kur, but when he shows it to me, I look at it and if I need I take it, if not I leave it. He (the Imam) said, 'It is bargaining and it is not harmful.' I then said that I then ask him to keep aside for me fifty kur or less or more according to his measurement then it comes extra or less and mostly it is extra. To whom the extra belongs? He (the Imam) said, 'It belongs to you.' He (the Imam) then said, 'I once sent Mu'attib or Salam who bought food for us and it came extra for two dinars and our family used it by the measurement that we knew.' I then asked, 'Did you find out who the seller was?' He (the Imam) replied, 'Yes, and we returned the extra to him.' I then said, 'May Allah be kind to you. In my case your fatwa is that the extra belongs to me and yourself return it to the seller because you knew that it belongs to him.' He (the Imam) said, 'Yes; it is a mistake that people make because what we bought was for eight or nine dirham.' He (the Imam) then said, 'In our case we, however, measured it again.'"

H 8784, Ch. 75, h 4

Muhammad ibn Yahya has narrated from Ahmad ibn Muhammad from Muhammad ibn 'Isma'il from Hanan who has said the following:

"Once I was sitting in the presence of abu 'Abd Allah, *'Alayhi al-Salam*, when Mu'ammar al-Zayyat said, 'We buy oil in Ziqaq (a certain container), they compensate it for deficit because of Ziqaq. He (the Imam) said, 'If it comes extra as well as in deficit, it is not harmful but if it comes extra and no deficit, then you must not go close to it.'"

Chapter 76 - Mixing of Foods of Various Kinds

H 8785, Ch. 76, h 1

Muhammad ibn Yahya has narrated from Muhammad ibn al-Husayn from Ali ibn al-Hakam from al-'Ala' from Muhammad ibn Muslim who has said the following:

"One of the two Imam, (abu Ja'far or abu 'Abd Allah), *'Alayhim al-Salam*, was asked about foodstuff of high and low quality mixed together. He (the Imam) said, 'If they see all of it, it is not harmful as long as that of good quality does not cover that of low quality.'"

H 8786, Ch. 76, h 2

Ali ibn Ibrahim has narrated from his father from ibn abu 'Umayr from Hammad from al-Halabiy who has said the following:

"This is concerning my question before abu 'Abd Allah, *'Alayhi al-Salam*, about the case of a man who has various kinds of the same item of foodstuff of the same price of which one is of high quality and one is of low quality but he mixes them together; then sells them for one kind of price. He (the Imam) said, 'It is not proper for him and it is cheating the Muslims unless he informs them of the condition.'"

H 8787, Ch. 76, h 3

Ibn abu 'Umayr has narrated from Hammad from al-Halabiy who has said the following:

"This is concerning my question before abu 'Abd Allah, *'Alayhi al-Salam*, about the case of a man who buys foodstuff and thinks is best for him and more sellable if he makes them moist but not intending to increase its quantity. He (the Imam) said, 'If it does not sell without moistening in other ways and it is without seeking to increase its weight, then it is not harmful, otherwise, it is cheating the Muslims.'"

Chapter 77 - Using Local Measuring Tools Is the only Valid Tools

H 8788, Ch. 77, h 1

Ali ibn Ibrahim has narrated from his father from ibn abu 'Umayr from Hammad from al-Halabiy who has said the following:

"Abu 'Abd Allah, *'Alayhi al-Salam*, has said, 'It is not proper to sell with a *Sa'* (a certain measuring device) which is not in use in the city (land).'"

H 8789, Ch. 77, h 2

Muhammad ibn Yahya has narrated from Ahmad ibn Muhammad from certain persons of his people from Aban from Muhammad al-Halabiy who have said the following:

"Abu 'Abd Allah, *'Alayhi al-Salam*, has said, 'It is not lawful for one to sell with a *Sa'* which is not in use in a city. A man may hire a camel man and measures with a device of his home which perhaps is smaller than the *mud* (a certain measurement) of the market- place. If he says it is smaller than the mud of the market he does not accept unless he guarantees and takes responsibility thereof.' He (the Imam) said, 'There must be one *mud*. Taking responsibility also serves this purpose.'"

H 8790, Ch. 77, h 3

Muhammad ibn Yahya has narrated from Muhammad ibn Khalid al-Barqiy from Sa'd ibn Sa'd who has narrated the following:

"I once asked abu al-Hassan, *'Alayhi al-Salam*, about a people who make *al-Qufzan* (measuring devices) small with which they sell. He (the Imam) said, 'They are of the people who cause losses in their belongings.'"

Chapter 78 - Purchase of Food in *Salam* (Advance Payment) Manner

H 8791, Ch. 78, h 1

Muhammad ibn Yahya has narrated from Ahmad ibn Muhammad from Muhammad ibn Yahya from Ghiyath ibn Ibrahim who has said the following:

"Abu 'Abd Allah, *'Alayhi al-Salam*, has said that 'Amir al-Mu'minin has said, 'Advance payment for a merchandise is not harmful if it is for known measures and appointed time. Advance payment is not made except for threshing and the time of harvest.'"

H 8792, Ch. 78, h 2

Abu Ali al-Ash'ariy has narrated from Muhammad ibn 'Abd al-Jabbar from Safwan from ibn Muskan from Muhammad al-Halabiy who has said the following:

"This is concerning my question before abu 'Abd Allah, *'Alayhi al-Salam*, about advance payment for foodstuff of a known measure and an appointed time. He (the Imam) said, 'It is not harmful.'"

H 8793, Ch. 78, h 3

Ali ibn Ibrahim has narrated from his father from 'Abd Allah ibn al-Mughirah from 'Abd Allah ibn Sinan who has said the following:

"This is concerning my question before abu 'Abd Allah, *'Alayhi al-Salam*, about the case of a man who makes advance payment to buy foodstuff from a man who does not have any farm or foodstuff or animals except that he at the appointed time buys the foodstuff and delivers it. He (the Imam) said, 'If he guarantees it within the appointed time then it is not harmful.' I then asked, 'If he delivers a certain amount and cannot deliver a certain amount, is it proper for me to demand from him the remaining of my capital? He (the Imam) said, 'Yes, that is very good.'"

H 8794, Ch. 78, h 4

Muhammad ibn Yahya has narrated from Ahmad ibn Muhammad from Ali al-Nu'man from ibn Muskan from Sulayman ibn Khalid who has said the following:

"This is concerning my question before abu 'Abd Allah, *'Alayhi al-Salam*, about the case of a man who makes advance payment for farms and takes a certain amount of his foodstuff and a certain amount remains. The other party offers him the remaining of his capital. He (the Imam) said, 'He must accept it; it is lawful.' I then said, 'He sells his foodstuff that he has received and it doubles.' He (the Imam) said, 'If he does, it is lawful.' I then asked him (the Imam) about a man who makes advance payment for what is not a farm or palm trees. He (the Imam) said, 'He must name something for an appointed time.'"

H 8795, Ch. 78, h 5

Muhammad ibn Yahya has narrated from Ahmad ibn Muhammad and Ali ibn Ibrahim has narrated from his father all from ibn abu 'Umayr from Hammad from al-Halabiy who has said the following:

"This is concerning my question before abu 'Abd Allah, *'Alayhi al-Salam*, about the case of a man to whom I made advance payment for foodstuff. When the time arrived he sent to me dirhams. He (the Imam) said, 'Buy foodstuff for yourself and compensate for your right.' He (the Imam) then said, 'I deem it proper that you appoint someone else for such work until you receive what belongs to you and you alone must not undertake the task and work.'"

H 8796, Ch. 78, h 6

Ahmad ibn Muhammad has narrated from ibn abu 'Umayr from Aban ibn 'Uthman from certain persons of our people who has said the following:

"About the case of a man who makes advance payment for foodstuff for an appointed time and when the foodstuff is ready he says, 'I do not have any foodstuff but consider what its price is and take it from me', abu 'Abd Allah, *'Alayhi al-Salam*, has said, 'It is not harmful.'"

H 8797, Ch. 78, h 7

Muhammad ibn Yahya has narrated from Muhammad ibn al-Husayn Ahmad ibn Muhammad from Muhammad ibn 'Isma'il has narrated from al-Fadl ibn Shadhan from Safwan from al-'Is ibn al-Qasim who has said the following:

"This is concerning my question before abu 'Abd Allah, *'Alayhi al-Salam*, about the case of a man who makes advance payment of dirhams in exchange for wheat until the appoint time comes and he does not have any foodstuff but has animals and other assets and slaves; if it is lawful for him to take from his assets in exchange for his foodstuff. He (the Imam) said, 'Yes, he must name such and such items for such and such *Sa'* (of foodstuff).'"

H 8798, Ch. 78, h 8

Humayd ibn Ziyad has narrated from al-Hassan ibn Muhammad ibn Sama'ah from more than one person from Aban ibn 'Uthman from Ya'qub ibn Shu'ayb and 'Ubayd ibn Zurarah who has said the following:

"We once asked abu 'Abd Allah, *'Alayhi al-Salam*, about the case of a man who sells foodstuff in exchange for dirhams for an appointed time. When the time comes and he demands it, the party says, 'I do not have dirhams. Take from me foodstuff.' He (the Imam) said, 'It is not harmful; his are dirhams in exchange, for which he can take whatever he likes.'"

H 8799, Ch. 78, h 9
Humayd has narrated from ibn Sama'ah from more than one person from Aban from 'Abd al-Rahman ibn abu 'Abd Allah who has said the following:
"This is concerning my question before abu 'Abd Allah, *'Alayhi al-Salam*, about the case of a man who makes advance payment of dirhams in exchange for foodstuff and the time comes but the party sends him dirhams. He (the Imam) said, 'He can buy foodstuff to compensate for his right. Do you see any problems in it?' He (the Imam) said, 'There must be someone else with him to work to make it happen.'"

H 8800, Ch. 78, h 10
Ali ibn Ibrahim has narrated from his father and Muhammad ibn Yahya has narrated from Ahmad ibn Muhammad all from ibn abu 'Umayr from Hammad from al-Halabiy who has said the following:
"Once abu 'Abd Allah, *'Alayhi al-Salam*, was asked about the case of a man who makes advance payment in exchange for five *Mukhatim* (a container) of wheat or barley for an appointed time but the party cannot deliver all that he owes on due time, and he asks the other party to accept half of the foodstuff or one-third or less or more and take the remaining of his capital back. He (the Imam) said, 'It is not harmful.' 'Can saffron be purchased through advance payment of twenty dirham for twenty *Mithqal* (a certain unit of weight) or less or more?' He (the Imam) said, 'It is not harmful. If the party cannot deliver all of saffron, the other party can take one-third or two-thirds of the remaining of his capital for his right.'"

H 8801, Ch. 78, h 11
Ali ibn Ibrahim has narrated from his father and Muhammad ibn 'Isma'il has narrated from al-Fadl ibn Shadhan from all from ibn abu 'Umayr from Hafs ibn al-Bakhtariy from Khalid ibn al-Hajjaj who has said the following:
"About the case of a man who buys foodstuff of a certain town, abu 'Abd Allah, *'Alayhi al-Salam*, has said, 'If the foodstuff of a certain town exactly is not mentioned he can give it from anywhere he likes.'"

H 8802, Ch. 78, h 12
Sahl ibn Ziyad has narrated from Mu'awiyah ibn Hakim from al-Hassan ibn Ali ibn Faddal who has said the following:
"I once wrote to abu al-Hassan, *'Alayhi al-Salam*, and asked, 'I make an advance payment deal with a man for foodstuff and when it is due time I do not have any foodstuff, if I can give him dirhams in exchange. He (the Imam) said, 'Yes, you can do so.'"

Chapter 79 - Exchange of One Kind of Food Items for another Kind

H 8803, Ch. 79, h 1
A number of our people have narrated from Sahl ibn Ziyad and Ahmad ibn Muhammad from ibn Mahbub from Hisham ibn Salim who has said the following:

"Once abu 'Abd Allah, *'Alayhi al-Salam*, was asked about the case of a man who sells foodstuff to another man in quantity of several kur but cannot deliver what he owes, and says to the other party to accept two *Qafiz* (a certain unit of measurement) of barley for one *Qafiz* of wheat to compensate for the deficit. He (the Imam) said, 'It is not valid; the origin of barley is from wheat, however, he can return his dirhams proportionate to the degree of deficit.'"

H 8804, Ch. 79, h 2
Abu Ali al-Ash'ariy has narrated from Muhammad ibn 'Abd al-Jabbar from Safwan from Mansur ibn Hazim from abu Basir and others who has said the following:
"Abu 'Abd Allah, *'Alayhi al-Salam*, has said, 'Wheat and barley are equal to each other; neither one of the two can be exchanged in excess of the other.'"

H 8805, Ch. 79, h 3
Ali ibn Ibrahim has narrated from his father from ibn abu 'Umayr from Hammad ibn 'Uthman from al-Halabiy who has said the following:
"Abu 'Abd Allah, *'Alayhi al-Salam*, has said, 'It is not permissible to sell two Makhtum (a container) of barley for one Makhtum of wheat. These items cannot be exchanged except in equal quantities of each other and so also is the date.' Abu 'Abd Allah, *'Alayhi al-Salam*, was asked about the case of a man who buys wheat but cannot find with his party anything except barley, if he can take two for one. He (the Imam) said, 'No, because the origin of the two is the same and Ali, *'Alayhi al-Salam*, would count barley for wheat.'"

H 8806, Ch. 79, h 4
Muhammad ibn Yahya has narrated from Ahmad ibn Muhammad from 'Uthman ibn 'Isa from Sama'ah who has said the following:
"I once asked him (the Imam), *'Alayhi al-Salam*, about wheat and barley. He (the Imam) said, 'If they are of equal measures it is not harmful.' He (the narrator) has said, 'I asked him (the Imam) about flour and wheat. He (the Imam) said, 'If they are of equal measures it is not harmful.'"

H 8807, Ch. 79, h 5
Muhammad ibn Yahya has narrated from Ahmad ibn Muhammad and a number of our people have narrated from Sahl ibn Ziyad from Ahmad ibn Muhammad from ibn abu Nasr from Aban from 'Abd al-Rahman ibn abu 'Abd Allah who has said the following:
"This is concerning my question before abu 'Abd Allah, *'Alayhi al-Salam*, if it is permissible to exchange one *Qafiz* (a certain unit of measurement) of wheat for two *Qafiz* of barley. He (the Imam) said, 'No, it is not permissible unless they are of equal quantities.' He (the Imam) then said, 'Barley is from wheat.'"

H 8808, Ch. 79, h 6
Ali ibn Ibrahim has narrated from his father from ibn abu 'Umayr from Hammad from al-Halabiy who has said the following:
"About the case of a man who asks another man to sell the fruits of his certain palm tree for two *Qafiz* (a certain unit of measurement) of dates or less or more that he names as he likes, abu 'Abd Allah, *'Alayhi al-Salam*, has said, 'It is not harmful.' He (the Imam) then said, 'Fresh dates and half-ripe dates from one

palm tree can be exchanged and it is not harmful but mixing of old dates and half-ripe dates is not valid and so also is the case of raisin and grape.'"

H 8809, Ch. 79, h 7
Ahmad ibn Muhammad has narrated from al-Hassan ibn Mahbub from Sayf al-Tammar who has said the following:

"I once asked abu Basir to ask abu 'Abd Allah, *'Alayhi al-Salam*, about the case of a man who exchanges two baskets of fresh half-ripe dates for one basket of *Mushaqaq* (stone-free) dates. Abu Basir asked him (the Imam) and he (the Imam) said, 'It is *Makruh* (detestable).' Abu Basir then asked, 'Why it is *Makruh* (detestable)?' He (the Imam) said, 'Ali ibn abu Talib, *'Alayhi al-Salam*, disliked to exchange one *wasaq* of dates of al-Madinah for two *wasaq* (a certain unit of measurement) of dates of Khaybar because dates of al-Madinah are of inferior quality and Ali, *'Alayhi al-Salam*, would not dislike lawful things.'"

H 8810, Ch. 79, h 8
Muhammad ibn Yahya has narrated from Ahmad ibn Muhammad from al-Washsha' from 'Abd Allah ibn Sinan who has said the following:

"I once heard abu 'Abd Allah, *'Alayhi al-Salam*, saying that 'Amir al-Mu'minin disliked exchanging of one *wasaq* (a certain unit of measurement) of dates of Khaybar with two *wasaq* of dates of al-Madinah because dates of Khaybar are of superior quality.'"

H 8811, Ch. 79, h 9
Muhammad ibn Yahya has narrated from Muhammad ibn al-Husayn from Ali ibn al-Hakam from al-'Ala' from Muhammad ibn Muslim who has said the following:

"I once asked abu Ja'far, *'Alayhi al-Salam*, about his opinion on wheat and the *sawiq* (mush made of wheat or barley). He (the Imam) said, 'Their exchange in equal measures is not harmful.' I then asked, 'What happens if one has a certain yield or preference over the other?' He (the Imam) said, 'Does it not have expenses and maintenance?' I replied, 'Yes, it has such overheads.' He (the Imam) said, 'This is for that.' He (the Imam) then said, 'If they are two different things then exchange of one for two at the same time is permissible.'"

H 8812, Ch. 79, h 10
A number of our people have narrated from Ahmad ibn Muhammad from al-Husayn ibn Sa'id from Jamil from Muhammad ibn Muslim and Zurarah who have said the following:

"Abu Ja'far, *'Alayhi al-Salam*, has said, 'It is permissible to exchange wheat with flour in equal measures and *sawiq* (mush) of wheat with mush and barley with wheat in equal measures, is not harmful.'"

H 8813, Ch. 79, h 11
Muhammad ibn Yahya has narrated from Ahmad ibn Muhammad from Ali ibn al-Hakam from al-'Ala' from Muhammad ibn Muslim who has said the following:

"I once asked abu Ja'far, *'Alayhi al-Salam*, about the case of a man who gives foodstuff to a flour man under a contract that requires him to return for every ten *Artal* (plural of *ritl*, a certain unit of measurement) twelve *Artal* of flour. He (the Imam) said, 'No, it is not permissible.' I then asked about sesame given under a contract to an oil man who guarantees for every *Sa'* a certain *Ritl* (a certain unit of measurement). He (the Imam) said, 'No, it is not permissible.'"

H 8814, Ch. 79, h 12
Ali ibn Ibrahim has narrated from his father from ibn abu 'Umayr from Hammad from al-Halabiy who has said the following:

"Abu 'Abd Allah, *'Alayhi al-Salam*, has said, 'Exchanging dry dates with fresh ones is not valid; dry dates are dry and fresh are not dry. When it dries it shrinks. Exchanging barley with wheat is also not valid unless it is in equal measures.' He (the Imam) said, 'Measuring is one and the same. It is detestable to exchange one *Qafiz* (a certain unit of measurement) of almond for two or one *Qafiz* of dates for two *Qafiz* of dates. However, it is valid to exchange one *Sa'* of wheat with two *Sa'* of dates and one *Sa'* of dates with two *Sa'* of raisins when they are different and in the form of dry fruits. It applies to foodstuff and fruits in the same manner.' Or that he (the Imam) said, 'It is not harmful if goods are exchanged as long as they are not exchanged in measurements and weighing.'"

H 8815, Ch. 79, h 13
A number of our people have narrated from Sahl ibn Ziyad and Ahmad ibn Muhammad from ibn Mahbub from Khalid ibn Jarir from abu al-Rabi' al-Shamiy who has said the following:

"Abu 'Abd Allah, *'Alayhi al-Salam*, disliked exchange of one *Qafiz* of almond with two *Qafiz* of almond and one *Qafiz* of dates with two *Qafiz* of dates.'"

H 8816, Ch. 79, h 14
A number of our people have narrated from Sahl ibn Ziyad and Ahmad ibn Muhammad from ibn Mahbub from 'Abd Allah ibn Sinan who has said the following:

"This is concerning my question before abu 'Abd Allah, *'Alayhi al-Salam*, about the case of a man who makes an advance payment for oil to receive ghee. He (the Imam) said, 'It is not valid.'"

H 8817, Ch. 79, h 15
Al-Husayn ibn Muhammad has narrated from Mu'alla' ibn Muhammad from al-Washsha' from 'Abd Allah ibn Sinan who has said the following:

"I once heard abu 'Abd Allah, *'Alayhi al-Salam*, saying, 'It is not valid for a man to make advance payment in the form of ghee to receive oil and vice versa.'"

H 8818, Ch. 79, h 16
Ibn Mahbub has narrated from abu Ayyub from Sama'ah who has said the following:

"Once abu 'Abd Allah, *'Alayhi al-Salam*, was asked about the exchange of grape with raisins and he (the Imam) replied, 'It is not permissible unless it is in equal measures.' I asked about exchange of dates and raisins. He (the Imam) said, 'It must be in equal measures.'"

H 8819, Ch. 79, h 17
In another Hadith through the same chain of narrators as that of the previous Hadith it is narrated that exchange of two different kinds of goods at the same time is not harmful.'"

H 8820, Ch. 79, h 18

Muhammad ibn Yahya has narrated from Ahmad ibn Muhammad from ibn Mahbub from Khalid from abu al-Rabi' who has said the following:

"This is concerning my question before abu 'Abd Allah, *'Alayhi al-Salam*, about dry dates and fresh dates exchanged in equal measures. He (the Imam) said, 'It is not harmful.' I then asked him (the Imam) about cooked juice and uncooked one exchanged in equal measures. He (the Imam) said, 'It is not harmful.'"

Chapter 80 - Exchange of Animals for Cloth or Other Items of Goods

H 8821, Ch. 80, h 1

Ali ibn Ibrahim has narrated from his father from ibn abu 'Umayr and Muhammad ibn 'Isma'il has narrated from al-Fadl ibn Shadhan from Safwan ibn Yahya and ibn abu 'Umayr from Jamil from Zurarah who has said the following:

"Abu Ja'far, *'Alayhi al-Salam*, has said, 'The exchange of one camel for two camels, one stumper for two at the same time is not harmful.'"

H 8822, Ch. 80, h 2

A number of our people have narrated from Ahmad ibn Muhammad from ibn abu 'Abd Allah al-Barqiy in a marfu' manner from 'Abd al-Rahman ibn abu 'Abd Allah who has said the following:

"This is concerning my question before abu 'Abd Allah, *'Alayhi al-Salam*, about the case of exchanging yarns for expanded fabrics while the yarn is heavier than fabrics in weight. He (the Imam) said, 'It is not harmful.'"

H 8823, Ch. 80, h 3

Muhammad ibn Yahya has narrated from 'Abd Allah ibn Muhammad from Ali ibn al-Hakam from Aban ibn 'Abd al-Rahman ibn abu 'Abd Allah who has said the following:

"This is concerning my question before abu 'Abd Allah, *'Alayhi al-Salam*, about exchanging one slave for two slaves and a slave for a slave and some dirhams. He (the Imam) said, 'It is not harmful in the case of all animals if it (the deal) is simultaneous.'"

H 8824, Ch. 80, h 4

Abu Ali al-Ash'ariy has narrated from al-Hassan ibn Ali al-Kufiy from 'Uthman ibn 'Isa from Sa'id ibn Yasar who has said the following:

"This is concerning my question before abu 'Abd Allah, *'Alayhi al-Salam*, about exchanging one camel for two camels in a hand in hand transaction and on credit. He (the Imam) said, 'Yes, it is permissible if you name it in terms of age, Jadh'ayn or Thaniyayn (kinds of camels in terms of age). He (the Imam) then commanded me to strike out the word 'al-Nisyah' (on credit perhaps because of Taqiyyah).

H 8825, Ch. 80, h 5

Ali ibn Ibrahim has narrated from his father from ibn abu Najran from 'Asim ibn Humayd from Muhammad ibn Qays who has said the following:

"Abu Ja'far, *'Alayhi al-Salam*, has said, 'The sale of one grown up camel in exchange for ten fetuses of camel to be born is not valid.'"

H 8826, Ch. 8, h 6

Al-Husayn from Muhammad has narrated from Mu'alla' ibn Muhammad from those whom he has mentioned from Aban from Muhammad who has said the following:

"Abu 'Abd Allah, *'Alayhi al-Salam*, has said, 'In the exchange of foodstuff of different kinds or other things with different quantities is not harmful in a hand in hand transaction but it is not valid on credit.'"

H 8827, Ch. 80, h 7

Muhammad ibn Yahya has narrated from Ahmad ibn Muhammad from Muhammad ibn Yahya from Ghiyath ibn Ibrahim who has said the following:

"Abu 'Abd Allah, *'Alayhi al-Salam*, has said that 'Amir al-Mu'minin, *'Alayhi al-Salam*, disliked exchange of meat for animals."

H 8828, Ch. 80, h 8

Muhammad ibn Yahya and others have narrated from Muhammad Ahmad from Ayyub ibn Nuh from al-'Abbas ibn 'Amir from Dawud ibn al-Husayn from Mansur who has said the following:

"I once asked him (the Imam), *'Alayhi al-Salam*, about exchange of one sheep for two sheep, one egg for two eggs. He (the Imam) said, 'It is not harmful as long as it is not in measures and weighing.'"

H 8829, Ch. 80, h 9

Humayd ibn Ziyad has narrated from al-Hassan ibn Muhammad from Ja'far ibn Sama'ah from Aban ibn 'Uthman from 'Isma'il ibn al-Fadl who has said the following:

"This is concerning my question before abu 'Abd Allah, *'Alayhi al-Salam*, about the case of a man who says to another man, 'Send your sheep and camels to be kept and when they give birth, if you like, I will exchange their male with female or vice versa.' He (the Imam) said, 'It is a detestable act unless the exchange takes place after they give birth and he knows them, which is which.'"

Chapter 81 - Exchange of Various Goods for Other Items of Goods

H 8830, Ch. 81, h 1

Ali ibn Ibrahim has narrated from his narrators whom he has mentioned the following:

"Exchange of gold for gold, silver for silver by weight in equal quantities is balanced. One does not have preference over the other. Silver can be exchanged for gold and gold can be exchanged for silver as you like in a hand in hand transaction and it is not harmful but it is not lawful on credit. Gold and silver can be sold in exchange for other things which are exchanged by weighing or measuring or numbering in a hand in hand transaction, and on credit all of such deals are not harmful. Things exchanged by measure or weight which are of the same origin do not have any preference over the other in measuring or weighing. If they are of different origins and are of things measured, it is not harmful to exchange two for one in a hand in hand deal but it is *Makruh* (detestable) on credit. Things of different origin which are exchanged by weight can be exchanged two for one in a hand in hand deal but on credit is *Makruh* (detestable). The exchange of things measured for what is weighed is not harmful in a hand in hand deal and on credit as well. The exchange of things

171

numbered and not measured or weighed is not harmful if it is two for one in a hand in hand deal but it is *Makruh* (detestable) on credit.

"He (Ali ibn Ibrahim) has said that this is if the origin is the same. If the origin of things numbered is different, then, it is not harmful to exchange two for one in a hand in hand deal or on credit as well, it all is not harmful. The exchange of things numbered or not numbered for what is measured or weighed in a hand in hand transaction or on credit is not harmful at all. Of things of the same origin and measured or weighed if then something comes out that is not measured or weighed, it is not harmful to exchange them in a hand in hand deal but it is *Makruh* (detestable) on credit. It is because cotton and al-Kattan originally are weighed and its yarn is weighed but fabrics are not weighed so cotton has no preference over yarn and its origin is one; so it is not valid unless it is in equal quantities by the same weight. When fabric is made out of it then in a hand in hand deal it is valid. In the case of fabrics it is valid to exchange one cloth for two cloths even though its origin is one in a hand in hand deal but it is *Makruh* (detestable) on credit. If it is cotton and al-Kattan then it is not harmful to exchange two for one in a hand in hand deal and it is *Makruh* on credit. If it is fabric of cotton and al-Kattan, it is not harmful to exchange two for one in a hand in hand deal or on credit; both deals are permissible. It is not harmful to exchange cotton and al-Kattan for wool in a hand in hand deal and on credit. The exchange of things from animals is not harmful if it is two for one, even if of one origin, in a hand in hand deal but it is *Makruh* (detestable) on credit. If the animals are of different origins it is not harmful to exchange two for one in a hand and hand deal but it is *Makruh* on credit. If animals are exchanged for goods and you take delivery of animal and leave the goods on credit, it is not harmful. If you take delivery of the goods and leave the animal it is *Makruh* (detestable). It is not harmful if you sell the animal in exchange for animal in addition with dirham also or goods. If you take delivery of animal and leave dirham on credit or one house for two houses, one *Jirib* of land for two *Jirib* of land it is not harmful in a hand in hand deal but it is *Makruh* (detestable) on credit.

"He (Ali ibn Ibrahim) has said, 'In the case of goods exchanged by measuring or weighing standard is the one which is common, not a special one, such as if a people measure meat and almonds it is not taken as standard because originally meat is weighed and almonds are counted in numbers.'""

(According to Mir`at al-'Uqul the above is fatwa of Ali ibn Ibrahim or his Shaykhs which is very strange to happen from people like him)

Chapter 82 - Selling Goods by Numbers and Estimate and Unknown Items

H 8831, Ch. 82, h 1
Ali ibn Ibrahim has narrated from his father from ibn abu 'Umayr from Hammad from al-Halabiy who has said the following:

"Abu 'Abd Allah, *'Alayhi al-Salam*, has said, 'In the case of foodstuff of known measurement venturous estimation is not valid and it is of undesirable matters in the case of foodstuff.'"

H 8832, Ch. 82, h 2
Muhammad ibn Yahya has narrated from Muhammad ibn al-Husayn from Safwan from Ya'qub ibn Shu'ayb who has said the following:

"This is concerning my question before abu 'Abd Allah, *'Alayhi al-Salam*, about the case of a man to whom another man owes one hundred *kur* of dates and he has palm trees. He comes and says, 'Give to me your palm trees for what you owe to me.' It seemed as if he (the Imam) disliked it. I then asked about two men who have palm trees. One of them says to the other, 'You can take the trees for such and such amount and give to me one-half more or less or I take the trees with the same condition. He (the Imam) said, 'It is not harmful.'"

H 8833, Ch. 82, h 3
Ali ibn Ibrahim has narrated from his father from ibn abu 'Umayr from Hammad from al-Halabiy who has said the following:

"Abu 'Abd Allah, *'Alayhi al-Salam*, was asked about walnuts that cannot be counted. The owner weighs a certain measurement, then counts the rest according to that measurement. He (the Imam) said, 'It is not harmful.'"

H 8834, Ch. 82, h 4
Humayd ibn Ziyad has narrated from al-Hassan ibn Muhammad ibn Sama'ah from those whom he has mentioned from Aban ibn 'Uthman from 'Abd al-Rahman ibn abu 'Abd Allah who has said the following:

"This is concerning my question before abu 'Abd Allah, *'Alayhi al-Salam*, about the case of a man who buys something which is sold by measure or weight and takes it according to that standard. He (the Imam) said, 'It is not harmful.'"

H 8835, Ch. 82, h 5
Muhammad ibn 'Isma'il has narrated from al-Fadl ibn Shadhan from Safwan ibn Yahya from 'Is ibn al-Qasim who has said the following:

"This is concerning my question before abu 'Abd Allah, *'Alayhi al-Salam*, about the case of a man who has cattle; if he can sell their milk without measurement. He (the Imam) said, 'Yes, he can do so until it stops (coming through the udder) or something similar.'"

H 8836, Ch. 82, h 6
Muhammad ibn Yahya has narrated from Ahmad ibn Muhammad from al-Husayn ibn Sa'id from his brother al-Hassan from Zurarah from Sama'ah who has said the following:

"I once asked him (the Imam), *'Alayhi al-Salam*, if milk which still is in the udder can be purchased. He (the Imam) said, 'No, until it is milked in *al-Sukurrujah* (a bowl) and the seller can say, "Buy what is in *al-Sukurruajah* and that which is in the udder for the named price" and if there is nothing in the udder that which is in *al-Sukurruajah* is what is sold.'"

H 8837, Ch. 82, h 7
Muhammad ibn Yahya has narrated from Muhammad ibn al-Husayn from Safwan from abu Sa'id from 'Abd al-Malik ibn 'Amr who has said the following:

"This is concerning my question before abu 'Abd Allah, *'Alayhi al-Salam*, about buying a hundred *Rawiyah* (a certain unit of measurement) of oil, then weigh one or two *Rawiyah* then accept the rest according to such weighing. He (the Imam) said, 'It is not harmful.'"

H 8838, Ch. 82, h 8
Muhammad ibn Yahya has narrated from Ahmad ibn Muhammad from ibn Mahbub Ibrahim al-Karkhiy who has said the following:
"This is concerning my question before abu 'Abd Allah, *'Alayhi al-Salam*, about the case of a man who buys wool of a hundred sheep from another man and what is in their womb for so amount of dirham. He (the Imam) said, 'It is not harmful; in case there is nothing in their womb he has his capital in the wool.'"

H 8839, Ch. 82, h 9
Ahmad ibn Muhammad has narrated from ibn Mahbub from Rifa'ah al-Nakhkhas who has said the following:
"I once asked abu al-Hassan, Musa, *'Alayhi al-Salam*, if my buying a runaway slave-girl from a people and paying them the price but myself search to find her, is valid. He (the Imam) said, 'It is not valid unless you buy from them a certain other item, like cloths or so and say to them, "I buy your so slave-girl and this item of goods for so and so amount of dirham." This is permissible.'"

H 8840, Ch. 82, h 10
A number of our people have narrated from Sahl ibn Ziyad from Muhammad ibn al-Hassan ibn Shammun from al-Assam from Misma' who has said the following:
"Abu 'Abd Allah, *'Alayhi al-Salam*, has said that 'Amir al-Mu'minin, *'Alayhi al-Salam*, prohibited buying the net of the fisherman by saying, 'Spread your net and whatever comes in is mine for so and so amount.'"

H 8841, Ch. 82, h 11
Sahl ibn Ziyad has narrated from Ahmad ibn Muhammad from ibn abu Nasr from certain persons of his people who has said the following:
"Abu 'Abd Allah, *'Alayhi al-Salam*, has said, 'If there is a bunch of trees without reeds with a few fish taken out along with what is in the bunch of trees, it can (lawfully) be sold.'"

H 8842, Ch. 82, h 12
Muhammad ibn Yahya has narrated from 'Abd Allah ibn Muhammad from Ali ibn al-Hakam from and Humayd ibn Ziyad from al-Hassan ibn Muhammad ibn Sama'ah from more than one person all from Aban ibn 'Uthman from 'Isma'il ibn al-Fadl al-Hashimiy who has said the following:
"About the case of a man who accepts in a transaction, in exchange for what he pays, the taxes due on non-Muslim taxpayers, taxes on palm trees, on groves, on birds and does not know if any such items exist or not, abu 'Abd Allah, *'Alayhi al-Salam*, has said, 'If he knows that at least one thing of it exists that he can have, he can buy and accept the deal with it.'"

H 8843, Ch. 82, h 13
Ali ibn Ibrahim has narrated from ibn Faddal from ibn Bukayr from a man from a certain persons of his people who has said the following:

"This is concerning my question before abu 'Abd Allah, *'Alayhi al-Salam*, about the case of a man who buys lime. He weighs a certain portion then accepts the rest without measurement. He (the Imam) said, 'He can accept all of it with his certification or measure all of it.'"

Chapter 83 - Buying and Selling Goods

H 8844, Ch. 83, h 1

Ali ibn Ibrahim has narrated from his father from ibn abu 'Umayr from Hammad ibn 'Uthman from al-Halabiy who has said the following:

"This is concerning my question before abu 'Abd Allah, *'Alayhi al-Salam*, about the case of a man who buys clothes without condition; then dislikes them and returns to the seller who does not accept the return without a certain amount of penalty. He (the Imam) said, 'He cannot charge any penalty but if he did it because of ignorance and then sold it to someone for more, he must return the extra to the first owner."

H 8845, Ch. 83, h 2

Ali ibn Ibrahim has narrated from his father from Hammad ibn 'Isa from Hariz from Muhammad ibn Muslim who has said the following:

"About the case of a man who says to another man, 'Sell my cloth for ten dirham, if you sold for more, then the extra is for you.' He (the Imam) said, 'It is not harmful.'"

H 8846, Ch. 83, h 3

Muhammad ibn Yahya has narrated from Ahmad ibn Muhammad from Muhammad ibn 'Isma'il has narrated from al-Fadl ibn Shadhan from abu al-Sabbah al-Kinaniy who has said the following:

"About the case of a man who carries goods for the people of a market who set a price on the goods and say, 'If you sold for more, the extra is for you', abu 'Abd Allah, *'Alayhi al-Salam*, has said, 'It is not harmful but he cannot sell it for them on the basis of profit sharing.'"

H 8847, Ch. 83, h 4

A number of our people have narrated from Ahmad ibn Muhammad from and Sahl ibn Ziyad from ibn Mahbub from abu Wallad from abu 'Abd Allah, *'Alayhi al-Salam*, and others from abu Ja'far, *'Alayhi al-Salam*, who has said the following:

"Abu Ja'far, *'Alayhi al-Salam*, has said, 'Brokerage fee is not unlawful; he only buys for people every now and then for a known amount. He in fact works on hire.'"

H 8848, Ch. 83, h 5

Humayd ibn Ziyad has narrated from Muhammad ibn Sama'ah from more than one person from Aban ibn 'Uthman from 'Abd al-Rahman ibn abu 'Abd Allah who has said the following:

"This is concerning my question before abu 'Abd Allah, *'Alayhi al-Salam*, about the case of a broker who buys for a fee. Notes are given to him with the condition that he brings the merchandise and the buyer accepts whatever he likes and leaves the rest. He then brings the goods and says, 'Take what you like and leave what you dislike.' He (the Imam) said, 'It is lawful.'"

H 8849, Ch. 83, h 6

Ali ibn Ibrahim has narrated from his father from 'Isma'il ibn Marrar from Yunus from Mu'awiyah ibn 'Ammar who has said the following:

"This is concerning my question before abu 'Abd Allah, *'Alayhi al-Salam*, about the case of a man who buys sacks made in Hirat, and in al-Quhiy. A man then buys from him ten cloths with the condition that he can choose every cloth, for a certain amount of profit, five or less or more. He (the Imam) said, 'I do not like this sale. Consider if he cannot find in choosing anything other than five cloths and finds the rest the same.' Imam's son, 'Isma'il said, 'They have set a condition on him to take ten pieces' and he repeated it several times. He (the Imam) said, 'He has set up a condition to take the best. Consider if there is nothing more than five cloths and he finds the rest the same.' He (the Imam) said, 'I do not like this deal.' He (the Imam) disliked it because of one party's suffering loss.'"

H 8850, Ch. 83, h 7

Muhammad ibn Yahya has narrated from certain persons of his people from al-Husayn ibn al-Hassan from Hammad who have said the following:

"Abu 'Abd Allah, *'Alayhi al-Salam*, has said, 'It is undesirable to buy something with dinar which is other than (a particular) dirham because he does not know the value of dinar in relation to the dirham.'"

Chapter 84 - Selling for Capital with an Additional Certain Percentage Profit (*Murabahah*) or a Certain Amount of Profit with Mention of Percentage Ratio

H 8851, Ch. 84, h 1

A number of our people have narrated from Ahmad ibn Muhammad from Ali ibn al-Hakam from Muhammad ibn Aslam from abu Hamzah who has said the following:

"I once asked abu Ja'far, *'Alayhi al-Salam*, about the case of a man who buys goods altogether for a certain price, then sets a price for each piece proportionately until all of his capital is covered; if he can sell it in the form of *Murabahah* (capital plus a certain percent profit). He (the Imam) said, 'No, he cannot do so until he makes it clear that the item has a fixed price.'"

H 8852, Ch. 84, h 2

Ali ibn Ibrahim has narrated from his father from ibn abu 'Umayr from Hammad from al-Halabiy who has said the following:

"Abu 'Abd Allah, *'Alayhi al-Salam*, has said that once goods for my father came from Egypt. He (the Imam) prepared food and invited the merchants. They said, 'We buy from you *Be dah dawazdah*. He (the Imam) asked, 'How much is that?' They replied, 'It is two thousand on every ten thousand.' My father said to them, 'I sell this to you for twelve thousand.' He (the Imam) sold it to them in the form of *Musawamah* (fixed price regardless of the capital)."

H 8853, Ch. 84, h 3

Muhammad ibn Yahya has narrated from Ahmad ibn Muhammad from al-Husayn ibn Sa'id from al-Nadr ibn Suwayd from al-Qasim ibn Sulayman from Jarrah al-Mada'iniy who has said the following:

"Abu 'Abd Allah, *'Alayhi al-Salam*, has said, 'I do not like the sale in the form of *dah, yaz dah*, and *dah dawazdah* but I sell for so and so (fixed price).'"

H 8854, Ch. 84, h 4
Al-Husayn from Muhammad has narrated from Mu'alla' ibn Muhammad from al-Hassan ibn Ali from Aban ibn 'Uthman from Muhammad who has said the following:

"Abu 'Abd Allah, *'Alayhi al-Salam*, has said, 'I do not like the sale of ten for eleven and ten for twelve and so on. I sell for so and so (fixed price) in the form of *Musawamah* (fixed price regardless of capital).' He (the Imam) then said, 'Once goods from Egypt came for me and I disliked selling it in that way (*Murabahah* (capital plus profit)) and it seemed greatly heavy, so I sold it in the form of *Musawamah* (fixed price regardless of capital).'"

H 8855, Ch. 84, h 5
Al-Husayn from Muhammad has narrated from Muhammad ibn Ahmad al-Nahdiy from Muhammad ibn Khalid from 'Isma'il ibn 'Abd al-Khaliq who has said the following:

"I once said to abu 'Abd Allah, *'Alayhi al-Salam*, 'We send dirham to Ahwaz where the price of dirham is different. With it goods are bought for us. We then wait until the goods are sold, the difference of price of dirham is deducted from it, if we sell. Is it necessary for us to mention the difference in prices in selling in the form of *Murabahah* (capital plus profit) on our part (of such difference)?' He (the Imam) said, 'No, you must mention it if it is in the form of *Murabahah* (capital plus profit), but if it is in the form of *Musawamah* (fixed price regardless of capital) then it is lawful.'"

H 8856, Ch. 84, h 6
Muhammad ibn Yahya has narrated from Ahmad ibn Muhammad from Muhammad ibn 'Isa from Yahya ibn al-Hajjaj who has said the following:

"This is concerning my question before abu 'Abd Allah, *'Alayhi al-Salam*, about the case of a man who said to me, 'Buy this cloth and this stumper from me, then in the form of *'Aynah* sell them to me (sell them to me and I will give you a profit of so and so amount).' He (the Imam) said, 'It is lawful.' He (the Imam) said, 'He should buy it but you must not make binding on him to sell before he makes it binding or you buy it.'"

H 8857, Ch. 84, h 7
Muhammad ibn Yahya has narrated from Muhammad ibn al-Husayn from Safwan from Ayyub ibn Rashid from Muyassir Bayya' al-Zuttiy who has said the following:

"I once said to abu 'Abd Allah, *'Alayhi al-Salam*, 'I buy goods with deferred payment for a certain time. A man comes to me and says, 'What is the price.' I say, 'It is so and so amount.' I then sell it to him with a certain amount of profit. He (the Imam) said, 'When you sell it in the form of *Murabahah* (capital plus profit) he has a share in the value of deferred payment also just as you have.' I then said *Istirja'* (the expression, 'To Allah we belong and to Him we all return') and said, 'We are destroyed.' He (the Imam) said, 'Because of what?' I replied, 'There is no cloth on earth that I buy without *Murabahah* (capital plus profit) and they are bought from me even if I reduce the capital to say it is for so and so amount. When he (the Imam) saw my difficulties he (the Imam) said, 'Do you want that I open a door for you to make things easier for you? Say, "It has costed me so and so and I sell it for so and so price;" do not say I sell it in the form of *Murabahah* (capital plus profit).'"

H 8858, Ch. 84, h 8
A number of our people have narrated from Sahl ibn Ziyad from Ali ibn Asbat from Asbat ibn Salim who has said the following:
"This is concerning my question before abu 'Abd Allah, *'Alayhi al-Salam*, about the case in which we buy a bundle of a hundred or so cloths in which there are good and bad ones *'dast shumar'* (farsi word for mixed). A man comes and takes ninety for the bundle with profit of one dirham for each. Is it proper for us to sell the rest as just we sold? He (the Imam) said, 'No, unless he alone buys the cloth.'"

Chapter 85 - Advance Payment in the Transaction of Goods

H 8859, Ch. 85, h 1
Ali ibn Ibrahim has narrated from his father from ibn abu 'Umayr from Jamil ibn Darraj who has said the following:
"Abu 'Abd Allah, *'Alayhi al-Salam*, has said, 'Advance payment to receive goods at an appointed time in the future is lawful if the length and width are fully described.'"

H 8860, Ch. 85, h 2
Muhammad ibn Yahya has narrated from Ahmad ibn Muhammad from 'Uthman ibn 'Isa from Sama'ah who has said the following:
"I once asked him (the Imam), *'Alayhi al-Salam*, about advance payment to receive goods on a date in future which is payment in advance for silk or goods made in the location where you live. He (the Imam) said, 'Yes, it is lawful if the time is known.'"

H 8861, Ch. 85, h 3
Ali ibn Ibrahim has narrated from his father from 'Isma'il ibn Marrar from Yunus from Mu'awiyah ibn 'Ammar who has said the following:
"Abu 'Abd Allah, *'Alayhi al-Salam*, has said, 'Advance payment to receive goods in future is lawful if the length and width is made known.'"

Chapter 86 - Selling an Item of Merchandise Which the Seller Does Not Yet Have in His Possession

H 8862, Ch. 86, h 1
A number of our people have narrated from Ahmad ibn Muhammad from Safwan from Musa ibn Bakr from Hadid ibn Hakim al-Azdiy who has said the following:
"This is concerning my question before abu 'Abd Allah, *'Alayhi al-Salam*, about the case of a man who comes to me and asks me for certain goods at the price of ten thousand dirham or less or more but I have only what is worth one thousand dirham. I then borrow from my neighbor and take from this and that person to complete the amount and sell to him; then buy from him or ask someone else to buy from him so that I then can return to the people from whom I had borrowed. He (the Imam) said, 'It is lawful.'"

H 8863, Ch. 86, h 2

Ahmad ibn Muhammad has narrated from Muhammad ibn 'Isa from Mansur from Hisham ibn Salim who has said the following:

"Once abu 'Abd Allah, *'Alayhi al-Salam*, was asked about the case of a man who makes a sale for an appointed time without having the merchandise with him and guarantees the sale for the buyer. He (the Imam) said, 'It is not unlawful.'".

H 8864, Ch. 86, h 3

Ahmad ibn Muhammad has narrated from Ali ibn al-Hakam from abu Hamzah who has said the following:

I once asked abu Ja'far, *'Alayhi al-Salam*, about the case of a man who has bought certain goods which are not exchanged by measurement or weighing; if he can sell them before receiving delivery. He (the Imam) said, 'It is lawful.'"

H 8865, Ch. 86, h 4

Ali ibn Ibrahim has narrated from his father from ibn abu 'Umayr from 'Abd al-Rahman ibn al-Hajjaj who has said the following:

"I once said to abu 'Abd Allah, *'Alayhi al-Salam*, 'A man comes to me and asks for certain goods. I contract with him for a certain profit, then buy it to sell to him. He (the Imam) asked, 'Does he have the choice to take or leave it?' I replied, 'Yes, he does.' He (the Imam) said, 'It is lawful.' I then said, 'There are those among us who destroy it.'. He (the Imam) asked, 'Why is that?' I replied, 'He sells what is not with him.' He (the Imam) asked, 'What does he say about advance payment to receive goods in future in which case he sells what is not with him?' I replied, 'Yes, it happens.' He (the Imam) said, 'It is valid because they call it advance payment. My father would say, "It is lawful to sell all kinds of goods that you can find at the time you sell."'"

H 8866, Ch. 86, h 5

A number of our people have narrated from Ahmad ibn Muhammad from al-Husayn ibn Sa'id from Fadalah ibn Ayyub from Mu'awiyah ibn 'Ammar who has said the following:

"This is concerning my question before abu 'Abd Allah, *'Alayhi al-Salam*, about the case of a man who comes to me and asks for certain goods of silk but I do not have anything as such, 'Consider if he finds a better deal than this; can he change and go for that deal instead of the deal with you and can the same thing apply to you also?' I replied, 'Yes, - that can happen.' He (the Imam) said, 'It then is lawful.'"

H 8867, Ch. 86, h 6

Ali ibn Ibrahim has narrated from his father from ibn abu 'Umayr from Yahya ibn al-Hajjaj from Khalid ibn Najih who has said the following:

"I once said to abu 'Abd Allah, *'Alayhi al-Salam*, 'A man comes to me and says, "Buy this cloth and I give you so and so much profit."' He (the Imam) asked, 'Can he take or leave it if he so wants?' I replied, 'Yes, he can do so.' He (the Imam) said, 'It is lawful. It is statements that make it lawful as well as unlawful.'"

H 8868, Ch. 86, h 7

Muhammad ibn Yahya has narrated from Ahmad ibn Muhammad from al-Husayn ibn Sa'id from al-Nadr ibn Suwayd from 'Abd Allah ibn Sinan who has said the following:

"Abu 'Abd Allah, *'Alayhi al-Salam*, has said, 'It is lawful for a man to sell goods which are not with him in the form of *Musawamah* (fixed price regardless of capital), then buy for him the goods he demands and make it necessary for yourself thereafter to ask him to sell it to you.'"

H 8869, Ch. 86, h 8

Ali ibn Ibrahim has narrated from his father from ibn abu 'Umayr from Hammad from al-Halabiy who has said the following:

"This is concerning my question before abu 'Abd Allah, *'Alayhi al-Salam*, about the case of a man who makes a sale and the merchandise is not with him for an appointed time but he guarantees the sale. He (the Imam) said, 'It is not unlawful.'"

H 8870, Ch. 86, h 9

Certain persons of our people have narrated from Ali ibn Asbat from abu Mukhallad al-Sarraj who has said the following:

"Once, we were with abu 'Abd Allah, *'Alayhi al-Salam*, when Mu'attib came in and said, 'There are two people at the door.' He (the Imam) said, 'Bring them inside.' The two men came inside and one of them said, 'I am a butcher. Can I sell the skin before I slaughter the sheep?' He (the Imam) said, 'It is not unlawful. However, say from the sheep is from so and so land.'"

Chapter 87 - Excellence of Excellent Merchandise to Sell

H 8871, Ch. 87, h 1

Abu Ali al-Ash'ariy has narrated from Muhammad ibn 'Abd al-Jabbar from certain persons of our people from Marwak ibn 'Ubayd from those whom he has mentioned who has said the following:

"Abu 'Abd Allah, *'Alayhi al-Salam*, has said, 'There are two expressions for each of good and bad merchandise: To the owner of good merchandise it is said, "May Allah grant you blessings and the one who sold it to you." To the owner of bad merchandise it is said, "Allah does not bless you and the one who sold it to you."'"

H 8872, Ch. 87, h 2

Muhammad ibn Yahya has narrated from Ahmad ibn Muhammad from Ya'qub ibn Yazid from al-Washsha' from 'Asem ibn Hamid who has said the following:

"Once, abu 'Abd Allah, *'Alayhi al-Salam*, asked me, 'How do you make a living?' I replied, 'I sell foodstuff.' He (the Imam) said to me, 'Buy those of good quality and sell of the good quality; if you sell that of good quality it is said, "Allah places blessings in you and the one who sold to you."'"

Chapter 88 - Merchandise Sold on Credit Is Purchased Back for Cash at a Lower Price Called (*'Aynah*)

(Note: Transactions in the form of *'Aynah* are like rescheduling a loan to extend payback time as in the case of Ahadith 10 and 11 below, or increasing the amount of loan on the debtor, extend the payback time and to generate cash, at the same time, for the creditor, as in Hadith 7 below, like a creditor's acting as cosigner to buy something from a third party on credit payable by the debtor then sell to a party for cash so that the debtor can pay the generated cash to his creditor of the previous loan.)

H 8873, Ch. 88, h 1

A number of our people have narrated from Ahmad ibn Muhammad ibn 'Isa from ibn abu 'Umayr from Hafs ibn Suwqah from al-Husayn ibn al-Mundhir who has said the following:

"I once said to abu 'Abd Allah, *'Alayhi al-Salam*, 'A man comes to me and asks for *'Aynah*. I then buy for him the merchandise in the manner of *Murabahah* (capital plus profit) then sell it to him, then buy it from him at the same place. He (the Imam) said, 'If he has the choice to sell if he likes or not to sell and you also have the choice to buy if you like or do not buy if you do not like, it is not unlawful.' I then said, 'People of the Masjid think it is not valid. They say, "If he brings it after few months it is valid."' He (the Imam) said, 'This is making early what is later and late what is early and it is not unlawful.'"

H 8874, Ch. 88, h 2

Ahmad ibn Muhammad has narrated from Ali ibn al-Hakam from 'Isma'il ibn 'Abd al-Khaliq who has said the following:

"I once asked abu al-Hassan, *'Alayhi al-Salam*, about *'Aynah* saying, 'Our merchants in general these days provide *'Aynah*. I like to explain how it is done. He (the Imam) said, 'Go on and explain.' I said, 'A man comes who works in *Musawamah* (fixed price regardless of capital) who wants merchandise on the basis of *Musawamah* but we do not have any goods and he says, "I give you a profit of *dah yazdah*" and I say "I give *dah dawazdah*." He continues bargaining and we also do so. When we complete I say to him, "Which merchandise you want me to buy for you?" He says, "I like silk because we do not find anything else less depreciating than silk." I agree and form a contract without selling.' He (the Imam) said, 'Is it possible that if you did not like you can refuse to give him and if he does not like he does not take from you?' I replied, 'Yes, it is possible. I then go and buy for him that silk and then bargain as much as I can and then I come to my home then sell it to him perhaps with an increase a little more than what is contracted, or perhaps give him for what is contracted, and perhaps we become difficult then nothing happens.

'Then if he buys from me he cannot find anyone else asking higher price than the one, from whom I bought it, to sell to him. He comes and takes the dirhams and gives it to him or perhaps he comes with an assignment on me.' He (the Imam) said, 'You must not give it to anyone else beside the owner of silk.' I then said, 'Perhaps the sale does not take place between us. I ask him and he agrees.' He (the Imam) said, 'Is it possible that if he likes, he does not do so and if you want you do not return?' I replied, 'Yes, it is possible. If he dies it is from my assets.' He (the Imam) said, 'It is lawful; if you do not violate the condition, then it is not unlawful.'"

H 8875, Ch. 88, h 3

Muhammad ibn Yahya has narrated from Ahmad ibn Muhammad from Ali ibn al-Hakam from Sayf ibn 'Amirah from Mansur ibn Hazim who has said the following:

"This is concerning my question before abu 'Abd Allah, *'Alayhi al-Salam*, about the case of a man who asks another man for a cloth on the basis of *'Aynah* and he says, 'I do not have it but take these dirhams and buy the cloth.' He takes the dirhams and buys a cloth as he wants, then comes to him so that he buys it from him. He (the Imam) said, 'Is it the case that if the cloth is lost it is from the assets of the one who gives dirham?' I replied, 'Yes, that is the case.' He (the Imam) asked, 'If it is possible that if he wants he buys it, if he does not want he does not buy, then it is not unlawful.'"

H 8876, Ch. 88, h 4

Ahmad ibn Muhammad has narrated from Ali ibn al-Hakam from Sayf ibn 'Amirah from abu Bakr al-Hadramiy who has said the following:

"This is concerning my question before abu 'Abd Allah, *'Alayhi al-Salam*, 'A man who is engaged in an *al-'Aynah* deal and the payment date has become due but he cannot find anything to pay back his debt; if he can arrange another al-*'Aynah* with the same creditor again.' He (the Imam) said, 'Yes, he can do so again.'"

H 8877, Ch. 88, h 5

Ahmad ibn Muhammad has narrated from ibn abu 'Umayr from Ali ibn 'Isma'il abu Bakr al-Hadramiy who has said the following:

"I once said to abu 'Abd Allah, *'Alayhi al-Salam*, 'A man owes me a certain amount of dirhams and he says, "Sell to me certain goods so I can pay what I owe to you." I then sell to him certain goods, then buy it from him and take what he owes me.' He (the Imam) said, 'It is not unlawful.'"

H 8878, Ch. 88, h 6

Muhammad ibn Yahya has narrated from Ahmad ibn Muhammad from Hanan ibn Sadir who has said the following:

"Once I was with abu 'Abd Allah, *'Alayhi al-Salam*, when Ja'far ibn Hanan asked him (the Imam), 'What do you say about al-*'Aynah* in the case of a man who sells certain goods to a man and says, "I sell to you *bah dah dawazdah* and *bah dah yazdah*?"' Abu 'Abd Allah, *'Alayhi al-Salam*, said, 'This is not valid. He must, however, say, "For all dirhams I give you so and so amount of dirham profit in the form of *Musawamah* (fixed price regardless of capital) in this deal;" then it is not unlawful.' He then asked, 'Can I make a deal in the form of *Musawamah* (fixed price regardless of capital) and I do not have any assets?' He (the Imam) said, 'It is not unlawful.'"

H 8879, Ch. 88, h 7

Ali ibn Ibrahim has narrated from his father from 'Abd Allah ibn al-Mughirah from 'Abd Allah ibn Sinan who has said the following:

"This is concerning my question before abu 'Abd Allah, *'Alayhi al-Salam*, about the case of a man who owes a certain amount of debts and he is a *Mu'sir* (unable to pay). Can I arrange for him to buy something from a man for an appointed time and guarantee in his favor so he can pay his debts (with the item just purchased for him) to me and then pay back what he owes? He (the Imam) said, 'It is lawful.'"

H 8880, Ch. 88, h 8

Abu Ali al-Ash'ariy has narrated from Muhammad ibn 'Abd al-Jabbar from Safwan ibn Yahya from Harun ibn Kharijah who has said the following:

"I once said to abu 'Abd Allah, *'Alayhi al-Salam*, 'I made an *al-'Aynah* deal with a man. I then asked him to pay back what he owes because of the deal. He replied, "I do not have anything to pay you back unless you arrange another *al-'Aynah* so I can pay you back."' He (the Imam) said, 'You can arrange another al-*'Aynah* for him so he can pay you back.'"

H 8881, Ch. 88, h 9

Muhammad ibn Yahya has narrated from Ahmad ibn Muhammad from Ali ibn Hadid from Muhammad ibn Ishaq ibn 'Ammar who has said the following:

"I once said to abu al-Hassan, *'Alayhi al-Salam*, 'Salsabil has asked me for a hundred thousand dirham which she will pay back with a ten thousand dirham profit. I gave her ninety thousand dirham loan with the sale of a cloth and something else worth a thousand dirham for ten thousand dirham (she now owes a total of one hundred thousand dirham).' He (the Imam) said, 'It is not unlawful.' In another Hadith it is said, 'It is not unlawful if you give her a hundred thousand and sell to her a cloth for ten thousand and write two contracts.'"

H 8882, Ch. 88, h 10

Abu Ali al-Ash'ariy has narrated from al-Hassan ibn 'Abd Allah from his uncle, Muhammad ibn 'Abd Allah from Muhammad ibn Ishaq ibn 'Ammar who has said the following:

"I once asked al-Rida', *'Alayhi al-Salam*, about the case of a man to whom someone owes a certain amount of goods and payback time becomes due. His party sells to him a pearl worth a hundred dirham for a thousand dirham and extends the payback time to another appointed time. He (the Imam) said, 'It is not unlawful. My father commanded me to do so and did such a deal.' He (the narrator) thinks that he had asked abu al-Hassan, *'Alayhi al-Salam*, about it and he (the Imam) had given a similar answer."

H 8883, Ch. 88, h 11

Muhammad ibn Yahya has narrated from Ahmad ibn Muhammad from ibn abu 'Umayr from Muhammad ibn Ishaq ibn 'Ammar who has said the following:

"I once asked abu al-Hassan, *'Alayhi al-Salam*, about the case of a man who owes me a certain amount of dirham and says to me, 'Extend the payback time and I will give you profit'. I then sell to him a gown worth a thousand dirham for ten thousand dirhams - or that he said, twenty thousand dirhams - and extend the payback time. He (the Imam) said, 'It is not unlawful.'"

H 8884, Ch. 88, h 12

Muhammad ibn Yahya has narrated from Ahmad ibn Muhammad from Ali ibn al-Hakam from 'Abd al-Malik ibn 'Utbah who has said the following:

"I once asked him (the Imam), *'Alayhi al-Salam*, about the case of a man with whom I like to arrange an *al-'Aynah*. He already owes me a certain amount of goods. He asks me for additional goods. Is it right to provide him additional goods and sell to him a pearl worth a hundred dirham for a thousand dirham and I say, 'I sell to you this pearl for a thousand dirham so I can extend the payback time for this and what you already owe to me up to so and so many months.' He (the Imam) said, 'It is not unlawful.'"

Chapter 89 - Merchandise Offered for Cash as Well as on Credit (Two Conditions in a Transaction)

H 8885, Ch. 89, h 1

Ali ibn Ibrahim has narrated from his father from ibn abu Najran from 'Asem ibn Hamid from Muhammad ibn Qays who has said the following:

"Abu Ja'far, *'Alayhi al-Salam*, has said that 'Amir al-Mu'minin has said, 'If one sells certain goods and says that its price in a hand in hand deal is so and so and in a deferred payment deal is so and so, so take which ever you like and makes it a package deal, he can only take what costs the least even if it is the deal with the deferred payment.' He (the Imam) said, 'If one finalizes a deal by the manner of *Musawamah* (fixed price regardless of capital) of immediate or deferred payment he must specify one of them before the package deal is final.'"

Chapter 90 - Finding Defect in Merchandise after the Sale

H 8886, Ch. 90, h 1

A number of our people have narrated from Ahmad ibn Muhammad from ibn abu 'Umayr from al-Hassan ibn 'Atiyyah from 'Umar ibn Yazid who has said the following:

"'Umar and I were in al-Madinah and 'Umar sold sacks made in Hirat, every cloth for so and so amount. They took them and divided among themselves but they found one defective piece and returned it. 'Umar said to them, 'I can pay you the price for which I sold to you.' He said, 'No, we take from you the price of the cloth.' 'Umar mentioned this before abu 'Abd Allah, *'Alayhi al-Salam*, and he (the Imam) said, 'He must do so (as he is asked to do).'" (The pronoun 'He' can apply to either one of seller or buyer but its applying to the buyer has greater support in the principles of the system of Shari'ah)

H 8887, Ch. 90, h 2

Ali ibn Ibrahim has narrated from his father from ibn abu 'Umayr from Jamil from certain persons of our people who has said the following:

"I once asked one of the two Imam, (abu Ja'far or abu 'Abd Allah), *'Alayhim al-Salam*, about the case of a man who buys cloths or goods and finds defects in it. He (the Imam) said, 'If the item is exactly as it was, he can return and get back what he has paid and if the cloth is cut or stitched or dyed he must pay for the loss.'"

H 8888, Ch. 90, h 3

A number of our people have narrated from Ahmad ibn Muhammad from al-Husayn ibn Sa'id from Fadalah from Musa ibn Bakr from Zurarah who has said the following:

"Abu Ja'far, *'Alayhi al-Salam*, has said, 'Whoever buys something and finds defect in it or injuries that does not get well which was not apparent to him (when buying) and he then does some changes in it after taking delivery then finds out about the defect or injury, he must approve the sale and ask for the refund of the cost of the defect or injury from the price of the item (he has paid).'"

Chapter 91 - Buying on Credit

H 8889, Ch. 91, h 1

A number of our people have narrated from Sahl ibn Ziyad from Ahmad ibn Muhammad from who has said the following:

"I once said to abu al-Hassan, *'Alayhi al-Salam*, 'I like to travel to certain areas of the mountains.' He (the Imam) said, 'This year people will not be able to avoid difficult times.' I then said, 'I pray to Allah to keep my soul in service for your cause, if we sell to them goods on credit with deferred payment it is more profitable. He (the Imam) said, 'Sell to them for one year deferred payment.' I asked, 'Can we defer payment for two years?' He (the Imam) said, 'Yes, you can do so.' I then asked, 'Can we defer payment for three years?' He (the Imam) said, 'No, you cannot do so.'"

H 8890, Ch. 91, h 2

Ali ibn Ibrahim has narrated from his father from ibn abu Najran from 'Asim ibn Hamid from Muhammad ibn Qays who has said the following:

"Abu Ja'far, *'Alayhi al-Salam*, has said that 'Amir al-Mu'minin, Ali, *'Alayhi al-Salam*, in the case of a man who was ordered by certain persons to ask to sell to them a camel and they had agreed to pay more if it was on credit with deferred payment, and he asked to sell to them a camel and certain ones of them were with him, judged to bar him from charging them more over the cash price with deferred payment.'"

H 8891, Ch. 91, h 3

Ali has narrated from his father Muhammad ibn 'Isma'il has narrated from al-Fadl ibn Shadhan all from ibn abu 'Umayr from Hisham ibn al-Hakam who has said the following:

"About the case of a man who buys certain goods with deferred payment for an appointed time, abu Ja'far, *'Alayhi al-Salam*, has said, 'He cannot buy it in the manner of *Murabahah* (capital plus profit) without deferment for an appointed time which is agreed upon; and if he sells in the manner of *Murabahah* (capital plus profit) without informing the party, then the one who has bought is entitled for a deferment of similar duration.'"

H 8892, Ch. 91, h 4

Muhammad ibn Yahya has narrated from Muhammad ibn al-Husayn from Muhammad ibn 'Isma'il from Mansur ibn Yunus from Shu'ayb ibn al-Haddad from Bashshar ibn Yasar who has said the following:

"This is concerning my question before abu 'Abd Allah, *'Alayhi al-Salam*, about the case of a man who sells goods on credit with deferred payment, then buys them from the party to whom he has sold. He (the Imam) said, 'It is not unlawful.' I then asked, 'Can I buy my own goods?' He (the Imam) said, 'It is not your property, your cow or your sheep.'"

Abu Ali al-Ash'ariy has narrated from Muhammad ibn 'Abd al-Jabbar from Safwan from Shu'ayb al-Haddad from Bashshar ibn Yasar from abu 'Abd Allah, *'Alayhi al-Salam*, a similar Hadith.

Chapter 92 - Buying Slaves

H 8893, Ch. 92, h 1
A number of our people have narrated from Sahl ibn Ziyad from ibn Mahbub from ibn Ri'ab who has said the following:

"I once asked abu al-Hassan, Musa, *'Alayhi al-Salam*, about the case of a man who is of my relatives who has left behind small children, slave-boys and slave-girls, and has not made any will. 'What do you say about one who buys from them a slave-girl for a mother of one's child and what do you say about selling them?' He (the Imam) said, 'If they have a guardian he looks after their affairs, sells for them, and looks after them, he will receive his reward from Allah.' I then asked, 'What do you say about one who buys from them a slave-girl to make her mother of his child.' He (the Imam) said, 'It is not unlawful if their guardian sells her for them who supervises for them in matters of their interest and they cannot revoke what the guardian has done to protect their interest.'"

H 8894, Ch. 92, h 2
Muhammad ibn Yahya has narrated from Ahmad ibn Muhammad from Muhammad ibn 'Isma'il who has said the following:

"A certain person of our people died without a will and his case was presented before a judge of al-Kufah. 'Abd al-Hamid was appointed as the supervisor over his affairs. The man had left behind small heirs, assets and slave-girls. 'Abd al-Hamid sold the assets and when he wanted to sell the slave-girls, His heart became weak in selling them because the deceased had not appointed him as executor of his will and his appointment was because of the order of the judge and it was a matter of *Furuj* (matters of reproductive issue). I then asked abu Ja'far, *'Alayhi al-Salam*, about it saying, 'If a man of our people dies without a will and leaves behind slave-girls, then the judge appoints a man from us as supervisor to sell the slave-girls or says that a man from us looks after this issue and his heart becomes weak because it is a matter of *Furuj*; what do you say about it?' He (the Imam) said, 'If the supervisor is like you or like 'Abd al-Hamid it is not unlawful.'"

H 8895, Ch. 92, h 3
Muhammad ibn Yahya has narrated from Ahmad ibn Muhammad from 'Uthman ibn 'Isa from Sama'ah who has said the following:

"I once asked him (the Imam), *'Alayhi al-Salam*, about the case of a man who buys a slave, who is a runaway one, from his people. He (the Imam) said, 'It is not valid unless he buys something else along with him and says, "I buy from you this thing and your slave so and so for so and so amount" and if he cannot find the slave his price (asset) will be in what he has paid for that thing.'"

H 8896, Ch. 92, h 4
A number of our people have narrated from Sahl ibn Ziyad and Ahmad ibn Muhammad all from al-Hassan ibn Mahbub from Rifa'ah al-Nakhkhas who has said the following:

"I once said to abu 'Abd Allah, *'Alayhi al-Salam*, 'I have made a deal with a man in the manner of *Musawamah* (fixed price regardless of capital) about his slave-girl. He sold her to me on my demand and I took possession on that basis, sent him a thousand dirham and said to him, 'This is a thousand because of my order.' He refused to accept it from me and I had already touched her before sending the thousand dirham. He (the Imam) said, 'I say that you must evaluate the slave-girl for a fair price. If her price is more than what you sent to him you must complete the deficit, and if the price is less than what you have sent to him it belongs to him.' I then said, 'What happens if I find a defect in her after touching her?' He (the Imam) said, 'You cannot return her. You can, however, demand for the difference of her prices as defect-free and defective condition.'"

H 8897, Ch. 92, h 5

Ali ibn Ibrahim has narrated from his father from ibn abu 'Umayr from Hammad from al-Halabiy who has said the following:

"This is about the case of a slave who is owned by several people and one of them sells his share and the other says, 'I am more rightful to buy it if his claim is right.' He (the Imam) said, 'It is a right if there is only one shareholder.' It then was asked if there is right of *al-Shuf'* (priority right over others to buy) in the sale of animals. He (the Imam) said, 'No, there is no right of *al-Shuf'* in the sale of animals.'"

H 8898, Ch. 92, h 6

Muhammad ibn 'Isma'il has narrated from al-Fadl ibn Shadhan from ibn abu 'Umayr from Ibrahim ibn 'Abd al-Hamid who has said the following:

"About the case of buying and the sale of Romans, abu al-Hassan, *'Alayhi al-Salam*, has said, '(If they are for sale), buy and sell them.'"

H 8899, Ch. 92, h 7

Humayd ibn Ziyad from al-Hassan ibn Muhammad ibn Sama'ah from more than one person from Aban ibn 'Uthman from 'Isma'il ibn al-Fadl who has said the following:

"This is concerning my question before abu 'Abd Allah, *'Alayhi al-Salam*, about buying slaves of tax payers if their government approves. He (the Imam) said, 'If the authority over them approves you can buy and marry them.'"

H 8900, Ch. 92, h 8

A number of our people have narrated from Ahmad ibn Muhammad from Muhammad ibn Sahl from Zakariya ibn Adam who has said the following:

"I once asked al-Rida', *'Alayhi al-Salam*, about the enemy people who make peace, then breach it because justice was not practiced with them; if it is permissible to buy their captives. He (the Imam) said, 'If they are open enemies you can buy but if they are exiled and treated unjustly, then do not buy their captives.' I asked him (the Imam) about captives from Daylam who steal from each other and the Muslims invade them without authorization from Imam; if buying them is permissible. He (the Imam) said, 'If they confess their slavery, then it is not unlawful.' I then asked him (the Imam) about taxpayer people who face famine and a man brings his children and says: this is for you feed him and he is for you. He (the Imam) said, 'You must not sell free people. It is not lawful for you as well as for the tax payers.'"

H 8901, Ch. 92, h 9

A number of our people have narrated from Sahl ibn Ziyad and Ahmad ibn Muhammad all from ibn Mahbub from Rifa'ah al-Nakhkhas who has said the following:

"I once asked abu al-Hassan, *'Alayhi al-Salam*, about Romans who invade al-Saqalibah (a people who lived between Bulgaria and Constantinople (Istanbul)), steal their children, slave-girls and slave-boys, then castrate the slave-boys, then send them to Baghdad for the merchants. What do you say about them and we know they are stolen and they were invaded wrongfully without declared war among them. He (the Imam) said, 'It is not unlawful to buy them because they have only taken them from paganism to al-Islam.'"

H 8902, Ch. 92, h 10

Humayd ibn Ziyad has narrated from al-Hassan ibn Muhammad ibn Sama'ah from more than one person from Aban from 'Abd al-Rahman ibn abu 'Abd Allah who has said the following:

"This is concerning my question before abu 'Abd Allah, *'Alayhi al-Salam*, about the slaves of the taxpayers; if I can buy from them. He (the Imam) said, 'You can buy them if they certify their slavery.'"

H 8903, Ch. 92, h 11

Aban has narrated from Zurarah who has said the following:

"This is concerning my question before abu 'Abd Allah, *'Alayhi al-Salam*, about the case of a man who buys a slave-girl for a certain price, then sells her (on credit) and makes a profit before paying the owner. The owner comes and demands payment but he does not pay. The owner says to those who have bought her to pay him what the person selling the slave-girl owes him and the profit that he has made is for them. He (the Imam) said, 'It is not unlawful.'"

H 8904, Ch. 92, h 12

Ali ibn Ibrahim has narrated from his father from ibn abu Najran from 'Asem ibn Hamid from Muhammad ibn Qays who has said the following:

"Abu Ja'far, *'Alayhi al-Salam*, has said that 'Amir al-Mu'minin, *'Alayhi al-Salam*, issued a judgment in the case of a slave-girl who is the mother of a child who is sold by the son of her master in the absence of his father. The buyer made her to become pregnant and a boy was born. Then her first master came and disputed the second master, saying: she was the mother of my child whom my son had sold without my permission. He (the Imam) said, 'The judgment gave him the mother and the child.' The one who had bought begged and pleaded before him (the Imam). He said, 'Take his son who sold to you the mother of the child until he pays you for the sale.' When he took him his father said, 'Allow my son to go.' He said, 'No, by Allah, I will not allow him to go until you allow my son to go.' When the master of the mother of the child saw this he authorized the sale of his son.'"

H 8905, Ch. 92, h 13

Ali ibn Ibrahim has narrated from his father from ibn abu 'Umayr from Jamil ibn Darraj from Hamzah ibn Humran who has said the following:

"I once said to abu 'Abd Allah, *'Alayhi al-Salam*, 'I go to the market to buy a slave-girl and she says that she is free. He (the Imam) said, 'You can buy her unless she presents proof of her freedom.'"

H 8906, Ch. 92, h 14

Ali ibn Ibrahim has narrated from his father from ibn abu 'Umayr from Zurarah who has said the following:

"Once I was sitting with abu 'Abd Allah, *'Alayhi al-Salam*, when a man came in with his son. Abu 'Abd Allah, *'Alayhi al-Salam*, asked, 'What kind of business does your son do?' He replied, 'He sells slaves.' Abu 'Abd Allah, *'Alayhi al-Salam*, said, 'You must not buy what is defective physically or morally. When you buy a head, you must not show its price on balance; whatever head sees its price in the balance it does not succeed. When you buy a head change its name, feed it something sweet and when you become the owner give four dirham charity for it.'"

H 8907, Ch. 92, h 15

A number of our people have narrated from Sahl ibn Ziyad from Ibrahim ibn 'Uqbah from Muhammad ibn Muyassir from his father who has said the following:

"Abu 'Abd Allah, *'Alayhi al-Salam*, has said, 'One who looks at his own price when he is weighed, he does not succeed.'"

H 8908, Ch. 92, h 16

Muhammad ibn Yahya has narrated from Ahmad ibn Muhammad from ibn Mahbub from Rifa'ah who has said the following:

"I once asked abu al-Hassan, Musa, *'Alayhi al-Salam*, about the case of a man who shares a slave-girl with another man and says, 'If we made profit half is for you, if it is a loss then there is nothing on you.' He (the Imam) said, 'I do not see anything unlawful in it if the owner of the slave-girl agrees without compulsion.'"

H 8909, Ch. 92, h 17

Ali ibn Ibrahim has narrated from his father from ibn abu 'Umayr from Hammad from al-Halabiy who has said the following:

"This is concerning my question before abu 'Abd Allah, *'Alayhi al-Salam*, about the case of slave-girls and conditions that say, 'She must not be sold or transferred in inheritance or given as gift.' He (the Imam) said, 'It is lawful except inheritance; she is inherited. Any condition against the book of Allah is rejected.'"

H 8910, Ch. 92, h 18

Muhammad ibn Yahya has narrated from Ahmad ibn Muhammad from Muhammad ibn 'Abd al-Hamid from abu Jamilah who has said the following:

"Once I visited abu 'Abd Allah, *'Alayhi al-Salam*, and he asked, 'Young man, what you do for a living?' I replied, 'It is slaves.' He (the Imam) said, 'I recommend you so keep my recommendations safe. You must not buy physically or morally defective ones. You must make the guarantees strong and firm.'"

Chapter 93 - Selling a Slave Who Owns Property

H 8911, Ch. 93, h 1

Ali ibn Ibrahim has narrated from his father from ibn abu 'Umayr from Jamil ibn Darraj from Zurarah who has said the following:

"This is concerning my question before abu 'Abd Allah, *'Alayhi al-Salam*, about the case of a man who buys a slave who owns assets; to whom such assets belong? He (the Imam) said, 'If the seller knows that the slave owns assets then such assets belong to the buyer but if he does not know then they belong to the seller.'"

H 8912, Ch. 93, h 2

A number of our people have narrated from Sahl ibn Ziyad and Ahmad ibn Muhammad all from ibn Mahbub from al-'Ala' from Muhammad ibn Muslim who has said the following:

"I once asked one of the two Imam, (abu Ja'far or abu 'Abd Allah), *'Alayhim al-Salam*, about the case of a man who sells a slave and finds out that the slave owns assets. He (the Imam) said, 'Such assets belong to the seller; he has sold the slave's person unless it is a condition in the contract of sale that says that whatever assets are there, they belong to him.'"

H 8913, Ch. 93, h 3

Muhammad ibn Yahya has narrated from Ahmad ibn Muhammad from Ali ibn Hadid from Jamil ibn Darraj from Zurarah who has said the following:

"This is concerning my question before abu 'Abd Allah, *'Alayhi al-Salam*, about the case of a man who buys a slave and his assets. He (the Imam) said, 'It is not unlawful.' I then asked, 'What happens if the assets of the slave are more than what is paid to buy the slave?' He (the Imam) said, 'It is not unlawful.'"

Chapter 94 - Buying Salves, Finding Defects, Returnable and Non-Returnable

H 8914, Ch. 94, h 1

A number of our people have narrated from Sahl ibn Ziyad and Ahmad ibn Muhammad all from ibn Mahbub from Malik ibn 'Atiyyah from Dawud ibn Farqad who has said the following:

"This is concerning my question before abu 'Abd Allah, *'Alayhi al-Salam*, about the case of a slave-girl who is well aware but does not experience Hayd (menses) for six month now with him and she is not pregnant. He (the Imam) said, 'If others similar to her experience and it is not because of old age, it is a defect, because of which she can be returned.'"

H 8915, Ch. 94, h 2

Ibn Mahbub has narrated from ibn Sinan who has said the following:

"This is concerning my question before abu 'Abd Allah, *'Alayhi al-Salam*, about the case of a man who buys a pregnant slave-girl and does not know that she is pregnant so he does sexual intercourse. He (the Imam) said, 'He must return to the one from whom he has purchased and he must return half of one-tenth of her price because of sexual intercourse. Ali, *'Alayhi al-Salam*, has said, 'A non-pregnant cannot be returned after the owner does sexual intercourse but proportionate to the defect her price is reduced if there is any defect in her.'"

H 8916, Ch. 94, h 3

Ali ibn Ibrahim has narrated from his father from ibn abu 'Umayr from Jamil ibn Salih from 'Abd al-Malik ibn 'Umayr who has said the following:

"Abu 'Abd Allah, *'Alayhi al-Salam*, has said, 'A non-pregnant slave-girl, after the owner does sexual intercourse cannot be returned but he can demand for loss because of defect. A pregnant one must be returned with half of one-tenth of her price.'" In another Hadith it is said that if she is virgin it is one-tenth of her price and if she is not virgin, it is half of one-tenth of her price.'"

H 8917, Ch. 94, h 4

Muhammad ibn Yahya has narrated from Ahmad ibn Muhammad from Muhammad ibn Yahya from Talhah ibn Zayd who has said the following:

"Abu 'Abd Allah, *'Alayhi al-Salam*, has said that 'Amir al-Mu'minin, in the case of a man who bought a slave-girl and did sexual intercourse with her, then found defect in her, issued a judgment that said, 'She must be evaluated as perfect as well as defective; then the seller must refund the difference of the two prices to the buyer.'"

H 8918, Ch. 94, h 5

Muhammad ibn Yahya has narrated from Muhammad ibn al-Husayn from Safwan from Mansur ibn Hazim who has said the following:

"About the case of a man who bought a slave-girl and did sexual intercourse, abu 'Abd Allah, *'Alayhi al-Salam*, has said, 'If he found a defect, he could not return her but ask for what the defect had reduced from her price.' I then asked, 'Is this how Ali, *'Alayhi al-Salam*, had judged?' He (the Imam) said, 'Yes, this is the way Ali, *'Alayhi al-Salam*, had judged.'"

H 8919, Ch. 94, h 6

Muhammad ibn Yahya has narrated from Muhammad ibn al-Husayn from Ali ibn al-Hakam from al-'Ala' from Muhammad ibn Muslim who has said the following:

"One of the two Imam, (abu Ja'far or abu 'Abd Allah), *'Alayhim al-Salam*, was asked about the case of a man who buys a slave-girl, then does sexual intercourse, then finds defect in her, and he (the Imam) said, 'She cannot be returned to her owner, but she can be evaluated as perfect and defective, and the difference of the two prices is returned to the buyer, may Allah grant protection against designating it as her wages.'"

H 8920, Ch. 94, h 7

Al-Husayn from Muhammad has narrated from Mu'alla' ibn Muhammad from al-Hassan ibn Ali from Aban from Zurarah who has said the following:

"Abu Ja'far, *'Alayhi al-Salam*, has said that Ali ibn al-Husayn, *'Alayhi al-Salam*, would not return a non-pregnant slave-girl after doing sexual intercourse but he (the Imam) would deduct from her price proportionate to the cost of the defect.'"

H 8921, Ch. 94, h 8

Humayd has narrated from al-Hassan ibn Muhammad from al-from more than one person from Aban from 'Abd al-Rahman ibn abu 'Abd Allah who has said the following:

"About the case of a man who buys a slave-girl, then does sexual intercourse, then finds her to be pregnant, abu 'Abd Allah, *'Alayhi al-Salam*, has said, 'He must return her with something.'"

H 8922, Ch. 94, h 9

Aban has narrated from Muhammad ibn Muslim who has said the following:

"About the case of a man who buys a pregnant slave-girl and does sexual intercourse with her when he did not know, abu Ja'far, *'Alayhi al-Salam*, has said, 'He must return her and clothe her.'"

H 8923, Ch. 94, h 10

Ali ibn Ibrahim has narrated from his father from ibn abu 'Umayr from Jamil ibn Darraj from certain persons of our people who has said the following:

"About the case of a man who buys a slave-girl and makes her to give birth, then finds her to be stolen, abu 'Abd Allah, *'Alayhi al-Salam*, has said, 'Her owner takes the slave-girl and the man takes the child.'"

H 8924, Ch. 94, h 11

Muhammad ibn Yahya has narrated from Ahmad ibn Muhammad from those whom he has mentioned from Zur'ah ibn Muhammad from Sama'ah who has said the following:

"This is concerning my question before abu 'Abd Allah, *'Alayhi al-Salam*, about the case of a man who sells a slave-girl as virgin but she is not found virgin. He (the Imam) said, 'He cannot return and there is nothing on him, it (virginity) may go away because of illness or something that affects it.'"

H 8925, Ch. 94, h 12

Al-Husayn from Muhammad has narrated from al-Sayyariy who has said that it is narrated from ibn abu Layla' to whom a man brought his disputing party and said, "This man has sold a slave-girl to me and I did not find any pubic hair on her when she uncovered as if it did not exist." Ibn abu Layla' said that people play tricks about it to remove. "What is it that you disliked?" The man said, "Judge, if it is defect judge in my favor." He said, "Wait until I come back because I feel trouble in my stomach." He went to Muhammad ibn Muslim al-Thaqafiy and asked, "What do you narrate from abu Ja'far, *'Alayhi al-Salam*, about a woman who has no pubic hair? Is it a defect?" Muhammad ibn Muslim replied, "I do not know of any exact text about it, however, abu Ja'far, *'Alayhi al-Salam*, would narrate from his ancestors from the Holy Prophet, *O Allah, grant compensation to Muhammad and his family worthy of their services to Your cause*, who has said that whatever due to the origin of the creation exists then increases or decreases it is a defect." Ibn abu Layla' then said, "This is enough." He returned to the people and issued a judgment accordingly.

H 8926, Ch. 94, h 13

A number of our people have narrated from Ahmad ibn Muhammad ibn 'Isa from abu 'Abd Allah, al-Farra' from Hariz from Zurarah who has said the following:

"I once asked abu Ja'far, *'Alayhi al-Salam*, about the case of a man who buys a slave-girl from the market and makes her to give birth. Then a man comes with proof that she is his slave-girl who is not sold or given as gift to anyone. He (the Imam) said, 'He must return his slave-girl to him along with the benefits he has received from her.' As if it means, it is the cost of the child."

H 8927, Ch. 94, h 14

Ali ibn Ibrahim has narrated from his father from 'Isma'il ibn Marrar from Yunus who has narrated the following:

"In the case of a man who buys a slave-girl that she is said to be a virgin but he does not find her to be as such, he (the Imam), *'Alayhi al-Salam*, said, 'He (the seller) must return the difference of the price if he can verify that what he says is true.'"

H 8928, Ch. 94, h 15

A number of our people have narrated from Sahl ibn Ziyad from ibn Faddal who has said the following:

"Abu al-Hassan, al-Rida', *'Alayhi al-Salam*, has said, 'A slave-girl can be returned because of four issues: Madness, leprosy, Bars (leprosy), al-*Qarn* (something in the vagina that prevents sexual intercourse) and al-Hadbah (convexity) which makes the chest go in and the back come out.'"

H 8929, Ch. 94, h 16

Al-Husayn from Muhammad has narrated from Mu'alla' ibn Muhammad from Ali ibn Asbat who has said the following:

"I once heard al-Rida', *'Alayhi al-Salam*, saying, 'The choice to revoke a contract of sale in the case of animals is for three days in favor of the buyer and in non-animal it is as long as they have not departed each other. The happenings of the year are returned after the year.' I asked, 'What is happening of the year?' He (the Imam) said, 'They are madness and leprosy, Bars (leprosy), and al-*Qarn*. One who buys and some of these things happen, then the rule is that it is returned to the owner up until the end of the year from the day of purchase.'"

H 8930, Ch. 94, h 17

Muhammad ibn Yahya and others have narrated from Ahmad ibn Muhammad from abu Hammam who has said the following:

"I once heard al-Rida', *'Alayhi al-Salam*, saying, 'Slaves, because of the happenings of the year are returned, such as madness, leprosy and Bars (leprosy).' We then asked, 'How is the return because of the happenings of the year?' He (the Imam) said, 'This is the beginning of the year. If you buy a slave with any of these things up to the month of Dhu al-Hajjah you can return to the owner.' Muhammad ibn Ali then asked, 'Are runaway slaves subject to this condition?' He (the Imam) said, 'Runaway is not so treated, unless proof is presented that he was a runaway with the owner.' It is narrated from Yunus also that the time for return in the case of madness, leprosy and Bars (leprosy) is one year. Al-Washsha' has narrated that time for returning due to madness alone is one year."

Chapter 95 - Rare Ahadith

H 8931, Ch. 95, h 1
Ali ibn Ibrahim has narrated from his father from ibn abu Habib from Muhammad ibn Muslim who has said the following:

"I once asked abu Ja'far, *'Alayhi al-Salam*, about the case of a man who buys a slave from another man who had two slaves and he says to the buyer, 'Take both of them then choose whichever you like and return the other' and he has received payment. The buyer takes both of them but one of them runs away from the location of the buyer. He (the Imam) said, 'He must return the one with him and take half of the price he has paid, then search for the runaway slave. If he finds him he then chooses either one that he likes and returns the other. If he does not find him the slave belongs to both of them in the manner of equal shares.'"

H 8932, Ch. 95, h 2
Ali ibn Ibrahim has narrated from his father from 'Isma'il ibn Marrar from Yunus from 'Abd Allah ibn Sinan who has said the following:

"This is concerning my question before abu 'Abd Allah, *'Alayhi al-Salam*, about the case of several men who share a slave-girl who is then entrusted to one of them and he does sexual intercourse with her. He (the Imam) said, 'His punishment is reduced proportionate to the amount of his share in the ownership of the slave-girl in the form of cash and he is punished proportionate to the amount that does not belong to him. The slave-girl is evaluated for the price that she is worth for. If such price is less than what is paid for her, then what is paid for her is her fair price; but if her price according to the evaluation is more than what is paid for her then this is her fair price and this man is held responsible for his act.' I then asked, 'What happens if another one of the shareholders wants to buy her?' He (the Imam) said, 'It is up to him but he cannot buy her before Istibra' (quarantine) and no one of them can buy her without payment.'"

H 8933, Ch. 95, h 3
Al-Husayn from Muhammad has narrated from Mu'alla' ibn Muhammad from al-Hassan ibn Ali from Ahmad ibn 'A'idh from abu Salmah who has said the following:

"About the case of two slaves who belong to two people and each is authorized to buy and sell with their properties. The two slaves disagree on something and each one runs to the other's owner, both of equal physical strength, and buy the other slave from his master. They return to their place each with the claim of buying the other from his master and each says, 'You are my slave because I have bought you from your master.' Abu 'Abd Allah, *'Alayhi al-Salam*, has said, 'From the place they separate from each other the distance is measured, then whoever was closer is the winner. If the distance is the same then whoever has reached the master of the other faster is the winner. He can then sell the other or keep, as he likes, but he cannot beat him up.' In another Hadith it is said that if the distance is the same the case is decided by casting raffle to find out who is the winner.'"

Chapter 96 - Separation of Slaves from their Relatives (Is Not Permissible)

H 8934, Ch. 96, h 1

Ali ibn Ibrahim has narrated from his father from Ahmad ibn Muhammad from Muhammad ibn 'Isma'il has narrated from al-Fadl ibn Shadhan from ibn abu 'Umayr from Mu'awiyah ibn 'Ammar who has said the following:

"I heard abu 'Abd Allah, *'Alayhi al-Salam*, saying, 'Once captives were brought to the Messenger of Allah, *O Allah, grant compensation to Muhammad and his family worthy of their services to Your cause*, from Yemen. When they arrived at al-Juhfah, their supplies depleted and they sold one girl from the captives whose mother was with them. When they came to the Holy Prophet, he heard her crying and he asked, 'What for is this crying?' They replied, 'O Messenger of Allah, our supplies depleted, so we sold her daughter.' He (the Messenger of Allah) sent what was paid for her and brought her back. He (the Messenger of Allah) said, 'You must sell them together or keep them together.'"

H 8935, Ch. 96, h 2

Muhammad ibn Yahya has narrated from Ahmad ibn Muhammad from 'Uthman ibn 'Isa from Sama'ah who has said the following:

"I once asked him (the Imam), *'Alayhi al-Salam*, about the case of two slaves who are brothers; if they can be separated from each other or a woman slave, if she can be separated from her children. He (the Imam) said, 'No, it is not lawful unless they want it.'"

H 8936, Ch. 96, h 3

Ali ibn Ibrahim has narrated from his father from Ahmad ibn Muhammad from Muhammad ibn 'Isma'il has narrated from al-Fadl ibn Shadhan all from ibn abu 'Umayr from Hisham ibn al-Hakam who has said the following:

"I once bought a slave-girl from al-Kufah for abu 'Abd Allah, *'Alayhi al-Salam*. He then went so she can do a certain task. She said, 'O mother!' Abu 'Abd Allah, *'Alayhi al-Salam*, asked, 'Do you have a mother?' She replied, 'Yes, I have a mother.' He (the Imam) commanded to return her and said, 'On keeping her I did not feel safe from seeing in my children what I dislike to see.'"

H 8937, Ch. 96, h 4

Muhammad ibn Yahya has narrated from Ahmad ibn Muhammad from al-'Abbas ibn Musa from Yunus from 'Arm ibn abu Nasr who has said the following:

"This is concerning my question before abu 'Abd Allah, *'Alayhi al-Salam*, if one can buy a small slave-girl. He (the Imam) said, 'If she is independent of her parents, it is not unlawful.'"

H 8938, Ch. 96, h 5

Muhammad has narrated from Ahmad ibn Muhammad from al-Husayn ibn Sa'id from al-Nadr ibn Suwayd from ibn Sinan who has said the following:

"About the case of a man who buys a slave-girl or a slave boy who has a brother or sister, or father or mother in a city of the cities, abu 'Abd Allah, *'Alayhi al-Salam*, has said, 'He must not take such slave out of that city to another city if the slave is a minor and must not buy such slaves but if the slave has a mother who agrees as well as the slave, then you can buy.'"

Chapter 97 - If the Slave Asks his Master to Sell him or Stipulates to Give him Something

H 8939, Ch. 97, h 1
Muhammad ibn Yahya has narrated from Ahmad ibn Muhammad from Ali ibn al-Hakam from Musa ibn Bakr from al-Fudayl who has said the following:
"Once, a slave said to abu 'Abd Allah, *'Alayhi al-Salam*, 'I had said to my master, "Sell me for seven hundred dirham, I pay you three hundred dirham."' Abu 'Abd Allah, *'Alayhi al-Salam*, said, 'If you owned something on the day you made the condition then you must pay, and if you did not have anything on that day, there is nothing on you.'"

H 8940, Ch. 97, h 2
A number of our people have narrated from Sahl ibn Ziyad from ibn Mahbub from Fudayl who has said the following:
"A Sindiy slave once said to abu 'Abd Allah, *'Alayhi al-Salam*, 'I said to my master, "Sell me for seven hundred dirham, I pay you three hundred dirham."' Abu 'Abd Allah, *'Alayhi al-Salam*, said, 'If you owned something on the day you made the condition then you must pay, and if you did not have anything on that day there is nothing on you.'"

Chapter 98 - Advance Payment for Buying Slaves and Animals

H 8941, Ch. 98, h 1
Muhammad ibn Yahya has narrated from Ahmad ibn Muhammad from Ali ibn al-Hakam from Ali ibn abu Hamzah from abu Basir who has said the following:
"This is concerning my question before abu 'Abd Allah, *'Alayhi al-Salam*, about the case of advance payment in buying animals. He (the Imam) said, 'It is not unlawful.' I then asked him (the Imam) if I can make an advance payment for known years or something known like slaves and I pay more or less than his stipulation with consent and happiness. He (the Imam) said, 'It is not unlawful.'"

H 8942, Ch. 98, h 2
Ali ibn Ibrahim has narrated from his father from 'Abd al-Rahman ibn abu Najran from 'Asim ibn Hamid from Muhammad ibn Qays who has said the following:
"Abu Ja'far, *'Alayhi al-Salam*, has said that 'Amir al-Mu'minin, about the case of a man who gave a note to another man for a servant for an appointed time and his party said, 'I could not find a servant for you, you take from me the cost of your servant today in the form of the value.' He ('Amir al-Mu'minin) has said, 'He can refuse to take anything other than his servant or the note that he had given him at first without any thing added.'"

H 8943, Ch. 98, h 3
Ali ibn Ibrahim has narrated from his father from ibn abu 'Umayr from Jamil ibn Darraj from Zurarah who has said the following:

"Abu 'Abd Allah, *'Alayhi al-Salam*, has said, 'Advance payment to buy an animal is not unlawful if the age of animals is clearly described.'"

H 8944, Ch. 98, h 4

Muhammad ibn Yahya has narrated from Ahmad ibn Muhammad from ibn Faddal from ibn Bukayr from 'Ubayd ibn Zurarah who has said the following:

"Abu 'Abd Allah, *'Alayhi al-Salam*, has said, 'Advance payment to buy an animals is not unlawful if it (the animal) is clearly made known.'"

H 8945, Ch. 98, h 5

Ahmad ibn Muhammad has narrated from Ali ibn al-Hakam from Sayf ibn 'Amirah from abu Maryam al-Ansariy who has said the following:

"Abu 'Abd Allah, *'Alayhi al-Salam*, has said that his father would not consider advance payment to buy an animal unlawful for a clearly known merchandise and time."

H 8946, Ch. 98, h 6

Ahmad ibn Muhammad from has narrated from Ali ibn al-Hakam from Qutaybah al-'A'sha' who has said the following:

"About the case of a man who makes advance payment for sheep of a certain age for an appointed time and the party gives him four years old in place of three years old, abu 'Abd Allah, *'Alayhi al-Salam*, asked, 'Is it not true that he has made advance payment for (animals of) known age and on an appointed time? I replied, 'Yes, that is true.' He (the Imam) said, 'It is not unlawful.'"

H 8947, Ch. 98, h 7

Ahmad ibn Muhammad from and Ali has narrated from his father all from ibn abu 'Umayr from abu al-Mighra' from al-Halabiy who has said the following:

"Once abu 'Abd Allah, *'Alayhi al-Salam*, was asked about the case of a man who made an advance payment for things of clearly described age and color; then the party gave him more or less than the set condition. He (the Imam) said, 'If it is with fine consent it is not unlawful.'"

H 8948, Ch. 98, h 8

Ali ibn Ibrahim has narrated from his father from ibn abu 'Umayr from Hammad from al-Halabiy who has said the following:

"Once abu 'Abd Allah, *'Alayhi al-Salam*, was asked about the case of a man who made and advance payment to buy sheep of three and less than three years old and others for an appointed time. He (the Imam) said, 'It is not unlawful if the one who must provide sheep cannot have all that he is responsible for; the buyer can have half, one-third, two-third with the capital of the rest of the sheep in the form of dirhams. They can take below their condition and not above the condition and this applies to sacks of wheat, barley and saffron and sheep also.'"

H 8949, Ch. 98, h 9

Ali ibn Ibrahim has narrated from his father from 'Isma'il ibn Marrar from Yunus from Mu'awiyah who has said the following:

"This is concerning my question before abu 'Abd Allah, *'Alayhi al-Salam*, about the case of a man who made an advance payment for things of clearly described age and appointed time and not clearly described ages; then he was given below the condition. He (the Imam) said, 'If it is with fine consent from him and from you it is not unlawful.' I then asked about a man who made an advance payment to buy sheep of three years and less than three years and others for an appointed time. He (the Imam) said, 'It is not harmful.' 'In case he cannot provide all of them, can he ask the party to accept half or one-third and take back the capital for the remaining sheep in the form of dirhams?' He (the Imam) said, 'It is not unlawful but they must not take up his condition without fine consent of the owner.'"

H 8950, Ch. 98, h 10
Humayd ibn Ziyad has narrated from al-Hassan ibn Muhammad ibn Sama'ah from more than one person from Aban from Hadid ibn Hakim who has said the following:
"This is concerning my question before abu 'Abd Allah, *'Alayhi al-Salam*, about the case of a man who bought skins from the butcher to give him every day something clearly known. He (the Imam) said, 'It is not unlawful.'"

H 8951, Ch. 98, h 11
Muhammad ibn Yahya has narrated from Ahmad ibn Muhammad from ibn Mahbub from abu Ayyub from Sama'ah who has said the following:
"Once abu 'Abd Allah, *'Alayhi al-Salam*, was asked about advance payment to buy animals. He (the Imam) said, 'The age must be clearly known and the numbers must be made known for the known time, then it is not unlawful.'"

H 8952, Ch. 98, h 12
Abu Ali al-Ash'ariy has narrated from certain persons of his people from Ahmad ibn al-Nadr from 'Amr ibn Shamir from Jabir who has said the following:
"I once asked abu Ja'far, *'Alayhi al-Salam*, about the case of advance payment for meat. He (the Imam) said, 'You must not go close to it because one time he gives you fatty, one time what is about to become spoiled and one time he gives you boney. Buy with examination and in hand in hand manner.' I then asked about advance payment for containers of water. He (the Imam) said, 'You must not go close to it because one time he gives you less and one time complete. Buy it with examination; it is safe for you and for him.'"

H 8953, Ch. 98, h 13
Muhammad ibn Yahya has narrated from Ahmad ibn Muhammad from ibn Mahbub from abu Wallad al-Hannat who has said the following:
"This is concerning my question before abu 'Abd Allah, *'Alayhi al-Salam*, about the case of a man saying, 'He has sheep that milks and the milk is abundant every day, if one can buy from him five hundred *Ritl* (a certain unit of measurement) or more and every one hundred *Ritl* for so and so much dirham then every day take certain *Ritl* until the deal is complete.' He (the Imam) said, 'It is not unlawful (for this) and similar things.'"

H 8954, Ch. 98, h 14
Muhammad ibn 'Isma'il has narrated from al-Fadl ibn Shadhan from Safwan ibn Yahya from Qutaybah al-`A'sha' who has said the following:
"Once abu 'Abd Allah, *'Alayhi al-Salam*, was asked, when I was present, by a man who said, 'My brother comes from and goes to the mountains, milks sheep

of known age for an appointed time; then he is given four years old in place of three years old.' He (the Imam) asked, 'Is it with fine consent of his party?' he replied, 'Yes, it is so.' He (the Imam) said, 'It is not unlawful.'"

Chapter 99 - Another Chapter on the Previous Subject

H 8955, Ch. 99, h 1

A number of our people have narrated from Ahmad ibn Muhammad ibn 'Isa from Mu'awiyah ibn Hakim from Muhammad ibn Hubab al-Jallab who has said the following:

"I once asked abu al-Hassan, '*Alayhi al-Salam*, about the case of a man who bought one hundred sheep; if so and so many of them were changed. He (the Imam) said, 'It is not permissible and it is not lawful.'"

H 8956, Ch. 99, h 2

Ahmad ibn Muhammad has narrated from ibn abu 'Umayr from 'Abd al-Rahman ibn al-Hajjaj from Minhal al-Qassab who has said the following:

"This is concerning my question before abu 'Abd Allah, '*Alayhi al-Salam*, about the case of my buying sheep or a group's buying sheep saying, 'They enter a house, then a man stands at the door counts one, two, three, four, and five, then calls it one share.' He (the Imam) said, 'It is not valid. Shares are valid only when they are equal.'"

H 8957, Ch. 99, h 3

A number of our people have narrated from Sahl ibn Ziyad and Ahmad ibn Muhammad from al-Hassan ibn Mahbub from Zayd al-Shahham who has said the following:

"This is concerning my question before abu 'Abd Allah, '*Alayhi al-Salam*, about the case of a man who bought the shares of butchers before the shares were taken out. He (the Imam) said, 'Nothing can be purchased until it is known where the shares come. If he buys like this he has the choice to buy or not to buy it.'"

Chapter 100 - Milk, Wool and Ghee of Sheep Given for their Maintenance

H 8958, Ch. 100, h 1

Ali ibn Ibrahim has narrated from his father from ibn abu 'Umayr from Hammad from al-Halabiy who has said the following:

"About the case of a man who owns sheep and gives them to be maintained and paid for their maintenance from their ghee a certain amount or a known amount of dirham for every sheep, abu 'Abd Allah, '*Alayhi al-Salam*, has said, 'Dirham is not unlawful but I do not like giving ghee.'"

H 8959, Ch. 100, h 2

Ali ibn Ibrahim has narrated from his father from ibn abu 'Umayr from abu al-Mighra' from Ibrahim ibn Maymun who has said the following:

"This is concerning my question before abu 'Abd Allah, '*Alayhi al-Salam*, about the case of a shepherd of sheep in the mountains to whom sheep were given to maintain them and use their milk and wool, in addition to a certain amount of dirham for every sheep. He (the Imam) said, 'It is not unlawful.' I then said that people of Masjid said, 'It was not permissible because certain ones among them did not have wool or milk.' Abu 'Abd Allah, *'Alayhi al-Salam*, said, 'Can there be other arrangements better than this? He takes certain ones and leaves others.'"

H 8960, Ch. 100, h 3

Humayd ibn Ziyad has narrated from al-Hassan ibn Muhammad ibn Sama'ah from certain persons of his people from Aban from Mudrik ibn al-Hazhaz who has said the following:

"This is concerning my question before abu 'Abd Allah, *'Alayhi al-Salam*, about the case of a man who had sheep and gave them for their maintenance in exchange for their wool or Ghee or dirham. He (the Imam) said, 'It is not unlawful.' He disliked ghee."

H 8961, Ch. 100, h 4

Ali ibn Ibrahim has narrated from his father from ibn Mahbub from 'Abd Allah ibn Sinan who has said the following:

"This is concerning my question before abu 'Abd Allah, *'Alayhi al-Salam*, about the case of a man who gave his sheep to a man for maintenance in exchange for Ghee and a certain amount of dirham for every sheep every month. He (the Imam) said, 'It is not unlawful in exchange for dirham, however, for ghee, I do not like unless they give milk.'"

Chapter 101 - Selling a Found Child and One Born Out of Wedlock

H 8962, Ch. 101, h 1

A number of our people have narrated from Ahmad ibn Muhammad from ibn Faddal from Muthanna' from Zurarah who has said the following:

"Abu 'Abd Allah, *'Alayhi al-Salam*, has said, 'One cannot buy or sell an abandoned child that is found.'"

H 8963, Ch. 101, h 2

Ahmad ibn Muhammad has narrated from ibn Faddal from Muthanna' from Hatim ibn 'Isma'il al-Mad'iniy who has said the following:

"Abu 'Abd Allah, *'Alayhi al-Salam*, has said, 'A discarded child who is found is free, if he likes to have a guardian other than the one who has brought him up, he can do so. If the one who has brought him up asks for his expenses, if he is affluent he must pay him back and if he is not affluent then whatever is spent is counted as charity.'"

H 8964, Ch. 101, h 3

Muhammad ibn Yahya has narrated from Ahmad ibn Muhammad ibn 'Isa from Ali ibn al-Hakam from 'Abd al-Rahman al-'Arzamiy who has said the following:

"Abu 'Abd Allah has narrated from his father, *'Alayhi al-Salam*, who has said, 'A discarded child is free. When he grows up, he can accept the one who picked him up as his guardian; otherwise, he must pay back what he has spent for him and he then can go to find a guardian of his choice.'"

H 8965, Ch. 101, h 4

Muhammad ibn Yahya has narrated from Ahmad ibn Muhammad from ibn Mahbub from Muhammad ibn Ahmad who has said the following:

"This is concerning my question before abu 'Abd Allah, *'Alayhi al-Salam*, about the case of a discarded child. He (the Imam) said, 'You cannot sell or buy him, but you can use his service to compensate for what you have spent for him.'"

H 8966, Ch. 101, h 5

Ali ibn Ibrahim has narrated from his father from Hammad from Hariz from Muhammad ibn Muslim who has said the following:

"I once asked abu Ja'far, *'Alayhi al-Salam*, about the case of a discarded child. He (the Imam) said, 'He is free but cannot be sold or given away as a gift.'"

H 8967, Ch. 101, h 6

A number of our people have narrated from Ahmad ibn abu 'Abd Allah from his father from abu al-Jahm from abu Khadijah who has said the following:

"I once heard abu 'Abd Allah, *'Alayhi al-Salam*, saying, 'One born out of fornication does not recover as well as his price. *Al-Mumraz* does not recover for seven generations. It was asked, 'What is *al-Mumraz*?' He (the Imam) said, 'One earns through unlawful ways and with such funds gets married or enjoys it, and a child is born for him. That child is *al-Mumraz*.'"

H 8968, Ch. 101, h 7

Al-Husayn from Muhammad has narrated from Mu'alla' ibn Muhammad from al-Hassan ibn Ali from Aban from those who narrated to him who has said the following:

"This is concerning my question before abu 'Abd Allah, *'Alayhi al-Salam*, saying, 'Can I buy, sell or use services of one born out of wedlock? He (the Imam) said, 'You can buy, sell, enslave or use his services but do not buy a discarded child that is found.'"

H 8969, Ch. 101, h 8

A number of our people have narrated from Ahmad ibn abu 'Abd Allah from ibn Faddal from Muthanna' al-Hannat from abu Basir who has said the following:

"This is concerning my question before abu 'Abd Allah, *'Alayhi al-Salam*, saying, 'I have a slave born out of wedlock; if I can perform al-Hajj with his price or spend it for my marriage.' He (the Imam) said, 'You must not perform al-Hajj with it and do not spend it for your marriage.'"

Chapter 102 - Comprehensive Heading on Goods That Are Lawful to Exchange in Transactions and Those Unlawful to Exchange

H 8970, Ch. 102, h 1

Abu Ali al-Ash'ariy has narrated from Muhammad ibn 'Abd al-Jabbar from Safwan ibn Yahya from 'Abd al-Hamid ibn Sa'd who has said the following:

"I once asked abu Ibrahim, *'Alayhi al-Salam*, about the bones of elephants; if it was permissible to sell or buy the combs which were made thereof. He (the Imam) said, 'It is not unlawful. My father, *'Alayhi al-Salam*, had such a comb or combs.'"

H 8971, Ch. 102, h 2

Ali ibn Ibrahim has narrated from his father from ibn abu 'Umayr from 'Umar ibn 'Udhaynah who has said the following:

"I once wrote to abu 'Abd Allah, *'Alayhi al-Salam*, and asked about a man who had a piece of wood and sold it to those who make barbat (musical tool) out of it. He (the Imam) said, 'It is not unlawful.' I asked about one who sold a piece of wood to those who made crosses with it. He (the Imam) said, 'It is not lawful.'"

H 8972, Ch. 102, h 3

Muhammad ibn Yahya has narrated from Ahmad ibn Muhammad from al-Hajjal from Tha'labah from Muhammad ibn Mudarib who has said the following:

"Abu 'Abd Allah, *'Alayhi al-Salam*, has said, 'Selling animal dung is not unlawful.'"

H 8973, Ch. 102, h 4

Abu Ali al-Ash'ariy has narrated from Muhammad ibn 'Abd al-Jabbar from Safwan from 'Is ibn al-Qasim who has said the following:

"This is concerning my question before abu 'Abd Allah, *'Alayhi al-Salam*, about Cheetah and predator birds; if business could be sought with them. He (the Imam) said, 'Yes, it is possible.'"

H 8974, Ch. 102, h 5

Muhammad ibn Yahya has narrated from Ahmad ibn Muhammad from ibn Mahbub from Aban from 'Isa al-Qummiy from 'Amr ibn Jarir who has said the following:

"This is concerning my question before abu 'Abd Allah, *'Alayhi al-Salam*, about my selling mulberry wood from which they made crosses and idols. He (the Imam) said, 'No, it is not permissible.'"

H 8975, Ch. 102, h 6

Ali ibn Ibrahim has narrated from his father from ibn abu 'Umayr from 'Umar ibn 'Udhaynah who has said the following:

"I once wrote to abu 'Abd Allah, *'Alayhi al-Salam*, and asked about the case of a man who rented his ship or stumper to those who carried wine and pigs on them. He (the Imam) said, 'It is not unlawful.'"

H 8976, Ch. 102, h 7

A number of our people have narrated from Sahl ibn Ziyad from Muhammad ibn al-Hassan ibn Shammun from Al-'Asamm from Misma' who has said the following:

"Abu 'Abd Allah, *'Alayhi al-Salam*, has said that the Messenger of Allah, *O Allah, grant compensation to Muhammad and his family worthy of their services to Your cause*, prohibited buying and selling of monkeys.'"

H 8977, Ch. 102, h 8

A number of our people have narrated from Ahmad ibn Muhammad from Muhammad ibn 'Isma'il from Ali ibn al-Nu'man from ibn Muskan from 'Abd al-Mu'min from Jabir who has said the following:

"This is concerning my question before abu 'Abd Allah, *'Alayhi al-Salam*, about the case of a man who rented his house to those who used it for selling wine. He (the Imam) said, 'Its rent is unlawful.'"

H 8978, Ch. 102, h 9

Certain persons of our people have narrated from A number of our people have narrated from abu Mukhallad al-Sarraj who has said the following:

"I once was with abu 'Abd Allah, *'Alayhi al-Salam*, when Mu'attib came in and said, 'There are two people at the door.' He (the Imam) said, 'Bring them inside.' They came inside and one of them said, 'I am a saddle maker and I sell skins of tigers.' He (the Imam) asked, 'Are they (skins) tanned?' He replied, 'Yes, they are tanned.' He (the Imam) said, 'It is not unlawful.'"

H 8979, Ch. 102, h 10

Muhammad ibn Yahya has narrated from Ahmad ibn Muhammad from Muhammad ibn Ahmad ibn 'Isa from abu al-Qasim al-Sayqal who has said the following:

"I once wrote to him (the Imam), *'Alayhi al-Salam*, and asked, 'There is a certain sheathing of swords called *al-Safan* (sandpaper) which is from skin of fish; if it is permissible to work with and we do not eat its meat.' He (the Imam) wrote back, 'It is not unlawful.'"

Chapter 103 - Buying Stolen Goods and Cheating

H 8980, Ch. 103, h 1

A number of our people have narrated from Sahl ibn Ziyad and Ahmad ibn Muhammad all from ibn Mahbub from abu Ayyub from abu Basir who has said the following:

"I once asked one of the two Imam, (abu Ja'far or abu 'Abd Allah), *'Alayhim al-Salam*, about buying goods from cheating and stealing. He (the Imam) said, 'No, it is not lawful unless it is mixed with other goods. The very substance of stolen goods cannot be purchased unless it is of the properties of the sultan in which case it is not unlawful.'"

H 8981, Ch. 103, h 2

Ibn Mahbub has narrated from Hisham ibn Salim from abu 'Ubayd who has said the following:

"I once asked abu Ja'far, *'Alayhi al-Salam*, about the case of one of our men who bought from the sultan of the camels of charity and sheep of charity and he knew that they took more than what is rightly due on them. He (the Imam) said, 'Camels and sheep are just like wheat and barley and other goods. It is not unlawful unless he recognizes the very substance of what is unlawful.' It was asked, 'What do you say about the charity collectors who come to us, collect the charity from our sheep, then we ask them to sell them to us and they sell them? What do you say about buying from them? He (the Imam) said, 'If he has taken them away, then it is not unlawful.' It was asked, 'What do you say about wheat and barley which the charity collector takes from us with his measurement and keeps it to one side: if we buy such foodstuff from him?' He (the Imam) said, 'If he has taken possession with a certain measurement, then it is not unlawful to buy from him without measuring.'"

H 8982, Ch. 103, h 3

Muhammad ibn Yahya has narrated from Ahmad ibn Muhammad from al-Hassan ibn Ali from Aban from Ishaq ibn 'Ammar who has said the following:

"This is concerning my question before abu 'Abd Allah, *'Alayhi al-Salam*, about the case of a man who bought from a charity collector who committed injustice.

He (the Imam) said, 'He can buy from him unless he learns that he has done injustice in collecting those goods.'"

H 8983, Ch. 103, h 4
Muhammad ibn Yahya has narrated from Ahmad ibn Muhammad from al-Husayn ibn Sa'id from al-Nadr ibn Suwayd from al-Qasim ibn Sulayman from Jarrah al-Mada'iniy who has said the following:

"Abu 'Abd Allah, *'Alayhi al-Salam*, has said, 'Buying and selling of goods obtained by cheating and stealing are not valid and not lawful.'"

H 8984, Ch. 103, h 5
Muhammad ibn Yahya has narrated from Ahmad ibn Muhammad from ibn abu 'Umayr from Jamil ibn Salih who has said the following:

"They wanted to sell the dates of 'Ayn of abu Ziyad (name of a place with farms that belonged to abu 'Abd Allah, *'Alayhi al-Salam)*, and I wanted to buy it but then I decided to ask permission from abu 'Abd Allah, *'Alayhi al-Salam*, so I asked Mu'adh and he asked him (the Imam) about it and he (the Imam) said, 'He can buy it because if he does not buy it someone else will buy it.'"

H 8985, Ch. 103, h 6
Al-Husayn ibn Muhammad has narrated from al-Nahdiy from ibn abu Najran from certain persons of his people who has said the following:

"Abu 'Abd Allah, *'Alayhi al-Salam*, has said, 'Whoever buys stolen goods when he knows it, he shares its shame and sin.'"

H 8986, Ch. 103, h 7
Ali has narrated from Salih al-Sindiy from Ja'far ibn Bashir from al-Husayn ibn abu al-'Ala' from abu 'Umar al-Sarraj who has said the following:

"About the case of a man with whom stolen goods were found, abu 'Abd Allah, *'Alayhi al-Salam*, has said, 'He is held responsible unless he presents testimony against the seller such as witnesses.'"

Chapter 104 - Buying Food from a People through Coercion

H 8987, Ch. 104, h 1
Muhammad ibn Yahya has narrated from Ahmad ibn Muhammad from al-Hassan ibn Ali from Ali ibn 'Uqbah from al-Husayn ibn Musa from Burayd and Muhammad ibn Muslim who has said the following:

"Abu 'Abd Allah, *'Alayhi al-Salam*, has said, 'If one buys the foodstuff of a people who dislike such purchase, on the Day of Judgment it will be recovered for them from his flesh.'"

Chapter 105 - Finding the Merchandise after Delivery to Be of Different Quality

H 8988, Ch. 105, h 1
Ali ibn Ibrahim has narrated from his father and Muhammad ibn Yahya has narrated from Ahmad ibn Muhammad from ibn abu 'Umayr and Ali ibn Hadid from Jamil ibn Darraj from Muyassir who has said the following:

"This is concerning my question before abu 'Abd Allah, *'Alayhi al-Salam*, about the case of a man who bought a skin sack of oil and found residue in it. He (the Imam) said, 'If he knew that the oil had such things in it, he cannot return; but if he did not know that the oil had such things in it he can return it to the owner.'"

H 8989, Ch. 105, h 2
Ali ibn Ibrahim has narrated from his father from ibn abu 'Umayr from Ibrahim ibn Ishaq al-Khudriy from abu Sadiq who has said the following:

"Once 'Amir al-Mu'minin, *'Alayhi al-Salam*, entered the market of the date sellers and saw a standing woman who was crying and disputing with a man who sold dates. He (the Imam) asked her, 'What is the matter with you?' She replied, 'O 'Amir al-Mu'minin, I bought dates from this man for one dirham and underneath it is of bad quality and it is not like what I had seen.' He (the Imam) told him to return her dirham but he refused until he (the Imam) said it three times, but he refused; then he (the Imam) raised the whip until he returned her dirham. Ali, *'Alayhi al-Salam*, disliked camouflaging dates.'"

Chapter 106 - Selling Juice and Wine

H 8990, Ch. 106, h 1
A number of our people have narrated from Sahl ibn Ziyad Ahmad ibn Muhammad from Ahmad ibn Muhammad ibn 'Isa from Ahmad ibn Muhammad from ibn abu Nasr who has said the following:

"I once asked abu al-Hassan, *'Alayhi al-Salam*, about selling juice that became wine before receiving the price. He (the Imam) said, 'If he sells fruits to one about whom the seller knows that he turns it into something unlawful, selling is not unlawful. If it is juice then it cannot be sold except for cash.'"

H 8991, Ch. 106, h 2
Ali ibn Ibrahim has narrated from his father from Hammad ibn 'Isa from Hariz from Muhammad ibn Muslim who has said the following:

"About the case of a man who has a slave whom he has left at a vineyard to sell grapes or juice, but the slave goes and squeezes wine and sells it, abu 'Abd Allah, *'Alayhi al-Salam*, has said, 'The price received is not useable.' He (the Imam) then said, 'Once a man from Thaqif presented to the Messenger of Allah, *O Allah, grant compensation to Muhammad and his family worthy of their services to Your cause*, two sacks of wine and the Messenger of Allah commanded to throw them away and said, "The One who has prohibited its drinking has prohibited to accept its price also."' Abu 'Abd Allah, *'Alayhi al-Salam*, then said, 'The best thing to do about what this slave has done is to give it as charity.'"

H 8992, Ch. 106, h 3
Muhammad ibn Yahya has narrated from Ahmad ibn Muhammad from al-Husayn ibn Sa'id from al-Qasim ibn Muhammad from Ali ibn abu Hamzah from abu Basir who has said the following:

"This is concerning my question before abu 'Abd Allah, *'Alayhi al-Salam*, about the price of juice before it boiled for one who wanted to buy it so he could cook or make wine out of it. He (the Imam) said, 'If you sell before it is wine and it is lawful, then selling is not unlawful.'"

H 8993, Ch. 106, h 4

Abu Ali al-Ash'ariy has narrated from Muhammad ibn 'Abd al-Jabbar from Safwan from ibn Muskan from Yazid ibn Khalifah who has said the following:

"Abu 'Abd Allah, *'Alayhi al-Salam*, disliked selling juice for deferred payment."

H 8994, Ch. 106, h 5

Ali ibn Ibrahim has narrated from his father from ibn abu Najran from Muhammad ibn Sinan from Mu'awiyah ibn Sa'd who has said the following:

"I once asked al-Rida', *'Alayhi al-Salam*, about the case of a Christian man who had become a Muslim and he, in his possession, had wine and pigs and he owed debts; if he could sell the wine and pigs to pay off his debts. He (the Imam) said, 'No, he cannot do so.'"

H 8995, Ch. 106, h 6

Safwan has narrated from ibn Muskan from Muhammad al-Halabiy who has said the following:

"This is concerning my question before abu 'Abd Allah, *'Alayhi al-Salam*, about selling grape juice to one who turned it into something unlawful. He (the Imam) said, 'It is not unlawful if you sell when it is lawful then he turns it into unlawful; may Allah keep him away and remotely distanced.'"

H 8996, Ch. 106, h 7

Al-Husayn from Muhammad has narrated from Mu'alla' ibn Muhammad from al-Hassan ibn Ali from Aban from abu Ayyub who has said the following:

"I once said to abu 'Abd Allah, *'Alayhi al-Salam*, 'A man asks his slave to sell his grapes as grape juice but he sells it as wine; then brings the price to him.' He (the Imam) said, 'The most beloved thing to me in this case is to give it (price) as charity.'"

H 8997, Ch. 106, h 8

Ali ibn Ibrahim has narrated from his father from ibn abu 'Umayr from 'Umar ibn 'Udhaynah who has said the following:

"I once wrote to 'Abd Allah, *'Alayhi al-Salam*, and asked about the case of a man who had a vineyard; if he could sell grapes and dates to someone who made wine or sugar out of them. He (the Imam) said, 'He has sold it as lawful when drinking, eating was lawful, thus it is not unlawful.'"

H 8998, Ch. 106, h 9

Ali ibn Ibrahim has narrated from his father from Hammad from Hariz from Muhammad ibn Muslim who has said the following:

"About the case of a man to whom another man owes a certain amount of dirham who sells wine or pig when he (the creditor) is looking, then pays him from such funds. He (the Imam) said, 'It is not unlawful. For the creditor it is lawful and for the seller it is unlawful.'"

H 8999 (a), Ch. 106, h 10

Muhammad ibn Yahya has narrated from Ahmad ibn Muhammad from ibn Faddal from Yunus ibn Ya'qub from Mansur who has said the following:

"I once said to abu 'Abd Allah, *'Alayhi al-Salam*, 'A non-Muslim taxpayer owes to me a certain amount of dirham. He sells wine and pig when I am present; if it is lawful for me to take it. He (the Imam) said, 'All he owes you are dirhams, and he has paid you dirhams.'"

H 8999 (b), Ch. 106, h 11
Ali ibn Ibrahim has narrated from his father from ibn abu 'Umayr from ibn 'Udhaynah from Zurarah who has said the following:

"This is concerning my question before abu 'Abd Allah, *'Alayhi al-Salam*, about the case of a man who owed me a certain amount of dirham with which he sold wine and pigs and with such business he paid me back. He (the Imam) said, 'It is not unlawful' or that he (the Imam) said, 'You can take it.'"

H 9000, Ch. 106, h 12
Muhammad ibn Yahya has narrated from Ahmad ibn Muhammad from 'Isma'il ibn Bazi' from Hanan from abu Kahmas who has said the following:

"A man once asked abu 'Abd Allah, *'Alayhi al-Salam*, about juice saying, 'I have a vineyard. 'Every year I squeeze juice and keep it in a large container, then sell it before it boils. He (the Imam) said, 'It is not harmful but if it boils then selling is not lawful.' He (the Imam) then said, 'We sell our dates knowing that they make wine out of it.'"

H 9001, Ch. 106, h 13
Ali ibn Ibrahim has narrated from his father from 'Isma'il ibn Marrar from Yunus who has said the following:

"About the case of a of Zoroastrian man who sold wine or pigs for an appointed time, then became a Muslim before due time for payment, he (the Imam), *'Alayhi al-Salam*, has said, 'He can have his dirhams.' He (the Imam) said, 'If one becomes a Muslim and owns wine and pigs, then dies while they are in his possession, and he owes a certain amount of debts, his creditor or guardian can sell his wine and pigs to non-Muslims to pay off his debts; but in his life time he cannot sell or keep them.'"

H 9002, Ch. 106, h 14
Ali ibn Ibrahim has narrated from his father from ibn abu 'Umayr from certain persons of our people who has said the following:

"I once asked al-Rida', *'Alayhi al-Salam*, about the case of a Christian man who became a Muslim and had wine and pigs and owed debts; if he could sell his wine and pigs to pay off his debts. He (the Imam) said, 'No, he cannot do so.'"

Chapter 107 - Non-Refundable Deposit

H 9003, Ch. 107, h 1
A number of our people have narrated from Ahmad ibn abu 'Abd Allah from his father from Wahab who has said the following:

"Abu 'Abd Allah, *'Alayhi al-Salam*, has said that 'Amir al-Mu'minin would say, 'Deposit or down payment is not permissible unless it is the cash portion of the price of the goods purchased.'"

Chapter 108 - Security Deposit (*Al-Rahn*) Mortgage

H 9004, Ch. 108, h 1
A number of our people have narrated from Ahmad ibn Muhammad from Ali ibn al-Hakam from Muhammad ibn Muslim from abu Hamzah who has said the following:

"I once asked abu Ja'far, *'Alayhi al-Salam*, about security deposit, mortgage and guarantor in transaction on credit. He (the Imam) said, 'It is not unlawful.'"

H 9005, Ch. 108, h 2
Muhammad ibn Yahya has narrated from Muhammad ibn al-Husayn from Safwan from Ya'qub ibn Shu'ayb who has said the following:

"I once asked him (the Imam), *'Alayhi al-Salam*, about the case of a man who bought something on credit with *al-Rahn* (security deposit). He (the Imam) said, 'It is not unlawful.'"

H 9006, Ch. 108, h 3
Ali ibn Ibrahim has narrated from his father from 'Isma'il ibn Marrar from Yunus from Mu'awiyah ibn 'Ammar who has said the following:

"This is concerning my question before abu 'Abd Allah, *'Alayhi al-Salam*, about the case of a man who contracted for purchasing an animal or foodstuff in the form of advance payment with *al-Rahn* (security deposit). He (the Imam) said, 'It is not unlawful to secure your asset.'"

H 9007, Ch. 108, h 4
Abu Ali al-Ash'ariy has narrated from Muhammad ibn 'Abd al-Jabbar from Safwan from Ishaq ibn 'Ammar who has said the following:

"I once asked abu Ibrahim, *'Alayhi al-Salam*, about the case of a man who had *al-Rahn* (security deposit) with him and did not know to whom it belonged. He (the Imam) said, 'I do not like his selling it until the owner comes.' I said, 'He does not know who the owner is.' He (the Imam) then asked, 'Is there any increase or decrease in it?' I then asked, 'What happens if there is increase or decrease in it?' He (the Imam) said, 'If there is decrease, it is easier. He can sell it and complete the reduction from his own property. If there is increase in it, it is more difficult because he sells it and must keep the increase until its owner comes.'"

H 9008, Ch. 108, h 5
A number of our people have narrated from Ahmad ibn Muhammad ibn Khalid from his father from ibn Bukayr from 'Ubayd ibn Zurarah who has said the following:

"This is concerning my question before abu 'Abd Allah, *'Alayhi al-Salam*, about the case of a man who held *al-Rahn* (security-deposit) for an unspecified time and his party disappeared; if he had a time limit within which he could sell *al-Rahn* (security deposit). He (the Imam) said, 'No, until his party comes.'"

H 9009, Ch. 108, h 6
Muhammad ibn Yahya has narrated from Muhammad ibn al-Husayn from Safwan from ibn Bukayr who has said the following:

"This is concerning my question before abu 'Abd Allah, *'Alayhi al-Salam*, about *al-Rahn* (security deposit). He (the Imam) said, 'If it is more than what mortgagee has provided and it is destroyed, the difference must be paid to the mortgager; but if it is less and is destroyed, the one who has the extra must pay the difference to the mortgagor, and if both sides are equal then there is nothing to dispute about.'"

H 9010, Ch. 108, h 7
A number of our people have narrated from Sahl ibn Ziyad Ahmad ibn Muhammad from Ahmad ibn Muhammad from ibn Mahbub from abu Hamzah who has said the following:

"I once asked abu Ja'far, *'Alayhi al-Salam*, about the words of Ali, *'Alayhi al-Salam*, about *al-Rahn* (security deposit and mortgage) 'both sides return the extra'. He (the Imam) said, 'Ali, *'Alayhi al-Salam*, indeed would say it.' I then asked, 'How both sides return?' He (the Imam) said, 'If what is mortgaged is more than the amount the mortgage has provided and it is destroyed, the mortgagee returns the difference to mortgager; if it is not equal the mortgager returns the difference to the mortgagee.' He (the Imam) said, 'This is how Ali, *'Alayhi al-Salam*, would say about animals and other goods.'"

H 9011, Ch. 108, h 8
Al-Husayn from Muhammad has narrated from Mu'alla' ibn Muhammad from al-Hassan ibn Ali al-Washsha' from Aban from those who narrated to him who has said the following:

"About *al-Rahn* (security deposit and mortgage), abu 'Abd Allah, *'Alayhi al-Salam*, has said, 'If loss takes place on the side of mortgagee without willingly consuming it, he asks the mortgager to provide compensation for his loss; but if he consumes it then both sides exchange the difference to each other.'"

H 9012, Ch. 108, h 9
A number of our people have narrated from Ahmad ibn Muhammad from and Sahl ibn Ziyad from Ahmad ibn Muhammad from ibn abu Nasr from Hammad ibn 'Uthman from Ishaq ibn 'Ammar who has said the following:

"I once asked abu Ibrahim, *'Alayhi al-Salam*, about the case of a man who made an *al-Rahn* (security deposit and mortgage) deal which is for one hundred dirham with a value of three hundred dirham and it was consumed; if he had to pay two hundred dirham to the other party. He (the Imam) said, 'Yes, because he has taken *al-Rahn* (security deposit) in which there is increase and loss.' I then asked, 'What happens if half is consumed?' He (the Imam) said, 'It is proportionate.' I then asked, 'Do they return to each other the extra?' He (the Imam) said, 'Yes, that it true.'"

H 9013, Ch. 108, h 10
Through the same chain of narrators as that of the previous Hadith the following is narrated:

"I once asked abu Ibrahim, *'Alayhi al-Salam*, about the case of a man who mortgaged a slave and the house and they suffered loss; if it was compensated by a particular party. He (the Imam) said, 'His master is responsible.' He (the Imam) then said, 'Suppose if someone is murdered who is responsible?' I replied, 'It is on the neck of the slave.' He (the Imam) said, 'Do you not consider that his property is not gone?' He (the Imam) then said, 'Consider, if his price was one hundred dinar and it increased up to two hundred dinars. To whom does it (the increase) belong?' I replied, 'It belongs to his master.' He (the Imam) said, 'In the same way it is on him just as it is for him.'"

H 9014, Ch. 108, h 11

Ali ibn Ibrahim has narrated from his father from ibn abu 'Umayr from Hammad from al-Halabiy who has said the following:

"About the case of a man who takes mortgage from another man, then it suffers loss or is lost. He (the Imam), *'Alayhi al-Salam*, has said, 'He can demand what is for him from the other party.'"

H 9015, Ch. 108, h 12

Muhammad ibn Yahya has narrated from Muhammad ibn al-Husayn from Safwan from Ishaq ibn 'Ammar who has said the following:

"I once asked abu Ibrahim, *'Alayhi al-Salam*, about the case of a man who left a slave, or clothes, or jewelries, or goods of the household as *al-Rahn* (security deposit) with someone, then said to mortgagee, 'You have permission to wear the clothes so wear them and benefit from the goods and use the services of the servant.' He (the Imam) said, 'It is lawful for him when he has made it lawful for him but I do not like if he did.' I asked, 'If one leaves a house as *al-Rahn* (security deposit) which has a certain amount of income. To whom such income belongs?' He (the Imam) said, 'It belongs to the owner of the house.' I then said, 'One has left his uncultivated land as *al-Rahn* (security deposit) saying to the party, "Farm it for yourself."' He (the Imam) said, 'This is not like that. He farms it for himself and it is lawful for him as he has made it lawful for him but he farms it with his own asset and establishes it.'"

H 9016, Ch. 108, h 13

Ali ibn Ibrahim has narrated from his father from 'Abd Allah ibn al-Mughirah from ibn Sinan who has said the following:

"Abu 'Abd Allah, *'Alayhi al-Salam*, has said that 'Amir al-Mu'minin had issued a judgment that said, 'Whoever leaves an income-producing *al-Rahn* (security deposit), such income is counted in favor of the owner of *al-Rahn* (security deposit) against what he owes.'"

H 9017, Ch. 108, h 14

Ali ibn Ibrahim has narrated from his father from ibn abu Najran from 'Asim ibn Humayd from Muhammad ibn al-Qays who has said the following:

Abu Ja'far, *'Alayhi al-Salam*, has said that 'Amir al-Mu'minin has said, 'If one holds a piece of barren land as *al-Rahn* (security deposit) which has no fruits and he farms it and incurs expenses on it, he keeps accounts of whatever he has spent and his work; then counts the share of the land to compensate for his assets with which he holds the land as *al-Rahn* (security deposit) until he compensates his assets, then returns the land to its owner.'"

H 9018, Ch. 108, h 15

Ali ibn Ibrahim has narrated from his father from ibn abu 'Umayr from Hammad from al-Halabiy who has said the following:

"This is concerning my question before abu 'Abd Allah, *'Alayhi al-Salam*, about the case of a man who left his slave-girl as *al-Rahn* (security deposit) with a people if it was lawful for him to do sexual intercourse with her. He (the Imam) said, 'Those who hold her as *al-Rahn* (security deposit) will bar him.' I then asked, 'What happens if he gets a chance? He (the Imam) said, 'Yes, I do not see it to be unlawful for him.'"

H 9019, Ch. 108, h 16
A number of our people have narrated from Sahl ibn Ziyad and Ahmad ibn Muhammad from ibn Mahbub from abu Wallad who has said the following:
"This is concerning my question before abu 'Abd Allah, *'Alayhi al-Salam*, about the case of a man who held a stumper and camels as *al-Rahn* (security deposit) against his assets; if he could ride them. He (the Imam) said, 'If he feeds them he can ride; but if the one who has left them as *al-Rahn* (security deposit) feeds them, then he cannot ride.'"

H 9020, Ch. 108, h 17
Muhammad ibn Yahya has narrated from certain persons of our people from Mansur ibn al-'Abbas from al-Hassan ibn Ali ibn Yaqtin from 'Amr ibn Ibrahim from Khalaf ibn Hammad from 'Isma'il ibn abu Qurrah from abu Basir who has said the following:
"About the case of a man, who borrows one hundred dinars and leaves as *al-Rahn* (security deposit) jewelries worth one hundred dinars, then comes to *al-Rahn* (security deposit) holder and asks him to lend him the gold which he has with him. *Al-Rahn* (security deposit) holder lends it to him and it is destroyed; if he owes anything to the man who has left *al-Rahn* (security deposit) with him. He (the Imam) said, 'It is on the one who left *al-Rahn* (security deposit) because he is the one who destroyed it and *al-Rahn* (security deposit) holder does not owe anything, not even a grain.'"

H 9021, Ch. 108, h 18
Muhammad ibn Ja'far al-Razzaz has narrated from Muhammad ibn 'Abd al-Hamid from Sayf ibn 'Amirah from Mansur ibn Hazim from Sulayman ibn Khalid who has said the following:
"Abu 'Abd Allah, *'Alayhi al-Salam*, has said, 'If you hold a slave or stumper as *al-Rahn* (security deposit) and they die; there is nothing upon you, but if the stumper is destroyed or the slave runs away you are responsible for it.'"

H 9022, Ch. 108, h 19
Abu Ali al-Ash'ariy has narrated from Muhammad ibn 'Abd al-Jabbar from Safwan from Muhammad ibn Riyah al-Qala' who has said the following:
I once asked abu al-Hassan, *'Alayhi al-Salam*, about the case of a man whose brother had died and left a box in which there were *al-Rahn* (security deposit) goods, of which certain ones had the name of the owner on them and others did not have any names on them and for how much they were left as *al-Rahn* (security deposit), and what do you say about that with an unknown owner. He (the Imam) said, 'It is like his own property.'"

H 9023, Ch. 108, h 20
Muhammad ibn Yahya has narrated from Ahmad ibn Muhammad from Safwan from al-'Ala' from Muhammad ibn Muslim who has said the following:
"I once asked abu Ja'far, *'Alayhi al-Salam*, about the case of a man who had left his slave-girl as *al-Rahn* (security deposit) with a people; if he could have sexual intercourse with her. He (the Imam) said, 'Those who hold her as *al-Rahn*

(security deposit) bar him from reaching her.' I asked, 'What happens if he gets a chance? He (the Imam) said, 'Yes, I do not see it as unlawful.'"

H 9024, Ch. 108, h 21
Ahmad ibn Muhammad has narrated from ibn Faddal from Ibrahim ibn 'Uthman who has said the following:
"I once said to abu 'Abd Allah, *'Alayhi al-Salam*, 'There is a man who owes to me a certain amount of dirhams and his house is as *al-Rahn* (security deposit) with me and I want to sell it. He (the Imam) said, 'Do you, by Allah, have the intention to take the roof away from the top of his head?'"

H 9025, Ch. 108, h 22
Ahmad ibn Muhammad has narrated from Muhammad ibn 'Isa from Mansur ibn Hazim from Hisham ibn Salim who has said the following:
"Once, abu 'Abd Allah, *'Alayhi al-Salam*, was asked about the case of a man to whom another man owed a certain amount of debts. He held *al-Rahn* (security deposit) if he could buy *al-Rahn* (security deposit). He (the Imam) said, 'Yes, he can do so.'"

Chapter 109 - Disputes Arising From *al-Rahn* (Security Deposit, Mortgage)

H 9026, Ch. 109, h 1
Humayd ibn Ziyad has narrated from al-Hassan ibn Muhammad from more than one person from Aban from ibn abu Ya'fur who has said the following:
"About the case of a dispute between the parties if one says that the amount of *al-Rahn* (security deposit) is one thousand dirham and the other says that it is one hundred dirham, abu 'Abd Allah, *'Alayhi al-Salam*, has said, 'The one who claims it to be one thousand dirham is asked to present proof and testimony. If he fails to do so, then the other party is asked to take an oath.' If the amount of *al-Rahn* (security deposit) is more or less but one party claims it to be *al-Rahn* (security deposit) and the party claims it to be *Wadi'ah* (safe deposit), abu 'Abd Allah, *'Alayhi al-Salam*, has said, 'The party who claims it to be *Wadi'ah* (safe deposit) is asked to present proof and testimony and upon his failure the other party is then asked to take an oath (to settle the dispute).'"

H 9027, Ch. 109, h 2
Muhammad ibn Yahya has narrated from Muhammad ibn al-Husayn from Ali ibn al-Hakam from al-'Ala' ibn Razin from Muhammad ibn Muslim who has said the following:
"It is the case of the parties of *al-Rahn* (security deposit) who dispute and there is no proof and testimony available for the parties involved. *Al-Rahn* (security deposit) holder claims it to be one thousand and the owner of *al-Rahn* (security deposit) claims it to be one hundred. Abu Ja'far, *'Alayhi al-Salam*, has said, '*Al-Rahn* (security deposit) holder who claims it to be one thousand is required to present proof and testimony and if he fails then the other party takes an oath.'"

H 9028, Ch. 109, h 3
Muhammad ibn Yahya has narrated from Ahmad ibn Muhammad from ibn abu 'Umayr from al-Husayn ibn 'Uthman from Ishaq ibn 'Ammar who has said the following:

"It is a case where one says that he is owed one thousand dirham and the other party says that it is *Wadi'ah* (safe deposit). Abu 'Abd Allah, *'Alayhi al-Salam*, has said, 'The words of the owner of the asset are accepted in addition to his taking oath.'"

H 9029, Ch. 109, h 4

Muhammad ibn Yahya has narrated from Ahmad ibn Muhammad from ibn Mahbub from 'Abbad ibn Suhayb who has said the following:

"This is concerning my question before abu 'Abd Allah, *'Alayhi al-Salam*, about the case of two men who disputed about an asset. One said that it was a *Wadi'ah* (safe deposit) and the other said that it was *al-Rahn* (security deposit). Abu 'Abd Allah, *'Alayhi al-Salam*, has said, 'The words of one who says that it is *al-Rahn* (security deposit) are accepted unless the other party presents witnesses who testify that it is *Wadi'ah* (safe deposit).'"

Chapter 110 - Liability for Safe Deposit and Borrowing

H 9030, Ch. 110, h 1

Ali ibn Ibrahim has narrated from his father from ibn abu 'Umayr from Hammad from al-Halabiy who has said the following:

"About the case of a man who claims that *Wadi'ah* (safe deposit) were entrusted assets, abu 'Abd Allah, *'Alayhi al-Salam*, has said, 'If a borrowed item is destroyed with the borrower he is not held liable unless it is stipulated.'"

In another Hadith it is said that if the borrower is a just Muslim he is not held liable.

H 9031, Ch. 110, h 2

Ali ibn Ibrahim has narrated from his father from 'Abd Allah ibn al-Mughirah from 'Abd Allah ibn Sinan who has said the following:

"Abu 'Abd Allah, *'Alayhi al-Salam*, has said, 'A borrower is not held liable for the item borrowed unless it is stipulated, except dinar which brings liability even if there is no stipulation.'"

H 9032, Ch. 110, h 3

Ali ibn Ibrahim has narrated from his father from ibn abu 'Umayr from Jamil from Zurarah who has said the following:

"This is concerning my question before abu 'Abd Allah, *'Alayhi al-Salam*, about the borrowed item; if the borrower was held liable for it. He (the Imam) said, 'If whatever you borrow is destroyed, you are not held liable except gold and silver; which bring liability unless it is stipulated that even on being destroyed you are not held liable. You are held liable for all that you borrow and it is stipulated that you are liable. Gold and silver bring liability, even if no stipulation is set.'"

H 9033, Ch. 110, h 4

Al-Husayn from Muhammad has narrated from Mu'alla' ibn Muhammad from al-Hassan ibn Ali from Aban (from Muhammad) who has said the following:

"I once asked abu Ja'far, *'Alayhi al-Salam*, about a borrowed item; if it was destroyed or was stolen. He (the Imam) said, 'If the borrower is trustworthy he is not held liable.' I then asked him (the Imam) about the case of a man who gave certain amount of assets to another person to use in business in which the worker had no share in the profit and the asset was destroyed or stolen; if this person was held responsible. He (the Imam) said, 'The man is not responsible for the loss after being found trustworthy.'"

H 9034, Ch. 110, h 5

Ali ibn Ibrahim has narrated from his father from 'Abd Allah ibn al-Mughirah from 'Abd Allah ibn Sinan who has said the following:

"This is concerning my question before abu 'Abd Allah, *'Alayhi al-Salam*, about the case of a borrowed item. He (the Imam) said, 'The borrower has no liability if the item is destroyed if he is trustworthy.'"

H 9035, Ch. 110, h 6

Al-Husayn from Muhammad has narrated from Mu'alla' ibn Muhammad from al-Hassan ibn Ali from Aban ibn 'Uthman from the one who narrated to him who has said the following:

"This is concerning my question before abu 'Abd Allah, *'Alayhi al-Salam*, about the case of a man who borrowed clothes, then left it as *al-Rahn* (security deposit) with someone; then the owner came to take it. He (the Imam) said, 'They can take their asset.'"

H 9036, Ch. 110, h 7

Ali ibn Ibrahim has narrated from his father from Hammad from Hariz from Zurarah who has said the following:

"This is concerning my question before abu 'Abd Allah, *'Alayhi al-Salam*, about the *Wadi'ah* (safe deposit) of gold and silver. He (the Imam) said, 'Whatever of *Wadi'ah* (safe deposit) for which liability is not stipulated does not make one liable.'"

H 9037, Ch. 110, h 8

A number of our people have narrated from Ahmad ibn Muhammad from and Sahl ibn Ziyad from Ahmad ibn Muhammad from ibn abu Nasr from Hammad ibn 'Uthman from Ishaq ibn 'Ammar who has said the following:

"I once asked abu al-Hassan, *'Alayhi al-Salam*, about the case of a man who borrowed one thousand dirham and it was lost and he said that it was *Wadi'ah* (safe deposit) with him and the other said that it was a debt on him. He (the Imam) said, 'He is responsible for it unless he presents proof that it was *Wadi'ah* (safe deposit).'"

H 9038, Ch. 110, h 9

Muhammad ibn Yahya has narrated from Muhammad ibn al-Husayn who has said the following:

"I wrote to abu Muhammad, *'Alayhi al-Salam*, and asked, 'A man leaves *Wadi'ah* (safe deposit) with another man who keeps it in the house of his neighbor and it is lost; if he is held liable for it after taking it out of his property against the instruction of the owner. He (the Imam) signed the answer that said, 'He is responsible for it, by the will of Allah.'"

H 9039, Ch. 110, h 10

Ali has narrated from his father from ibn abu Najran from 'Asim ibn Humayd from abu Basir who has said the following:

"I once heard abu 'Abd Allah, *'Alayhi al-Salam*, saying that the Messenger of Allah, *O Allah, grant compensation to Muhammad and his family worthy of their services to Your cause*, sent a message to Safwan ibn 'Umayyah asking him to borrow seventy pieces of coats of arms with their helmets. He asked, 'Is it forcibly, O Muhammad?' The Holy Prophet replied, 'It is borrowing with guarantee to return.'"

Chapter 111 - Liability for Profit Sharing, Its Profit and Expenses (*Al-Mudarabah*)

H 9040, Ch. 111, h 1
Ali ibn Ibrahim has narrated from his father from ibn abu 'Umayr from Hammad from al-Halabiy who has said the following:
"About the case of a man who gives a certain amount of asset to another man and tells him to go to so and so city and not beyond it then buy from it goods, abu 'Abd Allah, *'Alayhi al-Salam*, has said, 'If he goes beyond and the asset is destroyed, he is accountable and if he buys goods and it depreciates it is his responsibility; but if it makes profit it is for both parties.'"

H 9041, Ch. 111, h 2
Muhammad ibn Yahya ht Muhammad ibn al-Husayn from Ali ibn al-Hakam from al-'Ala' from Muhammad ibn Muslim who has said the following:
"I once asked one of the two Imam, (abu Ja'far or abu 'Abd Allah), *'Alayhim al-Salam*, about the case of a man who gave a certain amount of assets to another man for *Mudarabah* (profit sharing) and prohibited him from taking it out with him, but he went out. He (the Imam) said, 'He is held responsible for the assets and the profit is for both.'"

H 9042, Ch. 111, h 3
Ali ibn Ibrahim has narrated from his father from ibn abu Najran from 'Asim ibn Humayd from Muhammad ibn Qays who has said the following:
"Abu Ja'far, *'Alayhi al-Salam*, has said that 'Amir al-Mu'minin has said, 'If one uses a certain amount of assets in business with stipulation for half of the profit, he is not liable.' He (the Imam) also said, 'One who holds a merchant responsible he can only have his capital and has no share in the profit.'"

H 9043, Ch. 111, h 4
Ali ibn Ibrahim has narrated from his father from al-Nawfaliy from al-Sakuniy who has said the following:
"Abu 'Abd Allah, *'Alayhi al-Salam*, has said that about the case of a man who owed a certain amount of assets to another man who demanded it but he did not have it, then told him to keep it as capital for *Mudarabah* (profit sharing), 'Amir al-Mu'minin, has said, 'It is not valid until he takes possession.'"

H 9044, Ch. 111, h 5
Muhammad ibn Yahya has narrated from al-'Amrakiy ibn Ali from Ali ibn Ja'far from his brother who has said the following:
"About the case of *Mudarabah* (profit sharing) abu al-Hassan, *'Alayhi al-Salam*, has said, 'Whatever the trading party spends during his journey is from all of the

assets, but when he arrives home thereafter whatever he spends is from his own share.'"

H 9045, Ch. 111, h 6
Humayd ibn Ziyad has narrated from al-Hassan ibn Muhammad ibn Sama'ah from more than one person from Aban ibn 'Uthman from Ishaq ibn 'Ammar who has said the following:
"This is concerning my question before abu 'Abd Allah, *'Alayhi al-Salam*, about the case of a man who had a certain amount of assets for *Mudarabah* (profit sharing) with him but made very little profit; and was afraid of the other party's taking away the capital, so he paid him more than the amount stipulated, so that he would not take the capital away. He (the Imam) said, 'It is not unlawful.'"

H 9046, Ch. 111, h 7
Abu Ali al-Ash'ariy has narrated from Muhammad ibn 'Abd al-Jabbar from Muhammad ibn 'Isma'il from Ali ibn al-Nu'man from abu al-Sabbah al-Kinaniy who has said the following:
"About the case of a man who works for *Mudarabah* (profit sharing), abu 'Abd Allah, *'Alayhi al-Salam*, has said, 'He can have (his share of) the profit but is not liable for depreciation (loss) unless he violates the instructions of the owner of the assets.'"

H 9047, Ch. 111, h 8
Ali ibn Ibrahim has narrated from his father from ibn abu 'Umayr from Muhammad ibn Muyassir who has said the following:
"This is concerning my question before abu 'Abd Allah, *'Alayhi al-Salam*, about the case of a man who gave one thousand dirham to another man for *Mudarabah* (profit sharing) and he bought his father without knowing. He (the Imam) said, 'He is appraised, even if a single dirham remains extra (as profit), he is free while it has spread into the assets of the man.'"

H 9048, Ch. 111, h 9
Ali ibn Ibrahim has narrated from his father from al-Nawfaliy from al-Sakuniy who has said the following:
"Abu 'Abd Allah, *'Alayhi al-Salam*, has said that 'Amir al-Mu'minin, about *Mudarabah* (profit sharing), has said, 'Whatever he spends during his journey is from the whole of the capital, but when he is back home then whatever he spends is from his own share.'"

Chapter 112 - Liability of Technician or Person with a Certain Skill

H 9049, Ch. 112, h 1
Ali ibn Ibrahim has narrated from his father from ibn abu 'Umayr from Hammad from al-Halabiy who has said the following:
"Once abu 'Abd Allah, *'Alayhi al-Salam*, was asked about a cleaner who destroyed. He (the Imam) said, 'Everyone hired and paid for mending an item is liable if the item is destroyed.'"

H 9050, Ch. 112, h 2

It is narrated from the narrator of the previous Hadith from his father from ibn abu 'Umayr from Hammad from al-Halabiy who has said the following:

"Abu 'Abd Allah, *'Alayhi al-Salam*, has said, 'In the case of cleaners and dyers and the items stolen from them with no clear evidence that he has stolen, of small or large quantities, if it happens, there is nothing on him, if no evidence is presented to prove it to be his doing; but if he thinks the claimant has done it, he is liable if he fails to present evidence in support of what he says.'"

H 9051, Ch. 112, h 3

Through the same chain of narrators as that of the previous Hadith the following is narrated:

"Abu 'Abd Allah, *'Alayhi al-Salam*, has said that 'Amir al-Mu'minin, would hold a cleaner liable as well as a dyer as precautionary measures to protect the interests of the people but my father would deal with them more graciously if they were trusted ones.'"

H 9052, Ch. 112, h 4

Muhammad ibn Yahya has narrated from Ahmad ibn Muhammad from those whom he has mentioned from ibn Muskan from abu Basir who has said the following:

"This is concerning my question before abu 'Abd Allah, *'Alayhi al-Salam*, about the case of a cleaner to whom I gave a cloth and he thought it was stolen from his goods. He (the Imam) said, 'He is required to present evidence that it is stolen from his goods; then there is nothing on him and if all of his goods are stolen he is not liable for anything.'"

H 9053, Ch. 112, h 5

Ali ibn Ibrahim has narrated from his father from al-Nawfaliy from al-Sakuniy who has said the following:

"Abu 'Abd Allah, *'Alayhi al-Salam*, has said that 'Amir al-Mu'minin would hold cleaners, jewelers and dyers liable as precautionary measure to protect the interests of the people; but he would not hold them liable for things burnt or drowned. When a ship drowned with its contents and people found things thrown on shore, it was for the people of the area because of their being more rightful in the case. Whatever people found by diving and the owner had abandoned, it was considered their things.'"

H 9054, Ch. 112, h 6

Ali ibn Ibrahim has narrated from his father from ibn abu Najran from Safwan from al-Kahiliy who has said the following:

"This is concerning my question before abu 'Abd Allah, *'Alayhi al-Salam*, about the case of a cleaner man to whom I gave clothes with a condition to return at a given time. He (the Imam) said, 'If he violates the time and clothes are lost after the given time he is liable.'"

H 9055, Ch. 112, h 7

A number of our people have narrated from Ahmad ibn Muhammad ibn 'Isa from Ali ibn al-Hakam from 'Isma'il ibn abu al-Sabbah who has said the following:

"This is concerning my question before abu 'Abd Allah, *'Alayhi al-Salam*, about the case of a cleaner man to whom I gave clothes but he burnt them. He (the

Imam) said, 'You can make him compensate, you gave him for mending and not to destroy them.'"

H 9056, Ch. 112, h 8
Ahmad ibn Muhammad has narrated from Muhammad ibn Yahya from Ghiyath ibn Ibrahim who has said the following:
"Abu 'Abd Allah, *'Alayhi al-Salam*, has said that once the owner of a public bath house with whom clothes were left and were lost, was brought before 'Amir al-Mu'minin, *'Alayhi al-Salam*, who did not hold him liable and said that he was trusted.'"

H 9057, Ch. 112, h 9
Ali ibn Ibrahim has narrated from his father from al-Nawfaliy from al-Sakuniy who has said the following:
"Abu 'Abd Allah, *'Alayhi al-Salam*, has said that once a man who had hired another man to mend his door and who by driving a nail into the door had damaged it, came for judgment before 'Amir al-Mu'minin, and he ('Amir al-Mu'minin) held him liable for the door.'"

H 9058, Ch. 112, h 10
Ali ibn Ibrahim has narrated from his father from 'Isma'il ibn Marrar from Yunus who has said the following:
"I once asked al-Rida', *'Alayhi al-Salam*, about the case of a cleaner man and a jeweler if they were liable. He (the Imam) said, 'People do not behave well unless they are held liable.' Yunus would act accordingly and hold liable.'"

Chapter 113 - Liability of Carrier Animals and Owners of Ships

H 9059, Ch. 113, h 1
Ali ibn Ibrahim has narrated from his father from ibn abu 'Umayr from Hammad from al-Halabiy who has said the following:
"Once abu 'Abd Allah, *'Alayhi al-Salam*, was asked about the case of a man who hired a camel man to transport oil to another location and he thought that certain skin sacks were damaged and oil was lost. He (the Imam) said, 'If he likes he can accept the oil.' He (the Imam) said, 'Even if it is damaged he is not considered truthful without just witnesses and evidence.'"

H 9060, Ch. 113, h 2
A number of our people have narrated from Ahmad ibn Muhammad ibn 'Isa from Muhammad ibn Yahya from Yahya ibn al-Hajjaj from Khalid ibn al-Hajjaj who has said the following:
"This is concerning my question before abu 'Abd Allah, *'Alayhi al-Salam*, about the case of a man who transported people on the water to the other side and I carried foodstuff through him then received it from him and it was reduced. He (the Imam) said, 'If he is trusted, you must not hold him liable.'"

H 9061, Ch. 113, h 3
Ali ibn Ibrahim has narrated from his father from ibn abu 'Umayr from Hammad from al-Halabiy who has said the following:

"In the case of a man who carries foodstuff in the ship and it is reduced, abu 'Abd Allah, *'Alayhi al-Salam*, has said, 'He is liable.' I then asked, 'What if it is increased?' He (the Imam) said, 'Do you know it is increased?' I replied, 'No, I do not know.' He (the Imam) said, 'It is for you.'"

H 9062, Ch. 113, h 4

Muhammad ibn Yahya has narrated from Muhammad ibn al-Husayn from Ali ibn al-Hakam from Musa ibn Bakr who has said the following:

"I once asked abu al-Hassan, *'Alayhi al-Salam*, about the case of a man who hired a ship from a sailor and loaded it with foodstuff, with the condition that if it was reduced he was liable. He (the Imam) said, 'It is permissible.' I then said, 'Perhaps it increases.' He (the Imam) asked, 'Does the sailor claim that he has increased anything to it?' I replied, 'No, he does not claim.' He (the Imam) said, 'It belongs to the owner of the foodstuff and he is liable for reduction if it is stipulated.'"

H 9063, Ch. 113, h 5

Muhammad ibn Yahya has narrated from Ahmad ibn Muhammad from ibn abu 'Umayr from Ja'far ibn 'Uthman who has said the following:

"My father carried goods to al-Sham with a camel man, then he remembered that one load was lost. I mentioned it to abu 'Abd Allah, *'Alayhi al-Salam*, and he asked, 'Do you charge him?' I replied, 'No, I do not charge him.' He (the Imam) said, 'You must not hold him liable.'"

H 9064, Ch. 113, h 6

Muhammad ibn Yahya has narrated from Ahmad ibn Muhammad from al-'Abbas ibn Musa from Yunus from ibn Muskan from abu Basir who has said the following:

"About the case of a camel man who breaks what he carries or spills, abu 'Abd Allah, *'Alayhi al-Salam*, has said, 'If he is trusted, there is nothing on him; but if he is not trusted then he is liable.'"

H 9065, Ch. 113, h 7

A number of our people have narrated from Sahl ibn Ziyad from Muhammad ibn al-Hassan ibn Shammun from 'Abd Allah ibn 'Abd al-Rahman from Misma' ibn 'Abd al-Malik who has said the following:

"Abu 'Abd Allah, *'Alayhi al-Salam*, has said that 'Amir al-Mu'minin has said, 'One hired and a partner are liable unless it (the loss) is because of beasts, drowning, burning or a stubborn thief.'"

Chapter 114 - Currency Exchange

H 9066, Ch. 114, h 1

A number of our people have narrated from Ahmad ibn Muhammad ibn 'Isa from Muhammad ibn 'Isa from Yahya ibn al-Hajjaj from Khalid ibn al-Hajjaj who has said the following:

"I once asked him (the Imam), *'Alayhi al-Salam*, about the case of a man who owed me a hundred dirham in numbers and he paid me by weight. He (the Imam) said, 'It is not unlawful if it is not stipulated.' He (the Imam) said, *'Riba'* comes from stipulation; only stipulation destroys it.'"

H 9067, Ch. 114, h 2

A number of our people have narrated from Ahmad ibn Muhammad from and Sahl ibn Ziyad from ibn Mahbub from Ishaq ibn 'Ammar who has said the following:

"I once said to abu 'Abd Allah, *'Alayhi al-Salam*, 'A man had a certain amount of clear dirhams with me and in a meeting asked me about the rates of clear dirham on that day and I said, 'It is so and so much today.' He asked if he had so and so much thousand clear dirhams with me and I said that he was right and he asked me to change them with dinars with such rate and keep them with me. I wish to have your word about it. He (the Imam) said to me, 'If you checked the rate thoroughly for him on that day it is not unlawful.' I then said that I did not weigh or actually exchange them; it was only exchange of words between us. He (the Imam) asked, 'Is it not the case that dirhams are with you as well as dinars?' I replied, 'Yes, that is right.' He (the Imam) said, 'It is not unlawful.'"

H 9068, Ch. 114, h 3

A number of our people have narrated from Ahmad ibn Muhammad ibn 'Isa from Ali ibn al-Hakam from 'Abd al-Malik ibn 'Utbah al-Hashimiy who has said the following:

"I once asked abu al-Hassan, Musa, *'Alayhi al-Salam*, about the case of a man who had with him a certain amount of dinars that belonged to a person of his associates for which he took *wariq* (dirham) from him for his needs; and the rate on that day was seven and seven and a half dirham for dinar. The owner of the asset asked for a certain amount of *wariq* (dirham) for his needs and it was not present and he bought them for him from a money changer with this rate or so then the rate changed before they finalized the account until the *wariq* (dirham) became twelve dirhams for one dinar; if he could settle it with him and it was with the rate as it was at the beginning when he took possession which was seven and seven and a half for a dinar. He (the Imam) said, 'When he gave *wariq* (dirham) to him equal to the amount of dinars it is not harmful how the rates are and it is not harmful.'"

H 9069, Ch. 114, h 4

Ali ibn Ibrahim has narrated from his father from ibn abu 'Umayr from Hammad from al-Halabiy who has said the following:

"This is concerning my question before abu 'Abd Allah, *'Alayhi al-Salam*, about the case of a man who owed dinars. He (the Imam) said, 'It is not unlawful if he takes its price in the form of dirhams.'"

H 9070, Ch. 114, h 5

Ali ibn Ibrahim has narrated from his father from Hammad ibn 'Isa from Hariz from Muhammad ibn Muslim who has said the following:

"I once asked him (the Imam), *'Alayhi al-Salam*, about the case of a man to whom another man owed a certain amount of dinars and he assigned another man to collect it from him; if he could take it in the form of dirhams for the current rate. He (the Imam) said, 'Yes, if he wanted.'"

H 9071, Ch. 114, h 6

Abu Ali al-Ash'ariy has narrated from Muhammad ibn 'Abd al-Jabbar from Safwan from ibn Muskan from al-Halabiy who has said the following:

"This is concerning my question before abu 'Abd Allah, *'Alayhi al-Salam*, about the case of a man who owed a certain amount of dirham and the party asked him to accept from him in the form of dinar at the current rate. He (the Imam) said, 'It is not unlawful.'"

H 9072, Ch. 114, h 7

Abu Ali al-Ash'ariy has narrated from Muhammad ibn 'Abd al-Jabbar from Safwan ibn Yahya from Ishaq ibn 'Ammar who has said the following:

"I once asked abu Ibrahim, *'Alayhi al-Salam*, about the case of a man who sold to me *wariq* (dirham) for dinar and I weighed it from him. I weighed it for him until it was complete and there was no other work between us, except that his *wariq* (dirham) had invalid and unreal pieces, and what was not permissible in them. He asked me to find and return such pieces. He (the Imam) said, 'It is not unlawful; however, you must not delay it more than one day or two, because it is exchange.' I then asked, 'What happens if I find extra in them equal to the amount of invalid ones?' He (the Imam) said, 'This is precautionary measure and I like it more.'"

H 9073, Ch. 114, h 8

Safwan has narrated from Ishaq ibn 'Ammar who has said the following:

"This is concerning my question before abu 'Abd Allah, *'Alayhi al-Salam*, if exchange of dirham for dirham and lead was permissible. He (the Imam) said, 'Lead is not valid.'"

H 9074, Ch. 114, h 9

Muhammad ibn Yahya has narrated from Muhammad ibn al-Husayn from Safwan from 'Abd al-Rahman ibn al-Hajjaj who has said the following:

"I once asked him (the Imam), *'Alayhi al-Salam*, about currency exchange saying, 'The comrades perhaps hurry and I go with them but cannot find al-Dimishqiyah (dirham) or al-Basriyah; they only allow only Sabur of al-Dimishqiyah and al-Basriyah. He (the Imam) asked, 'What is comrade?' I replied, 'A group of people get together to travel and when they hurry we may not find al-Dimishqiyah and al-Basriyah; then we send invalid dirham and they exchange it one thousand and fifteen for one thousand al-Dimishqiyah and al-Basriyah.' He (the Imam) said, 'There is nothing good in it. Why you do not place gold instead of the extra?' I then asked, 'Can I buy one thousand dinar for two thousand dirhams?' He (the Imam) said, 'It is not unlawful. My father was more influential than me among the people of al-Madinah and he would say this. People would say it is running away. If a man comes with dinar he does not give it for a thousand dirham, and if he comes with one thousand dirham, he does not give one thousand dinar. He (the Imam) would say to them, 'Yes, running away from unlawful matters to lawful ones is the best policy.'"

Ali ibn Ibrahim has narrated from his father and Muhammad ibn 'Isma'il has narrated from al-Fadl ibn Shadhan from Safwan ibn Yahya and ibn abu 'Umayr from 'Abd al-Rahman, a similar Hadith.

H 9075, Ch. 114, h 10

Ali ibn Ibrahim has narrated from his father from ibn abu 'Umayr from 'Abd al-Rahman ibn al-Hajjaj who has said the following:

"Abu 'Abd Allah, *'Alayhi al-Salam*, has said that Muhammad ibn al-Munkadir would say to my father, 'O abu Ja'far, Allah has granted you kindness, by Allah, we know, if you take a dinar and the rate is eighteen and you go around the whole of al-Madinah to find one who would give you twenty, you will not find and this is no more than running away. My father would say, 'You are right, by Allah, however, it is running away from falsehood to the truth.'"

H 9076, Ch. 114, h 11

Abu Ali al-Ash'ariy has narrated from Muhammad ibn 'Abd al-Jabbar from Safwan from ibn Muskan from Muhammad al-Halabiy who has said the following:

"This is concerning my question before abu 'Abd Allah, *'Alayhi al-Salam*, about the case of a man who exchanged al-Kufiy (dirham) for al-Shamiy in equal weight, and the exchanger said, 'I will not exchange it for you unless you exchange for me invalid Yusufiyah in equal weight.' He (the Imam) said, 'It is not unlawful.' We then said, 'The exchanger asked for the extra of invalid al-Yusufiyah only.' He (the Imam) said, 'It is not unlawful.'"

H 9077, Ch. 114, h 12

Muhammad ibn Yahya has narrated from Ahmad ibn Muhammad from Muhammad ibn 'Isma'il from Mansur ibn Yunus from Ishaq ibn 'Ammar from 'Ubayd ibn Zurarah who has said the following:

"This is concerning my question before abu 'Abd Allah, *'Alayhi al-Salam*, about the case of a man with whom I had a certain amount of dinars; I asked him to change them to dirhams and keep them with himself. I did not take possession of any of them.' He (the Imam) said, 'It is not unlawful.'"

H 9078, Ch. 114, h 13

Ali ibn Ibrahim has narrated from his father from ibn abu 'Umayr from Hammad from al-Halabiy who has said the following:

"This is concerning my question before abu 'Abd Allah, *'Alayhi al-Salam*, about the case of a man who bought from another man with a dinar; half in the form of certain goods, and with the half in the form of dirham. He (the Imam) said, 'It is not unlawful.' I then asked, 'Can he take half in the form of goods or dirham and leave the rest until he comes back and takes it in the form of dirham or goods?' He (the Imam) said, 'I do not like his leaving anything without taking it all at once.'"

H 9079, Ch. 114, h 14

Abu Ali al-Ash'ariy has narrated from Muhammad ibn 'Abd al-Jabbar from Safwan from Ishaq ibn 'Ammar who has said the following:

"I once asked abu Ibrahim, *'Alayhi al-Salam*, about the case of a man who came to me with dirham and I bought them from him with dinars; then I because of manner of weighing, cashing and the difference in between, I gave him dinars and said, 'It is not a sale between us; I change what is between us in the form of sale. Your dirham with me is in the form of loan and my dinar with you is in the form of loan until you come tomorrow, then I sell.' He (the Imam) said, 'It is not unlawful.'"

H 9080, Ch. 114, h 15
Ali ibn Ibrahim has narrated from his father and Muhammad ibn 'Isma'il has narrated from al-Fadl ibn Shadhan from all from ibn abu 'Umayr from 'Abd al-Rahman ibn al-Hajjaj who has said the following:
"About the case of buying *al-Asrub* with silver, abu 'Abd Allah, *'Alayhi al-Salam*, has said, 'If *al-Asrub* is more prevalent then it is not unlawful.'"

H 9081, Ch. 114, h 16
Abu Ali al-Ash'ariy has narrated from Muhammad ibn 'Abd al-Jabbar from Safwan from Ishaq ibn 'Ammar who has said the following:
"I once asked abu Ibrahim, *'Alayhi al-Salam*, about the case of a man who owed me a certain amount of assets and paid me back a certain amount in dinars and others in dirhams. He came to finalize the account to pay me the difference because of the exchange in rate of dinar. Was it necessary to pay according to the rate in the day he paid me dinars or the day of accounting? He (the Imam) said, 'He must pay you according to the rate of the day he gave you dinars because you counted the profit from that day.'"

H 9082, Ch. 114, h 17
Safwan has narrated from Ishaq ibn 'Ammar who has said the following:
"This is concerning my question before abu 'Abd Allah, *'Alayhi al-Salam*, about the case of a man who came to me with dirham to sell them to me for the dirhams with me. He certainly did not want dinars but he wanted the dirham and he did not leave until he took my dirham. I bought from him dirham in exchange for dinars. His dinars were not with me in complete form so I borrowed from my neighbor and gave to him and perhaps I did not pay attention how much it weighed. He (the Imam) said, 'Is it not the case that he takes it to offset what belongs to him?' I replied, 'Yes, that is true. He (the Imam) said, 'It is not unlawful.'"

H 9083, Ch. 114, h 18
Ali ibn Ibrahim has narrated from his father from ibn abu 'Umayr from Hammad from al-Halabiy who has said the following:
"Abu 'Abd Allah, *'Alayhi al-Salam*, has said, 'My father purchased a piece of land and stipulated with the owner to pay him *wariq* (dirham) and dinar for ten dirham.'"

H 9084, Ch. 114, h 19
A number of our people have narrated from Ahmad ibn Muhammad from al-Husayn ibn Sa'id from Fadalah from abu al-Mighra' from abu Basir who has said the following:
"I once said to abu 'Abd Allah, *'Alayhi al-Salam*, 'I go to the money changer with dirhams and buy from him dinars. He weighs for me more than my right. I then at the same place buy from him with it dirhams. He (the Imam) said, 'It is not unlawful but do not weigh less than your right.'"

H 9085, Ch. 114, h 20

Muhammad ibn Yahya has narrated from Ahmad ibn Muhammad from Muhammad ibn 'Isma'il from Muhammad ibn al-Fudayl from abu al-Sabbah al-Kinaniy who has said the following:

"This is concerning my question before abu 'Abd Allah, *'Alayhi al-Salam*, about the case of a man who said to a jeweler, 'Make for me this ring in exchange for one fresh dirham with one mixed dirham.' He (the Imam) said, 'It is not unlawful.'"

H 9086, Ch. 114, h 21

Ali ibn Ibrahim has narrated from his father from 'Abd Allah ibn al-Mughirah from 'Abd Allah ibn Sinan who has said the following:

"This is concerning my question before abu 'Abd Allah, *'Alayhi al-Salam*, about buying gold in which there was silver, mercury and soil in exchange for dinars and *wariq* (dirham). He (the Imam) said, 'You must not change except with *wariq* (dirham).' I then asked him (the Imam) about buying silver in which there was lead and *wariq* (dirham). If it was pure it was reduced by two or three dirhams of each ten. He (the Imam) said, 'It is not valid except for gold.'"

H 9087, Ch. 114, h 22

A number of our people have narrated from Ahmad ibn Muhammad from al-Husayn ibn Sa'id from 'Abd Allah ibn Yahya from ibn Muskan from abu 'Abd Allah, Mawla ''Abd Rabbihi who has said the following:

"This is concerning my question before abu 'Abd Allah, *'Alayhi al-Salam*, about the case of a substance that was taken from the mine in which there were gold, silver and zinc. How could we buy it? He (the Imam) said, 'You can buy it with both gold and silver.'"

H 9088, Ch. 114, h 23

Ahmad ibn Muhammad has narrated from al-Husayn ibn Sa'id from Hammad ibn 'Isa from Shu'ayb al-'Aqarqufiy from abu Basir who has said the following:

"This is concerning my question before abu 'Abd Allah, *'Alayhi al-Salam*, about selling the sword decorated with cash (gold or silver). He (the Imam) said, 'It is not unlawful.' I then asked about selling on credit. He (the Imam) said, 'If what is sold for cash is like what it is for its silver, then is not unlawful; or give foodstuff.'"

H 9089, Ch. 114, h 24

A number of our people have narrated from Ahmad ibn abu 'Abd Allah from Ali ibn Hadid from Ali ibn Maymun al-Sa'igh who has said the following:

"I (jewelry maker) once asked abu 'Abd Allah, *'Alayhi al-Salam*, about what was swept from the soil (in his shop) and I sold it and what to do about it. He (the Imam) said, 'Give it as charity; it is your thing or that of your family.' I then said, 'There is gold, silver and iron in it. How should I sell?' He (the Imam) said, 'Sell it in exchange for foodstuff.' I then asked, 'Can I give it to my needy relatives?' He (the Imam) said, 'Yes, you can do so.'"

H 9090, Ch. 114, h 25

Humayd ibn Ziyad has narrated from al-Hassan ibn Muhammad ibn Sama'ah from more than one person from Aban ibn 'Uthman from Muhammad who has said the following:

"Once he (the Imam), *'Alayhi al-Salam*, was asked about the decorated sword and sword of iron which was gilded and was sold for dirhams. He (the Imam) said, 'Yes, and it can be sold for gold also.' He (the Imam) said, 'It is *Makruh* (detestable) to sell it on credit.' He (the Imam) said, 'If the price is more than silver, it is not unlawful.'"

H 9091, Ch. 114, h 26

Ali ibn Ibrahim has narrated from his father from ibn Faddal from Ali ibn 'Uqbah from Hamzah from Ibrahim ibn Hilal who has said the following:

"This is concerning my question before abu 'Abd Allah, *'Alayhi al-Salam*, about a bowl in which there were gold and silver; if I could buy it with gold or silver. He (the Imam) said, 'If you can purify it, it is not lawful; but if you cannot purify, then it is lawful.'"

H 9092, Ch. 114, h 27

Muhammad ibn Yahya has narrated from Ahmad ibn Muhammad from Muhammad ibn 'Isa from 'Uthman ibn 'Isa from Ishaq ibn 'Ammar who has said the following:

"I once said to him (the Imam), *'Alayhi al-Salam*, 'We receive dirhams of different weight, then we buy them with *al-Fulus*,' He (the Imam) said, 'It is not lawful. Find the difference, then weigh copper and the difference then place it in good dirhams then take in equal weight.'"

H 9093, Ch. 114, h 28

Ali ibn Ibrahim has narrated from his father from 'Isma'il ibn Marrar from Yunus from Mu'awiyah or others who has said the following:

"This is concerning my question before abu 'Abd Allah, *'Alayhi al-Salam*, about the case of the substance of *al-'Usrub* which when purified had silver in it; if one could buy it for advance payment for a known amount of dirhams. He (the Imam) said, 'If people know it as *al-'Usrub* only then it is not unlawful.'"

H 9094, Ch. 114, h 29

Abu Ali al-Ash'ariy has narrated from Muhammad ibn 'Abd al-Jabbar and Muhammad ibn 'Isma'il has narrated from al-Fadl ibn Shadhan from all from Safwan from 'Abd al-Rahman ibn al-Hajjaj who has said the following:

"I once asked him (the Imam); *'Alayhi al-Salam*, about the case of decorated swords in which there was silver sold for gold for an appointed time. He (the Imam) said, 'People do not differ that on credit; it is *Riba'* (unlawful additional payment). They differ about the deal of hand in hand.' I then asked, 'Can he buy it with dirhams in cash?' He (the Imam) said, 'My father would say, "I like it to be along with something."' I then asked, 'What happens if dirhams given are more than the silver in it?' He (the Imam) said, 'How can they maintain precaution in it?' I said that they think they know it. He (the Imam) said, 'If they know it then it is not unlawful, otherwise, if they include something else along with it, is more desirable to me.'"

H 9095, Ch. 114, h 30

Muhammad ibn Yahya has narrated from Ahmad ibn Muhammad from Muhammad ibn 'Isa from abu Muhammad al-Ansariy from 'Abd Allah ibn Sinan who has said the following:

"This is concerning my question before abu 'Abd Allah, *'Alayhi al-Salam*, about the case of a man who owed me a certain amount of dirham and gave me a container of al-Kohl. He (the Imam) said, 'Silver is for silver and al-Kohl in it is a debt on him until he returns it to you on the Day of Judgment.'"

H 9096, Ch. 114, h 31

Ali ibn Ibrahim has narrated from his father from ibn abu Najran from 'Asim ibn Humayd from Muhammad ibn Qays who has said the following:

"Abu Ja'far, *'Alayhi al-Salam*, has said that 'Amir al-Mu'minin has said, 'One must not sell silver for gold unless it is in a hand in hand deal; and gold is not sold in exchange for silver unless it is in a hand in hand deal.'"

H 9097, Ch. 114, h 32

Abu Ali al-Ash'ariy has narrated from Muhammad ibn 'Abd al-Jabbar Ahmad ibn Muhammad from Muhammad ibn 'Isma'il has narrated from al-Fadl ibn Shadhan from all from Safwan ibn Yahya from 'Abd al-Rahman ibn al-Hajjaj who has said the following:

"I once asked him (the Imam), *'Alayhi al-Salam*, about the case of a man who bought dirhams in exchange for dinars; then weighed them, cashed them and counted their prices to find the amount of dinar, then said to him to send his slave so he gave him dinars. He (the Imam) said, 'I do not like his separation before taking dinars.' I then said, 'It is only in the same house and their places are close to each other and this becomes difficult for them.' He (the Imam) said, 'When he completes weighing and cashing he must instruct the slave that he wants to send, to become the seller and give the *wariq* (dirham) to him and receive dinars from him as he delivers to him the *wariq* (dirham).'"

H 9098, Ch. 114, h 33

Humayd ibn Ziyad has narrated from al-Hassan ibn Muhammad from more than one person from Aban ibn 'Uthman from 'Abd al-Rahman ibn abu 'Abd Allah who has said the following:

"This is concerning my question before abu 'Abd Allah, *'Alayhi al-Salam*, about selling gold in exchange for dirham. He (the Imam) said, 'Send a messenger to receive the price saying, 'Give that and take this.'"

Chapter 115 - Another Chapter about the Previous Topic

H 9099, Ch. 115, h 1

Ali ibn Ibrahim has narrated from Muhammad ibn 'Isa from Yunus who has said the following:

"I once wrote to al-Rida', *'Alayhi al-Salam*, and asked, 'A man owes to me three thousand dirham which were in circulation at that time among people, but today they are not in circulation among people; if he still owes me the very substance of those dirham or what is currently in circulation today. He (the Imam) wrote to me, 'You have the right to be paid what is current in circulation today as you had given him what was current in circulation among people in those days.'"

Chapter 116 - Impure Dirhams (Certain Silver or Gold Coins)

H 9100, Ch. 116, h 1

Ali ibn Ibrahim has narrated from his father from ibn abu 'Umayr from Hammad ibn 'Uthman from 'Umar Yazid who has said the following:

"This is concerning my question before abu 'Abd Allah, *'Alayhi al-Salam*, about spending dirhams with impurities. He (the Imam) said, 'If the amount of silver is overwhelming in it, it is not unlawful.'"

H 9101, Ch. 116, h 2
Ali ibn Ibrahim has narrated from his father from ibn abu 'Umayr from ibn Ri'ab who has that I know this Hadith through Muhammad ibn Muslim only who has said the following:

"This is concerning my question before abu 'Abd Allah, *'Alayhi al-Salam*, about the case of a man who worked with dirhams that had copper in them or such other things and he then sold them. He (the Imam) said, 'If that is what is among people then it is not harmful.'"

H 9102, Ch. 116, h 3
Muhammad ibn Yahya has narrated from those who narrated to him from Jamil from Hariz ibn 'Abd Allah who has said the following:

"I once was with abu 'Abd Allah, *'Alayhi al-Salam*, when a people from Sajistan came to him (the Imam) and asked about dirham with impurities. He (the Imam) said, 'It is not harmful if they currently are in circulation in a city.'"

H 9103, Ch. 116, h 4
Muhammad ibn Yahya has narrated from Ahmad ibn Muhammad from al-Barqiy from al-Fadl ibn al-'Abbas who has said the following:

"This is concerning my question before abu 'Abd Allah, *'Alayhi al-Salam*, about dirhams with impurities. He (the Imam) said, 'If you spend what is permissible to spend among people in a city, it is not unlawful; but if you spend what is not lawful to spend among the people of a land, then it is not permissible.'"

Chapter 117 - Borrowing Dirhams (Coins) to Keep the Good ones Among them

H 9104, Ch. 117, h 1
Ali ibn Ibrahim has narrated from his father from ibn abu 'Umayr from Hammad from al-Halabiy who has said the following:

"This is concerning my question before abu 'Abd Allah, *'Alayhi al-Salam*, about the case of a man who took a loan of white dirham by numbers, then gave black ones, knowing that they are heavier than what he had taken and he was pleased to make the extra for him. He (the Imam) said, 'It is not unlawful if there is no stipulation or if he gives it as a gift; all is valid.'"

H 9105, Ch. 117, h 2
A number of our people have narrated from Sahl ibn Ziyad Ahmad ibn Muhammad from Ahmad ibn Muhammad all from ibn Mahbub from Khalid ibn Jarir from abu al-Rabi' who has said the following:

"Once abu 'Abd Allah, *'Alayhi al-Salam*, was asked about the case of a man who gave a loan to another man who paid it back with better dirhams without compulsion, and the creditor knew it as well as the debtor that the loan was given to receive payment with the better dirhams. He (the Imam) said, 'It is not unlawful.'"

H 9106, Ch. 117, h 3

Ali ibn Ibrahim has narrated from his father from ibn abu 'Umayr from Hammad from al-Halabiy who has said the following:

"Abu 'Abd Allah, *'Alayhi al-Salam*, has said, 'If you give dirhams as a loan, then the party pays you back with better ones, it is not unlawful, if there is no stipulation between you.'"

H 9107, Ch. 117, h 4

Muhammad ibn Yahya has narrated from Muhammad ibn al-Husayn from Safwan from Ya'qub ibn Shu'ayb who has said the following:

"This is concerning my question before abu 'Abd Allah, *'Alayhi al-Salam*, about the case of a man who gave impure dirhams as a loan to another man, who then paid him back with better dirhams without compulsion. He (the Imam) said, 'It is not unlawful and it is from Ali, *'Alayhi al-Salam.*'"

H 9108, Ch. 117, h 5

Muhammad ibn Yahya has narrated from Ahmad ibn Muhammad from ibn Faddal from Yunus ibn Ya'qub from abu Maryam who has said the following:

"Abu 'Abd Allah, *'Alayhi al-Salam*, has said that the Messenger of Allah, *O Allah, grant compensation to Muhammad and his family worthy of their services to Your cause*, whenever owing something to someone would pay back heavier.'"

H 9109, Ch. 117, h 6

Abu Ali al-Ash'ariy has narrated from Muhammad ibn 'Abd al-Jabbar and Muhammad ibn 'Isma'il has narrated from al-Fadl ibn Shadhan from Safwan from 'Abd al-Rahman ibn al-Hajjaj who has said the following:

"This is concerning my question before abu 'Abd Allah, *'Alayhi al-Salam*, about the case of a man who borrowed from another man dirham and returned with a *Mithqal* (a certain unit of weight) or borrowed a *Mithqal* and paid back with dirham. He (the Imam) said, 'If there is no stipulation it is not unlawful, it is only extra. My father would borrow dirhams of low quality and pay back with dirhams of high quality and say to me, "My son, pay it back to the one from whom I have borrowed." I would say, "Father, the dirhams you borrowed were of low quality and these are better." He (the Imam) would say, 'My son, it is an extra favor. Give it back to him.'"

H 9110, Ch. 117, h 7

Abu Ali al-Ash'ariy has narrated from Muhammad ibn 'Abd al-Jabbar from Ali ibn al-Nu'man from Ya'qub ibn Shu'ayb who has said the following:

"This is concerning my question before abu 'Abd Allah, *'Alayhi al-Salam*, about the case of a man who owed a basket of dry dates and got back a basket of fresh dates which was less. He (the Imam) said, 'It is not unlawful.' I then asked, 'What will happen if he owes to me a basket of dry dates and I take from him a basket of fresh dates which is more?' He (the Imam) said, 'It is not unlawful if it is a known practice between the two of you.'"

Chapter 118 - Loan That Brings Profit

H 9111, Ch. 118, h 1

Ali ibn Ibrahim has narrated from his father from ibn abu 'Umayr from abu Ayyub from Muhammad ibn Muslim and others who has said the following:

"This is concerning my question before abu 'Abd Allah, *'Alayhi al-Salam*, about the case of a man who asked for a loan. He left *al-Rahn* (security deposit) like a servant or utensils or cloths. The party needed to benefit from them, so he asked permission and he gave permission. He (the Imam) said, 'If permission is given without compulsion it is not unlawful.' I then said, 'In our area people see it as if every loan brings benefits. Is it invalid?' He (the Imam) said, 'Is it not a fact that the best loans are those which attract benefits?'"

H 9112, Ch. 118, h 2

Muhammad ibn Yahya has narrated from Muhammad ibn al-Husayn from Safwan from ibn Bukayr from Muhammad ibn 'Abdah who has said the following:

"This is concerning my question before abu 'Abd Allah, *'Alayhi al-Salam*, if loan attracted benefits. He (the Imam) said, 'The best loan is that which attracts benefits.'"

H 9113, Ch. 118, h 3

Ali ibn Ibrahim has narrated from his father from ibn abu 'Umayr from Bishr ibn Muslimah from more than one person who reported who has said the following:

"Abu Ja'far, *'Alayhi al-Salam*, has said, 'The best loan is that which attracts benefits.'"

H 9114, Ch. 118, h 4

Abu Ali al-Ash'ariy has narrated from Muhammad ibn 'Abd al-Jabbar from Safwan from 'Abd al-Rahman ibn al-Hajjaj who has said the following:

"I once asked abu al-Hassan, *'Alayhi al-Salam*, about the case of a man who came to me; I bought for him goods from people and guaranteed payment on his behalf. Then he came to me with dirham. I took and withheld them from their owner, then took the good quality dirhams and gave them of lower quality. He (the Imam) said, 'He guaranteed payment, perhaps it became severe upon him so he hurried to pay before he (the guarantor) asks for payment. He (the guarantor) withholds payment after receiving, it is not unlawful.'"

Chapter 119 - The Case of one Who Gives Dirhams to Receive them in another City

H 9115, Ch. 119, h 1

Abu Ali al-Ash'ariy has narrated from Muhammad ibn 'Abd al-Jabbar from Afi ibn al-Nu'man from Ya'qub Shu'ayb who has said the following:

"This is concerning my question before abu 'Abd Allah, *'Alayhi al-Salam*, about the case of a man who made an advance payment with the *wariq* (dirham) so that the other could pay him in cash in another land and make it a condition. He (the Imam) said, 'It is not unlawful.'"

H 9116, Ch. 119, h 2

Ali ibn Ibrahim has narrated from his father from al-Nawfaliy from al-Sakuniy who has said the following:

"Abu 'Abd Allah, *'Alayhi al-Salam,* has said that 'Amir al-Mu'minin has said, 'It is not unlawful if a man takes dirhams in Makkah and writes for them (his people) notes to pay them in al-Kufah.'"

H 9117, Ch. 119, h 3

Muhammad ibn Yahya has narrated from Ahmad ibn Muhammad from Ali ibn al-Nu'man from abu al-Sabbah who has said the following:

"About the case of a man who wants to send goods to a land, if the one with whom he wants to send says, 'Give this to me as a loan and I will pay you when you reach that land, abu 'Abd Allah, *'Alayhi al-Salam,* has said, 'It is not unlawful.'"

Chapter 119 - Journey in the Sea for Business

H 9118, Ch. 120, h 1

A number of our people have narrated from Ahmad ibn Muhammad from ibn Khalid from ibn abu Najran from al-'Ala' from Muhammad ibn Muslim who has said the following:

"Abu Ja'far, and abu 'Abd Allah, *'Alayhim al-Salam,* have said, 'We dislike sailing on the sea for business.'"

H 9119, Ch. 120, h 2

Ali ibn Ibrahim has narrated in a marfu' manner the following:

"Amir al-Mu'minin, Ali, *'Alayhi al-Salam,* 'has said, 'How beautiful is the quest for trade to sail on the sea!'"

[Note: H 9118 and H 9119 appear to occur during two different eras, perhaps of safe and unsafe sailing times]

H 9120, Ch. 120, h 3

Ali ibn Ibrahim has narrated from his father from Ali ibn Asbat who has said the following:

"I had carried goods with me to Makkah. I faced severe competition there so I went to visit abu al-Hassan, al-Rida', *'Alayhi al-Salam,* and told him (the Imam) that I had carried goods to Makkah but I faced competition and I decided to travel to Egypt. Should I travel by land or by sea? He (the Imam) said, 'Egypt is destructive. It wrecks the youngest in age. The Messenger of Allah, *O Allah, grant compensation to Muhammad and his family worthy of their services to Your cause,* has said, "How beautiful is sailing on the sea in quest for trade."' He (the Imam) said, 'It will not be against you if you go to the shrine of the Messenger of Allah, *O Allah, grant compensation to Muhammad and his family worthy of their services to Your cause,* perform near him two Rak'at *Salat* (prayer) and ask Allah for what is good, one hundred times; then whatever decision comes to your mind follow that decision. When you ride say, "All praise belongs to Allah who has made it possible for us when we were not able to reach it. To our Lord, we return." After you sail on the sea in the ship say, "In the name of Allah who has made it to flow and sail. My Lord is forgiving and merciful." If waves agitate on you, lean to your left and make a gesture to your right to the waves and say, "Calm down through the calmness of Allah and be tranquil through tranquility of Allah. There is no means and power except the power and means of Allah, the most High, most Great.'"

"Ali ibn Asbat has said, 'I sailed on the sea and waves rose. I would say what I was told to say. It would break into pieces as if there was nothing.' Ali ibn Asbat has said, 'I asked him (the Imam) saying I pray to Allah to keep my soul in service for your cause, what is *al-Sakinah*?' He (the Imam) said, 'It is a wind from paradise with a face like the face of the human being, more sweet smelling than musk, and it is the one Allah sent to the Messenger of Allah, *O Allah, grant compensation to Muhammad and his family worthy of their services to Your cause*, in Hunayn (name of a place) which defeated the pagans.'"

H 9121, Ch. 120, h 4
A number of our people have narrated from Ahmad ibn abu 'Abd Allah from his father from Hammad from Hariz from Muhammad ibn Muslim who has said the following:

"Abu Ja'far, *'Alayhi al-Salam*, has said, 'In sailing on the sea for trade one is deceived in his religion.'"

H 9122, Ch. 120, h 5
It is narrated from him from his father from Safwan from Mu'alla' abu 'Uthman from Mu'alla' ibn al-Khunayth who has said the following:

"This is concerning my question before abu 'Abd Allah, *'Alayhi al-Salam*, about the case of a man who traveled and sailed on the sea. He (the Imam) said, 'My father would say that it causes harms to one's religion. There are people who find their livelihood and sustenance.'"

H 9123, Ch. 120, h 6
It is narrated from him from Muhammad ibn Ali from 'Abd al-Rahman ibn abu Hashim from Husayn ibn abu al-'Ala' who has said the following:

"Abu 'Abd Allah, *'Alayhi al-Salam*, has said that once a man came to abu Ja'far, *'Alayhi al-Salam*, and said, 'We work for business in these mountains and come upon areas where we cannot perform *Salat* (prayer) except on snow. He (the Imam) said, 'Why can you not be like so and so who is happy with less and does not demand such things because of which he cannot performing *Salat* (prayer) except on snow.'"

Chapter 121 - Having a Business Where one Lives Is a Good Fortune

H 9124, Ch. 121, h 1
A number of our people have narrated from Ahmad ibn Muhammad from 'Uthman ibn 'Isa from ibn Muskan from certain persons of his people who has said the following:

"Ali ibn Al-Husayn, *'Alayhi al-Salam*, has said, 'It is of a man's good fortune to have his place of business where he lives, to have virtuous associates and children who support him.'"

H 9125, Ch. 121, h 2

Ahmad ibn Muhammad has narrated from Ali ibn Al-Husayn al-Tamimiy from Ja'far ibn Bakr from 'Abd Allah ibn abu Sahl ibn 'Abd al-Karim who has said the following:

"Abu 'Abd Allah, *'Alayhi al-Salam*, has said, 'Three factors help a man enjoy good fortune: One is a cooperating wife, virtuous and kind children, and he finds his living where he lives and is present in his family every morning and evenings.'"

H 9126, Ch. 121, h 3

A number of our people have narrated from Sahl ibn Ziyad from Ibrahim ibn 'Abd al-Hamid from 'Uthman ibn 'Isa from ibn Muskan from certain persons of our people who has said the following:

"Ali ibn Al-Husayn, *'Alayhi al-Salam*, has said, 'It is of a man's good fortune to have his place of business where he lives, to have virtuous associates and children who support him. It is misfortune of a man to have a conceited wife who is treacherous toward him.'"

Chapter 122 - Mutual Settlement

H 9127, Ch. 122, h 1

Ali ibn Ibrahim has narrated from his father from ibn abu 'Umayr from Hammad from al-Halabiy from abu 'Abd Allah, *'Alayhi al-Salam*, who has said the following:

"This is about the two men who had a business partnership with a certain amount of asset in which they made a certain amount of profit, there, however, was a loan against that asset which both had to pay. One of them asked the other to give him the capital in exchange for the profit and payment of loan. The Imam said, 'There is no offense in such deal provided they had established such condition, however, if the condition is against the book of Allah it then is a rejection of the book of Allah.'"

H 9128, Ch. 122, h 2

Ali ibn Ibrahim has narrated from his father from Hammad from Hariz from Muhammad ibn Muslim who has said the following:

"About two men who each had a certain amount of grain in the possession of the other but no one of them knew how much was the amount, and each one of them had said to the other one, 'You can have whatever amount of grain is with you and I will have the amount which is with me,' one of the two Imam, (abu Ja'far or abu 'Abd Allah), *'Alayhim al-Salam*, has said, 'There is no offense in such settlement upon which both have mutually agreed.'"

H 9129, Ch. 122, h 3

Al-Husayn ibn Muhammad has narrated from Mu'alla ibn Muhammad from al-Hassan ibn Ali from Aban from those who narrated to him who has said the following:

"I once asked the Imam, *'Alayhi al-Salam*, about the case of a man to whom another man owed a certain amount of loan who before the due date asked the borrower to pay him half of the loan so he then might cancel the other half in favor of the borrower. He (the Imam) said, 'Such settlement is lawful.'"

H 9130, Ch. 122, h 4

Ali ibn Ibrahim has narrated from his father from ibn abu 'Umayr from Hammad from al-Halabiy who has said the following:

"I once asked the Imam about one who before due date of payment, asked a man who owed him a certain amount, to pay him a certain amount and he might write off the rest or extend the due date for payment in his favor. He (the Imam) said, 'I do not see any offense in such deal as long as he does not increase his capital. Allah, most Majestic, most Glorious, has said, "Your capital belongs to you. (In a deal where you) receive your capital you are not doing any injustice nor is any injustice done to you." (2:279)'"

H 9131, Ch. 122, h 5

Ali ibn Ibrahim has narrated from his father from ibn abu 'Umayr from Hafs al-Bakhtariy who has said the following:

"Abu 'Abd Allah, *'Alayhi al-Salam*, has said, 'Settlement by means of mutual agreement is permissible for people.'"

H 9132, Ch. 122, h 6

Ali ibn Ibrahim has narrated from his father from ibn abu 'Umayr from Ali ibn abu Hamzah who has said the following:

"I once asked abu al-Hassan, *'Alayhi al-Salam.* 'There are four thousand dirhams of a Jew or a Christian and he has died. Is it permissible to reach a settlement about it with his heirs without informing them of the amount?' He (the Imam) said, 'No, until you inform them of the amount.'"

H 9133, Ch. 122, h 7

Muhammad ibn Yahya has narrated from Ahmad ibn Muhammad ibn 'Isa, from Muhammad ibn 'Isa from ibn Bukayr from 'Umar ibn Yazid who has said the following:

"I once asked abu 'Abd Allah, *'Alayhi al-Salam*, about a man who has bailed out another man and has reached a settlement with him.' He (the Imam) said, 'He can only have the actual amount the man owes to him.'"

H 9134, Ch. 122, h 8

A number of our people have narrated from Ahmad ibn Muhammad from Muhammad ibn 'Isma'il from Muhammad ibn 'Adhafir from 'Umar ibn Yazid who has said the following:

"Abu 'Abd Allah, *'Alayhi al-Salam*, has said, 'If one owes a certain amount of debts to another person and he delays payment until the creditor dies and then he reaches a settlement with such person's heirs whatever they receive belongs to them and the remaining belongs to the deceased who will acquire from him in the next life; but if he does not reach any settlement with the heirs of the deceased all of the loan belongs to the deceased for which the borrower will be held responsible.'"

Chapter 123 - Excellence of Farming

H 9135, Ch. 123, h 1

A number of our people have narrated from Ahmad ibn Muhammad ibn Khalid from certain persons of his people from Muhammad ibn Sinan from Muhammad ibn 'Atiyyah who has said the following:

"I heard abu 'Abd Allah, *'Alayhi al-Salam*, saying, 'Allah, most Majestic, most Glorious, has chosen farming and plantation for His prophets so that they will not dislike the drops falling from the sky.'"

H 9136, Ch. 123, h 2

Ali ibn Muhammad has narrated from Sahl ibn Ziyad in a marfu' manner the following:

"Abu 'Abd Allah, *'Alayhi al-Salam*, has said, 'Allah has placed means of the sustenance of His prophets in agriculture and stock farming so that they will not dislike drops falling from the sky.'"

H 9137, Ch. 123, h 3

Muhammad ibn Yahya has narrated from Ahmad ibn Muhammad from Muhammad ibn Khalid from Sayabah who has said the following:

"A man once asked abu 'Abd Allah, *'Alayhi al-Salam*, saying, 'I pray to Allah to keep my soul in service for your cause, I hear a people who say that farming is *Makruh* (detestable).' He (the Imam) said, 'You must farm and plant, by Allah, there is no work that people do which is sweeter and fine than farming. By Allah, farming will be done as well as plantations even after the emergence of al-Dajjal.'"

H 9138, Ch. 123, h 4

A number of our people have narrated from Sahl ibn Ziyad from ibn Mahbub from al-Hassan ibn 'Umarah from Misma' who has said the following:

"Abu 'Abd Allah, *'Alayhi al-Salam*, has said, 'When Adam descended to earth he needed food and drinks and he complained to Jibril. Jibril said to him, 'O Adam, be a farmer.' He said, 'Teach me a prayer.' Jibril said, 'Say: "O Lord, protect me against the worldly impediments and all horrors that are before reaching paradise and dress me in good health so life becomes pleasant for me.'"

H 9139, Ch. 123, h 5

A number of our people have narrated from Ahmad ibn abu 'Abd Allah from certain persons of our people who has said the following:

"Abu Ja'far, *'Alayhi al-Salam*, has said, 'My father, *'Alayhi al-Salam*, would say, "The best work is farming in which you plant, and the virtuous as well as sinful ones eat. The virtuous on eating asks forgiveness for you and the sinful one on eating it is condemned; and even animals and birds eat thereof.'"

H 9140, Ch. 123, h 6

Ali ibn Ibrahim has narrated from his father from al-Nawfaliy from al-Sakuniy who has said the following:

"Abu 'Abd Allah, *'Alayhi al-Salam*, has said that the Messenger of Allah, *O Allah, grant compensation to Muhammad and his family worthy of their services to Your cause*, was asked, 'Are assets (belongings) good?' He (the Messenger of Allah) said, 'An owner farms and maintains it, then pays the dues on it on the day of harvest. What asset is better than farms?' He (the Messenger of Allah) said, 'A man tends sheep, takes them to pasture, performs *Salat* (prayer), pays Zakat. What asset is better than sheep?' He (the Messenger of Allah) said, 'Cows go out safely and come back in the evening safely. What asset is better than cows?' He (the Messenger of Allah) said, 'Firmly established palm trees reach moisture, the grafted ones produce sweet. How good is palm tree! One who sells them must notice that its price is like dust on a high place in a stormy windy day unless one replaces it.' It was asked, 'O Messenger of Allah, *O Allah, grant compensation to Muhammad and his family worthy of their services to Your cause*, what kind of asset is better after palm trees?' He (the Messenger of Allah) remained calm for a while. A man then stood up and said, 'O Messenger of Allah, what about camel? He (the Messenger of Allah) said, 'In it there are misfortune, injustice, fatigue and farness from home. In the morning it is a loss and in the evening it is a loss. Its benefit comes only from its unfortunate side. It always is with the wicked sinful ones.'"

It is narrated from abu 'Abd Allah, *'Alayhi al-Salam*, that farming is the great alchemy.

H 9141, Ch. 123, h 7
Ali ibn Muhammad has narrated from Ibrahim ibn Ishaq from al-Hassan ibn al-Sariy from al-Hassan ibn Ibrahim from Yazid ibn Harun who has said the following:
"I once heard abu 'Abd Allah, *'Alayhi al-Salam*, saying, 'Farmers are the mines of living creatures. They farm goodness that Allah, most Majestic, most Glorious, makes to grow and on the Day of Judgment they will have the best position and the closest place and they are called the blessed ones.'"

Chapter 124 - Another Chapter on the Previous Subject

H 9142, Ch. 124, h 1
Muhammad ibn Yahya has narrated from Salmah ibn al-Khattab from Ibrahim ibn 'Uqbah from Salih ibn Ali ibn 'Atiyyah from a whom he has mentioned who has said the following:
"Abu 'Abd Allah, *'Alayhi al-Salam*, once passed by a people of al-Ansar who were farming and he (the Imam) said to them, 'Continue farming; the Messenger of Allah, *O Allah, grant compensation to Muhammad and his family worthy of their services to Your cause*, has said, "Allah causes it to grow by wind as He does so by water."' They farmed and their farm turned out good."

H 9143, Ch. 124, h 2
Muhammad ibn Yahya has narrated from Ahmad ibn Muhammad from Muhammad ibn Sinan from ibn Muskan from Sadir who has said the following:
"I once heard abu 'Abd Allah, *'Alayhi al-Salam*, saying, 'The Israelites went to Moses and asked him to ask Allah to make the sky rain on them only when they wanted and stop it from raining when they wanted. Moses asked Allah, most Majestic, most Glorious, and Allah, most Majestic, most Glorious, said, 'O Moses, they can have it as they wanted.' Moses informed them about it and they cultivated and farmed all they wanted. They then asked for rain whenever they wanted and stopped it as they wanted. Their farms grew like mountains and thick brushwood. They then harvested, threshed and exposed it to the wind (to separate the grain from the hay) but did not find anything. They expressed their anger to Moses and said, 'We only asked you to ask Allah to send rain for us when we wanted and He agreed, but then He made it harmful to us.' Moses then said, 'O Lord, the Israelites have shown exasperation for what You have done to

them.' Allah asked, 'What is it that I have done to them, O Moses?' Moses said, 'They asked me to ask You to send rain on them only when they wanted and stop it when they wanted. You agreed but then made it harmful to them.' Allah said, 'O Moses, I was measuring it for the Israelites but they were not happy with My measurement for them, then I agreed to leave it to their will, then it happened as you have seen.'"

Chapter 125 - Words to Say at the Time of Plantation

H 9144, Ch. 125, h 1
Ali ibn Ibrahim has narrated from his father from ibn abu 'Umayr from ibn 'Udhaynah from ibn Bukayr who has said the following:

"Abu 'Abd Allah, *'Alayhi al-Salam*, has said, 'When you like to plant something, take a handful of seed, face al-Qiblah (al-Ka'bah) and say, "Have you seen what you cultivate? Do you cultivate it or We are the ones who cultivate." (56:62-63) Then say, "In fact Allah is the cultivator" three times then say, "O Lord, make it blessed grain and provide us safety in it." Then spread the handful from your hand on the plain ground.'"

H 9145, Ch. 125, h 2
A number of our people have narrated from Ahmad ibn Muhammad ibn Khalid from Ali ibn al-Hakam from Shu'ayb al-'Aqarqufiy who has said the following:

"Abu 'Abd Allah, *'Alayhi al-Salam*, has said, 'At the time of spreading seed say, "O Lord, I have spread the seed and You are the cultivator; so make it to produce plentiful grains."'"

H 9146, Ch. 125, h 3
Muhammad ibn Yahya has narrated from Ahmad ibn Muhammad from Muhammad ibn 'Isa from Ahmad 'Umar al-Jallab from al-Hudayniy from ibn 'Arfah who has said the following:

"Abu 'Abd Allah, *'Alayhi al-Salam*, has said, 'If one wants to pollinate palm trees which are not good in their conception and do not accept pollens, he can take small fish, crush them between the two grinding plates and place a little of it in every sprouting element, keep the remaining in a bag and place in the center of the tree, it will be useful by the permission of 'Allah.'"

H 9147, Ch. 125, h 4
Muhammad ibn Yahya has narrated from Muhammad ibn al-Husayn from Muhammad ibn 'Isma'il from Salih ibn 'Uqbah who has said the following:

"Abu 'Abd Allah, *'Alayhi al-Salam*, once said to me, 'I saw your garden, have you planted anything in it yet?' I said, 'I wanted to take small stems from your garden and plant them.' He (the Imam) said, 'Allow me to tell you what is better than this and quicker.' I replied, 'Yes please do so.' He (the Imam) said, 'When dates ripen and you are about to pick them as fresh dates, plant them, it (the crop) will produce just like what you planted.' I followed the instruction and it (the crop) grew exactly like it.'"

H 9148, Ch. 125, h 5
Ali ibn Muhammad has narrated from in a marfu' manner the following:

"He (the Imam), *'Alayhi al-Salam*, has said, 'When you plant a tree or plantation, say with every twig or deed, "Free of all defect is One who raises and inherits", it then cannot fail, by the will of Allah.'"

H 9149, Ch. 125, h 6

Muhammad ibn Yahya has narrated from in a marfu' manner the following:

"One of the two Imam, (abu Ja'far or abu 'Abd Allah), *'Alayhim al-Salam*, has said, 'When you plant or cultivate read, "The likeness of the blessed word is like that of a blessed tree with firmly established roots and branches that rise into the sky. It produces fruits all the time, by the will of its Lord."'"

H 9150, Ch. 125, h 7

Muhammad ibn Yahya has narrated from Ahmad ibn Muhammad from Ahmad ibn Muhammad from ibn abu Nasr who has said the following:

"I once asked abu al-Hassan, *'Alayhi al-Salam*, about cutting down a lotus tree. He (the Imam) said, 'One of your people asked me about it and I wrote to him that abu al-Hassan, *'Alayhi al-Salam*, once cut down a lotus tree and planted in its place grape-vines.'"

H 9151, Ch. 125, h 8

Muhammad ibn Yahya has narrated from Muhammad ibn Ahmad from Ahmad ibn al-Hassan from 'Amr ibn Sa'id from Musaddiq ibn Sadaqah from 'Ammar ibn Musa who has narrated the following:

"Abu 'Abd Allah, *'Alayhi al-Salam*, has said that cutting down of palm trees is detestable. He (the Imam) was asked about cutting down of trees. He (the Imam) replied, 'It is not unlawful.' I then asked about cutting down of lotus trees. He (the Imam) said, 'It is not unlawful. It is detestable to cut them down in the wilderness because it is very rare there, however, here it is plentiful.'"

H 9152, Ch. 125, h 9

It is narrated from ibn abu 'Umayr from Al-Husayn ibn Bashir from ibn Mudarib who has narrated the following:

"Abu 'Abd Allah, *'Alayhi al-Salam*, has said, 'You must not cut down a fruit bearing tree; Allah will send on you a great suffering.'"

Chapter 126(a) - Matters Permissible or Otherwise in Renting Land

H 9153, Ch. 126a, h 1

A number of our people have narrated from Ahmad ibn Muhammad from and Sahl ibn Ziyad from Ahmad ibn Muhammad from ibn abu Nasr from 'Abd al-Karim from Sama'ah from abu Basir who has said the following:

"Abu 'Abd Allah, *'Alayhi al-Salam*, has said, 'You must not rent land in exchange for wheat, barley, dates, canals or small amount of water, but you can do so in exchange for gold or silver; gold and silver are guaranteed and those are not guaranteed.'"

H 9154, Ch. 126a, h 2

Muhammad ibn Yahya has narrated from Muhammad ibn al-Husayn from Safwan from Ishaq ibn 'Ammar from abu Basir who has said the following:

"Abu 'Abd Allah, *'Alayhi al-Salam*, has said, 'You must not rent land in exchange for dates, wheat, barley, al-Arbi'a' or al-Nitaf.' I then asked, 'What is al-Arbi'a?' He (the Imam) said, 'It is a small amount of water and al-Nitaf means extra water, but rent it in exchange for gold or silver, for half of the produce, one-third or one-fourth.'"

H 9155, Ch. 126a, h 3
Abu Ali al-Ash'ariy has narrated from Muhammad ibn 'Abd al-Jabbar from Safwan from ibn Muskan from al-Halabiy who has said the following:

"Abu 'Abd Allah, *'Alayhi al-Salam*, has said, 'You must not rent land in exchange for wheat where you plant wheat.'"

H 9156, Ch. 126a, h 4
Muhammad ibn Yahya has narrated from Ahmad ibn Muhammad from Tha'labah ibn Maymun from Burayd who has said the following:

"About the case of a man who accepts dinar or dirham for (the rent of) land, abu Ja'far, *'Alayhi al-Salam*, has said, 'It is not unlawful.'"

H 9157, Ch. 126a, h 5
A number of our people have narrated from Ahmad ibn Muhammad from Sahl ibn Ziyad all from Ahmad ibn Muhammad from ibn abu Nasr from Dawud ibn Sarhan who has said the following:

"About the case of a man who has a piece of land for which he pays a certain amount of tax that may increase or decrease; and he gives it to another man to pay its taxes and two hundred dirham every year. He (the Imam) said, 'It is not unlawful.'"

H 9158, Ch. 126a, h 6
Ali has narrated from Salih al-Sindiy from Ja'far ibn Bashir from Musa ibn Bakr from al-Fudayl ibn Yasar who has said the following:

"I once asked abu Ja'far, *'Alayhi al-Salam*, about renting land in exchange for foodstuff. He (the Imam) said, 'If it is of the produce of the same land, there is nothing good in it.'"

H 9159, Ch. 126a, h 7
Humayd ibn Ziyad has narrated from al-Hassan ibn Muhammad ibn Sama'ah from more than one person from Aban ibn 'Uthman ibn al-Fadl who has said the following:

"This is concerning my question before abu 'Abd Allah, *'Alayhi al-Salam*, about the case of a man who rented a piece of land from another man saying, 'I rent this piece of land to cultivate, and if I will not cultivate I will still pay you the rent'; and he does not cultivate it. He (the Imam) said, 'He has the right to collect the rent whether he cultivates it or not.'"

H 9160, Ch. 126a, h 8
Al-Husayn from Muhammad has narrated from Mu'alla' ibn Muhammad and Muhammad ibn Yahya has narrated from Ahmad ibn Muhammad all from al-Washsha' who has said the following:

"I once asked al-Rida', *'Alayhi al-Salam*, about the case of a man who bought a certain piece of land from another man in exchange for one hundred *Kur* (a certain unit of measurement) to be paid from the land. He (the Imam) said, 'It is unlawful.' I then asked, 'I pray to Allah to keep my soul in service for your cause, what do you say if I buy from him the land for a known measure of wheat from other sources. He (the Imam) said, 'It is not unlawful.'"

H 9161, Ch. 126a, h 9

Muhammad ibn Yahya has narrated from Ahmad ibn Muhammad from Muhammad ibn Sahl from his father who has said the following:

"I once asked abu al-Hassan, *'Alayhi al-Salam*, about the case of a man for whom the farmers cultivate saffron and guarantee to give him a certain amount by the weight of dirham for every *Jirib* (a certain unit of measurement) that is cultivated and then it may produce less thus, he is in loss or may produce more, thus, he gains. He (the Imam) said, 'It is not unlawful if they mutually agree.'"

H 9162, Ch. 126a, h 10

Ahmad ibn Muhammad from has narrated from Muhammad ibn Sahl from his father from 'Abd Allah ibn Bukayr who has said the following:

"This is concerning my question before abu 'Abd Allah, *'Alayhi al-Salam*, about the case of a man for whom saffron was cultivated and the farmers guaranteed to give him one *Mann* (a certain unit of weight) out of every forty *Mann* fresh saffron and made a settlement about the dried saffron. Dried saffron reduces by three-fourth from fresh kind and one-fourth remains and this is experimented. He (the Imam) said, 'It is not valid.' I then said, 'If he appoints trusted people for protection, he cannot do so because it is worked upon during the night, it is not difficult to protect.' He (the Imam) said, 'He can contract the land first in which he must say that from every forty *Mann* it is one *Mann*.'"

Chapter 126(b) - Renting (Qabala) Land for Farming in Exchange for a Certain Percentage of Produce

H 9163, Ch. 126b, h 1

Ali ibn Ibrahim has narrated from his father from ibn abu 'Umayr from Hammad from al-Halabiy who has said the following:

"Abu 'Abd Allah, *'Alayhi al-Salam*, informed me that his father, *'Alayhi al-Salam*, has narrated that the Messenger of Allah, *O Allah, grant compensation to Muhammad and his family worthy of their services to Your cause*, gave the land of Khaybar and its palm trees for half. When fruits ripened he (the Messenger of Allah) delegated 'Abd Allah ibn Rawahah who appraised and said to them, 'You can take it and pay me half of the appraised value or I pay you half of the appraised value and take the produce.' They said, 'This is (justice) the fact upon which the skies and earth are maintained.'"

H 9164, Ch. 126b, h 2

A number of our people have narrated from Ahmad ibn Muhammad and Sahl ibn Ziyad from al-Hassan ibn Mahbub from Mu'awiyah ibn 'Ammar from abu al-Sabbah who has said the following:

"I once heard abu 'Abd Allah, *'Alayhi al-Salam*, saying, 'When the Holy Prophet, *O Allah, grant compensation to Muhammad and his family worthy of their services to Your cause*, liberated Khaybar he left it in their hand for half. When fruits ripened he (the Messenger of Allah) delegated 'Abd Allah ibn Rawahah who estimated the value and they came to the Holy Prophet, and said,

'He has charged us more.' He (the Messenger of Allah) sent someone to ask 'Abd Allah if there was reason for which they complained. He replied, 'I estimated and they can take or we take it.' A Jewish man then said, 'This is (justice) the fact upon which the skies and earth are maintained.'"

H 9165, Ch. 126b, h 3
Ali ibn Ibrahim has narrated from his father from ibn abu 'Umayr from Hammad from al-Halabiy who has said the following:

"Abu 'Abd Allah, *'Alayhi al-Salam*, has said, 'Land cannot be accepted for specified wheat, however, it is accepted for one-half, one-third, one-fourth or one-fifth.' He (the Imam) said, 'Sharecropping for one-third, one for-fourth or one-fifth is not unlawful.'"

H 9166, Ch. 126b, h 4
A number of our people have narrated from Ahmad ibn Muhammad from al-Hassan ibn Mahbub from al-Husayn ibn Sa'id from al-Nadr ibn Suwayd from 'Abd Allah ibn Sinan who has said the following:

"About the case of a man who works in sharecropping, cultivates the land of another man and says, 'One third for the bulls, one-third for the seed and one-third for the land', he (the Imam) *'Alayhi al-Salam*, has said, 'Things like bulls, seeds and so on must not be mentioned, instead he must say, "You must cultivate so and so items, if you want for one-half or if you want for one-third."'"

H 9167, Ch. 126b, h 5
Muhammad ibn Yahya has narrated from Ahmad ibn Muhammad from Ali ibn al-Nu'man from ibn Muskan from Sulayman ibn Khalid who has said the following:

"This is concerning my question before abu 'Abd Allah, *'Alayhi al-Salam*, about the case of a man who cultivated the land of another man; if he could set the condition of one-third for the seed, one-third for the bull. He (the Imam) said, 'It is not proper to mention seed or bull. It is statement that makes it unlawful.'"

H 9168, Ch. 126b, h 6
Ali ibn Ibrahim has narrated from his father from ibn abu 'Umayr from Hammad from al-Halabiy who has said the following:

"Once abu 'Abd Allah, *'Alayhi al-Salam*, was asked about the case of a man who cultivated a land with the condition of one-third for the seed and one-third for the bull. He (the Imam) said, 'It is not proper to designate anything, because it is statements that makes it unlawful.'"

Chapter 127 - Partnership in Farming with Taxpayers and Others and Conditions Between Them

H 9169, Ch. 127, h 1
A number of our people have narrated from Ahmad ibn Muhammad from Sahl ibn Ziyad from al-Hassan ibn Mahbub from Ibrahim al-Karkhiy who has narrated the following:

"I once said to abu 'Abd Allah, *'Alayhi al-Salam*, 'I become a partner of an al-'ilj (a great non-Muslim person). I provide land, seed, and the bull. Al-'ilj does the plantation and other works for the farm. When the wheat or barely comes, the produce is divided; al-Sultan takes away his right, one-third is for al-'ilj and the remaining is for me. He (the Imam) said, 'It is not unlawful.' I then asked if the seed can be given to me from the produce of the land and the rest is divided. He (the Imam) said, 'You have formed a partnership which required you to provide the seed and he must provide water and other works.'"

H 9170, Ch. 127, h 2

Muhammad ibn Yahya has narrated from Muhammad ibn Al-Husayn from Safwan from Ya'qub ibn Shu'ayb who has narrated the following:

"This is concerning my question before abu 'Abd Allah, *'Alayhi al-Salam*, about the case of a man who had a land of al-Kharaj (of government) which he had given to a man to develop, pay its taxes and the extra of its produce were to be shared by the two of them. He (the Imam) said, 'It is not unlawful.' I asked abu 'Abd Allah, *'Alayhi al-Salam*, about the case of a man who gave his land to a man which had pomegranate, palm trees or fruit bearing trees. He told him to water and develop it for one-half of the produce thereof. He (the Imam) said, 'It is not unlawful.' This is concerning my question before abu 'Abd Allah, *'Alayhi al-Salam*, about the case of a man who told a man to have his land for three or five years or as Allah wills. He (the Imam) said, 'It is not unlawful.' I then asked about sharecropping. He (the Imam) then said, 'The expenses are from you and the land is from the land-owner. Its produce is divided in portions. This is how the Messenger of Allah, *O Allah, grant compensation to Muhammad and his family worthy of their services to Your cause*, gave the people of Khaybar when they came to him. He (the Messenger of Allah) gave it to them to develop for one-half of its produce.'"

H 9171, Ch. 127, h 3

Ali ibn Ibrahim has narrated from his father from ibn abu 'Umayr from Hammad from al-Halabiy who has narrated the following:

"Abu 'Abd Allah, *'Alayhi al-Salam*, has said, 'In a land contract you can have it for twenty years or less from its people to develop it and pay its expenses; such contract is not unlawful.'"

H 9172, Ch. 127, h 4

A number of our people have narrated from Ahmad ibn Muhammad from 'Uthman ibn 'Isa from Sama'ah who has narrated the following:

"This is concerning my question before abu 'Abd Allah, *'Alayhi al-Salam*, about sharecropping of a Muslim and a pagan in which the Muslim provides seed and bull, the land, water, taxes and work is by the al-'ilj. He (the Imam) said, 'It is not unlawful.' I then asked about sharecropping saying that a man spreads seed on one hundred *Jirib* (acre) or less or more for grain or other produce. A man then comes and says to take one-half of the value of the seed from me and one-half of the expenses and give me a share in it. He (the Imam) then said, 'It is not unlawful.' I then asked, 'What happens if he has not bought the seed, it just was with him?' He (the Imam) then said, 'He must appraise it with that day's prices, then take one-half of its value and one-half of his expenses and then share the farm with him.'"

Chapter 128 - Contracting Taxpayers' Land and the Tax on their Person; Contracting Land from Al-Sultan and then Contracting it to Others

H 9173, Ch. 128, h 1

A number of our people have narrated from Sahl ibn Ziyad and Ahmad ibn Muhammad from ibn Mahbub from Ibrahim al-Kharkhiy who has said the following:

"This is concerning my question before abu 'Abd Allah, *'Alayhi al-Salam*, about the case of a man who had a large town in which he had taxpayer infidels from whom al-Sultan collected taxes and they paid to him fifty or thirty or more or less, each one. The owner of the town reached a settlement for them with al-Sultan and he collected more from them than what he paid to al-Sultan. He (the Imam) said, 'It is unlawful.'"

H 9174, Ch. 128, h 2

Humayd ibn Ziyad has narrated from al-Hassan ibn Muhammad from Ahmad ibn al-Hassan al-Mithamiy who has said that narrated to him abu Najih al-Misma'iy from al-Fayd ibn al-Mukhtar who has said the following:

"This is concerning my question before abu 'Abd Allah, *'Alayhi al-Salam*, saying, 'I pray to Allah to keep my soul in service for your cause, what do you say about a land that I rent from al-Sultan, then rent it to my tenants for, whatever Allah makes to grow, one-half or one-third after excluding the share of al-Sultan. He (the Imam) said, 'It is not unlawful and that is how I deal with my tenants.'"

H 9175, Ch. 128, h 3

Ali ibn Ibrahim has narrated from his father from ibn abu 'Umayr from Hammad from al-Halabiy who has said the following:

"Abu 'Abd Allah, *'Alayhi al-Salam*, has said, 'It is not unlawful to reach an agreement with the owners of the land for twenty years or less or more, then revive it and pay what he spends on it; but one must not include al-'ilj (the infidels) in the agreement because it is not lawful.'"

H 9176, Ch. 128, h 4

A number of our people have narrated from Ahmad ibn Muhammad from 'Uthman ibn 'Isa from Sama'ah who has said the following:

"I once asked him (the Imam), *'Alayhi al-Salam*, about the case of a man who formed a contract for a land without compulsion on the owners, with the condition with them that if he did certain repairs or built a building, that he would have the rent of such homes except what was in the hands of the farmers from before. He (the Imam) said, 'If he has entered into contract for a known matter, he must not bother with farmers unless he has set a condition with the owner to include what is in the hands of the farmers also.'"

H 9177, Ch. 128, h 5

Ali ibn Ibrahim has narrated from his father from ibn abu 'Umayr from Hammad from Ibrahim ibn Maymun who has said the following:

"This is concerning my question before abu 'Abd Allah, *'Alayhi al-Salam*, about a town that belonged to non-Muslim taxpayers and I did not know if they were the original owners or not, except that it was in their hands and they paid Kharaj (taxes). Al-Sultan infringed on them and they asked me to take over their town and land to suffice them against al-Sultan with more or less. A certain amount of extra remained with me after whatever al-Sultan took away. He (the Imam) said, 'It is not unlawful for you to have such extra remainders.'"

Chapter 129 - The Case of Tenant of Land Who Dies Before Expiration of Lease

H 9178, Ch. 129, h 1

Muhammad ibn Yahya has narrated from Ahmad ibn Muhammad from Ali ibn Ahmad from Yunus who has said the following:

'I once wrote to al-Rida', *'Alayhi al-Salam*, and asked about the case of a man who formed a contract with another man about land or something else for several known years and the landlord then decided to sell the land before the end of the contract; if the tenant could stop the sale before the end of the time of agreement and if so, what was the tenant's responsibility. He (the Imam) wrote back the answer that said, 'He can sell it if he sets a condition upon the buyer that requires him to allow the tenant to use his years according to the contract of tenancy.'"

H 9179, Ch. 129, h 2

A number of our people have narrated from Sahl ibn Ziyad and Ahmad ibn Muhammad from Ali ibn Mahziyar from Ibrahim ibn Muhammad al-Hamadaniy and Muhammad ibn Ja'far al-Raziy from Muhammad ibn 'Isa from Ibrahim al-Hamadaniy who has said the following:

"I once wrote to abu al-Hassan, *'Alayhi al-Salam*, and asked about the case of a woman who had rented her asset for ten years, that the rent had to be paid at the end of every year and there would be no rent before the end of such time; but she died before three years or after it; if it was necessary for her heirs to continue with the terms of the contract or that the contract terminated because of the death of the woman. He (the Imam) wrote the answer that said, 'If the time was specified which was not complete yet and she died, her heir could have the rent. If the time was not complete or one-third or half or so was complete, the heirs could have the rent proportionate to the time used, by the will of Allah.'"

H 9180, Ch. 129, h 3

Sahl ibn Ziyad has narrated from Ahmad ibn Ishaq al-Raziy who has said the following:

"A man once wrote to abu al-Hassan, the third, *'Alayhi al-Salam*, and asked about the case of a man who rented an asset from another man and the owner sold that asset in the presence of the tenant who did not raise any objection against the sale while he was present with witness and the buyer died; if the asset became of the legacy or remained in the hand of the tenant until the time of tenancy ended. He (the Imam) wrote the answer that said, 'It remains until the time of tenancy ends.'"

Chapter 130 - One's Renting a House or Land and His Renting to another Tenant for Higher Price

H 9181, Ch. 130, h 1
A number of our people have narrated from Sahl ibn Ziyad and Ahmad ibn Muhammad from all from ibn Mahbub from Khalid ibn Jarir from abu al-Rabi' al-Shamiy who has said the following:

"This is concerning my question before abu 'Abd Allah, *'Alayhi al-Salam*, about the case of a man who contracted land from farmers, then rented it for more to others and undertook the share of al-Sultan. He (the Imam) said, 'It is not unlawful because land is not like wages or a house. The increase of wages and house rent is unlawful.'"

H 9182, Ch. 130, h 2
Muhammad ibn Yahya has narrated from 'Abd Allah ibn Muhammad from Ali ibn al-Hakam from Aban from 'Isma'il ibn al-Fadl al-Hashimiy who has said the following:

"This is concerning my question before abu 'Abd Allah, *'Alayhi al-Salam*, about the case of a man who leased from al-Sultan al-Kharaj (tax) land for a known amount of dirham or foodstuff of known amount, then rented to someone with the condition to cultivate it and to divide the produce in half and half or more or less and still something extra remained for him from the land; if it was valid for him. He (the Imam) said, 'Yes it is valid, provided, he digs a canal or a certain work to help them, then it is for him.' I then asked him (the Imam) about the case of a man who leased a piece of land of Kharaj (tax) land for a certain amount of dirham or foodstuff, then rented it in pieces or by *Jirib* (a certain unit of measurement) for a known amount, then a certain amount extra remained for him after payment to al-Sultan but he did not spend anything, or that he leased that land in pieces with the condition to give them seed and expenses, then extra remained for him over the rent; if the soil was for him or not. He (the Imam) said, 'If you rent a land and spend on it or do mending work in it, then the matters you have mentioned are not unlawful.'"

H 9183, Ch. 130, h 3
Ali ibn Ibrahim has narrated from his father from ibn abu 'Umayr from abu al-Mighra' who has said the following:

"About the case of a man who leases a piece of land, then rents it to someone for more than what he has leased for, he (the Imam), *'Alayhi al-Salam*, said, 'It is not unlawful because it is not like a shop or wages; increase of wages and rent of shop is not lawful.'"

H 9184, Ch. 130, h 4
Ali ibn Ibrahim has narrated from his father from ibn abu 'Umayr from Hammad from al-Halabiy who has said the following:

"Abu 'Abd Allah, *'Alayhi al-Salam*, has said, 'If a man rents a house for ten dirham and lives in it, but uses only two-thirds and rents the other one-third for ten dirhams, it is not unlawful but he must not rent out for more than what has rented (which is ten dirham) unless he introduces something in it.'"

H 9185, Ch. 130, h 5

A number of our people have narrated from Sahl ibn Ziyad from ibn Faddal from abu al-Mighra' from Ibrahim ibn Maymun who has said the following:

"Ibrahim ibn al-Muthanna' once asked abu 'Abd Allah, *'Alayhi al-Salam*, this, when I was listening, 'A man leases land, then rents to someone else for more than what he pays.' He (the Imam) said, 'It is not unlawful because land is not like a house or a worker on hire. Extra in the rent of a house is unlawful and extra in hiring is unlawful.'"

H 9186, Ch. 130, h 6

Sahl ibn Ziyad has narrated from Ahmad ibn Muhammad from 'Abd al-Karim from al-Halabiy who has said the following:

"This is concerning my question before abu 'Abd Allah, *'Alayhi al-Salam*, about leasing saying, 'There is a piece of land and it leased for one-third or one-fourth, then to someone else for one-half.' He (the Imam) said, 'It is not unlawful.' I then asked, 'What happens if I lease for one thousand dirhams and then lease it to someone else for two thousand dirhams?' He (the Imam) said, 'It is not lawful.' I then asked, 'How is it that it is lawful in the first case and unlawful in the second case?' He (the Imam) said, 'It is because in this case it is guaranteed and in that case it is not guaranteed.'"

H 9187, Ch. 130, h 7

Muhammad ibn Yahya has narrated from Muhammad ibn al-Husayn from Safwan from Ishaq ibn 'Ammar who has said the following:

"Abu 'Abd Allah, *'Alayhi al-Salam*, has said, 'If you lease a piece of land in exchange for gold or silver, then do not lease it to someone else for more than what you have leased; but if you lease it in exchange for one-half or one-third of the produce you can lease it to someone else for more, because gold and silver are guaranteed.'"

H 9188, Ch. 130, h 8

Ali ibn Ibrahim has narrated from his father from ibn abu 'Umayr from Hammad from al-Halabiy who has said the following:

"About the case of a man who leases a house then rents to someone else for more than what he has rented for, abu 'Abd Allah, *'Alayhi al-Salam*, has said, 'It is not valid unless he introduces something in it.'"

H 9189, Ch. 130, h 9

A number of our people have narrated from Ahmad ibn Muhammad from 'Uthman ibn 'Isa from Sama'ah from abu Basir who has said the following:

"Abu 'Abd Allah, *'Alayhi al-Salam*, has said, 'I dislike renting a grinding stone, then renting it out to someone else for more than what I has rented for, unless some improvement is made or loss has taken place.'"

H 9190, Ch. 130, h 10

Muhammad ibn Yahya has narrated from Ahmad ibn Muhammad from al-Husayn ibn Sa'id from his brother, al-Hassan from Zur'ah ibn Muhammad from Sama'ah who has said the following:

"Upon asking him (the Imam), *'Alayhi al-Salam*, about the case of a man who buys a pasture for fifty dirham or less or more and he wants to allow entering the pasture whoever wants to enter so that he charges them for it. He (the Imam) said, 'He can allow whomever he wants with a payment of part of what he has paid. If he enters the pasture with a payment of forty-nine and his sheep (graze) for one dirham, it is not unlawful. He cannot receive payment of fifty dirham and his sheep graze along with them or for more than fifty but his sheep do not graze with them, unless he has done a certain work in the pasture, like digging a well, or a canal or has experienced fatigue in it with the consent of the owners of the pasture, in which case it is not unlawful to sell it for more than for what he has bought, because he has done certain work in it and with this it becomes valid for him.'"

Chapter 131 - The Case of one Who Contracts for a Work for a Certain Amount and then Contracts with another Person for More

H 9191, Ch. 131, h 1

Muhammad ibn Yahya has narrated from Muhammad ibn al-Husayn from Safwan from al-'Ala' from Muhammad ibn Muslim who has said the following:

"Upon my asking one of the two Imam, (abu Ja'far or abu 'Abd Allah), *'Alayhim al-Salam*, about the case of a man who forms a contract for a certain work with another man but he does not do the work, instead he gives it to someone else and makes a certain amount of profit. He (the Imam) said, 'No, he cannot do so unless he does certain work in it.'"

H 9192, Ch. 131, h 2

Abu Ali al-Ash'ariy has narrated from Muhammad ibn 'Abd al-Jabbar from Safwan from al-Hakam al-Khayyat who has said the following:

"Upon my asking abu 'Abd Allah, *'Alayhi al-Salam*, about the case of a cloth (for tailoring) that I accept for a dirham and then give it to another person on credit for more than a dirham without doing anything more than cutting. He (the Imam) said, 'It is not unlawful.' He (the Imam) then said, 'It is not unlawful if you accept a work then seek increase in it.'"

H 9193, Ch. 131, h 3

Muhammad ibn Yahya has narrated from Ahmad ibn Muhammad from Ali ibn al-Hakam from Ali ibn Maymun al-Sa'igh (jeweler) who has said the following:

"Upon my asking abu 'Abd Allah, *'Alayhi al-Salam*, about a goldsmith work in which there is engraving and I stipulate with an engraver; but when it is time to finalize our account, I ask him to reduce from what was stipulated. He (the Imam) asked, 'Is it without compulsion on his part?' I replied, 'Yes, it is without compulsion.' He (the Imam) said, 'It is not unlawful.'"

Chapter 132 - Selling Vegetables and So On

H 9194, Ch. 132, h 1

Ali ibn Ibrahim has narrated from his father from ibn abu 'Umayr from Hammad from al-Halabiy who has said the following:

"Abu 'Abd Allah, *'Alayhi al-Salam*, has said, 'It is not unlawful to buy a plantation when it is green, then leave it until the harvest time, if you like or use it for animal feed before wheat ears appear when it is only grass.' He (the Imam) has said, 'It is not unlawful to buy plantations in which the ears have appeared and wheat has formed.'"

H 9195, Ch. 132, h 2

Ali has narrated from his father from Hammad from Hariz from Bukayr ibn 'A'yan who has said the following:

"Upon my asking abu 'Abd Allah, *'Alayhi al-Salam*, about buying a plantation when it only is green, he (the Imam) said, 'It is not unlawful.'"

H 9196, Ch. 132, h 3

It is narrated from the narrator of the previous Hadith from Zurarah a similar Hadith.

"He (the Imam), *'Alayhi al-Salam*, has said, 'It is not unlawful to buy a plantation or greenery, then leave it, if you like, until the ears appear, then harvest, or if you like use it as animal feed as grass and it is not unlawful before ears appear, and when the ears appear then do not use it (ears) as animal feed because it is destroying.'"

H 9197, Ch. 132, h 4

A number of our people have narrated from Sahl ibn Ziyad from Ahmad ibn Muhammad from ibn abu Nasr from Muthanna' al-Hannat from Zurarah who has said the following:

"About the case of a plantation which is sold when it is only grass, abu 'Abd Allah, *'Alayhi al-Salam*, has said, 'It is not unlawful if he says, "I buy from you what comes out of this plantation." If he buys it when it is only grass he can use it or if he likes he can wait (until harvest time).'"

H 9198, Ch. 132, h 5

Muhammad ibn Yahya has narrated from Ahmad ibn Muhammad from Safwan from Aban from 'Abd al-Rahman ibn abu 'Abd Allah who has said the following:

"Abu 'Abd Allah, *'Alayhi al-Salam*, has said that the Messenger of Allah, *O Allah, grant compensation to Muhammad and his family worthy of their services to Your cause*, prohibited *al-Muhaqalah* and *al-Muzabanah*.' I then asked, 'What are they?' He (the Imam) said, 'It is selling what a palm tree has just conceived in exchange for dates and green plantation for wheat.'"

H 9199, Ch. 132, h 6

A number of our people have narrated from Ahmad ibn Muhammad from 'Uthman ibn 'Isa from Sama'ah who has said the following:

"Upon my asking abu 'Abd Allah, *'Alayhi al-Salam*, about a man who buys green plantation, then he decides to leave it until ears appear as barley or wheat when basically he had purchased as such that the tax is on the infidel to pay. He (the Imam) said, 'If he has bought it with the condition at the time of purchase that if he likes he can leave it as it is until the ears appear, otherwise, it is not proper for him to leave it until the ears appear.'"

H 9200, Ch. 132, h 7

A number of our people have narrated from Ahmad ibn Muhammad from ibn Mahbub from abu Ayyub from Sama'ah who has said the following:

"Sama'ah has narrated a similar Hadith from abu 'Abd Allah, *'Alayhi al-Salam*, with this addition, 'If he leaves it until ears appear, he is responsible for its maintenance and expenses and he can have whatever comes out thereof.'"

H 9201, Ch. 132, h 8
'Uthman ibn 'Isa has narrated from Sama'ah who has said the following:
"Upon my asking him (the Imam), *'Alayhi al-Salam*, about the case of a man who establishes a plantation, who is a Muslim or tax payer, maintains it and incurs expenses on it, then he decides to sell it because of his relocating or other needs. He (the Imam) said, 'He can buy it (with al-*wariq*, as leaves not as grains) because its origin is from foodstuff.'"

H 9202, Ch. 132, h 9
Ali ibn Ibrahim has narrated from his father from al-Nawfaliy from al-Sakuniy who has said the following:
"Abu 'Abd Allah, *'Alayhi al-Salam*, has said that the Messenger of Allah, *O Allah, grant compensation to Muhammad and his family worthy of their services to Your cause*, granted permission for the sale of *al-'Ara'ya'* by estimating it as dates. *Al-'Ara'ya'* is a palm tree that belongs to someone but it is in other person's house, in this case it is permissible to sell it by estimation and it is not permissible in other things.'"

Chapter 133 - Selling Pastures

H 9203, Ch. 133, h 1
Ali ibn Ibrahim has narrated from his father from 'Isma'il ibn Marrar from Yunus from certain persons of our people who has said the following:
"Regarding my question before abu 'Abd Allah, *'Alayhi al-Salam*, about the case of a man who is Muslim and has an asset in the mountains which is sold and his Muslim brother comes who has sheep and needs a mountain, if it is lawful to sell the mountain as he sells to others or deny him use of the mountain if he asks without payment and how is his condition and what he takes. He (the Imam) said, 'It is not lawful for him to sell his mountain to his brother because the mountain is not his mountain, he can only sell it to non-Muslims.'"

H 9204, Ch. 133, h 2
A number of our people have narrated from Ahmad ibn Muhammad from and Sahl ibn Ziyad from Ahmad ibn Muhammad from ibn abu Nasr from Idris ibn Zayd who has said the following:
"Regarding my question before abu al-Hassan, *'Alayhi al-Salam*, - after saying, 'I pray to Allah to keep my soul in service for your cause, we have a property that has boundaries and a pasture – about a man from us who has sheep and camel. He needs those pastures for his camel and sheep if it is permissible for him to preserve and protect the pastures for his needs.' He (the Imam) said, 'If the land is his land he has the right to reserve and keep it for his needs.' I then asked, 'Can the man sell the pastures?' He (the Imam) said, 'If the land is his land, it is not unlawful to do so.'"

H 9205, Ch. 133, h 3

Ahmad ibn Muhammad from ibn abu Nasr has narrated from Muhammad ibn 'Abd Allah who has said the following:

"This is concerning my question before al-Rida', *'Alayhi al-Salam*, about the case of a man who has a property which has boundaries that extend for about twenty miles or less or more and a man comes and says, 'If you give to me from your pastures I will give you so and so amount of dirham. He (the Imam) said, 'If the property is his property it is not unlawful.'"

H 9206, Ch. 133, h 4

Humayd ibn Ziyad has narrated from al-Hassan ibn Muhammad ibn Sama'ah from Ja'far ibn Sama'ah from Aban from 'Isma'il ibn al-Fadl who has said the following:

"This is concerning my question before abu 'Abd Allah, *'Alayhi al-Salam*, about a man's selling pastures which needs watering. He works to provide water for its grass and he is the one who has dug the well and canal and he has water for the plantation of whatever he likes to cultivate. He (the Imam) said, 'If water belongs to him he can cultivate whatever he likes and sell to whoever he likes.' I then asked him (the Imam) about selling the remaining portions of wheat or barley stems after harvest. He (the Imam) said, 'It is lawful, thus, he can sell if he wants.'"

H 9207, Ch. 133, h 5

A number of our people have narrated from Sahl ibn Ziyad from 'Ubayd Allah al-Dihqan from Musa ibn Ibrahim who has said the following:

"This is concerning my question before abu al-Hassan, *'Alayhi al-Salam*, about selling grass and pastures. He (the Imam) said, 'It is not unlawful, the Messenger of Allah, *O Allah, grant compensation to Muhammad and his family worthy of their services to Your cause*, had reserved al-Naqi' (name of a place) for the horses of the Muslims.'"

Chapter 134 - Selling Water for Agriculture and Preserving Extra Water of Valleys and Floods

H 9208, Ch. 134, h 1

Abu Ali al-Ash'ariy has narrated from Muhammad ibn 'Abd al-Jabbar from Safwan from Sa'id al-A'raj who has said the following:

"This is concerning my question before abu 'Abd Allah, *'Alayhi al-Salam*, about the case of a man who has a share of water with a people in a canal as partners and certain ones among them stand free of need of their share of water; if he can sell his share. He (the Imam) said, 'Yes, he can do so, he can sell it in exchange for *wariq* (dirham) or if he likes, he can sell for a measure of wheat.'"

H 9209, Ch. 134, h 2

Muhammad ibn Yahya has narrated from 'Abd Allah ibn Muhammad from Ali ibn al-Hakam from and Humayd ibn Ziyad from al-Hassan ibn Sama'ah from Ja'far ibn Sama'ah all from Aban who has said the following:

"Abu 'Abd Allah, *'Alayhi al-Salam*, has said that the Messenger of Allah, *O Allah, grant compensation to Muhammad and his family worthy of their services to Your cause*, prohibited *al-Nitaf* and *al-Arbi'a'*. He said, '*Al-Arbi'a'* is constructing, something as a dam, to hold water to water the land, then he stands free of need for such water.' He said, 'You must not sell it but allow your neighbor to use it.' *Al-Nitaf* is a share that one has in a body of water, then he stands free of need for such a share. And he (the Messenger of Allah) would say, 'You must not sell it but allow your neighbor to use it or your brother.'"

H 9210, Ch. 134, h 3

Muhammad ibn Yahya has narrated from Ahmad ibn Muhammad and Ali ibn Ibrahim has narrated from his father all from my from Hakam ibn Ayman from Ghiyath ibn Ibrahim who has said the following:

"I once heard abu 'Abd Allah, *'Alayhi al-Salam*, saying, 'The Messenger of Allah once issued a judgment about the flood of the valley of Mahzur (name of a place). The amount of water that those of higher areas can hold is up to the anklebones for palm trees and up to one's shoelaces for plantation. Thereafter water must be allowed for those below that; for plantation up to the shoelace and for the palm trees up to the anklebone, then allow water for those yet lower.' Ibn abu 'Umayr has made a statement that *Mahr*zur is the name of an area in the valley."

H 9211, Ch. 134, h 4

Muhammad ibn Yahya has narrated from Ahmad ibn Muhammad from Muhammad ibn Yahya from Ghiyath ibn Ibrahim who has said the following:

"Abu 'Abd Allah, *'Alayhi al-Salam*, has said that the Messenger of Allah, *O Allah, grant compensation to Muhammad and his family worthy of their services to Your cause*, issued a judgment about the flood water of valley of Mahzur by which those of higher area could hold water for palm trees up to the anklebones and for plantation up to shoelaces."

H 9212, Ch. 134, h 5

A number of our people have narrated from Sahl ibn Ziyad from Ali ibn Asbat from Ali ibn Shajarah Hafs ibn Ghiyath who has said the following:

"Abu 'Abd Allah, *'Alayhi al-Salam*, has said that the Messenger of Allah, *O Allah, grant compensation to Muhammad and his family worthy of their services to Your cause*, issued a judgment about the flood water of valley of Mahzur for palm trees up to the anklebones and for plantation up to shoelaces."

H 9213, Ch. 134, h 6

Muhammad ibn Yahya has narrated from Muhammad ibn al-Husayn from Muhammad ibn 'Abd Allah ibn Hilal from 'Uqbah ibn Khalid who has said the following:

"Abu 'Abd Allah, *'Alayhi al-Salam*, has said that the Messenger of Allah, *O Allah, grant compensation to Muhammad and his family worthy of their services to Your cause*, issued a judgment about water for palm trees from flood water that said, 'Those of the higher area drink before the lower ones, and water is left up to the anklebones; then water is allowed for the lower ones which is next until all gardens' needs are met and water is depleted.'"

Chapter 135 - Reviving Barren Land

H 9214, Ch. 135, h 1
Ali ibn Ibrahim has narrated from his father from ibn abu 'Umayr from Muhammad ibn Humran from Muhammad ibn Muslim who has said the following:

"I once heard abu Ja'far, *'Alayhi al-Salam*, saying, 'Whoever of people revive a land and build it, they are more deserving to have it and it is for them.'"

H 9215, Ch. 135, h 2
A number of our people have narrated from Sahl ibn Ziyad Ahmad ibn Muhammad from Ahmad ibn Muhammad all from ibn Mahbub from Mu'awiyah ibn 'Ammar who has said the following:

"I once heard abu 'Abd Allah, *'Alayhi al-Salam*, saying, 'Whoever comes upon a ruined barren place, then finds out and digs its canals and builds it, he owes charity. If the land belonged to a man before him who has disappeared, abandoned it and ruined it, then came thereafter, he has to take notice that the land belongs to Allah and to those who build it.'"

H 9216, Ch. 135, h 3
Ali ibn Ibrahim has narrated from his father from Hammad from Hariz from Zurarah who has said the following:

" Abu Ja'far, *'Alayhi al-Salam*, has said that the Messenger of Allah, *O Allah, grant compensation to Muhammad and his family worthy of their services to Your cause*, has said, 'One who revives a barren (dead) land, it becomes his land.'"

H 9217, Ch. 135, h 4
Hammad has narrated from Hariz from Zurarah and Muhammad ibn Muslim and abu Basir and Fudayl and Bukayr and Humran and 'Abd al-Rahman ibn abu 'Abd Allah who has said the following:

"Abu Ja'far, and abu 'Abd Allah, *'Alayhim al-Salam*, have said that the Messenger of Allah, *O Allah, grant compensation to Muhammad and his family worthy of their services to Your cause*, has said, 'Whoever revives a barren (dead) land, it becomes his land.'"

H 9218, Ch. 135, h 5
Muhammad ibn Yahya has narrated from Ahmad ibn Muhammad from ibn Mahbub from Hisham ibn Salim from abu Khalid al-Kabuliy who has said the following:

"Abu Ja'far, *'Alayhi al-Salam*, has said, 'We have found in the book of Ali, *'Alayhi al-Salam*, that the land belongs to Allah which He makes whomever of His servant He wants to inherit; and the end result is in favor of the pious people. We and the people of the House have inherited the earth and we are the pious ones. All of the earth belongs to us. Whoever of the Muslims revives and builds it and pays taxes to the Imam from the people of the House, he can eat thereof. If he abandons and ruins it and then another person of the Muslims takes it after him, builds it and revives it, he then is more rightful than the one who has abandoned it. So he pays taxes to the Imam from the House and he can eat thereof until the reappearance of al-Qa'im from the people of my house with the sword to control and protect it. He sends them in exile just as the Messenger of Allah, *O Allah, grant compensation to Muhammad and his family worthy of their services to Your cause*, protected it, except for what is in the hands of our followers who will then contract with him for what is in their hands and he, *'Alayhi al-Salam*, will leave it in their hands.'"

H 9219, Ch. 135, h 6
Ali ibn Ibrahim has narrated from his father from al-Nawfaliy from al-Sakuniy who has said the following:
"Abu 'Abd Allah, *'Alayhi al-Salam*, has said that the Messenger of Allah, *O Allah, grant compensation to Muhammad and his family worthy of their services to Your cause*, has said, 'Whoever plants a tree or digs a valley as the first one before anyone else and revives a land which is barren (dead), it becomes his land from Allah and the Messenger of Allah, *'O Allah, grant compensation to Muhammad and his family worthy of their services to Your cause.'"*

Chapter 136 - *Al-Shuf'* One's Rights of Pre-emption

H 9220, Ch. 136, h 1
Muhammad ibn Yahya has narrated from Ahmad ibn Muhammad ibn 'Isa from Ali ibn Hadid from Jamil ibn Darraj from certain persons of our people who has said the following:
"One of the two Imam, (abu Ja'far or abu 'Abd Allah), *'Alayhim al-Salam*, has said, 'The right of *al-Shuf'ah* (pre-emption) of an asset belongs to a business partner who has not yet departed partnership.'"

H 9221, Ch. 136, h 2
Ali ibn Ibrahim has narrated from his father from ibn abu 'Umayr from Jamil ibn Darraj from Mansur ibn Hazim who has said the following:
"Regarding my question before 'Abd Allah, *'Alayhi al-Salam*, about a house which is among the houses that have one driveway through a courtyard and one of them sells to a man, if the people sharing the driveway can apply their *al-Shuf'* (one's rights of pre-emption). He (the Imam) said, 'If he has sold his house and has changed its driveway to another driveway then such right is not applicable; but if he has sold the house along with its driveway then they can apply such right.'"

H 9222, Ch. 136, h 3
Ali ibn Muhammad has narrated from Ibrahim ibn Ishaq from 'Abd Allah ibn Hammad from Jamil ibn Darraj from Muhammad ibn Muslim who has said the following:
"Abu Ja'far, *'Alayhi al-Salam*, has said, 'When division takes place, *al-Shuf'* (one's rights of pre-emption) ceases to apply.'"

H 9223, Ch. 136, h 4
Muhammad ibn Yahya has narrated from Muhammad ibn al-Husayn from Muhammad ibn 'Abd Allah ibn Hilal from 'Uqbah ibn Khalid who has said the following:
"Abu 'Abd Allah, *'Alayhi al-Salam*, has said, 'The Messenger of Allah, *O Allah, grant compensation to Muhammad and his family worthy of their services to Your cause*, issued a judgment in favor of *al-Shuf'* (one's rights of pre-emption) in the case of partners in the ownership of land and houses, saying, "Harming and causing harm because of suffering harm is not lawful." He (the Messenger

of Allah) also said, "Once division takes place and boundaries are set *al-Shuf'* (one's rights of pre-emption) ceases to exist.""""

H 9224, Ch. 136, h 5

Muhammad ibn Yahya has narrated from Muhammad ibn al-Husayn from Yazid ibn Ishaq Sh'ir from Harun ibn abu Hamzah al-Ghanaviy who has said the following:

"This is concerning my question before abu 'Abd Allah, *'Alayhi al-Salam*, about *al-Shuf'* (one's rights of pre-emption) in the case of houses; if it is obligatory on the neighbor to offer to the neighbor because of his priority right to buy. He (the Imam) said, '*Al-Shuf'* (one's rights of pre-emption) is applicable in selling if one is a partner; he is more rightful to buy with payment.'"

H 9225, Ch. 136, h 6

Ali ibn Ibrahim has narrated from his father from al-Nawfaliy from al-Sakuniy who has said the following:

"Abu 'Abd Allah, *'Alayhi al-Salam*, has said, '*Al-Shuf'* (one's rights of pre-emption) does not apply in the case of Jews and Christians. It only applies to a partner who has not concluded the partnership.' He (the Imam) has said, that 'Amir al-Mu'minin, *'Alayhi al-Salam*, has said, 'The Executor of the will for an orphan is like his father who applies *al-Shuf'* if it is in his interest', and he (the Imam) said that *al-Shuf'* applies in favor of and absent person also."

H 9226, Ch. 136, h 7

Ali ibn Ibrahim has narrated from his father from Muhammad ibn 'Isa ibn 'Ubayd from Yunus ibn 'Abd al-Rahman from 'Abd Allah ibn Sinan who has said the following:

"Abu 'Abd Allah, *'Alayhi al-Salam*, has said, '*Al-Shuf'* (one's rights of pre-emption) is applicable only between two partners who have not concluded the partnership. If they become three then one of them does not have such right.'"

H 9227, Ch. 136, h 8

Yunus has narrated from certain persons of his people who have said the following:

"This is concerning my question before abu 'Abd Allah, *'Alayhi al-Salam*, about *al-Shuf'* (one's rights of pre-emption), in whose favor it is, in what it is, in whose favor it is proper, if in the case of animals it applies and how it is. He (the Imam) said, '*Al-Shuf'* is applicable to animals, land or assets if it is between two partners and not more than two. When one of them sells his share then his partner has such right more than others, but if they are more than two it does not apply to one of them.' It is also narrated that it does not apply to anything other than land and houses."

H 9228, Ch. 136, h 9

Muhammad ibn Yahya has narrated from Ahmad ibn Muhammad from Ali ibn al-Hakam from al-Kahiliy from Mansur ibn Hazim who has said the following:

"This is concerning my question before abu 'Abd Allah, *'Alayhi al-Salam*, about the case of a house which a certain people divided, each one took a piece, built and left in between a courtyard with the driveway on it. A man came and bought the share of someone among them; if he can do so. He (the Imam) said, 'Yes, he can do so but he must close his door and open a door to a driveway or climb down from the top of the house and close its door. When the owner of the driveway decides to sell, they have the right more than others, otherwise, it is the pathway through which he comes to set on that door.'"

H 9229, Ch. 136, h 10
Humayd ibn Ziyad has narrated from al-Hassan ibn Muhammad ibn Sama'ah from Ahmad ibn al-Hassan al-Mithamiy from Aban from abu al-'Abbas and 'Abd al-Rahman ibn abu 'Abd Allah who has said the following:
"We heard abu 'Abd Allah, *'Alayhi al-Salam*, saying, *'Al-Shuf'* (one's rights of pre-emption) is applicable only between two partners who have not concluded their partnership.'"

H 9230, Ch. 136, h 11
Ali ibn Ibrahim has narrated from his father from al-Nawfaliy from al-Sakuniy who has said the following:
"Abu 'Abd Allah, *'Alayhi al-Salam*, has said that the Messenger of Allah, *O Allah, grant compensation to Muhammad and his family worthy of their services to Your cause*, has said, *'Al-Shuf'* (one's rights of pre-emption) does not apply to ship, canal or road.'"

Chapter 137 - Buying Al-Kharaj Land From Al-Sultan When Owners Are Coerced . . .

H 9231, Ch. 137, h 1
Muhammad ibn Yahya has narrated from 'Abd Allah ibn Muhammad from Ali ibn al-Hakam and Humayd ibn Ziyad from al-Hassan ibn Muhammad from more than one person from Aban ibn 'Uthman from 'Isma'il ibn al-Fadl al-Hashimiy who has said the following:
"This is concerning my question before abu 'Abd Allah, *'Alayhi al-Salam*, about the case of a man who rents, from al-Sultan a piece of land of al-Kharaj that belongs to tax payers, because of the failure of the owners. He (the Imam) said, 'If the owners fail, you can take such land unless it is harmful to the owners. If you pay a certain amount to the owners and it helps to make them agree, then you can have such land.' I then asked him (the Imam) about the case of a man who bought a piece of al-Kharaj land, then built in it or not except that tax payer people arrived therein, if he could receive the rent of houses from them if they pay taxes on their persons. He (the Imam) said, 'He must stipulate it with them and after stipulation it is lawful.'"

H 9232, Ch. 137, h 2
Al-Husayn ibn Muhammad has narrated from Mu'alla' ibn Muhammad from al-Hassan ibn Ali from Aban from Zurarah who has said the following:
"He (the Imam), *'Alayhi al-Salam*, has said, 'It is not unlawful if tax payers buy land, if they build and revive it, it becomes their land.'"

H 9233, Ch. 137, h 3
Ali ibn Ibrahim has narrated from his father from Hammad ibn 'Isa from Hariz from Muhammad ibn Muslim from abu Ja'far, *'Alayhi al-Salam*, and from al-Sabatiy and from Zurarah who has said the following:
"This is regarding their question before one of the two Imam, (abu Ja'far or abu 'Abd Allah), *'Alayhim al-Salam*, about buying the land of farmers of al-Kharaj

land. He (the Imam), *'Alayhi al-Salam*, said, 'On its coming (the time of the rise of al-Mahdiy with Divine Authority and Power) the land will be taken away or you pay what is due on it of al-Kharaj.' 'Ammar has said that he (the Imam) then turned to me and said, "You can buy it because your right on it is more than that of others."'"

H 9234, Ch. 137, h 4

A number of our people have narrated from Sahl ibn Ziyad and Ahmad ibn Muhammad from ibn Mahbub from al-'Ala' from Muhammad ibn Muslim who has said the following:

"This is concerning my question before abu Ja'far, *'Alayhi al-Salam*, about buying the land of tax payers (non-Muslims). He (the Imam) said, 'It is not unlawful. On its coming (the time of the rise of al-Mahdiy with Divine Authority and Power) you will pay what they pay.' I then asked him (the Imam) about the case of a man from people of al-Nil and a land that he had bought at the outlet of al-Nil about which people of that area said it was their land and people of al-'Ustan said it was of their land. He (the Imam) said, 'You must not buy it without agreement of its owner.'"

H 9235, Ch. 137, h 5

Ali ibn Ibrahim has narrated from his father from 'Isma'il ibn Marrar from Yunus from 'Abd Allah ibn Sinan from his father who has said the following:

"I once said to abu 'Abd Allah, *'Alayhi al-Salam*, that I had a piece of land of al-Kharaj which had caused to me great difficulties. He (the Imam) remained quiet for a while, then said, 'On its coming (the time of the rise of al-Mahdiy with Divine Authority and Power) your share of the land will be greater than this and on such time 'Ustan will be more ideal piece of land than their pieces.'"

Chapter 138 - Using Labors of *Al-'Aluj* (infidel) for Free

H 9236, Ch. 138, h 1

Humayd ibn Ziyad has narrated from al-Hassan ibn Muhammad ibn Sama'ah from more than one person from Aban Ahmad ibn Muhammad from Muhammad ibn Yahya from 'Abd Allah ibn Muhammad from Ali ibn al-Hakam from Aban from 'Isma'il al-Fadl al-Hashimiy who has said the following:

"This is concerning my question before abu 'Abd Allah, *'Alayhi al-Salam*, about free labor in villages and what is taken of *al-'Aluj* (infidels) and laborers on hire. He (the Imam) said, 'Stipulate with them. Whatever you have stipulated with them like dirhams, their free labor and other things, then it is for you; but you cannot take from them anything without stipulating, even if you are almost certain (of its lawfulness) that whoever comes to that village that much is taken from him.' I then asked him (the Imam) about a man who built on his land next to his neighbor, houses or a house, then the people of the house became his neighbors; if he could remove them despite their dislike. He (the Imam) said, 'They are free to disembark wherever they like and move wherever they like.'"

H 9237, Ch. 138, h 2

Ali ibn Ibrahim has narrated from his father from ibn abu 'Umayr from Jamil ibn Darraj from Ali al-Azraq who has said the following:

"I once heard abu 'Abd Allah, *'Alayhi al-Salam*, saying, 'The Messenger of Allah, *O Allah, grant compensation to Muhammad and his family worthy of their services to Your cause*, said, when he was about to leave this world to Ali, *'Alayhi al-Salam*, "O Ali, you must not allow that farmers be oppressed before you; and you must not allow taxes on land to increase and you must not allow free labor on a Muslim" (meaning free labor when he is hired).'"

H 9238, Ch. 138, h 3

Abu Ali al-Ash'ariy has narrated from Muhammad ibn 'Abd al-Jabbar from Safwan from ibn Muskan from al-Halabiy who has said the following:

"Abu 'Abd Allah, *'Alayhi al-Salam*, has said that 'Amir al-Mu'minin, would write to his agents, 'You must not make Muslims to perform free labor. Whoever of you asks for what is not obligatory, he has committed transgression and you must not give him anything.' He ('Amir al-Mu'minin) would write and recommend about farmers good advice, about them and laborers on hire.'"

H 9239, Ch. 138, h 4

A number of our people have narrated from and Sahl ibn Ziyad from ibn Mahbub from ibn Sinan who has said the following:

"Abu 'Abd Allah, *'Alayhi al-Salam*, has said, 'The duration of stay to demand al-Kharaj (taxes) from people of al-Kharaj is three days.'"

H 9240, Ch. 138, h 5

Ali ibn Ibrahim has narrated from his father from ibn abu 'Umayr from Hammad from al-Halabiy who has said the following:

"Abu 'Abd Allah, *'Alayhi al-Salam*, has said, 'He (the tax collector agent) stays to demand al-Kharaj from the people of al-Kharaj for three days.'"

Chapter 139 - Brokerage and Brokerage Fees

H 9241, Ch. 139, h 1

Muhammad ibn Yahya has narrated from Ahmad ibn Muhammad from Al-Husayn ibn al-Bashshar who has said the following:

"About the case of a broker who shows houses and assets for a certain amount of fee, abu al-Hassan, *'Alayhi al-Salam*, said it is not unlawful.'"

H 9242, Ch. 139, h 2

Muhammad ibn Yahya has narrated from Ahmad ibn Muhammad from Ali ibn al-Hakam from and others from 'Abd Allah ibn Sinan who has said the following:

"Once abu 'Abd Allah, *'Alayhi al-Salam*, was asked, when I was listening, 'We order a man to buy land, slave, a house or a servant for us and assign a certain amount for him. He (the Imam) said, 'It is not unlawful.'"

H 9243, Ch. 139, h 3

Ahmad ibn Muhammad has narrated from ibn abu 'Umayr from certain persons of our people of slave traders who has said the following:

"I once bought a slave-girl for abu 'Abd Allah, *'Alayhi al-Salam*, and he (the Imam) gave me four dinars but I declined. He (the Imam) said, 'You must take it' and I took it and he (the Imam) said, 'You must not take anything from the seller.'"

H 9244, Ch. 139, h 4

A number of our people have narrated from Sahl ibn Ziyad and Ahmad ibn Muhammad from ibn Mahbub from 'Abd Allah ibn Sinan who has said the following:

"Once, a man asked abu 'Abd Allah, *'Alayhi al-Salam*, when I was listening, 'We perhaps order a man to buy for us land, house, slave or slave-girl and assign for him a certain amount. He (the Imam) said, 'It is not unlawful.'"

H 9245, Ch. 139, h 5

It is narrated from the two of them from ibn Mahbub from abu Wallad and others who has said the following:

"They have said that abu Ja'far, *'Alayhi al-Salam*, has said, 'Payment for brokerage fee to a broker who buys goods for people day after day is not unlawful.'"

Chapter 140 - Partnership with *al-Dhimmiy* (non-Muslim Tax payer)

H 9246, Ch. 140, h 1

A number of our people have narrated from Ahmad ibn Muhammad from ibn Mahbub from ibn Ri'ab who has said the following:

"Abu 'Abd Allah, *'Alayhi al-Salam*, has said, 'It is not proper for a Muslim man to become a partner of *al-Dhimmiy* (non-Muslim tax payer) and not to give him goods for business, leave safe deposit with him and not to have pure friendly relationship with him.'"

H 9247, Ch. 140, h 2

Ali ibn Ibrahim has narrated from his father from al-Nawfaliy from al-Sakuniy who has said the following:

"Abu 'Abd Allah, *'Alayhi al-Salam*, has said that 'Amir al-Mu'minin did not like partnership with Jews, Christians, al-Majusiy, unless it was a hand in hand business deal in the presence of the Muslim.'"

Chapter 141 - Asking for Reduction of Price After Concluding a Deal

H 9248, Ch. 141, h 1

Ali ibn Ibrahim has narrated from his father from ibn abu 'Umayr from Ibrahim al-Kharkhiy who has said the following:

"I once bought a slave-girl for abu 'Abd Allah, *'Alayhi al-Salam*, and went to get dirhams and I asked him (the Imam), 'Can I ask to reduce the price?' He (the Imam) said, 'No, because the Messenger of Allah, *O Allah, grant compensation to Muhammad and his family worthy of their services to Your cause*, prohibited asking for reduction after the deal is finalized.'"

H 9249, Ch. 141, h 2

A number of our people have narrated from Ahmad ibn Muhammad from certain persons of our people from Mu'awiyah ibn 'Ammar from Zayd al-Shahham who has said the following:

"I once took a slave-girl to abu 'Abd Allah, *'Alayhi al-Salam*. He (the Imam) bargained and I also bargained very hard. I then sold her to him (the Imam) and he (the Imam) shook my hand and I said, 'I pray to Allah to keep my soul in service for your cause, I bargained hard to see if it was permissible or not and I said, "I reduce the price by ten dinar."' He (the Imam) said, 'Never, however, this could have happened before shaking hands. Have you not heard the words of the Holy Prophet, *O Allah, grant compensation to Muhammad and his family worthy of their services to Your cause*, "Asking for reduction after handshake is unlawful"?"'

Chapter 142 - Estimating Produce of Plantation

H 9250, Ch. 142, h 1
Ali ibn Muhammad has narrated from Muhammad ibn Ahmad from Muhammad ibn 'Isa from certain persons of his people who has said the following:
"This is concerning my question before abu al-Hassan, *'Alayhi al-Salam*, about the people who work for hire and we make a deal with them to farm for us and they say, 'We have estimated this farm for so and so much and if you give it to us we guarantee your share according to our estimation.' He (the Imam) asked, 'Is it completed?' I replied, 'Yes, it is complete.' He (the Imam) said, 'It is not unlawful.' I then asked, 'He afterward comes and says that estimation is not as it was supposed to be and it is less.' He (the Imam) said, 'Do they return to you if it is more than estimated?' I replied, 'No, they do not return to us anything.' He (the Imam) said, 'You have the right to take according to the estimation, just as when it is more than estimation, they keep the extra, so also it is on them if it is less than estimation.'"

Chapter 143 - Rent From Tenant and His Responsibilities

H 9251, Ch. 143, h 1
Abu Ali al-Ash'ariy has narrated from Muhammad ibn 'Abd al-Jabbar from Safwan from Ishaq ibn 'Ammar who has said the following:
"This is concerning my question before abu Ibrahim, *'Alayhi al-Salam*, about the case of a man who hires a man for a certain amount of wages and sends him to work; but he gives dirhams to another man and asks him, 'Buy such and such things; we will share the profit.' He (the Imam) said, 'If the one who has hired gives permission, it is not unlawful.'"

H 9252, Ch. 143, h 2
Muhammad ibn Yahya has narrated from Ahmad ibn Muhammad from al-'Abbas ibn Musa from Yunus from Sulayman ibn Salim who has said the following:
"This is concerning my question before abu al-Hassan, *'Alayhi al-Salam*, about the case of a man who hires another man for a certain amount of wages and dirham to send him to a certain land. When he arrives in that land one of his friends invites him with who he stays for one or two months where he does not need to spend from the supplies of his employer. After calculating he finds out that the amount his employer had provided is not enough and that his expenses have been taken care of by the resources of his friend; if the shortages in his expenses is the responsibility of the employee or the employer. He (the Imam) said, 'It is on the employer if it serves his interests, but if it does not serve his

interest then it is on the employee.' I then asked about the case of a man who hired another man for a certain amount of wages and did not explain anything about his sending him (the employee) to another land, and then whose responsibility was his expenses such as washing clothes and bathing? He (the Imam) said, 'It is the responsibility of the employer.'"

H 9253, Ch. 143, h 3

Ahmad ibn Muhammad has narrated from ibn abu 'Umayr from Ali ibn 'Isma'il ibn 'Ammar from 'Ubayd ibn Zurarah who has said the following:

"This is concerning my question before abu 'Abd Allah, *'Alayhi al-Salam*, about the case of a man who comes to another man and says, 'Write for me for a few dirham.' He says, 'I take from you and write (in your presence).' He (the Imam) said, 'It is not unlawful.' I then asked about a man who hires a slave who says, 'Make my master agree for whatever amount you like but so and so much dirham will be for me', if this becomes binding upon the employer and if it is lawful for the slave. He (the Imam) said, 'It does not become binding upon the employer and it is not lawful for the slave.'"

Chapter 144 - Detestability of Using the Labor of a Worker before Agreeing on Wages and Delay Payment of His Wages

H 9254, Ch. 144, h 1

Muhammad ibn Yahya has narrated from Ahmad ibn Muhammad from Sulayman ibn Ja'far al-Ja'fariy who has said the following:

"I once was with al-Rida', *'Alayhi al-Salam*, because of a certain work and I wanted to leave for my home but he (the Imam) said, 'Come with me and stay for the night with me.' I went with him (the Imam), he entered in his house with al-Mu'attib and looked at his slaves who worked with clay, in the animal barn and other things and with them there was a black man who was not one of them. He (the Imam) asked, 'Who is this man with you?' They replied, 'He is helping us and we will give him something.' He (the Imam) then asked, 'Have you determined how much you must pay him?' They replied, 'No, because he will agree with whatever we will give him.' He (the Imam) turned upon them using a whip, expressing intense anger. I then said, 'I pray to Allah to keep my soul in service for your cause, please do not take it upon yourself.' He (the Imam) said, 'I have prohibited them many times from allowing anyone to work with them without determining his wages. I know that there is no one who works for you in anything without determining his wages; then you pay him three times more than what his work is worth for, he still thinks that you have paid him less than his wages; but if you determine his wages first, then pay his wages he will be grateful to you for keeping your promise and if you increase even by one grain he will recognize it as your favor and see that you have paid him extra.'"

H 9255, Ch. 144, h 2

Ali ibn Ibrahim has narrated from his father from ibn abu 'Umayr from Hisham ibn al-Hakam who has said the following:

"About the case of porters and a man working for hire, abu 'Abd Allah, *'Alayhi al-Salam*, has said, 'You must pay him before his perspiration dries up.'"

H 9256, Ch. 144, h 3

Muhammad ibn Yahya has narrated from Ahmad ibn Muhammad from Muhammad ibn 'Isma'il from Hanan from Shu'ayb who has said the following:

"We once hired a people for abu 'Abd Allah, *'Alayhi al-Salam*, to work in his garden and they were suppose to work until the time of al-'Al-'Asr. When they finished, he (the Imam) said to Mu'attib, 'Pay them their wages before their perspiration dries up.'"

H 9257, Ch. 144, h 4

Ali ibn Ibrahim has narrated from his father from Harun ibn Muslim from Mas'adah ibn Sadaqah who has said the following:

"Abu 'Abd Allah, *'Alayhi al-Salam*, has said, 'Whoever believes in Allah and on Day of Judgment must not make a person work for him on hire until he knows how much his wages are, and if one hires a person and keeps him from Friday, he is held responsible for his sin; and if he allows him to attend Friday they will share the reward.'"

Chapter 144 - Hiring an Animal and Using Beyond Limit

H 9258, Ch. 145, h 1

Al-Husayn ibn Muhammad has narrated from Mu'alla' ibn Muhammad from al-Hassan ibn Ali from Aban ibn 'Uthman from al-Hassan al-Sayqal who has said the following:

"This is concerning my question before abu 'Abd Allah, *'Alayhi al-Salam*, about the case of a man who hires a stumper to a certain place but he goes beyond such place. He (the Imam) said, 'He must pay for the extra distance; and if the donkey is destroyed, he is held responsible.'"

H 9259, Ch. 145, h 2

A number of our people have narrated from Ahmad ibn Muhammad from Ali ibn al-Hakam from al-'Ala' from Muhammad ibn Muslim from abu Hamzah who has said the following:

"This is concerning my question before abu Ja'far, *'Alayhi al-Salam*, about the case of a man who rents a stumper and says, 'I rent it from you to so and so place; if I went beyond such place you will be paid so and so much extra which he mentions.' He (the Imam) said, 'All of it is permissible.'"

H 9260, Ch. 145, h 3

Ahmad ibn Muhammad has narrated from a man from abu al-Mighra' from al-Halabiy who has said the following:

"This is concerning my question before abu 'Abd Allah, *'Alayhi al-Salam*, about the case of a man who rents a stumper to a certain place but it dies. He (the Imam) said, 'If he has violated the stipulation he is responsible, if he enters a valley where he is not confident for its safety, he then is responsible, if it falls in a well where for its safety he is not confident, he is responsible.'"

H 9261, Ch. 145, h 4

Muhammad ibn Yahya has narrated from al-Husayn from Muhammad from Safwan from al-'Ala' from Muhammad ibn Muslim who has said the following:

"I once heard abu Ja'far, *'Alayhi al-Salam*, saying, 'I was sitting near the judge in al-Madinah when two men came to him. One of them said, 'I hired this person to appear in the market on such and such day but he did not appear.' The judge said, 'He does not deserve payment.' He (the Imam) has said, 'I then called him and said, "O servant of Allah, you cannot take away his right." To the other man I said, "You cannot take all that he owes. You must reach a settlement and be lenient toward each other."'"

H 9262, Ch. 146, h 5

Muhammad ibn Yahya has narrated from Ahmad ibn Muhammad from Muhammad ibn 'Isma'il from Mansur ibn Yunus from Muhammad al-Halabiy who has said the following:

"I once was sitting with the judge and abu Ja'far, *'Alayhi al-Salam*, was also there, when two men came to him and one of them said, 'I rented a camel from this man to carry my goods to the mine and I stipulated with him to come to me to the mine on so and so day because that was the market day and I was afraid of missing it. If you will be held up I will reduce the rent for each day that you are held up so and so much amount. He kept me on hold for so and so many days.' The judge said, 'This is an invalid stipulation. You must pay his rent.' When the man stood up he came to abu Ja'far, *'Alayhi al-Salam*, who said, 'His stipulation is permissible as long as he does not drop all of the rent.'"

H 9263, Ch. 146, h 6

A number of our people have narrated from Ahmad ibn Muhammad from ibn Mahbub from abu Wallad al-Hannat who has said the following:

"I once rented a mule to Qasr ibn Hubayrah for both ways for so and so much amount. I left in search of my debtor and when I reached near the bridge of al-Kufah, I was informed that my debtor had gone to al-Nil. I then moved to al-Nil. When I went to al-Nil I was informed that my debtor had gone to Baghdad. I then followed him, found him and finalized whatever was between him and me and we returned to al-Kufah. Going and coming took me fifteen days. I informed the owner of the mule of my reasons for the delay. I wanted to make it a lawful deal and make him agree so I paid him fifteen dirham but he refused to accept it. We then agreed to go to abu Hanifah for judgment. I told my side of the story to him and the man also told his side of the story. He asked me, 'What did you do to the mule?' I replied, 'I have returned it to him safely.' He (owner) said, 'Yes, after fifteen days.' He asked, 'What do you want from the man?' He replied, 'I want the rent for the mule which he kept for fifteen days.' He said, 'I do not see any such right in your favor because he rented it to Qasr ibn Hubayrah, and he then violated the agreement and rode it to al-Nil and to Baghdad, so he became responsible for the price of the mule and the rent became void. He then returned the mule safely to you and you have it in your possession so he is not responsible for rent.' We came out of his office and the owner of mule kept saying, 'To Allah we belong and to Him we all return.' I felt sympathy for him because of the fatwa of abu Hanifah against him and I gave him something and asked him not to hold me responsible. I went for al-Hajj in that year and informed abu 'Abd Allah, *'Alayhi al-Salam*, about the fatwa of abu Hanifah. He (the Imam) said, 'It is because of this kind of judgments that the sky stops sending water and the earth denies its blessings.' I then asked abu 'Abd Allah, *'Alayhi al-Salam*, 'What do you say about it?' I say that you must pay him a similar rent that is charged for a mule from al-Kufah to al-Nil, a similar rent for a mule that is charged from al-Nil to Baghdad, a similar rent that is charged for a mule from Baghdad to al-Kufah. You must pay him.' I then said, 'I pray to Allah to keep my soul in service for your cause, I fed the mule with a cost of many dirhams so he must pay for the feed.' He (the Imam) said, 'No, because you usurped it.' I then said, 'What could happen if the mule died and was damaged, would he not hold me responsible?' He (the Imam) said, 'Yes, he could do so for the value of the mule on the day you went against the stipulation.' I then asked, 'What could happen if the mule became damaged, sustained injuries or so?' He (the Imam) said, 'You would owe the price between healthy and damaged mule on the day you returned to him.' I then asked, 'Who could determine it?' He (the Imam) said, 'You and he (owner of mule) could do so. Either he had to take an oath to confirm the value for which you were responsible. If he turned the oath to you, you then had to take an oath about the value and it became binding on him or the owner of the mule had to present testimony and witness to prove how much the value of the mule was when it was rented and it became binding upon you.' I then said, 'I gave him a certain amount of dirham, he agreed and made it lawful in my favor.' He (the Imam) said, 'He agreed and made it lawful for you because of the fatwa of abu Hanifah, unjustly. However, you must go to him and inform him of my fatwa on this matter to see if he still agrees after knowing it, thereafter there will be nothing on you.' Abu Wallad al-Hannat has said, 'As soon as I returned I met al-Mukariy and informed him of the fatwa of abu 'Abd Allah, '*Alayhi al-Salam*, and I said to him, "Now say what you want to say so I pay you." He said, "I feel love for Ja'far ibn Muhammad in my heart and my heart says he has preference over the others. You do not owe me anything even though I love to return what I have taken from you, I still can do so."'"

H 9264, Ch. 145, h 7
Muhammad ibn Yahya has narrated from al-'Amrakiy ibn Ali from Ali ibn Ja'far from his who has said the following:

"This is concerning my question before abu al-Hassan, '*Alayhi al-Salam*, about the case of a man who rents a stumper but he gives it to another one and it dies. He (the Imam) said, 'If he had stipulated that no one else except him ride it, then he is responsible; if such thing is not mentioned then he is not responsible.'"

Chapter 146 - Renting a House or Ship

H 9265, Ch. 146, h 1
A number of our people have narrated from Ahmad ibn Muhammad from al-Hassan ibn Ali ibn Yaqtin from his brother al-Husayn from Ali ibn Yaqtin who has said the following:

"This is concerning my question before abu al-Hassan, '*Alayhi al-Salam*, about the case of a man who rents a ship for a year or less or more. He (the Imam) said, 'The lease is binding up to the end of its term. Receiving payment of rent is up to the owner who may accept it or leave it.'"

H 9266, Ch. 146, h 2
Ahmad ibn Muhammad has narrated from Muhammad ibn Sahl from his father who has said the following:

"Regarding my question before abu al-Hassan, Musa, *'Alayhi al-Salam*, about the case of a man who rents a ship or house from another man for a year or more or less. He (the Imam) said, 'Payment of rent up to the end of the term is incumbent, but accepting payment of rent or leaving it is up to the owner who may like to receive or leave it.'"

Chapter 147 - Causing Losses (*Dirar*)

H 9267, Ch. 147, h 1

Muhammad ibn Yahya has narrated from Ahmad ibn Muhammad from Muhammad ibn Yahya from Talhah ibn Zayd who has said the following:

"Abu 'Abd Allah, *'Alayhi al-Salam*, has said, 'A neighbor (in matters of immunity) is like a soul which is not harmed or has not committed sins.'"

H 9268, Ch. 147, h 2

A number of our people have narrated from Ahmad ibn Muhammad from ibn Khalid from his father from 'Abd Allah ibn Bukayr from Zurarah who has said the following:

"Abu Ja'far, *'Alayhi al-Salam*, has said, 'Samrah ibn Jundab had a fruit bearing palm tree in the garden of another man from al-Ansar whose house was at the door of the garden and he (Samrah) would pass by when going to his palm tree without permission. The man from al-Ansar spoke to him and asked him to ask for permission whenever he comes. Samrah refused to do so. When he refused the man from al-Ansar went to the Messenger of Allah, *O Allah, grant compensation to Muhammad and his family worthy of their services to Your cause*, complained before him and informed him of the condition. The Messenger of Allah, *O Allah, grant compensation to Muhammad and his family worthy of their services to Your cause*, sent someone to call Samrah, informed him of the complaints of the man from al-Ansar and asked him to ask permission whenever going to his palm tree but he refused. When he refused, he (the Messenger of Allah) bargained with him and offered him a huge price but he still refused. He (the Messenger of Allah) then said, "In exchange for this you can have a fruit bearing palm trees in paradise", but he refused to accept. The Messenger of Allah, *O Allah, grant compensation to Muhammad and his family worthy of their services to Your cause*, then asked the man from al-Ansar to go, uproot that palm tree and throw it to him; harming and leading to harm is not lawful.'"

H 9269, Ch. 147, h 3

Ali ibn Ibrahim has narrated from his father from Muhammad ibn Hafs from a man who has said the following:

"This is concerning my question before abu 'Abd Allah, *'Alayhi al-Salam*, about the case of a people whose water fountains in a land are near each other, one of them decides to make his fountain below its original place in which case is harmful to the other fountains but certain ones do not harm due to solidity of earth. He (the Imam) said, 'Whatever is in solid land it does not harm but whatever is in soft land and sandy, it harms. One can ask his neighbor to keep his fountain at the same level as his and if they agreed it does not harm.' He (the

Imam) said, 'The distance between two fountains must be kept at one thousand Dhira' (hands or arms length).'"

H 9270, Ch. 147, h 4
Muhammad ibn Yahya has narrated from al-Husayn ibn Muhammad from Yazid ibn Ishaq, Sha'Ir from Harun ibn Hamzah al-Ghanaviy who has said the following:

"About the case of a man who found a sick camel for sale and bought it for ten dirham, then another man came and asked to share for the head and skin for two dirham, but then it was found that the camel was fine and not sick and its price reached many dinars. He then asked the owner of two dirham to take one-fifth of the price, but he refused and said that he wanted the head and skin. Abu 'Abd Allah, 'Alayhi al-Salam, has said, 'He does not have such right; it is harming. His right was made available when one-fifth was offered to him.'"

H 9271, Ch. 147, h 5
Muhammad ibn Yahya has narrated from Muhammad ibn al-Husayn who has said the following:

"I once wrote to abu Muhammad, 'Alayhi al-Salam, and asked, 'A man had a canal in a village and another man wanted to dig another canal in a village that belonged to him. How much distance is required between the two so that they do not harm each other when the land is solid or soft? He (the Imam) signed the answer that said, 'It is according to a measure that does not cause one to harm the other, by the will of Allah.' I wrote to him (the Imam), 'Alayhi al-Salam, about a man who had a flour mill on the canal of a village that belonged to a man and the owner of the village wanted to divert the water to his village in another canal and put the flour mill out of work; if he can do so. He (the Imam), 'Alayhi al-Salam, signed the answer that said, 'He must be pious before Allah and act according to what is acceptable among people and must not cause harm to his believing brother.'"

H 9272, Ch. 147, h 6
Muhammad ibn Yahya has narrated from Muhammad ibn al-Husayn from Muhammad ibn 'Abd Allah ibn Hilal from 'Uqbah ibn Khalid al-Husayn from Muhammad who has said the following:

"About the case of a man who dug a canal in a hill and it dried up another canal, abu 'Abd Allah, 'Alayhi al-Salam, has said, 'They can divide and find out which one is harming the other by closing the flow of water of each canal and leave the other open and alternate by one night between the two (to measure the difference of increase and decrease of the level of water in each one).'"

H 9273, Ch. 147, h 7
Muhammad ibn Yahya has narrated from Muhammad ibn Al-Husayn from Muhammad ibn 'Abd Allah ibn Hilal from 'Uqbah ibn Khalid who has narrated the following:

"Abu 'Abd Allah, 'Alayhi al-Salam, has said that if a man digs a well (a canal) in a hill which reduces the water of an existing well or canal, they must be examined closely. Such tests must be conducted every night to find out which one reduces the water of the other. If it is found out that the second one reduces the water of the existing, one then it must be closed.'"

H 9274, Ch. 147, h 8

Ali ibn Muhammad ibn Bandar has narrated from Ahmad ibn abu 'Abd Allah from his father from certain persons of his people from 'Abd Allah ibn Muskan from Zurarah who has said the following:

"Abu Ja'far, *'Alayhi al-Salam,* has said, 'Samrah ibn Jundab had a fruit bearing palm tree and his path way was through the inside section of the house of a man from al-Ansar. He would come and enter to go to his palm tree without permission. The man from al-Ansar said to him, 'O Samrah, you continue to take us off guard in a condition that we do not like you to take us off guard. Please, when you come ask for permission. He said, 'I do not need permission for the path that is the path to my palm tree.' He (the Imam) said that the man from al-Ansar went to the Messenger of Allah, *O Allah, grant compensation to Muhammad and his family worthy of their services to Your cause,* complained before him and informed him of the condition. The Messenger of Allah, *O Allah, grant compensation to Muhammad and his family worthy of their services to Your cause,* sent someone to call Samrah, informed him that so and so complains and thinks that you pass by him and his family without permission so you must ask for permission when you want to go to your palm tree.' He said, 'O Messenger of Allah, why must I ask permission for the pathway of my palm tree?' The Messenger of Allah, *O Allah, grant compensation to Muhammad and his family worthy of their services to Your cause,* said, 'Leave that palm tree in exchange for a palm tree in such and such place.' He said, 'No, I do not want to exchange.' He (the Messenger of Allah) said, 'Exchange for two.' He said, 'No.' He (the Messenger of Allah) went on up to offering ten palm trees and he refused to accept. He (the Messenger of Allah) said, 'Exchange it for ten palm trees in so and so place.' He refused. He (the Messenger of Allah) said, 'Exchange it for a palm tree in paradise.' He refused and said, 'I do not want it.' The Messenger of Allah, *O Allah, grant compensation to Muhammad and his family worthy of their services to Your cause,* then said, 'You are a harmful man. Harming and causing to lead to harm is not lawful against a believing man.' He (the Imam) said that the Messenger of Allah, *O Allah, grant compensation to Muhammad and his family worthy of their services to Your cause,* commanded to uproot that palm tree and threw it to him. The Messenger of Allah, *O Allah, grant compensation to Muhammad and his family worthy of their services to Your cause,* said to him, 'Go plant it wherever you want.'"

Chapter 148 - Comprehensive Chapter on Limits of Rights

H 9275, Ch. 148, h 1

Ali ibn Ibrahim has narrated from his father from al-Nawfaliy from al-Sakuniy who has said the following:

"Abu 'Abd Allah, *'Alayhi al-Salam,* has said that the Messenger of Allah, *O Allah, grant compensation to Muhammad and his family worthy of their services to Your cause,* issued a judgment, in the case of a man who sold a garden with the exception of one tree, that gave it a path to go to and come out and for its twigs.'"

H 9276, Ch. 148, h 2

A number of our people have narrated from Sahl ibn Ziyad from Muhammad ibn al-Hassan ibn Shammun from 'Abd Allah ibn 'Abd al-Rahman al-Asamm from Misma' ibn 'Abd al-Malik who has said the following:

"Abu 'Abd Allah, *'Alayhi al-Salam*, has said that the Messenger of Allah, *O Allah, grant compensation to Muhammad and his family worthy of their services to Your cause*, assigned the distance between two wells for drinking water to be forty *Dhira'* (arms length) and between two irrigating wells sixty *Dhira'* and between two water fountains five hundred *Dhira'* and the width of a road when people disputed was seven *Dhira'*.'"

H 9277, Ch. 148, h 3

Ali ibn Ibrahim has narrated from his father from ibn abu 'Umayr from abu al-Mighra' from Mansur ibn Hazim who has said the following:

"This is concerning my question before abu 'Abd Allah, *'Alayhi al-Salam*, about the yard between two houses and he (the Imam) expressed certainty about the judgment of Ali, *'Alayhi al-Salam*, in such case in favor of the house toward which the fence is facing.'"

H 9278, Ch. 148, h 4

Muhammad ibn Yahya has narrated from Muhammad ibn al-Husayn from Muhammad ibn 'Abd Allah ibn Hilal from 'Uqbah ibn Khalid who has said the following:

"The Holy Prophet, *O Allah, grant compensation to Muhammad and his family worthy of their services to Your cause*, issued a judgment about the size of the area around one or two palm trees that a man may have in a garden which is disputed for each tree to be an area covered by its longest branch or twig.'"

H 9279, Ch. 148, h 5

A number of our people have narrated from Ahmad ibn Muhammad from al-Barqiy from Muhammad ibn Yahya from Hammad ibn 'Uthman who has said the following:

"I once heard abu 'Abd Allah, *'Alayhi al-Salam*, saying, 'The distance between two old wells must be forty *Dhira'* around it and between two wells for drinking water fifty *Dhira'* unless it is near the road, in which case it is less than twenty five *Dhira'*.'"

H 9280, Ch. 148, h 6

Muhammad ibn Yahya has narrated from Muhammad ibn al-Husayn from Muhammad ibn 'Abd Allah ibn Hilal from 'Uqbah ibn Khalid who has said the following:

"Abu 'Abd Allah, *'Alayhi al-Salam*, has said, 'The necessary distance between two wells if the land is solid must be five hundred *Dhira'* and if the land is soft then it must be one thousand *Dhira'*.'"

H 9281, Ch. 148, h 7

Ali ibn Ibrahim has narrated from his father in a marfu' manner the following:

"He (the Imam), *'Alayhi al-Salam*, has said, the restricted area around a canal is up to its edge and that which adjoins it."

H 9282, Ch. 148, h 8

Ali ibn Ibrahim has narrated from his father from al-Nawfaliy from al-Sakuniy who has said the following:

"Abu 'Abd Allah, *'Alayhi al-Salam*, has said that the Messenger of Allah, *O Allah, grant compensation to Muhammad and his family worthy of their services to Your cause*, assigned the distance between two wells for drinking water to be forty *Dhira'* (arms length) and between two irrigating wells sixty *Dhira'* and between two water fountains five hundred *Dhira'* and the width of a road when people disputed was seven *Dhira'*.'"

H 9283, Ch. 148, h 9
Abu Ali al-Ash'ariy has narrated from Muhammad ibn 'Abd al-Jabbar from Safwan ibn Yahya from Mansur ibn Hazim who has said the following:

"This is concerning my question before abu 'Abd Allah, *'Alayhi al-Salam*, about the case of a fence between two houses, he (the Imam), *'Alayhi al-Salam*, expressed certainty about the judgment of Ali, *'Alayhi al-Salam*, which was in favor of the house toward which the fence was facing.'"

Chapter 149 - The Case of One Who Farms on Other's Land

H 9284, Ch. 149, h 1
Muhammad ibn Yahya has narrated from Muhammad ibn al-Husayn from Muhammad ibn 'Abd Allah ibn Hilal from 'Uqbah ibn Khalid who said the following:

"This is concerning my question before abu 'Abd Allah, *'Alayhi al-Salam*, about the case of a man who comes to the land of another man and cultivates it without the permission of the owner until it is time of harvests; and the owner comes and says, 'You have cultivated my land without my permission so your plantation belongs to me and I owe what you have spent'; if he is right. He (the Imam) said, 'Plantation belongs to the farmer and the owner of the land deserves to receive the rent for his land.'"

H 9285, Ch. 149, h 2
Ali ibn Ibrahim has narrated from his father from ibn Faddal from Ali ibn 'Uqbah from Musa ibn 'Ukayl al-Numayriy from Muhammad ibn Muslim who has said the following:

"About the case of a man who rents a house in which there is a garden, in the garden he plants palm trees and other fruit bearing trees and fruits and so on without permission from the owner of the garden. He (the Imam) said, 'He must pay the rent and the owner of the garden evaluates the plantation in a fair manner and pays to the man who had planted them. Had he asked permission he had to pay the rent and the plantation belonged to him, which he had to cut off and take whenever he wanted.'"

H 9286, Ch. 149, h 3
Muhammad ibn Yahya has narrated from Muhammad ibn Yahya from Yazid ibn Ishaq from Harun ibn Hamzah who has said the following:

"This is concerning my question before abu 'Abd Allah, *'Alayhi al-Salam*, about the case of a man who purchases the palm tree to cut for its branches, but he disappears and leaves the palm tree in its original condition without doing anything about it, he comes only when the tree has already pollinated. He (the Imam) said, 'The pollinated palm tree is his and he can do whatever he wants unless the owner of the garden has been watering it and looking after it.'"

Chapter 150 - Rare Ahadith

H 9287, Ch. 150, h 1
A number of our people have narrated from Sahl ibn Ziyad from Al-Rayyan ibn al-Salt or a man from Rayyan from Yunus from the virtuous servant (of Allah) who has said the following:

"He (the Imam), *'Alayhi al-Salam*, has said, 'The earth belongs to Allah who has made it an endowment for His servants. Whoever keeps a land out of use for three consecutive years without good reason, loses its ownership and it will be given to others, and one who does not demand his right for ten years, then his right ceases to exist.'"

H 9288, Ch. 150, h 2
Ali ibn Ibrahim has narrated from his father from 'Isma'il ibn Marrar from Yunus from a man who has said the following:

"Abu 'Abd Allah, *'Alayhi al-Salam*, has said, 'If you take a land from someone who does not demand it back for three years he loses the right to demand it thereafter.'"

Chapter 151 - Lending Without Witness

H 9289, Ch. 151, h 1
Muhammad ibn Yahya has narrated from Ahmad ibn Muhammad ibn 'Isa from Ali ibn al-Hakam from 'Umar ibn abu 'Asem who has said the following:

"Abu 'Abd Allah, *'Alayhi al-Salam*, has said, 'The prayers of four kinds of people are not heard and accepted, one is a man who has an asset which he gives to someone without the presence of any witness and Allah, most Majestic, most Glorious, says, 'Did I not command you to secure the witness?'"

H 9290, Ch. 151, h 2
Ahmad ibn Muhammad al-'Asemiy has narrated from Ali ibn al-Hassan al-Tamimiy from ibn Baqqah from abu 'Abd Allah al-Mu'min from 'Ammar ibn abu 'Asem who has said the following:

"Abu 'Abd Allah, *'Alayhi al-Salam*, has said, 'The prayers of four kinds of people are not heard and accepted and he (the Imam) said that the fourth one is he who has an asset which he lends it to someone without the presence of witness and testimony; and Allah, most Majestic, most Glorious, then says, "Did I not command you to secure witness and testimony."'"

H 9291, Ch. 151, h 3
A number of our people have narrated from Ahmad ibn abu 'Abd Allah from Muhammad ibn Ali from Musa ibn Sa'dan from 'Abd Allah ibn al-Qasim from 'Abd Allah ibn Sinan who has said the following:

"Abu 'Abd Allah, *'Alayhi al-Salam*, has said, 'One who loses his right just because of not having witnesses, does not receive any reward.'"

Muhammad ibn Yahya has narrated from Muhammad ibn al-Husayn from Musa ibn Sa'dan from 'Abd Allah ibn Sinan abu 'Abd Allah, *'Alayhi al-Salam*, a similar Hadith.

Chapter 152 - Rare Ahadith

H 9292, Ch. 152, h 1

A number of our people have narrated from Sahl ibn Ziyad from Harun ibn Muslim from Mas'adah ibn Sadaqah who has said the following:

"Abu 'Abd Allah, *'Alayhi al-Salam*, has said, 'You cannot accuse one whom you trust and you must not trust a treacherous person when you have already tried him.'"

H 9293, Ch. 152, h 2

Sahl ibn Ziyad has narrated from Muhammad ibn al-Hassan ibn Shammun from Muhammad ibn Harun al-Jallab who has said the following:

"I once heard abu al-Hassan, *'Alayhi al-Salam*, saying, 'When injustice is more than the truth, it is not lawful for anyone to think good of anyone until he finds it out to be the case.'"

H 9294, Ch. 152, h 3

Ali ibn Muhammad has narrated from Ahmad ibn abu 'Abd Allah from Muhammad ibn 'Isa from Khalaf ibn Hammad Zakariya ibn Ibrahim in a marfu' manner who has said the following:

"Abu Ja'far, once said to abu 'Abd Allah, *'Alayhi al-Salam*, 'One who trusts an untrustworthy one, he does not have good reason and ground before Allah.'"

H 9295, Ch. 152, h 4

Muhammad ibn Yahya has narrated from Ahmad ibn Muhammad from Mu'ammar ibn Khallad who has said the following:

"I once heard abu al-Hassan, *'Alayhi al-Salam*, saying, 'Abu Ja'far, *'Alayhi al-Salam*, would say, "A trustworthy person has not betrayed you but you have trusted a treacherous one."'"

H 9296, Ch. 152, h 5

Abu Ali al-Ash'ariy has narrated from Muhammad ibn 'Abd al-Jabbar from al-Hassan ibn Ali al-Kufiy from 'Ubays ibn Hisham from abu Jamilah from abu Hamzah who has said the following:

"Abu Ja'far, *'Alayhi al-Salam*, has said, 'If one learns that a servant of the servants of Allah has lied in what he had said, disregarded his promise and betrayed his trust with what he was entrusted, then considers such person trustworthy, it becomes a right before Allah, most High to afflict him with it without any recompense or give him any reward for his suffering.'"

Chapter 153 - Another Chapter about Previous Subject, Protection of Property and Detestability of Wasting

H 9297, Ch. 153, h 1

Ali ibn Ibrahim has narrated from his father from ibn abu 'Umayr from Hammad ibn 'Isa from Hariz who has said the following:

"'Isma'il, son of abu 'Abd Allah, *'Alayhi al-Salam*, had a certain amount of dinar and a man from Quraysh wanted to travel to Yemen, so 'Isma'il asked his father, 'Father, so and so wants to go to Yemen and I have so and so amount of dinar. Do you think I should give it to him to bring for me goods from Yemen?' Abu 'Abd Allah, *'Alayhi al-Salam*, said, 'Are you not aware that he drinks wine?' 'Isma'il replied, 'Yes, this is what people say about him.' He (the Imam) then said, 'Son, do not give him your dinars.' 'Isma'il disobeyed his father and gave the dinars to him. He used them and did not bring anything. 'Isma'il traveled, so also abu 'Abd Allah, *'Alayhi al-Salam*, for al-Hajj in that year. 'Isma'il, when performing Tawaf would say, 'O Lord, grant me reward and replace for me what I have lost.' Abu 'Abd Allah, *'Alayhi al-Salam*, approached him and tapped him with his hand and said, 'Hold it my son, by Allah, you have no ground for your argument before Allah and you have no right for receiving any reward or replacement for what you have lost, when you knew that he drank wine and you still trusted him.' 'Isma'il said, 'O father, I did not see him drinking wine. I only heard people say so.' He (the Imam) said, 'My son, Allah, most Majestic, most Glorious, says in His book, "He believes in Allah and in the believers," (9:62) meaning he accepts (the words of) Allah (as true words) and accepts (the words of) the believers (as true words). When the believers testify before you then accept their words as true and do not trust one who drinks wine; Allah, most Majestic, most Glorious, says in His book, "You must not give your assets to dimwitted ones." (4:5) Who can be more dimwitted than one who drinks wine? The speech (advice) of one who drinks wine has no beneficial effect, his intercession is useless and he is not trusted in matters of trust. Whoever entrusts him with his assets and he destroys it, such person does not deserve any reward from Allah for his loss or replacement from Allah.'"

H 9298, Ch. 153, h 2

Ali ibn Ibrahim has narrated from his father from Muhammad ibn 'Isa from Yunus and A number of our people have narrated from Ahmad ibn abu 'Abd Allah from his father all from Yunus from 'Abd Allah ibn Sinan and ibn Muskan from abu al-Jarud who has said the following:

"Abu Ja'far, *'Alayhi al-Salam*, has said, 'When you speak to me, ask me about the book of Allah.' He (the Imam) then in his Hadith said, 'Allah has prohibited from *qil* (it was said so), *qal* (he said so and so on . . .), destruction of assets and a great deal of questions.' They then asked, 'O child of the Messenger of Allah, where in the Quran is what you just said?' He (the Imam) then said, 'Allah, most Majestic, most Glorious, says in His book, "There is nothing good in many of their whispering conversations." (4:114) He has also said, "You must not give your assets to the dimwitted ones, upon which Allah has made you a keeper," (4:5) and He has said, "You must not ask about all kinds of things because if revealed to you can make you feel bad." (5:101)'"

H 9299, Ch. 153, h 3

A number of our people have narrated from Ahmad ibn Muhammad from ibn Mahbub from Khalid ibn Jarir from abu al-Rabi' who has said the following:

"Abu 'Abd Allah, *'Alayhi al-Salam*, has said that the Holy Prophet, *O Allah, grant compensation to Muhammad and his family worthy of their services to Your cause*, has said, 'If one trusts one who drinks wine, about a trust after knowing that he drinks wine, he has no guarantee for it before Allah or any reward or replacement for his loss.'"

H 9300, Ch. 153, h 4

A number of our people have narrated from Sahl ibn Ziyad from Ali ibn Asbat from certain persons of our people from 'Amr ibn abu al-Miqdam who has said the following:

"Abu 'Abd Allah, *'Alayhi al-Salam*, has said, 'One's trusting a treacherous person and wasting assets is a worthless act.'"

H 9301, Ch. 153, h 5

Al-Husayn from Muhammad has narrated from Mu'alla' ibn Muhammad from al-Washsha' who has said the following:

"I once heard abu al-Hassan, *'Alayhi al-Salam*, saying, 'Allah, most Majestic, most Glorious, hates *qil* (it was said so), *qal* (he said so and so on . . .), wasting assets and asking a great deal of questions.'"

Chapter 154 - Liability for Animal's Causing Losses

H 9302 (a), Ch. 154, h 1

Muhammad ibn Yahya has narrated from Muhammad ibn al-Husayn from Yazid ibn Ishaq Sha'ir from Harun ibn Hamzah who has said the following:

"This is concerning my question before abu 'Abd Allah, *'Alayhi al-Salam*, about the case of cows, sheep and camels in a pasture which destroy certain things; if anyone is held responsible for anything. He (the Imam) said, 'If they destroy during the day there is no responsibility; the owners must protect them (their belongings); but if they destroy during the night then the owner of cattle is held responsibility.'"

H 9302 (b), Ch. 154, h 2

A number of our people have narrated from Ahmad ibn Muhammad from al-Husayn ibn Sa'id from certain persons of our people from Mu'alla' abu 'Uthman from abu Basir who has said the following:

"I once asked abu 'Abd Allah, *'Alayhi al-Salam*, about the words of Allah, most Majestic, most Glorious, '. . . and Dawud and Sulayman who judged about the plantation which was damaged by the sheep of the people.' (21:78) Abu 'Abd Allah, *'Alayhi al-Salam*, has said, 'Such damage can happen only during the night. It is the responsibility of the owner of plantation to protect it during the day. The owner of cattle is not required to protect them during the day. During the day it is grazing and feeding. What is damaged is not the responsibility of its owner. The owner of the cattle is responsible to guard them during the night against destroying the people's plantation. Whatever they may destroy during the night is the responsibility of the owner of cattle and that is what is called *al-Nafsh* (grazing). Dawud issued judgment in favor of the one whose plantation was damaged against the owner of sheep. Sulayman issued his judgment to pay for the damage in the form of one year's milk and wool of the sheep to the owner of the plantation.'"

H 9303, Ch. 154, h 3

Ahmad ibn Muhammad from has narrated from 'Isa from al-Husayn ibn Sa'id from 'Abd Allah ibn Bahr from ibn Muskan from abu Basir who has said the following:

"I once said abu 'Abd Allah, *'Alayhi al-Salam*, 'What is the meaning of the words of Allah, most Majestic, most Glorious, "Dawud and Sulayman who issued judgment about the plantation.'" I asked, 'Was it one issue about which they gave judgment?' He (the Imam) said, 'Allah, most Majestic, most Glorious, had sent revelation to the prophets before Dawud about such issue. To Dawud Allah revealed that whatever of sheep graze on a plantation, the owner of the plantation receives the necks of the sheep and such grazing must be that which takes place during the night; the owner of the plantation must protect it during the day; and the owner of the sheep must guard them during the night, therefore, Dawud judged as the prophets had judged before. To Sulayman Allah, most Majestic, most Glorious, sent revelation that required the owner of the plantation to ask only for what comes out of the belly of the sheep. This tradition continued after Sulayman and that is mentioned in the words of Allah, most High, "To everyone of them We give command and knowledge," (22:79) thus, everyone of them judged according to the command of Allah, most Majestic, most Glorious.'"

Chapter 155 - Another Chapter

H 9304, Ch. 155, h 1

Ali ibn Ibrahim has narrated from his father from ibn abu 'Umayr from ibn Muskan from Zurarah and abu Basir who has said the following:

"Abu 'Abd Allah, *'Alayhi al-Salam*, has said that 'Amir al-Mu'minin, issued judgment in favor of a man whose slave was hired by a goldsmith or another man. The judgment said, 'If he has caused certain damage or has run away with something, the masters are held responsible.'"

H 9305, Ch. 155, h 2

A number of our people have narrated from Ahmad ibn Muhammad ibn Khalid from his father from Wahab who has said the following:

"Abu 'Abd Allah, *'Alayhi al-Salam*, has said that 'Amir al-Mu'minin has said, 'If one uses the services of the slave of a people and causes damage to him, he is responsible. If one uses the works of a small free person and causes damage to that person, he is responsible.'"

Chapter 156 - A Slave Does Business Who Becomes Indebted

H 9306, Ch. 156, h 1

Certain persons of our people have narrated Muhammad ibn al-Husayn from 'Uthman ibn 'Isa from Zarif al-Akfaniy who has said the following:

"This is about the case of a man who authorizes his slave to buy and sell and who becomes bankrupt and is taken by the creditor for the debt which is more than his price. I asked abu 'Abd Allah, *'Alayhi al-Salam*, about it. He (the Imam) said, 'If you sell him you are responsible for the debt, but if you set him free you are not responsible for the debt.' He set him free and he was not held responsible for anything."

H 9307, Ch. 156, h 2

Humayd ibn Ziyad has narrated from al-Hassan ibn Muhammad from ibn Mahbub from ibn Ri'ab from Zurarah who has said the following:

"This is concerning my question before abu 'Abd Allah, *'Alayhi al-Salam*, about the case of a man who dies owing a certain amount of debts and leaves behind a slave who has his assets in business and a son. In the hand of the slave he leaves the assets, goods and debts owed by the slave which he had incurred during the lifetime of his master for business. The heir and creditors dispute about what is in the hand of the slave, the slave himself and the assets and goods. He (the Imam) said, 'In my view the heirs have no say about the slave or about what is in his hand of assets and goods, except if they take responsibility for the debt for all the creditors. Thereafter the slave and what is in his hand of the assets and goods all go in the hands of the heirs; but if they refuse to take responsibility, the slave and all that is in his hand go to the creditors. The slave and whatever is in his hand of the assets are distributed among the creditors proportionate to their shares. If the slave and the asset could not pay the debts the creditors can ask the heirs for the remaining liabilities if the deceased has left anything. If the slave and assets exceed the debts the remaining goes to the heirs.'"

H 9308, Ch. 156, h 3
Muhammad ibn Yahya has narrated from Muhammad ibn al-Husayn from Ahmad ibn Muhammad from ibn abu Nasr from 'Asem ibn Hamid from abu Basir who has said the following:
"This is concerning my question before abu Ja'far, *'Alayhi al-Salam*, about the case of a man who authorizes his slave to do business but he becomes indebted. He (the Imam) said, 'If his master had authorized him to borrow; then he is responsible for the debts, but if he had not authorized him to borrow, he is not responsible for anything but the slave is made to work to pay the debts.'"

Chapter 157 - Rare Ahadith

H 9309, Ch. 157, h 1
Ali ibn Ibrahim has narrated from his father from al-Nawfaliy from al-Sakuniy who has said the following:
"Abu 'Abd Allah, *'Alayhi al-Salam*, has said that once two people brought their dispute before 'Amir al-Mu'minin, *'Alayhi al-Salam*. One of them had purchased a camel from the other one, and the seller had excluded the head and the skin. The buyer then decided to sell it. He (the Imam) said to the buyer, 'His share in the camel is proportionate to the head and skin.'"

H 9310, Ch. 157, h 2
Ali ibn Muhammad has narrated from Salih ibn abu Hammad from Ahmad ibn Hammad who has said that Murazim narrated to me from his father or his uncle who has said the following:
"I once saw abu 'Abd Allah, *'Alayhi al-Salam*, examine an account with his agent who very often said, 'By Allah, I have not committed treachery, by Allah I have not committed treachery.' Abu 'Abd Allah, *'Alayhi al-Salam*, then said, 'O you, wasting my assets and your committing treachery is the same; the wickedness of treachery is on you.' He (the Imam) then said, 'The Messenger of Allah has said, *O Allah, grant compensation to Muhammad and his family worthy of their services to Your cause*, has said, "If one of you runs away from his share of sustenance, it follows him just as one who runs away from his death

which follows him until it finds him. If one commits treachery it is counted (taken) against his sustenance and its sin is written on him.""""

H 9311, Ch. 157, h 3

Muhammad ibn Yahya has narrated from Ahmad ibn Muhammad from ibn Faddal from abu 'Umarah al-Tayyar who has said the following:

"I once said to abu 'Abd Allah, *'Alayhi al-Salam*, that my assets are gone, my belongings have scattered and I have a large family. Abu 'Abd Allah, *'Alayhi al-Salam*, then said, 'When you arrive in al-Kufah, open your shop, set up your display and balance and engage in (earning) sustenance from your Lord.' Upon his arrival he opened his shop, set up his display and balance. People around found it strange knowing that there was nothing in his home of assets or with him. A man came to him and asked (and paid) him to buy for him cloths. He bought it (perhaps on credit) for him and received the payment for it which remained with him. Then another man came and said, 'Buy for me a cloth.' He searched in the market for him, and then bought it for him and the payment for it remained in his hand. This was how business people exchanged goods among themselves. Then another man came and said, 'O abu 'Ummarah, I have a bundle of Kattan. Do you want to buy it to pay me after one year?' He replied, 'Yes, load it and deliver to me.' It was delivered to him and he bought it to pay after one year. The man then left and a man from the market came and asked, 'O abu 'Ummarah, what is this bundle?' He replied, 'I have purchased this bundle.' He asked, 'Can you sell to me one-half of it and keep the price with you?' He then purchased it and he gave him one-half of the goods for a payment of one-half of the price which remained in his hand for one year. He then would buy cloths with that fund, put one or two cloths on display, buy and sell, until he became affluent, able to show his face and find fame.'"

H 9312, Ch. 157, h 4

Ali ibn Muhammad has narrated from Salih ibn abu Hammad from Muhammad ibn Sinan from abu Ja'far al-Ahwal who has said the following:

"Abu 'Abd Allah, *'Alayhi al-Salam*, once asked me, 'How do you make a living?' I replied, 'I have two slaves and two camels.' He (the Imam) said, 'You must not speak about it to your brothers (in belief); if they do not harm, they do not benefit you either.'"

H 9313, Ch. 157, h 5

Abu Ali al-Ash'ariy has narrated from certain persons of our people from Ibrahim ibn 'Abd al-Hamid from al-Walid ibn Sabiyh who has said the following:

"I once heard abu 'Abd Allah, *'Alayhi al-Salam*, saying, 'The sustenance of certain people is in trading, others have it in their sword and certain ones in their tongue.'"

H 9314, Ch. 157, h 6

Ali ibn Ibrahim has narrated from his father from ibn abu 'Umayr from Hisham ibn al-Muthanna' who has said the following:

"Abu 'Abd Allah, *'Alayhi al-Salam*, has said, 'One who faces constraint in his living' —or he (the Imam) said 'in his sustenance— should buy small ones (of animal) and sell large ones.'"

It is also narrated from him (the Imam) that if one's plans do not work he should work in al-kursuf (a certain kind of fabric).

H 9315, Ch. 157, h 7

Muhammad ibn Yahya has narrated from Ahmad ibn Muhammad from Muhammad ibn Khalid from Sa'd ibn Sa'd from Muhammad ibn al-Fudayl who has said the following:

"Abu al-Hassan, *'Alayhi al-Salam*, has said, 'With whatever (lawful) means one opens the door to his sustenance it is business and trade.'"

H 9316, Ch. 157, h 8

Muhammad ibn Yahya has narrated from certain persons of our people from Mansur ibn al-'Abbas from al-Hassan ibn Ali ibn Yaqtin from al-Husayn ibn Mayyah from 'Umayyah ibn 'Amr form al-Sha'iyriy who has said the following:

"Abu 'Abd Allah, *'Alayhi al-Salam*, has said that 'Amir al-Mu'minin, *'Alayhi al-Salam*, would say, 'If one is calling to what he sells, you do not have to increase; only announcing makes increasing unlawful and remaining silent makes the increase lawful.'"

H 9317, Ch. 157, h 9

Muhammad ibn Yahya has narrated from Ahmad ibn Muhammad or others from ibn Mahbub from 'Abd al-'Aziz al-'Abdiy from 'Abd Allah ibn abu Ya'fur who has said the following:

"I once heard abu 'Abd Allah, *'Alayhi al-Salam*, saying, 'If one plants wheat in a land and it does not come pure or the plantation grows with a great deal of barley, it is because of the injustice of his work to the piece of land that he owns or it is because of the injustice of his workers. Allah, most Majestic, most Glorious, says, '. . . because of the injustice of Jews We made certain good things that were lawful, unlawful for them.' (4:158) It was meat of camel, cow and sheep. He (the Imam) said, 'Israel when eating the meat of camel would suffer pain in his lower back, thus he made eating of the meat of camel unlawful for himself, and this was before the coming of the Torah. When Torah came it did not make it unlawful but he did not eat.'"

H 9318, Ch. 157, h 10

Muhammad ibn Yahya has narrated from Ahmad ibn Muhammad ibn 'Isa from Ja'far ibn Muhammad ibn abu al-Sabbah from his father from his grandfather who has said the following:

"This is concerning my question before abu 'Abd Allah, *'Alayhi al-Salam*, about the case of a man who becomes a friend of a young woman who gives him four thousand dirham and says, 'If our friendship is destroyed you can return the dirhams to me.' He works with it and makes profits. The young man marries and wants to repent, what should he do? He (the Imam) said, 'He must return the dirhams and the profit belongs to him.'"

H 9319, Ch. 157, h 11

Ali ibn Ibrahim has narrated from his father from ibn abu 'Umayr from Hammad from al-Halabiy who has said the following:

"Abu 'Abd Allah, *'Alayhi al-Salam*, has said that the Messenger of Allah prohibited eating of what ants carry in their mouth or with their legs."

H 9320, Ch. 157, h 12

Al-Husayn from Muhammad has narrated from Mu'alla' ibn Muhammad from al-Washsha' who has said the following:

"I once heard him (the Imam), *'Alayhi al-Salam*, saying, 'The skillfulness of a man is for his earning a living.'"

H 9321, Ch. 157, h 13

A number of our people have narrated from Ahmad ibn Muhammad from ibn Mahbub from al-Ribatiy from abu al-Sabbah Mawla' Ale Sam from Jabir who has said the following:

"This is concerning my question before abu 'Abd Allah, *'Alayhi al-Salam*, about the case of a man who becomes friends with a woman who gives him a certain amount of asset which remains in his hands for as long as Allah wants; then he spends from it. He (the Imam) said, 'He must return it to her and if anything extra is left it is for him.'"

H 9322, Ch. 157, h 14

Muhammad ibn Yahya has said that Muhammad once wrote to abu Muhammad, *'Alayhi al-Salam*, about a man to whom another man owed one hundred dirham. He demanded for payment but the debtor said, 'I will come back to you in ten days after completing my work. If I will not come back, you will have one thousand dirham on me at once without any condition and I appoint witnesses for it.' He then calls for witnesses. He (the Imam) signed the answer that said, 'They must only testify to what is true and the creditor must only take what is his right, by the will of Allah.'"

H 9323, Ch. 157, h 15

It is narrated from the narrator of the previous Hadith from Ahmad ibn Muhammad from ibn Faddal from 'Abd Allah ibn 'Abd al-Rahman from Yahya al-Halabiy from al-Thumaliy who has said the following:

"I once passed with abu 'Abd Allah, *'Alayhi al-Salam*, through the copper market and I asked, 'I pray to Allah to keep my soul in service for your cause, what is the origin of the copper?' He (the Imam) said, 'It is silver but the land spoils it and if one can take away the invalidity, he can benefit from it.'"

H 9324, Ch. 157, h 16

A number of our people have narrated from Ahmad ibn Muhammad from ibn Faddal from Tha'labah ibn Maymun from 'Abd al-Malik ibn 'Utbah who has said the following:

"'I still give goods to this man and he says that it is destroyed or is spent, so what kind of plan can help it?' He (the planner) said, 'You can give the man one thousand dirham and give it to him as loan; then give him twenty dirham to work with the asset and say to him, "This is my capital and that is your capital. Whatever you gain thereof is between both of us."' I asked about it from 'Abd Allah, *'Alayhi al-Salam*, who said, 'It is not unlawful.'"

H 9325, Ch. 157, h 17

A number of our people have narrated from Ahmad ibn abu 'Abd Allah from his father from 'Abd Allah ibn al-Fadl from certain persons of our people who has said the following:

"We complained before abu 'Abd Allah, *'Alayhi al-Salam*, about the loss of our clothes with the cleaners. He (the Imam) said, 'Write on them, "Blessing for us."' We did so and did not lose any cloth thereafter."

H 9326, Ch. 157, h 18

Muhammad ibn Yahya has narrated from Muhammad ibn al-Husayn from Muhammad ibn 'Isma'il ibn Bazi' from al-Khaybariy from al-Husayn ibn Thuwayri who has said the following:

"Abu 'Abd Allah, *'Alayhi al-Salam*, has said, 'When you are hungry play (eat slowly) with raisins.'"

H 9327, Ch. 157, h 19

It is narrated from the narrator of the previous Hadith from Muhammad ibn Ahmad from al-Sindiy ibn Muhammad from abu al-Bakhtariy who has said the following:

"Abu 'Abd Allah, *'Alayhi al-Salam*, has said that 'Amir al-Mu'minin, *'Alayhi al-Salam*, has said, 'It is not lawful to deny salt and fire (to those who ask for it).'"

H 9328, Ch. 157, h 20

It is narrated from the narrator of the previous Hadith from Musa ibn Ja'far al-Baghdadiy from 'Ubayd Allah ibn 'Abd Allah from Wasil ibn Sulayman from 'Abd Allah ibn Sinan who has said the following:

"Abu 'Abd Allah, *'Alayhi al-Salam*, has said that the Holy Prophet, *O Allah, grant compensation to Muhammad and his family worthy of their services to Your cause*, had an occasional companion from the time of ignorance. When he (the Messenger of Allah) was commissioned as the Holy Prophet, he met him and said to the Holy Prophet, *O Allah, grant compensation to Muhammad and his family worthy of their services to Your cause*, 'As a companion I pray to Allah to give you good because you agreed and did not argue.' The Holy Prophet said to him, 'So also from me, may Allah give you good for a companion; you did not refuse any benefit and did not grind your teeth (you were not stingy).'"

H 9329, Ch. 157, h 21

Ali ibn Ibrahim has narrated from (his father) from Ali ibn Muhammad al-Qasaniy from al-Qasim ibn Muhammad from Sulayman ibn Dawud from a man who has said the following:

"This is concerning my question before abu 'Abd Allah, *'Alayhi al-Salam*, about the case of a Muslim man with whom a thieving man leaves a certain amount of dirham and he is a Muslim also; if he must return it to him. He (the Imam) said, 'No, he must not return it. If he can find the owner he must give it to him; otherwise, he must deal with it as what is found as a lost item and announce about it in public for one year. If the owner is found it is fine; otherwise, it is given as charity. If the owner comes thereafter he is given the choice to leave it for charity and reward or claim the loss. If he chooses charity he receives the reward; if he chooses compensation for the loss, the reward goes to one who pays compensation.'"

H 9330, Ch. 157, h 22

Ali has narrated from Muhammad ibn 'Isa from Yunus ibn 'Abd al-Rahman who has said the following:

"This is concerning my question before the virtuous servant of Allah saying, 'I pray to Allah to keep my soul in service for your cause, we in Makkah had travel-mates, and when they left and we also left we carried certain items of their goods without knowing and they had gone. We did not know their places and the goods were left with us. What should we do about them? He (the Imam) said, 'Take them with you to meet them in al-Kufah.' I (Yunus) said, 'I do not know them and we do not know how to find them.' He (the Imam) said, 'Sell the items and give its price to your people.' I then asked, 'I pray to Allah to keep my soul in service for your cause, should I give them to *Ahl al-Walayah* (people who believe in the Divine Authority of 'A'immah)? He (the Imam) said, 'Yes, give it to them.'"

H 9331, Ch. 157, h 23

Al-Husayn from Muhammad has narrated from Mu'alla' ibn Muhammad from al-Washsha' from Ahmad ibn 'A'idh from abu Khadijah who has said the following:

"This is concerning my question of Dhariyh al-Muharibiy before abu 'Abd Allah, *'Alayhi al-Salam*, about a slave who takes an item that is found. He (the Imam) said, 'What a slave has to do with an item found! He does not own anything for himself. A slave must not have bothered about it. He must announce it in public for one year. If the owner comes it must be given to him, otherwise, it remains in his belongings; and if he dies it becomes of his legacy for his children and those who inherit him. If no one comes to demand it, it remains in their belongings and it becomes their property; but if someone comes asking for it they must give it to him.'"

H 9332, Ch. 157, h 24

Ali ibn Ibrahim has narrated from his father from al-Nawfaliy from al-Sakuniy who has said the following:

"Abu 'Abd Allah, *'Alayhi al-Salam*, has said that the Messenger of Allah, *O Allah, grant compensation to Muhammad and his family worthy of their services to Your cause*, prohibited exposing a she-camel before a he-camel for breeding, unless the young is given in charity or is slaughtered as well as a donkey to leap (mount) over an old one.'"

H 9333, Ch. 157, h 25

Ali ibn Ibrahim has narrated from his father from al-Hassan ibn al-Husayn al-Lu'luwiy from Safwan ibn Yahya from 'Abd al-Rahman ibn al-Hajjaj who has said the following:

"A certain person of our people lived in al-Madinah and he suffered severe constraints. Abu 'Abd Allah, *'Alayhi al-Salam*, said to him, 'You must go to find a shop in the market, set up your display and keep a jar of water with you and guard the door of your shop. He (the narrator) has said that he followed the instruction and remained in that condition as long as Allah wanted. Then a company of people came from Egypt. Every one of them left their goods with people whom each one knew until shops became full. Only one man was left who did not find a shop to store his goods. People of the market told him that there is man who has no problems and there are no goods in his shop. You can store your goods in his shop. He went to him and asked him, 'Can I store my goods in your shop?' He replied, 'Yes, you can do so.' He stored his goods in his shop and he began to sell his goods one by one until it was time for his companions to leave and of his goods very little was left. He did not like to stay, so he said to our friend, 'I leave these goods with you to sell and send the proceeds to me.' He agreed. The company left as well as the man along with them, leaving the goods with him. Our companion sold the goods and sent the proceeds to him. He (the narrator) has said that when the company from Egypt left, he sent goods to this man and he sold them and sent the proceeds to him. When he experienced this he stayed in Egypt and would send goods to him prepared. He (the narrator) has said that he was set at the right course, thus, he became affluent and rich."

H 9334, Ch. 157, h 26
A number of our people have narrated from Ahmad ibn Muhammad from ibn Faddal from Tha'labah from 'Abd al-Hamid ibn 'Awwad al-Ta'iy who has said the following:
"I once said to abu 'Abd Allah, *'Alayhi al-Salam*, that I owned a flour mill and that it had become my assembly place where my companions came together. He (the Imam) said, 'That is a blessing from Allah, most Majestic, most Glorious.'"

H 9335, Ch. 157, h 27
Al-Husayn ibn Muhammad has narrated from Mu'alla' ibn Muhammad from al-Hassan ibn Ali from Hammad ibn 'Uthman who has said the following:
"I once heard abu 'Abd Allah, *'Alayhi al-Salam*, saying, 'A man's sitting for follow-up prayer, after the morning *Salat* (prayer) at his prayer place until sunrise is better for his business than sailing on the ocean in search for sustenance.' I then asked, 'What happens if he has an urgent work which he is afraid to miss?' He (the Imam) said, 'He can leave for it and he is considered doing the follow-up prayer as long as he has a valid wudu.'"

H 9336, Ch. 157, h 28
A number of our people have narrated from Sahl ibn Ziyad and Ahmad ibn Muhammad from ibn Faddal from Mu'awiyah ibn Wahab who has said the following:
"Abu 'Abd Allah, *'Alayhi al-Salam*, has said, 'There will come a biting time upon people. Everyone will keep tight with whatever is in his hand and forget about generosity. Allah, most Majestic, most Glorious, has said, 'You must not forget generosity among yourselves.' (2:239) At that time a people appears who deals (unjustly) with helpless people and they are the wicked ones.'"

H 9337, Ch. 157, h 29
Sahl ibn Ziyad has narrated from Ya'qub ibn Yazid from Muhammad ibn Murazim from a man from Ishaq ibn 'Ammar who has said the following:
"I once heard abu 'Abd Allah, *'Alayhi al-Salam*, saying, 'If one searches for little amounts of sustenance it leads to attract greater amounts of sustenance, and if one gives up small amounts of sustenance it leads to going away of the greater amount of sustenance.'"

H 9338, Ch. 157, h 30
Ali ibn Muhammad ibn Bandar has narrated from Ahmad ibn abu 'Abd Allah from Muhammad ibn 'Isa from a man whom has named from al-Husayn al-Jammal who has said the following:

"One day I saw Ishaq ibn 'Ammar pack his bag, ready to move, when a man came asking to exchange dirham with dinar. He opened his bag, gave him dirham and took the dinar. I then said, 'Allah is free of all defects, how dinar can be better?' Ishaq said, 'I did not do it because of my interest in dinar, but I heard abu 'Abd Allah, *'Alayhi al-Salam*, saying, "One who considers a small amount of sustenance little becomes deprived of a great deal of sustenance."'"

H 9339, Ch. 157, h 31
Ahmad ibn Muhammad from has narrated from Muhammad ibn 'Isa from abu Muhammad al-Ghifariy from 'Abd Allah ibn Ibrahim from those who narrated to him who has said the following:
"Abu 'Abd Allah, *'Alayhi al-Salam*, has said that the Messenger of Allah, *O Allah, grant compensation to Muhammad and his family worthy of their services to Your cause*, has said, 'One who is tired of power must cherish small ones.'"

Muhammad ibn 'Isa thinks that al-Ghifariy is of the children of abu Dharr, may Allah be pleased with him.

H 9340, Ch. 157, h 32
Ahmad ibn Muhammad from has narrated from 'Uthman ibn 'Isa from abu Zuhrah from 'Umm al-Hassan who has said the following:
"Once, 'Amir al-Mu'minin, *'Alayhi al-Salam*, passed by and asked, 'What are you doing O 'Umm al-Hassan?' I replied, 'I am spinning to make yarn.' He (the Imam) said, 'That is a very sweet way of earning' –or that he said– 'of the sweetest way of earning.'"

H 9341, Ch. 157, h 33
Ahmad ibn Muhammad has narrated from Muhammad ibn Ali from Ali ibn Asbat from those who narrated to him from Jahm ibn Hamid al-Rawasiy who has said the following:
"Abu 'Abd Allah, *'Alayhi al-Salam*, has said, 'When you see a man who takes out from his assets in obedience to Allah, most Majestic, most Glorious, then you must be certain that he has earned it by lawful ways, and when he takes it in disobedience to Allah, most Majestic, most Glorious, you must rest assured that he has earned it in unlawful ways.'"

H 9342, Ch. 157, h 34
Ahmad ibn Muhammad ibn 'Isa has narrated from those who narrated to him who has said the following:
"I once said to abu 'Abd Allah, *'Alayhi al-Salam*, a man traveled and then came back with a great deal of assets and we did not know if he had earned it in a lawful or unlawful ways. He (the Imam) said, 'If such is the case, look how he spends it. If he spends in ways that he is not supposed to spend or is of the sinful ways it then is from unlawful ways.'"

H 9343, Ch. 157, h 35
Ali ibn Ibrahim has narrated from his father from al-Nawfaliy from al-Sakuniy who has said the following:
"Abu 'Abd Allah, *'Alayhi al-Salam*, has said that the Holy Prophet, *O Allah, grant compensation to Muhammad and his family worthy of their services to Your cause*, once passed by a man who sold clothes. The man was tall and the

cloth was short. He (the Messenger of Allah) said, 'Sit down; it is more useful for your commodity.'"

H 9344, Ch. 157, h 36

A number of our people have narrated from Ahmad ibn Muhammad from Muhammad ibn Khalid from Ja'far ibn Muhammad al-Ash'ariy from ibn Qaddah who has said the following:

"Abu 'Abd Allah, *'Alayhi al-Salam*, has said, 'I once took a letter to my father that a man had sent and I took it out of my sleeves. He (the Imam) said, 'My son, do not keep anything in your sleeves; it causes loss of things.'"

H 9345, Ch. 157, h 37

Ali ibn Ibrahim has narrated from his father from Ahmad ibn abu Nadr from 'Amr ibn Shamir from Jabir who has said the following:

"Abu Ja'far, *'Alayhi al-Salam*, has said that the Messenger of Allah, *O Allah, grant compensation to Muhammad and his family worthy of their services to Your cause*, has said, 'There will come a time when people complain before their Lord.' I then asked, 'How they will complain before their Lord?' He (the Imam) replied, 'A man will say, "By Allah, I have not gained anything since so and so much time and ate or drank except from my capital." Fie upon you, is your capital or its peak from any source other than from your Lord!'"

H 9346, Ch. 157, h 38

Muhammad ibn Yahya has narrated from Ahmad ibn Muhammad ibn 'Isa from al-Hassan ibn Mahbub from Hisham ibn Salim from abu Basir who has said the following:

"I once heard abu Ja'far, *'Alayhi al-Salam*, saying, 'During the time of the Messenger of Allah, *O Allah, grant compensation to Muhammad and his family worthy of their services to Your cause*, there was a believing man, poor and very needy of the people of the platform (in front of Masjid). He always kept very close to the Messenger of Allah, *O Allah, grant compensation to Muhammad and his family worthy of their services to Your cause*, at the times of all *Salat* (prayer) and did not miss any of them. The Messenger of Allah, *O Allah, grant compensation to Muhammad and his family worthy of their services to Your cause*, sympathized with him greatly, looked after his needs and his poverty and said, 'O Sa'd, if something comes to me I will make you self-sufficient.' It so happened that for a long time the Messenger of Allah, *O Allah, grant compensation to Muhammad and his family worthy of their services to Your cause*, did not get a chance and he (the Messenger of Allah) became depressed for Sa'd. Allah, most Majestic, noticed how the Messenger of Allah felt about Sa'd and Jibril came to the Messenger of Allah with two dirham and said, 'O Muhammad, Allah has noticed how you feel about Sa'd. Do you want to make him rich?' He (the Messenger of Allah) replied, 'Yes, I want to make him rich. Jibril gave him two dirhams and told him to give them to Sa'd and instruct him to do business with them. The Messenger of Allah, *O Allah, grant compensation to Muhammad and his family worthy of their services to Your cause*, took the two dirham then went out for *Salat* (prayer) and Sa'd was standing at the door of the chambers of the Messenger of Allah waiting for him. When the Messenger of Allah saw him he said, 'O Sa'd, are you good at trading?' Sa'd replied, 'By Allah, I do not own anything to do trading. The Messenger of Allah, *O Allah, grant compensation to Muhammad and his family worthy of their services to Your cause*, gave him the two dirham and told him to use them in trading and work for sustenance from Allah.' Sa'd took them and went with the Holy Prophet, until they performed al-Zuhr and al-'Asr *Salat* (prayer). The Holy Prophet, said, 'Go in search for sustenance; I was worried about your condition, O Sa'd.' Whatever Sa'd bought for one he then sold it for two dirham and whatever he bought for two dirham he sold for four dirham and the worldly things began to move to him. His assets grew larger and his business became great. At the door of the Masjid he found a place where he sat and operated his trade. The Messenger of Allah, *O Allah, grant compensation to Muhammad and his family worthy of their services to Your cause*, came out for *Salat* (prayer) when Bilal said Adhan but Sa'd was busy with the worldly things without wudu and unprepared unlike the way he did before he was engaged in trading. The Holy Prophet, *O Allah, grant compensation to Muhammad and his family worthy of their services to Your cause*, asked, 'O Sa'd, the worldly things have kept you busy and away from *Salat* (prayer).' He replied, 'What can I do? I do not want to waste my assets. From this man I must receive payment and to this man I must pay.' He (the Imam) said that the Messenger of Allah began to feel sadder about Sa'd than about his poverty. Jibril came and said, 'O Muhammad, Allah has noticed your feeling about Sa'd. Of his conditions which one you like: this condition or that one before?' The Holy Prophet said, 'O Jibril, I like his condition before because his worldly things have taken away his hereafter. Jibril then said, 'The love of the world and its asset is a trial and deviates one from the hereafter. You must ask Sa'd to return your two dirham that you gave him. His condition will change to that he had before.' He (the Imam) said, 'The Messenger of Allah, *O Allah, grant compensation to Muhammad and his family worthy of their services to Your cause*, went out, passed by Sa'd and asked, 'Do you not want to return the two dirham I had given to you?' Sa'd replied, 'Yes, indeed, I can give two hundred dirham.' He (the Messenger of Allah) said, 'I just want the two dirham.' Sa'd gave two dirham to the Messenger of Allah, *O Allah, grant compensation to Muhammad and his family worthy of their services to Your cause*. He (the Imam) said that the worldly things turned away from Sa'd until all that he had collected were gone and he returned to the condition he had before.'"

H 9347, Ch. 157, h 39
A number of our people have narrated from Sahl ibn Ziyad and Ahmad ibn Muhammad all from ibn Mahbub from 'Abd Allah ibn Sinan who has said the following:
"Abu 'Abd Allah, *'Alayhi al-Salam*, has said, 'All things that exist in lawful and unlawful forms are considered lawful for you until you recognize it (the unlawful one) to be exactly the unlawful item, then you must avoid it.'"

H 9348, Ch. 157, h 40
Ali ibn Ibrahim has narrated (from his father) from Harun ibn Muslim from Mas'adah ibn Sadaqah who has said the following:
"I once heard abu 'Abd Allah, *'Alayhi al-Salam*, saying, 'All things are lawful for you until you recognize it to be exactly an unlawful item which you must avoid from your own side. One such example is a cloth which you may have

purchased and it is proved a stolen cloth; or a slave who is with you and perhaps he is free who has sold himself or is tricked and sold or is compelled; or a woman whom you have married and she is your sister or is one who is fed with milk from your wife or mother or sister or daughter and things likewise; until it becomes clear that they are otherwise or testimony proves otherwise.'"

H 9349, Ch. 157, h 41
A number of our people have narrated from Sahl ibn Ziyad from al-Haytham ibn abu Masruq al-Nahdiy from Musa ibn 'Umar ibn Bazi' who has said the following:
"I once asked al-Rida', *'Alayhi al-Salam*, saying, 'I pray to Allah to keep my soul in service for your cause, people narrate that the Messenger of Allah, *O Allah, grant compensation to Muhammad and his family worthy of their services to Your cause*, whenever he walked on a road would not return from the same, if this is how it was. He (the Imam) said, 'Yes, that is how it was and very often I also do so and you should also do it.' He (the Imam) said, 'It gives you a greater chance to increase your sustenance.'"

H 9350, Ch. 157, h 42
It is narrated from the narrator of the previous Hadith from al-'Abbas ibn 'Amir from abu 'Abd al-Rahman al-Mas'udiy from Hafs ibn al-Bakhtariy ibn 'Umar al-Bajaliy who has said the following:
"I once complained before abu 'Abd Allah, *'Alayhi al-Salam*, against my worsening condition and mounting difficulties. He (the Imam) said, 'When you arrive in al-Kufah, sell a piece of pillow from your home for ten dirham, invite your brothers, prepare food for them and ask them to pray for you to Allah.' He (the narrator) has said, 'I followed the instruction but it was not possible without selling the piece of pillow to prepare food as he (the Imam) had instructed me. So I sold the pillow and asked them to pray for me before Allah.' He has said, 'By Allah I waited only very little that one of my debtors came at the door and knocked at it. He made a settlement with me about a large amount of assets that I counted at ten thousand dirham.' He has said that thereafter things began to come to him.'"

H 9351, Ch. 157, h 43
A number of our people have narrated from Sahl ibn Ziyad and Ahmad ibn Muhammad from 'Abd Allah from ibn Mahbub from Sama'ah who has said the following:
"Abu 'Abd Allah, *'Alayhi al-Salam*, has said, 'One who consumes the assets of a believing person in unlawful ways is not of my follower and friends.'"

H 9352, Ch. 157, h 44
Muhammad ibn Ja'far has narrated from al-'Abbas al-Kufiy from Muhammad ibn 'Isa ibn 'Ubayd and Ali ibn Ibrahim all from Ali ibn Muhammad al-Qasaniy who has said the following:
"I once wrote to him (the Imam) (abu al-Hassan, al-Thalith) from al-Madinah in the year two hundred thirty-one, saying, 'I pray to Allah to keep my soul in service for your cause, a man commands another man to buy goods for him or other things which he buys but the goods are stolen or are looted on the way, from whose asset is this loss, is it from the assets of the commander or the one commanded? He (the Imam) *'Alayhi al-Salam*, wrote the answer that said, 'It is from the asset of the commander.'"

H 9353, Ch. 157, h 45

A number of our people have narrated from Sahl ibn Ziyad and Ya'qub ibn Yazid from the son of the sister of al-Walid ibn Sabih from his maternal uncle, al-Walid who has said the following:

"Abu 'Abd Allah, *'Alayhi al-Salam*, has said, 'Of the people there are those who earn their living from the sword, others from trade and still others earn by their tongue.'"

H 9354, Ch. 157, h 46

Sahl ibn Ziyad has narrated from Yahya ibn al-Mubarak from Ibrahim ibn Salih from a man from al-Ja'fariy who has said the following:

"In al-Madinah there was a man with us, called abu al-Qamqa'm who was unfortunate. He went to abu al-Hassan, *'Alayhi al-Salam*, and complained before him against his condition and informed him (the Imam) that wherever he goes for something he fails. Abu al-Hassan, *'Alayhi al-Salam*, said, 'In your last prayer in the morning, say, 'Free of all defect is Allah, most Great. I ask forgiveness from Allah and plead before Him for help through His generosity', ten times.' Abu Qamqa'm has said, 'I kept doing it and after very little time a people from village came to me and told me that a man from my people has died and there no heir is found for him except me. I went with them and received his legacy which made me rich.'"

H 9355, Ch. 157, h 47

It is narrated from the narrator of the previous Hadith from ibn Mahbub from Sa'dan from Mu'awiyah ibn 'Ammar who has said the following:

"Abu 'Abd Allah, *'Alayhi al-Salam*, has said, 'You must not deny loaning yeast for bread-making and taking fire to start a fire; because it attracts sustenance to the family along with high moral manners.'"

H 9356, Ch. 157, h 48

A number of our people have narrated from Ahmad ibn abu 'Abd Allah from his father from those who narrated to him from 'Amr ibn abu al-Miqdam from al-Harith ibn Hadirah al-Azdiy who has said the following:

"A man during the time of 'Amir al-Mu'minin, *'Alayhi al-Salam*, had found a treasure and my father bought it from him for three hundred dirham and one hundred sheep followed by their young; and my mother blamed him for it, saying, 'You have bought it for three hundred sheep; one hundred of their young, one hundred sheep and one hundred in their womb.' My father regretted and went to ask for a reduced price. He refused and said, 'Take from me ten sheep, take from me twenty sheep' and made him tired. My father then took the treasure and made a price for one thousand sheep from it. The other man came back and said, 'Take your sheep back and give me whatever you like.' But he refused. He tried until he was exhausted and said, 'I can harm you.' He complained before 'Amir al-Mu'minin, *'Alayhi al-Salam*, against my father. When my father told his side of the story before 'Amir al-Mu'minin, *'Alayhi al-Salam*, he (the Imam) said to the owner of treasure, 'Pay one-fifth of what you have received because it is on you as the finder of the treasure and there is nothing on him because he has taken the price of his sheep.'"

H 9357, Ch. 157, h 49

Ali ibn Ibrahim has narrated from his father from Harun ibn Muslim from Mas'adah ibn Sadaqah who has said the following:

"Once abu 'Abd Allah, *'Alayhi al-Salam*, was asked about the case of a man to whom another man owed a certain amount of assets because of *'Aynah* deal. When payment time was due he did not have anything to pay so he wanted to turn it over on him for profit; if he can sell a pearl or something else worth a hundred dirham for a thousand so he can defer payment. He (the Imam) said, 'It is not unlawful because my father, may Allah be pleased with him, had done so and he commanded me to do so because of something that he owed.'"

H 9358, Ch. 157, h 50

A number of our people have narrated from Sahl ibn Ziyad from Ali ibn Sulayman from Ahmad ibn al-Fadl (from) abu 'Amr al-Hadhdha' who has said the following:

"I faced a difficult condition and wrote to abu Ja'far, *'Alayhi al-Salam*, about it and he (the Imam) wrote to me, 'Continue reading, "We sent Noah to his people . . . to the end."' (Chapter 71) I read it for one year but did not see any change. I wrote to him again to inform him (the Imam) of my difficult condition and that I have been reading the Chapter for one year as the Imam had instructed and that I did not experience any change. He (the Imam) then wrote to me saying, 'One year is passed, now read Chapter 97.' I then read it for a very short time that ibn abu Dawud sent me something and paid off my debts and sent me and my family to al-Basrah as an agent to Bab Kala' (name of a place) with a salary of five hundred dirham; and from al-Basra I wrote through Ali ibn Mahziyar to abu al-Hassan, *'Alayhi al-Salam*, explaining, 'I had written to your father about so and so issues and had complained against so and so matters, I have found what I liked. I like to ask you about what I should do about reading Chapter 97, if I must continue reading it in my obligatory *Salat* (prayer) and others or there is a limit of time for it.' He (the Imam) signed the answer and I read the signature that said, 'You must not leave from Quran, short or long passages. Of Chapter 97 it is enough to read one hundred times in one day and night.'"

H 9359, Ch. 157, h 51

Sahl ibn Ziyad has narrated from Mansur ibn al-'Abbas from 'Isma'il ibn Sahl who has said the following:

"I once wrote to abu Ja'far, *'Alayhi al-Salam*, and said, 'Debts are holding me down and they are heavy.' He (the Imam) wrote to me, 'Ask forgiveness from Allah a great deal and moisten you tongue by reading, "Inna Anzalna" Chapter 97.'"

H 9360, Ch. 157, h 52

Sahl ibn Ziyad has narrated from Muhammad ibn 'Isa ibn 'Ubayd from al-Hassan ibn Ali ibn Yaqtin from al-Fadl ibn Kathir al-Mada'iniy from those whom he has mentioned who has said the following:

"Once a certain person of the followers of abu 'Abd Allah, *'Alayhi al-Salam*, came to visit him (the Imam) and he saw his shirt had a patch on it, so he kept looking at it. Abu 'Abd Allah, *'Alayhi al-Salam*, asked, 'Why are you looking?' He replied, 'I pray to Allah to keep my soul in service for your cause, there is a patch on your shirt.' He (the Imam) said, 'Pick up this book and read what is there' – there was a book in front of him (the Imam) or nearby. The man looked in the book and it was written there, 'One who does not feel shy has no faith, one who does not plan has no wealth and one who does not have anything old cannot have anything new.'"

H 9361, Ch. 157, h 53

Abu Ali al-Ash'ariy has narrated from al-Hassan ibn Ali al-Kufiy from al-'Abbas ibn Ma'ruf from a man from Mandal ibn Ali al-'Anziy from Muhammad ibn Mutarrif from Misma' from al-Asbagh ibn Nubatah who has said the following:

"'Amir al-Mu'minin, *'Alayhi al-Salam*, has said that the Messenger of Allah, *O Allah, grant compensation to Muhammad and his family worthy of their services to Your cause*, has said, 'When Allah becomes angry with a people on whom He has not sent any suffering, He makes their prices to become costly, shortens their life span, takes away profit from their trade, their fruits do not become clean, their canals do not over-flow and He withholds their rain and makes their wicked ones to dominate them.'"

H 9362, Ch. 157, h 54

Ali ibn Ibrahim has narrated from his father from ibn abu 'Umayr from Ibrahim ibn 'Abd al-Hamid from Mus'ab ibn 'Abd Allah al-Nawfaliy from the one who has narrated in a marfu' manner who has said the following:

"Once an Arab came on his camel in the time of the Messenger of Allah, *O Allah, grant compensation to Muhammad and his family worthy of their services to Your cause*, and said, 'O Messenger of Allah, sell my (herd of) camels for me.' The Messenger of Allah, *O Allah, grant compensation to Muhammad and his family worthy of their services to Your cause*, said, 'I am not a camel seller in the market.' He then said, 'Give me an idea.' The Messenger of Allah said, 'Sell this he-camel for so and so much and this she-camel for so and so much until he (the Messenger of Allah) explained for him about every camel there. The Arab man went to the market and sold them. He then came back to the Messenger of Allah, *O Allah, grant compensation to Muhammad and his family worthy of their services to Your cause*, and said, 'I swear by the One who has sent you with truth, not one dirham was less or more than what you had said it was, so accept my gift, O Messenger of Allah.' He (the Messenger of Allah) said, 'No, I do not accept.' He said, 'Yes, O Messenger of Allah, accept it.' They continued speaking until he (the Messenger of Allah) said, 'You must give us a she-camel as a gift and you must not separate it from its young.'"

H 9363, Ch. 157, h 55

A number of our people have narrated from Sahl ibn Ziyad from Ya'qub Yazid from Zakariya' al-Khazzaz from Yahya al-Hadhdha' who has said the following:

"I once said to abu al-Hassan *'Alayhi al-Salam*, 'I may buy certain things in the presence of my father and I see certain things in him that make me depressed.' He (the Imam) said, 'Avoid buying in his presence. When you have a right on a man say to him, "Write down, 'So and so has written in his handwriting, assigning Allah as witness upon himself and Allah is sufficient witness.'" He will certainly pay in his life time or after his death.'"

H 9364, Ch. 157, h 56
Sahl ibn Ziyad has narrated from Ali ibn Bilal from al-Hassan ibn Bassam al-Jammal who has said the following:

"I once was with Ishaq ibn 'Ammar al-Sayrafiy when a man came and he wanted something for a dinar but he had closed the shop and had sealed the sack. He then gave him the item for a dinar. I then said, 'Fie on you, O Ishaq! I could have picked up for you a hundred thousand dirham from the ship.' He said to me, 'I had the same attitude but I heard abu 'Abd Allah, *'Alayhi al-Salam*, saying, "Whoever belittles a small amount of sustenance is deprived of its greater amount." Then he (the Imam) turned to me and said, "O Ishaq, do not belittle small amounts of sustenance; otherwise, you will be deprived of its greater amount.""

H 9365, Ch. 157, h 57
Humayd ibn Ziyad has narrated from 'Ubayd Allah ibn Ahmad ibn abu 'Umayr from al-Husayn ibn Ahmad al-Minqariy from Zurarah who has said the following:

"Abu 'Abd Allah, *'Alayhi al-Salam*, has said, 'Earning certain kinds of sustenance dries up one's skin on his bones (very hard to earn).'"

H 9366, Ch. 157, h 58
Ahmad ibn Muhammad al-'Asemiy has narrated from Ali ibn al-Hassan al-Tamimiy from Ali ibn Asbat from a man who has said the following:

"I once mentioned Egypt to abu 'Abd Allah, *'Alayhi al-Salam*. He (the Imam) said that the Messenger of Allah, *O Allah, grant compensation to Muhammad and his family worthy of their services to Your cause*, has said, 'You can seek to earn sustenance from it but you must not seek to stay there.' Abu 'Abd Allah, *'Alayhi al-Salam*, then said, 'Egypt is harsh; young ones break down there.'"

H 9367, Ch. 157, h 59
Ahmad ibn Muhammad al-'Asemiy has narrated from Muhammad ibn Ahmad al-Nahdiy from Muhammad ibn Ali from Sharif ibn Sabiq from al-Fadl ibn abu Qurrah who has said the following:

"Abu 'Abd Allah, *'Alayhi al-Salam*, has said that once *al-Mawaliy* (non-Arab Muslims) came to 'Amir al-Mu'minin, *'Alayhi al-Salam*, and said, 'We complain before you against these Arabs. The Messenger of Allah, *O Allah, grant compensation to Muhammad and his family worthy of their services to Your cause*, would give us gifts along with them equally. He (the Messenger of Allah) arranged marriage for Salman, Bilal and Suhayb but these have denied it for us saying, "We do not do so."' 'Amir al-Mu'minin, *'Alayhi al-Salam*, went to them and spoke to them and Arabs shouted, 'We have denied them, O abu al-Hassan, we have denied them O abu al-Hassan.' He (the Imam) came out angry with his gown dragging behind him, saying, 'O Mawaliy people, they have equaled you with Jews and Christians. They marry from you but do not allow you to marry from them and do not give you what they take. You must do business, may Allah grant you blessings. I heard the Messenger of Allah, *O Allah, grant compensation to Muhammad and his family worthy of their services to Your cause*, saying, "Sustenance has ten parts, of which nine are in trade and one part is in other things."""

End of Book of Commerce of the book al-Kafi followed by the Book of Marriage and thanks to Allah who opens the morning

In the Name of Allah, the Beneficient, the Merciful

Part Three: The Book of Marriage

Chapter 1 - Love of Women

H 9368 (a), Ch. 1, h 1
Ali ibn Ibrahim ibn Hashim has narrated from his father from Muhammad ibn abu 'Umayr from Ishaq ibn 'Ammar who has said the following:

"Abu 'Abd Allah, *'Alayhi al-Salam*, has said, 'Love for women is of the moral manners of the Prophets.'"

H 9368 (b), Ch. 1, h 2
Muhammad ibn Yahya al-'Attar has narrated from 'Abd Allah ibn Muhammad from Ali ibn al-Hakam from Aban ibn 'Uthman from 'Umar ibn Yazid who has said the following:

"Abu 'Abd Allah, *'Alayhi al-Salam*, has said, 'I do not think a man can increase anything good in his belief except that he increases his love for women.'"

H 9369, Ch. 1, h 3
Muhammad ibn Yahya has narrated from Ahmad ibn Muhammad ibn 'Isa from Mu'ammar ibn Khallad who has said the following:

"I once heard al-Rida', *'Alayhi al-Salam*, saying, 'Three things are of the traditions of the Messengers (of Allah): use of perfume, trimming hairs and ampleness of (relation in) marriage.'"

H 9370, Ch. 1, h 4
Muhammad ibn 'Isma'il has narrated from al-Fadl ibn Shadhan from and Ali ibn Ibrahim from his father all from ibn abu 'Umayr from Ibrahim ibn 'Abd al-Hamid who has narrated the following:

"Sukayn al-Nakha'iy worshipped and had given up women, perfume and food. He wrote to abu 'Abd Allah, *'Alayhi al-Salam*, and asked him (the Imam) about it. He (the Imam) wrote to him in answer, 'About your words concerning women, take notice about the Messenger of Allah, *O Allah, grant compensation to Muhammad and his family worthy of their services to Your cause*, how many women he (the Messenger of Allah) had, and about food you must take notice that the Messenger of Allah ate meat with honey.'"

H 9371, Ch. 1, h 5
Ali ibn Ibrahim has narrated from his father from Salih al-Sindiy from Ja'far ibn Bashir from Aban from 'Umar ibn Yazid who has said the following:

"Abu 'Abd Allah, *'Alayhi al-Salam*, has said, 'I do not think anyone increases goodness in this issue (belief in the Divine Authority of 'A'immah) without his increasing love for women.'"

H 9372, Ch. 1, h 6
Ali ibn Ibrahim has narrated from his father from ibn abu 'Umayr from Hafs ibn al-Bakhtariy who has said the following:

"Abu 'Abd Allah, *'Alayhi al-Salam*, has said that the Messenger of Allah, *O Allah, grant compensation to Muhammad and his family worthy of their services*

to Your cause, has said, 'I do not love anything from your world except women and perfume.'"

H 9373, Ch. 1, h 7
Muhammad ibn abu 'Umayr has narrated from Bakkar ibn Kardam from more than one person who has said the following:
"Abu 'Abd Allah, *'Alayhi al-Salam*, has said that the Messenger of Allah, *O Allah, grant compensation to Muhammad and his family worthy of their services to Your cause*, has said, 'The delight for my eyes is placed in *Salat* (prayer) and my pleasure in women.'"

H 9374, Ch. 1, h 8
Muhammad ibn Yahya has narrated from Salmah ibn al-Khattab from Ali ibn Hassa'n from certain persons of our people who has said the following:
"We once asked abu 'Abd Allah, *'Alayhi al-Salam*, 'What is the most enjoyable thing?' We said other things. He (the Imam) said, 'The most enjoyable of things is sexual intercourse with women.'"

H 9375, Ch. 1, h 9
Al-Husayn from Muhammad has narrated from Mu'alla' ibn Muhammad from al-Hassan ibn Ali from Hammad ibn 'Uthman from 'Umar ibn Yazid who has said the following:
"Abu 'Abd Allah, *'Alayhi al-Salam*, has said that the Messenger of Allah, *O Allah, grant compensation to Muhammad and his family worthy of their services to Your cause*, has said, 'The delight of my eyes is placed in *Salat* (prayer), my enjoyment of the world in women and my comfort and relief with al-Hassan and al-Husayn, *'Alayhi al-Salam*.'"

H 9376, Ch. 1, h 10
A number of our people have narrated from Ahmad ibn abu 'Abd Allah al-Barqiy from al-Hassan ibn abu Qatadah from a man from Jamil ibn Darraj who has said the following:
"Abu 'Abd Allah, *'Alayhi al-Salam*, has said, 'The most enjoyable thing people experience in this world and in the hereafter is enjoyment with women and it is in the words of Allah, most Majestic, most Glorious, 'The love and enjoyment for women and children is made attractive for people.' (3:13) He (the Imam) then said, 'People of paradise will not enjoy from anything else as much as they will with marriage, but not from food or drink.'"

Chapter 2 - Domination of Women

H 9377, Ch. 2, h 1
A number of our people have narrated from Ahmad ibn abu 'Abd Allah from his father from Sulayman ibn Ja'far al-Ja'fariy from those whom he has mentioned who has said the following:
"Abu 'Abd Allah, *'Alayhi al-Salam*, has said that the Messenger of Allah, *O Allah, grant compensation to Muhammad and his family worthy of their services to Your cause*, has said, 'I never saw anyone more snatching from an intelligent person, than these weak in religion, deficient of reason; you women are.'"

H 9378, Ch. 2, h 2
Ahmad ibn al-Hajjal has narrated from Ghalib ibn 'Uthman from "Uqbah ibn Khalid who has said the following:

"I once went to see abu 'Abd Allah, *'Alayhi al-Salam*, and he (the Imam) came to me saying, 'O 'Uqbah, the women held us back from meeting you.'"

Chapter 3 - Kinds of Women

H 9379, Ch. 3, h 1
Ali ibn Ibrahim has narrated from his father from al-Nawfaliy from al-Sakuniy who has said the following:
"Abu 'Abd Allah, *'Alayhi al-Salam*, has said that the Messenger of Allah, *O Allah, grant compensation to Muhammad and his family worthy of their services to Your cause*, or 'Amir al-Mu'minin has said, 'Women are of four kinds: a universal goodness, a fountain of breeding, an oppressive over-burdening or feed for parasites.'"

H 9380, Ch. 3, h 2
A number of our people have narrated from Sahl ibn Ziyad from Ali ibn Asbat from Muhammad ibn al-Sabbah from 'Abd al-Rahman ibn al-Hajjaj from 'Abd Allah ibn Mus'ab al-Zubayriy who has said the following:
"I once I heard abu al-Hassan, Musa ibn Ja'far, *'Alayhi al-Salam* - while we were sitting in the Masjid of the Messenger of Allah, *O Allah, grant compensation to Muhammad and his family worthy of their services to Your cause* - discussing issues about women and we delved in it a great deal but he (the Imam) was quiet and did not enter in our discussion not even with one word; but when we became quiet then I heard him (the Imam) saying, 'As far as free ones are concerned you must not speak about them, however, the best slave-girl is one whom you love, who has power of reason and moral discipline so you do not need to command or prohibit. Next to this is the one whom you love but does not have moral discipline and you need to command and prohibit. Next to this is the one whom you love but who does not have the power of reason and moral discipline and you have to exercise patience because of your love. Next to this is the slave-girl whom you do not love, she does not have the power of reason or moral discipline and you keep between yourself and her, the green ocean.' He (the narrator) has said, 'I then held my beard and wanted to make the sound of loud flatus because of our so much delving and without reaching any meaningful point and for his comprehensive words. He (the Imam) said, 'Hold it, if you did it I will not sit with you.'"

H 9381, Ch. 3, h 3
A number of our people have narrated from Sahl ibn Ziyad Ahmad ibn Muhammad from Ahmad ibn Muhammad from all ibn Mahbub from Ibrahim al-Karkhiy who has said the following:
"I once said to abu 'Abd Allah, *'Alayhi al-Salam*, 'My wife who lived in complete harmony with me has died and I want to marry.' He (the Imam) said, 'Think where you want to place yourself and whom you are making your partner in your assets, inform of your religion and secrets. If you must marry find a virgin who is spoken of with goodness and of good moral discipline. You must take notice that women are as it is said:

'Women are of various moral manners; among them are gains and losses. Among them are lawful when she shines for her companion and among them is darkness. Whoever succeeds in finding the righteous among them is a sure fortunate but one who is cheated cannot revenge.

'They are of three kinds; one kind is a child bearing and loving who helps her husband all the time in the worldly as well as the matters of the hereafter and the world does not work against her. The other kind is woman who is barren without beauty and moral manners and does not help her husband in anything good, she is loud and noisy, roaming around and faultfinding who considers a great deal very little and does not accept things of lesser amount.'"

H 9382, Ch. 3, h 4
Muhammad ibn Yahya has narrated from Salmah ibn al-Khattab from Sulayman ibn Sama'ah from al-Hadhdha' from his uncle, 'Asem who has said the following:
"Abu 'Abd Allah, *'Alayhi al-Salam*, has said that the Messenger of Allah, *O Allah, grant compensation to Muhammad and his family worthy of their services to Your cause*, has said, 'Women are of four kinds: Goodness in all respects, a child bearing fountain, a dimwitted destructive one and feed for parasites.'"

Chapter 4 - Best Kinds of Women

H 9383, Ch. 4, h 1
A number of our people have narrated from Sahl ibn Ziyad and Muhammad ibn Yahya has narrated from Ahmad ibn 'Isa and Ali ibn Ibrahim has narrated from his father from all from al-Hassan ibn Mahbub from Ali ibn Ri'ab from abu Hamzah who has said the following:
"I once heard Jabir ibn 'Abd Allah saying, 'Once we were with the Holy Prophet, *O Allah, grant compensation to Muhammad and his family worthy of their services to Your cause*, when he said, "The best of your women are the child bearing, loving and chaste who are dear at home, humble with her husband, showing her beauty to her husband, fortressed from strangers, who listens to his words and obeys his orders and in private offers to him what he wants and she does not display vulgar manners as man does."'"

H 9384, Ch. 4, h 2
A number of our people have narrated from Ahmad ibn Muhammad ibn Khalid al-Barqiy from Ahmad ibn abu Nasr from Hammad ibn 'Isa from abu Basir who has said the following:
"Abu 'Abd Allah, *'Alayhi al-Salam*, has said, 'The best of your women are those who in privacy removes the shield of shyness before her husband and when dressed up dresses with him the shield of shyness.'"

H 9385, Ch. 4, h 3
Al-Husayn ibn Muhammad has narrated from Mu'alla' ibn Muhammad from certain persons of his people from Aban ibn 'Uthman from Yahya ibn abu al-'Ala' and al-Fadl ibn 'Abd al-Malik who has said the following:
"Abu 'Abd Allah, *'Alayhi al-Salam*, has said that the Messenger of Allah, *O Allah, grant compensation to Muhammad and his family worthy of their services to Your cause*, has said, 'The best of your women is the chaste and full of carnal appetite.'"

H 9386, Ch. 4, h 4

Ali ibn Ibrahim has narrated from his father from al-Nawfaliy from al-Sakuniy who has said the following:

"Abu 'Abd Allah, *'Alayhi al-Salam*, has said that the Messenger of Allah, *O Allah, grant compensation to Muhammad and his family worthy of their services to Your cause*, has said, 'The best of the women of my followers are those who have a beautiful face and the least amount of *Mahr* (dowry).'"

H 9387, Ch. 4, h 5

A number of our people have narrated from Ahmad ibn Muhammad from al-Barqiy from 'Isma'il ibn Mehran from Sulayman al-Ja'fariy who has said the following:

"Abu al-Hassan al-Rida', *'Alayhi al-Salam*, has said that 'Amir al-Mu'minin, *'Alayhi al-Salam*, has said, 'The best of your women are five.' It was asked, 'O 'Amir al-Mu'minin what kind of five are they?' He (the Imam) replied, 'Simple, nice and suitable, when her husband becomes angry, does not neglect him until he is pleased, and when he is absent she protects him in his absence and that is a worker from Allah and the worker from Allah does not fail.'"

H 9388, Ch. 4, h 6

It is narrated from the narrator of the previous Hadith from Muhammad ibn Sinan from certain persons of his people who has said the following:

"Abu 'Abd Allah, *'Alayhi al-Salam*, has said, 'The best of your women are those who smell nice, cook nice and when spending she spends what is proper and withholds what is proper. That is a worker from Allah and a worker from Allah does not fail or become regretful.'"

H 9389, Ch. 4, h 7

Humayd ibn Ziyad has narrated from al-Hassan ibn Musa al-Khashshab from al-Hassan ibn Ali ibn Yusuf ibn Baqqah from Mu'adh al-Jawhariy from '(Belief in the Divine Authority of 'A'immah) ibn Jami' who has said the following:

"Abu 'Abd Allah, *'Alayhi al-Salam*, has said that the Messenger of Allah, *O Allah, grant compensation to Muhammad and his family worthy of their services to Your cause*, has said, 'The best of your women are those who cook nice, smell nice, when spending she spends what is proper and withholds what is proper. That is a worker from Allah and a worker from Allah does not fail.'"

Chapter 5 - Worst Kinds of Women

H 9390, Ch. 5, h 1

A number of our people have narrated from Sahl ibn Ziyad and Muhammad ibn Yahya has narrated from Ahmad ibn Muhammad and Ali ibn Ibrahim has narrated from his father all from ibn Mahbub from ibn Ri'ab from abu Hamzah from Jabir who has said the following:

"I once heard abu 'Abd Allah, *'Alayhi al-Salam*, saying that the Messenger of Allah, *O Allah, grant compensation to Muhammad and his family worthy of their services to Your cause*, has said, 'If you like I can tell you who are of the worst kind of your women. She is the one who is undignified in her family, flattered by her husband, barren, spiteful, who does not abstain from indecency, roams around to show off in the absence of her husband and very reserved when her husband is present. She does not listen to his words and does not obey his orders and in private she refuses to yield to him like recalcitrant animal who refuses to allow riding. She does not accept any of his excuses and does not forgive any of his sins.'"

H 9391, Ch. 5, h 2

A number of our people have narrated from Ahmad ibn Muhammad ibn Khalid from certain persons of his people from Milhan from 'Abd Allah ibn Sinan who has said the following:

"Abu 'Abd Allah, *'Alayhi al-Salam*, has said that the Messenger of Allah, *O Allah, grant compensation to Muhammad and his family worthy of their services to Your cause*, has said, 'The wicked ones of your women is one who is barren, filthy, quarrelsome, disobedient, undignified among her people and honored to herself, reserved in the presence of her husband but shows others to be of great carnal appetite.'"

H 9392, Ch. 5, h 3

Ali ibn Ibrahim has narrated from his father from al-Nawfaliy from al-Sakuniy who has narrated the following:

"Abu 'Abd Allah, *'Alayhi al-Salam*, has said that of the prayers of the Messenger of Allah, *O Allah, grant compensation to Muhammad and his family worthy of their services to Your cause*, was this, 'I seek refuge with You, O Lord, against a woman who makes me become old before my becoming old.'"

Chapter 6 - Excellence of Women of Quraysh

H 9393, Ch. 6, h 1

Ali ibn Ibrahim has narrated from his father from ibn abu 'Umayr from Hammad ibn 'Uthaman who has said the following:

"Abu 'Abd Allah, *'Alayhi al-Salam*, has said that the Messenger of Allah, *O Allah, grant compensation to Muhammad and his family worthy of their services to Your cause*, has said, 'The best of women who ever rode a camel on their wedding to the house of their husband are the women of Quraysh who are most compassionate to their children and are the best of them for their husband.'"

H 9394, Ch. 6, h 2

A number of our people have narrated from Ahmad ibn abu 'Abd Allah al-Barqiy from more than one person from Ziyad al-Qandiy from abu Waki' from abu Ishaq al-Sabi'i from al-Harith al-A'war who has said the following:

"'Amir al-Mu'minin, *'Alayhi al-Salam*, has said that the Messenger of Allah, *O Allah, grant compensation to Muhammad and his family worthy of their services to Your cause*, has said, 'The best of your women are the women of Quraysh who are very kind to their husbands, most compassionate to their children, *al-Majun* with her husband and very reserved before the others.' We asked, 'What is *al-Majun*?' He (the Messenger of Allah) said, 'It is the one who does not deny her husband.'"

H 9395, Ch. 6, h 3

Abu Ali al-Ash'ariy has narrated from Muhammad ibn 'Abd al-Jabbar from Safwan from Ishaq ibn 'Ammar from abu Basir who has said the following:

"One of the two Imam, (abu Ja'far or abu 'Abd Allah), *'Alayhi al-Salam*, has said, 'When the Holy Prophet, *O Allah, grant compensation to Muhammad and his family worthy of their services to Your cause*, proposed for marriage to 'Umm Haniy daughter of abu Talib, she said, 'O Messenger of Allah, I am a grieved widow and I have orphans in my lap, thus, the most suitable for you is a woman who is free.' The Messenger of Allah, *O Allah, grant compensation to Muhammad and his family worthy of their services to Your cause*, said, 'No women have ever ridden a camel on their wedding to the house of their husbands more compassionate to their children and caring for their husbands than the women of Quraysh.'"

Chapter 7 - Virtuous Women are Fortunate Chance for a Man

H 9396, Ch. 7, h 1

A number of our people have narrated from Sahl ibn Ziyad from Ja'far ibn Muhammad al-Ash'ariy from 'Abd Allah ibn Maymun al-Qaddah who has said the following:

"Abu 'Abd Allah, *'Alayhi al-Salam*, has said that the Holy Prophet, *O Allah, grant compensation to Muhammad and his family worthy of their services to Your cause*, has said, 'There is not anything more beneficial to a man after his accepting Islam than a Muslim woman who pleases him when he looks at her, gives when he asks and protects his interests in his absence.'"

H 9397, Ch. 7, h 2

A number of our people have narrated from Ahmad ibn Muhammad from ibn Faddal from Ali ibn 'Uqbah from Burayd ibn Mu'awiyah al-'Ijliy who has said the following:

"Abu Ja'far, *'Alayhi al-Salam*, has said that the Messenger of Allah, *O Allah, grant compensation to Muhammad and his family worthy of their services to Your cause*, has said, 'Allah, most Majestic, most Glorious, has said, "When I want to bring together for a Muslim the goodness of this and the next life, I place in him a heart that shows reverence (to Me), a tongue that speaks (of Me), a body that bears patience in hardships and a believing wife who gives him joy when he looks to her and who protects his interest in his absence.'"

H 9398, Ch. 7, h 3

Muhammad ibn 'Isma'il has narrated from al-Fadl ibn Shadhan from Safwan ibn Yahya who has said the following:

"Abu al-Hassan, al-Rida', *'Alayhi al-Salam*, has said, 'A servant (of Allah) never gains a benefit better than a virtuous wife who gives him joy when he looks to her and who protects his interest in his absence.'"

H 9399, Ch. 7, h 4

Ali ibn Ibrahim has narrated from his father from al-Nawfaliy from al-Sakuniy who has said the following:

"Abu 'Abd Allah, *'Alayhi al-Salam*, has said that the Messenger of Allah, *O Allah, grant compensation to Muhammad and his family worthy of their services to Your cause*, has said, 'Having a virtuous wife is a good fortune that a man enjoys.'"

H 9400, Ch. 7, h 5

Muhammad ibn Yahya has narrated from Ahmad ibn Muhammad from 'Isma'il ibn Hanan ibn Sadir from his father who has said the following:

"Abu Ja'far, *'Alayhi al-Salam*, has said that the Messenger of Allah, *O Allah, grant compensation to Muhammad and his family worthy of their services to Your cause*, has said, 'Of the shares forming the well-being of a Muslim one is a wife who makes him delightful when he looks at her and in his absence protects his interests and obeys his orders.'"

H 9401, Ch. 7, h 6

Al-Husayn ibn Muhammad has narrated from Mu'alla' ibn Muhammad from Mansur ibn al-'Abbas from Shu'ayb ibn Junah from Matar Mawla' Ma'n who has said the following:

"Abu 'Abd Allah, *'Alayhi al-Salam*, has said, 'Three issues provide comfort for a believing person: a spacious house which provides privacy and in bad condition keeps him out of the sight of people, a virtuous wife who helps him in his worldly affairs and those of the life hereafter and a daughter whom he escorts out of the house on her death or on her wedding.'"

Chapter 8 - Encouragement to Get Married

H 9402, Ch. 8, h 1

Muhammad ibn Yahya has narrated from Ahmad ibn Muhammad ibn 'Isa from Ali ibn al-Hakam from Safwan ibn Mehran who has said the following:

"Abu 'Abd Allah, *'Alayhi al-Salam*, has said that the Messenger of Allah, *O Allah, grant compensation to Muhammad and his family worthy of their services to Your cause*, has said, 'It is of the share of good fortune of a Muslim that female members of his family find marriage early on and there is nothing more beloved to Allah, most Majestic, most Glorious, than a home that is established in Islam with marriage and there is nothing more hated to Allah, most Majestic, most Glorious, than a home that is destroyed in Islam because of division, – divorce.' Abu 'Abd Allah, *'Alayhi al-Salam*, then said, 'Allah, most Majestic, most Glorious, has stressed on His hating divorce in repeated ways because of His extreme dislike of division.'"

Chapter 9 - The Detestability of Living Single

H 9403, Ch. 9, h 1

A number of our people have narrated from Ahmad ibn Muhammad from ibn Faddal from ibn al-Qaddah who has said the following:

"Abu 'Abd Allah, *'Alayhi al-Salam*, has said, 'Two Rak'at *Salat* (prayer) performed by a married person is more virtuous than seventy Rak'at *Salat* (prayer) performed by a non-married person.'"

"A number of our people have narrated from Sahl ibn Ziyad from Ja'far ibn Muhammad al-Ash'ariy from ibn al-Qaddah from abu 'Abd Allah, *'Alayhi al-Salam*, a similar Hadith."

H 9404, Ch. 9, h 2

Ali ibn Muhammad ibn Bandar has narrated from Ahmad ibn Muhammad from ibn Khalid from al-Jamuraniy from al-Hassan ibn Ali ibn abu Hamzah from Kulayb ibn Mu'awiyah al-Asadiy who has said the following:

"Abu 'Abd Allah, *'Alayhi al-Salam*, has said that the Messenger of Allah, *O Allah, grant compensation to Muhammad and his family worthy of their services to Your cause*, has said, 'By getting married one secures one-half of his religion.' In another Hadith it is said that one must thereafter maintain piety before Allah about the other one-half."

H 9405, Ch. 9, h 3

It is narrated from the narrator of the previous Hadith from Muhammad ibn Ali from 'Abd al-Rahman ibn Khalid from Muhammad al-Asamm who has said the following:

"Abu 'Abd Allah, *'Alayhi al-Salam*, has said that the Messenger of Allah, *O Allah, grant compensation to Muhammad and his family worthy of their services to Your cause*, has said, 'The worthless dead among you are the unmarried ones.'"

H 9406, Ch. 9, h 4

Ali ibn Ibrahim has narrated from his father from ibn abu 'Umayr from 'Abd Allah ibn Sinan who has said the following:

"Abu 'Abd Allah, *'Alayhi al-Salam*, has said, 'When Yusuf met his brother, he asked, "How did you marry women after me?" He replied, "My father commanded me to do so and said, 'If you can have so many children who will load the earth heavily with *Tasbih* (Allah is free of all defects), then you must do so.'"""

H 9407, Ch. 9, h 5

Muhammad ibn Yahya has narrated from Ahmad ibn Muhammad from al-Qasim ibn Yahya from his grandfather, al-Hassan ibn Rashid from Muhammad ibn Muslim who has said the following:

"Abu 'Abd Allah, *'Alayhi al-Salam*, has said that 'Amir al-Mu'minin, *'Alayhi al-Salam*, has said, 'You must become married because the Messenger of Allah, *O Allah, grant compensation to Muhammad and his family worthy of their services to Your cause*, has said, "Whoever wants to follow my Sunnah, must take notice that of my Sunnah is marriage."""

H 9408, Ch. 9, h 6

Ali ibn Muhammad has narrated and others have narrated from Ahmad ibn abu 'Abd Allah al-Barqiy form ibn Faddal and Ja'far ibn Muhammad from ibn al-Qaddah who has said the following:

"Once, a man came to abu 'Abd Allah, *'Alayhi al-Salam*, and he (the Imam) asked, 'Are you married?' The man replied, 'No, I am not married.' My father said, 'I do not like to have the whole world but spend one night without wife.' He (the Imam) then said, 'Two Rak'at *Salat* (prayer) performed by a married man is better than an unmarried man's performing *Salat* (prayer) the whole night and fasting during the day.' My father gave him seven dinars and said, 'You must get married with this.' My father then said that the Messenger of Allah, *O Allah, grant compensation to Muhammad and his family worthy of their services to Your cause*, has said, 'Find a wife because it is helpful to increase your sustenance.'"

H 9409, Ch. 9, h 7

It is narrated from the narrator of the previous Hadith from his father from 'Abd Allah ibn al-Mughirah who has said the following:

"'Abd Allah ibn al-Mughirah has narrated from abu al-Hassan, *'Alayhi al-Salam*, a similar Hadith and added the following: Muhammad ibn 'Ubayd said, 'I pray to Allah to keep my soul in service for your cause, I am not married.' He (the Imam) asked, 'Do you not have slave-girls' or that he (the Imam) asked, 'Do you not have mothers of your children?' He replied, 'Yes, I have.' He (the Imam) said, 'You then are not an unmarried man.'"

Chapter 10 - With Marriage Sustenance Increases

H 9410, Ch. 10, h 1

Ali ibn Ibrahim has narrated from his father from ibn abu 'Umayr from Aban ibn 'Uthman from Hariz from Walid ibn Sabih who has said the following:

"One who neglects marriage for fear of failure to feed his family has become distrustful of Allah.'"

H 9411, Ch. 10, h 2

Muhammad ibn Yahya has narrated from Ahmad and 'Abd Allah sons of Muhammad ibn 'Isa from Ali ibn al-Hakam from Hisham ibn Salim who has said the following:

"Abu 'Abd Allah, *'Alayhi al-Salam*, has said, 'Once a man came to the Holy Prophet, *O Allah, grant compensation to Muhammad and his family worthy of their services to Your cause*, and complained about his financial condition. He (the Messenger of Allah) told him to become married and he did so after which he became affluent.'"

H 9412, Ch. 10, h 3

Ali ibn Ibrahim has narrated from his father from Salih al-Sindiy from Ja'far ibn Bashir from Ali ibn abu Hamzah from abu Basir who has said the following:

"Abu 'Abd Allah, *'Alayhi al-Salam*, has said, 'Once a young man from al-Ansar (people of al-Madinah) came to the Messenger of Allah, *O Allah, grant compensation to Muhammad and his family worthy of their services to Your cause*, and complained about his needs. He (the Messenger of Allah) told him to become married. The young man said, "I feel shy to come to the Messenger of Allah to ask for help again." A man from al-Ansar (people of al-Madinah) followed him and said, "I have a beautiful daughter." He gave her in marriage to him. Allah granted increase in his sustenance. The young man came to the Holy Prophet, informed him of his condition and the Messenger of Allah, *O Allah, grant compensation to Muhammad and his family worthy of their services to Your cause*, said, "You, the young people, must get married."'"

H 9413, Ch. 10, h 4

A number of our people have narrated from Ahmad ibn abu 'Abd Allah from abu 'Abd Allah al-Jamuraniy from al-Hassan ibn Ali ibn abu Hamzah from al-Mu'min from Ishaq ibn 'Ammar who has said the following:

"This is concerning my question before abu 'Abd Allah, *'Alayhi al-Salam*, about the truth in Hadith which people narrate that a man came to the Holy Prophet, *O Allah, grant compensation to Muhammad and his family worthy of their services to Your cause*, and complained about his financial condition. He (the Messenger of Allah) commanded him to get married. He married but then came to complain again. He (the Messenger of Allah) commanded him to get married and so on up to three times.' Abu 'Abd Allah, *'Alayhi al-Salam*, has said, 'Yes, it (Hadith) is true.' He (the Imam) then said, 'Sustenance is with women and with the dependents to feed.'"

H 9414, Ch. 10, h 5

It is narrated from the narrator of the previous Hadith from al-Jamuraniy from al-Hassan ibn Ali ibn abu Hamzah from Muhammad ibn Yusuf al-Tamimiy from Muhammad ibn Ja'far from his father from ancestors who has said the following:

"He (the Imam), *'Alayhi al-Salam*, has said that the Messenger of Allah, *O Allah, grant compensation to Muhammad and his family worthy of their services to Your cause*, has said, 'One who neglects marriage because of his fear to feed his dependents has become cynical about Allah, most Majestic, most Glorious, who has said, "If they are poor Allah makes rich through His generosity."'" (24: 32)

H 9415, Ch. 10, h 6

It is narrated from the narrator of the previous Hadith from Muhammad ibn Ali from Hamdwayh ibn 'Imran from ibn abu Layla' who has said that 'Asem ibn Humayd narrated to me saying the following:

"Once I was with abu 'Abd Allah, *'Alayhi al-Salam*, when a man came and complained before him (the Imam) about his financial conditions. He (the Imam) commanded him to get married but his needs became more pressing and he came back again to abu 'Abd Allah, *'Alayhi al-Salam*, who asked about his conditions. He replied that it has worsened. He (the Imam) told him to separate. The man came back again and he (the Imam) asked about his conditions. The man replied, 'I have become affluent and my conditions are better.' He (the Imam) said, 'I commanded you as I did because of the two commandments with which Allah, most Majestic, most Glorious, has commanded: "Marry the single ones among you and the virtuous of your slaves and slave-girls and if you are poor Allah through His generosity will make you self-sufficient." (24:32) "If they depart each other Allah will make each one self-sufficient through His vast resources." (4:129)'"

H 9416, Ch. 10, h 7

Abu Ali al-Ash'ariy has narrated from certain persons of his people from Safwan ibn Yahya from Mu'awiyah ibn Wahab who has said the following:

"About the words of Allah, most Majestic, most Glorious, 'Those who cannot find marriage must remain chaste until Allah through His generosity makes them self-sufficient,' (24:33) he (the Imam), *'Alayhi al-Salam*, has said, 'They must become married so that (when) Allah makes them self-sufficient through His generosity.'"

Chapter 11 - Hard Work for Marriage

H 9417, Ch. 11, h 1
Ali ibn Ibrahim has narrated from his father from al-Nawfaliy from al-Sakuniy who has said the following:
"Abu 'Abd Allah, *'Alayhi al-Salam*, has said that 'Amir al-Mu'minin has said, 'The best intercession and mediation is that between two people until Allah unites them in marriage.'"

H 9418, Ch. 11, h 2
A number of our people have narrated from Ahmad ibn Muhammad from 'Uthman ibn 'Isa from Sama'ah ibn Mehran who has said the following:
"Abu 'Abd Allah, *'Alayhi al-Salam*, has said, 'One who arranges a marriage for an unmarried person is of those to whom Allah, most Majestic, most Glorious, will look on Day of Judgment.'"

Chapter 12 - Choosing a Wife

H 9419, Ch. 12, h 1
A number of our people have narrated from Ahmad ibn Muhammad from 'Uthman ibn 'Isa from 'Abd Allah ibn Muskan from certain persons of his people who has said the following:
"I once heard abu 'Abd Allah, *'Alayhi al-Salam*, saying, 'A woman is a necklace, so consider what you are placing around your neck.' I (the narrator) also heard him (the Imam) saying, 'Women are priceless and it applies to both, virtuous and otherwise, among them. Gold and silver cannot become the price for a virtuous woman because she is better than gold and silver. The price of the wicked ones among women is not even worth a piece of dirt because dirt is better than them.'"

H 9420, Ch. 12, h 2
Ali ibn Ibrahim has narrated from his father from al-Nawfaliy from al-Sakuniy who has said the following:
Abu 'Abd Allah, *'Alayhi al-Salam*, has said that the Holy Prophet, *O Allah, grant compensation to Muhammad and his family worthy of their services to Your cause*, has said, 'Choose for your seed (the best ground) thus, maternal uncle is one of the two bedfellows (close associates).'"

H 9421, Ch. 12, h 3
Through the same chain of narrators as that of the previous Hadith the following is narrated:
"The Messenger of Allah has said, 'Get married but the party must be a proper match, so marry from them (proper matches) and choose (proper environment) for your seeds.'"

H 9422, Ch. 12, h 4
Through the same chain of narrators as that of the previous Hadith the following is narrated:
"The Messenger of Allah, *O Allah, grant compensation to Muhammad and his family worthy of their services to Your cause*, one day stood up to give a speech and said, 'O people, I warn you against *Khadra' al-Deman* (a green plant that grows on the dump-site).' It was asked, 'What is *Khadra' al-Deman* O

Messenger of Allah?' He (the Messenger of Allah) replied, 'It is the good looking women who have grown in a wicked environment.'"

Chapter 13 - Excellence of Marriage with a Religious Spouse and the Detestability of Marriage for the Sake of Wealth

H 9423, Ch. 13, h 1

A number of our people have narrated from Sahl ibn Ziyad from Ali ibn Asbat from his uncle Ya'qub ibn Salim from Muhammad ibn Muslim who has said the following:

"Abu Ja'far, *'Alayhi al-Salam*, has said, 'Once a man came to the Holy Prophet, *O Allah, grant compensation to Muhammad and his family worthy of their services to Your cause*, requesting instruction for getting married. The Messenger of Allah said to him, 'You must marry one who is religious beyond questions.'"

H 9424, Ch. 13, h 2

Ali ibn Muhammad ibn Bandar has narrated from Ahmad ibn abu 'Abd Allah from his father from Ahmad ibn al-Nadr from certain persons of his people from Ishaq ibn 'Ammar who has said the following:

"I once heard abu 'Abd Allah, *'Alayhi al-Salam*, saying, 'If one marries a woman for the sake of her wealth, Allah makes that wealth his (only) refuge.'"

H 9425, Ch. 13, h 3

Ali ibn Ibrahim has narrated from his father from and Muhammad ibn 'Isma'il has narrated from al-Fadl ibn Shadhan from all from ibn abu 'Umayr from Hisham ibn al-Hakam who has said the following:

"Abu 'Abd Allah, *'Alayhi al-Salam*, has said, 'If one marries a woman for the sake of her beauty or wealth he will be left alone with such things; but if one marries for the sake of her religion, Allah provides him beauty and wealth.'"

Chapter 14 - The Detestability of Marriage with Barren Women

H 9426, Ch. 14, h 1

A number of our people have narrated from Ahmad ibn Muhammad from and Sahl ibn Ziyad all from ibn Mahbub from 'Abd Allah ibn Sinan who has said the following:

"Abu 'Abd Allah, *'Alayhi al-Salam*, has said, 'Once a man came to the Messenger of Allah and said, "O the Holy Prophet of Allah, I have the daughter of an uncle whose beauty, goodness and religion I like; but she is barren."' He (the Messenger of Allah) said, 'You must not marry her; Yusuf after meeting his brother asked him, "How did you manage to get married after me." He replied, "Because my father said, 'If you can have such a great number of children whose *Tasbih* (Allah is free of all defects) can become a heavy load for the earth then do it.'"' He (the Imam) has said, that the next day another man came who said a similar thing and he (the Messenger of Allah) said, 'Marry al-Su'a and child bearing because I will express pride for the greater number of my followers among the nations on the Day of Judgment.' I (the narrator) then asked abu 'Abd Allah, *'Alayhi al-Salam*, 'What is *al-Su'a*?' He (the Imam) said, 'It means an ugly looking woman.'"

H 9427, Ch. 14, h 2
Al-Hassan ibn Mahbub has narrated from al-'Ala' ibn Razin from Muhammad ibn Muslim who has said the following:

"Abu Ja'far, *'Alayhi al-Salam*, has said that the Messenger of Allah, *O Allah, grant compensation to Muhammad and his family worthy of their services to Your cause*, has said, 'You must marry virgin and child bearing women, but you must not marry good a looking but barren woman because I will express pride because of you among nations on the Day of Judgment.'"

H 9428, Ch. 14, h 3
Ali ibn Ibrahim has narrated from his father from ibn abu 'Umayr from Ahmad ibn 'Abd al-Rahman from 'Isma'il ibn 'Abd al-Khaliq from those whom he has mentioned who has said the following:

"I once complained before abu 'Abd Allah, *'Alayhi al-Salam*, for not having enough children and that I have no child. He (the Imam) said to me, 'When you arrive in Iraq, marry a woman and do not mind if she is *al-Su'a*.' I then asked, 'I pray to Allah to keep my soul in service for your cause, what is *al-Su'a*?' He (the Imam) said, 'It is a woman who has certain degrees of ugliness because such woman bears more children.'"

H 9429, Ch. 14, h 4
A number of our people have narrated from Sahl ibn Ziyad from Ali ibn Sa'id al-Riqqiy to whom narrated Sulayman ibn Ja'far al-Ja'fariy who has said the following:

"Abu al-Hassan, al-Rida', *'Alayhi al-Salam*, has said that the Messenger of Allah, *O Allah, grant compensation to Muhammad and his family worthy of their services to Your cause*, once said to a man, 'Marry *al-Su'a*' and child bearing woman but do not marry a good looking barren woman. I will express pride because of you among nations on the Day of Judgment. Have you taken notice that children under the Throne ask forgiveness for their parents? Ibrahim and Sara are the custodians of these children in a mountain of musk, ambergris and saffron.'"

Chapter 15 - Excellence of Virgins

H 9430, Ch. 15, h 1
A number of our people have narrated from Sahl ibn Ziyad and Ahmad ibn Muhammad from ibn Mahbub from ibn Ri'ab from 'Abd al-'Ala' ibn 'A'yan Mawla' Ale Sam who has said the following:

"Abu 'Abd Allah, *'Alayhi al-Salam*, has said that the Messenger of Allah, *O Allah, grant compensation to Muhammad and his family worthy of their services to Your cause*, has said, 'Marry virgins; they are of the finest mouth.' In another Hadith it is said that, their uterus most dry, their posterior most round, and their womb most open. Have you taken notice that I will express pride among the nations on the Day of Judgment even because of a miscarried child who, filled with anger, stands at the door of paradise? Allah, most Majestic, most Glorious, then says, 'Enter paradise.' The child says, 'No, I will not enter until my parents enter before I enter.' Allah, most Blessed, most High, says to an angel of the angels, 'Bring to Me his parents.' He then commands to admit them in paradise, and then He says, 'This is because of My mercy upon you.'"

Chapter 16 - Signs of Praiseworthiness of Women

H 9431, Ch. 16, h 1

A number of our people have narrated from Sahl ibn Ziyad from Ahmad ibn Muhammad from ibn abu Nasr from 'Abd Allah ibn al-Mughirah who has said the following:

"I once heard abu al-Hassan, *'Alayhi al-Salam*, saying, 'You must marry women of large hips because they are most fertile for child bearing.'"

H 9432, Ch. 16, h 2

Muhammad ibn Yahya has narrated from Ahmad ibn Muhammad ibn 'Isa from Malik ibn 'Ushaym certain persons of his people who have said the following:

"Abu 'Abd Allah, *'Alayhi al-Salam*, has said, 'Marry woman of brunette color, wide buttocks and of medium height. If you disliked, her *mahr* (dowry) is on me.'"

H 9433, Ch. 16, h 3

Al-Husayn from Muhammad has narrated from Mu'alla' ibn Muhammad from Ahmad ibn Muhammad from ibn 'Abd Allah who has said the following:

"Al-Rida', *'Alayhi al-Salam*, once said to me, 'If you want to marry, marry a woman of large buttocks.'"

H 9434, Ch. 16, h 4

A number of our people have narrated from Ahmad ibn abu 'Abd Allah from certain persons of our people in a marfu' manner has said the following:

"When the Holy Prophet, *O Allah, grant compensation to Muhammad and his family worthy of their services to Your cause*, wanted to marry a woman he would send a woman to examine her with the instruction, 'Smell her neck; if it smells fine her scent smells fine, and if her soles are full, her knees are large.'"

H 9435, Ch. 16, h 5

Ahmad has narrated from his father from Ali ibn al-Nu'man from his brother from Dawud ibn al-Nu'man from abu Ayyub al-Khazzaz who has said the following:

"Abu 'Abd Allah, *'Alayhi al-Salam*, has said, 'I have put to the test white and dark color slave-girls. There is a great difference between them.'" (It may also mean both kinds are good)

H 9436, Ch. 16, h 6

Ali ibn Ibrahim has narrated from his father from al-Nawfaliy from al-Sakuniy who has said the following:

"Abu 'Abd Allah, *'Alayhi al-Salam*, has said that the Messenger of Allah, *O Allah, grant compensation to Muhammad and his family worthy of their services to Your cause*, has said, 'Marry blue colored eyes; it is a sign of good fortune.'"

H 9437, Ch. 16, h 7

A number of our people have narrated from Sahl ibn Ziyad from Bakr ibn Salih from certain persons of his people who have said the following:

"Abu al-Hassan, *'Alayhi al-Salam,* has said, 'It is of the well-being of a man who on moving aside the veil of a woman finds her white.'"

H 9438, Ch. 16, h 8

Sahl has narrated from Bakr ibn Salih from Malik ibn 'Ushaym from certain persons of his people who has said the following:

"Abu 'Abd Allah, *'Alayhi al-Salam,* has said that 'Amir al-Mu'minin has said, 'Marry a woman of large eyes, of brunette color, wide buttocks and of medium height; and if you disliked, her *mahr* (dowry) is on me.'"

Chapter 17 - Rare Ahadith

H 9439, Ch. 17, h 1

Muhammad ibn Yahya has narrated from Muhammad ibn abu al-Qasim from his father in a marfu' manner who has said the following:

"Abu 'Abd Allah, *'Alayhi al-Salam,* has said, 'A good looking woman cuts down phlegm and an ugly looking woman excites black bile.'"

H 9440, Ch. 17, h 2

Al-Husayn from Muhammad from al-Sayyariy from Ali ibn Muhammad from Muhammad ibn 'Abd al-Hamid from certain persons of his people who has said the following:

"He (the narrator) once complained before abu 'Abd Allah, *'Alayhi al-Salam,* against phlegm and he (the Imam) asked, 'Do you not have a slave-girl who can make you laugh?' I (the narrator) said, 'No, I do not have one.' He (the Imam) said, 'Find one; she will cut down phlegm.'"

Chapter 18 - Allah, Most Blessed, Most High, Has Created for People Similarities

H 9441, Ch. 18, h 1

Ali ibn Muhammad has narrated from Salih ibn abu Hammad from Harun ibn Muslim from Burayd ibn Mu'awiyah who has said the following:

"Abu 'Abd Allah, *'Alayhi al-Salam,* has said that once a man came to the Holy Prophet, *O Allah, grant compensation to Muhammad and his family worthy of their services to Your cause,* and said, 'O Messenger of Allah, I carry the largest thing that man carry, if I can make use of the animals that I own, like a donkey or she-camel, because women cannot bear what I have.' The Messenger of Allah said, 'Allah has not created your thing without creating what can match your kind.' The man went and very shortly came back to the Messenger of Allah and repeated what he had said before. The Messenger of Allah, *O Allah, grant compensation to Muhammad and his family worthy of their services to Your cause,* said, 'Why do you not find the black woman with a tall neck and healthy body?' He went and very shortly came back and said, 'I testify that you are the Messenger of Allah in all truth. I searched for what you commanded me to do and found her to be of my kind and match and I am satisfied.'"

Chapter 19 - The Desirability of Marriage for Women at Puberty and Fortifying them with Marriage

H 9442, Ch. 19, h 1

Muhammad ibn Yahya has narrated from Ahmad ibn Muhammad ibn 'Isa from certain persons of his people who has said the following:

"Abu 'Abd Allah, *'Alayhi al-Salam*, has said, 'It is of the good fortune of a man whose daughter does not experience Hayd (menses) in his home.'"

H 9443, Ch. 19, h 2

Certain persons of our people whose chain of narrators I have missed have narrated the following:

"Abu 'Abd Allah, *'Alayhi al-Salam*, has said that Allah, most Majestic, most Glorious, has taught to His Prophet, *O Allah, grant compensation to Muhammad and his family worthy of their services to Your cause*, everything that is needed. Of such teachings is what he spoke one day from the pulpit. He (the Messenger of Allah) praised Allah and spoke of His glory, then said, 'O people, Jibril came to me from the most Subtle, most Aware One and said, "The virgins are like ripe fruit on the tree which if not plucked up become spoiled because of the sun, and winds scatter them away. So also are virgins when they experience what women experience; then there is no medicine for them except husbands, otherwise, one is not safe from their getting spoiled because they are human beings."' One man then stood up and said, 'O Messenger of Allah, *O Allah, grant compensation to Muhammad and his family worthy of their services to Your cause*, to whom must we give in marriage?' He (the Messenger of Allah) said, 'Give them in marriage to their matches.' He then asked, 'Who is a match?' He (the Messenger of Allah) replied, 'The believers are each other's match.'"

H 9444, Ch. 19, h 3

Muhammad ibn Yahya has narrated from 'Abd Allah ibn Muhammad from Ali ibn al-Hakam from Aban ibn 'Uthman from 'Abd al-Rahman ibn Sayabah who has said the following:

"Abu 'Abd Allah, *'Alayhi al-Salam*, has said, 'Allah created the creatures from Eve and Adam. The ambition of women is for men and their fortresses are the homes.'"

H 9445, Ch. 19, h 4

Aban has narrated from al-Wasitiy who has said the following:

"Abu 'Abd Allah, *'Alayhi al-Salam*, has said, 'Allah created Adam from water and clay so the ambition of the sons of Adam is in water and clay. He created Eve from Adam so the ambition of women is for men and their fortress is in the houses.'"

H 9446, Ch. 19, h 5

Ali ibn Muhammad has narrated from ibn Jumhur from his father in a marfu' manner who has said the following:

"'Amir al-Mu'minin, *'Alayhi al-Salam*, in certain parts of his speech has said, 'The ambition of beasts is to fill their stomach, and the ambition of women is to find men.'"

H 9447, Ch. 19, h 6

A number of our people have narrated from Ahmad ibn abu 'Abd Allah from his father from Wahab who has said the following:

"Abu 'Abd Allah, *'Alayhi al-Salam*, has said that 'Amir al-Mu'minin has said, 'Men are created from earth, their ambition is in earth, and women are created from men and their ambition is to find men; so keep your women, O community of men.'"

H 9448, Ch. 19, h 7

Abu 'Abd Allah al-Ash'ariy has narrated from certain persons of our people from Ja'far ibn 'Anbasah from 'Ubadah ibn Ziyad from 'Amr ibn abu al-Miqdam from abu Ja'far, *'Alayhi al-Salam*, and Ahmad ibn Muhammad al-'Asemiy from those who narrated to him from al-'Ala' from Ali ibn Hassan from 'Abd al-Rahman ibn al-Kathir who has said the following:

"Abu 'Abd Allah, *'Alayhi al-Salam*, has said that 'Amir al-Mu'minin has said, in his letter to al-Hassan, *'Alayhi al-Salam*: 'You must never consult women because their opinion is weak in reason and their aim is not durable. They must keep their eye cast down by means of your barrier, because strict privacy is better for you and for them and away from doubts. Their going out is not more difficult than entering of one to their place whom you do not trust about them. If you can, do something that no man other than you can know them; then do so.'"

Ahmad ibn Muhammad from ibn Sa'id from Ja'far ibn Muhammad al-Husayniy from Ali ibn 'Abdakin from al-Hassan ibn Tarif ibn Nasih from al-Husayn ibn 'Ulwan from Sa'd ibn Tarif from al-Asbagh ibn Nubatah from 'Amir al-Mu'minin, *'Alayhi al-Salam*, a similar Hadith except that he has said 'Amir al-Mu'minin wrote it to his son Muhammad (bin al-Hanafiyah).

H 9449, Ch. 19, h 8

A number of our people have narrated from Ahmad ibn Muhammad from ibn Khalid from Nuh ibn Shu'ayb in a marfu' manner who has said the following:

"Abu 'Abd Allah, *'Alayhi al-Salam*, has said that Ali ibn al-Husayn, *'Alayhi al-Salam*, would spread his gown as furnishing when the husband of his daughter or sister would come to him (the Imam) and would say, 'Welcome to the one who has taken good care of a need and the one who protected the privacy.'"

Chapter 20 - Women's Desire More Intense than Men's

H 9450, Ch. 20, h 1

A number of our people have narrated from Ahmad ibn Muhammad ibn 'Isa from al-Husayn ibn Sa'id ibn 'Ulwan from Sa'd ibn Tarif from al-Asbagh ibn Nubatah who has said the following:

"'Amir al-Mu'minin, *'Alayhi al-Salam*, has said, 'Allah created desire of ten parts, of which nine parts are placed in women and only one part in men. If He did not place shyness in women of a similar (nine out of ten) amount in women like desire, nine women would attach themselves to one man.'"

H 9451, Ch. 20, h 2

A number of our people have narrated from Ahmad ibn Muhammad from ibn Khalid from Ahmad ibn Muhammad from ibn abu Nasr from those who narrated to him from Ishaq ibn 'Ammar who has said the following:

"Abu 'Abd Allah, *'Alayhi al-Salam*, has said, 'Allah has placed in women a degree of patience which is ten times greater than the patience of men. If excited she has a force of desire which is equal to ten men.'"

H 9452, Ch. 20, h 3

A number of our people have narrated from Ahmad ibn Muhammad ibn 'Isa from Muhammad ibn Sinan from abu Khalid al-Qammat from Durays who has said the following:

"I once heard abu 'Abd Allah, *'Alayhi al-Salam*, saying, 'Women are given desires of twelve parts and patience of twelve parts.'"

H 9453, Ch. 20, h 4

Ahmad ibn Muhammad has narrated from Ali ibn al-Hakam from Durays who has said the following:

"I once heard abu 'Abd Allah, *'Alayhi al-Salam*, saying, 'Women are given desires of twelve parts and patience of twelve parts.'"

H 9454, Ch. 20, h 5

Muhammad ibn Yahya has narrated from certain persons of his people from Marwak ibn 'Ubayd from Zur'ah ibn Muhammad from Sama'ah ibn Mehran from abu Basir who has said the following:

"I once heard abu 'Abd Allah, *'Alayhi al-Salam*, saying, 'Women have an additional ninety-nine parts of enjoyment above men but Allah has placed shyness upon them.'"

H 9455, Ch. 20, h 6

Ali has narrated from Harun ibn Muslim from Mas'adah ibn Sadaqah who has said the following:

"Abu 'Abd Allah, *'Alayhi al-Salam*, has said, 'Allah has placed ten times more patience in women above men, but when grown (excited) she has the force (of desire) like ten men.'"

Chapter 21 - Believers Are Good Match of Believing Women

H 9456, Ch. 21, h 1

Muhammad ibn Yahya has narrated from Ahmad ibn Muhammad ibn 'Isa from al-Hassan ibn Mahbub from Malik ibn 'Atiyyah from abu Hamzah al-Thumaliy who has said the following:

"I once was with abu Ja'far when a man asked permission for a meeting. He came in and offered Salam (the phrase of offering greeting of peace). Abu Ja'far, *'Alayhi al-Salam*, said welcome to him, gave him a place nearby and asked about his condition. The man said, 'I pray to Allah to keep my soul in service for your cause, I proposed marriage to your Mawla', so and so ibn abu Rafi' for his daughter so and so but he refused, turned away from me, considered me worthless, because of my ugliness, poverty and alienation, which attacked and broke my heart and I wished death to approach me.' Abu Ja'far, *'Alayhi al-Salam*, said, 'You must go; you are my messenger to him and say to him that Muhammad ibn Ali ibn al-Husayn and ibn Ali ibn abu Talib says, "You must give your daughter so and so in marriage to my Mawla' Munjih ibn Rabah and do not refuse."' Abu Hamzah has said that the man jumped out with joy with the letter from abu Ja'far, *'Alayhi al-Salam*. When he left abu Ja'far, *'Alayhi al-Salam*, said, 'There was a man from the people of Yamamah called Juwayabir who came to the Messenger of Allah, *O Allah, grant compensation to*

Muhammad and his family worthy of their services to Your cause, seeking success through Islam. He became a Muslim and a good Muslim. He was of short height, ugly looking, poor, naked and he was of the ugly looking people of Sudan. The Messenger of Allah associated with him closely because of his alienation and nakedness and had assigned one *Sa'* of dates by the measure of the first *Sa'* food for him, clothed him with two pieces of sheets, commanded him to stay in Masjid and sleep there during the night. He lived that way as long as Allah wanted until the number of emigrants grew of those who accepted Islam of the poor people in al-Madinah and the Masjid became smaller and congested. Allah, most Majestic, most Glorious, sent revelation to His holy prophet, to clean the Masjid, move from it those who slept there in the night, commanded to block all doors that opened to the Masjid except the door of Ali and the door to the living-quarter of Fatimah, *'Alayha al-Salam.* Everyone after sexual relation and before Ghusl (bath) was barred from entering the Masjid, and no alien could sleep in the Masjid. So the Messenger of Allah commanded to blocking all doors that opened to the Masjid except the door of Ali, and allowed the door of the living-quarter of Fatimah, *'Alayha al-Salam,* to remain as they were before.' He (the Imam) said, 'The Messenger of Allah, *O Allah, grant compensation to Muhammad and his family worthy of their services to Your cause,* then commanded to build a canopy for the Muslims which was built and that was the platform or the edge. He (the Messenger of Allah) then commanded the emigrants and the poor ones to stay there for the night and days. They made it their home and gathered therein. The Messenger of Allah, *O Allah, grant compensation to Muhammad and his family worthy of their services to Your cause,* would come to see them, bring for them wheat, dates, barley and raisins whenever available. The Muslims sympathized with them because the Messenger of Allah sympathized with them and spent their charity on them. The Messenger of Allah one day looked at Juwayabir with kindness and sympathy and said to him, "I wish you to get married with a woman to safeguard your chastity and receive help for your worldly affairs as well as those of the hereafter." Juwayabir then said, "O Messenger of Allah, I pray to Allah to keep my soul and the souls of my parents in service for your cause, who will want me? By Allah, I do not have any good position and social standing, or wealth, or physical beauty. No woman will ever pay attention to me." The Messenger of Allah then said, "O Juwayabir, Allah by means of Islam has removed those who were called noble in pre-Islamic time of darkness and ignorance and has honored them with Islam. To those who did not have any social position before Islam, Allah has granted honor as well as to those who were considered low in the time of ignorance. With Islam He has removed the pride of the time of ignorance and people's expressing pride because of tribes and strong genealogy. Today (we say) all people, white and black, those from Quraysh, Arab, non-Arab are all from Adam, and Adam was created by Allah from clay. The most beloved in the sight of Allah, most Majestic, most Glorious, on the Day of Judgment will be those who are most obedient to Him and most pious before Him. O Juwayabir, I do not see any of the Muslims as better than you except because of his being more pious and more obedient to Allah than you."' He (the

Messenger of Allah) said, 'O Juwayabir, you must go to Ziyad ibn Labid; he is an honorable man of the tribe of Bayadah, due to social standards and say to him, "I am the messenger of the Messenger of Allah to you and the Messenger of Allah says, 'You must give your daughter al-Dhalfa' in marriage to Juwayabir.'"' He (the Imam) said that Juwayabir left with the message from the Messenger of Allah, *O Allah, grant compensation to Muhammad and his family worthy of their services to Your cause,* to Ziyad ibn Labid when he was at home with a group from his people. Juwayabir asked permission. He was informed and permission was granted. He entered and offered his greeting of peace, then said, 'I am a messenger from the Messenger of Allah to you for a certain issue: if you like I can convey it to you in private or if you want I can say it in public.' He said, 'Say it in public; it is an honor for me and a privilege.' Juwayabir said, 'The Messenger of Allah says to you, "You must give your daughter al-Dhalfa' in marriage to Juwayabir."' Ziyad then asked him, 'Has the Messenger of Allah sent you with this?' Juwayabir replied, 'Yes, I never want to speak a lie against the Messenger of Allah.' Ziyad said, 'We do not give our young girls in marriage to anyone, unless he is a good match for us of the people of al-Ansar (people of al-Madinah); so you must go back, O Juwayabir, until I meet the Messenger of Allah and inform him of my excuse.' Juwayabir returned back saying, 'By Allah, this is not what the Quran is all about or Prophet Muhammad, *O Allah, grant compensation to Muhammad and his family worthy of their services to Your cause,* has appeared for it.' Al-Dhalfa', daughter of Ziyad in her living-quarter heard what Juwayabir said. She sent someone to her father to ask him to come to her room and he went to her. She asked, 'What were the words that I heard you spoke to Juwayabir?' He said to her, 'He told me that the Messenger of Allah had sent him and he (the Messenger of Allah) said, "You must give your daughter, al-Dhalfa' in marriage to Juwayabir."' She then said, 'By Allah Juwayabir cannot lie against the Messenger of Allah, *O Allah, grant compensation to Muhammad and his family worthy of their services to Your cause,* in his presence. You must now send a messenger to call him back.' Ziyad sent a messenger to call Juwayabir and approached him and said. 'O Juwayabir, you are welcome. You must not be worried and wait until I come back.' Ziyad went to the Messenger of Allah and said, 'I pray to Allah to keep my soul and the souls of my parents in service for your cause, Juwayabir has brought your message to me that says, "The Messenger of Allah commands you to give your daughter al-Dhalfa' in marriage to Juwayabir." I was not so soft speaking to him. We do not give our young women in marriage to anyone except to our match of al-Ansar (people of al-Madinah).' The Messenger of Allah said to him, 'O Ziyad, Juwayabir is a believing person. A believing man is a match of a believing woman. A Muslim is a match of a female Muslim. Therefore you must give her in marriage to him. O Ziyad, you must give her in marriage to him and you must not refuse.' He (the Imam) said that Ziyad returned back to his home, went to his daughter and said to her what he had heard from the Messenger of Allah, *O Allah, grant compensation to Muhammad and his family worthy of their services to Your cause,* She said to him, 'If you disobey the Messenger of Allah, you will become an unbeliever, so you must give in marriage to

Juwayabir.' Ziyad came out, held the hand of Juwayabir, took him before his people, gave her to him in marriage according to the tradition of Allah and the tradition of the Messenger of Allah and took responsibility of *mahr* (dower). He (the Imam) has said, 'They prepared al-Dhalfa' for her wedding, sent for Juwayabir and asked him, 'Do you have any house so we escort her to your house?' he replied, 'No, by Allah, I do not have any house.' He (the Imam) said, 'They prepared her for her wedding, prepared for them a house, furnishings, household necessities, dressed Juwayabir with two dresses, brought al-Dhalfa' to her house, and admitted Juwayabir also there. Juwayabir went in the house after *al-'Isha' Salat* (prayer). He looked at the house, the furnishings, the sweet smelling fragrance, thus, he moved to a corner of the house and began to recite from the Quran, in *Ruku'* (bowing down on one's knees) and in *Sajdah* (prostration) until it was dawn. He heard the call for *Salat* (prayer), so he went out for *Salat* (prayer) as well as his wife. She made wudu and performed *Salat* (prayer) of the morning and she was asked about being touched. She replied, 'He continued reciting the Quran in *Ruku'* and *Sajdah* until the call for *Salat* (prayer) was said then he went out.' In the second night he did just as he had done the night before but they did not tell it to Ziyad. In the third night he again did as he had done before, then her father was informed. He went to the Messenger of Allah and said, 'I pray to Allah to keep my soul and the souls of my parents in service for your cause, O Messenger of Allah, you commanded me to give my daughter in marriage to Juwayabir and by Allah we did not want to do so; but obedience to you made it necessary on us to do so.' The Holy Prophet, *O Allah, grant compensation to Muhammad and his family worthy of their services to Your cause,* asked, 'What is it that you disliked about him?' he replied, 'We prepared a house for him with furnishings, household necessities, sent my daughter to that house, he also was admitted there after *al-'Isha' Salat* (prayer) but he did not speak to her, did not look at her and did not go close to her, instead he stood in one corner of the house, continued reciting al-Quran, in *Ruku'* and *Sajdah* (prostration) until the call for *Salat* (prayer) was said. He went out for *Salat* (prayer); he did it again in the second, and in the third nights. He did not go close to her and did not speak to her until the time of my coming to you. We did not find him to be interested in women. Please look into our problem.' Ziyad went back and the Messenger of Allah sent for Juwayabir and asked him, 'Is it the case that you do not go close to women?' Juwayabir replied, 'A male person I am O Messenger of Allah and I indeed have intense desire and passion for women.' The Messenger of Allah said, to him, 'I am informed otherwise about what you are telling to me. I am told that they prepared for you a house, furnishings, the necessities of a household and she was brought to you in that house, a beautiful young woman and rich with sweet smelling perfumes. You went after performing your *al-'Isha' Salat* (prayer) but did not look at her, did not speak to her, and did not go close to her. What was your wisdom in it?' Juwayabir replied, 'O Messenger of Allah, when I entered the vast house, saw the furnishings, the household necessities, the young beautiful girl, rich in sweet smelling perfumes, remembered my condition in which I lived, my alienation, my poverty, and lowliness, my clothes with the emigrants and the destitute people; I then loved at first to thank Allah for what He had given to me and tried to become closer to Him. I then went to one corner of the house and continued in *Salat* (prayer) reciting al-Quran in *Ruku'* (bowing down on one's knees) and *Sajdah* (prostration) thanking Allah until I heard the call for *Salat* (prayer), then I went out. In the day I decided to fast that day and did so for three days and nights and I thought to do that for what Allah had given to me although my thanks were very little, however, I will make her happy and make them happy tonight, by the will of Allah.' The Messenger of Allah then sent a message to Ziyad who came to the Messenger of Allah and he (the Messenger of Allah) informed him about Juwayabir. They became delighted. Juwayabir kept his promise. Thereafter, the Messenger of Allah went out for an armed expedition, Juwayabir was with him and he became a martyr, may Allah, most High grant him mercy. In the community of al-Ansar (people of al-Madinah) there was no single woman in such a great demand than her (al-Dhalfa') after Juwayabir.'"

H 9457, Ch. 21, h 2

Certain persons of our people have narrated from Ali ibn al-Husayn ibn Salih al-Taymuliy from Ayyub ibn Nuh from Muhammad ibn Sinan from a man who has said the following:

"Abu 'Abd Allah, *'Alayhi al-Salam*, has said that once a man came to the Holy Prophet, *O Allah, grant compensation to Muhammad and his family worthy of their services to Your cause*, and said, 'O Messenger of Allah, I have *Mahirah al-'Arab* (the girl with highest amount of dower among Arabs); will you accept her and she is my daughter?' He (the Messenger of Allah) replied, 'I accept her.' The man said, 'Another (characteristic) O Messenger of Allah.' He (the Messenger of Allah) asked, 'What is that?' He said, 'She has never suffered any hardships at all.' He (the Messenger of Allah) said, 'I do not need her but give her in marriage to Jilbib.' He (the Imam) said, 'Both legs of the man almost failed because of the shock, then her mother came and when she was informed she also felt the same condition as her father. When the girl heard the words and saw the condition her parents were in, she said to them, 'Please be happy for me with what Allah and His Messenger have chosen for me.' He (the Imam) said, 'What the girl said comforted her parents. Her father came to the Holy Prophet, and informed him of her words. The Messenger of Allah, *O Allah, grant compensation to Muhammad and his family worthy of their services to Your cause,* said, 'I have made paradise for her *mahr* (dower).' Safwan has added, 'Her husband (Jilbib) died and her *mahr* reached one hundred thousand dirham.'"

Chapter 22 - Another Chapter about the Previous Topic

H 9458, Ch. 22, h 1

Ali ibn Ibrahim has narrated from his father from al-Hassan ibn Ali ibn Faddal from Tha'labah ibn Maymun from 'Umar ibn abu Bakkar from ibn abu Bakr al-Hadramiy who has said the following:

"Abu 'Abd Allah, *'Alayhi al-Salam*, has said that the Messenger of Allah, *O Allah, grant compensation to Muhammad and his family worthy of their services to Your cause*, arranged a marriage between Miqdad ibn al-Aswad and Duba'ah daughter of al-Zubayr ibn 'Abd al-Muttalib. He (the Messenger of Allah) did so only to explain the rules of marriage so that people follow the foot-steps of the Messenger of Allah, *O Allah, grant compensation to Muhammad and his family worthy of their services to Your cause,* and take notice that the most excellent in the sight of Allah are the most pious people.'"

H 9459, Ch. 22, h 2
A number of our people have narrated from Ahmad ibn Muhammad ibn 'Isa from Ali ibn al-Hakam from Hisham ibn Salim from a man who has said the following:

"Abu 'Abd Allah, *'Alayhi al-Salam,* has said that the Messenger of Allah, *O Allah, grant compensation to Muhammad and his family worthy of their services to Your cause,* arranged a marriage between Miqdad ibn al-Aswad and Duba'ah daughter of al-Zubayr ibn 'Abd al-Muttalib.' He (the Imam) then said, 'He (the Messenger of Allah) arranged this marriage for Miqdad only to explain the rules of marriage so that people follow the foot-steps of the Messenger of Allah, *O Allah, grant compensation to Muhammad and his family worthy of their services to Your cause,* and take notice that the most excellent in the sight of Allah are the most pious people. Al-Zubayr was brother of 'Abd Allah and abu Talib from both father and mother's side.'"

H 9460, Ch. 22, h 3
Muhammad ibn Yahya has narrated from Ahmad ibn Muhammad and Ali ibn Ibrahim has narrated from his father from all from al-Hassan ibn Ali from ibn Faddal from 'Abd Allah ibn Bukayr from Zurarah ibn 'A'yan who has said the following:

"Abu Ja'far, *'Alayhi al-Salam,* has said, 'Once a man from Basrah, a Shaybaniy man called 'Abd al-Malik ibn Harmalah visited Ali ibn al-Husayn, *'Alayhi al-Salam.* Ali ibn al-Husayn, *'Alayhi al-Salam,* asked, 'Do you have a sister? He replied, 'Yes, I have a sister.' He (the Imam) then asked, 'Will you give her in marriage to me?' He replied, 'Yes, I agree.' The man left and a man of the companions of Ali ibn Al-Husayn, *'Alayhi al-Salam,* followed him to his house, asked about him and it was said that he is so and so, the master of his tribe. He returned to Ali ibn al-Husayn, *'Alayhi al-Salam,* and said, 'Your brother in-law to be appears to be the master of his tribe.' Ali ibn al-Husayn, *'Alayhi al-Salam,* said, 'I can explain to you, O so and so about what I see and what I hear. Have you not taken notice that Allah, most Majestic, most Glorious, through Islam has removed the lowliness and has completed the shortcomings, has honored with it those blamed before Islam, thus there is no blame on a Muslim; the only blame is the blame of the time of ignorance.'"

H 9461, Ch. 22, h 4
A number of our people have narrated from Ahmad ibn Muhammad from ibn Khalid from his father from 'Abd al-Rahman ibn Muhammad from Yazid ibn Hatim who has said the following:

"'Abd al-Malik ibn Marwan had a spy in al-Madinah who reported to him from time to time about things that happened there. Ali ibn al-Husayn, *'Alayhi al-Salam,* set free one of his slave-girls and then married with her. The spy reported this to 'Abd al-Malik who wrote to Ali ibn al-Husayn, *'Alayhi al-Salam,* in a letter that said, 'Thereafter, it has been reported to me that you have married one of your slave-girls, when you know very well that among Quraysh there are your match for whose marital relation; one can take pride and privilege and give birth to noble offspring. You have neglected yourself as well as your offspring, and al-Salam (greeting of peace).' Ali ibn al-Husayn, *'Alayhi al-Salam*, wrote to him in answer a letter that said, 'Thereafter, I received your letter in which you have used harsh words against me because of my marriage to my slave-girl and you think that among Quraysh there are women for whose marital relation one can assume pride and privilege because of their giving birth to noble children. (You must take notice) that no one can ever have a glorious position higher than that of the Messenger of Allah, *O Allah, grant compensation to Muhammad and his family worthy of their services to Your cause*, or any more grace. She was in my possession and went out of my possession when Allah, most Majestic, most Glorious, wanted me to set her free for the sake of good rewards from Him. I then returned her according to the Sunnah. Whoever is clean in the religion of Allah, nothing is able to disturb him in any of his affairs. Allah through Islam has removed lowliness, has completed the shortcomings and has taken away the blame. So there is no blame on a Muslim man and the only blame is the blame of ignorance.' When he read the letter he threw it to his son Sulayman who read it and said, 'O 'Amir al-Mu'minin, Ali ibn al-Husayn, *'Alayhi al-Salam*, has strengthened his pride over you.' 'Abd al-Malik said, 'My son do not say that; it is the tongues of banu Hashim that can tear down rocks and scoop the sea. My son, Ali ibn al-Husayn, *'Alayhi al-Salam*, rises where people go down.'"

H 9462 (a), Ch. 22, h 5

Al-Husayn ibn al-Hassan al-Hashimiy has narrated from Ibrahim ibn Ishaq al-Ahmar and Ali ibn Muhammad ibn Bandar from al-Sayyariy from certain person of Baghdad from Ali Bilal, who has said the following:

"Hisham ibn al-Hakam once met a man of Khawarij (a certain sect) who said, 'O Hisham, what do you say if al-'Ajam (non-Arab) marries from Arab?' Hisham said, 'Yes, they can marry.' He asked, 'Can Arabs marry from Quraysh?' He replied, 'Yes, they can marry.' He then asked, 'Can Quraysh marry from banu Hashim?' He replied, 'Yes, they can marry.' He then asked, 'From whom have you taken this?' He replied, 'I have taken this from Ja'far ibn Muhammad, *'Alayhi al-Salam*. I heard him (the Imam) saying, "How can it be (accepted) that your lives match as equals but not your reproductive organs?"' He (the narrator) has said that the Kharijiy man left and went to abu 'Abd Allah, *'Alayhi al-Salam*, and said, 'I met Hisham and asked him so and so questions and he answered me so and so, saying that he has heard it from you.' He (the Imam) said, 'Yes, I have said so.' He then said, 'Here I have come with a marriage proposal.' Abu 'Abd Allah, *'Alayhi al-Salam*, said, 'You are a match of members of your community in matters of life and social issues. Allah, most Majestic, most Glorious, however, has protected us from charity which is the dirt of the hands of people and we dislike to share what preference Allah has given to us with those to whom Allah has not given such preference as He has set it for us.' The Kharijiy man left saying, 'By Allah, I have never seen any man like him. He repulsed me with a disgracing response and without contradicting his companion.'"

H 9462 (b), Ch. 22, h 6
Ali ibn Ibrahim has narrated from his father from ibn Faddal from Tha'labah ibn Maymun from those who narrated to him who has said the following:
"Abu 'Abd Allah, *'Alayhi al-Salam*, has said that Ali ibn al-Husayn, *'Alayhi al-Salam*, married a slave-girl who belonged to al-Hassan ibn Ali *'Alayhi al-Salam*, and 'Abd al-Malik ibn Marwan was informed about it. He wrote a letter to him (the Imam) that said, 'I have heard that you have become the husband of a slave-girl!' Ali ibn al-Husayn wrote back to him saying, 'With Islam Allah has removed the lowliness and has completed the shortcomings, exonerated of the blame and there is no blame on a Muslim. Blame certainly is the blame of ignorance. The Messenger of Allah, *O Allah, grant compensation to Muhammad and his family worthy of their services to Your cause,* arranged marriage for his male slave and married with his slave-girl.' When the letter reached 'Abd al-Malik he asked those near him, 'Tell me who is such a man that when something that makes people low and humiliating, comes to him it increases for him nothing other than honor?' They replied, 'That is 'Amir al-Mu'minin ('Abd al-Malik).' He ('Abd al-Malik) said, 'No, by Allah that is not it.' They then said, 'We do not know anyone to be as such except 'Amir al-Mu'minin.' He said, 'No, by Allah, he is not 'Amir al-Mu'minin but he is Ali ibn al-Husayn, *'Alayhi al-Salam*.'"

Chapter 23 - Marriage of 'Umm Kulthum

H 9463, Ch. 23, h 1
Ali ibn Ibrahim has narrated from his father from ibn abu 'Umayr from Hisham ibn Salim and Hammad from Zurarah who has said the following:
"Abu 'Abd Allah, *'Alayhi al-Salam*, about the marriage of 'Umm Kulthum has said, 'It was a rape we suffered.'"

H 9464, Ch. 23, h 2
Muhammad ibn abu 'Umayr has narrated from Hisham ibn Salim who has said the following:
"Abu 'Abd Allah, *'Alayhi al-Salam*, has said, 'When he proposed marriage with 'Umm Kulthum, 'Amir al-Mu'minin, *'Alayhi al-Salam*, said, 'She is yet just a child.' He (the Imam) has said that he saw al-'Abbas and asked, 'What is wrong with me, is there something wrong with me?' He al-'Abbas asked, 'What is the matter?' He replied saying, 'I proposed marriage before the son of your brother for his daughter but he rejected my proposal. I swear by Allah, I will shut down Zamzam, leave no honor for you without being destroyed; I will prove him guilty of theft through two witnesses and cut off his right hand.' Al-'Abbas went to him (the Imam) and informed him of what he had said and asked him (the Imam) to authorize him to settle the matter and he (the Imam) agreed.'"

Chapter 24 - Another Chapter

H 9465, Ch. 24, h 1
A number of our people have narrated from Sahl ibn Ziyad from al-Husayn ibn Bashshar al-Wasitiy who has said the following:

"I once wrote to abu Ja'far, *'Alayhi al-Salam*, and asked him about marriage. He (the Imam) wrote back to me the answer that said, 'If one proposes marriage and if you are happy with that person's religion and trust, then accept his proposal. If you do not do so there will be mischief in the land and a great destruction.'"

H 9466, Ch. 24, h 2

Sahl ibn Ziyad Ahmad ibn Muhammad from Muhammad ibn Yahya has narrated from Ahmad ibn Muhammad from all from Ali ibn Mahziyar from who has said the following:

"Ali ibn Asbat once wrote to abu Ja'far, *'Alayhi al-Salam*, about the issue of his daughters and that he cannot find anyone as equal match for them. He (the Imam), *'Alayhi al-Salam*, wrote to him, 'I understood what you have written about the issue of your daughters that you do not find anyone as their equal match, you must not see to it, may Allah grant you kindness, because the Messenger of Allah, *O Allah, grant compensation to Muhammad and his family worthy of their services to Your cause,* has said, "If one proposes marriage and you are happy with his health and religion, then accept his proposal." If you do not do so mischief and great destruction can take place in the land.'"

H 9467, Ch. 24, h 3

A number of our people have narrated from Ahmad ibn abu 'Abd Allah from Ibrahim ibn Muhammad al-Hamadaniy who has said the following:

"I once wrote to abu Ja'far, *'Alayhi al-Salam*, about marriage then his letter came to me with his handwriting that said, 'The Messenger of Allah, *O Allah, grant compensation to Muhammad and his family worthy of their services to Your cause,* has said, "If one proposes marriage and you are happy with his health and religion then accept his proposal. If you do not do so mischief and great destruction may take place in the land.'"

Chapter 25 - Proper Match for Marriage

H 9468, Ch. 25, h 1

A number of our people have narrated from Ahmad ibn Muhammad from Ali ibn al-Hakam from Aban from a man who has said the following:

"Abu 'Abd Allah, *'Alayhi al-Salam*, has said, 'Proper match is one who is chaste and affluent.'"

Chapter 26 - The Detestability of Marriage with a Drunkard

H 9469, Ch. 26, h 1

A number of our people have narrated from Ahmad ibn Muhammad from in a marfu' manner has said the following:

"Abu 'Abd Allah, *'Alayhi al-Salam*, has said, 'If one gives his daughter in marriage to a man who drinks wine, he has cut off the relation that relatives are commanded to maintain.'"

H 9470, Ch. 26, h 2

Ali ibn Ibrahim has narrated from his father from ibn abu 'Umayr from certain persons of his people who has said the following:

"Abu 'Abd Allah, *'Alayhi al-Salam*, has said that the Messenger of Allah, *O Allah, grant compensation to Muhammad and his family worthy of their services to Your cause*, has said, 'If one who drinks wine proposes for marriage, it must not be accepted.'"

H 9471, Ch. 26, h 3
Muhammad ibn Yahya has narrated from Ahmad ibn Muhammad from al-Hassan ibn Mahbub from Khalid ibn Jarir from abu al-Rabi' who has said the following:
"Abu 'Abd Allah, *'Alayhi al-Salam*, has said that the Messenger of Allah, *O Allah, grant compensation to Muhammad and his family worthy of their services to Your cause*, has said, 'If one who after knowing that Allah has, through my words, made wine unlawful, drinks wine, his proposal for marriage must not be accepted.'"

Chapter 27 - Marriage of Fanatic (Enemy of 'A'immah) and Skeptics

H 9472, Ch. 27, h 1
A number of our people have narrated from Sahl ibn Ziyad Ahmad ibn Muhammad from ibn abu Nasr from 'Abd al-Karim ibn '(Belief in the Divine Authority of 'A'immah) from abu Basir who has said the following:
"Abu 'Abd Allah, *'Alayhi al-Salam*, has said, 'You can marry a skeptic but do not give in marriage to a skeptic because a woman follows the manners of her husband, and he compels her into his religion.'"

H 9473, Ch. 27, h 2
Abu Ali al-Ash'ariy has narrated from Muhammad ibn 'Abd al-Jabbar from Safwan ibn Yahya from 'Abd Allah ibn Muskan from Yahya al-Halabiy from 'Abd al-Hamid al-Ta'iy from Zurarah ibn 'A'yan who has said the following:
"This is concerning my question before abu 'Abd Allah, *'Alayhi al-Salam*, if I can marry a Murji'ah or Harawriyah (two sects). He (the Imam) said, 'No, but you must marry simple hearted woman.' I then said, 'By Allah, it is only a believer or unbeliever.' Abu 'Abd Allah, *'Alayhi al-Salam*, said, 'What is the position of Thanawiy (a sect) people about Allah, most Majestic, most Glorious? The words of Allah, most Majestic, most Glorious, are truer than what you say ". . . except the weak ones of man, woman and children who cannot plan or find guidance to the right path. . . '" (4:101)

H 9474, Ch. 27, h 3
Muhammad ibn Yahya has narrated from Ahmad ibn Muhammad from ibn Mahbub from Jamil ibn Salih from Fudayl ibn Yasar who has said the following:
"Abu 'Abd Allah, *'Alayhi al-Salam*, has said, 'A believer must not marry one who is hostile to 'A'immah, *'Alayhim al-Salam*, and his hostility is well known.'"

H 9475, Ch. 27, h 4
Muhammad ibn 'Isma'il has narrated from al-Fadl ibn Shadhan from ibn abu 'Umayr from Rib'iy from Fudayl ibn Yasar who has said the following:

"This is concerning my question before abu 'Abd Allah, *'Alayhi al-Salam*, if I can marry al-Nasibah (one hostile to 'A'immah). He (the Imam) said, 'No, it is not an honor.' I then said, 'I pray to Allah to keep my soul in service for your cause, I just say it but even if she comes to me with a whole house full of dirham I will not do so.'"

H 9476, Ch. 27, h 5

Muhammad ibn Yahya has narrated from Ahmad ibn Muhammad from Ali ibn al-Hakam from Musa ibn Bakr from Zurarah ibn 'A'yan who has said the following:

"Abu 'Abd Allah, *'Alayhi al-Salam*, has said, 'You can marry a skeptic but do not give in marriage to a skeptic; women follow their husband and he compels her into his religion.'"

H 9477, Ch. 27, h 6

Ahmad ibn Muhammad has narrated from ibn Faddal from Ali ibn Ya'qub from Marwan ibn Muslim from al-Husayn ibn Musa al-Hannat from Fudayl ibn Yasar who has said the following:

"This is concerning my question before abu 'Abd Allah, *'Alayhi al-Salam*, about the case of the sister of my wife who is of the same belief as we are; but in Basra very few people believe as we do; if we can give her in marriage to those who do not believe as we do. He (the Imam) said, 'No, it is not a bounty or honor. Allah, most Majestic, most Glorious, says, "You must not return them to unbelievers; they (women) are not lawful for them (unbelievers) and they are not lawful for them (women)." (6:10)'"

H 9478, Ch. 27, h 7

Ali ibn Ibrahim has narrated from his father from ibn abu 'Umayr from Jamil ibn Darraj from Zurarah who has said the following:

"I once said to abu Ja'far, *'Alayhi al-Salam*, 'I am afraid that my getting married to one who does not believe as I do is not lawful. He (the Imam) said, 'Your marriage with a simple-minded woman is not unlawful.' I then asked, 'Who is a simple-minded one? He (the Imam) said, 'They are those who are weak and who are not hostile (to 'A'immah) and do not know what you believe in.'"

H 9479, Ch. 27, h 8

Muhammad ibn Yahya has narrated from Ahmad ibn Muhammad from 'Abd al-Rahman ibn abu Najran from 'Abd Allah ibn Sinan who has said the following:

"This is concerning my question before abu 'Abd Allah, *'Alayhi al-Salam*, about the case of al-Nasib (one hostile to 'A'immah) who is well known for his hostility; if we can give a believing woman in marriage to him. He (the guardian of the believing woman) is capable to disprove his (Nasib's) belief but he (Nasib) is not able to prove himself right. He (the Imam) said, 'A believing man must not marry a Nasibah and a believing woman must not be given in marriage to him and a believing woman must not marry a man of weak understanding.'"

H 9480, Ch. 27, h 9

Ahmad ibn Muhammad from has narrated from al-Hassan ibn Ali ibn Faddal from Yunus ibn Ya'qub from Humran ibn 'A'yan who has said the following:

"Someone in my family wanted to get married but could not find a suitable Muslimah and I mentioned it to abu 'Abd Allah, *'Alayhi al-Salam*, who said, 'Why does he not find simple-minded women who do not know anything.'"

H 9481, Ch. 27, h 10

Al-Husayn from Muhammad has narrated from Mu'alla' ibn Muhammad from al-Hassan ibn Ali al-Washsha' from Jamil from Zurarah who has said the following:

"I once said to abu 'Abd Allah, *'Alayhi al-Salam*, 'I pray to Allah to keep you well, I am afraid it is not lawful for me to get married with those who do not believe in the Divine Authority of 'A'immah. He (the Imam) said, 'Why do you not marry with one of the simple minded women?' He (the Imam) said, 'They are who are weak, who are not hostile to 'A'immah and do not know what you believe in.'"

H 9482, Ch. 27, h 11

Humayd ibn Ziyad has narrated from al-Hassan ibn Muhammad from more than one person from Aban ibn 'Uthman from Fudayl ibn Yasar who has said the following:

"This is concerning my question before abu 'Abd Allah, *'Alayhi al-Salam*, about giving in marriage to one hostile to 'A'immah. He (the Imam) said, 'No, by Allah, it is not lawful.' I (Fudayl) then asked him (the Imam) again saying, 'I pray to Allah to keep my soul in service for your cause, what do you say about their marriage?' He (the Imam) asked, 'Is the woman knowledgeable?' I replied, 'Yes, she is knowledgeable.' He (the Imam) said, 'Knowledgeable lives only with knowledgeable.'"

H 9483, Ch. 27, h 12

Muhammad ibn Yahya has narrated from Ahmad ibn Muhammad from ibn Faddal from ibn Bukayr from Zurarah who has said the following:

"This is concerning my question before abu Ja'far, *'Alayhi al-Salam*, about the marriage of people. 'I, as you can see, of this age have not married yet.' He (the Imam) asked, 'What holds you back from getting married?' I replied, 'The only thing that holds me back is that I am afraid marrying them is not lawful and I wish to see what you command me to do.' He (the Imam) said, 'What you want to do and you are young, can you bear patience without it?' I then asked, 'Can I find slave-girls?' He (the Imam) said, 'That is fine but how you make them lawful?' I said, 'Slaves are not like free people and if a slave-girl causes me to doubt about an issue, I can sell her or stay away from her.' He (the Imam) asked, 'Tell me on what basis you make her lawful.' He (the narrator) has said, I did not have any answer and I said, 'I pray to Allah to keep my soul in service for your cause, instruct me about marriage.' He (the Imam) said, 'I do not mind if you get married.' I then said, 'Consider your words, "I do not mind if you get married" which may have two meanings: "I do not mind if you sinned without a command from me", so I asked what is your command? Do you command me to get married?' He (the Imam) said, 'The Messenger of Allah, *O Allah, grant compensation to Muhammad and his family worthy of their services to Your cause*, married, there was the woman of Nuh and the woman of Lot as Allah, most Majestic, most Glorious, has stated it, "Allah has given the example of the unbelievers, the woman of Nuh and the woman of Lot who were married to two virtuous ones of our servants but they committed treachery.'" (66:11) I then said, 'I am not of the position of the Messenger of Allah, *O Allah, grant compensation to Muhammad and his family worthy of their services to Your cause.* She was in his control and she acknowledged his commands, expressed her belief in his religion.' 'O yes, by Allah, in the words of Allah, most Majestic, most Glorious, "the two committed treachery" do not mean anything else other than . . . The Messenger of Allah married so and so.' I then asked, 'I pray to Allah to keep you well, do you command me to go and marry by your command?' He (the Imam) said, 'If you want to marry, then marry the simple-minded ones.' I asked, 'Who are simple minded ones?' He (the Imam) said, 'They are those who maintain privacy and chastity.' I then asked, 'What about those who are in the religion of Salim abu Hafs?' He (the Imam) said, 'No, it is not from them.' I then asked about those who are in the religion of Rabi'a al-Ra'iy?' He (the Imam) said, 'No, but she is of the young ones who are not hostile to 'A'immah and do not know what you believe in.'"

H 9484, Ch. 27, h 13
Ahmad ibn Muhammad has narrated from ibn Faddal from ibn Bukayr from Zurarah who has said the following:

"Abu Ja'far, *'Alayhi al-Salam*, had a wife from the people of Thaqif and from her he (the Imam) had a son called Ibrahim. A slave-girl from Thaqif came to her and asked, 'Who is your husband?' She replied, 'He is Muhammad ibn Ali.' She then said, 'That is why in al-Kufah there are people who insult the ancestors and say...' He (the narrator) has said that he (the Imam) divorced and allowed her to go. He (the narrator) has said that I saw him afterward. The effect of it was clear on him and he had lost a little weight. I said that the effect of her separation is apparent on you. He (the Imam) said, 'I can see it.' I said, 'Yes, it is so.'"

H 9485, Ch. 27, h 14
Ahmad ibn Muhammad has narrated from ibn Faddal from ibn Bukayr from Zurarah who has said the following:

"Abu Ja'far, *'Alayhi al-Salam*, has said, 'Once a man came to Ali ibn al-Husayn, *'Alayhi al-Salam*, and said, "Your wife from al-Shayban people is of Kharijiy sect who vilify Ali, *'Alayhi al-Salam*. If you like I can manage for you to hear what she says." He (the Imam) said, 'Yes, I agree.' He (man) said, 'Tomorrow as you come out of your home as you normally do, wait on the side of the house.' Next day he (the Imam) waited on the side of the house and the man came. He spoke to her and it (vilification) became clear from her. He (the Imam) divorced her although he liked her quite well.'"

H 9486, Ch. 27, h 15
Ali ibn Ibrahim has narrated from his father from Muhammad ibn abu 'Umayr from 'Abd Allah ibn Sinan who has said the following:

"My father once asked abu 'Abd Allah, *'Alayhi al-Salam*, about marriage with the Jews and Christians when I was listening. He (the Imam) said, 'Marriage with them in my view is better than marriage with al-Nasibah (people hostile to 'A'immah) and I do not like a Muslim man's marriage with a Jewish woman or a Christian woman because of fear that she can convert his children to Judaism or Christianity.'"

H 9487, Ch. 27, h 16
Ali ibn Ibrahim has narrated from his father from ibn abu 'Umayr from Ali ibn abu Hamzah from abu Basir who has said the following:

"Abu 'Abd Allah, *'Alayhi al-Salam*, has said, 'Marriage with a Jewish or Christian women is preferable' - or He (the Imam) said that it is better- 'than marriage with al-Nasibah (people hostile to 'A'immah).'"

H 9488, Ch. 27, h 17
Ali ibn Ibrahim has narrated from his father from ibn abu 'Umayr from Hammad from al-Halabiy who has said the following:

"Once, a people from Khurasan, from Transoxiana came to abu 'Abd Allah, *'Alayhi al-Salam*. He (the Imam) asked them, 'Do you shake hands with the people of your country and marry them? If you shake hands with them a ring of the rings of Islam is cut and if you marry them the privacy between you and Allah is violated.'"

Chapter 28 - Marriage with Kurds and Sudan

H 9489, Ch. 28, h 1
Ali has narrated from Harun ibn Muslim from Mas'adah ibn Ziyad who has said the following:

"Abu 'Abd Allah, *'Alayhi al-Salam*, has said that 'Amir al-Mu'minin has said, 'You must remain on your guard against marriage with people of al-Zanj because it is a distorted creature.'"

H 9490, Ch. 28, h 2
Ali ibn Ibrahim has narrated from 'Isma'il ibn Muhammad al-Makkiy from Ali ibn al-Husayn from 'Amr ibn 'Uthman from al-Husayn ibn Khalid from those whom he has mentioned from abu Rabi' al-Shamiy who has said the following:

"Abu 'Abd Allah, *'Alayhi al-Salam*, once said to me, 'You must not buy anyone from al-Sudan, but if you must buy, then buy from al-Nawbah; they are of those about whom Allah, most Majestic, most Glorious, has said, "Of those who have said, 'We are helpers', We took a covenant from them; then they forgot the share of what they were reminded." (5:14) However, they will remember that share and they, a group of them, will come out with the rise of al-Qa'im with divine authority from us. You must not marry anyone of the Kurds; they are a species of Jinn from which the cover is removed.'"

H 9491, Ch. 28, h 3
A number of our people have narrated from Sahl ibn Ziyad from Musa ibn Ja'far from 'Amr ibn Sa'id from Muhammad al-Hashimiy from Ahmad ibn Yusuf from Ali ibn Dawud al-Haddad who has said the following:

"Abu 'Abd Allah, *'Alayhi al-Salam*, has said, 'You must not marry, al-Zanj and al-Khazar; they have such wombs that indicate disloyalty.' He (the Imam) said, 'Of Indians, al-Sind and al-Qand - meaning al-Qandahar - a hybrid does not exist among them.'"

Chapter 29 - Marriage of one Born out of Wedlock

H 9492, Ch. 29, h 1

Ali ibn Ibrahim has narrated from his father from Hammad ibn 'Isa from Hur ibn 'Abd Allah from Muhammad ibn Muslim who has said the following:

"This is concerning my question before abu Ja'far, *'Alayhi al-Salam*, if I can marry the filthy (prostitute). He (the Imam) said, 'No, you cannot do so.'"

H 9493, Ch. 29, h 2

Ali ibn Ibrahim has narrated from his father from Muhammad ibn abu 'Umayr from Jamil ibn Darraj from Muhammad ibn Muslim who has said the following:

"One of the two Imam, (abu Ja'far or abu 'Abd Allah), *'Alayhim al-Salam*, about the case of a man who buys a slave-girl or marries her without proper wedlock and keeps her for his own self, he (the Imam) has said, 'If he is not afraid of the stigma for his children, it is not unlawful.'"

H 9494, Ch. 29, h 3

Muhammad ibn Yahya has narrated from Ahmad ibn Muhammad Ahmad ibn Muhammad from certain persons of our people from Sahl ibn Ziyad from al-Hassan ibn Mahbub from 'Abd Allah ibn Sinan who has said the following:

"This is concerning my question before abu 'Abd Allah, *'Alayhi al-Salam*, about marriage with one born out of wedlock. He (the Imam) said, 'Yes, but her children are not wanted.'"

H 9495, Ch. 29, h 4

Muhammad ibn Yahya has narrated from Ahmad ibn Muhammad from Ali ibn al-Hakam from al-'Ala' ibn Razin from Muhammad ibn Muslim who has said the following:

"I once asked abu Ja'far, *'Alayhi al-Salam*, about the case of a man if he could marry the filthy (prostitute). He (the Imam) said, 'No, he cannot do so.' He (the Imam) said, 'If he has a slave-girl with whom he has gone to bed but she must not be taken as the mother of his children.'" (He must use contraceptives)

H 9496, Ch. 29, h 5

Ali ibn Ibrahim has narrated from his father from Muhammad ibn abu 'Umayr from Hammad from al-Halabiy who has said the following:

"Once abu 'Abd Allah, *'Alayhi al-Salam*, was asked about the case of a man who has a servant born out of wedlock; if he can go to bed with her. He (the Imam) said, 'No, if he stays clean of that, it is more likeable to me.'"

Chapter 30 - Detestability of Marriage with Dimwitted and Insane People

H 9497, Ch. 30, h 1

Ali ibn Ibrahim has narrated from his father from al-Nawfaliy from al-Sakuniy who has said the following:

"Abu 'Abd Allah, *'Alayhi al-Salam*, has said that 'Amir al-Mu'minin has said, 'Beware of marriage with dimwitted ones, living with her is a tragedy and her children are a loss.'"

H 9498, Ch. 30, h 2

A number of our people have narrated from Ahmad ibn abu 'Abd Allah from his father from those who narrated to him who has said the following:

"Abu 'Abd Allah, *'Alayhi al-Salam*, has said, 'You can give in marriage to a dimwitted man but do not marry a dimwitted woman; a dimwitted man can have children (healthy ones) but a dimwitted woman cannot.'"

H 9499, Ch. 30, h 3

Muhammad ibn Yahya has narrated from Ahmad ibn Muhammad from ibn Mahbub abu Ayyub al-Khazzaz from Muhammad ibn Muslim who has said the following:

"Certain persons of our people once asked abu Ja'far, *'Alayhi al-Salam*, about the case of a Muslim man who likes a beautiful woman; if he can marry her and she is insane. He (the Imam) said, 'No, however, if he has an insane slave-girl he can go to bed with her but must not seek her children (he must use contraceptives).'"

Chapter 31 - Fornicator Man and Women

H 9500, Ch. 31, h 1

A number of our people have narrated from Sahl ibn Ziyad from Ahmad ibn Muhammad from ibn abu Nasr from Dawud ibn Sarhan from Zurarah who has said the following:

"Once I asked abu 'Abd Allah, *'Alayhi al-Salam*, about the meaning of the words of Allah, most Majestic, most Glorious. 'A prostitute man cannot marry but a prostitute woman or a pagan.' (24:4) He (the Imam) said, 'They were well-known prostitute females, and males. Today people who are convicted for fornication and punished (by the qualified court) are of the same status. No one must marry them unless it is known that they have repented.'"

H 9501, Ch. 31, h 2

Muhammad ibn Yahya has narrated from Ahmad ibn Muhammad from Muhammad ibn 'Isma'il from Muhammad ibn al-Fudayl from abu al-Sabbah al-Kinaniy who has said the following:

"This is concerning my question before abu 'Abd Allah, *'Alayhi al-Salam*, about the word of Allah, most Majestic, most Glorious, 'A prostitute man cannot marry but a prostitute woman or a pagan.' (24:4) He (the Imam) said, 'They were well-known prostitute females and males. Today people who are convicted for fornication and punished (by the qualified court) are of the same status. No one must marry them unless it is known that they have repented.'"

H 9502, Ch. 31, h 3

Al-Husayn from Muhammad has narrated from Mu'alla' ibn Muhammad al-Hassan ibn Ali from Aban ibn 'Uthman from Muhammad ibn Muslim who has said the following:

"Abu Ja'far, *'Alayhi al-Salam*, about the word of Allah, most Majestic, most Glorious, 'A prostitute man cannot marry but a prostitute woman or a pagan,' (24:4) has said, 'During the time of the Messenger of Allah, *O Allah, grant compensation to Muhammad and his family worthy of their services to Your cause*, there were well-known prostitutes female and male. Allah, most Majestic, most Glorious, has prohibited forming marriage contract with such men and women. Today people who become known as such or are convicted for fornication and punished (by the qualified court) are of the same status. No one must marry them unless it is known that they have repented.'"

H 9503, Ch. 31, h 4
Muhammad ibn Yahya has narrated from Ahmad ibn Muhammad from Ali ibn al-Hakam from Mu'awiyah ibn Wahab who has said the following:

"This is concerning my question before abu 'Abd Allah, *'Alayhi al-Salam*, about the case of a man who marries a woman and afterwards finds out that she had committed fornication. He (the Imam) said, 'If the husband wants he can take back from her guardian the *mahr* that he has paid, but she deserves the *mahr* because of which her marriage was made lawful, and if he wants he can separate from her (by means of divorce).'"

H 9504, Ch. 31, h 5
Muhammad ibn Yahya has narrated from Ahmad ibn Muhammad from ibn Faddal from ibn Bukayr from Zurarah ibn 'A'yan who has said the following:

"I once heard abu Ja'far, *'Alayhi al-Salam*, saying, 'There is no goodness in one who is born out of wedlock, not in his skin, his hair, his flesh, his blood and not in anything of him, the Ark (of Noah) failed to carry him even though dogs and pigs had embarked therein.'"

H 9505, Ch. 31, h 6
Humayd ibn Ziyad has narrated from al-Hassan ibn Muhammad ibn Sama'ah from Ahmad ibn al-Hassan al-Mithamiy from Aban from Hakam ibn Hakim who has said the following:

"About the words of Allah, most Majestic, most Glorious, 'A prostitute man cannot marry but a prostitute woman or a pagan,' (24:4) abu 'Abd Allah, *'Alayhi al-Salam*, has said, 'This is about well-known, and openly committing prostitution.' He (the Imam) then said, 'If one after committing fornication repents he can marry as he wants.'"

Chapter 32 - Marriage after Conjugal Relations Out of Wedlock

H 9506, Ch. 32, h 1
Muhammad ibn Yahya has narrated from Ahmad ibn Muhammad from Ahmad ibn al-Hassan from 'Amr ibn Sa'id from Musaddiq ibn Sadaqah from 'Ammar ibn Musa who has said the following:

"This is concerning my question before abu 'Abd Allah, *'Alayhi al-Salam*, about the case of a man who has committed fornication with a woman; if he can marry her. He (the Imam) said, 'If he finds her to have gained wisdom then he can do so, otherwise, he can try her by offering unlawful choices; if she follows then it is unlawful for him to marry; but if she refuses he then can marry her.'"

H 9507, Ch. 32, h 2
Ali ibn Ibrahim has narrated from his father from Muhammad ibn abu 'Umayr from Hammad ibn 'Uthman from 'Ubayd Allah ibn Ali al-Halabiy who has said the following:

"Abu 'Abd Allah, *'Alayhi al-Salam*, has said, 'If a man commits indecent act (goes to bed with her out of wedlock) with a woman and then decides to marry her, it is a case of indecency in the beginning and then marriage, like a palm tree that one uses its fruit in an unlawful manner then buys the whole tree in a lawful manner and it thereafter is all lawful.'"

H 9508, Ch. 32, h 3
Muhammad ibn Yahya has narrated from Ahmad ibn Muhammad from Ali ibn al-Hakam from Ali ibn abu Hamzah from abu Basir who has said the following:
"This is concerning my question before abu 'Abd Allah, *'Alayhi al-Salam*, about the case of a man who commits an indecent act (goes to bed with her out of wedlock), then decides to marry her. He (the Imam) said, 'It is lawful, although in the beginning, it is indecency, and at the end is marriage; in the beginning, (it is) unlawful and in the end becomes lawful.'"

H 9509, Ch. 32, h 4
Muhammad ibn Yahya has narrated from certain persons of our people from 'Uthman ibn 'Isa from Ishaq ibn Jarir who has said the following:
"This is concerning my question before abu 'Abd Allah, *'Alayhi al-Salam*, about the case of a man who commits an indecent act (goes to bed with her out of wedlock) with a woman and then decides to marry her; if it is lawful for him. He (the Imam) said, 'Yes, it is lawful if he waits until her waiting period is complete to cleans her womb from indecent activities; then he can marry her and it is only when he ascertains that she has repented.'"

Chapter 33 - Marriage with a Taxpayer Female

H 9510, Ch. 33, h 1
Muhammad ibn Yahya has narrated from Ahmad ibn Muhammad from al-Hassan ibn Mahbub from Mu'awiyah ibn Wahab and others who has said the following:
"About the case of a man who marries a Jewish or a Christian woman, abu 'Abd Allah, *'Alayhi al-Salam*, has said, 'What has he to do with a Jewish or Christian woman if he can find a Muslim woman?' I (the narrator) asked, 'What happens if he loves her?' He (the Imam) said, 'If he marries, he must stop her from drinking wine and eating pork and you must take notice that he will have deficiency in his religion.'"

H 9511, Ch. 33, h 2
Al-Husayn from Muhammad has narrated from Mu'alla' ibn Muhammad from al-Hassan ibn Ali al-Washsha' from Aban ibn 'Uthman from Zurarah ibn 'A'yan who has said the following:
"I once asked abu Ja'far, *'Alayhi al-Salam*, about marriage with a Jewish or Christian woman. He (the Imam) said, 'It is not proper for a Muslim to marry a Jewish or Christian woman; only with the simple-minded ones of them marriage is lawful.'"

H 9512, Ch. 33, h 3
A number of our people have narrated from Sahl ibn Ziyad from al-Hassan ibn Mahbub from al-'Ala' ibn Razin from Muhammad ibn Muslim who has said the following:
"I once asked abu Ja'far, *'Alayhi al-Salam*, if it is lawful to marry a Zoroastrian woman. He (the Imam) said, 'No, however, she can be his slave-girl.'"

H 9513, Ch. 33, h 4

Muhammad ibn Yahya has narrated from Ahmad ibn Muhammad from Ali ibn al-Hakam from al-'Ala' ibn Razin from Muhammad ibn Muslim who has said the following:

"Abu Ja'far, *'Alayhi al-Salam*, has said, 'A Jewish or a Christian woman cannot become a second wife, the first being a Muslim woman.'"

H 9514, Ch. 33, h 5

A number of our people have narrated from Ahmad ibn Muhammad from ibn Khalid al-Barqiy from 'Uthman ibn 'Isa from Sama'ah ibn Mehran who has said the following:

"This is concerning my question before him (the Imam), *'Alayhi al-Salam*, if one can marry a Jewish or a Christian woman as a second wife, the first being a Muslim woman. He (the Imam) said, 'No, but a Muslim woman can become a second wife, the first being a Jewish or a Christian woman.'"

H 9515, Ch. 33, h 6

Muhammad ibn Yahya has narrated from Ahmad ibn Muhammad from ibn Faddal from al-Hassan ibn al-Jahm who has said the following:

"Abu al-Hassan, al-Rida', *'Alayhi al-Salam*, once said to me, 'O abu Muhammad, what do you say about a man who marries a Jewish or a Christian woman, as a second wife, the first being a Muslim woman?' I replied, 'I pray to Allah to keep my soul in service for your cause, my words have no meaning in your presence.' He (the Imam) said, 'You must say it; with it my words will come to light.' I said, 'It is not lawful to marry a Christian woman as a second wife, the first being a Muslim woman or non-Muslim woman.' He (the Imam) asked, 'Why is it so?' I replied, 'It is because of the words of Allah, most Majestic, most Glorious, "You must not marry the pagan women until they become believers."' (2:221) He (the Imam) then asked, 'What do you say about, "Marry of the chaste woman of the followers of the book (bible) which was before you" (5:5)?' I replied, 'Verse 221 of Chapter 2 has cancelled verse 5:5.' He (the Imam) smiled and remained quiet.'"

H 9516, Ch. 33, h 7

Muhammad ibn Yahya has narrated from Ahmad ibn Muhammad from ibn Faddal from Ahmad ibn 'Umar from Durust al-Wasitiy from ibn Ri'ab from Zurarah ibn 'A'yan who has said the following:

"Abu Ja'far, *'Alayhi al-Salam*, has said, 'It is not proper to marry a woman of the people of the book (bible).' I then asked, 'I pray to Allah to keep my soul in service for your cause, where is its unlawfulness mentioned?' He (the Imam) said, 'It is in His words, 'You must not hold on to your unbelieving wives.' (60:10)"

H 9517, Ch. 33, h 8

Ali ibn Ibrahim has narrated from his father from ibn Mahbub from ibn Ri'ab from Zurarah ibn 'A'yan who has said the following:

"I once asked abu Ja'far, *'Alayhi al-Salam*, about the words of Allah, most Majestic, most Glorious, 'Marry of the chaste women of those to whom the book was given before you.' (5:5) He (the Imam) said, 'It is cancelled by, 'You must not hold on to your unbelieving wives.' (60:10)"

H 9518, Ch. 33, h 9

Ali ibn Ibrahim has narrated from his father from ibn abu 'Umayr from certain persons of his people from Muhammad ibn Muslim who has said the following:

"Abu Ja'far, *'Alayhi al-Salam*, has said, 'Of the non-Muslim taxpayers, if one spouse becomes a Muslim, their marriage remains valid and he cannot take her out of the Muslim domain to other areas or spend a night with her but he can meet her during the day. The pagans, like Arab pagans or others live with their marriage until the time the waiting period is complete. If the woman becomes a Muslimah then the man becomes a Muslim before the waiting period is over. She remains his wife; but if he did not become a Muslim before the waiting period is complete then she becomes stranger for him and he cannot approach her. This applies to all non-tax payers. It is not proper for a Muslim to marry a Jewish or a Christian woman if he can find a Muslim woman.'"

H 9519, Ch. 33, h 10

Ali ibn Ibrahim has narrated from his father from 'Isma'il ibn Marrar from Yunus ibn 'Abd al-Rahman from Muhammad ibn Muslim who has said the following:

"Abu Ja'far, *'Alayhi al-Salam*, has said, 'It is not proper for a Muslim to marry a Jewish or a Christian woman if he can find a free Muslim woman or a slave-girl.'"

H 9520, Ch. 33, h 11

Ali ibn Ibrahim has narrated from his father from ibn Mahbub from ibn Ri'ab from abu Basir who has said the following:

"I once asked abu Ja'far, *'Alayhi al-Salam*, about the case of a man who has a Christian wife; if he can marry a Jewish woman as a second wife. He (the Imam) said, 'People of the book are under the domain of the Imam and there is permission from us for you especially, so it is not unlawful to marry.' I then asked, 'Can he marry a slave-girl?' He (the Imam) said, 'It is not proper to marry three slave-girls. If he marries a Muslim woman who does not know about his non-Muslim wives and he goes to bed with her, she can demand the *mahr* (dower) whatever it is, and it is up to her to live with him or go to her family. If she decides to go; after three cycles of menses or three months she can lawfully marry.' I then asked, 'Can he bring her back if he divorces the Jewish and Christian women before her waiting periods is complete?' He (the Imam) said, 'Yes, he can do so.'"

Chapter 34 - Marriage of a Free Man with a Slave

H 9521, Ch. 34, h 1

A number of our people have narrated from Ahmad ibn Muhammad from 'Uthman ibn 'Isa from Sama'ah from abu Basir who has said the following:

"About the case of a free man who marries a slave-girl, abu 'Abd Allah, *'Alayhi al-Salam*, has said, 'It is not unlawful if it is an emergency.'"

H 9522, Ch. 34, h 2

Ali ibn Ibrahim has narrated from his father from ibn abu 'Umayr from Hammad from al-Halabiy who has said the following:

"Abu 'Abd Allah, *'Alayhi al-Salam*, has said, 'A free woman can become a second wife, the first wife being a slave-girl; but a slave-girl cannot become a second wife, the first wife being a free woman. If one marries a slave-girl as a second wife, the first being a free woman, such marriage is invalid.'"

H 9523, Ch. 34, h 3

Muhammad ibn Yahya has narrated from Ahmad ibn Muhammad ibn 'Isa from al-Husayn ibn Sa'id from al-Qasim ibn Muhammad from Ali ibn abu Hamzah from abu Basir who has said the following:

"This is concerning my question before abu 'Abd Allah, *'Alayhi al-Salam*, about the marriage with a slave-girl. He (the Imam) said, 'One can marry a free woman as a second wife, the first being a slave-girl, but he cannot marry a slave-girl as a second wife, the first being a free woman, and the marriage contract of slave-girl as a second wife, the first being a free woman, is invalid. If you have a free and a slave-girl wife, for the free wife are two days and for the slave-girl one day and it is not proper to marry a slave-girl without the permission of the master.'"

H 9524, Ch. 34, h 4

Muhammad ibn Yahya has narrated from Ahmad ibn Muhammad ibn Mahbub from Yahya al-Lahham from Sama'ah who has said the following:

"About the case of a man who marries a free woman and he has a wife who is a slave-girl and the free woman does not know that he has a slave-girl wife, abu 'Abd Allah, *'Alayhi al-Salam*, has said, 'If the free woman wants to live with his slave-girl wife, she can do so and if she wants she can go to her family.' I then asked, 'If she did not like to live with his slave-girl wife and went to her family, is there a way for him to bring her back?' He (the Imam) said, 'He has no way to bring her back if she does not agree when she finds out.' I then asked, 'Is her going to her family her divorce?' He (the Imam) said, 'Yes, when she goes out of his house, she commences her waiting period for three months or three cycles of menses then she can marry if she so chooses.'"

H 9525, Ch. 34, h 5

Muhammad ibn Yahya has narrated from 'Abd Allah ibn Muhammad from Ali ibn al-Hakam from Aban ibn 'Uthman from 'Abd al-Rahman ibn abu 'Abd Allah who has said the following:

"This is concerning my question before abu 'Abd Allah, *'Alayhi al-Salam*, if a man can marry a Christian woman as a second wife, the first being a Muslim woman or a slave-girl as a second wife, the first being a free woman. He (the Imam) said, 'He cannot marry anyone of them as a second wife, the first being a Muslim woman. One can marry a Muslim woman as a second wife, the first being a slave-girl or a Christian woman. The Muslim woman will have two-thirds of the time, the slave-girl and the Christian woman one-third of the time.'"

H 9526, Ch. 34, h 6

Aban has narrated from Zurarah ibn 'A'yan who has said the following:

"I once asked abu Ja'far, *'Alayhi al-Salam*, about the marriage of a slave-girl. He (the Imam) said, 'No, unless it is an emergency.'"

H 9527, Ch. 34, h 7

Muhammad ibn Yahya has narrated from Ahmad ibn Muhammad from ibn Faddal from ibn Bukayr from certain persons of our people who have said the following:

"Abu 'Abd Allah, *'Alayhi al-Salam*, has said, 'It is not proper today for a free man to marry a slave-girl. It was permissible as Allah, most Majestic, most Glorious, has said, 'If one cannot find resources. . . .' (4:25) Resources is a reference to *mahr* (dower). Today *mahr* (dower) is like the *mahr* (dower) of slave-girls or less.'"

H 9528, Ch. 34, h 8

Ali ibn Ibrahim has narrated from his father from 'Isma'il ibn Marrar and others from Yunus from 'A'immah who has said the following:

"He (the Imam), *'Alayhi al-Salam*, has said, 'It is not proper for an affluent Muslim man to marry a slave-girl unless he cannot find a free woman. So also, it is not proper for him to marry a woman from the people of the book unless it is an emergency when he cannot find a free Muslim woman or a slave-girl.'"

H 9529, Ch. 34, h 9

Ali ibn Ibrahim has narrated from his father from 'Isma'il ibn Marrar from Yunus from ibn Muskan from abu Basir who has said the following:

"Abu 'Abd Allah, *'Alayhi al-Salam*, has said, 'It is not proper for a free man to marry a slave-girl when he is able to marry a free woman, and it is not proper for him to marry a slave-girl as a second wife, the first being a free woman but it is not unlawful to marry a free woman as a second wife, the first being a slave-girl; and if he did so, two days of time is for the free woman and one day for the slave-girl.'"

Chapter 25 - Marriage in the form of Al-Shighar

H 9530, Ch. 35, h 1

Muhammad ibn Yahya has narrated from Ahmad ibn Muhammad from ibn Faddal from ibn Bukayr from certain persons of our people who have said the following:

"Abu 'Abd Allah, or abu Ja'far, *'Alayhi al-Salam*, prohibited marriage of two women without assigning any *mahr* (dower) for anyone of them except that this agrees for marriage because of the other woman's agreeing to marry because she (the other woman) has done so.'"

H 9531, Ch. 35, h 2

Ali ibn Ibrahim has narrated from Salih ibn al-Sindiy from Ja'far ibn Bashir from Ghiyath ibn Ibrahim who has said the following:

"I once heard abu 'Abd Allah, *'Alayhi al-Salam*, saying that the Messenger of Allah, *O Allah, grant compensation to Muhammad and his family worthy of their services to Your cause*, has said, 'In Islam al-Jalb, al-Janb and Shighar are not permissible. Shighar is one man's giving in marriage his daughter or sister to another man to marry this man's daughter or sister without any amount of *mahr* (dower) being assigned to anyone of them except that this person marries that person and the other person marries the other person.'"

Al-Jalb means that a tax collector commands the tax payers to deliver what they owe to him even if he is far away.

Al-Janb means in horse racing keeping of a spare horse on the side so that when one horse is exhausted the second horse can continue the race.

H 9532, Ch. 35, h 3

Ali ibn Muhammad has narrated from ibn Jumhur from his father in a marfu' manner who has said the following:

"Abu 'Abd Allah, *'Alayhi al-Salam*, has said that the Messenger of Allah, *O Allah, grant compensation to Muhammad and his family worthy of their services to Your cause*, prohibited marriage in the manner of Shighar which is giving away and it is done by one man's saying to the other man, 'Give your daughter in marriage to me so that I give my daughter in marriage to you and that there will be no *mahr* (dower) for anyone of them.'"

Chapter 36 - Marriage with a Woman and 'Umm Walad of Her Father

H 9533, Ch. 36, h 1

Ali ibn Ibrahim has narrated from his father from Ahmad ibn Muhammad from ibn abu Nasr who has said the following:

"I once asked al-Rida', *'Alayhi al-Salam*, about the case of a man who marries a woman then marries the mother of the child of her father. He (the Imam) said, 'It is not unlawful.' I then asked, 'It is narrated to us from your father, *'Alayhi al-Salam*, that Ali ibn al-Husayn, *'Alayhi al-Salam*, married, daughter of al-Hassan ibn Ali, *'Alayhi al-Salam*, and mother of the child of al-Hassan because a certain person of our people asked me to ask you about it. He (the Imam) said, 'It is not that way. Ali ibn al-Husayn, *'Alayhi al-Salam*, had married daughter of al-Hassan, *'Alayhi al-Salam*, and mother of the child of Ali ibn al-Husayn who was murdered with you. It was reported to 'Abd al-Malik ibn Marwan who blamed Ali ibn al-Husayn, *'Alayhi al-Salam*, about it and Ali ibn al-Husayn, *'Alayhi al-Salam*, wrote to him the answer. After reading the letter he said, 'Ali ibn al-Husayn lowers himself but Allah raises him up.'"

H 9534, Ch. 36, h 2

Muhammad ibn Yahya has narrated from Muhammad ibn al-Husayn from Muhammad ibn Sinan who has said the following:

"I once asked abu al-Hassan, *'Alayhi al-Salam*, about the case of a man who marries a woman and a mother of the child of her father. He (the Imam) said, 'It is not unlawful.'"

H 9535, Ch. 36, h 3

Abu Ali al-Ash'ariy has narrated from al-Hassan ibn Ali al-Kufiy ibn Jabalah from Ishaq ibn 'Ammar who has said the following:

"I once asked abu al-Hassan, *'Alayhi al-Salam*, about the case of a man who gives as a gift his slave-girl with whom he has gone to bed, to his son in-law; if his son in-law can go to bed with this slave-girl. He (the Imam) said, 'It is not unlawful.'"

H 9536, Ch. 36, h 4
It is narrated from the narrator of the previous Hadith from 'Imran ibn Musa from Muhammad ibn 'Abd al-Hamid from Muhammad ibn al-Fudayl who has said the following:
"Once I was with al-Rida', *'Alayhi al-Salam*, when Safwan asked about a man who has married the daughter of a man and the man has a woman and a mother of child. The father of the girl dies; if this man can marry the wife and mother of the child of the deceased. He (the Imam) said, 'It is not unlawful.'"

H 9537, Ch. 36, h 5
Abu Ali al-Ash'ariy has narrated from al-Hassan ibn Ali al-Kufiy from 'Ubays ibn Hisham from Muhammad ibn abu Hamzah who has said the following:
"This is concerning my question before abu 'Abd Allah, *'Alayhi al-Salam*, about the case of a man who marries a woman and her father gives her a slave-girl with whom he has gone to bed, as a gift; if her husband can go to bed with the slave-girl. He (the Imam) said, 'It is not unlawful.'"

H 9538, Ch. 36, h 6
Muhammad ibn Yahya has narrated from Ahmad ibn Muhammad from ibn Mahbub from abu Ayyub from Sama'ah who has said the following:
"This is concerning my question before abu 'Abd Allah, *'Alayhi al-Salam*, about the case of a man who marries the mother of the child of a man and her master dies. The deceased has a child from a woman other than his mother of the child; if the man who has married the mother of the child can marry the daughter of her master who has set her free so he will have both the daughter of the master who set her free and the slave-girl. He (the Imam) said, 'It is not unlawful.'"

Chapter 37 - Women Whom Allah, Most Majestic, Most Glorious, Made Lawful for Marriage

H 9539, Ch. 37, h 1
Ali ibn Ibrahim has narrated from his father from Nuh ibn Shu'ayb and Muhammad ibn al-Hassan who has said the following:
"Once, ibn abu al-'Awja' asked Hisham ibn al-Hakam, 'Is not Allah wise?' Hisham ibn al-Hakam replied, 'Yes, He is. He is the most firm of the judges.' He (ibn abu al-'Awja') then asked, 'Tell me about the words of Allah, most Majestic, most Glorious, "Marry whomever of women you like, two, three or four and if you fear of failure to maintain justice then marry only one." (4:3) Is not it obligatory?' He replied, 'Yes, it is.' He then asked, 'Tell me about the words of Allah, most Majestic, most Glorious, "You can never maintain justice among women no matter how strongly you desire, so do not incline completely to a particular side." (4:128) What kind of a wise person makes such statements?' Hisham ibn al-Hakam did not have an answer for it so he traveled to al-Madinah to abu 'Abd Allah, *'Alayhi al-Salam*. He (the Imam) asked, 'O Hisham, this is not the season of Hajj or 'Umrah.' Hisham replied, 'Yes, I pray to Allah to keep my soul in service for your cause, I have come for what is very

important for me. Ibn abu al-'Awja' asked me a question and I did not have any answer to it.' He (the Imam) asked, 'What is the question?' He explained the story and abu 'Abd Allah, *'Alayhi al-Salam*, said, 'The words of Allah, most Majestic, most Glorious, "Marry whomever of women you like, two, three or four and if you fear of failure to maintain justice then marry only one," (4:3) are about maintenance and expenses and the words of Allah, most Majestic, most Glorious, "You can never maintain justice among women no matter how strongly you desire, so do not incline completely to a particular side to leave her in suspense," (4:128) are about love.' He (the narrator) has said that when Hisham ibn al-Hakam came back with this answer he (ibn abu al-'Awja') said, 'By Allah, this is not from you.'"

H 9540, Ch. 37, h 2

Ali ibn Ibrahim has narrated from Muhammad ibn 'Isa from Yunus from Hisham ibn al-Hakam who has said the following:

"He (the Imam), *'Alayhi al-Salam*, has said, 'Allah, most High has made marriage lawful on the basis of His servants' ability to pay *mahr* (dower) and their ability to provide maintenance, so He has said, "Marry whomever of women you like, two, three or four and if you fear of failure to maintain justice then marry only one or a slave-girl that you own." (4:3) Allah has also said, "Anyone of you who is not able to pay *mahr* (dower) to marry chaste believing woman he can marry of the slave-girls that you own of the young believing woman." (4:128) Allah has said, "If you seek advantage from the women then pay their compensation as an obligation and it is not unlawful if you settle among yourselves." (4:24) Allah has made marriage lawful for those who are able to pay *mahr* (dower) according to their financial resources and their ability to provide maintenance for four or for three or two or just one. Those who cannot provide expenses for one they can marry slave-girls whom they own. If one cannot maintain women, marry free women or buy a slave-girl; Allah has made *al-Mut'ah* lawful by means of whatever is easy of *mahr* (dower) to pay in which providing maintenance and all expenses is not necessary. Allah makes each one self-sufficient by means of whatever He has given them in the form of their abilities to pay *mahr* (dower) with (or without) constraint in expenses for maintenance and the ability to refrain from indecent activities and the ability to refrain. From Allah, most Majestic, most Glorious, are good resources, capabilities and guidance to lawful goals by means of what He has given them so they can maintain chastity, remain away from unlawful matters by means of what He has given them and has made them free of needing unlawful matters and by whatever He has given them and has explained to them. Thus He has set limits upon them, like punishment by lashing and stoning, Li'an (condemnation) and separation. Had Allah not met the needs of each group by the resources that are made available to them and the lawful ways He would not set any of such limitation upon them.

"The permanent manner of marriage and owning slave-girls are well-known among people because of being practiced so often. The issue of *al-Mut'ah* is not clear for many people because of the prohibition of the One who prohibited it even though permission for it exists in the revelation (al-Quran) and is mentioned in the universal Sunnah for those who may like to find the reason and like to know it. Marriage in the manner of *al-Mut'ah* is permissible for rich and poor with equal measure of lawfulness of marriage as they are equal in completing the obligation of al-Hajj and *al-Mut'ah* in al-Hajj. The offering animal is for both rich and poor to offer. In this respect rich and poor are equal. It is because obligatory matters are sanctioned on the basis of the ability of those with the least amount of abilities to include both rich and poor. It is not fair to sanction obligatory matters on the basis of the abilities of people, otherwise, weakness and strength become confused. They are sanctioned on the basis of the least amount of abilities, thereafter the stronger ones are exhorted to compete in good deeds in optional matters because of their strength in their persons and wealth. *Al-Mut'ah* is lawful for rich and poor, for those with limited abilities and for those with four wives or those who are married with slave-girls, if one likes. It is lawful for those who can only find enough for *mahr* (dower) of *al-Mut'ah* and *mahr* (dower) is whatever they agree on within the limits of marriage for rich and poor regardless of being very little or a great deal.'"

Chapter 38 - Kinds of Marriage

H 9541, Ch. 38, h 1
Ali ibn Ibrahim has narrated from his father from al-Nawfaliy from al-Sakuniy who has said the following:
"Abu 'Abd Allah, *'Alayhi al-Salam*, has said, 'Marriage is of three conditions: It is with right for inheritance, or without the right for inheritance, or it is marriage with the right of ownership.'"

H 9542, Ch. 38, h 2
Muhammad ibn Yahya has narrated from Ahmad ibn Muhammad from al-'Abbas ibn Musa from Muhammad ibn Ziyad from al-Husayn ibn Zayd who has said the following:
"I once heard abu 'Abd Allah, *'Alayhi al-Salam*, saying, 'Marriage becomes lawful with three conditions: marriage with the right for inheritance, without inheritance, and with the right for ownership.'"

H 9543, Ch. 38, h 3
Ali ibn Ibrahim has narrated from Muhammad ibn 'Isa from Yunus from al-Husayn ibn Zayd who has said the following:
"I once heard abu 'Abd Allah, *'Alayhi al-Salam*, saying, 'Marriage becomes lawful with three conditions: marriage with the right for inheritance, without inheritance, and with the right for ownership.'"

Chapter 39 - Looking at a Woman with Intention to Marry

H 9544, Ch. 39, h 1
Ali ibn Ibrahim has narrated from his father from ibn abu 'Umayr from abu Ayyub al-Khazzaz from Muhammad ibn Muslim who has said the following:

"I once asked abu Ja'far, *'Alayhi al-Salam*, about the case of a man who wanted to marry a woman if he could look at her. He (the Imam) said, 'Yes, he can do so because he wants to pay a high price.'"

H 9545, Ch. 39, h 2
It is narrated from the narrator of the previous Hadith from ibn abu 'Umayr from Hisham ibn Salim and Hammad ibn 'Uthman and Hafs ibn al-Bakhtariy all have said the following:
"Abu 'Abd Allah, *'Alayhi al-Salam*, has said, 'It is not unlawful for a man to look at her face and hands to wrists, if he wants to marry her.'"

H 9546, Ch. 39, h 3
Abu Ali al-Ash'ariy has narrated from Muhammad ibn 'Abd al-Jabbar from Safwan from ibn Muskan from al-Hassan al-Sariy who has said the following:
"This is concerning my question before abu 'Abd Allah, *'Alayhi al-Salam*, about the case of a man who wants to marry a woman; if he can think about her, look behind her and to her face. He (the Imam) said, 'Yes, it is lawful for a man to look at the woman, if he wants to marry, behind her and to her face.'"

H 9547, Ch. 39, h 4
Al-Husayn from Muhammad has narrated from Mu'alla' ibn Muhammad from certain persons of our people from Aban ibn 'Uthman from al-Hassan al-Sariy who has said the following:
"This is concerning my question before abu 'Abd Allah, *'Alayhi al-Salam*, about the case of a man who looks at a woman before he marries her. He (the Imam) said, 'Yes, he can do so; then what for he gives his assets?'"

H 9548, Ch. 39, h 5
A number of our people have narrated from Ahmad ibn Muhammad from ibn Khalid from his father from 'Abd Allah ibn al-Fadl from a man who has said the following:
"This is concerning my question before abu 'Abd Allah, *'Alayhi al-Salam*, about the case of a man who wants to marry a woman; if he can look to her hairs and beauty. He (the Imam) said, 'It is lawful if it is not with lust.'"

Chapter 40 - Detestability of Marriage Ceremony at Certain Times

H 9549, Ch. 40, h 1
Ahmad ibn Muhammad has narrated from Ali ibn al-Hassan ibn Ali from al-'Abbas ibn 'Amir and Muhammad ibn Yahya al-Khath'amiy from Durays ibn 'Abd al-Malik who has said the following:
"When it was mentioned to abu Ja'far, *'Alayhi al-Salam*, that a man married a woman during the heat of the midday, abu Ja'far, *'Alayhi al-Salam*, said, 'I do not see they can agree.' They then separated from each other (as he (the Imam) had mentioned)."

H 9550, Ch. 40, h 2
Muhammad ibn Yahya has narrated from Ahmad ibn Muhammad from ibn Faddal from ibn Bukayr from Zurarah who has said the following:
"Abu Ja'far, *'Alayhi al-Salam*, said to me, 'I wanted to marry a woman but my father disliked it. I went and married her and afterwards I went to see her. I looked at her and did not see anything attractive to me. I stood up to leave but

her guard with her went to the door to close it on me. I told her not to do so and she could have what she wanted. When I returned home to my father and informed him about it, he said, 'You only owe to her half of the *mahr* (dower).' He said, 'You married her during a hot hour.'"

H 9551, Ch. 40, h 3
Humayd ibn Ziyad has narrated from al-Hassan ibn Sama'ah from Ahmad ibn al-Hassan al-Mithamiy from Aban ibn 'Uthman from 'Ubayd ibn Zurarah and abu al-'Abbas who has said the following:
"Abu 'Abd Allah, *'Alayhi al-Salam*, has said, 'A man must not go to bed with a woman in a Wednesday night.'"

Chapter 41 - Matters Preferable to Do During the Night of Marriage

H 9552, Ch. 41, h 1
Al-Husayn from Muhammad has narrated from Mu'alla' ibn Muhammad from al-Hassan ibn Ali al-Washsha' who has said the following:
"I once heard al-Rida', *'Alayhi al-Salam*, saying, 'It is of the Sunnah to become married during the night because Allah has made the night for rest and comfort and women are (to provide) ease and comfort.'"

H 9553, Ch. 41, h 2
Ali ibn Ibrahim has narrated from his father from al-Nawfaliy from al-Sakuniy who has said the following:
"Abu 'Abd Allah, *'Alayhi al-Salam*, has said, 'Conduct your marriages during the night and serve food during the day.'"

H 9554, Ch. 41, h 3
Muhammad ibn Yahya has narrated from Ahmad ibn Muhammad from al-Hassan ibn Ali from ibn Faddal from Ali ibn 'Uqbah from his father from Muyassir ibn 'Abd al-'Aziz who has said the following:
"Abu Ja'far, *'Alayhi al-Salam*, once said to me, 'O Muyassir, marry during the night because Allah has made the night for comfort and do not seek for any of your needs during the night; the night is dark. He (the narrator) has said, that he (the Imam) then said, 'One who comes during the night has a great right and the companion has a great right.'"

Chapter 42 - Serving Food in Marriage Ceremony

H 9555, Ch. 42, h 1
A number of our people have narrated from Sahl ibn Ziyad and al-Husayn from Muhammad from Mu'alla' ibn Muhammad all from al-Hassan ibn Ali al-Washsha' who has said the following:
"I once heard al-Rida', *'Alayhi al-Salam*, saying, 'When al-Najashiy proposed marriage on behalf of the Messenger of Allah to Aminah daughter of abu Sufyan and pronounced them wife and husband, he called for food and said, 'It is of the Sunnah of the prophets to serve food at the time of getting married.'"

H 9556, Ch. 42, h 2

Ali ibn Ibrahim has narrated from his father from ibn abu 'Umayr from Hisham ibn Salim who has said the following:

"Abu 'Abd Allah, *'Alayhi al-Salam,* has said that when the Messenger of Allah, *O Allah, grant compensation to Muhammad and his family worthy of their services to Your cause,* married Maymunah, daughter of al-Harith, he served food to people and it was mashed dates with the stones removed, with ghee.'"

H 9557, Ch. 42, h 3

A number of our people have narrated from Ahmad ibn Muhammad from ibn Faddal in a marfu' manner who has said the following:

"Abu Ja'far, *'Alayhi al-Salam,* has said, 'Serving food in a wedding ceremony for one or two days is an honor ; but for three days (it) is a show-off and for the sake of publicity.'"

H 9558, Ch. 42, h 4

Ali ibn Ibrahim has narrated from his father from al-Nawfaliy from al-Sakuniy who has said the following:

"Abu 'Abd Allah, *'Alayhi al-Salam,* has said that the Messenger of Allah, *O Allah, grant compensation to Muhammad and his family worthy of their services to Your cause,* has said, 'Serving food in a wedding ceremony for the first day is a right, the second day is reasonable, and for more than this is a show-off and publicity.'"

Chapter 43 - Marriage without Khutbah Speech before (Solemnizing) a Marriage

H 9559, Ch. 43, h 1

Muhammad ibn Yahya has narrated from Ahmad ibn Muhammad from al-Hassan ibn Ali from ibn Faddal from Ali ibn Ya'qub from Harun ibn Muslim from 'Ubayd ibn Zurarah who has said the following:

This is concerning my question before abu 'Abd Allah, *'Alayhi al-Salam,* about the case of a marriage without formal proposal (Khutbah). He (the Imam) said, 'Is it not the case in general that when our young people marry, we prepare food and at the table we say, "O so and so, do you give so and so in marriage to so and so" and he says, "Yes, I have done so"?'"

H 9560, Ch. 43, h 2

A number of our people have narrated from Sahl ibn Ziyad from Ja'far ibn Muhammad al-Ash'ariy from 'Abd Allah ibn Maymun al-Qaddah who has said the following:

"Abu 'Abd Allah, *'Alayhi al-Salam,* has said that Ali ibn al-Husayn, *'Alayhi al-Salam,* when solemnizing a marriage at the table of food would say no more than his saying, 'All praise belongs to Allah, *O Allah, grant compensation to Muhammad and his family worthy of their services to Your cause,* he would ask forgiveness from Allah and say, 'We have given to you in marriage on the condition of Allah.' Then Ali ibn Al-Husayn, *'Alayhi al-Salam,* would say, 'If Allah is praised then Khutbah is complete (proposal, or the speech before solemnization).'"

Chapter 44 - The Sermon for Marriage

H 9561, Ch. 44, h 1

A number of our people have narrated from Ahmad ibn Muhammad ibn 'Isa from ibn Mahbub from ibn Ri'ab who has said the following:

"Abu 'Abd Allah, *'Alayhi al-Salam*, has said that one day a group of banu 'Umayyah during the time of the government of 'Uthman came together in Masjid of the Messenger of Allah, *O Allah, grant compensation to Muhammad and his family worthy of their services to Your cause*, on a Friday and they wanted to solemnize marriage for one of their people and 'Amir al-Mu'minin, *'Alayhi al-Salam*, was nearby. They said to each other. If you want to embarrass Ali, call him now to give a speech and we will keep talking. He will feel embarrassed and will not be able to speak. They went to him (the Imam) and said, 'O abu al-Hassan we want you to deliver for us a speech.' He (the Imam) asked, 'Are you waiting for someone?' They replied, 'No, we are not waiting for anyone.' He (the Imam) by Allah, without delay said, 'All praise belongs to Allah who is special in oneness, who advances with warning, who does whatever He wants, who is curtained with light from His creatures, who has aspiring horizon, who in mystification is lofty, whose Kingdom is high and is worshipped for His bounties, Lord of the earth and sky. I praise Him for His good trial, generous charity, and abundant favor and for our Lord's diverting afflictions from us. I praise Him in a way that servants worship Him, lands become fertile and I testify that no one deserves worship except Allah alone who has no partner. There was nothing before Him and there will be nothing after Him. I testify that Muhammad, *O Allah, grant compensation to Muhammad and his family worthy of their services to Your cause*, is His servant and His Messenger whom He chose with excellence and guided through him people from straying. He chose him especially for Himself and sent him to His creatures with His message, and statements. He calls people to worship Him, believe in His oneness, and acknowledge that He is the Lord and confirm that he is His Holy Prophet, *O Allah, grant compensation to Muhammad and his family worthy of their services to Your cause*, whom He has sent at a time of lapse of the presence of the messengers of Allah among people, when people had turned away from the truth, had become ignorant about their Lord, denied the resurrection and warnings. He delivered His message, strove hard for His cause, gave good advice to his followers and worshipped Him until death approached him, *O Allah, grant compensation to Muhammad and his family worthy of their services to Your cause*, a great deal. I advise you and myself to become pious before Allah, most Great. Allah, most Majestic, most Glorious, has assigned a way out for the pious ones out of what they dislike, and sustenance from sources that they do not expect. So complete the promise of Allah and seek what is with Him through worshipping Him and working for what He loves because goodness cannot be achieved without Him and nothing that is with Him can be achieved without obeying Him. There is no protection against the creatures except His protection and there is no means and power without the power of Allah.

'Thereafter, Allah has settled things and has approved them in measures and they do not stop in their channels without reaching their goals as they are determined for them. Of the things He had determined of His inevitable issues and His decisions measured and determined is that the successors come in branches and the means continue. He has determined the end of issues to take place about us and you to be present here in this gathering for which He has given us the opportunity that we speak of His bounties and of His good trial and describe His blessings. We ask blessings from Allah for you and for us. It is the blessing which has made us to come together here for its benefits. Thereafter, so and so has mentioned so and so and he as far as his status is as you know him and as matters of genealogy is not unknown to you. He has paid *mahr* (dower) of an amount that you know so return good, you will be praised for it and ascribe to it (good), *O Allah, grant compensation to Muhammad and his family worthy of their services to Your cause.*

H 9562, Ch. 44, h 2

Ahmad ibn Muhammad has narrated from 'Isma'il ibn Mehran from 'Ayman ibn Muhriz from 'Amr ibn Shamir from Jabir who has said the following:

"Abu Ja'far, *'Alayhi al-Salam*, has said that 'Amir al-Mu'minin once gave a woman from banu 'Abd al-Muttalib in marriage, solemnized her marriage and said, 'All praise belongs to Allah, most Majestic, most Powerful, the Forbearing, the Forgiving, the one Dominant, the most Great, most High – no matter whatever anyone of you says of words in secrecy or in public, when hidden in the night or conspicuous in the day - I praise Him, ask assistance from Him, believe in Him, and place my trust with Him; Allah is sufficient legal representative. Whomever Allah guides no one is able to mislead him and whomever Allah causes to go astray, no one is able to guide him and you can never find anyone other than Him as true guide. I testify that no one deserves worship except Allah alone who has no partners, the kingdom belongs to Him and all praise and He has power over all things. I testify that Muhammad, *O Allah, grant compensation to Muhammad and his family worthy of their services to Your cause,* is His servant and His Messenger whom He sent with His book and Authority over His servants. Whoever obeys him has obeyed Allah and one has disobeyed Allah if he has disobeyed him, *O Allah, grant compensation to Muhammad and his family worthy of their services to Your cause,* and peace a great deal. He is the Imam of guidance and the chosen prophet. I thereafter advise you to become pious before Allah; it is the advice from Allah in the past and bygone.' Then he (the Imam) pronounced them wife and husband."

H 9563, Ch. 44, h 3

Ahmad ibn 'Isma'il ibn Mehran has said that narrated to us 'Abd al-Malik ibn abu al-Harith from Jabir who has said the following:

"Abu Ja'far, *'Alayhi al-Salam*, has said that 'Amir al-Mu'minin, *'Alayhi al-Salam*, once addressed with the following speech: 'All praise belongs to Allah, I praise Him, beg assistance from Him, ask forgiveness from Him, seek His guidance, believe in Him and place my trust with Him and I testify that no one deserves worship except Allah alone who has no partners and I testify that Muhammad, *O Allah, grant compensation to Muhammad and his family worthy of their services to Your cause,* is His servant and His Messenger. He sent him with guidance and true religion to make it dominant over all other religions, as a guide to Him and calling to Him. So he destroyed the pillars of disbelief and lit up the beacon of belief. Whoever obeys Allah and the Messenger of Allah, the right guidance becomes his path and the light of piety becomes his guide. Whoever disobeys Allah and His Messenger misses the straight path altogether and harms no one except himself. I recommend you, O servants of Allah, to become pious before Allah with an advice from an adviser and a preaching of one who delivers and strives. Thereafter, Allah, most Majestic, most Glorious, has made Islam the bright landmarks with shining light houses. In it hearts come together and on its basis are brotherhood and what is between us and you, of such facts are to love Him and old memories among us and everyone knowing everyone else of that on which we are based. May Allah forgive us and you and peace be with you and the blessing of Allah and His kindness.'"

H 9564, Ch. 44, h 4

Ahmad ibn Muhammad has narrated from ibn al-'Arzamiy from his father who has said the following:

"When 'Amir al-Mu'minin, *'Alayhi al-Salam,* wanted to solemnize a marriage he would say, 'All praise belongs to Allah, I praise Him, beg assistance from Him, believe in Him and place my trust with Him and I testify that no one deserves worship except Allah alone who has no partners and I testify that Muhammad, *O Allah, grant compensation to Muhammad and his family worthy of their services to Your cause,* is His servant and His Messenger. He sent him with guidance and true religion to make it dominant over all other religions, even though the pagans dislike it. *O Allah, grant compensation to Muhammad and his family worthy of their services to Your cause,* may peace and blessings of Allah be with you. I recommend you, O servants of Allah, to become pious before Allah, who is the Owner of bounties and mercy, the Creator of the people and the Planner of all issues in it with power over it and firmness, to Allah, belongs all praise for the matters of the past and the bygone. All praise belongs to Allah alone and glorification is purely for Him for His favor that He has done to us as a beautiful bounty on us with grace and has beautified it to us. He is the Creator that never runs out of resources, humbles down all difficult issues, softens what is hard and achieves with ease. He is the Inventor of the creation which He began first on the day He created the sky when it was smoke and said to it and the earth, "Come voluntarily or by force." They responded, "We come voluntarily." Then He made them seven heavens in two days. He never runs out of resources and no runaway can go faster than Him and no perishing thing is lost for Him. There will be the day when every soul will receive what it has earned without any injustice being done to it. Thereafter so and so . . .'"

H 9565, Ch. 44, h 5

Muhammad ibn Yahya has narrated from Ahmad ibn Muhammad ibn 'Isa who has said that narrated to me al-'Abbas ibn Musa al-Baghdadiy in a marfu' manner has said the following:

"Abu 'Abd Allah, *'Alayhi al-Salam,* as response in Khutbah for marriage has said, 'All praise belongs to Allah who chooses praise especially for Himself, glorified is thereby His mention and facilitated thereby is His command. We praise Him without any doubt in it; we see what we prepare in the hope for success and as key to its benefit. We receive what we need from Him and we seek guidance from Allah, a safe guidance and strong means of safety and the determination for piety. We seek protection with Allah against blindness after guidance and against working in misleading desires. I testify that no one other than Allah alone, who has no partners, deserves worship and I testify that Muhammad is His servant and His Messenger, a servant who never worshipped anyone other than Him. He chose him by His knowledge and entrusted him with His revelation, as a messenger to His creatures, *O Allah, grant compensation to Muhammad and his family worthy of their services to Your cause.* Thereafter, we have heard your words and you are the nearest generation with whom we like to have marital relationship and assist you in your needs. We are greedy for your brotherhood. We have accepted the mediation of your mediator and given in marriage to the one from you who have proposed for marriage for the designated *mahr* (dower) and we ask Allah who decides all issues with His power to make the consequences of our meeting towards His love; He is the guardian thereof and has power thereat.'"

H 9566, Ch. 44, h 6

A number of our people have narrated from Ahmad ibn Muhammad from ibn Khalid from 'Abd al-'Azim ibn 'Abd Allah who has said the following:

"I heard abu al-Hassan, *'Alayhi al-Salam*, give the following as Khutbah (sermon) when solemnizing a marriage: 'All praise belongs to Allah who knows what is to come into being before anyone of His creatures with the ability to recognize (and know) can recognize it (the being that is to come into being). He is the Inventor of the skies and earth, harmonizer of the means about which the Pen has moved and the determination has been made in His knowledge of the past and measures of His wisdom. I praise Him for His bounties, and seek protection with Him against His dislikes, appeal before Allah for guidance, seek His protection against straying and destruction. Whomever Allah guides has found guidance, has walked on the right path and has earned the great benefit. Whomever Allah causes to go astray, misses guidance and is headed to destruction. I testify that no one other than Allah alone, who has no partners, deserves worship and I testify that Muhammad is His servant and His chosen messenger and His friend with whom He is pleased, His Messenger with guidance whom He sent at a time of lapse of the existence of His Messengers, when differences among nations were a great deal, cutting off of the roads, decadence of wisdom, wiped out landmarks of guidance and clear signs, were all everywhere. He preached and delivered the message of his Lord, executed His commands, fulfilled the right he owed and left this world and he is very much missed. *O Allah, grant compensation to Muhammad and his family worthy of their services to Your cause.*

'All issues are in the hands of Allah. He allows them to run by their means and measures. The command of Allah applies to His measures and His measures work to the appointed time and His appointed time works to His record; for every appointed time there is a record. Allah deletes whatever He wants and establishes whatever He wants; He has the original record and *'Umm al-Kitab* (mother book). Thereafter, Allah, most Majestic, most Glorious, has made marriage to bring the hearts close together and a relation for the relationship, to interlace a relationship among relatives. He has made it for compassion and kindness and in this there are signs (of existence of Allah) for the worlds. He in His firmly established book has said, "It is He who has created man from water and has designed them for marriage and offspring." (25:56) He has also said, "Arrange marriage for your unmarried ones and the virtuous ones of your servants and slave-girls." (24:32) So and so is of those whom you know for his status, position, religion and discipline and he is interested in your participation and likes to establish marital relationship with you and has come with marriage proposal to the young lady from you so and so daughter of so and so and has offered a *mahr* (dower) of such and such amount for immediate payment and such and such amount payable on credit. Accept our mediation and give in marriage to our proposing gentleman who has arrived at a beautiful arriving place, and say to him good words and I ask Allah to grant forgiveness to me and you and all Muslims.'"

H 9567, Ch. 44, h 7

Ahmad ibn Muhammad has narrated from Mu'awiyah ibn Hakim who has said the following:

"Al-Rida', *'Alayhi al-Salam*, once read the following as Khutbah (sermon) when solemnizing a marriage: 'All praise belongs to Allah who has praised Himself in the book and has opened His book with it, has made it the first reward of the recipient of His bounties and the last words of the dwellers of His paradise. I testify that no one other than Allah alone, who has no partners, deserves worship, a testimony that I present purely for Him and save in reserve with Him. *O Allah, grant compensation to Muhammad and his family worthy of their services to Your cause.* He is the last in the line of prophets and the best of the people, and his family is the family of mercy and kindness, the tree of bounties, the source of Divine message, the junction of coming and going of the angels. All praise belongs to Allah who had it in His eternal knowledge and in His speaking book and true statements that the most deserving means, for compensation and preference and the foremost issue to be interested in is the means that involves a means and issue that is followed by freedom from want. Allah, most Majestic, most Glorious, has said, "It is He who has created the human being from water to have relationships of both lineage and wedlock. Your Lord has all power." (25:54) "Marry the single people among you and the righteous slaves and slave-girls. If you are poor, Allah will make you rich through His favor; He is Bountiful and All-knowing." (24:32) Had there been no clear verse of the Quran about marriage or texts of Sunnah which are followed or any other source of law unanimously accepted, it (marriage) would have been of what Allah has made of the very close and nearby good deeds and of the facts that bring far away things close and bring the hearts near together, to intermingle rights and to multiply numbers of children to help in difficult conditions of time and happenings of issues. It is of the facts in which people of reason are interested, fortunate people strive to achieve and skillful people of the field of discipline feel greedy about. People close to Allah are those who obey His command, execute His orders, approve His decision and hope for His reward. So and so son of so and so is one whose condition and excellence are well known to you. His soul has agreed to give preference to you over the others and to choose proposing marriage to so and so daughter of so and so, your graceful daughter and has decided to pay such and such amount as *mahr* (dower), so please welcome him with acceptance, respond to him with interest and ask Allah to show what is in your interest and well-being in your affairs. He will decide for you what is reasonable, if Allah so wills and we ask Allah to bring harmony among you by means of piety and virtuous manners, bring him close with affection and love and complete for him with agreement and pleasure; He listens to the prayers and is subtle in what He wishes.'"

Certain persons of our people have narrated from Ali ibn al-Hassan ibn Faddal from 'Isma'il ibn Mehran from Ahmad ibn Muhammad from ibn abu Nasr who has narrated the following: "I heard abu al-Hassan, al-Rida', *'Alayhi al-Salam*, saying, '. . . he then has mentioned this sermon just as Mu'awiyah ibn Hakam has narrated, which is a similar sermon.'"

H 9568, Ch. 44, h 8
Muhammad ibn Ahmad has narrated from certain persons of our people who have said the following:
"Al-Rida', *'Alayhi al-Salam*, when solemnizing a marriage would read a Khutbah as follows:

"All praise belongs to Allah. It is to glorify His power, and no one other than Allah deserves worship. Worship is to express humbleness before His Majesty. *O Allah, grant compensation to Muhammad and his family worthy of their services to Your cause*, whenever he is mentioned. 'Allah has created man from water, then designed him in offspring and marriage . . . to the end of the verse. . . .'"

H 9569, Ch. 44, h 9
Certain persons of our people have narrated from Ali ibn al-Husayn from Ali ibn Hassan from 'Abd al-Rahman ibn Kathir who has said the following:
"When the Messenger of Allah, *O Allah, grant compensation to Muhammad and his family worthy of their services to Your cause*, decided to marry Khadijah daughter of Khuwaylid, abu Talib with his family and certain individuals of Quraysh went to the house of Waraqah ibn Nawfal, uncle of Khadijah. Abu Talib began speaking and said, 'All praise belongs to the Lord of this House, (al-Ka'bah) who has made us of the offspring of Ibrahim and 'Isma'il and has given us accommodation in the secure sanctuary, has made us judges for people and has blessed for us our land in which we live. The son of my brother, this one, meaning the Messenger of Allah, *O Allah, grant compensation to Muhammad and his family worthy of their services to Your cause*, is as such that he cannot be compared with any man from Quraysh, He is above them and he is greater (in excellence) than whomever he is compared with. There is no one as his equal among the creatures even though he is not wealthy because wealth is a favor (from Allah) that comes and goes. He is interested in Khadijah and she is

interested in him and we have come to you to propose (on his behalf) marriage (to Khadijah) if she agrees. Her order and *mahr* (dower) for her is on my assets of whatever amount you ask for advance payment and on credit. His share (the share of the Messenger of Allah) by the Lord of this House is great, his religion is publicly known and his opinion is perfect.' Abu Talib then remained quiet and her uncle began to speak but he stuttered and could not give complete answer to abu Talib, his words became disconnected and he was overwhelmed. He was a clergyman. Khadijah then began saying, 'Uncle, even though you are my guardian in public, I have more control of myself. O Muhammad, I have given myself in marriage to you and *mahr* (dower) is on me from my assets. Ask your uncle to slaughter a camel for the wedding ceremony and you can join your family (wife).' Abu Talib then said, 'O people, bear witness to her accepting Muhammad (as her husband) and her taking responsibility of *mahr* (dower) from her wealth.' A certain person from Quraysh said, 'This is strange. *Mahr* (dower) is paid by women for men!' It made abu Talib very much upset and he stood up on his feet. People feared his anger and he said, 'If they were like the son of my brother such people are sought with the highest price and the greatest amount of *mahr* (dower), and if they are of the like of your kind they cannot marry without paying a large amount for *mahr* (dower).' Abu Talib slaughtered a she-camel for the wedding ceremony and the Messenger of Allah, *O Allah, grant compensation to Muhammad and his family worthy of their services to Your cause*, joined his family (wife). A man from Quraysh, called 'Abd Allah ibn Ghanm, composed the following lines:

'Congratulations and blessings! O Khadijah, the bird (of your good luck) has flown for you to the one happier than you.

You have married the best of all the people. There is no one among people like Muhammad (in excellence). Happy news about him was given to all people by Jesus son of Mary as well as by Moses, son of 'Imran and how close the promised time is!

Writers of long ago in time had determined that from al-Batha there will come a messenger (of Allah) for guidance well guided.'"*

Chapter 45 - The Sunnah about *Mahr*

H 9570, Ch. 45, h 1
A number of our people have narrated from Sahl ibn Ziyad from Ahmad ibn Muhammad from ibn abu Nasr from Hammad ibn 'Uthman and Jamil ibn Darraj from Hudhayfah ibn Mansur who has said the following:
"Abu 'Abd Allah, *'Alayhi al-Salam*, has said, 'The amount of *mahr* (dower) the Messenger of Allah, *O Allah, grant compensation to Muhammad and his family worthy of their services to Your cause*, paid was twelve *Awqiyah* and one *Nashsha*. Al-Awqiyah is equal to forty dirham and one *al-Nashsha* is equal to twenty dirham and it is equal to one-half of *al-Awqiyah*.'"

H 9571, Ch. 45, h 2

Muhammad ibn Yahya has narrated from Ahmad ibn Muhammad ibn 'Isa from Ali ibn al-Hakam from Mu'awiyah ibn Wahab who has said the following:

"I once heard abu 'Abd Allah, *'Alayhi al-Salam*, saying, 'The amount of *mahr* (dower) the Messenger of Allah, *O Allah, grant compensation to Muhammad and his family worthy of their services to Your cause*, paid to his wives was twelve *Awqiyah* and one *Nashsha*. *Al-Awqiyah* is equal to forty dirham and one *al-Nashsha* is equal to one-half of *al-Awqiyah*. It was five hundred dirham.' I then asked, 'Was it according to our weighing system?' He (the Imam) said, 'Yes, that is how it was.'"

H 9572, Ch. 45, h 3

A number of our people have narrated from Sahl ibn Ziyad from Ahmad ibn Muhammad from ibn abu Nasr from Dawud ibn al-Husayn from abu al-'Abbas who has said the following:

"This is concerning my question before abu 'Abd Allah, *'Alayhi al-Salam*, about *mahr* (dower); if there is an appointed time to pay it. He (the Imam) said, 'No, there is no particular time for it.' He (the Imam) then said, 'The amount of *mahr* (dower) the Messenger of Allah paid was twelve *Awqiyah* and one *Nashsha*. One *al-Nashsha* is equal to one-half of *al-Awqiyah* and *al-Awqiyah* is equal to forty dirham and it was five hundred dirham.'"

H 9573, Ch. 45, h 4

Muhammad ibn Yahya has narrated from Ahmad ibn Muhammad ibn 'Isa from ibn Faddal from ibn Bukayr from 'Ubayd ibn Zurarah who has said the following:

"I once heard abu 'Abd Allah, *'Alayhi al-Salam*, saying, 'The amount of *mahr* (dower) the Messenger of Allah, *O Allah, grant compensation to Muhammad and his family worthy of their services to Your cause*, paid to his wives was twelve *Awqiyah* and one *Nashsha*. *Al-Awqiyah* is equal to forty dirham and one *al-Nashsha* is equal to one-half of *al-Awqiyah* which is twenty dirham.'"

H 9574, Ch. 45, h 5

Ali ibn Ibrahim has narrated from his father from Hammad ibn 'Isa who has said the following:

"I once heard abu 'Abd Allah, *'Alayhi al-Salam*, saying that my father has said, 'The Messenger of Allah, *O Allah, grant compensation to Muhammad and his family worthy of their services to Your cause*, did not give in marriage any of his daughters or marry any of his wives for a *mahr* (dower) of more than twelve *Awqiyah* and one *Nashsha*. *Awqiyah* is equal to twelve dirham and one *Nashsha* is equal to twenty dirham.'"

H 9575, Ch. 45, h 6

And Hammad has narrated from Ibrahim ibn abu Yahya who has said the following:

"Abu 'Abd Allah, *'Alayhi al-Salam*, has said, 'The weight of dirham in those days was six.'"

H 9576, Ch. 45, h 7

Muhammad ibn Yahya has narrated from Ahmad ibn Muhammad from ibn abu Nasr from al-Husayn ibn Khalid and Ali ibn Ibrahim has narrated from his father from ibn abu 'Umayr from 'Uthman al-Khazzaz from a man from al-Husayn ibn Khalid who has said the following:

"I once asked abu al-Hassan, *'Alayhi al-Salam*, about *mahr* (dower) according to Sunnah and how it has become five hundred. He (the Imam) said, 'Allah, most Blessed, most High, has made obligatory upon Himself that if any believing person says one hundred times *Takbir* (Allah is great beyond description), one hundred times, *Tasbih* (Allah is free of all defects), one hundred times, *Tahmid*, (all praise belongs to Allah), one hundred times, *Tahlil*, (no one deserves worship except Allah) one hundred times and one hundred times, *O Allah, grant compensation to Muhammad and his family worthy of their services to Your cause*, and then says, 'O Allah pair me up with *Hur al-'In.*' Allah pairs him up with a *Hawra' al-'In* and makes this (things he has said) as *mahr* (dower). Then Allah, most Majestic, most Glorious, sent revelation to His Holy prophet, *O Allah, grant compensation to Muhammad and his family worthy of their services to Your cause*, to set *mahr* (dower) for the believing women at five hundred dirham. The Messenger of Allah followed the instruction and if any believing man proposes marriage to his brother in belief for his graceful daughter with five hundred dirham as *mahr* (dower) and he does not agree, he has caused a suspension and he will not deserve from Allah, most Majestic, most Glorious, to pair him with *Hur al-'In.*'"

Chapter 46 - *Mahr* of the Marriage of Amir Al-Mu'minin, *'Alayhi al-Salam*

H 9577, Ch. 46, h 1

A number of our people have narrated from Sahl ibn Ziyad from Ahmad ibn Muhammad from ibn abu Nasr from 'Abd al-Karim ibn 'Amr al-Khath'amiy from ibn abu Ya'fur who has said the following:

"I once heard abu 'Abd Allah, *'Alayhi al-Salam*, saying that Ali, *'Alayhi al-Salam*, married Fatimah, *'Alayha al-Salam*, for a *mahr* (dower) from the price of a single gown, a shield and a bed which was made of the hide of a ram.'"

H 9578, Ch. 46, h 2

Muhammad ibn Yahya has narrated from Ahmad ibn 'Isa from ibn Faddal from ibn Bukayr who has said the following:

"I once heard abu 'Abd Allah, *'Alayhi al-Salam*, saying, 'The Messenger of Allah, *O Allah, grant compensation to Muhammad and his family worthy of their services to Your cause*, arranged the marriage of Fatimah and Ali, *'Alayhim al-Salam*, for a *mahr* (dower) from one shield made by Hatmiyah (a certain people) valued at thirty dirham.'"

H 9579, Ch. 46, h 3

Ahmad ibn Muhammad has narrated from Ali ibn al-Hakam from Mu'awiyah ibn Wahab who has said the following:

"Abu 'Abd Allah, *'Alayhi al-Salam*, has said, 'The Messenger of Allah, *O Allah, grant compensation to Muhammad and his family worthy of their services to Your cause*, arranged marriage of Ali and Fatimah, *'Alayhim al-Salam*, with a *mahr* (dower) from a shield made by Hatmiyah and their bed was made of the hide of ram and when sleeping they would turn its fury face under their side.'"

H 9580, Ch. 46, h 4

Certain persons of our people have narrated from Ali ibn al-Husayn from al-'Abbas ibn 'Amir 'Abd Allah ibn Bukayr who has said the following:

"Abu 'Abd Allah, *'Alayhi al-Salam*, has said, 'The Messenger of Allah, *O Allah, grant compensation to Muhammad and his family worthy of their services to Your cause*, arranged the marriage of Fatimah and Ali, *'Alayhim al-Salam*, for a *mahr* (dower) from one shield made by Hatmiyah (a certain people) valued at thirty dirham.'"

H 9581, Ch. 46, h 5

A number of our people have narrated from Sahl ibn Ziyad from Muhammad ibn walid al-Khazzaz from Yunus ibn Ya'qub from abu Maryam al-Ansariy who has said the following:

"Abu Ja'far, *'Alayhi al-Salam*, has said that *mahr* (dower) of Fatimah, *'Alayha al-Salam*, was from a gown which was patched, a shield of Hatmiyah and her bed was of hide of a ram which the wife and husband used as floor covering and bed on which they would sleep.'"

H 9582, Ch. 46, h 6

A number of our people have narrated from Ahmad ibn Muhammad ibn Khalid from Ali ibn Asbat from Dawud from Ya'qub ibn Shu'ayb who has said the following:

"He (the Imam), *'Alayhi al-Salam*, has said, 'When the Messenger of Allah, *O Allah, grant compensation to Muhammad and his family worthy of their services to Your cause*, arranged the marriage of Ali and Fatimah, *'Alayhim al-Salam*, he went to see her but found her weeping. He (the Messenger of Allah) asked her, 'What has made you weep, by Allah, had there been anyone better in my family than him I would not have given you in marriage to him, and I have not given you in marriage to him but it is Allah who has given you in marriage to him with a *mahr* (dower) of al-Khums (one-fifth), for as long as there are the skies and earth.'"

H 9583, Ch. 46, h 7

Ali ibn Muhammad has narrated from 'Abd Allah ibn Ishaq from al-Hassan ibn Ali ibn Sulayman from those who narrated to him who has said the following:

"Abu 'Abd Allah, *'Alayhi al-Salam*, has said, 'Fatimah, *'Alayha al-Salam*, said to the Messenger of Allah, *O Allah, grant compensation to Muhammad and his family worthy of their services to Your cause*, 'You have given me in marriage for a very little *mahr* (dower).' The Messenger of Allah said, 'I have not given you in marriage but it is Allah who has given you in marriage from the heaven and has assigned one-fifth of the world as your *mahr* (dower) for as long as there are the skies and the earth.'"

Chapter 47 - Amount of *Mahr* today is the Mutually Agreed Amount

H 9584, Ch. 47, h 1

Muhammad ibn Yahya has narrated from Ahmad ibn Muhammad ibn 'Isa from Muhammad ibn 'Isma'il from Muhammad ibn al-Fudayl from abu al-Sabbah al-Kinaniy who has said the following:

"This is concerning my question before abu 'Abd Allah, *'Alayhi al-Salam*, about *mahr* (dower) and its amount. He (the Imam) said, 'Whatever amount people agree upon is *mahr* (dower).'"

H 9585, Ch. 47, h 2

Ali ibn Ibrahim has narrated from his father from ibn abu 'Umayr from Jamil ibn Darraj who has said the following:

"Abu 'Abd Allah, *'Alayhi al-Salam*, has said, '*Mahr* (dower) is what people agree upon or twelve *Awqiyah* and one *Nashsha* or five hundred dirham.'"

H 9586, Ch. 47, h 3

Ali ibn Ibrahim has narrated from his father from ibn abu 'Umayr from 'Umar ibn 'Udhaynah from Fudayl ibn Yasar who has said the following:

"Abu Ja'far, *'Alayhi al-Salam*, has said, 'The amount of *mahr* (dower) is what people agree upon which can be little or a great deal, that is *mahr* (dower).'"

H 9587, Ch. 47, h 4

Ali ibn Ibrahim has narrated from his father from 'Isma'il ibn Marrar from Yunus al-Nadr ibn Suwayd from Musa ibn Bakr from Zurarah ibn 'A'yan who has said the following:

"Abu Ja'far, *'Alayhi al-Salam*, has said, 'The amount of *mahr* (dower) is that upon which people agree and it can be little or a great deal, in an advantageous marriage or non-advantageous marriage.'"

H 9588, Ch. 47, h 5

Ali ibn Ibrahim has narrated from his father from ibn abu 'Umayr from Hammad from al-Halabiy who has said the following:

"This is concerning my question before abu 'Abd Allah, *'Alayhi al-Salam*, about *mahr* (dower). He (the Imam) said, 'It is the amount upon which people agree or twelve *Awqiyah* and one *Nashsha* or five hundred dirham.'"

Chapter 48 - Rare Ahadith about *Mahr*

H 9589, Ch. 48, h 1

A number of our people have narrated from Sahl ibn Ziyad Ahmad ibn Muhammad from Muhammad ibn Yahya has narrated from Ahmad ibn Muhammad ibn 'Isa from ibn Mahbub from Hisham ibn Salim from al-Hassan ibn Zurarah from his father who has said the following:

"This is concerning my question before abu Ja'far, *'Alayhi al-Salam*, about the case of a man who marries a woman following her command to form the marriage contract. He (the Imam) said, 'Her command in the matters of *mahr* (dower) must stay within the amount of *mahr* (dower) of the family of Muhammad, *O Allah, grant compensation to Muhammad and his family worthy of their services to Your cause*, which is twelve *Awqiyah* and one *Nashsha* and it weighs five hundred dirham of silver.' I then asked, 'What will happen if he forms the marriage contract according to his own command and she agrees with it?' He (the Imam) said, 'Whatever he commands is lawful and binding on her whether the amount is very little or more.' I then asked, 'How is it that her command is not binding on him and his command is binding upon her?' He (the Imam) said, 'It is because according to her own command she could not go beyond the Sunnah of the Messenger of Allah, *O Allah, grant compensation to*

Muhammad and his family worthy of their services to Your cause, upon which he married his wives, she must act according to the Sunnah because she appointed him as the agent to form the contract and settle *mahr* (dower) and she agreed to his decision so she must accept his decision and command about the amount whether it is less or more.'"

H 9590, Ch. 48, h 2

Al-Hassan ibn Mahbub has narrated from abu Ayyub from Muhammad ibn Muslim who has said the following:

"About the case of a man who marries a woman on her command and decision or according to his decision and command then he or she dies before they go to bed with each other, abu Ja'far, *'Alayhi al-Salam*, has said, 'She can have advantage and inheritance but has no *mahr* (dower).' I then asked what happens if he divorces her after marriage according to her command and decision?' He (the Imam) said, 'If he divorces her after marriage according to her command and decision her *mahr* (dower) is not more than the weight of five hundred dirham of silver which is the *mahr* (dower) of the women of the Messenger of Allah, *O Allah, grant compensation to Muhammad and his family worthy of their services to Your cause.*'"

H 9591, Ch. 48, h 3

Al-Hassan ibn Mahbub has narrated from abu Jamilah from Mu'alla' ibn Khunayth who has said the following:

"Once abu 'Abd Allah, *'Alayhi al-Salam*, was asked, when I was present, about the case of a man who married a woman as the second wife, the first being al-Mudabbarah, a slave-girl (a slave whose freedom is agreed to take place after the death of the master) which was known to the woman but she executed the marriage and then he divorced her before going to bed with her. He (the Imam) said, 'In my view the woman can have half of the services of al-Mudabbarah, that is one day of her service for the woman and one day of her service for her master.' It was asked, 'What happens if she dies before the woman and the master and who will have her legacy?' He (the Imam) said, 'One-half is for the woman and one-half is for the master.'"

H 9592, Ch. 48, h 4

Ibn Mahbub has narrated from al-Harith ibn Muhammad ibn al-Nu'man al-Ahwal from Burayd al-'Ijliy who has said the following:

"I once asked abu Ja'far, *'Alayhi al-Salam*, about the case of a man who married a woman to teach her a chapter from the book of Allah, most Majestic, most Glorious. He (the Imam) said, 'I do not like his going with her to bed before teaching her the Chapter and giving her something.' I then asked if giving dates or raisins is enough. He (the Imam) said, 'It is not unlawful if she agrees with whatever it is.'"

H 9593, Ch. 48, h 5

Muhammad ibn Yahya has narrated from Ahmad ibn Muhammad from Ali ibn al-Hakam from al-'Ala' ibn Razin from Muhammad ibn Muslim who has said the following:

"Abu Ja'far, *'Alayhi al-Salam*, has said that once a woman came to the Holy Prophet, *O Allah, grant compensation to Muhammad and his family worthy of their services to Your cause*, and said, 'You must give me in marriage.' The Messenger of Allah, asked, 'Is there anyone for her?' A man stood up and said, 'I am for her, O Messenger of Allah, give her in marriage to me.' He (the Messenger of Allah) asked, 'What do you want to give her?' He replied, 'I do not have anything.' He (the Messenger of Allah) said, 'No, I will not give her in marriage to you.' She repeated and the Messenger of Allah also repeated his question to people, but no one other than that man said anything. She repeated again and on the third time the Messenger of Allah asked that man, 'Do you know something from the Quran well?' He replied, 'Yes, I know from the Quran.' He (the Messenger of Allah) said, 'I give her in marriage to you to teach her what you know well of the Quran.'"

H 9594, Ch. 48, h 6
Muhammad ibn Yahya has narrated from Ahmad ibn Muhammad from al-Hassan ibn Mahbub from Jamil ibn Salih from al-Fudayl who has said the following:

"This is concerning my question before abu 'Abd Allah, *'Alayhi al-Salam*, about the case of a man who marries a woman for one thousand dirham. He then gives her a runaway slave and a gown made of silk for one thousand dirham for her *mahr* (dower). He (the Imam) said, 'If she agrees for the slave and knows his condition, then it is not unlawful if she takes possession of the clothes and has agreed for the slave.' I then asked, 'What happens if he divorces her before going to bed with her?' He (the Imam) said, 'She will have no *mahr* (dower) and has to return five hundred dirham and the slave is for her.'"

H 9595, Ch. 48, h 7
Ali ibn Ibrahim has narrated from his father from ibn abu 'Umayr from Ali ibn abu Hamzah who has said the following:

"I once asked al-Rida', *'Alayhi al-Salam*, about the case of a man who marries a woman and her *mahr* (dower) is a servant. He (the Imam) said, 'The servant must be of average and medium condition.' I then asked, 'What happens if it is a house?' He (the Imam) said, 'It must be of average and medium condition.'"

H 9596, Ch. 48, h 8
Muhammad ibn Yahya has narrated from Ahmad ibn Muhammad from Ali ibn al-Hakam from Ali ibn abu Hamzah who has said the following:

"I once asked abu Ibrahim, *'Alayhi al-Salam*, about the case of a man who gave his daughter in marriage to the son of his brother with a *mahr* (dower) of a house and a servant and the man died. He (the Imam) said, '*Mahr* (dower) is paid from medium kinds of assets.' I (the narrator) than asked, 'What is the condition of the house and servant?' He (the Imam) said, 'The house must be of a medium condition and the servant must be of a medium condition.' I then asked, 'Can it be thirty or forty dinar? The house is about that much.' The Imam said, 'This is seventy-eighty dinar or one hundred dinar or so.'"

H 9597, Ch. 48, h 9
Muhammad ibn Yahya has narrated from Ahmad ibn Muhammad from Ali ibn al-Hakam from 'Abd Allah al-Kahiliy who has said that narrated to me daughter of al-Hassan sister of abu 'Ubaydah al-Hadhddha' who has said the following:

"This is concerning my question before abu 'Abd Allah, *'Alayhi al-Salam*, about the case of a man who marries a woman with a condition not to marry any other woman with her and she agrees for that as her *mahr* (dower). He (the Imam) said, 'This condition is not valid because *mahr* (dower) can only be like one or two dirham.'"

H 9598, Ch. 48, h 10

Humayd ibn Ziyad has narrated from al-Hassan ibn Muhammad ibn Sama'ah from more than one person from Aban ibn 'Uthman from 'Abd al-Rahman ibn abu 'Abd Allah who has said the following:

"About the case of a man who marries a woman without assigning any *mahr* (dower) and goes to bed with her, abu 'Abd Allah, *'Alayhi al-Salam*, has said, 'She has a *mahr* (dower) similar to that for the women of her family.'"

H 9599, Ch. 48, h 11

Muhammad ibn Yahya has narrated from Ahmad ibn Muhammad from Muhammad ibn Yahya from Ghiyath ibn Ibrahim who has said the following:

"About the case of a man who marries a woman for a *mahr* (dower) payable immediately and a part of it on credit, abu 'Abd Allah, *'Alayhi al-Salam*, has said, 'The due date for payment of what is on credit of *mahr* (dower) is on their separation or death.'"

H 9600, Ch. 48, h 12

Abu Ali al-Ash'ariy has narrated from Muhammad ibn 'Abd al-Jabbar from Safwan from Musa ibn Bakr from Zurarah who has said the following:

"About the case of a man who hides the amount of *mahr* (dower) and in public shows it more, abu Ja'far, *'Alayhi al-Salam*, has said, 'It (*mahr* (dower)) is what he hides.'"

H 9601, Ch. 48, h 13

Ali ibn Ibrahim has narrated from his father from Hammad from Hariz from Muhammad ibn Muslim who has said the following:

"Abu Ja'far, *'Alayhi al-Salam*, once asked, 'Do you know why *mahr* (dower) of women has become four thousand?' I replied, 'No, I do not know.' He (the Imam) said, "Umm Habibah, daughter of abu Sufyan was in al-Habashah (Ethiopia) and the Holy Prophet, *O Allah, grant compensation to Muhammad and his family worthy of their services to Your cause,* proposed marriage. Al-Najashiy paid four thousand. For this reason they take it, however, the actual *mahr* (dower) is twelve *Awqiyah* and one *Nashsha*.'"

H 9602, Ch. 48, h 14

Muhammad ibn Yahya has narrated from Muhammad ibn Ahmad from Musa ibn Ja'far from Ahmad ibn Bashir from Ali ibn Asbat from al-Bitkhiy from ibn Bukayr from Zurarah who has said the following:

"About the case of a man who marries a woman for teaching her a chapter from the book of Allah, then divorces her before going to bed with her and what she must receive, abu Ja'far, *'Alayhi al-Salam*, has said, 'He owes to teach her half as much of that chapter.'"

H 9603, Ch. 48, h 15

Ali ibn Ibrahim has narrated from his father from al-Nawfaliy from al-Sakuniy who has said the following:

"Abu 'Abd Allah, *'Alayhi al-Salam*, has said that the Holy Prophet, *O Allah, grant compensation to Muhammad and his family worthy of their services to Your cause*, has said, 'If a woman gives her *mahr* (dower) as charity to her husband before going to bed with her, Allah writes for her for every dinar freeing of a slave.' It was asked, 'O Messenger of Allah, What is for gifting it after going to bed?' He (the Messenger of Allah) said, 'That is because of affection and kindness.'"

H 9604, Ch. 48, h 16

Abu Ali al-Ash'ariy has narrated from Muhammad ibn 'Abd al-Jabbar from Safwan from ibn Muskan from abu Ayyub al-Khazzaz from Muhammad ibn Muslim who has said the following:

"This is concerning my question before abu 'Abd Allah, *'Alayhi al-Salam*, about the minimum amount of *mahr* (dower). He (the Imam) said, 'It can be a figure of sugar.'"

H 9605, Ch. 48, h 17

Ali ibn Ibrahim has narrated from his father from al-Nawfaliy from al-Sakuniy who has said the following:

"Abu 'Abd Allah, *'Alayhi al-Salam*, has said that the Messenger of Allah, *O Allah, grant compensation to Muhammad and his family worthy of their services to Your cause*, has said, 'Allah forgives every sin on the Day of Judgment except non-payment of *mahr* (dower), usurpation of wages and selling free people.'"

H 9606, Ch. 48, h 18

A number of our people have narrated from Ahmad ibn Muhammad from ibn Khalid from Muhammad ibn 'Isa from al-Mashriqiy from a group who narrated to him who has said the following:

"Abu 'Abd Allah, *'Alayhi al-Salam*, has said, 'Imam pays debts of believing people except *mahr* (dower) of women.'"

Chapter 49 - The Effect of Conjugal Relation on *Mahr*

H 9607, Ch. 49, h 1

Ali ibn Muhammad has narrated from Salih ibn abu Hammad from ibn Faddal from ibn Bukayr from 'Ubayd ibn Zurarah who has said the following:

"Abu 'Abd Allah, *'Alayhi al-Salam*, has said, 'A man's going to bed with his woman destroys immediate payability of *mahr* (dower) which was for immediate payment.'"

H 9608, Ch. 49, h 2

A number of our people have narrated from Sahl ibn Ziyad from 'Abd al-Rahman ibn abu Najran from al-'Ala' ibn Razin from Muhammad ibn Muslim who has said the following:

"About the case of a man who marries a woman and goes to bed with her, then she asks for payment of *mahr* (dower), abu Ja'far, *'Alayhi al-Salam*, has said, 'His going to bed with her destroys immediate payability of *mahr* (dower) which was for immediate payment.'"

H 9609, Ch. 49, h 3

Muhammad ibn Yahya has narrated from Ahmad ibn Muhammad from ibn Faddal from ibn Bukayr from 'Ubayd ibn Zurarah who has said the following:

"About the case of a man who goes to bed with a woman, then she asks for payment of *mahr* (dower), abu 'Abd Allah, *'Alayhi al-Salam*, has said, 'When he goes to bed with her the condition of immediate payment is destroyed.'"

Chapter 50 - One's Intention about Payment of *Mahr*

H 9610, Ch. 50, h 1

Ali ibn Muhammad has narrated from Salih ibn abu Hammad from ibn Faddal from certain persons of our people who has said the following:

"Abu 'Abd Allah, *'Alayhi al-Salam*, has said, 'If one agrees to pay *mahr* (dower) then decides not to pay it, he is like a thief.'"

H 9611, Ch. 50, h 2

Al-Husayn from Muhammad has narrated from Mu'alla' ibn Muhammad from al-Hassan ibn Ali from Hammad ibn 'Uthaman who has said the following:

"Abu 'Abd Allah, *'Alayhi al-Salam*, has said, 'If one marries a woman and then decides in his soul not to pay her *mahr* (dower), he has committed fornication.'"

H 9612, Ch. 50, h 3

A number of our people have narrated from Ahmad ibn abu 'Abd Allah from his father from Khalaf ibn Hammad from ibn Rib'iy ibn 'Abd Allah from al-Fudayl ibn Yasar who has said the following:

"Abu 'Abd Allah, *'Alayhi al-Salam*, has said, 'If a man marries a woman and does not tell his soul to pay her *mahr* (dower) it is fornication.'"

Chapter 51 - The Case of a Certain amount of *Mahr* for a Woman and a Payment to Her Father

H 9613, Ch. 51, h 1

Al-Husayn from Muhammad has narrated from Mu'alla' ibn Muhammad Ahmad ibn Muhammad from Muhammad ibn Yahya from Ahmad ibn Muhammad from all from al-Washsha' who has said the following:

"I once heard al-Rida', *'Alayhi al-Salam*, saying, 'If a man marries a woman for a *mahr* (dower) of twenty thousand of which ten thousand is for her father, *mahr* (dower) is permissible but that which is for her father is invalid.'"

Chapter 52 – A Woman offers Herself as a Gift to a Man

H 9614, Ch. 52, h 1

Abu Ali al-Ash'ariy has narrated from Muhammad ibn 'Abd al-Jabbar from Safwan and Muhammad ibn 'Isma'il has narrated from al-Fadl ibn Shadhan from Safwan Ahmad ibn Muhammad and Muhammad ibn Sinan all from ibn Muskan from al-Halabiy who has said the following:

"This is concerning my question before abu 'Abd Allah, *'Alayhi al-Salam*, about the case of a woman who gives herself as a gift to a man for marriage. He (the Imam) said, 'This was only for the Holy Prophet, *O Allah, grant compensation to Muhammad and his family worthy of their services to Your cause*, but for others it is not proper without something in exchange before going to bed with her; a small or large amount even a cloth or dirham.' He (the Imam) said, 'Dirham is enough.'"

H 9615, Ch. 52, h 2
A number of our people have narrated from Sahl ibn Ziyad from Ahmad ibn Muhammad from ibn abu Nasr from Dawud ibn Sarhan from Zurarah who has said the following:
"I once asked abu Ja'far, *'Alayhi al-Salam*, about the words of Allah, most Majestic, most Glorious, 'A believing woman who gifts herself to the Holy Prophet. . . .' (33:50) He (the Imam) said that such gift is not lawful except for the Messenger of Allah, *O Allah, grant compensation to Muhammad and his family worthy of their services to Your cause*, In the case of other people marriage without *mahr* (dower) is not proper.'"

H 9616, Ch. 52, h 3
Muhammad ibn Yahya has narrated from Ahmad ibn Muhammad from Muhammad ibn 'Isma'il has narrated from al-Fadl ibn Shadhan from abu al-Sabbah al-Kinaniy who has said the following:
"Abu 'Abd Allah, *'Alayhi al-Salam*, has said, '(A woman's) gifting herself is not lawful except to the Messenger of Allah, *O Allah, grant compensation to Muhammad and his family worthy of their services to Your cause*, and in other people's case, marriage is not proper without *mahr* (dower).'"

H 9617, Ch. 52, h 4
Ali ibn Ibrahim has narrated from his father from certain persons of his people from 'Abd Allah ibn Sinan who has said the following:
"About the case of a woman who gifts herself or her guardian gifts her to a man, abu 'Abd Allah, *'Alayhi al-Salam*, has said, 'No, it was only for the Messenger of Allah, *O Allah, grant compensation to Muhammad and his family worthy of their services to Your cause*, and not for others unless it is in exchange for something, little or more.'"

H 9618, Ch. 52, h 5
A number of our people have narrated from Ahmad ibn Muhammad from abu al-Qasim al-Kufiy from 'Abd Allah ibn al-Mughirah from a man who has said the following:
"About the case of a woman who gifts herself to a Muslim man, abu 'Abd Allah, *'Alayhi al-Salam*, has said, 'If it is in exchange for something it then is correct.'"

Chapter 53 - Dispute between Man, Woman and Her Family about *Mahr*

H 9619, Ch. 53, h 1
Muhammad ibn Yahya has narrated from Ahmad ibn Muhammad and Ali ibn Ibrahim has narrated from his father from all from ibn Mahbub from ibn Ri'ab from abu 'Ubaydah and Jamil ibn Salih from al-Fudayl who has said the following:
"About the case of a man who marries a woman, goes to bed with her, makes her to give birth to children, then dies and she asks something of her *mahr* (dower) from the heirs of the deceased as well as her share of inheritance, abu Ja'far, *'Alayhi al-Salam*, has said, 'She can ask for her share of inheritance but *mahr* (dower) is what she had received from her husband before going to bed with him and that is which made their marriage lawful, whether little or more as

she took possession and accepted and he went to bed with her but thereafter she has nothing to ask for.'"

H 9620, Ch. 53, h 2

Abu Ali al-Ash'ariy has narrated from Muhammad ibn 'Abd al-Jabbar from Safwan from 'Abd al-Rahman ibn al-Hajjaj who has said the following:

"This is concerning my question before abu 'Abd Allah, *'Alayhi al-Salam*, about the case of a husband and wife who both die and the heirs of the woman ask the heirs of the man to pay her *mahr* (dower). He (the Imam) said, 'There is no such right for them.' I then asked, 'What happens if woman is living and after his death comes and asks for her *mahr* (dower)?' He (the Imam) said, 'There is nothing for her; she lived with him until his death.' I then asked, 'What happens if she dies and he lives and her heirs come and ask for her *mahr* (dower)?' He (the Imam) said, 'She lived with him until her death and did not ask.' I said that that is true. He (the Imam) said, 'They have no right.' I then asked, 'What happens if he divorces her and she asks for her *mahr* (dower).' He (the Imam) said, 'She had lived with him and did not ask for her *mahr* (dower), so there is nothing for her.' I then asked, 'When has she the right to ask for her *mahr* (dower)?' He (the Imam) said, 'When she is led to his house until she arrives, her demand thereafter is nothing for her, such time is a great deal. She can ask him to take an oath by Allah saying that he does not owe her any *mahr* (dower), small or large.'"

H 9621, Ch. 53, h 3

Ali ibn Ibrahim has narrated from his father from ibn Mahbub from abu Ayyub from abu 'Ubaydah who has said the following:

"About the case of a man who marries a woman but he does not go to bed with her and she claims that her *mahr* (dower) is one hundred dinar while the husband says that it is fifty dinar and there is no witness, abu Ja'far, *'Alayhi al-Salam*, has said, 'The words of the husband are accepted on oath.'"

H 9622, Ch. 53, h 4

Muhammad ibn Yahya has narrated from Muhammad ibn Ahmad from Muhammad ibn 'Abd al-Hamid from abu Jamilah from al-Hassan ibn Ziyad who has said the following:

"Abu 'Abd Allah, *'Alayhi al-Salam*, has said, 'When a man goes to bed with his wife then she asks for her *mahr* (dower) and he says that he has paid, he must present testimony and take an oath.'"

Chapter 54 - Marriage without Witness

H 9623, Ch. 54, h 1

Ali ibn Ibrahim has narrated from his father from ibn abu 'Umayr from 'Umar ibn 'Udhaynah from Zurarah ibn 'A'yan who has said the following:

"Once abu 'Abd Allah, *'Alayhi al-Salam*, was asked about the case of a man who married a woman without witness. He (the Imam) said, 'It is not unlawful at all between him and Allah. Witness in marriage is for the sake of children, if that is not the concern then it is not unlawful.'"

H 9624, Ch. 54, h 2

Ali ibn Ibrahim has narrated from his father from and Muhammad ibn Yahya has narrated from 'Abd Allah ibn Muhammad all from ibn abu 'Umayr from Hisham ibn Salim who has said the following:

"Abu 'Abd Allah, *'Alayhi al-Salam*, has said, 'Witness and testimony (for marriage) is only for the sake of children and inheritance.' In another Hadith it is said, 'and it is for the sake of criminal issues.'"

H 9625, Ch. 54, h 3

Ali ibn Ibrahim has narrated from his father from and Muhammad ibn 'Isma'il has narrated from al-Fadl ibn Shadhan from ibn abu 'Umayr from Hafs ibn al-Bakhtariy who has said the following:

"About the case of a man who marries without witness, abu 'Abd Allah, *'Alayhi al-Salam*, has said, 'It is not unlawful.'"

H 9626, Ch. 54, h 4

A number of our people have narrated from Sahl ibn Ziyad from Dawud al-Nahdiy from ibn abu Najran from Muhammad ibn al-Fudayl who has said the following:

"Abu al-Hassan, Musa, *'Alayhi al-Salam*, once said to abu Yusuf, al-Qadi, 'Allah, most Blessed, most High, has commanded in His book about divorce and He has placed strong emphasis on the presence of two witnesses. He has not accepted anyone as witness other than two just ones. He has commanded in His book about marriage but He has left it (presence of witness) as overlooked. You, however, have established firmly the need for the presence of witnesses where He has overlooked, but you have invalidated the need for the presence of witnesses where He has placed strong emphasis (which is divorce).'"

Chapter 55 - Woman Lawful in Marriage for the Holy Prophet

H 9627, Ch. 55, h 1

Ali ibn Ibrahim has narrated from his father from and Muhammad ibn Yahya has narrated from Ahmad ibn Muhammad all from ibn abu 'Umayr from Hammad from al-Halabiy who has said the following:

"This is concerning my question before abu 'Abd Allah, *'Alayhi al-Salam*, about the words of Allah, most Majestic, most Glorious, 'O Holy prophet, we have made your wives lawful for you' (33:50) and that how many wives has He made lawful for him (the Holy Prophet)? He (the Imam) said, 'As many as he wanted were lawful for him.' I then asked about His words, 'Thereafter women are not lawful for you and it also is not lawful to exchange with wives.' (33:53) He (the Imam) said, 'The Messenger of Allah, *O Allah, grant compensation to Muhammad and his family worthy of their services to Your cause*, had permission to marry as many as he wanted of the daughters of his uncle, daughters of his aunts, daughters of his maternal uncles daughters of his maternal aunts and his wives who migrated with him and it was made lawful for him to marry whoever of believing women presented themselves to him without *mahr* (dower) as a gift and that such a gift is not lawful for people other than the Messenger of Allah, *O Allah, grant compensation to Muhammad and his family worthy of their services to Your cause*. For people other than the Messenger of Allah marriage without *mahr* (dower) is not valid and that is the meaning of the words of the most High, "and a believing woman who gifts herself to the Holy Prophet." (33:49) I then asked about the meaning of His words, 'You can defer whoever you like and accommodate whoever you like.' (33:51) He (the Imam) said, 'Whoever came forward he married and those who did not he did not marry.' I then asked about the meaning of, 'Thereafter women are not lawful for you.' He (the Imam) said, 'It refers to the women mentioned in this verse, "Unlawful to you for marriage are your mothers, daughters, sisters . . ." (4:23) Had it been as they say it is, it became lawful for you those who are not lawful for him, that one of you could exchange whenever he wanted but it is not as they say. Allah, most Majestic, most Glorious, made it lawful for His Holy prophet, *O Allah, grant compensation to Muhammad and his family worthy of their services to Your cause*, whatever he wanted of women except those unlawful in this verse.' (4:23)"

H 9628, Ch. 55, h 2

A number of our people have narrated from Sahl ibn Ziyad from abu Najran from 'Asem ibn Hamid from abu Basir who has said the following:

"This is concerning my question before abu 'Abd Allah, *'Alayhi al-Salam*, about the words of Allah, most Majestic, most Glorious, 'Other than these women are not lawful or to exchange wives even though their beauty may attract you except what your right hands possess.'(33:52) He (the Imam) said, 'I see that you think it is lawful for you what is unlawful for the Messenger of Allah, *O Allah, grant compensation to Muhammad and his family worthy of their services to Your cause*, when Allah, most High has made lawful for His Messenger, to marry as many as he wanted. He has said, "other than these 'woman'" are not lawful for you after that he has made unlawful to you meaning the "women" mentioned in the following verse, "Unlawful to you for marriage are your mothers, daughters . . ." (4:23)'"

H 9629, Ch. 55, h 3

Al-Husayn from Muhammad has narrated from Mu'alla' ibn Muhammad from al-Hassan ibn Ali al-Washsha' from Jamil ibn Darraj Ahmad ibn Muhammad from Muhammad ibn Humran who has said the following:

"We once asked abu 'Abd Allah, *'Alayhi al-Salam*, 'How many women were lawful for the Messenger of Allah, *O Allah, grant compensation to Muhammad and his family worthy of their services to Your cause*. He (the Imam) said, 'As many as he (the Messenger of Allah) wanted' - making a hand gesture by keeping it closed he (the Imam) said - 'it was lawful for him.'"

H 9630, Ch. 55, h 4

A number of our people have narrated from Sahl ibn Ziyad from ibn abu Najran from 'Abd al-Karim ibn 'Amr from abu Bakr al-Hadramiy who has said the following:

"This is concerning my question before abu 'Abd Allah, *'Alayhi al-Salam*, about the words of Allah, most Majestic, most Glorious, to His the Holy Prophet, *O Allah, grant compensation to Muhammad and his family worthy of their services to Your cause*, 'O prophet, we have made your wives lawful for you.' (33:50) and that how many wives has He made lawful for him (the Holy Prophet)? He (the Imam) said, 'As many as he wanted were lawful for him.' I then asked about His words, '. . . and the believing woman who gifts herself for the Holy Prophet,' He (the Imam) said, 'Such a gift is not lawful for people, except the

Messenger of Allah; people other than the Messenger of Allah cannot marry without *mahr* (dower); it is not valid.' I then asked about the meaning of '. *. .* thereafter women are not lawful for you.' He (the Imam) said, 'It refers to the women mentioned in this verse, "Unlawful to you for marriage are your mothers, daughters, sisters . . ." (4:23) Had it been as they say it is, those who are not lawful for him became lawful for you, that one of you could exchange whenever he wanted. It is not as they say. Allah, most Majestic, most Glorious, made it lawful for His Holy prophet, *O Allah, grant compensation to Muhammad and his family worthy of their services to Your cause*, as many as he wanted of women except those unlawful in this verse (4:23). The Messenger of Allah had permission to marry as many as he wanted of women except those unlawful in this verse (4:23).'"

H 9631, Ch. 55, h 5

It is narrated from the narrator of the previous Hadith from 'Asem ibn Hamid from abu Basir and others about the names of the wives of the Holy Prophet, and their relations and qualities has said the following:

"The names of the wives of the Holy Prophet, were: 'A'ishah, Hafsah, 'Umm Habib daughter of abu Sufyan ibn Harb, Zaynab daughter of Jahash, Sawdah daughter of Zam'ah, Maymunah daughter of al-Harith, Safiyah daughter of Hay ibn Akhtab, 'Umm Salamah daughter of abu 'Umayyah and Juwayriyah daughter of al-Harith. 'A'ishah was from the tribe of Tamim, Hafsah from the tribe of 'Adiy, 'Umm Salamah was from tribe of banu Makhzum. Sawdah was from tribe of banu Asad ibn 'Abd al-'Uzza', Zaynab daughter of Jahash was from the tribe of banu Asad, certain ones were from banu 'Umayyah, 'Umm Habib daughter of abu Sufyan was from the tribe of banu 'Umayyah, Maymunah daughter of al-Harith was from the tribe of banu Hilal and Safiyah daughter Hay Akhtab was from banu Israel. He (the Messenger of Allah), *O Allah, grant compensation to Muhammad and his family worthy of their services to Your cause*, died and he had nine wives. Besides these there were those who had given themselves as a gift to the Holy Prophet. Khadijah daughter of Khuwaylid was (his first wife and) the mother of his children. Also of his wives were Zaynab daughter of abu al-Jawn who was deceived and al-Kindiyah."

H 9632, Ch. 55, h 6

Ali ibn Ibrahim has narrated from his father from ibn abu 'Umayr from Hammad from al-Halabiy who has said the following:

"Abu 'Abd Allah, *'Alayhi al-Salam*, has said, 'The Messenger of Allah, *O Allah, grant compensation to Muhammad and his family worthy of their services to Your cause*, did not marry a second wife in Khadijah's lifetime.'"

H 9633, Ch. 55, h 7

Muhammad ibn Yahya has narrated from Salmah ibn al-Khattab from al-Hassan Ali ibn Yaqtin from 'Asem ibn Hamid from Ibrahim ibn abu Yahya who has said the following:

"Abu 'Abd Allah, *'Alayhi al-Salam*, has said, 'The Messenger of Allah married 'Umm Salamah and she was given in marriage to him (the Messenger of Allah) by 'Umar ibn abu Salmah who was small and was not mature yet.'"

H 9634, Ch. 55, h 8

Ahmad ibn Muhammad al-'Asemiy has narrated from abu al-Hassan ibn Faddal from Ali ibn Asbat from his uncle Ya'qub ibn Salim from abu Basir who has said the following:

"This is concerning my question before abu 'Abd Allah, *'Alayhi al-Salam*, about the meaning of the words of Allah, most Majestic, most Glorious, 'Thereafter women are not lawful for you. . . .' (33:53) He (the Imam) said, 'Unlawful for him were the women mentioned in the verse, "Unlawful for you to marry are your mothers, daughters. . ." (4:23) Had it been as they say it is, those who are not lawful for him became lawful for you, that one of you could exchange whenever he wanted. It is not as they say. Ahadith of Ale Muhammad, *O Allah, grant compensation to Muhammad and his family worthy of their services to Your cause*, are different from the Ahadith of people. Allah, most Majestic, most Glorious, made it lawful for His Holy prophet to marry as many as he wanted of women except those unlawful in this verse (4:23).'"

Chapter 56 - Marriage Without Guardian

H 9635, Ch. 56, h 1

Ali ibn Ibrahim has narrated from his father from ibn abu 'Umayr from 'Umar ibn 'Udhaynah from al-Fudayl ibn Yasar and Muhammad ibn Muslim and Zurarah ibn 'A'yan and Burayd ibn Mu'awiyah who has said the following:

"Abu Ja'far, *'Alayhi al-Salam*, has said, 'A woman who has control over herself and is not dimwitted and has no master over her, her marriage without guardian is lawful.'"

H 9636, Ch. 56, h 2

Al-Husayn from Muhammad has narrated from Mu'alla' ibn Muhammad from al-Hassan ibn Ali from Aban ibn 'Uthman from abu Maryam who has said the following:

"Abu 'Abd Allah, *'Alayhi al-Salam*, has said, 'The virgin girl who has her father must not marry without his permission.' He (the Imam) said, 'If she has control over her affairs she can marry whenever she wants.'"

H 9637, Ch. 56, h 3

Aban has narrated from 'Abd al-Rahman ibn abu 'Abd Allah who has said the following:

"Abu 'Abd Allah, *'Alayhi al-Salam*, has said, 'A woman who has control of her affairs can marry whomever she likes or she can appoint someone as her guardian.'"

H 9638, Ch. 56, h 4

Muhammad ibn Yahya has narrated from Ahmad ibn Muhammad from al-Husayn ibn Sa'id from Fadalah ibn Ayyub from 'Umar ibn Aban al-Kalbiy from Maysarah who has said the following:

"This is concerning my question before abu 'Abd Allah, *'Alayhi al-Salam*, about the case of a woman whom I meet in the wilderness and I ask her if she has a husband and she says, 'No; I do not have a husband' if I can marry her. He (the Imam) said, 'Yes, her words about herself are accepted as true.'"

H 9639, Ch. 56, h 5

Ali ibn Ibrahim has narrated from his father from Ahmad ibn Muhammad from Muhammad ibn Yahya has narrated from Ahmad ibn Muhammad all from ibn abu 'Umayr from Hammad ibn 'Uthaman from al-Halabiy who has said the following:

"About the case of a woman's second marriage if she can propose for marriage, abu 'Abd Allah, *'Alayhi al-Salam*, has said, 'She has more control over her affairs and she can appoint someone to act as her guardian if the man is a proper match and it is her second marriage.'"

H 9640, Ch. 56, h 6
Abu Ali al-Ash'ariy has narrated from Muhammad ibn 'Abd al-Jabbar from Yahya from ibn Muskan from al-Hassan ibn Ziyad who has said the following:

"This is concerning my question before abu 'Abd Allah, *'Alayhi al-Salam*, about the case of a woman if she can propose for marriage. He (the Imam) said, 'She has more control over her affairs; she can appoint whomever she likes to act as her guardian if it is her second marriage.'"

H 9641, Ch. 56, h 7
Muhammad ibn Yahya has narrated from Ahmad ibn Muhammad from ibn Mahbub from ibn 'Abd al-'Aziz al-'Abdiy from 'Ubayd ibn Zurarah who has said the following:

"This is concerning my question before abu 'Abd Allah, *'Alayhi al-Salam*, about the case of a slave-girl who belongs to me and an heir (one who has a share in her price as part of his legacy) with me. We set her free. She has a brother who is absent and she is virgin; if it is permissible for me to marry her or it is not permissible without the permission of her brother. He (the Imam) said, 'Yes, it is permissible for you to marry.' I then asked, 'Can I marry her if I wanted?' He (the Imam) said, 'Yes, you can do so.'"

H 9642, Ch. 56, h 8
Ahmad ibn Muhammad has narrated from ibn Mahbub from ibn Ri'ab from Zurarah ibn 'A'yan who has said the following:

"I once heard abu Ja'far, *'Alayhi al-Salam*, saying, 'No one other than a father can revoke a marriage.'"

Chapter 57 - Fathers Permission for a Girl's Marriage

H 9643, Ch. 57, h 1
Muhammad ibn Yahya has narrated from Ahmad ibn Muhammad from Ali ibn al-Hakam from al-'Ala' ibn Razin from ibn abu ibn abu Ya'fur who has said the following:

"Abu 'Abd Allah, *'Alayhi al-Salam*, has said, 'A virgin woman who has her father must not marry without his permission.'"

H 9644, Ch. 57, h 2
Muhammad ibn Yahya has narrated from Ahmad ibn Muhammad from Ali ibn al-Hakam from al-'Ala' ibn Razin from Muhammad ibn Muslim who has said the following:

"One of the two Imam, (abu Ja'far or abu 'Abd Allah), *'Alayhim al-Salam*, has said, 'A virgin girl when living with her parents cannot appoint anyone to solemnize her marriage. In the absence of her father anyone can ask her to be appointed as her guardian.'"

H 9645, Ch. 57, h 3
A number of our people have narrated from Sahl ibn Ziyad from Ahmad ibn Muhammad from ibn abu Nasr from Dawud ibn Sarhan who has said the following:

"This is concerning my question before abu 'Abd Allah, *'Alayhi al-Salam*, about the case of a man who wants to give his sister in marriage. He (the Imam) said, 'He must have her permission and if she remains quiet it is her affirmation. If she refuses he must not give her in marriage, if she says, "Give me in marriage to so and so" then he must give her in marriage to whom she has chosen. An orphan in the care of a man must not be given in marriage without her agreement.'"

H 9646, Ch. 57, h 4

Ali ibn Ibrahim has narrated from his father from ibn abu 'Umayr from Hammad ibn 'Uthaman from al-Halabiy who has said the following:

"This is concerning my question before abu 'Abd Allah, *'Alayhi al-Salam*, about the case of a man who gives his daughter in marriage to someone without her permission. He (the Imam) said, 'With the existence of her father she has no say and commandments. If he gives her in marriage it is permissible even if she dislikes.' He (the Imam) was asked about the case of a man who wants to give his sister in marriage. He (the Imam) said, 'He must have her commandment, permission and if she remains quiet it is her affirmation and if she refuses he cannot give her in marriage.'"

H 9647, Ch. 57, h 5

Humayd ibn Ziyad has narrated from al-Hassan ibn Muhammad ibn Sama'ah from Ja'far ibn Sama'ah from Aban from ibn Fadl ibn 'Abd al-Malik who has said the following:

"Abu 'Abd Allah, *'Alayhi al-Salam*, has said, 'The girl who is with her parents cannot appoint someone (to solemnize her marriage) when her father wants to give her in marriage; he is more careful than her. A woman for her second marriage must be asked for her permission if she lives with her parents and they want to give her in marriage.'"

H 9648, Ch. 57, h 6

A number of our people have narrated from Ahmad ibn Muhammad from al-Husayn ibn Sa'id from 'Abd Allah ibn al-Salt who has said the following:

"I once asked al-Rida', *'Alayhi al-Salam*, about the case of a small girl whose father wanted to give her in marriage: if she had any commandment. He (the Imam) said, 'No, with the existence of her father she has no commandments.' I then asked about a virgin who has grown like other woman; if she has any commandment with her father. He (the Imam) said, 'No, she does not have any commands with her father until she grows up.'"

H 9649, Ch. 57, h 7

Muhammad ibn Yahya has narrated from Ahmad ibn Muhammad from Ali ibn Mahziyar from Muhammad ibn al-Hassan al-Ash'ariy who has said the following:

"Certain ones of sons of my uncle wrote to abu Ja'far al-Thaniy, *'Alayhi al-Salam*, asking about the small girl whom her uncle gave in marriage to someone and when she grew up she disagreed with the marriage. He (the Imam) wrote back in his own handwriting, 'She must not be forced, and the command is her command.'"

H 9650, Ch. 57, h 8

Muhammad ibn Yahya has narrated from Ahmad ibn Muhammad and Ahmad ibn Muhammad from ibn abu Nasr who has said the following:

"Abu al-Hassan, *'Alayhi al-Salam*, has said, 'In the case of a virgin, her remaining quiet is her permission, and a woman for her second marriage has her own command and power of decision-making.'"

H 9651, Ch. 57, h 9

Muhammad ibn Yahya has narrated from Ahmad ibn Muhammad from Muhammad ibn 'Isma'il ibn Bazi' who has said the following:

"I once asked abu al-Hassan, *'Alayhi al-Salam*, about the case of a small girl whose father gave her in marriage, but he died before her husband went to bed with her; if her marriage was permissible or it was it up to her to decide. He (the Imam) said, 'Her father's giving in marriage is permissible.'"

Chapter 58 - A Man Wants to Marry one's Daughter and the Father Intends to Give Her to Another Man

H 9652, Ch. 58, h 1

Muhammad ibn Yahya has narrated from Ahmad ibn Muhammad from ibn Faddal from ibn Bukayr from 'Ubayd ibn Zurarah who has said the following:

"This is concerning my question before abu 'Abd Allah, *'Alayhim al-Salam*, about the case of a girl whose father wants to give her in marriage to one man and her grandfather wants to give her in marriage to another man. He (the Imam) said, 'Grandfather is preferred above the father as long as it is not harmful to the girl and that the father has not given her in marriage before the grandfather. Both father and grandfather's giving her in marriage is permissible.'"

H 9653, Ch. 58, h 2

Ahmad ibn Muhammad has narrated from Ali ibn al-Hakam from al-'Ala' ibn Razin from Muhammad ibn Muslim who has said the following:

"One of the two Imam, (abu Ja'far or abu 'Abd Allah), *'Alayhi al-Salam*, has said, 'If a man gives in marriage his granddaughter to a man, it is binding upon his son and his son also can give her in marriage.' I then asked, 'What happens if her father likes one man and her grandfather prefers another man?' He (the Imam) said, 'Grandfather has greater priority.'"

H 9654, Ch. 58, h 3

A number of our people have narrated from Sahl ibn Ziyad from Ahmad ibn Muhammad from ibn abu Nasr from abu al-Mighra' from 'Ubayd ibn Zurarah who has said the following:

"Abu 'Abd Allah, *'Alayhi al-Salam*, has said, 'One day I was with Ziyad ibn 'Ubayd Allah al-Harithiy when a man came and complained saying, "My father has given my daughter in marriage without my permission." Ziyad then asked the people in his meeting about their views in the matter. They said, "His marriage is invalid."' He (the Imam) has said, 'He then asked, "What do you say, O 'Abd Allah?" When he asked me I then turned to those who had given him an answer and asked them, 'Of the matters that you narrate from the Messenger of Allah, *O Allah, grant compensation to Muhammad and his family worthy of their services to Your cause*, is there the case of the man who came to him (the Messenger of Allah) and complained against his father like this man and the Messenger of Allah told him that you and your assets belong to your father?' They replied, 'Yes, we narrate.' I then asked them, 'Why is it that even he and his assets belong to his father but his father's giving in marriage is not permissible?' He (the Imam) said, 'He accepted their words and ignored my words.'"

H 9655, Ch. 58, h 4

Ali ibn Ibrahim has narrated from his father from and Muhammad ibn 'Isma'il has narrated from al-Fadl ibn Shadhan from all from ibn abu 'Umayr from Hisham ibn Salim and Muhammad ibn Hakim who has said the following:

"Abu 'Abd Allah, *'Alayhi al-Salam*, has said, 'If both father and grandfather give in marriage, the first one's marriage is effective and if both happens at the same time, the grandfather has the priority.'"

H 9656, Ch. 58, h 5

Humayd ibn Ziyad has narrated from al-Hassan ibn Muhammad ibn Sama'ah from Ja'far ibn Sama'ah from Aban from al-Fadl ibn 'Abd al-Malik who has said the following:

"Abu 'Abd Allah, *'Alayhi al-Salam*, has said, 'If a grandfather gives his granddaughter in marriage and his son is living but grandfather is ill, still marriage is binding.' We then asked, 'What happens if the father loves one and grandfather loves another man and they both are equal in justice and agreement?' He (the Imam) said, 'I love if she agrees with her grandfather.'"

H 9657, Ch. 58, h 6

A number of our people have narrated from Sahl ibn Ziyad from Ahmad ibn Muhammad from ibn abu Nasr from Dawud ibn al-Husayn from al-'Abbas who has said the following:

"Abu 'Abd Allah, *'Alayhi al-Salam*, has said, 'If a man marries, then his father rejects it, giving in marriage by the father is permissible; if the grandfather dislikes it, it is not like the case where grandfather gives in marriage, then father wants to reverse it.'"

Chapter 59 - Two Guardians, Each Gives a Girl to a Different Man in Marriage

H 9658, Ch. 59, h 1

Ali ibn Ibrahim has narrated from his father from ibn abu Najran from 'Asem ibn Hamid from Muhammad ibn Qays who has said the following:

"Abu Ja'far, *'Alayhi al-Salam*, has said that 'Amir al-Mu'minin, *'Alayhi al-Salam*, issued a judgment. It was about the case of a woman whose brother gave her in marriage to one man and her mother gave her in marriage to another man, her maternal uncle or her brother were younger. He went to bed with her and she became pregnant and the two men sought judgment in the case. The first presented witnesses so she was joined with the first man. Two *mahr* (dowers) were assigned for her altogether; the Imam stopped the husband who won from going to bed with her until the birth of the child and related the child to the father (the winner of the case).'"

H 9659, Ch. 59, h 2

Abu Ali al-Ash'ariy has narrated from Muhammad ibn 'Abd al-Jabbar and Muhammad ibn 'Isma'il has narrated from al-Fadl ibn Shadhan from all from Safwan from ibn Muskan from Walid Bayya' al-Asfat who has said the following:

"Once abu 'Abd Allah, *'Alayhi al-Salam*, was asked about the case of a girl, when I was present, who had several brothers. The elder brother gave her in marriage in al-Kufah and the younger brother gave her in marriage in another land and he (the Imam) said, 'The first has priority unless the other one has gone to bed with her, and if he has gone to bed she is his wife and his marriage is binding.'"

H 9660, Ch. 59, h 3

Muhammad ibn Yahya has narrated from Ahmad ibn Muhammad from Muhammad ibn 'Isma'il ibn Bazi' who has said the following:

"Once a man asked him (the Imam), *'Alayhi al-Salam*, about the case of a man who dies and leaves behind two brothers and a daughter who is small. One brother becomes the executor of the will and gives the girl in marriage to his son. The father of the boy married to the girl dies and thereafter the other brother says that his brother did not give the girl in marriage to his son so he gives the girl in marriage to his son and the girl is asked, 'Which one of the (two) husbands is more beloved to you?' She says, 'The other one (son of the second brother) is more beloved to me.' Then the second brother dies and the other brother has left behind another son older than the son who was married to the girl. He asks the girl to choose whichever of the two she likes. He (the narrator) has said that Hadith about this case says that she is for the second husband because she at that time was able to discern when she was given in marriage and it is not lawful for her to disregard the marriage which is formed after her gaining the ability to discern.'"

Chapter 60 - A Woman's Attorney Gives Her in Marriage to a Man Other Than What She Wanted

H 9661, Ch. 60, h 1

Ali ibn Ibrahim has narrated from his father and Muhammad ibn Yahya has narrated from Ahmad ibn Muhammad all from ibn abu 'Umayr from Hammad ibn 'Uthaman from al-Halabiy who has said the following:

"About the case of a woman who appoints a man to form her marriage with so and so and he says, 'I will do so only if you testify that I am your attorney;' she testifies for him and at the time of ceremony he says to the man who has proposed marriage, 'O so and so you owe such and such amount' and he says, 'Yes, I agree.' He (her attorney) says to people, 'Bear witness that this amount for her is on me and I give her in marriage to myself.' She then says, 'No, it is not an honor. The control of my affairs is in my own hand and I have not appointed you as the person in charge of my affairs. It was only because of not to verbally be embarrassed before people.' He (the Imam) said, 'He is removed from her. He deserves only a headache.'"

Muhammad ibn Yahya has narrated from Ahmad ibn Muhammad from Ali ibn al-Nu'man from abu al-Sabbah al-Kinaniy from abu 'Abd Allah, *'Alayhi al-Salam*, a similar Hadith.

Chapter 61 - Marriage of Minors Does Not Bring them Love

H 9662, Ch. 61, h 1

Muhammad ibn 'Isma'il has narrated from al-Fadl ibn Shadhan from and Ali ibn Ibrahim has narrated from his father from all from ibn abu 'Umayr from Hisham ibn al-Hakam who has said the following:

"It was once said to abu 'Abd Allah, or abu al-Hassan, *'Alayhi al-Salam*, 'We give our children in marriage when they are small children.' He (the narrator) has said that he (the Imam) said, 'If they are given in marriage when they are small, they may fail to develop loving relationships.'"

Chapter 62 - Age Limit of Conjugal Relations (Consult Fatwah about the contents of this chapter)

H 9663, Ch. 62, h 1

A number of our people have narrated from Sahl ibn Ziyad from Ahmad ibn Muhammad from ibn abu Nasr from 'Abd al-Karim ibn 'Amr from abu Basir who has said the following:

(...Consult Fatwah about this Hadith)

H 9664, Ch. 62, h 2

Ali ibn Ibrahim has narrated from his father from and Muhammad ibn Yahya has narrated from Ahmad ibn Muhammad all from ibn abu 'Umayr from Hammad from al-Halabiy who has said the following:

(...Consult Fatwah about this Hadith)

H 9665, Ch. 62, h 3

Humayd ibn Ziyad has narrated from al-Hassan ibn Muhammad ibn Sama'ah from Safwan ibn Yahya from Musa ibn Bakr from Zurarah who has said the following:

(...Consult Fatwah about this Hadith)

H 9666, Ch. 62, h 4

It is narrated from the narrator of the previous Hadith from Zakariya al-Mu'min or between him and him there is a man whom I do not know except that he narrated to me from 'Ammar al-Sajistaniy who has said the following:

(...Consult Fatwah about this Hadith)

Chapter 63 - Father Marries a Woman and His Son Marries Her Daughter

H 9667, Ch. 63, h 1

Abu Ali al-Ash'ariy has narrated from Muhammad ibn 'Abd al-Jabbar from Safwan ibn Yahya from 'Is ibn al-Qasim who has said the following:

"This is concerning my question before abu 'Abd Allah, *'Alayhi al-Salam*, about the case of a man who divorces his wife who marries another man and gives birth from the second man; if her children from the second husband are lawful for the children of the first husband from his wife other than her. He (the Imam)

363

said, 'Yes, it is lawful.' I then asked him about the case of a man who frees his slave-girl who marries another man and gives birth from the second man; if her children are lawful for the children of the man who freed her. He (the Imam) said, 'Yes, they are lawful.'"

H 9668, Ch. 63, h 2
Muhammad ibn Yahya has narrated from Muhammad ibn al-Husayn from Safwan and Ahmad ibn Muhammad from al-'Asemiy from Ali ibn al-Hassan Faddal from al-'Abbas ibn 'Amir from Safwan ibn Yahya from Shu'ayb al-'Aqarqufiy who has said the following:
"This is concerning my question before abu 'Abd Allah, *'Alayhi al-Salam*, about the case of a man who has a slave-girl with whom he goes to bed seeking to have a child, but does not become fortunate to have a child and gives her to his brother as a gift or sells her and she gives birth to several children; if his children from a woman other than her can marry the children of his brother from her. He (the Imam) asked me to say it again. I said it again and he (the Imam) said, 'Yes, it is not unlawful.'"

H 9669, Ch. 63, h 3
It is narrated from the narrator of the previous Hadith from al-Husayn ibn Khalid al-Sayrafiy who has said the following:
"I once asked abu al-Hassan, *'Alayhi al-Salam*, about this case and he asked me to say it again and I said, 'I had a slave-girl and I was not fortunate to have a child from her so I sold her and she give birth to a child from someone other than me and I have a child from a woman other than her; if I can give in marriage my child from another woman to her child.' He (the Imam) said, 'You can give in marriage to her children who were before you, before she became yours.'"

H 9670, Ch. 63, h 4
It is narrated from the narrator of the previous Hadith from Zayd ibn al-Juhaym al-Hilaliy who has said the following:
"This is concerning my question before abu 'Abd Allah, *'Alayhi al-Salam*, about the case of a man who marries a woman and his son marries the daughter of that woman. He (the Imam) said, 'If her daughter was there before she married him, it is not unlawful.'"

Chapter 64 - Giving Children in Marriage and Arranging Marriage for Them

H 9671, Ch. 64, h 1
Muhammad ibn Yahya has narrated from 'Abd Allah ibn Muhammad ibn Ali ibn al-Hakam from Aban 'Uthman fro al-Fadl ibn 'Abd al-Malik who has said the following:
"This is concerning my question before abu 'Abd Allah, *'Alayhi al-Salam*, about the case of a man who arranges marriage for his son who is small. He (the Imam) said, 'It is not unlawful.' I asked if divorce is permissible. He (the Imam) said, 'No, it is not permissible.' I asked, 'Who must pay *mahr* (dower)?' He (the Imam) said, 'The father must pay *mahr* (dower) if he has taken responsibility for it; but if he has not taken the responsibility on himself then the boy must pay unless the boy has no assets, then still he is responsible even if he has not taken

the responsibility.' He (the Imam) then said, 'If a man arranges marriage for his son it is up to him but if he gives his daughter in marriage it is binding.'"

H 9672, Ch. 64, h 2

Muhammad ibn Yahya has narrated from Ahmad ibn Muhammad from al-Hassan ibn Ali ibn Faddal from 'Abd Allah ibn Bukayr from 'Ubayd ibn Zurarah who has said the following:

"This is concerning my question before abu 'Abd Allah, *'Alayhi al-Salam*, about the case of a man who arranges marriage for his son who is small. He (the Imam) said, 'If his son has any assets *mahr* (dower) is on him but if the son does not have any asset then the father is responsible for *mahr* (dower) whether he accepts such responsibility or not.'"

H 9673, Ch. 64, h 3

Muhammad ibn Yahya has narrated from Ahmad ibn Muhammad from Ali ibn al-Hakam from al-'Ala' ibn Razin from Muhammad ibn Muslim who has said the following:

"I once asked one of the two Imam, (abu Ja'far or abu 'Abd Allah), *'Alayhim al-Salam*, about the case of a man who had sons and he arranged marriage for two of them and assigned *mahr* (dower) then he died; who was to pay *mahr* (dower); was it to be from all of the legacy or from the share of the two sons. He (the Imam) said in such case, 'It is from the whole of the legacy because it is like debts.'"

H 9674, Ch. 64, h 4

A number of our people have narrated from Sahl ibn Ziyad and Muhammad ibn Yahya has narrated from Ahmad ibn Muhammad and Ali ibn Ibrahim has narrated from his father from all from ibn Mahbub from ibn Ri'ab from abu 'Ubaydah al-Hadhdha' who has said the following:

"This is concerning my question before abu Ja'far, *'Alayhi al-Salam*, about the case of a boy and a girl for whom marriage is arranged by their guardians and they are not mature yet. He (the Imam) said, 'Marriage is binding and whichever becomes mature has a choice but if they die before maturity there will be no inheritance between them and no *mahr* (dower) unless they become mature and agree with the marriage.' I then asked, 'What happens if one of them becomes mature before the other?' He (the Imam) said, 'It becomes binding on him if he agrees.' I then asked, 'What happens if he becomes mature before the girl and agrees with the marriage, then he dies before the girl becomes mature; if she can inherit him.' He (the Imam) said, 'Yes, her share of inheritance is kept aside until she becomes mature, then she is made to take an oath that nothing has made her to claim the inheritance except her agreement with the marriage, then it is given to her as well as one-half of the *mahr* (dower).' I then asked, 'What happens if the girl dies before becoming mature and if the husband who has become mature can inherit her.' He (the Imam) said, 'No, because she had the choice upon her becoming mature.' I then asked, 'What happens if her father is the one who gives her in marriage before her becoming mature?' He (the Imam) said, 'Marriage which is arranged for her by her father becomes binding on her and on the boy and *mahr* (dower) is on the father in favor of the girl.'"

Chapter 65 - A Man Loves a Woman, His Parents Want Another Woman

H 9675, Ch. 65, h 1

Humayd ibn Ziyad has narrated from al-Hassan ibn Muhammad ibn Sama'ah from al-Hassan Ribat from Habib al-Khath'amiy from ibn abu Ya'fur who has said the following:

"I once said to abu 'Abd Allah, *'Alayhi al-Salam*, 'I want to marry with a woman but my father wants another one. He (the Imam) said, 'Marry the one you love, not the one your parents love.'"

H 9676, Ch. 65, h 2

Abu Ali al-Ash'ariy has narrated from Muhammad ibn 'Abd al-Jabbar from 'Isma'il ibn Sahl from al-Hassan ibn Muhammad al-Hadramy from al-Kahily from Muhammad ibn Muslim who has said the following:

"Once, abu Ja'far, *'Alayhi al-Salam*, was asked about the case of a man whose mother arranged marriage for him in his absence. He (the Imam) said, 'Marriage is permissible, the husband may agree or disagree; and if he disagrees payment of *mahr* (dower) becomes due on his mother.'"

Chapter 66 - Stipulations in Marriage: The Permissible and Impermissible ones

H 9677, Ch. 66, h 1

A number of our people have narrated from Sahl ibn Ziyad from ibn abu Najran from Ahmad ibn Muhammad from ibn abu Nasr fro 'Asem ibn Hamid from Muhammad ibn Qays who has said the following:

"About the case of a man who marries a woman for an appointed time that if within that time he pays *mahr* (dower) she is his wife and if he does not pay *mahr* (dower) within the appointed time he will have no way to the woman because such is their condition of the time of forming marriage, abu Ja'far *'Alayhi al-Salam*, has said, 'He has his wife in his hand and their condition falls void.'"

H 9678, Ch. 66, h 2

Muhammad ibn Yahya has narrated from Ahmad and 'Abd Allah sons of Muhammad ibn 'Isa have narrated from ibn abu 'Umayr from Hisham ibn Salim from abu al-'Abbas who has said the following:

"About the case of a man who marries a woman with the condition that he will not take her out of her town, abu 'Abd Allah, *'Alayhi al-Salam*, has said, 'He must keep that promise' or that he (the Imam) said, 'It is binding upon him.'"

H 9679, Ch. 66, h 3

Al-Husayn from Muhammad has narrated from Mu'alla' ibn Muhammad from al-Hassan ibn Ali from Aban ibn 'Uthman from 'Abd al-Rahman ibn abu 'Abd Allah who has said the following:

"This is concerning my question before abu 'Abd Allah, *'Alayhi al-Salam*, about the case of a man who marries a woman with the condition to come to her whenever he wants and pays her an agreed upon amount every month. He (the Imam) said, 'It is not unlawful.'"

H 9680, Ch. 66, h 4

Muhammad ibn Yahya has narrated from Ahmad ibn Muhammad from Ali ibn al-Hakam from Musa ibn Bakr from Zurarah who has said the following:

"Abu Abu Ja'far, *'Alayhi al-Salam*, was asked about the case of a man who married a woman who could only be visited during the day because of a condition at the time of forming marriage that he could visit her whenever he wants, like every month, every week one day with so and so amount for expenses. He (the Imam) said, 'Such condition is not meaningful. If one marries a woman she must have what a woman must have for her expenses as well as her share of her time. However, if a woman marries and is afraid of his neglecting or that he may marry another woman or divorce her and she reaches a settlement in exchange for her rights like expenses or share of her time, such points are valid, and it is not unlawful.'"

H 9681, Ch. 66, h 5

Muhammad ibn Yahya has narrated from Muhammad ibn al-Husayn from Safwan from al-'Ala' ibn Razin from Muhammad ibn Muslim who has said the following:

"About the case of a man who has a slave to whom he says, 'I set you free with the condition that I will give my daughter in marriage to you and if you married a second wife on her or did something secretly against her you must pay one hundred dinar', and he sets him free on such condition but he does secretly and marries. One of the two Imam, (abu Ja'far or abu 'Abd Allah), *'Alayhim al-Salam*, has said, 'He must stand by his condition.'"

H 9682, Ch. 66, h 6

Muhammad ibn Yahya has narrated from Ahmad ibn Muhammad from Ali ibn al-Hakam from Musa ibn Bakr from Zurarah who has said the following:

"Durays was married to the daughter of Humran with the condition that he will not marry a second wife on her and will never do anything secretly against her in her lifetime and after her death and a condition on her not to marry anyone after him. They set upon each other the condition of offering sacrifice, al-Hajj, and al-Budn and if anyone of them violated such conditions all of his or her assets go to the destitute. Then they came to abu 'Abd Allah, *'Alayhi al-Salam*, and informed him (the Imam) of the story. He (the Imam) said, 'The daughter of Humran has her rights and such rights will not make us to say that you have no rights. Go and marry and do things secretly because the conditions are not congenial and you or she is not obliged for anything and what you have done is not meaningful.' He did secretly certain things and many children were born for him.'"

H 9683, Ch. 66, h 7

Muhammad ibn Yahya has narrated from Ahmad ibn Muhammad from ibn Faddal from ibn Bukayr from certain persons of our people who have said the following:

"About the case of a woman who marries a man and she as part of her *mahr* (dower) says that going to bed will be in her control as well as divorce, abu 'Abd Allah, *'Alayhi al-Salam*, has said, 'It is against the Sunnah and has entrusted the right with one who is not the right person for it. Judgment requires

367

that the man must pay *mahr* (dower). He has the right to go to bed and divorce and that is the Sunnah.'"

H 9684, Ch. 66, h 8

Muhammad ibn Yahya has narrated from Muhammad ibn al-Husayn from Muhammad ibn 'Isma'il ibn Bazi' from Mansur ibn Buzurj who has said the following:

"I once said to abu al-Hassan, Musa, *'Alayhi al-Salam*, when I was standing, 'I pray to Allah to keep my soul in service for your cause, my partner had a wife. He divorced her and became stranger to her then he wanted to go back to her and she said, 'No, by Allah, I will never marry you until you make it binding on yourself from Allah not to divorce me and not to marry a second wife.' He (the Imam) asked, 'Did he do so?' I replied, 'Yes, he did, I pray to Allah to keep my soul in service for your cause.' He (the Imam) said, 'What he has done is terrible, ignoring the fact that what may fall in his heart in the middle of the night or day.' He (the Imam) then said, 'Now, however, say to him to complete the condition for the woman because the Messenger of Allah, *O Allah, grant compensation to Muhammad and his family worthy of their services to Your cause*, has said, "Muslims stand by their conditions."' I then said, 'I pray to Allah to keep my soul in service for your cause, I have doubts about the words (of the stipulation).' He (the Imam) said, 'He is 'Imran who meets you, is he not with you in al-Madinah?' I replied, 'Yes, that is true.' He (the Imam) then said, 'Tell him to write it and send it to me.' 'Imran afterwards came to us and we wrote them to him (the Imam) and there was no addition in it or reduction. He came back and met with me in the market of flours and touched my shoulder saying, 'He (the Imam) says Salam (the phrase of offering greeting of peace) to you and says to you to tell the man to stand by his condition.'"

H 9685, Ch. 66, h 9

A number of our people have narrated from Sahl ibn Ziyad Ahmad ibn Muhammad from Ali ibn Ibrahim has narrated from his father from all from ibn Mahbub from ibn Ri'ab who has said the following:

"This is concerning a question before abu al-Hassan, Musa, *'Alayhi al-Salam*, in my presence, about the case of a man who marries a woman for one hundred dinar with the condition that she will go with him to his town. If she will not go with him to his town her *mahr* (dower) will be fifty dinar. He (the Imam) said, 'If he wants to take her to the lands of pagans, then such condition is not valid and the one hundred dinar belongs to her which is her *mahr* (dower) but if he wants to take her to the lands of the Muslims within the Muslim domain then the condition is valid in his favor; Muslims must stand by their conditions. He cannot take her out of her town without first paying her *mahr* (dower) or make her agree with whatever amount, it then is permissible.'"

Chapter 67 - Cheating in Marriage

H 9686, Ch. 67, h 1

Muhammad ibn Yahya has narrated from Ahmad ibn Muhammad Ahmad ibn Muhammad from Ali ibn Ibrahim has narrated from his father from all from ibn Mahbub from al-'Abbas ibn Walid from al-Walid ibn Sabih who has said the following:

"About the case of a man who marries a free woman and finds her to be a slave who has disguised herself before him, abu 'Abd Allah, *'Alayhi al-Salam*, has said, 'If the one who has given her in marriage is not one of her masters, the marriage is invalid.' I then asked, 'What should he do about *mahr* (dower) that she has taken?' He (the Imam) said, 'If he finds with her something of what he has given to her, he can take it back, but if he does not find then she does not owe him anything. If a guardian has given her in marriage to him he can demand from such guardian what he has paid and her masters can demand from him one-tenth of her price if she is virgin; and if she is not virgin then it is half of one-tenth of her price which has made the marriage lawful.' He (the Imam) said, 'She must complete the waiting period for a slave.' I then asked, 'What happens if she gives birth to a child?' He (the Imam) said, 'Her children from him are free, if marriage is without the permission of the masters.'"

H 9687, Ch. 67, h 2
Muhammad ibn Yahya has narrated from Ahmad ibn Muhammad from al-Husayn ibn Sa'id from his brother al-Hassan from Zur'ah from Sama'ah who has said the following:

"This is concerning my question before him (the Imam); *'Alayhi al-Salam*, about the case of a slave-girl of a people who goes to a tribe other than her tribe and tells that she is free. A man marries her and she gives birth for him. He (the Imam) said, 'Her children are slaves unless testimony is established to prove that a witness had testified in favor of her being free, then her children cannot be owned; they remain free.'"

H 9688, Ch. 67, h 3
Ahmad ibn Muhammad has narrated from al-Husayn ibn Sa'id from 'Abd Allah ibn Bahr from Hariz from Zurarah who has said the following:

"This is concerning my question before abu 'Abd Allah, *'Alayhi al-Salam*, about the case of a slave girl who runs away from her masters, comes to another tribe and claims that she is free. A man in a hurry comes forward, marries her and her master then succeeds to find her out when she has already given birth to children. He (the Imam) said, 'If he can establish testimony that he has married her as a free woman her children are free, otherwise, he has caused himself a back pain and his children become slaves.'"

H 9689, Ch. 67, h 4
A number of our people have narrated from Sahl ibn Ziyad from Ahmad ibn Muhammad from ibn abu Nasr from Muhammad ibn Sama'ah from 'Abd al-Hamid from Muhammad ibn Muslim who has said the following:

"This is concerning my question before abu Ja'far, *'Alayhi al-Salam*, about the case of a man who proposes marriage to a man for his daughter for a certain amount of *mahr* (dower) but in the night of their going to bed he sends his other daughter who is from a slave-girl. He (the Imam) said, 'He returns her to her father who must send his wife to him and her *mahr* (dower) is on her father.'"

H 9690, Ch. 67, h 5
Ali ibn Ibrahim has narrated from his father from Hammad ibn 'Isa from Hariz from Muhammad ibn Muslim who has said the following:

"This is concerning my question before abu 'Abd Allah, *'Alayhi al-Salam*, about the case of a man who proposes marriage to a man for his daughter for a certain amount of *mahr* (dower) but he sends someone other than her. He (the Imam) said, 'The one identified in marriage must be sent to him with *mahr* (dower) paid by her father and the *mahr* (dower) which was set first belongs to the woman with whom he has gone to bed.'"

H 9691, Ch. 67, h 6
Ali ibn Ibrahim has narrated from his father from ibn abu 'Umayr from Hammad ibn 'Uthaman from al-Halabiy who has said the following:

"This is concerning my question before abu 'Abd Allah, *'Alayhi al-Salam*, about the case of a man who marries from a people but finds out that his wife is blind about which he was not informed. He (the Imam) said, 'Marriage is revoked only because of *al-Bars* (albino), leprosy, insanity and *al-'Afal* (growth of something in woman's vagina that does not allow sexual intercourse).'"

H 9692, Ch. 67, h 7
Muhammad ibn Yahya has narrated from Ahmad ibn Muhammad from al-Hassan ibn Ali ibn Faddal from 'Abd Allah ibn Bukayr from certain persons of his people who has said the following:

"This is concerning my question before abu 'Abd Allah, *'Alayhi al-Salam*, about the case of a man who marries a woman who is insane or has leprosy and so on. He (the Imam) said, 'He is responsible for *mahr* (dower).'"

H 9693, Ch. 67, h 8
A number of our people have narrated from Sahl ibn Ziyad from Ahmad ibn Muhammad from ibn abu Nasr from abu Jamilah from Zayd al-Shahham who has said the following:

"Abu 'Abd Allah, *'Alayhi al-Salam*, has said, 'Marriage of a woman with illness of *al-Bars* (albino), insanity and leprosy is revoked and invalid.' I asked about a blind. He (the Imam) said, 'No, it does not apply to her.'"

H 9694, Ch. 67, h 9
Sahl has narrated from Ahmad ibn Muhammad from Rifa'ah who has said the following:

"I once asked him (the Imam), *'Alayhi al-Salam*, about the case of a woman who suffers from *al-Bars* (albino). He (the Imam) said, ''Amir al-Mu'minin, *'Alayhi al-Salam*, issued a judgment, in the case of a woman who was given in marriage by her guardian when she suffered from *al-Bars*, that she deserves *mahr* (dower) which must be paid by the one who gave her in marriage. *Mahr* (dower) is on him because he cheated. If a man marries a woman and a man who does not know about her cheating gives her in marriage he does not owe anything but she must return the *mahr* (dower) back.'"

H 9695, Ch. 67, h 10
Sahl has narrated from Ahmad ibn Muhammad from Dawud ibn Sarhan and Ali ibn Ibrahim has narrated from his father from ibn abu 'Umayr from Hammad from al-Halabiy all who have said the following:

About the case of a man who is appointed by a woman to manage her affairs or a relative or a neighbor who does not know about her cheating and he finds her as cheating about a defect which exists in her. He (the Imam) said, 'She must pay back the *mahr* (dower) and the one who has given her in marriage does not owe anything.'"

H 9696, Ch. 67, h 11

Muhammad ibn Yahya has narrated from Ahmad ibn Muhammad and Ali ibn Ibrahim has narrated from his father from all from al-Hassan ibn Mahbub from Jamil ibn Salih from certain persons of abu 'Abd Allah, *'Alayhi al-Salam*, who has said the following:

"In the case of two sisters who were given (in marriage) as a gift to two brothers and who in the night of going to bed with them each one went to bed with the woman of the other one, abu 'Abd Allah, *'Alayhi al-Salam*, has said, 'Each one must pay *mahr* (dower) because of going to bed and if their guardians had known it and ignored they are liable for payment of *mahr* (dower). No one of them must go close to his wife until the waiting periods are complete, thereafter, each one can go to her husband according to the first marriage.' He (the Imam) was asked, 'What happens if they both die before completion of waiting period?' He (the Imam) said, 'Their husbands demand for half of *mahr* (dower) from their (women's) heir and both men have their shares in the legacy of the dead women.' It was asked, 'What happens if both men die and they are in their waiting period?' He (the Imam) said, 'They inherit them and they can have half of the *mahr* (dower) which was assigned and they must complete a waiting period after completing the waiting period before, the second being the waiting period for the death of their husbands.'"

H 9697, Ch. 67, h 12

Humayd ibn Ziyad has narrated from al-Hassan ibn Muhammad ibn Sama'ah from more than one person from Aban ibn 'Uthman from 'Abd al-Rahman ibn abu 'Abd Allah who has said the following:

"About the case of a man who marries a woman and finds *Qarn* or *al-'Afal* (growth of a substance in her vagina that prevents sexual intercourse) with her or whiteness or leprosy, he (the Imam), *'Alayhi al-Salam*, has said that he can revoke the marriage if he has not gone to bed with her.'"

H 9698, Ch. 67, h 13

Muhammad ibn Yahya has narrated from Muhammad ibn al-Husayn from Muhammad ibn Sinan from 'Isma'il ibn Jabir who has said the following:

"This is concerning my question before abu 'Abd Allah, *'Alayhi al-Salam*, about the case of a man who looks at a woman, likes her, asks about her and it is said that she is daughter of so and so. He goes to her father and asks him to give his daughter in marriage to him but he gives another woman in marriage to him and she gives birth for him but later he finds out that she is someone other than his daughter; instead she is his slave-girl. He (the Imam) said, 'He must return the mother to her master and the child is his. The masters of slave-girl must pay the cost and the price of the child to the man because of their cheating the man.'"

H 9699, Ch. 67, h 14

A number of our people have narrated from Sahl ibn Ziyad and Muhammad ibn Yahya has narrated from Ahmad ibn Muhammad all from al-Hassan ibn Mahbub from ibn Ri'ab from abu 'Ubaydah who has said the following:

"About the case of a man who marries a woman by the approval of her guardian and finds a defect in her after going to bed with her, abu Ja'far, *'Alayhi al-Salam*, has said, 'If the defect is *al-'Afal, al-Bars* (albino), insanity, or *'Ifda'* (an injury that cuts into her feces and urine passages), one who has an apparent defect and illness, such defective people's marriage is revoked and they are returned to their families without divorce. The husband demands for *mahr* (dower) from her guardian who has cheated about her, and if her guardian did not know about it then there is nothing on him (the guardian) and she is returned to her family.' He (the Imam) said, 'If the husband receives back what he had given, it belongs to him but if he did not get back anything then there is nothing for him.' He (the Imam) said, 'She must complete a waiting period which is for divorce if he has gone to bed with her but if he has not gone to bed with her then she does not need to complete a waiting period.'"

H 9700, Ch. 67, h 15
Ali ibn Ibrahim has narrated from his father from ibn abu 'Umayr from Hammad ibn 'Uthaman from al-Halabiy who has said the following:

"This is concerning my question before abu 'Abd Allah, *'Alayhi al-Salam*, about the case of a woman who gives birth because of going to bed with a man out of wedlock and no one except her guardian knows it, if it is proper for him to give her in marriage and remain quiet about it, provided, he has seen her repenting or good deeds. He (the Imam) said, 'If he does not mention it to her husband and later he (the husband) comes to know it, if he wants to demand her *mahr* (dower) from her guardian who cheated, he can do so and the *mahr* (dower) that he had received, he cannot collect it back from her because of marriage and if her husband wants to keep her it is not unlawful.'"

H 9701, Ch. 67, h 16
Abu Ali al-Ash'ariy has narrated from Muhammad ibn 'Abd al-Jabbar from Safwan ibn Yahya from 'Abd al-Rahman ibn abu 'Abd Allah who has said the following:

"Abu 'Abd Allah, *'Alayhi al-Salam*, has said, 'A woman can be returned because of four things: *al-Bars* (albino, a form of leprosy), leprosy, insanity and al-*Qarn* which is *al-'Afal*, (growth of a substance in her vagina that prevents sexual intercourse) if he has not yet gone to bed with her, and if so then she cannot be returned.'"

H 9702, Ch. 67, h 17
Muhammad ibn Yahya has narrated from Ahmad ibn Muhammad from ibn Mahbub from al-Hassan ibn Salih who has said the following:

"This is concerning my question before abu 'Abd Allah, *'Alayhi al-Salam*, about the case of a man who marries and finds *Qarn* in her. He (the Imam) said, 'She cannot become pregnant, so she is returned to her family and the husband abstains from going to bed with her to return her to her family.' I then asked, 'What happens if he has gone to bed with her?' He (the Imam) said, 'If he knew about it before going to bed with her then went to bed, he has agreed and if he comes to know it after going to bed then he can keep if he so wishes, or return her and she can have what she has received as *mahr* (dower).'"

H 9703, Ch. 67, h 18

Muhammad ibn Yahya has narrated from Ahmad ibn Muhammad from ibn Mahbub from abu Ayyub from abu al-Sabbah who has said the following:

"This is concerning my question before abu 'Abd Allah, *'Alayhi al-Salam*, about the case of a man who marries and finds *Qarn* in her. He (the Imam) said, 'She cannot become pregnant and her husband cannot go to bed with her, so she is compelled to return to her family and she has no *mahr* (dower).' I then asked, 'What happens if he has gone to bed with her?' He (the Imam) said, 'If he knew about it before going to bed with her then went to bed, he has agreed and if he comes to know it after going to bed then he can keep if he so wishes, or return her and she can have what she has received as *mahr* (dower).'"

H 9704, Ch. 67, h 19

Muhammad ibn Yahya has narrated from Ahmad ibn Muhammad from ibn Mahbub from Hisham ibn Salim from Burayd al-'Ijliy who has said the following:

"This is concerning my question before abu Ja'far, *'Alayhi al-Salam*, about the case of a man who marries a woman but her sister who is older than her goes to the house of the man, takes away the clothes of his wife, wears them, lies down in her room, moves her away and switches off the light. The girl cannot speak because of shyness. The man comes to the room and goes to bed with her thinking her as his wife and in the morning his wife comes to him saying, 'I am your wife so and so whom you married and my sister plotted to take away my clothes, sat in my room and removed me from there.' The man considers it and finds it to be true just as she said. He (the Imam) said, 'In my view the woman who cheated has no *mahr* (dower) and she must be punished in the form of punishment for fornication of an unmarried person and her husband must not go to bed with her until waiting period for the cheating is complete and when waiting period is complete he can join his wife.'"

Chapter 68 - Cheating from Man's Side in Marriage

H 9705, Ch. 68, h 1

Ali ibn Ibrahim has narrated from his father from ibn abu Najran from 'Asem ibn Hamid from Muhammad ibn Qays who has said the following:

"Abu Ja'far, *'Alayhi al-Salam*, has said that 'Amir al-Mu'minin, *'Alayhi al-Salam*, issued a judgment about the case of a free woman who was cheated by a slave who married her and she did not know him to be other than a free man. He (the Imam) said, 'They must be separated if the woman so wanted.'"

H 9706, Ch. 68, h 2

Muhammad ibn Yahya has narrated from Ahmad ibn Muhammad from Ali ibn al-Hakam from al-'Ala' ibn Razin from Muhammad ibn Muslim who has said the following:

"This is concerning my question before abu Ja'far, *'Alayhi al-Salam*, about the case of a woman who is free and marries a slave thinking that he is free and then finds out that he is a slave. He (the Imam) said, 'She has all the control of herself; if she wants she can stay with him or not stay with him. If he has gone to be bed with her she has the *mahr* (dower) and if he has not gone to bed with her she does not have any *mahr* (dower). If he goes to bed with her after her knowing that he is a slave and confirms it then he has more of her control.'"

H 9707, Ch. 68, h 3

A number of our people have narrated from Sahl ibn Ziyad from and Muhammad ibn Yahya has narrated from Ahmad ibn Muhammad from al-Hassan ibn Mahbub from ibn Ri'ab from ibn Bukayr from his father who has said the following:

"About the case of a castrated man who cheats and marries a Muslim woman, one of the two Imam, (abu Ja'far or abu 'Abd Allah), *'Alayhim al-Salam*, has said, 'They are separated from each other if she wants and he will have a headache, but if she agrees and stays with him, after her agreement she cannot deny him.'"

H 9708, Ch. 68, h 4

Abu Ali al-Ash'ariy has narrated from Muhammad ibn 'Abd al-Jabbar from Safwan ibn Yahya from Aban from 'Abbad al-Dabbiy who has said the following:

"About the case of a man who is impotent, abu 'Abd Allah, *'Alayhi al-Salam*, has said, 'When it is found out that he is impotent and cannot sleep with women, they are separated from each other; and if he goes to bed with her even once then they are not separated from each other; man is not turned away because of defect.'"

H 9709, Ch. 68, h 5

It is narrated from the narrator of the previous Hadith from Safwan ibn Yahya from ibn Muskan from abu Basir who has said the following:

"This is concerning my question before abu 'Abd Allah, *'Alayhi al-Salam*, about the case of a woman who tries her husband but he is not able to go to bed with her; if they must be separated from each other. He (the Imam) said, 'Yes, if she wants separation.' Ibn Muskan has said that in another Hadith he (the Imam) has said that she must wait for one year and if he still is not able to go to bed with her, she can leave him, but if she likes to stay with him she can do so.'"

H 9710, Ch. 68, h 6

A number of our people have narrated from Ahmad ibn Muhammad from al-Hassan ibn Sa'id from his brother al-Hassan ibn Zur'ah ibn Muhammad ibn Sama'ah who has said the following:

"About the case of a man who is castrated but he cheats and marries a woman, abu 'Abd Allah, *'Alayhi al-Salam*, has said, 'They are separated from each other and the women takes her *mahr* (dower) from him and he will have a backache (punishment) because of his cheating.'"

H 9711, Ch. 68, h 7

A number of our people have narrated from Sahl ibn Ziyad and Muhammad ibn Yahya has narrated from Ahmad ibn Muhammad all from ibn Mahbub from ibn Ri'ab from abu Hamzah who has said the following:

"I once heard abu Ja'far, *'Alayhi al-Salam*, saying, 'If a man marries a woman who was married before to another man and she alleges that the man has not come close to her from the time he entered with her in such case, the words of the man are accepted on oath by Allah that he has gone to bed with her because she is a plaintiff.' He (the Imam) has said, 'If he marries her as a virgin and she alleges that he never approached her, it then is the job of trustworthy women who can examine her and if they say that she is virgin then the Imam gives him one year's time during which if he is able to reach her, otherwise, they are separated from each other and she is given half of the *mahr* (dower) and no waiting period is required.'"

H 9712, Ch. 68, h 8

A number of our people have narrated from Ahmad ibn Muhammad from ibn Khalid from his father from 'Abd Allah ibn al-Fadl al-Hashimiy from certain persons of his teachers who have said the following:

"It is about the case of a woman before abu 'Abd Allah, *'Alayhi al-Salam*, when a man asked him (the Imam) about a man against whom his wife alleges that he is impotent but the man denies it, abu 'Abd Allah, *'Alayhi al-Salam*, said, 'She must allow the nurse to fill her with al-Khaluq (a certain perfume) without allowing the man to know. He then goes to bed with her; if perfume is found on his penis he has told the truth, otherwise, she has spoken the truth and he has lied.'"

H 9713, Ch. 68, h 9

Muhammad ibn Yahya has narrated from Ahmad ibn Muhammad from Ahmad ibn al-Hassan from 'Amr ibn Sa'id from Musaddiq ibn Sadaqah from 'Ammar ibn Musa who has said the following:

"Once abu 'Abd Allah, *'Alayhi al-Salam*, was asked about the case of a man who is held back (by magic) and cannot go to bed with his wife. He (the Imam) said, 'If he cannot go to bed with other woman also, he must not keep her on hold without her consent; but if he is able to go to bed with other women then it is not unlawful to keep her.'"

H 9714, Ch. 68, h 10

Ali ibn Ibrahim has narrated from his father from al-Nawfaliy from al-Sakuniy who has said the following:

"Abu 'Abd Allah, *'Alayhi al-Salam*, has said that 'Amir al-Mu'minin, *'Alayhi al-Salam*, has said, 'If a man only once goes to bed with his wife then is held back (by magic), no choice then remains for her (to revoke the marriage).'"

H 9715, Ch. 68, h 11

Al-Husayn from Muhammad has narrated from Hamdan al-Qalanisiy from Ishaq ibn Bunan from ibn Baqqah from Ghiyath ibn Ibrahim who has said the following:

"Abu 'Abd Allah, *'Alayhi al-Salam*, has said that during the time of 'Amir al-Mu'minin, *'Alayhi al-Salam*, a woman alleged that her husband is not able to go to bed with her and he denied it. 'Amir al-Mu'minin commanded her to fill up herself with saffron and that he then washes his penis; if the water takes the color of saffron his words are accepted, otherwise, he is commanded to divorce her.'"

Chapter 69 - Rare Ahadith

H 9716, Ch. 69, h 1

Muhammad ibn Yahya has narrated from Ahmad ibn Muhammad and Ali ibn Ibrahim has narrated from his father all from ibn Mahbub from Jamil ibn Salih from abu 'Ubaydah who has said the following:

"About the case of a man who has three virgin daughters and gives one of them in marriage to a man without identifying the girl for the husband or to the witnesses. The husband assigns a *mahr* (dower) for her. At the time for him to meet the girl he is informed that it is the oldest girl. He then says to the father, 'I married the youngest of your daughters.' Abu Ja'far, *'Alayhi al-Salam*, has said, 'If the husband had seen them and did not identify one of them the words of the father are accepted between him and Allah to give in marriage the girl that he had intended at the time forming marriage terms. If the husband had not seen all of them and had not identified any one of them at the time of forming the terms of marriage, the marriage then is invalid.'"

Chapter 70 - Marriage with Virginity Stipulation

H 9717, Ch. 70, h 1
Muhammad ibn Yahya has narrated from Ahmad ibn Muhammad ibn Khalid from Sa'd ibn Sa'd from Muhammad ibn al-Qasim ibn Fudayl who has said the following:
"About the case of a man who marries a woman as a virgin but finds that she is not virgin; if it is permissible to live with her, abu al-Hassan has said, 'At certain times it is torn because of riding or jumping.'"

H 9718, Ch. 70, h 2
Muhammad ibn Yahya has narrated from 'Abd Allah ibn Ja'far from Muhammad ibn Jazzak who has said the following:
"I once wrote to abu al-Hassan, *'Alayhi al-Salam*, and asked about the case of a man who married a virgin girl but found out that she was not virgin if it was obligatory to pay complete *mahr* (dower) or less. He (the Imam) answered, 'It is less.'"

Chapter 71 - Conjugal Relation without Paying *Mahr*

H 9719, Ch. 71, h 1
Muhammad ibn Yahya has narrated from Muhammad ibn al-Husayn from Muhammad ibn 'Isma'il from Mansur ibn Yunus from 'Abd al-Hamid ibn 'Awwad who has said the following:
"This is concerning my question before abu 'Abd Allah, *'Alayhi al-Salam*, about forming marriage terms with a woman; if I can go to bed with her without paying her anything in cash of her *mahr* (dower). He (the Imam) said, 'Yes, you can do so, it is only a debt on you.'"

H 9720, Ch. 71, h 2
A number of our people have narrated from Sahl ibn Ziyad and Ali ibn Ibrahim has narrated from his father all from Ahmad ibn Muhammad from ibn abu Nasr who has said the following:
"This is concerning my question before abu al-Hassan, *'Alayhi al-Salam*, about the case of a man who marries a woman for a certain amount of *mahr* (dower) and goes to bed with her without paying anything. He (the Imam) said, 'He must pay in advance a little or more unless he has a certain asset which is enough to pay her *mahr* (dower) in case something happens to him, then it is not unlawful.'"

H 9721, Ch. 71, h 3

Ali ibn Ibrahim has narrated from his father from ibn abu 'Umayr from certain persons of his people from 'Abd al-Hamid al-Ta'iy who has said the following:

"This is concerning my question before abu 'Abd Allah, *'Alayhi al-Salam,* if I can marry and go to bed with her without paying anything. He (the Imam) said, 'Yes, you can do so and it is a debt on you.'"

H 9722, Ch. 71, h 4

Ali ibn Ibrahim has narrated from Muhammad ibn 'Isa from Yunus from 'Abd al-Hamid ibn 'Awwad al-Ta'iy who has said the following:

"This is concerning my question before abu 'Abd Allah, *'Alayhi al-Salam,* about the case of a man who marries a woman and does not have anything to pay her and then goes to bed with her. He (the Imam) said, 'It is not unlawful; it is a debt on him.'"

Chapter 72 - Working for Hire as Payment for *Mahr*

H 9723, Ch. 72, h 1

A number of our people have narrated from Sahl ibn Ziyad and Ali ibn Ibrahim has narrated from his father all from Ahmad ibn Muhammad from ibn abu Nasr who has said the following:

"I once asked abu al-Hassan, *'Alayhi al-Salam,* about the meaning of the words of Shu'ayb, '(Shu'ayb) said to (Moses), "I want to give one of my daughters to you in marriage on the condition that you will work for me for eight years, but you may continue for two more years only out of your own accord"' (28:27) and that which one of the terms he completed. He (the Imam) said, 'Completion was of the longest term which was ten years.' I then asked, 'Did he go to bed before completing the term or afterwards?' He (the Imam) said, 'It was before completing the terms.' I then asked, 'If a man marries a woman and stipulates with her father for the wages of two months if it is permissible.' He (the Imam) said, 'Moses knew that he will complete the terms. How can this man know that he remains alive until the time of paying? At the time of the Messenger of Allah, *O Allah, grant compensation to Muhammad and his family worthy of their services to Your cause,* people married women for teaching a chapter of al-Quran, for one dirham and for one handful of wheat.'"

H 9724, Ch. 72, h 2

Ali ibn Ibrahim has narrated from his father from al-Nawfaliy from al-Sakuniy who has said the following:

"Abu 'Abd Allah, *'Alayhi al-Salam,* has said, 'Marriage is not lawful in Islam for hiring and saying, 'I will work for you up to so and so many years and you give to me in marriage your daughter or sister.' He (the Imam) said, 'It is unlawful because it is the price of her neck and in fact she is the rightful person for her *mahr* (dower).'"

Chapter 73 - Death Before Consummation of Marriage

H 9725, Ch. 73, h 1

Muhammad ibn Yahya has narrated from Ahmad ibn Muhammad from al-Hassan ibn Ali from 'Abd Allah ibn Bukayr from certain persons of our people who has said the following:

"About the case of a man who sends a proposal for marriage and he is absent. They give her in marriage to one who is absent and assign *mahr* (dower) but then news comes that he is dead after assigning *mahr* (dower). He (the Imam) said, 'If his earning is after his death she has no *mahr* (dower) or inheritance but if his earning is before his death then she deserves half of *mahr* (dower) and she inherits him.'"

Chapter 74 - One's Marriage with a Mother or Sister of a Woman after out of Wedlock Conjugal Relation With Her Or going to Bed with One's Mother-in-Law Or Stepdaughter

H 9726, Ch. 74, h 1
Muhammad ibn Yahya has narrated from Ahmad ibn Muhammad from Ali ibn al-Hakam from al-'Ala' ibn Razin from Muhammad ibn Muslim who has said the following:
"One of the two Imam, (abu Ja'far or abu 'Abd Allah), *'Alayhim al-Salam*, was asked about the case of a man who went to bed with a woman out of wedlock; if he could marry her daughter. He (the Imam) said, 'No, however, if a woman is his wife and he goes to bed with her mother or her daughter or sister, his wife does not become unlawful for him because unlawful does not destroy what is lawful.'"

H 9727, Ch. 74, h 2
Abu Ali al-Ash'ariy has narrated from Muhammad ibn 'Abd al-Jabbar and Muhammad ibn 'Isma'il has narrated from al-Fadl ibn Shadhan from all from Safwan ibn Yahya from 'Is ibn al-Qasim who has said the following:
"This is concerning my question before abu 'Abd Allah, *'Alayhi al-Salam*, about the case of a man who associates with a woman and kisses her but does not go to bed with her; if he can marry her daughter. He (the Imam) said, 'If he has not gone to bed with the mother, it is not unlawful to marry her but if he has gone to bed with her mother then he must not marry her (the daughter).'"

H 9728, Ch. 74, h 3
Ali ibn Ibrahim has narrated from his father from ibn abu 'Umayr from Hammad from al-Halabiy who has said the following:
"About the case of a man who marries a girl then goes to bed with her, then due to wickedness goes to bed with her mother; if she becomes unlawful for him, abu Ja'far, *'Alayhi al-Salam*, has said, 'His wife does not become unlawful for him.' He (the Imam) then said, 'Unlawful never makes a lawful thing unlawful.'"

H 9729, Ch. 74, h 4
Ali ibn Ibrahim has narrated from his father from ibn abu 'Umayr from ibn 'Udhaynah from Zurarah who has said the following:
"About the case of a man who goes to bed with his mother-in-law or his stepdaughter or her sister, abu Ja'far *'Alayhi al-Salam*, has said, 'This does not make his wife unlawful for him.' He (the Imam) then said, 'Unlawful does not make a lawful thing unlawful.'"

H 9730, Ch. 74, h 5

Abu Ali al-Ash'ariy has narrated from Muhammad ibn 'Abd al-Jabbar from Safwan from Mansur ibn Hazim who has said the following:

"About the case of a man and a woman who are involved in sinful activities; if he can marry her daughter, abu 'Abd Allah, *'Alayhi al-Salam*, has said, 'If such activities are in the form of kissing or similar things he can marry her daughter; but if it is sexual intercourse then he must not marry her daughter, he can, however, marry the woman if he wants.'"

H 9731, Ch. 74, h 6

A number of our people have narrated from Sahl ibn Ziyad from ibn Mahbub from ibn Ri'ab from Zurarah who has said the following:

"This is concerning my question before abu Ja'far, *'Alayhi al-Salam*, about the case of a man who goes to bed with the mother of his wife or her sister. He (the Imam) said, 'This does not make his wife unlawful for him; unlawful does not destroy or make lawful ones unlawful.'"

H 9732, Ch. 74, h 7

Al-Husayn from Muhammad has narrated from Mu'alla' ibn Muhammad from certain persons of his people from Aban ibn 'Uthman from Mansur ibn Hazim who has said the following:

"This is concerning my question before abu 'Abd Allah, *'Alayhi al-Salam*, about the case of a man and a woman who are involved in sinful acts. He (the Imam) said, 'If such activities are in the form of kissing or similar things he can marry her daughter; but if it is sexual intercourse then he must not marry her daughter, he can, however, marry the woman if he wants.'"

H 9733, Ch. 74, h 8

Muhammad ibn Yahya has narrated from Ahmad ibn Muhammad from Ali ibn al-Hakam from al-'Ala' ibn Razin from Muhammad ibn Muslim who has said the following:

"I once asked one of the two Imam, (abu Ja'far or abu 'Abd Allah), *'Alayhim al-Salam*, about the case of a man who had committed sinful acts with a woman if he could marry her breastfeeding mother or daughter. He (the Imam) said, 'No, he cannot do so.'

Muhammad ibn Yahya has narrated from Ahmad ibn Muhammad from ibn Mahbub from al-'Ala' ibn Razin from Muhammad ibn Muslim a similar Hadith."

H 9734, Ch. 74, h 9

Ibn Mahbub has narrated from Hisham ibn Salim from Yazid al-Kunnasiy who has said the following:

"A certain person of our people married a woman and said to me, 'I like if you ask abu 'Abd Allah, *'Alayhi al-Salam*, about the case of a man from our people who has married a woman and thinks that he may have played with her mother like kissing without sexual intercourse.' He (the narrator) has said, 'I asked abu 'Abd Allah, *'Alayhi al-Salam*, about it and he said, 'He has lied. Tell him to separate from her.' I returned from my journey and informed the man of what abu 'Abd Allah, *'Alayhi al-Salam*, had said. By Allah, he did not defend himself and sent her to go away.'"

H 9735, Ch. 74, h 10

Ali ibn Ibrahim has narrated from his father from ibn abu 'Umayr from abu Ayyub al-Khazzaz from Muhammad ibn Muslim who has said the following:

"Once, a man asked abu 'Abd Allah, *'Alayhi al-Salam*, when I was sitting, about the case of a man who when young was involved with his maternal aunt then refrained, if he could marry her daughter. He (the Imam) said, 'No, he cannot do so.' He then asked, 'What happens if there was no sexual intercourse, but it was something near the thing?' He (the Imam) said, 'No, his words are not accepted, and it is not honorable.'"

Chapter 75 - The Case of Sinful Relation of a Man with a Boy and Marriage with His Daughter or Sister

H 9736, Ch. 75, h 1

Al-Husayn from Muhammad has narrated from Mu'alla' ibn Muhammad from al-Hassan ibn Ali from Hammad ibn 'Uthaman who has said the following:

"This is concerning my question before abu 'Abd Allah, *'Alayhi al-Salam*, about the case of a man who commits sinful act with a boy; if he can marry his sister. He (the Imam) said, 'If he made a hole, then he cannot do so (marry).'"

H 9737, Ch. 75, h 2

Ali ibn Ibrahim has narrated from his father from ibn abu 'Umayr from certain persons of our people who has said the following:

"About the case of a man who plays with a boy, abu 'Abd Allah, *'Alayhi al-Salam*, has said, 'If he makes hole in him, his daughter and sister become unlawful for him.'"

H 9738, Ch. 75, h 3

Ali ibn Ibrahim has narrated from his father or from Muhammad ibn Ali from Musa ibn Sa'dan from certain persons of his people who have said the following:

"Once I was with abu 'Abd Allah, *'Alayhi al-Salam*, when a man came and said, 'I pray to Allah to keep my soul in service for your cause, if two young men slept together and one has a son and the other has a daughter; if his son could marry the other man's daughter.' He (the narrator) has said that he (the Imam) said, 'Yes, Allah is free of all defects, why can it be unlawful?' The man said they were friends. He (the Imam) said, 'Even if such is the case it is not unlawful.' The man said, 'He was doing to him.' He (the Imam) turned away his face then, while covering his face with his arms, said, 'Even if it was what it was without doing the hole it is not unlawful to marry but if *awqaba* (made a hole in him) then marriage is not lawful.'"

H 9739, Ch. 75, h 4

Ali ibn Ibrahim has narrated from his father from ibn abu 'Umayr from certain persons of his people who have said the following:

About the case of a man who goes to his brother-in-law, abu 'Abd Allah, *'Alayhi al-Salam*, has said, 'If he has made hole in him his wife becomes unlawful for him.'"

Chapter 76 - Because of Marriage People Who Become Unlawful to Marry

H 9740, Ch. 76, h 1

Ali ibn Ibrahim has narrated from his father from ibn abu 'Umayr from Hammad from al-Halabiy who has said the following:

"This is concerning my question before abu 'Abd Allah, *'Alayhi al-Salam*, about the case of a man who marries a woman and has touched her. He (the Imam) said, 'Her *mahr* (dower) is obligatory and she becomes unlawful for marriage to his father and his son.'"

H 9741, Ch. 76, h 2

Muhammad ibn Yahya has narrated from Ahmad ibn Muhammad from Muhammad ibn 'Isma'il who has said the following:

"I once asked al-Rida', *'Alayhi al-Salam*, about the case of a man who had a slave-girl and he kissed her; if she was lawful for his sons. He (the Imam) asked, 'Was it with lust?' I replied, 'Yes, it was with lust.' He (the Imam) said, 'He then has left nothing if he has kissed with lust.' He (the Imam) then initiating said, 'If he makes her bare and looks at her with lust she becomes unlawful to marry for his father and his son.' I then asked, 'What happens if he looks at her body?' He (the Imam) said, 'If he looks at her vagina and body with lust she becomes unlawful for him.'"

H 9742, Ch. 76, h 3

Ali ibn Ibrahim has narrated from his father from ibn abu 'Umayr from Jamil ibn Darraj who has said the following:

"This is concerning my question before abu 'Abd Allah, *'Alayhi al-Salam*, about the case of a man who looks at a slave-girl whom he wants to buy; if she is lawful for his son. He (the Imam) said, 'Yes, she is lawful unless he has looked at her private organs.'"

H 9743, Ch. 76, h 4

Muhammad ibn Yahya has narrated from Ahmad ibn Muhammad from Ali ibn al-Hakam from 'Abd Allah ibn Yahya al-Kahiliy who has said the following:

"Once abu 'Abd Allah, *'Alayhi al-Salam*, was asked, when I was with him (the Imam), about the case of a man who bought a slave-girl but did not touch her. His wife commanded his son, who was ten years old, to fall on her (for sexual intercourse) and he did it, now what do you say about it. He (the Imam) said, 'The boy has sinned as well as his mother and it is not permissible for the father, after his son's going near her, to fall on her.' I then asked him (the Imam) about the case of a man who has a slave-girl and his father places his hand on her with lust or looks where it is not permissible to look with lust. He (the Imam) disliked his son's touching her.'"

H 9744, Ch. 76, h 5

Muhammad ibn 'Isma'il has narrated from al-Fadl ibn Shadhan from ibn abu 'Umayr from Rib'iy ibn 'Abd Allah from Muhammad ibn Muslim who has said the following:

"Abu 'Abd Allah, *'Alayhi al-Salam*, has said, 'If a man makes a slave-girl bare and places his hand on her she becomes unlawful for his son.'"

H 9745, Ch. 76, h 6

Abu Ali al-Ash'ariy has narrated from Muhammad ibn 'Abd al-Jabbar from Safwan ibn Yahya from ibn Muskan from al-Hassan ibn Ziyad from Muhammad ibn Muslim who has said the following:

"This is concerning my question before abu 'Abd Allah, *'Alayhi al-Salam*, about the case of a man who has married a woman and has touched her. He (the Imam), *'Alayhi al-Salam*, said, 'She is unlawful to his father and her *mahr* (dower) is obligatory.'"

H 9746, Ch. 76, h 7

Muhammad ibn Yahya has narrated from Ahmad ibn Muhammad from Ali ibn al-Hakam from Musa ibn Bakr from Zurarah who has said the following:

"Abu Ja'far, *'Alayhi al-Salam*, has said, 'If a man commits fornication with the woman of his father or his slave-girl, it does not make her unlawful to her husband or the slave-girl unlawful to her master. If he goes to bed with a slave-girl who is lawful thereafter she becomes unlawful forever to his son and father. If a man marries a woman in a lawful way, that woman is not lawful for his father and son for marriage.'"

H 9747, Ch. 76, h 8

A number of our people have narrated from Sahl ibn Ziyad from Ahmad ibn Muhammad from ibn abu Nasr from Hammad ibn 'Uthaman from Murazim who has said the following:

"I once heard abu 'Abd Allah, *'Alayhi al-Salam*, saying, when he (the Imam) was asked about the case of a woman who commanded her son to fall on the slave-girl of his father and he did, 'She has sinned and so has her son and certain ones of these people asked me about it and I said, "You can keep her because unlawful does not make lawful ones unlawful."'"

H 9748, Ch. 76, h 9

A number of our people have narrated from Sahl ibn Ziyad from Musa ibn Ja'far from "Amr ibn Sa'id from Musaddiq ibn Sadaqah from 'Ammar who has said the following:

"About the case of a man who has a slave-girl and his grandson falls on her (does sexual intercourse) before his grandfather or that a man commits fornication with a woman; if she is lawful for his father to marry, abu 'Abd Allah, *'Alayhi al-Salam*, said, 'No, it is not permissible. Only if the man marries her and goes to bed with her then his son commits fornication with her it does not harm him because unlawful does not make lawful ones unlawful and so also is the case of the slave-girl.'"

Chapter 77 - Another Chapter and a Mention of the Wives of the Holy Prophet

H 9749, Ch. 77, h 1

Muhammad ibn Yahya has narrated from Ahmad ibn Muhammad from Ali ibn al-Hakam from al-'Ala' ibn Razin from Muhammad ibn Muslim who has said the following:

"One of the two Imam, (abu Ja'far or abu 'Abd Allah), *'Alayhim al-Salam*, has said, 'If the wives of the Holy Prophet, *O Allah, grant compensation to Muhammad and his family worthy of their services to Your cause*, were not made unlawful for people to marry because of the words of Allah, most Majestic, most Glorious, "You must not cause pain to the Messenger of Allah

382

and never marry his wives after him" (33:53) they were unlawful for al-Hassan and al-Husayn, *'Alayhi al-Salam*, because of the words of Allah, most Majestic, most Glorious, "You must not marry whoever your fathers have married." (4:22)'"

H 9750, Ch. 77, h 2

Al-Husayn from Muhammad has narrated from Mu'alla' ibn Muhammad from al-Hassan ibn Ali from Aban ibn 'Uthman from abu al-Jarud who has said the following:

"I once heard abu 'Abd Allah, *'Alayhi al-Salam*, saying, when this verse was mentioned, 'We advised the man about his (two fathers) parents', (29:7) 'The Messenger of Allah is one of the (two fathers) parents.' 'Who is the other (father) parent?' 'Abd Allah ibn 'Ajalan then asked. He (the Imam) replied 'Ali, *'Alayhi al-Salam*, is the other (father) parent. His women are unlawful to us and this (verse) is especially for us.'"

H 9751, Ch. 77, h 3

Ali ibn Ibrahim has narrated from his father from ibn abu 'Umayr from 'Umar ibn 'Udhaynah who has said the following:

"Sa'd ibn abu 'Urwah narrated to me from al-Hassan al-Basriy that the Messenger of Allah, *O Allah, grant compensation to Muhammad and his family worthy of their services to Your cause*, married a woman from the tribe of banu 'Amir ibn Sa'sa'ah called Sana' and she was the most beautiful among women of her time. When 'A'ishah and Hafsah looked at her they said that she will dominate them before the Messenger of Allah because of her beauty. They said to her, 'The Messenger of Allah does not show any interest in you.' When she went to the Messenger of Allah, *O Allah, grant compensation to Muhammad and his family worthy of their services to Your cause*, he (the Messenger of Allah) took her in his hand and she said, 'I seek refuge with Allah.' The hand of the Messenger of Allah moved away from her and he divorced her and sent her to her family. The Messenger of Allah, *O Allah, grant compensation to Muhammad and his family worthy of their services to Your cause*, married a woman from Kindah who was a daughter of abu al-Jawn. When Ibrahim, son of the Messenger of Allah from Maria the Coptic died, she said, 'Had he been a prophet, his son would not die.' The Messenger of Allah, *O Allah, grant compensation to Muhammad and his family worthy of their services to Your cause*, sent her to her family before going to bed with her. When the Messenger of Allah passed away and abu Bakr took charge of the affairs of the people; al-'Amiriyah and al-Kindah women who had proposed for marriage came to him. Abu Bakr and 'Umar had a meeting and they said to the women, 'You can choose the veil or sexual satisfaction.' They chose sexual satisfaction and married but one of the men contracted leprosy and the other man became insane. 'Umar ibn 'Udhaynah has said, 'I narrated this Hadith to Zurarah and al-Fudayl and they narrated it from abu Ja'far, *'Alayhi al-Salam*, who has said, 'Whatever Allah, most Majestic, most Glorious, prohibited He is disobeyed in it so much so that they even married the wives of the Holy Prophet, *O Allah, grant compensation to Muhammad and his family worthy of their services to Your cause*, after him and he (the Imam) mentioned the two women, al-'Amiriyah and al-Kindiyah. Abu Ja'far, *'Alayhi al-Salam*, then said, 'If you ask them about the case of a man who marries a woman then divorces her before going to bed with her if she is lawful for his son, they will say, 'No. It is not lawful.' The Messenger of Allah, *O Allah, grant compensation to Muhammad and his family worthy of their services to Your cause*, is greater than their fathers in matters of unlawfulness in such case.'"

H 9752, Ch. 77, h 4
Muhammad ibn Yahya has narrated from Ahmad ibn Muhammad from Ali ibn al-Hakam from Musa ibn Bakr from Zurarah ibn 'A'yan who has said the following:
"Zurarah has narrated a Hadith similar to the previous Hadith from Abu Ja'far, *'Alayhi al-Salam*, and he (the Imam) has said, 'They do not consider it lawful to marry their mothers if they are believers. The wives of the Messenger of Allah, *O Allah, grant compensation to Muhammad and his family worthy of their services to Your cause*, in the matter of the above unlawfulness are like their mothers.'"

Chapter 78 - A Marriage and Divorce or Death before or after the Consummation of Marriage then Marries Her Mother or Daughter

H 9753, Ch. 78, h 1
Ali ibn Ibrahim has narrated from his father from ibn abu 'Umayr from Jamil ibn Darraj and Hammad ibn 'Uthaman who has said the following:
"Abu 'Abd Allah, *'Alayhi al-Salam*, has said, 'A mother and daughter are the same if one has not gone to bed with her, that is, if one marries a woman then divorces her before going to bed with her, in such case it is permissible to marry her mother or her daughter."

H 9754, Ch. 78, h 2
Muhammad ibn Yahya has narrated from Ahmad ibn Muhammad ibn 'Isa from Ahmad ibn Muhammad from ibn abu Nasr who has said the following:
"I once asked abu al-Hassan, *'Alayhi al-Salam*, about the case of a man who married a woman in manner of *al-Mut'ah*; if it is permissible for him to marry her daughter. He (the Imam) said, 'No, it is not permissible.'"

H 9755, Ch. 78, h 3
Muhammad ibn Yahya has narrated from Ahmad ibn Muhammad from Ali ibn al-Hakam from al-'Ala' ibn Razin from Muhammad ibn Muslim who has said the following:
"I once asked one of the two Imam, (abu Ja'far or abu 'Abd Allah), *'Alayhim al-Salam*, about the case of a man who married a woman and looks at her head and a few places of her body; if he could marry her daughter. He (the Imam) said, 'No, he cannot do so when he has seen what is unlawful for people other than him to look at. It is not lawful for him to marry her daughter.'"

H 9756, Ch. 78, h 4
Abu Ali al-Ash'ariy has narrated from Muhammad ibn 'Abd al-Jabbar and Muhammad ibn 'Isma'il has narrated from al-Fadl ibn Shadhan from Safwan ibn Yahya from Mansur ibn Hazim who has said the following:

"Once I was with abu 'Abd Allah, *'Alayhi al-Salam*, when a man came and asked about the case of a man who married a woman but she died before going to bed with her; if he could marry her mother. Abu 'Abd Allah, *'Alayhi al-Salam*, said, 'A man from us had done so, thus I do not see it as unlawful.' I then said, 'I pray to Allah to keep my soul in service for your cause, al-Shi'ah are only proud of the judgment of Ali, *'Alayhi al-Salam*, on the issue of al-Shamakhiyah about which ibn Mas'ud had given a Fatwa that said, "It is not harmful", then he went to Ali, *'Alayhi al-Salam*, and asked him (the Imam) and Ali, *'Alayhi al-Salam*, asked, "From what source did you take it?" He (ibn Mas'ud) replied, "I took it from the words of Allah, most Majestic, most Glorious, '. . . and those who grow in your care from your women with whom you have gone to bed but if you have not gone to bed with them (their mother) then it is not harmful for you . . .' (4:23)" Ali, *'Alayhi al-Salam*, said, "This (the case in this verse) is an exception (from woman married in general with or without sexual intercourse) and this one is free of such exceptions (that is she is divorced and there is no question about sexual intercourse) and 'the mother of your women' in the above verse.'" Abu 'Abd Allah, *'Alayhi al-Salam*, said to the man, 'Do you hear what this man is narrating from Ali, *'Alayhi al-Salam*.' When I stood up I regretted and said to myself, 'What did I do?' He (the Imam) said, 'A man from us has done so, thus I do not see it as harmful,' and I say, 'Ali, *'Alayhi al-Salam*, judged the issue.' I then met him (the Imam) afterwards and said, 'I pray to Allah to keep my soul in service for your cause, about the question of that man, my saying that "he says so and so" was a slip from me. What do you say about it?' He (the Imam) said, 'O Shaykh, when you narrate to me that Ali, *'Alayhi al-Salam*, judged the issue then why do you ask me about what I say on the case?'" (One must consult fatwa about the above Hadith)

H 9757, Ch. 78, h 5
Muhammad ibn Yahya has narrated from Ahmad ibn Muhammad from ibn Mahbub from Khalid ibn Jarir from abu al-Rabi' who has said the following:
"About the case of a man who marries a woman and lives with her for many days, unable to do anything except that he has seen from her what is unlawful for others to see; then he divorces her; if he can marry her daughter. He (the Imam) said, 'How can it be proper for him when he has seen of her mother what he has seen?'"

Chapter 79 - Marriage with a Woman Divorced Against the Sunnah

H 9758, Ch. 79, h 1
Muhammad ibn Yahya has narrated from Muhammad ibn al-Husayn from 'Uthman ibn 'Isa from certain persons of our people who have said the following:
"Abu 'Abd Allah, *'Alayhi al-Salam*, has said, 'You must remain on your guard in the case of married women who are divorced against the Sunnah.' I asked him (the Imam) that a man has divorced his wife and I am interested. He (the Imam) said, 'Meet him after he divorces her and waiting period is complete with him then ask him, 'Have you divorced so and so?' If he said, 'Yes, I have divorced

her', this is one divorce during a menses free period. From the time he has divorced her until waiting period is complete then you can marry and divorce has made them complete strangers to each other.'"

H 9759, Ch. 79, h 2
A number of our people have narrated from Ahmad ibn Muhammad ibn 'Isa from al-Husayn ibn Sa'id from al-Nadr ibn Suwayd from Muhammad ibn abu Hamzah from Shu'ayb al-Hadad who has said the following:
"I once said to abu 'Abd Allah, *'Alayhi al-Salam,* 'One of your followers offers greetings of peace to you and he wants to marry a woman who has agreed and he likes her due to certain matters about her and she has a husband who has divorced her three times on non-Sunnah basis. He dislikes marrying her without your instruction so you command him to do so. Abu 'Abd Allah, *'Alayhi al-Salam,* said, 'It is an issue of marriage and the matter of marriage is severe because from marriage are children and we maintain precaution, so he must not marry her.'"

H 9760, Ch. 79, h 3
Ali ibn Ibrahim has narrated from his father from ibn abu 'Umayr from Hafs ibn al-Bakhtariy from Ishaq ibn 'Ammar who has said the following:
"About the case of a man who divorces his wife three times and then another man wants to marry her and about what he must do, abu 'Abd Allah, *'Alayhi al-Salam,* has said, 'He must wait until she experiences one cycle of menses; then he must go to the man who has divorced her and ask him in the presence of two people, 'Have you divorced so and so?' If he said, 'Yes, I have divorced her, then he must leave her alone for three months, then propose to her for marriage.'"

H 9761, Ch. 79, h 4
Muhammad ibn Yahya has narrated from Ahmad ibn Muhammad from Ali ibn al-Hakam from Musa ibn Bakr from Ali ibn Hanzalah who has said the following:
"Abu 'Abd Allah, *'Alayhi al-Salam,* has said, 'Beware of the case of a woman divorced three times in one meeting; they are married women."

Chapter 80 - Marriage with a Woman and Her Maternal or Paternal Aunt

H 9762, Ch. 80, h 1
Muhammad ibn Yahya has narrated from Ahmad ibn Muhammad ibn 'Isa from al-Hassan ibn Ali ibn Faddal from ibn Bukayr from Muhammad ibn Muslim who has said the following:
"Abu Ja'far, *'Alayhi al-Salam,* has said, 'You must not marry a daughter of a brother or daughter of a sister as a second wife, the first being her paternal or maternal aunt without their permission and you must not marry a paternal or maternal aunt as a second wife, the first being a daughter of her brother or a daughter of her sister, without their permission.'"

H 9763, Ch. 80, h 2
A number of our people have narrated from Sahl ibn Ziyad from al-Hassan ibn Mahbub from ibn Ri'ab from abu 'Ubaydah al-Hadhdha' who has said the following:

"I once heard abu Ja'far, *'Alayhi al-Salam*, saying, 'You must not marry a woman as a second wife, the first being her paternal or maternal aunt, without her permission.'"

Chapter 81 - Legalizing a Divorced Woman to Her Husband

H 9764, Ch. 81, h 1

Ali ibn Ibrahim has narrated from his father from Hammad ibn 'Isa from Hariz from Muhammad ibn Muslim who has said the following:

"I once asked one of the two Imam, (abu Ja'far or abu 'Abd Allah), *'Alayhim al-Salam*, about the case of a man who divorced his wife three times; then another man formed *Mut'ah* with her if thereafter she can become lawful for him. He (the Imam) said, 'No, it (*Mut'ah*) is not enough.'"

H 9765, Ch. 81, h 2

A number of our people have narrated from Sahl ibn Ziyad from Ahmad ibn Muhammad from ibn abu Nasr from 'Abd al-Karim from al-Hassan al-Sayqal who has said the following:

"This is concerning my question before abu 'Abd Allah, *'Alayhi al-Salam*, about the case of a man who divorces his wife as such that thereafter he cannot marry her without her marriage with another man but a man marries her in the manner of *Mut'ah*; if thereafter he can marry her. He (the Imam) said, 'No, until she enters into what is similar to what from which she has come out.'"

H 9766, Ch. 81, h 3

Sahl ibn Ziyad has narrated from Ahmad ibn Muhammad from ibn abu Nasr from al-Muthanna' from Ishaq ibn 'Ammar who has said the following:

"This is concerning my question before abu 'Abd Allah, *'Alayhi al-Salam*, about the case of a man who divorces his wife in such a way that he cannot remarry her before her marriage with another man, then a slave marries and divorces her; if divorce is destroyed (restriction due to three divorces). He (the Imam) said, 'Yes, because of the words of Allah, most Majestic, most Glorious, in His book, ". . . until she marries a husband other than him." (2:230) He (the Imam) said, 'He is one of the husbands.'"

H 9767, Ch. 81, h 4

Sahl ibn Ziyad has narrated from Muthanna' from abu Hatim who has said the following:

"This is concerning my question before abu 'Abd Allah, *'Alayhi al-Salam*, about the case of a man who divorces his wife in such a way for which he cannot remarry her without her marriage with another man, then another man marries her and does not go to bed with her. He (the Imam) said, 'No, it is not enough until he tastes her honey.'"

H 9768, Ch. 81, h 5

Ali ibn Ibrahim has narrated from his father from ibn abu 'Umayr from Hammad from al-Halabiy who has said the following:

"This is concerning my question before abu 'Abd Allah, *'Alayhi al-Salam*, about the case of a man who divorces his wife once, then leaves her alone until waiting period is complete; then another man marries her, then the man dies or divorces her and the first husband comes back to her. He (the Imam) said, 'She can live with him for the two remaining divorces.'"

H 9769, Ch. 81, h 6
Muhammad ibn Yahya has narrated from Ahmad ibn Muhammad from Ali ibn Mahziyar from who has said the following:

"'Abd Allah ibn Muhammad once wrote to abu al-Hassan, *'Alayhi al-Salam*, saying that certain persons of our people have narrated from abu 'Abd Allah, *'Alayhi al-Salam*, about the case of a man who divorces his wife according to the book and Sunnah and she becomes stranger for him after the first divorce; then marries another man who dies or divorces her and she goes back to her first husband to live with him for the two remaining divorces when one (divorce) has passed. He (the Imam) signed with his handwriting, 'What they have narrated is true.' A certain ones of them have narrated that she can live with him for three divorces in future and this divorce is not counted because she married another husband. He (the Imam) signed the answer in his handwriting, 'No, that is not the case.'"

Chapter 82 - Women who Become Unlawful for Marriage Forever

H 9770, Ch. 82, h 1
A number of our people have narrated from Sahl ibn Ziyad and Muhammad ibn Yahya has narrated from Ahmad ibn Muhammad all from Ahmad ibn Muhammad from ibn abu Nasr from al-Muthanna' from Zurarah ibn 'A'yan from Dawud ibn Sarhan from abu 'Abd Allah, *'Alayhi al-Salam*, and 'Abd Allah ibn Bukayr from 'Udaym Bayya' al-Harawiy who has said the following:

"Abu 'Abd Allah, *'Alayhi al-Salam*, has said, 'A woman who because of *al-Mula'inah* (condemnation) when it (condemnation) is from the husband becomes unlawful for marriage for him forever; a woman who is married during her waiting period knowing all about her condition becomes unlawful for him forever; a woman divorced three times in a way whereafter he can only marry her again after her marriage with another man, remarry her three times, each time after the above process, she then becomes unlawful for him forever and a woman whom one marries in the state of Ihram knowing that it is unlawful becomes unlawful for him forever.'"

H 9771, Ch. 82, h 2
Ali ibn Ibrahim has narrated from his father from ibn abu 'Umayr from Hammad from al-Halabiy who has said the following:

"Abu 'Abd Allah, *'Alayhi al-Salam*, has said, 'If one marries a woman during her waiting period and goes to bed with her, she becomes unlawful for him forever, regardless, he knows or not, but if he has not gone to bed with her, she is lawful for the one ignorant of her condition and is unlawful for the other (one who knows her condition).'"

H 9772, Ch. 82, h 3
Abu Ali al-Ash'ariy has narrated from Muhammad ibn 'Abd al-Jabbar and Muhammad ibn 'Isma'il has narrated from al-Fadl ibn Shadhan all from Safwan from 'Abd al-Rahman ibn al-Hajjaj who has said the following:

"I once asked abu Ibrahim, *'Alayhi al-Salam*, about the case of a man who married a woman during her waiting period because of ignorance; if she became unlawful for him forever. He (the Imam) said, 'No, if marriage is because of ignorance he must marry her again after the waiting period is complete; people due to ignorance are sometimes forgiven even for an issue bigger than this.' I then asked, 'Of the two which ignorance is excused, ignorance of its unlawfulness or ignorance of her being in the waiting period?' He (the Imam) said, 'Of the two the ignorance which is easier is excused, and it is ignorance of the fact that Allah has made it unlawful because with it he cannot maintain precaution.' I then asked, 'Will he because of such ignorance be excused on the Day of Judgment?' He (the Imam) said, 'Yes, when her waiting period is complete he is excused if he marries her.' I then asked, 'What happens if one knows and the other is ignorant?' He (the Imam) said, 'The one who knowingly has done it can never return to his companion.'"

H 9773, Ch. 82, h 4
Ali ibn Ibrahim has narrated from his father from ibn abu 'Umayr from Hammad from al-Halabiy who has said the following:
"This is concerning my question before abu 'Abd Allah, *'Alayhi al-Salam*, about the case of a woman who is pregnant and her husband dies. She gives birth and marries before the passing of four months and ten days. He (the Imam) said, 'If he has gone to bed with her, they must be separated from each other and she will be unlawful for him forever. She must complete the remaining of her waiting period and complete another waiting period from the end of that for three cycles of menses, but if he has not gone to bed with her, they must separated from each other and she must complete the remaining of her waiting period and he then is one of the people who can propose to her for marriage.'"

H 9774, Ch. 82, h 5
A number of our people have narrated from Sahl ibn Ziyad and Muhammad ibn Yahya has narrated from Ahmad ibn Muhammad all from Ahmad ibn Muhammad from ibn abu Nasr from 'Abd al-Karim from Muhammad ibn Muslim who has said the following:
"I once asked abu Ja'far, *'Alayhi al-Salam*, about the case of a woman who was pregnant and her husband died. She gave birth and married before the passing of four months and ten days. He (the Imam) said, 'If the one who has married has gone to bed with her, they must separate from each other and she is not lawful for him forever. She must complete the remaining of her first waiting period and complete another waiting period in future for three cycles of menses; but if he has not gone to bed with her, they must separate from each other and she must complete the remaining of her waiting period. He then is one of those who can propose to her for marriage.'"

H 9775, Ch. 82, h 6
Muhammad ibn Yahya has narrated from Ahmad ibn Muhammad and Muhammad ibn al-Husayn from 'Uthman ibn 'Isa from Sama'ah and ibn Muskan from Sulayman ibn Khalid who has said the following:
"I once asked him (the Imam), *'Alayhi al-Salam*, about the case of a man who married a woman during her waiting period. He (the Imam) said, 'They must

separate from each other; and if he has gone to bed with her he must pay *mahr* (dower) for making his going to bed with her lawful. They must separate from each other and she is not lawful for him forever. If he has not gone to bed with her she does not have any *mahr* (dower).'"

H 9776, Ch. 82, h 7

Muhammad ibn 'Isma'il has narrated from al-Fadl ibn Shadhan from and Ali ibn Ibrahim has narrated from his father all from ibn abu 'Umayr from Jamil ibn Darraj from abu 'Abd Allah, *'Alayhi al-Salam*, and Ibrahim ibn 'Abd al-Hamid from abu 'Abd Allah, and abu al-Hassan, recipients of divine supreme covenant, who has said the following:

"Abu 'Abd Allah, and abu al-Hassan, *'Alayhim al-Salam*, have said, 'If a man (1) divorces a woman then remarries her, then (2) he divorces and the same husband marries her, then (3) divorces her and another man marries her then this man divorces her and the first man marries her then the first husband divorces her in the same way up to three times, she thereafter becomes unlawful for him forever.'"

H 9777, Ch. 82, h 8

Ahmad ibn Muhammad al-'Asemiy has narrated from Ali ibn al-Hassan ibn Faddal from Ali ibn Asbat from his uncle, Ya'qub ibn Salim from Muhammad ibn Muslim who has said the following:

"I once asked abu Ja'far, *'Alayhi al-Salam*, about the case of a man who married a woman during her waiting period. He (the Imam) said, 'If he has gone to bed with her, they must separate from each other and she is not lawful for him forever. She must complete the remaining time of the first waiting period and complete another waiting period thereafter, but if he has not gone to bed with her they must separate from each other and she must complete the first waiting period and he can be of those who can propose to her for marriage.'"

H 9778, Ch. 82, h 9

Muhammad ibn Yahya has narrated from Ahmad ibn Muhammad from Ali ibn al-Hakam from Ali ibn abu Hamzah from abu Basir who has said the following:

"About the case of a man who marries a woman during her waiting period, abu 'Abd Allah, *'Alayhi al-Salam*, has said, 'They must separate from each other and she must complete her waiting period. If he has gone to bed with her he must pay *mahr* (dower) for his going to bed and they must separate from each other. If he has not gone to bed with her then she has no *mahr* (dower). He (the narrator) has said, 'I then asked him (the Imam) about the case of a man who divorced then returned to his wife then divorced and then returned then divorced.' He (the Imam) said, 'She is not lawful for him until she marries another man and who divorces her according to the Sunnah then she returns to her first husband who divorces her three times according to the Sunnah then she marries another man then she marries. Such woman is the one who becomes unlawful for him forever and because of *al-Mula'inah* (condemnation) also she becomes unlawful for him forever.'"

H 9779, Ch. 82, h 10

Ali ibn Ibrahim has narrated from his father from Safwan from Ishaq ibn 'Ammar who has said the following:

"I once said to abu Ibrahim, *'Alayhi al-Salam,* 'It is narrated to us from your father that if a man marries a woman during her waiting period she becomes unlawful for him forever.' He (the Imam) said, 'That is the case if he knows about it, but if he is ignorant he must separate from her and she must complete the waiting period then he can marry her anew.'"

H 9780, Ch. 82, h 11
A number of our people have narrated from Ahmad ibn Muhammad in a marfu' manner has said the following:
"He (the Imam), *'Alayhi al-Salam,* has said, 'If a man marries a woman and knows that she has a husband, they must separate from each other and she becomes unlawful for him forever.'"

H 9781, Ch. 82, h 12
A number of our people have narrated from Sahl ibn Ziyad from Ya'qub ibn Yazid from certain persons of our people who have said the following:
(...Consult Fatwah about this Hadith)

H 9782, Ch. 82, h 13
Ali ibn Ibrahim has narrated from his father from ibn abu 'Umayr from Jamil ibn Darraj who has said the following:
"Abu 'Abd Allah, *'Alayhi al-Salam,* has said, 'If a man divorces a woman, then she marries a man then he divorces her then she marries the first man then divorces her and she marries a man then divorces her then she marries the first man then he divorces her, she becomes unlawful for him forever.'"

Chapter 83 - The Case of Four Wives and Divorcing one to Marry another before the end of the *'Iddah* (waiting period) or Marries Five Women at one Time

H 9783, Ch. 83, h 1
Ali ibn Ibrahim has narrated from his father from ibn abu 'Umayr from Jamil ibn Darraj from Zurarah ibn 'A'yan and Muhammad ibn Muslim who has said the following:
"Abu 'Abd Allah, *'Alayhi al-Salam,* has said, 'If a man accumulates four wives then divorces one, he cannot marry the fifth before the end of waiting period of the woman whom he has divorced.' He (the Imam) said, 'A man cannot deposit his water in five.'"

H 9784, Ch. 83, h 2
Muhammad ibn Yahya has narrated from Ahmad ibn Muhammad from Ali ibn al-Hakam from Ali ibn abu Hamzah who has said the following:
"This is concerning my question before abu Ibrahim, *'Alayhi al-Salam,* about the case of a man who has four wives; if he can divorce one and marry in her place another one. He (the Imam) said, 'No, he cannot do so until her waiting period is complete.'"

H 9785, Ch. 83, h 3
A number of our people have narrated from Sahl ibn Ziyad from Ahmad ibn Muhammad from ibn abu Nasr from 'Asem ibn Hamid from Muhammad ibn Qays who has said the following:

"About the case of a man who has four wives, who divorces one and marries another one in her place before the waiting period of the one just divorced is complete, I once heard abu Ja'far, *'Alayhi al-Salam*, saying, 'He must join her with her family until the one just divorced completes her waiting period and the other one must complete a waiting period and she deserves her *mahr* (dower), if he has gone to bed with her; but if he has not gone to bed with her he has his assets and there is no waiting period on her; thereafter if she asks her family to arrange marriage for her they can do so or if they want they will not do so.'"

H 9786, Ch. 83, h 4

A number of our people have narrated from Sahl ibn Ziyad and Muhammad ibn Yahya has narrated from Ahmad ibn Muhammad all from al-Hassan ibn Mahbub from ibn Ri'ab from 'Anbasah ibn Mus'ab who has said the following:

"This is concerning my question before abu 'Abd Allah, *'Alayhi al-Salam*, about the case of a man who had three wives and he married two more women. He went to bed with one of them, then died. He (the Imam) said, 'The marriage of the woman whom he first married and mentioned her name at the time of pronouncing the terms, is permissible. She deserves inheritance and she must complete waiting period; but if he had gone to bed with the woman who was named and mentioned after the mention of the first woman, her marriage is invalid, she does not deserve inheritance and *mahr* (dower), but she must complete the waiting period.'"

H 9787, Ch. 83, h 5

Ali ibn Ibrahim has narrated from his father from ibn abu 'Umayr from Jamil ibn Darraj who has said the following:

"About the case of a man who marries five women in one contract, abu 'Abd Allah, *'Alayhi al-Salam*, has said, 'He can keep any four and allow anyone of them to go.'"

Chapter 84 - Marriage with Two Sisters at the Same Time: Free or Slave-girls

H 9788, Ch. 84, h 1

Ali ibn Ibrahim has narrated from his father and A number of our people have narrated from Sahl ibn Ziyad all from ibn abu Najran and Ahmad ibn Muhammad from ibn abu Nasr from 'Asem ibn Hamid from Muhammad ibn Qays who has said the following:

"Abu Ja'far, *'Alayhi al-Salam*, has said that 'Amir al-Mu'minin, *'Alayhi al-Salam*, issued a judgment about the case of two sisters, of whom one had married a man who divorced her, and she was pregnant, then proposed marriage to her sister and married her before her divorced sister gave birth, he (the Imam) commanded them to separate from the one married last until her sister gives birth, then he can propose marriage to her and assign *mahr* (dower) for her twice.'"

H 9789, Ch. 84, h 2

Abu Ali al-Ash'ariy has narrated from Muhammad ibn 'Abd al-Jabbar from Safwan ibn Yahya from ibn Muskan from abu Bakr al-Hadramiy who has said the following:

"I once asked abu Ja'far, *'Alayhi al-Salam*, about the case of a man who marries a woman and then comes to a land where he marries her sister but he does not know. He (the Imam) said, 'He can keep whichever he wants and allow the other one to go.'"

H 9790, Ch. 84, h 3

Ali ibn Ibrahim has narrated from his father from ibn abu 'Umayr from Jamil ibn Darraj from certain persons of his people who have said the following:

"About the case of a man who marries two sisters in one marriage, one of the two Imam, (abu Ja'far or abu 'Abd Allah), *'Alayhim al-Salam*, has said, 'He has the choice to keep whichever he wants and allow the other one to go.' About the case of a man who had a slave-girl with whom he went to bed, then bought her mother or her daughter, he (the Imam) said, 'She is unlawful for him forever.'"

H 9791, Ch. 84, h 4

Muhammad ibn Yahya has narrated from Ahmad ibn Muhammad from al-Hassan ibn Mahbub from ibn Bukayr and Ali ibn Ri'ab from Zurarah ibn 'A'yan who has said the following:

"This is concerning my question before abu Ja'far, *'Alayhi al-Salam*, about the case of a man who marries in Iraq a woman; then goes to al-Sham (Syria) and marries another there who is the sister of the one in Iraq. He (the Imam) said, 'He must separate from the one in al-Sham and must not go close to the woman until waiting period of the woman in al-Sham is complete.' I then asked, 'What happens if one marries a woman then marries her mother in ignorance?' He (the Imam) said, 'Allah has exempted people in their ignorance.' Then he (the Imam) said, 'When he comes to know that she is her mother he must not go close to her as well as to her daughter until waiting period of the mother is complete and when waiting period of mother is complete marriage with daughter becomes lawful.' I then asked, 'What happens if the mother gives birth?' He (the Imam) said, 'He is his child and thus his son becomes brother of his wife.'"

H 9792, Ch. 84, h 5

Ali ibn Ibrahim has narrated from his father from 'Isma'il ibn Marrar from Yunus who has said the following:

"I read in the letter of a man to al-Rida', *'Alayhi al-Salam*, that said, 'I pray to Allah to keep my soul in service for your cause, if a man marries a woman in the manner of *Mut'ah* for an appointed time which expires; if he can marry her sister before her sister completes her waiting period.' He (the Imam) had written to him, 'It is not lawful for him to marry before her waiting period is complete.'"

H 9793, Ch. 84, h 6

Muhammad ibn Yahya has narrated from Ahmad ibn Muhammad ibn 'Isa from Muhammad ibn 'Isma'il ibn Bazi' from Muhammad ibn al-Fadl from abu al-Sabbah al-Kinaniy who has said the following:

"This is concerning my question before abu 'Abd Allah, *'Alayhi al-Salam*, about the case of a man whose wife divorces him in the manner of al-Khula'(payment for divorce); if it is permissible to propose marriage to her sister before her waiting period is complete. He (the Imam) said, 'Since she has set herself free and there is no chance to go back, it is lawful for him to propose marriage to her sister.' He (the narrator) has said that he (the Imam) was asked about the case of a man who had two sisters as his slave-girls. He goes to bed with one of them then he goes to bed with the other one. He (the Imam) said, 'When he goes to bed with the other one, the first one becomes unlawful for him until the other one dies.' I then asked, 'What happens if he sells her?' He (the Imam) said, 'If he sells her because of a reason without anything in his mind about the other slave-girl, then I do not see it as harmful, but if he sells her so he can go to the first one, then it is not permissible.'"

H 9794, Ch. 84, h 7
Ali ibn Ibrahim has narrated from his father from ibn abu 'Umayr from Hammad from al-Halabiy who has said the following:

"About the case of a man who divorces his wife or she arranges for Khul' (payment for divorce) or she becomes a stranger to him; if he can marry her sister. He (the Imam) said, 'When she has freed herself from responsibility and he is not able to go back to her, it then is permissible for him to propose marriage to her sister.' He (the narrator) has said that he (the Imam) was asked about the case of a man who has two sisters as his slave-girls. He goes to bed with one of them, then he goes to bed with the other one. He (the Imam) said, 'When he goes to bed with the other one the first one becomes unlawful for him until the other one dies.' I then asked, 'What happens if he sells her?' He (the Imam) said, 'If he sells her because of a reason without anything in his mind about the other slave-girl, then I do not see it as harmful; but if he sells her so he can go to the first one, then it is not permissible and it is not honorable.'"

H 9795, Ch. 84, h 8
Al-Husayn from Muhammad has narrated from Mu'alla' ibn Muhammad from al-Hassan ibn Ali from Zurarah who has said the following:

"About the case of a man who divorces his wife and she is pregnant; if he can marry her sister before she gives birth, he (the Imam), 'Alayhi al-Salam, has said, 'He must not marry her until her time is complete.'"

H 9796, Ch. 84, h 9
Muhammad ibn Yahya has narrated from Ahmad ibn Muhammad from Ali ibn al-Hakam from Ali ibn abu Hamzah who has said the following:

"This is concerning my question before abu al-Hassan, 'Alayhi al-Salam, about the case of a man who divorces a woman; if he can marry her sister. He (the Imam) said, 'No, he cannot do so until her waiting period is complete.' He (the narrator) has said, 'I asked him (the Imam) about the case of a man who owns two sisters; if he can go to bed with both of them. He (the Imam) said, 'He can go to bed with one of them. When he goes to bed with the second one, the first one becomes unlawful for him until the second one dies or separates from her and he cannot sell the second in order to go to the first one unless he sells for a reason or gives her in charity or she dies.' He (the narrator) has said, 'I asked him (the Imam) about the case of a man who had a woman who died; if he could marry her sister. He (the Imam) said, 'He can do so at the same hour if he likes.'"

H 9797, Ch. 84, h 10

Muhammad ibn Yahya has narrated from Ahmad ibn Muhammad from Ali ibn al-Hakam from al-'Ala' ibn Razin from Muhammad ibn Muslim who has said the following:

"This is concerning my question before abu 'Abd Allah, *'Alayhi al-Salam*, about the case of a man who has a slave-girl and sets her free. She then marries and gives birth; if her first master can marry her daughter. He (the Imam) said, 'She is unlawful for him because she is his daughter, free and slaves are the same in this issue.' Then he (the Imam) read this verse, ". . . the ones who grow in your care from your wives.' (4:23)"

Muhammad ibn Yahya has narrated from Ahmad ibn Muhammad from ibn Mahbub from al-'Ala' ibn Razin from Muhammad ibn Muslim from one of the two Imam, (abu Ja'far or abu 'Abd Allah), *'Alayhi al-Salam*, a similar Hadith.

H 9798, Ch. 84, h 11

Ahmad ibn Muhammad has narrated from those whom he has mentioned from al-Husayn ibn Bishr who has said the following:

"I once asked al-Rida', *'Alayhi al-Salam*, about the case of a man who had a slave-girl who had a daughter. He falls on her (for sexual intercourse); if he could fall on her daughter. He (the Imam) said, 'Does a man of good deeds marry his own daughter?'"

H 9799, Ch. 84, h 12

Ahmad ibn Muhammad from has narrated from al-Husayn ibn Sa'id from al-Nadr ibn Suwayd from al-Qasim ibn Sulayman from 'Ubayd ibn Zurarah who has said the following:

"About the case of a man who has a slave-girl with whom he has gone to bed; if he can marry her daughter, he (the Imam) said, 'No, he cannot do so because of the words of Allah, most Majestic, most Glorious, ". . . those who grow in your care . . ." (4:23)'"

H 9800, Ch. 84, h 13

Abu Ali al-Ash'ariy has narrated from Muhammad ibn 'Abd al-Jabbar from Safwan ibn Yahya from ibn Muskan from abu Basir who has said the following:

"This is concerning my question before abu 'Abd Allah, *'Alayhi al-Salam*, about the case of a man who divorces his wife and they become strangers to each other. She has a daughter who is a slave and he buys her; if he can go to bed with her. He (the Imam) said, 'No, he cannot do so.' I asked him (the Imam) about the case of a man who has a slave-girl and her daughter and he goes to bed with one of them, then she dies and the other is living; if he can go to bed with her. He (the Imam) said, 'No, he cannot do so.'"

H 9801, Ch. 84, h 14

Muhammad ibn Yahya has narrated from Ahmad ibn Muhammad from ibn Mahbub from ibn Ri'ab from al-Halabiy who has said the following:

"This is concerning my question before abu 'Abd Allah, *'Alayhi al-Salam*, about the case of a man who buys two sisters and goes to bed with one of them, then goes to bed with the other due to ignorance. He (the Imam) said, 'If he has gone to bed with the other due to ignorance the first one does not become unlawful for him but if he goes to bed with the other knowing that it is unlawful, both of them become unlawful for him.'"

Chapter 85 - About the Words of Allah, Most Majestic, Most Glorious, 'You must not Make Secret Dates . . .

H 9802, Ch. 85, h 1
Ali ibn Ibrahim has narrated from his father from ibn abu 'Umayr from Hammad from al-Halabiy who has said the following:

"This is concerning my question before abu 'Abd Allah, *'Alayhi al-Salam*, about the meaning of the words of Allah, '. . . but you must not secretly date (make secret appointment with) such women (during their waiting period) unless you speak to them in a lawful manner.' (2:235) He (the Imam) said, 'He is a man who speaks to the woman before she completes her waiting period saying, "I invite you for a date in the house of so and so" and to propose marriage to her and His word, "Unless you speak to them in a lawful way" is a reference to "proposing marriage", ". . . but you must not decide for marriage until the appointed waiting period is complete..." (2:235)'"

H 9803, Ch. 85, h 2
A number of our people have narrated from Sahl ibn Ziyad and Muhammad ibn Yahya has narrated from Ahmad ibn Muhammad ibn 'Isa from Ahmad ibn Muhammad from ibn abu Nasr from 'Abd Allah ibn Sinan who has said the following:

"This is concerning my question before abu 'Abd Allah, *'Alayhi al-Salam*, about the words of Allah, most Majestic, most Glorious, '. . . but you must not secretly date such women (during their waiting period) unless you speak to them in a lawful manner and you must not decide to form terms of marriage until the appointed time is complete.' (2:235). He (the Imam) said, 'The word "secret" means his saying, "The place of your date is the house of so and so", then calls her to that place then asks her not to decide to get married with someone else before him when waiting period is complete.' I then asked about, 'Except if you speak in a lawful manner.' He (the Imam) said, 'It is seeking lawful matters without determination for marriage until the appointed time of waiting period is complete.'"

H 9804, Ch. 85, h 3
Muhammad ibn Yahya has narrated from Ahmad ibn Muhammad from Ali ibn al-Hakam from Ali ibn abu Hamzah who has said the following:

"I once asked abu al-Hassan, *'Alayhi al-Salam*, about the words of Allah, most Majestic, most Glorious, '. . . but you must not secretly date such women (during their waiting period).' (2:235). He (the Imam) said, 'It is his saying, "The place for your date (with me) is the house of the family of so and so where he asks her for *rafath* (sexual intercourse) and performs it, and Allah, most Majestic, most Glorious, says, "Unless you speak in a lawful manner." Speaking in a lawful manner is proposing for marriage the way it should be in a lawful manner which is, "You must not decide forming the terms of marriage until the appointed time of waiting period is complete."'"

H 9805, Ch. 85, h 4

Humayd ibn Ziyad from al-Hassan ibn Muhammad from more than one person from Aban from 'Abd al-Rahman ibn abu 'Abd Allah who has said the following:

"About the words of Allah, most Majestic, most Glorious, '. . . unless you speak in a lawful manner;' (2:235) he (the Imam) said, 'He meets her and says, "I am interested in you, I respect women, so you must not decide about yourself (to marry someone else) before me." In "secret" dating he does not meet her as he had promised.'"

Chapter 86 - Marriage with Taxpayers and Pagans of Whom Certain Ones Become Muslims and other do not Become Muslims or all of them Become Muslims

H 9806, Ch. 86, h 1

Ali ibn Ibrahim has narrated from his father from ibn abu 'Umayr from Hammad from al-Halabiy who has said the following:

"This is concerning my question before abu 'Abd Allah, *'Alayhi al-Salam*, about the case of a man who migrates and leaves his wife with the pagans, then afterward she joins him; if he can keep her with first marriage or her safety is cut off. He (the Imam) said, 'He can keep her and she is his wife.'"

H 9807, Ch. 86, h 2

Muhammad ibn Yahya has narrated from Ahmad ibn Muhammad from al-Hassan ibn Mahbub from 'Abd Allah ibn Sinan who has said the following:

"Abu 'Abd Allah, *'Alayhi al-Salam*, has said, 'If a woman becomes Muslim and she is married in a way that is an un-Islamic way, they must be separated.' I then asked him (the Imam) about the case of a man who migrates and leaves his wife among the pagans, then she joins him; if he can keep her with the first marriage or that her safety is cut off. He (the Imam) said, 'He can keep her; she is his wife.'"

H 9808, Ch. 86, h 3

Muhammad ibn Yahya has narrated from 'Abd Allah ibn Muhammad from Ali ibn al-Hakam from Aban from Mansur ibn Hazim who has said the following:

"This is concerning my question before abu 'Abd Allah, *'Alayhi al-Salam*, about the case of a man who is a *Majusiy* (Zoroastrian) or a pagan, other than the people of the book, who had a woman, he becomes a Muslim or she become a Muslim. He (the Imam) said, 'He waits for completion of waiting period if he is a Muslim or she becomes a Muslim before waiting period is complete then they remain with their first marriage; and if he does not become a Muslim when the waiting period is complete, she becomes stranger to him.'"

H 9809, Ch. 86, h 4

Muhammad ibn Yahya has narrated from Ahmad ibn Muhammad from al-Hassan ibn Mahbub from 'Abd al-Rahman ibn al-Hajjaj who has said the following:

"About the case of a man who is a Christian and marries a Christian woman who then becomes a Muslim before his going to bed with her, abu al-Hassan, *'Alayhi al-Salam*, has said, 'The hindrance from him on her way is removed, she has no *mahr* (dower) and no waiting period because of him.'"

H 9810, Ch. 86, h 5

Ahmad ibn Muhammad has narrated from Muhammad ibn Yahya from Talhah ibn Zayd who has said the following:

"A man once asked abu 'Abd Allah, *'Alayhi al-Salam*, about the case of two men of taxpayers or of those in the state of war who each married a woman and assigned a *mahr* (dower) in the form of wine and pigs; then they became Muslims. He (the Imam) said, 'Marriage is permissible and lawful and it does not become unlawful because of wine and pigs.' He (the Imam) then said, 'If they both become Muslims he must pay her something, that is, he must pay her *mahr* (dower).'"

H 9811, Ch. 86, h 6

Ali ibn Ibrahim has narrated from his father from al-Nawfaliy from al-Sakuniy who has said the following:

"Abu 'Abd Allah, *'Alayhi al-Salam*, has said that about the case of a Zoroastrian woman who became a Muslim before he went to bed with her 'Amir al-Mu'minin, *'Alayhi al-Salam*, said to her husband to become a Muslim, but he refused so he (the Imam) judged in her favor half of the *mahr* (dower) and said, 'Islam has not brought to her anything but honor.'"

H 9812, Ch. 86, h 7

Muhammad ibn Yahya has narrated from Muhammad ibn al-Husayn from Muhammad ibn 'Abd Allah ibn Hilal from 'Uqbah ibn Khalid who has said the following:

"About the case of a Zoroastrian man who became a Muslim and he had seven wives who also became Muslims, abu 'Abd Allah, *'Alayhi al-Salam*, has said, 'He could keep four and divorce three of them.'"

H 9813, Ch. 86, h 8

A number of our people have narrated from Sahl ibn Ziyad from Muhammad ibn 'Isa from Yunus who has said the following:

"I once asked him (the Imam), *'Alayhi al-Salam*, about the case of a taxpayer man who had a taxpayer wife and she became a Muslim, he (the Imam) said, 'She is his wife who stays with him during the day but not during the night.' He (the Imam) said, 'If the man becomes a Muslim he stays with her during the night as well as the day.'"

H 9814, Ch. 86, h 9

A number of our people have narrated from Ahmad ibn Muhammad ibn Khalid from his father from al-Qasim ibn Muhammad al-Jawhariy from Rumiy ibn Zurarah who has said the following:

'This is concerning my question before abu 'Abd Allah, *'Alayhi al-Salam*, about the case of a man who is a Christian and marries a Christian woman for thirty sacks of wine and thirty pigs; then they become Muslims and he has not yet gone to bed with her. He (the Imam) said, 'He must find out how much the value of wine and pigs is. He must send them to her, then he can go to bed with her and they remain with their first marriage.'"

Chapter 87 - Breastfeeding

H 9815, Ch. 87, h 1
Ali ibn Ibrahim has narrated from his father from ibn abu Najran from 'Abd Allah ibn Sinan who has said the following:
"I once heard abu 'Abd Allah, *'Alayhi al-Salam*, saying, 'Whoever is unlawful for marriage due to blood relationship becomes unlawful for marriage because of breastfeeding also.'"

H 9816, Ch. 87, h 2
Muhammad ibn Yahya has narrated from Ahmad ibn Muhammad from Muhammad ibn 'Isma'il from Muhammad ibn al-Fudayl from abu al-Sabbah al-Kinaniy who has said the following:
"Once abu 'Abd Allah, *'Alayhi al-Salam*, was asked about breastfeeding. He (the Imam) said, 'Because of breastfeeding, whoever is unlawful for marriage because of being a relative (blood relationship), becomes unlawful for marriage.'"

H 9817, Ch. 87, h 3
A number of our people have narrated from Sahl ibn Ziyad and Ahmad ibn Muhammad from ibn abu Nasr from Dawud ibn Sarhan who has said the following:
"Abu 'Abd Allah, *'Alayhi al-Salam*, has said, 'Because of breastfeeding, whoever is unlawful for marriage because of being a relative (blood relationship), becomes unlawful for marriage.'"

H 9818, Ch. 87, h 4
Al-Husayn from Muhammad has narrated from Mu'alla' ibn Muhammad from al-Hassan ibn Ali from Aban ibn 'Uthman from those who narrated to him who has said the following:
"Abu 'Abd Allah, *'Alayhi al-Salam*, has said that 'Amir al-Mu'minin, *'Alayhi al-Salam*, has said, 'The daughter of Hamzah was proposed to the Messenger of Allah, *O Allah, grant compensation to Muhammad and his family worthy of their services to Your cause*, for marriage and he (the Messenger of Allah) said, "Did you not know that she is a daughter of my brother because of breastfeeding?"'"

H 9819, Ch. 87, h 5
Ali ibn Ibrahim has narrated from his father from ibn abu 'Umayr from Hammad from al-Halabiy who has said the following:
"Abu 'Abd Allah, *'Alayhi al-Salam*, has said that 'Amir al-Mu'minin, *'Alayhi al-Salam*, has said, 'In the case of a daughter of a brother because of breastfeeding I do not command anyone or prohibit. I only refrain myself and my sons.' He ('Amir al-Mu'minin) said, 'The daughter of Hamzah was proposed to the Messenger of Allah for marriage and he (the Messenger of Allah), *O Allah, grant compensation to Muhammad and his family worthy of their services to Your cause*, refused and said, "She is a daughter of my brother because of breastfeeding."'"

Chapter 88 - Limits of Breastfeeding to Take Effect

H 9820, Ch. 88, h 1
Al-Husayn from Muhammad has narrated from Mu'alla' ibn Muhammad from al-Hassan ibn Ali al-Washsha' from 'Abd Allah ibn Sinan who has said the following:
"I once heard abu 'Abd Allah, *'Alayhi al-Salam*, saying, 'Breastfeeding does not bring unlawfulness unless it makes the flesh to grow and the bones to strengthen.'"

H 9821, Ch. 88, h 2
Muhammad ibn Yahya has narrated from Ahmad ibn Muhammad from ibn Faddal from Ali ibn Ya'qub from Muhammad ibn Muslim from 'Ubayd ibn Zurarah who has said the following:
"This is concerning my question before abu 'Abd Allah, *'Alayhi al-Salam*, about the case of breastfeeding and its minimum limit that brings unlawfulness. He (the Imam) said, 'It is an amount of breastfeeding that makes the flesh or blood grow.' He (the Imam) then asked, 'Do you think once can do it?' I replied, 'I pray to Allah to keep you well, I ask you, can twice do it?' He (the Imam) said, 'No, it cannot do it.' I kept counting up to ten times breastfeeding."

H 9822, Ch. 88, h 3
It is narrated from the narrator of the previous Hadith from ibn Faddal from Ali ibn 'Uqbah from 'Ubayd ibn Zurarah who has said the following:
"This is concerning my question before abu 'Abd Allah, *'Alayhi al-Salam*, about breastfeeding and its minimum limit that makes marriage unlawful. He (the Imam) said, 'It is an amount that grows flesh and blood.' He (the Imam) then asked, 'Do you think once can do it?' I replied, 'I pray to Allah to keep you well, I ask you, can twice do it?' He (the Imam) said, 'No, it cannot do so.' I continued counting until ten times breastfeeding.'"

H 9823, Ch. 88, h 4
Abu Ali al-Ash'ariy has narrated from Muhammad ibn 'Abd al-Jabbar and Muhammad ibn 'Isma'il has narrated from al-Fadl ibn Shadhan from all from Safwan ibn Yahya from Mu'awiyah ibn Wahab from Sabah ibn Sayabah who has said the following:
"Abu 'Abd Allah, *'Alayhi al-Salam*, has said, 'Breastfeeding once, twice or three times does not bring unlawfulness.'"

H 9824, Ch. 88, h 5
Ali ibn Ibrahim has narrated from his father from ibn abu 'Umayr from Hammad ibn 'Uthman who has said the following:
"Abu 'Abd Allah, *'Alayhi al-Salam*, has said, 'Breastfeeding does not bring unlawfulness unless it grows flesh and blood.'"

H 9825, Ch. 88, h 6
Ali ibn Ibrahim has narrated from his father from ibn abu 'Umayr from Ziyad al-Qandiy from 'Abd Allah ibn Sinan who has said the following:
"I once asked abu al-Hassan, *'Alayhi al-Salam*, if breastfeeding once or twice brought unlawfulness or three times. He (the Imam) said, 'No, until it strengthens bones and grows flesh.'"

H 9826, Ch. 88, h 7

Abu Ali al-Ash'ariy has narrated from Muhammad ibn 'Abd al-Jabbar and Muhammad ibn 'Isma'il has narrated from al-Fadl ibn Shadhan from all from Safwan ibn Yahya who has said the following:

"This is concerning my question before abu al-Hassan, *'Alayhi al-Salam*, about breastfeeding and who becomes unlawful for marriage thereby. He (the Imam) said, 'A man once asked my father, *'Alayhi al-Salam*, about it and he said that once has no affect, and twice until he counted up to ten times breastfeeding.' I then asked, 'Are they one after the other or suckle after suckle?' He (the Imam) said, 'That is how he said to him and another man asked him (the Imam) about it and he (the Imam) counted up to nine times and said, "A great many times I am asked about breastfeeding."' I then said, 'I pray to Allah to keep my soul in service for your cause, tell me about your own words on this issue. What is the maximum limit according to you?' He (the Imam) said, 'I just told you what my father had answered.' I then said, 'I took notice of what your father has said but I thought perhaps there is a limit for it which he did not inform, thus you inform me about it.' He (the Imam) said, 'This is how my father has said.' I then asked, 'My mother breastfed a girl with my milk.' He (the Imam) said, 'She is your sister because of breastfeeding.' I then asked, 'Is she lawful for marriage for my brother from whose milk she was not breastfed?' He (the Imam) asked, 'Is the father (whose going to bed has its effect on the milk) one?' I replied, 'Yes, he is my brother from my father and mother.' He (the Imam) said, 'Milk is because of the effect of father's going to bed. Your father becomes her father and your mother becomes her mother.'"

H 9827, Ch. 88, h 8

Al-Husayn from Muhammad has narrated from Mu'alla' ibn Muhammad from al-Hassan ibn Ali ibn Faddal from 'Abd Allah ibn Sinan from 'Umar ibn Yazid who has said the following:

"This is concerning my question before abu 'Abd Allah, *'Alayhi al-Salam*, about the case of a boy who is breastfed once and twice. He (the Imam) said, 'It does not cause unlawfulness.' I counted up to ten times breastfeeding. He (the Imam) said, 'If they are on different times they do not cause unlawfulness.'"

H 9828, Ch. 88, h 9

Muhammad ibn Yahya has narrated from Ahmad ibn Muhammad from Ali ibn al-Hakam from Mu'awiyah ibn Wahab from 'Ubayd ibn Zurarah who has said the following:

"I once said to abu 'Abd Allah, *'Alayhi al-Salam*, 'I belong to a large family. On different occasions of happiness and sorrow during which men and women come together women feel shy removing their head scarf before men between whom there is breastfeeding relationship or men fear looking to that, so who becomes unlawful because of breastfeeding. He (the Imam) said, 'It is what grows flesh and blood.' I then asked, 'What grows flesh and blood?' He (the Imam) said, 'It has been said that it is ten times breastfeeding.' I then asked, 'Does ten times bring unlawfulness?' He (the Imam) said, 'Leave that alone.' He (the Imam) said, 'Whoever is unlawful for marriage because of being a relative becomes unlawful because of breastfeeding.'"

H 9829, Ch. 88, h 10

Ali ibn Ibrahim has narrated from Harun ibn Muslim from Mas'adah ibn Sadaqah who has said the following:

"Abu 'Abd Allah, *'Alayhi al-Salam*, has said, 'Breastfeeding does not bring unlawfulness unless it strengthens the bones and grows flesh, and one or two or three times breastfeeding even up to ten times on different times does not bring the unlawfulness affect.'"

Chapter 89 - Meaning of Milk from Impregnating Agent (the Father)

H 9830, Ch. 89, h 1

Muhammad ibn Yahya has narrated from Ahmad ibn Muhammad from ibn Mahbub from 'Abd Allah ibn Sinan who has said the following:

"This is concerning my question before abu 'Abd Allah, *'Alayhi al-Salam*, about the milk of 'impregnating agent'. He (the Imam) said, 'It is the milk from your wife from your milk and the milk of your children given to the child of another woman and that child is unlawful (for marriage).'"

H 9831, Ch. 89, h 2

Muhammad ibn Yahya has narrated from Muhammad ibn al-Husayn from 'Uthman ibn 'Isa from Sama'ah who has said the following:

"This is concerning my question before abu 'Abd Allah, *'Alayhi al-Salam*, about the case of a man who has two women, each of whom gives birth; and he divorces one of the two who has breastfed a girl of the people; if the son of this man can marry that girl. He (the Imam) said, 'No, because she has given milk from the milk of the shaykh (man of the family).'"

H 9832, Ch. 89, h 3

Ali ibn Ibrahim has narrated from his father from ibn abu Najran from 'Abd Allah ibn Sinan who has said the following:

"This is concerning my question before abu 'Abd Allah, *'Alayhi al-Salam*, about the milk of 'impregnating agent'. He (the Imam) said, 'It is the milk from your wife from your milk and the milk of your children given to the child of another woman and that child is unlawful (for marriage).'"

H 9833, Ch. 89, h 4

A number of our people have narrated from Sahl ibn Ziyad and Ali ibn Ibrahim has narrated from his father from Ahmad ibn Muhammad from ibn abu Nasr who has said the following:

"I once asked abu al-Hassan, *'Alayhi al-Salam*, about the case of a woman who breastfeeds a girl and her husband has a son from another woman if it is lawful for this boy, the son of her husband to marry the girl she has breastfed. He (the Imam) said, 'The milk is from 'impregnating agent' her husband.'"

H 9834, Ch. 89, h 5

Muhammad ibn Yahya has narrated from Ahmad ibn Muhammad from al-Hassan ibn Mahbub from Jamil ibn Salih from abu Basir who has said the following:

"About the case of a man who marries a woman who gives birth from him to a girl, then the woman dies and he marries another woman who gives birth to a boy, then she breastfeeds a boy; if this boy can marry the daughter of the woman who was the wife of the man before this woman. He (the Imam) said, 'I do not like for him to marry the daughter of the 'impregnating agent' from whose milk he is breastfed.'"

H 9835, Ch. 89, h 6

Ali ibn Ibrahim has narrated from his father from ibn abu 'Umayr from Hammad from al-Halabiy who has said the following:

"This is concerning my question before abu 'Abd Allah, *'Alayhi al-Salam*, about the mother of the child of a man who has breastfed a child and he had a daughter from another woman; if the girl is lawful for that child. He (the Imam) said, 'I do not like the marriage of the daughter of a man to one who is breastfed from the milk of his children.'"

H 9836, Ch. 89, h 7

Ali ibn Ibrahim has narrated from his father from and Muhammad ibn Yahya has narrated from Ahmad ibn Muhammad from ibn abu Najran from Muhammad ibn 'Ubayd al-Hamadaniy who has said the following:

"Al-Rida', *'Alayhi al-Salam*, once asked me, 'What do your people say about breastfeeding?' I replied, 'They called it the milk of the 'impregnating agent' (husband) until a Hadith from you came to them that said, "Because of breastfeeding whoever is unlawful for marriage, as being a relative, becomes unlawful" then they returned to your words.' He (the narrator) has said that he (the Imam) said, 'It is because 'Amir al-Mu'minin, (the Caliph, Mamun) asked me last night about it and said, "Explain to me the milk of Fahl ('impregnating agent', husband) and I do not like words." Then he said to me, "Bear with me as you are, so I can ask you about it which is what you have said about the case of a man who has several mothers of his children and one of them breastfeeds a stranger boy. Are all of the children of this man from all of the mothers of his children not lawful for marriage to this boy?" I said, "Yes they are unlawful for him."' He (the narrator) has said, 'Abu al-Hassan, *'Alayhi al-Salam*, then said, 'How is it that breastfeeding because of the milk of the 'impregnating agent' has an unlawfulness affect but not because of the breastfeeding of the mothers even though breastfeeding is by the mothers; still the milk of the 'impregnating agent' (husband), also brings unlawfulness.'"

H 9837, Ch. 89, h 8

Muhammad ibn Yahya has narrated from Ahmad ibn Muhammad from Ali ibn Mahziyar from who has said that 'Isa ibn Ja'far ibn 'Isa who has said the following:

"This is concerning my question before abu Ja'far, al-Thaniy, *'Alayhi al-Salam*, about a woman who breastfeeds a child for me: if it is lawful for me to marry a daughter of her husband. He (the Imam) said, 'It is a very good question. It is because of this that people say, 'His wife has become unlawful because of the milk of 'impregnating agent' (husband).' This is the milk of 'impregnating agent' and nothing else. I then asked, 'The girl is not a daughter of the woman who breastfed her. She is a daughter of another woman.' He (the Imam) said, 'Even if they were ten different women, no one of them would have been lawful for you because of being as like your daughters.'"

H 9838, Ch. 89, h 9

Muhammad ibn Yahya has narrated from Ahmad ibn Muhammad and Ali ibn Ibrahim has narrated from his father all from ibn Mahbub from Hisham ibn Salim from Burayd al-'Ijliy who has said the following:

"I once asked abu Ja'far, *'Alayhi al-Salam*, about the words of Allah, most Majestic, most Glorious, 'He is the one who has created human beings from water, then made him into lineage and in-law relationship.' (25:54) He (the Imam) said, 'Allah, most High, created Adam from sweet water and He created his spouse of his kind and carved her from his lower ribs, because of that rib, in-law and lineage relationship came into being. Lineage, O brother of banu 'Ijl, is when the means are men; and in-laws are when the means are women.' He (the narrator) has said, 'I then asked about the meaning of the words of the Messenger of Allah, *O Allah, grant compensation to Muhammad and his family worthy of their services to Your cause,* "Because of breastfeeding whoever is unlawful for marriage due to kinship becomes unlawful for marriage."' He (the Imam) said, 'Every woman who breastfeeds from the milk of her "impregnating agent" (husband) the child of another woman, girls or boys, it then is the kind of breastfeeding which is mentioned in the words of the Messenger of Allah, *O Allah, grant compensation to Muhammad and his family worthy of their services to Your cause,* "Because of breastfeeding unlawful becomes whoever is unlawful because of kinship relations." However, if a woman breastfeeds a child with the milk of two impregnating agents that she may have had one after the other, and the child being a boy or a girl, it then is not of the kind of breastfeeding which is mentioned in the Hadith of the Messenger of Allah which says that what is unlawful because of the lineage is unlawful because of breastfeeding. It, because of the lineage of the in-law, is breastfeeding and it does not make anything unlawful when it is not for reason of breastfeeding from the side of the milk of 'impregnating agent' (husband) which makes it unlawful.'"

H 9839, Ch. 89, h 10

Ibn Mahbub has narrated from Hisham ibn Salim from 'Ammar al-Sabatiy who has said the following:

"This is concerning my question before abu 'Abd Allah, *'Alayhi al-Salam*, about the case of a boy who is breastfed by a woman; if it is lawful for him to marry her sister because of breastfeeding who is from her father's side. He (the narrator) has said that he (the Imam) said, 'No, because all are breastfed from the milk of one "impregnating agent" (husband).' He asked, 'Can he marry her sister because of breastfeeding who is from her mother's side?' He (the narrator) has said, that he (the Imam) said, 'It is not unlawful because in the case of his sister who is breastfed, her "impregnating agent" (husband) is different from the one that has breastfed the boy so the two "impregnating agents" are different, thus it is not unlawful.'"

H 9840, Ch. 89, h 11

Ibn Mahbub has narrated from abu Ayyub al-Khazzaz from ibn Muskan from al-Halabiy who has said the following:

"This is concerning my question before abu 'Abd Allah, *'Alayhi al-Salam*, about the case of a man who is breastfed when a child by a woman; if it is lawful for him to marry her sister because of breastfeeding from her mother's side. He (the Imam) said, 'If the two women are breastfed by one woman from the milk of one "impregnating agent" (husband), then it is unlawful but if the two women are breastfed by one woman with milk of two "impregnating agents" (husbands), then it is not unlawful.'"

Chapter 90 - After Weaning Breastfeeding does not have any Effect

H 9841, Ch. 90, h 1
Ali ibn Ibrahim has narrated from his father from ibn abu 'Umayr from Hammad from al-Halabiy who has said the following:
"Abu 'Abd Allah, *'Alayhi al-Salam*, has said, 'Breastfeeding after weaning is not effective.'"

H 9842, Ch. 90, h 2
Muhammad ibn Yahya has narrated from Ahmad ibn Muhammad from Ali ibn al-Hakam from Aban ibn 'Uthman from al-Fadl ibn 'Abd al-Malik who has said the following:
"Abu 'Abd Allah, *'Alayhi al-Salam*, has said, 'Breastfeeding is effective before completion of two years of a child before weaning him.'"

H 9843, Ch. 90, h 3
A number of our people have narrated from Sahl ibn Ziyad from Ahmad ibn Muhammad from ibn abu Nasr from Hammad ibn 'Uthaman who has said the following:
"I once heard abu 'Abd Allah, *'Alayhi al-Salam*, saying, 'Breastfeeding after weaning is not effective.' I then said, 'I pray to Allah to keep my soul in service for your cause, what is *al-Fatam* (weaning)?' He (the Imam) said, 'It is the two years that Allah, most Majestic, most Glorious, has mentioned (in His book).' (2:233)"

H 9844, Ch. 90, h 4
Ali ibn Ibrahim has narrated from his father and a number of our people have narrated from Sahl ibn Ziyad all from ibn abu Najran from 'Asem ibn Hamid from Muhammad ibn Qays who has said the following:
"I once asked him (the Imam), *'Alayhi al-Salam*, about the case of a woman who drained her milk and made her husband to drink it so that she could become unlawful to him. He (the Imam) said, 'He keeps her and makes her feel a backache.'" (Such expression is used for a flogging implemented by a judicial body.)

H 9845, Ch. 90, h 5
Ali ibn Ibrahim has narrated from his father from ibn abu 'Umayr from Mansur ibn Yunus from Mansur ibn Hazim who has said the following:
"Abu 'Abd Allah, *'Alayhi al-Salam*, has said that the Messenger of Allah, *O Allah, grant compensation to Muhammad and his family worthy of their services to Your cause*, has said, 'Breastfeeding after weaning is not effective, continuous fasting is not valid, one is not an orphan after experiencing wet-dream, vowing

to remain silent for the whole day until the night is not valid, going back to disbelief after migrating to Islam is not permissible, migration after the conquest is not applicable, divorce before marriage is not valid, setting free of slaves before owning a slave is not valid, oath by the son against his father or of a slave against his master, or a wife against her husband is not valid, a vow for unlawful matters is not valid. Swearing to disregard good relation with relatives is not permissible. The meaning of the words of the Messenger of Allah, 'Breastfeeding after weaning is not effective' means that if a boy drinks the milk of a woman after he is weaned, such breastfeeding does not make marriage unlawful.'"

Chapter 91 - Rare Ahadith

H 9846, Ch. 91, h 1
Ali ibn Ibrahim has narrated from his father from ibn abu 'Umayr from 'Abd Allah ibn al-Mughirah who has said the following:
"I once said to abu al-Hassan, al-Madiy (previous), *'Alayhi al-Salam*, that I have married a woman and found out that she had breastfed me and had breastfed her sister. He (the narrator) has said that he (the Imam) asked, 'How much had she done so?' I replied, 'It was a little.' He (the Imam) said, 'May Allah make it a blessing for you.'"

H 9847, Ch. 91, h 2
Ali ibn Ibrahim has narrated from his father from ibn abu 'Umayr from more than one person from Ishaq ibn 'Ammar who has said the following:
"About the case of a man who married the sister of his brother of breastfeeding, abu 'Abd Allah, *'Alayhi al-Salam*, has said, 'I do not like one's marriage to the sister of his brother of breastfeeding.'"

H 9848, Ch. 91, h 3
Muhammad ibn 'Isma'il has narrated from al-Fadl ibn Shadhan from Safwan ibn Yahya who has said the following:
"This is concerning my question before Allah's virtuous servant, *'Alayhi al-Salam*, about the case of my mother who has breastfed a girl along with me. He (the Imam) said, 'She is your sister of breastfeeding.' I then asked if she is lawful for my brother from my mother's side whom she has not breastfed with his milk, that is not from this pregnancy but from another pregnancy. He (the Imam) asked, 'Is the 'impregnating agent' (husband) one?' I replied, 'Yes, she is my sister from my parents.' He (the Imam) said, 'Because of the milk of "impregnating agent" your father has become her father and your mother her mother.'"

H 9849, Ch. 91, h 4
Ali ibn Ibrahim has narrated from his father from ibn abu 'Umayr from Hammad from al-Halabiy who has said the following:
"Abu 'Abd Allah, *'Alayhi al-Salam*, has said, 'If a man marries a small girl and she is breastfed by his wife his marriage becomes invalid.' I then asked about the case of woman of a man who breastfeeds a girl; if her sons from another husband can marry her (the girl). He (the Imam) said, 'No, they cannot do so.' I

then asked, 'Is she like a sister of breastfeeding?' He (the Imam) said, 'Yes, from the side of the father.'"

H 9850, Ch. 91, h 5

Ali ibn Ibrahim has narrated from his father from ibn abu 'Umayr from Hammad from al-Halabiy who has said the following:

"Abu 'Abd Allah, *'Alayhi al-Salam*, has said that once a man came to 'Amir al-Mu'minin, and said, 'O 'Amir al-Mu'minin, my wife drained her milk in a bowl and made my slave-girl to drink it.' He (the Imam) said, 'Make your woman suffer (judicially applicable punishment) and keep your slave-girl'. This is how it is in the judgment of Ali, *'Alayhi al-Salam*.'"

H 9851, Ch. 91, h 6

Ali ibn Ibrahim has narrated from his father from ibn abu 'Umayr from Hammad from al-Halabiy from 'Abd Allah ibn Sinan who has said the following:

"About the case of a man who marries a small girl and his wife breastfeeds her or the mother of his children, abu 'Abd Allah, *'Alayhi al-Salam*, has said, 'She becomes unlawful for him.'"

H 9852, Ch. 91, h 7

Ali has narrated from his father from ibn abu 'Umayr from certain persons of our people who has said the following:

"Abu 'Abd Allah, *'Alayhi al-Salam*, has said, 'Breastfeeding that grows flesh and blood is the one that he drinks until he feels weary and disinterested and his breath ends.'"

H 9853, Ch. 91, h 8

Muhammad ibn Yahya has narrated from Ahmad ibn Muhammad from ibn Faddal from ibn Bukayr from abu Yahya al-Hannat who has said the following:

"I once said to abu 'Abd Allah, *'Alayhi al-Salam*, that my son and the daughter of my brother are in my care and I want to arrange marriage between them but certain ones of my family has said that she has breastfed both of them. He (the Imam) asked, 'How much breastfeeding has taken place?' I replied, 'I do not know.' He (the Imam) said, 'Inform me so then I determine.' He (the narrator) has said, that I then said, 'I do not know.' He (the Imam) said, 'You can arrange marriage between them.'"

H 9854, Ch. 91, h 9

Ali ibn Ibrahim has narrated from his father from ibn abu 'Umayr from Hammad from al-Halabiy who has said the following:

"This is concerning my question before abu 'Abd Allah, *'Alayhi al-Salam*, about the case of a woman who alleges that she has breastfed a woman and a boy, then she denies. He (the Imam) asked, 'Do you accept her words of denial?' I replied, 'She said it and alleged that she has breastfed them.' He (the Imam) said, 'You must not accept or say yes to her words.'"

H 9855, Ch. 91, h 10

Ali has narrated from his father from ibn abu 'Umayr from 'Abd Allah ibn Sinan who has said the following:

"Abu 'Abd Allah, *'Alayhi al-Salam*, has said, 'It is not proper for a woman to get married to her paternal or maternal uncle of breastfeeding.'"

H 9856, Ch. 91, h 11

Muhammad ibn Yahya has narrated from Ahmad ibn Muhammad from ibn Mahbub from ibn Ri'ab from abu 'Ubaydah who has said the following:

"I once heard abu 'Abd Allah, *'Alayhi al-Salam*, saying, 'You must not marry a woman as a second wife, the first being her paternal aunt, maternal aunt of breastfeeding or her sister of breastfeeding. He (the Imam) said that Ali *'Alayhi al-Salam*, has said that daughter of Hamzah was mentioned before the Messenger of Allah, *O Allah, grant compensation to Muhammad and his family worthy of their services to Your cause*, and he (the Messenger of Allah) said, "Do you not know that she is daughter of my brother of breastfeeding?" The Messenger of Allah and his uncle Hamzah were breastfed by one woman.'"

H 9857, Ch. 91, h 12

Humayd ibn Ziyad has narrated from al-Hassan ibn Muhammad from Ahmad ibn al-Hassan al-Mithamiy from Yunus ibn Ya'qub who has said the following:

"This is concerning my question before abu 'Abd Allah, *'Alayhi al-Salam*, about the case of a woman who allows her milk without giving birth and breastfeeds a girl or a boy with that milk; if because of such milk the unlawfulness on account of breastfeeding comes into existence. He (the Imam) said, 'No, unlawfulness does not come into existence.'"

H 9858, Ch. 91, h 13

Ali ibn Muhammad has narrated from Salih ibn abu Hammad from Ali ibn Mahziyar from who has said the following:

"Once abu Ja'far, *'Alayhi al-Salam*, was asked about the case of a man who married a small girl, then his wife breastfed her, then his other woman breastfed her. Ibn Shubramah has said that the girl and both of his wives become unlawful for him. Abu Ja'far, *'Alayhi al-Salam*, has said, 'Ibn Shubramah has made a mistake. The girl and his wife who first breastfed her become unlawful but his other wife is not unlawful because her case is like her breastfeeding her own daughter.'"

H 9859, Ch. 91, h 14

Ali ibn Ibrahim has narrated from his father from al-Nawfaliy from al-Sakuniy who has said the following:

"Abu 'Abd Allah, *'Alayhi al-Salam*, has said that 'Amir al-Mu'minin has said, 'Prohibit your wives from breastfeeding many children, left and right, because they forget.'"

H 9860, Ch. 91, h 15

Muhammad ibn Yahya has narrated from Ahmad ibn Muhammad from ibn Mahbub from Ali ibn al-Hassan ibn Ribat from ibn Muskan from Muhammad ibn Muslim who has said the following:

"One of the two Imam, (abu Ja'far or abu 'Abd Allah), *'Alayhim al-Salam*, has said, 'If a boy is breastfed by different women and it is up to the required number or his flesh and blood grow, the daughters of all of them become unlawful for him for marriage.'"

408

H 9861, Ch. 91, h 16

It is narrated from the narrator of the previous Hadith from ibn Sinan from a man who has said the following:

"This is concerning a question before abu 'Abd Allah, *'Alayhi al-Salam*, when I was present, about the case of a woman who has breastfed her own slave boy from her milk until weaning; if she can sell him. He (the narrator) has said, that he (the Imam) said, 'No, because he is her son of breastfeeding. Selling him and consuming his price is unlawful for her.' He (the Imam) then said, 'Has the Messenger of Allah, *O Allah, grant compensation to Muhammad and his family worthy of their services to Your cause*, not said, "Whoever is unlawful for marriage because of lineage is unlawful because breastfeeding."'"

H 9862, Ch. 91, h 17

Muhammad ibn Yahya has narrated from Salmah ibn al-Khattab from 'Abd Allah ibn Khidash from Salih ibn 'Abd Allah al-Khath'amiy who has said the following:

"This is concerning my question before abu al-Hassan, Musa, *'Alayhi al-Salam*, about the case of mother of my child who is truthful and who alleges that she has breastfed my slave-girl: if I must accept her word. He (the Imam) said, 'No, do not accept her word.'"

H 9863, Ch. 91, h 18

Muhammad ibn Yahya has narrated from 'Abd Allah ibn Ja'far who has said the following:

"I once wrote to abu Muhammad, *'Alayhi al-Salam*, and asked, 'A woman has breastfed the son of a man; if the man can marry the daughter of breastfeeding woman. He (the Imam) signed the answer, 'No, he cannot marry because it is not lawful for him.'"

Chapter 92 - Another Chapter About the Previous Subject

H 9864, Ch. 92, h 1

A number of our people have narrated from Sahl ibn Ziyad from Muhammad ibn al-Hassan ibn Shammun from 'Abd Allah ibn 'Abd al-Rahman al-Asamm from Misma' ibn 'Abd al-Malik who has said the following:

"Abu 'Abd Allah, *'Alayhi al-Salam*, has said that 'Amir al-Mu'minin has said, 'In the following eight cases marriage is not permissible: Your slave-girl whose mother is your slave-girl, or her sister is your slave-girl, your slave-girl who is your paternal aunt of breastfeeding, your slave-girl who is your maternal aunt of breastfeeding, your slave-girl who has breastfed you, your slave-girl who has gone to bed with someone until passing of one menses cycle, your slave-girl who is pregnant from another man, your slave-girl whose value is being assessed and is not yet purchased and your slave-girl who has a husband.'"

Chapter 93 - Marriage with Nurse (*al-Qabilah*)

H 9865, Ch. 93, h 1

Ali ibn Ibrahim has narrated from his father from ibn abu 'Umayr from Khallad al-Sindiy from "Amr ibn Shamir from (Jabir) who has said the following:

"This is concerning my question before abu 'Abd Allah, *'Alayhi al-Salam*, if one can marry his al-Qabilah (special nurse who helps one's mother during her giving birth and thereafter). He (the Imam) said, 'No, and not her daughter also.'"

H 9866, Ch. 93, h 2
Muhammad ibn Yahya has narrated from Ahmad ibn Muhammad ibn 'Isa from abu Muhammad al-Ansariy from ''Amr ibn Shamir from Jabir ibn Yazid who has said the following:
"This is concerning my question before abu Ja'far, *'Alayhi al-Salam*, about *al-Qabilah* (special nurse who helps one's mother during her giving birth and thereafter); if the child can marry her. He (the Imam) said, 'No, not her daughter also, because she is one of his mothers.'

Mu'awiyah ibn 'Ammar has narrated the following:
"Abu 'Abd Allah, *'Alayhi al-Salam*, has said, 'If she just helps to give birth and moves on, then such nurses are many; but if she helps during birth, and brings him up, then she is unlawful for marriage.'"

H 9867, Ch. 93, h 3
Humayd ibn Ziyad has narrated from 'Abd Allah ibn Ahmad from Ali ibn al-Hassan from Muhammad ibn Ziyad ibn 'Isa Bayya' al-Sabiriy from Aban ibn 'Uthman from Ibrahim who has said the following:
"Abu 'Abd Allah, *'Alayhi al-Salam*, has said, 'If the child feels compassion toward *al-Qabilah* (special nurse who helps one's mother during her giving birth and thereafter) she becomes unlawful to him for marriage as well as her children.'"

Chapter 94 - *Al-Mut'ah* (Advantageous Marriage)

H 9868, Ch. 94, h 1
A number of our people have narrated from Sahl ibn Ziyad and Ali ibn Ibrahim has narrated from his father from all from ibn abu Najran from 'Asem ibn Hamid from abu Basir who has said the following:
"In response to my question before abu Ja'far, *'Alayhi al-Salam*, about *al-Mut'ah* (advantageous marriage), he (the Imam) said, 'It is mentioned in al-Quran, "If you marry them for *al-Mut'ah* (advantageous marriage) you must pay their dowries. There is no harm if you reach an understanding among yourselves about *mahr* (the dowry). Allah is All-knowing and All-wise."'" (4:24)

H 9869, Ch. 94, h 2
Muhammad ibn 'Isma'il has narrated from al-Fadl ibn Shadhan from Safwan ibn Yahya from ibn Muskan from 'Abd Allah ibn Sulayman who has said the following:
"I once heard abu Ja'far, *'Alayhi al-Salam*, saying that Ali, *'Alayhi al-Salam*, would say, 'Had banu al-Khattab not prohibited *al-Mut'ah* (advantageous marriage) before (the beginning of my administration) no one would commit fornication except the wicked ones.'"

H 9870, Ch. 94, h 3
Ali ibn Ibrahim has narrated from his father from ibn abu 'Umayr from those whom he has mentioned who has said the following:

"Abu 'Abd Allah, *'Alayhi al-Salam*, has said, 'It was revealed as "If you marry them [for an appointed time] for *al-Mut'ah* (advantageous marriage) you must pay their dowries." (4:24)'"

H 9871, Ch. 94, h 4

Ali ibn Ibrahim has narrated from his father from ibn abu 'Umayr from 'Umar ibn 'Udhaynah from Zurarah who has said the following:

"Once 'Abd Allah ibn 'Umayr al-Laythiy came to abu Ja'far, *'Alayhi al-Salam*, and asked, 'What do you say about *al-Mut'ah* (advantageous marriage) of women?' He (the Imam) said, 'Allah has made it lawful in His book by the tongue of His Holy prophet, *O Allah, grant compensation to Muhammad and his family worthy of their services to Your cause*, thus it will remain lawful up to the Day of Judgment.' He then said, 'O abu Ja'far, how can someone like you say this, when 'Umar made it unlawful and prohibited it?' He (the Imam) said, 'Even if he has done so.' He said, 'I ask Allah to protect you against a thing that 'Umar has made unlawful.' He (the narrator) has said that he (the Imam) then said, 'So you can stand by the words of your friend but I stand by the words of the Messenger of Allah, *O Allah, grant compensation to Muhammad and his family worthy of their services to Your cause*, and I am prepared for *al-Mula'inah* (ask Allah to condemn the party on the side of falsehood) that the word is what the Messenger of Allah, *O Allah, grant compensation to Muhammad and his family worthy of their services to Your cause*, has said; and that falsehood is what your friend has said.' He (the narrator) has said that 'Abd Allah ibn 'Umayr then said, 'Will it make you happy that your women, daughters, sisters, daughters of your aunts do?' He (the narrator) has said that abu Ja'far, *'Alayhi al-Salam*, when he mentioned his women and daughters of his aunts turned away from him.'"

H 9872, Ch. 94, h 5

Muhammad ibn Yahya has narrated from 'Abd Allah ibn Muhammad from Ali ibn al-Hakam from Aban ibn 'Uthman from abu Maryam who has said the following:

"Abu 'Abd Allah, *'Alayhi al-Salam*, has said, '*Al-Mut'ah* (advantageous marriage) is mentioned in al-Quran and the Sunnah of the Messenger of Allah, *O Allah, grant compensation to Muhammad and his family worthy of their services to Your cause*, has followed it.'"

H 9873, Ch. 94, h 6

Ali ibn Ibrahim has narrated from his father from ibn abu 'Umayr from Ali ibn al-Hassan ibn Ribat from Hariz from 'Abd al-Rahman ibn abu 'Abd Allah who has said the following:

"I heard abu Hanifah ask abu 'Abd Allah, *'Alayhi al-Salam*, about *al-Mut'ah* (advantageous matters). He (the Imam) asked, 'Are you asking about the two *al-Mut'ah* (advantageous matters)?' He said, 'I asked you about *al-Mut'ah* (advantageous matters of al-Hajj) and you inform me about *al-Mut'ah* (advantageous marriage) is it true?' He (the Imam) said, 'Allah is free of all defects, have you not read the book of Allah, most Majestic, most Glorious, "If you marry them for *al-Mut'ah* (advantageous marriage) you must pay their dowries. . . ."' (4:24). Abu Hanifah said, 'By Allah, it is as if I have never read this verse.'"

411

H 9874, Ch. 94, h 7

Ali ibn Ibrahim has narrated from his father from ibn Mahbub from al-Sa'iy who has said the following:

"I once said to abu al-Hassan, *'Alayhi al-Salam*, 'I pray to Allah to keep my soul in service for your cause, I would marry in the manner of *al-Mut'ah* (advantageous marriage), I then disliked it and had bad omens about it; then I promised before Allah between the corner of al-Ka'bah and the Station of Ibrahim, *'Alayhi al-Salam*, kept a vow upon myself and fasting not to do such marriage again. It became difficult for me, I regretted because of my swearing and I was not able to marry publicly. He (the Imam) said, 'You promised Allah not to obey Him. By Allah, if you do not obey Him you sin against Him.'"

H 9875, Ch. 94, h 8

Ali has narrated from in a marfu' manner saying:

"Abu Hanifah once asked abu Ja'far, Muhammad ibn al-Nu'man Sahib al-Taq saying, 'O abu Ja'far, what do you say about *al-Mut'ah* (advantageous marriage)? Do you think it is lawful?' He replied, 'Yes, it is lawful.' He then said, 'Why then do you not ask your women to go for *al-Mut'ah* (advantageous marriage) and earn for you?' Abu Ja'far said, 'All kinds of skills are not desirable even if they are lawful, because people have their values and positions which raise their values. However, what do you say O abu Hanifah, about al-Nabidh (wine from dates)? Do you think it is lawful?' He replied, 'Yes, it is lawful.' He then said, 'What prevents you from making your women sit in shops as al-Nabidh sellers to sell al-Nabidh to earn for you?' Abu Hanifah said, 'This is one for one and your share is more effective.' He then said, 'O abu Ja'far, the verse in which there is "one asking a question asked" (Chapter 70) speaks of unlawfulness of *al-Mut'ah* (advantageous marriage) and Hadith from the Holy Prophet, *O Allah, grant compensation to Muhammad and his family worthy of their services to Your cause*, has come to cancel it.' Abu Ja'far said, 'O abu Hanifah, the chapter "one asking a question asked" was revealed in Makkah and the verse that speaks of *al-Mut'ah* (advantageous marriage) was revealed in al-Madinah and Hadith you spoke of is atypical and refuted.' Abu Hanifah then said, 'The verse about inheritance also speaks of cancellation of *al-Mut'ah* (advantageous marriage).' Abu Ja'far, said, 'Proof of lawfulness of marriage is without inheritance.' Abu Hanifah said, 'On what basis you say so?' Abu Ja'far, asked, 'If a Muslim marries a woman from the people of the book then he dies what do you say about her?' He said, 'She will not inherit him.' Abu Ja'far, said, 'So marriage is proved without inheritance. They then departed each other.'"

(Because of marriage spouses inherit each other. In *Mut'ah* inheritance is not applicable thus *Mut'ah* is not a marriage, according to the argument of abu Hanifah, if inheritance between the spouses is not applicable it is not a marriage. Abu Ja'far, proved one case where there is marriage but inheritance is not applicable).

Chapter 95 - Such Wives Are Like Slave-girls, Not Like any of Four Wives

H 9876, Ch. 95, h 1

Ali ibn Ibrahim has narrated from his father from ibn abu 'Umayr from 'Umar ibn 'Udhaynah who has said the following:

"This is concerning my question before abu 'Abd Allah, *'Alayhi al-Salam*, about how many are lawful for *al-Mut'ah* (advantageous marriage). He (the Imam) said, 'Their case is similar to slave-girls.'"

H 9877, Ch. 95, h 2

Al-Husayn from Muhammad has narrated from Ahmad ibn Ishaq al-Ash'ariy from Bakr ibn Muhammad al-Azdiy who has said the following:

"In response to my question before abu 'Abd Allah, *'Alayhi al-Salam*, about *al-Mut'ah* (advantageous marriage) if it is one of the four, he (the Imam) said, 'No, it is not one of the four.'"

H 9878, Ch. 95, h 3

Muhammad ibn Yahya has narrated from Ahmad ibn Muhammad from ibn Mahbub from ibn Ri'ab from Zurarah ibn 'A'yan who has said the following:

"I once asked him (the Imam), *'Alayhi al-Salam*, 'How many is lawful for *al-Mut'ah* (advantageous marriage)?' He (the Imam) said, 'It is as many as you wish.'"

H 9879, Ch. 95, h 4

Al-Husayn from Muhammad has narrated from Mu'alla' ibn Muhammad from al-Hassan ibn Ali from Hammad ibn 'Uthaman from abu Basir who has said the following:

"This is concerning my question before abu 'Abd Allah, *'Alayhi al-Salam*, if *al-Mut'ah* (advantageous marriage) is of four. He (the Imam) said, 'No, even seventy is not unlawful.'"

H 9880, Ch. 95, h 5

Muhammad ibn Yahya has narrated from Ahmad ibn Muhammad ibn 'Isa from al-Husayn ibn Sa'id Ahmad ibn Muhammad from Muhammad ibn Khalid al-Barqiy from al-Qasim ibn 'Urwah from 'Abd al-Hamid from Muhammad ibn Muslim who has said the following:

"Abu Ja'far, *'Alayhi al-Salam*, has said, '*Al-Mut'ah* (advantageous marriage) is not of four because it has no divorce or inheritance; she is only hired.'"

H 9881, Ch. 95, h 6

Ali ibn Ibrahim has narrated from his father from ibn abu 'Umayr from 'Umar ibn 'Udhaynah from 'Isma'il ibn al-Fadl al-Hashimiy who has said the following:

"This is concerning my question before abu 'Abd Allah, *'Alayhi al-Salam*, about *al-Mut'ah* (advantageous marriage). He (the Imam) said, 'Meet 'Abd al-Malik ibn Jurayh and ask him about it; he has information about it.' I met him and he dictated a great deal of issues about its lawfulness. Among the matters that ibn Jurayh narrated to me was that he said, 'There is no particular time limit for it or a particular number. The case is similar to that of the slave-girls. One may marry as many as he wishes and one with four wives can marry in this manner, as many as he wishes, without the presence of guardian or witness. When the time

413

expires she becomes a stranger to him without divorce and he may give her something very little. Her waiting period is two cycles of menses but if she does not experience Hayd (menses) her waiting period is forty five days.' I brought the book to abu 'Abd Allah, *'Alayhi al-Salam*, and displayed it before him (the Imam). He (the Imam) said, 'He has spoken the truth and has made it easy.' Ibn 'Udhaynah has said, that Zurarah ibn 'A'yan would say so and swear that it is true except that he would say, 'If she experiences Hayd (menses) her waiting period is one cycle of Hayd (menses) and if she does not experience Hayd (menses) her waiting period is one and a half month.'"

H 9882, Ch. 95, h 7
Al-Husayn from Muhammad has narrated from Ahmad ibn Ishaq from Sa'dan ibn Muslim from 'Ubayd ibn Zurarah from his father who has said the following:
"I once mentioned *al-Mut'ah* (advantageous marriage) before abu 'Abd Allah, *'Alayhi al-Salam*, and asked if it is one of four (wives). He (the Imam) said, 'You may marry a thousand of them; they are on hire.'"

Chapter 96 - It (*Mut'ah*) Must Not Be Practiced if Not Urgently Needed

H 9883, Ch. 96, h 1
Ali ibn Ibrahim has narrated from his father from ibn abu 'Umayr from Ali ibn Yaqtin who has said the following:
"I once asked abu al-Hassan, Musa, *'Alayhi al-Salam*, about *al-Mut'ah* (advantageous marriage). He (the Imam) said, 'What do you have to do with it when Allah has made you free of need for it?' I then said, 'I only wanted to know about it.' He (the Imam) said, 'It is in the book of Ali, *'Alayhi al-Salam*.' I then asked, 'Can we extend and they women extend (the time)?' He (the Imam) said, 'What else makes him happy?'"

H 9884, Ch. 96, h 2
Ali ibn Ibrahim has narrated from al-Mukhtar ibn Muhammad al-Mukhtar and Muhammad ibn al-Hassan from 'Abd Allah ibn al-Hassan al-'Alawiy all from al-Fath ibn Yazid who has said the following:
"I once asked abu al-Hassan, *'Alayhi al-Salam*, about *al-Mut'ah* (advantageous marriage). He (the Imam) said, 'It is lawful, permissible and available for those whom Allah has not made free of need for marriage, so he can maintain chastity by means of *al-Mut'ah* (advantageous marriage), and when he is free of such need by means of marriage, then it is permissible in the absence of his wife.'"

H 9885, Ch. 96, h 3
A number of our people have narrated from Sahl ibn Ziyad from Muhammad ibn al-Hassan ibn Shammun who has said the following:
"Abu al-Hassan, *'Alayhi al-Salam*, once wrote to certain ones of his followers and it (the letter) said, 'You must not insist on *al-Mut'ah* (advantageous marriage). You only have to maintain the Sunnah. You must not involve in it to ignore your bed (wives) and your free ones to cause them turn to disbelief, disowning and claim against the command for it (*al-Mut'ah* (advantageous marriage)) and condemn us.'"

H 9886, Ch. 96, h 4

Ali ibn Muhammad has narrated from Salih ibn abu Hammad from ibn Sinan from al-Mufaddal ibn 'Umar who has said the following:

"I once heard abu 'Abd Allah, *'Alayhi al-Salam*, saying about *al-Mut'ah* (advantageous marriage), 'Stay away from it. Do you not feel ashamed of being seen in a place for which your virtuous brothers in belief and friends feel embarrassed?'"

Chapter 97 - *Al-Mut'ah* (advantageous marriage) Is Not Permissible With Non-Chaste Women

H 9887, Ch. 97, h 1

Muhammad ibn Yahya has narrated from Ahmad ibn Muhammad from ibn Mahbub from Aban from abu Maryam who has said the following:

"Once, abu Ja'far, *'Alayhi al-Salam*, was asked about *al-Mut'ah* (advantageous marriage). He (the Imam) said, *'Al-Mut'ah* (advantageous marriage) today is not like it was before this day. Women in those days believed in it but today they do not believe in it and you can ask them.'"

H 9888, Ch. 97, h 2

It is narrated from the narrator of the previous Hadith from Ahmad ibn Muhammad from al-'Abbas ibn Musa from Ishaq from abu Sarah who has said the following:

"This is concerning my question before abu 'Abd Allah, *'Alayhi al-Salam*, about it (*al-Mut'ah* (advantageous marriage)). He (the Imam) said to me, 'It is lawful but you must not marry except those who possess chastity; Allah, most Majestic, most Glorious, says, ". . .those who protect their private organs."(23:5) Therefore, do not marry one whom you cannot trust about your dirham.'"

H 9889, Ch. 97, h 3

Muhammad ibn Yahya has narrated from Ahmad ibn Muhammad from Muhammad ibn 'Isma'il who has said the following:

"A man once asked al-Rida', *'Alayhi al-Salam*, when I was listening, about the case of a man who married a woman in the manner of *al-Mut'ah* (advantageous marriage) with the condition that he was not to support her child. She thereafter brought a child to him and he strongly denied the child. He (the Imam) said, 'Does he deny it because of its greatness?' The man replied, 'He accuses her (of wrong doing).' He (the Imam) said, 'It is not proper for you to marry anyone other than believing, Muslim female because Allah, most Majestic, most Glorious, says, "The fornicator cannot marry but a female fornicator or a female pagan and a female fornicator cannot marry anyone other than a male fornicator or a pagan and it is unlawful to believing people." (23:3)'"

H 9890, Ch. 97, h 4

Ali ibn Ibrahim has narrated from his father from ibn abu 'Umayr from in a marfu' manner from 'Abd Allah ibn abu Ya'fur who has said the following:

"This is concerning my question before abu 'Abd Allah, *'Alayhi al-Salam*, about the case of a woman whose condition is not known; if a man can marry her in the manner of *al-Mut'ah* (advantageous marriage). He (the Imam) said, 'He can propose unlawful activities; if she agreed, he then must stay away from her.'"

H 9891, Ch. 97, h 5

A number of our people have narrated from Ahmad ibn Muhammad from al-Barqiy from Dawud ibn Ishaq al-Hadhdha' from Muhammad ibn al-Fayd who has said the following:

"This is concerning my question before abu 'Abd Allah, *'Alayhi al-Salam*, about *al-Mut'ah* (advantageous marriage). He (the Imam) said, 'Yes, if she is knowledgeable.' We then asked him (the Imam), 'We pray to Allah to keep our souls in service for your cause, what happens if she is not knowledgeable?' He (the Imam) said, 'Propose to her if she agrees then marry her, if she refuses to accept your words then stay away from her. You must remain on your guard against *al-Kawashif*, *al-Dawa'iy*, *al-Baghaya'* and *Dhawat al-Azwaj*.' I then asked who are *al-Kawashif*?' He (the Imam) said, 'They are those whose houses are known to people and people go to them.' I asked about *al-Dawa'iy* and he (the Imam) said, 'They are those women who call people to themselves and who are known for indecent acts.' I then asked about *al-Baghaya'* and he (the Imam) said, 'They are those who are known for their committing fornication.' I then asked about *Dhawat al-Azwaj* and he (the Imam) said, 'They are those who are not divorced according to the Sunnah.'"

H 9892, Ch. 97, h 6

Ali ibn Ibrahim has narrated from Muhammad ibn 'Isa from Yunus from Muhammad ibn al-Fudayl who has said the following:

"I once asked abu al-Hassan, *'Alayhi al-Salam*, about the case of a woman who was beautiful but was involved in indecent acts if it was permissible to form *al-Mut'ah* (advantageous marriage) with her for a day or more. He (the Imam) said, 'If she is known as a fornicator then *al-Mut'ah* (advantageous marriage) is not proper with her as well as marriage.'"

Chapter 98 - Conditions of *al-Mut'ah* (Advantageous Marriage)

H 9893, Ch. 98, h 1

A number of our people have narrated from Sahl ibn Ziyad and Muhammad ibn Yahya has narrated from Ahmad ibn Muhammad all from ibn Mahbub from Jamil ibn Salih from Zurarah who has said the following:

"Abu 'Abd Allah, *'Alayhi al-Salam*, has said, '*Al-Mut'ah* (advantageous marriage) cannot take place without two issues: they are the duration of time and the amount of *mahr* (dower).'"

H 9894 (a), Ch. 98, h 2

Muhammad ibn Yahya has narrated from Muhammad ibn al-Husayn and a number of our people have narrated from Ahmad ibn Muhammad from 'Uthman ibn 'Isa from Sama'ah from abu Basir who has said the following:

"He (the Imam), *'Alayhi al-Salam*, has said, 'It is necessary that in marriage in the manner of *al-Mut'ah* (advantageous marriage) and its conditions one must say, "I form marriage with you in the manner of *al-Mut'ah* (advantageous marriage) for so and so many days with such and such amount of dirham as *mahr* (dower), a marriage free of indecency according to the book of Allah, most Majestic, most Glorious, and the Sunnah of Allah's Holy prophet, *O Allah, grant compensation to Muhammad and his family worthy of their services to*

Your cause, that you will not inherit me and I will not inherit you and that you must complete forty-five days of waiting period'" and certain ones have said that it is one cycle of Hayd (menses)."

H 9894 (b), Ch. 98, h 3

Ali ibn Ibrahim has narrated from his father from "Amr ibn 'Uthman from Ibrahim ibn al-Fadl from Aban ibn Taghlib and Ali ibn Muhammad from Sahl ibn Ziyad from 'Isma'il ibn Mehran and Muhammad ibn Muslim from Ibrahim ibn al-Fadl from Aban ibn Taghlib who has said the following:

"This is concerning my question before abu 'Abd Allah, *'Alayhi al-Salam*, about what I should say when I am with her. He (the Imam) said, 'Say I marry you in the manner of *al-Mut'ah* (advantageous marriage) according to the book of Allah and the Sunnah of His Holy prophet, *O Allah, grant compensation to Muhammad and his family worthy of their services to Your cause*, and that there is no inheritor or inherited in it, for so and so many days or if you wished, for so and so many years, for so and so much amount of dirham as *mahr* (dower),' mention the amount you both have agreed, little or more, then if she said, "Yes," it means she has agreed. She is your wife and you are the nearest of all people to her.' I then said, 'I feel embarrassed to mention the condition of days.' He (the Imam) said, 'It (such feeling) is more harmful to you.' I then asked, 'Why is it as such?' He (the Imam) said, 'If you do not mention, marriage is permanent, you must pay her expenses during waiting period, there will be inheritance and you cannot divorce her except in the form of divorce according to the Sunnah.'"

H 9895, Ch. 98, h 4

Ali ibn Ibrahim has narrated from his father from ibn abu Nasr from Tha'labah who has said the following:

"He (the Imam), *'Alayhi al-Salam*, has said, say, 'I marry you in the manner of *al-Mut'ah* (advantageous marriage) according to the book of Allah and the Sunnah of His Holy prophet, *O Allah, grant compensation to Muhammad and his family worthy of their services to Your cause*, a marriage which is not indecency and that you will not inherit me and I will not inherit you, for so and so amount of dirham as *mahr* (dower) and that you must complete the waiting period.'"

H 9896, Ch. 98, h 5

Muhammad ibn Yahya has narrated from 'Abd Allah ibn Muhammad ibn abu 'Umayr from Hisham ibn Salim who has said the following:

"I once asked him (the Imam), *'Alayhi al-Salam*, about how *al-Mut'ah* (advantageous marriage) is formed?' He (the Imam) said that you must say, 'O female servant of Allah, I marry you for so and so many days for such and such amount of dirham as *mahr* (dower).' When the days pass her divorce is her condition and she does not need waiting period.'"

Chapter 99 - The Need to Mention Conditions after Nikah

H 9897, Ch. 99, h 1

Ali ibn Ibrahim has narrated from his father from ibn abu 'Umayr from 'Abd Allah ibn Bukayr who has said the following:

"Any condition before marriage becomes invalid by marriage and the condition after marriage is permissible.' He (the Imam) said, 'If time limit is mentioned it is *al-Mut'ah* (advantageous marriage) and if time limit is not mentioned it is permanent.'"

H 9898, Ch. 99, h 2

A number of our people have narrated from Sahl ibn Ziyad from ibn Mahbub from ibn Ri'ab from Muhammad ibn Muslim who has said the following:

"This is concerning my question before abu 'Abd Allah, *'Alayhi al-Salam*, about the words of Allah, most Majestic, most Glorious, '. . . it is not harmful for you if you agree upon it after marriage.' (4:24) He (the Imam) said, 'Whatever they agree upon after marriage is permissible and whatever is before marriage is not permissible except with her agreement and with something given to her to make her agree.'"

H 9899, Ch. 99, h 3

A number of our people have narrated from Ahmad ibn abu 'Abd Allah from his father from Sulayman ibn Salim from ibn Bukayr who has said the following:

"Abu 'Abd Allah, *'Alayhi al-Salam*, has said, 'When you settle the conditions of *al-Mut'ah* (advantageous marriage) with a woman and she agrees and marriage becomes binding, you can bring your prior condition after marriage; if she agrees it is permissible, if she does not agree, it does not apply effectively to her; it was before marriage.'"

H 9900, Ch. 99, h 4

Muhammad ibn Yahya has narrated from Ahmad ibn Muhammad from ibn Faddal from ibn Bukayr from Muhammad ibn Muslim who has said the following:

"I once heard abu Ja'far, *'Alayhi al-Salam*, saying, about the case of a man who marries in the manner of *al-Mut'ah* (advantageous marriage) 'They inherit each other if they do not set a condition because condition is effective after marriage.'"

H 9901, Ch. 99, h 5

Ali ibn Ibrahim has narrated from Muhammad ibn 'Isa from Sulayman ibn Salim from ibn Bukayr ibn 'A'yan who has said the following:

"Abu 'Abd Allah, *'Alayhi al-Salam*, has said, 'When you settle the conditions of *al-Mut'ah* (advantageous marriage) with a woman and she agrees, marriage becomes binding; you can bring your prior condition after marriage, if she agrees it is permissible; if she does not agree it does not apply effectively to her; it was before marriage.'"

Chapter 100 - *Mahr* (dower) in this form of Marriage, *al-Mut'ah*

H 9902, Ch. 100, h 1

A number of our people have narrated from Sahl ibn Ziyad from Ahmad ibn Muhammad from ibn abu Nasr and 'Abd al-Rahman ibn abu Najran from 'Asem ibn Hamid from Muhammad ibn Muslim who has said the following:

"In response to my question before abu 'Abd Allah, *'Alayhi al-Salam*, about how much *mahr* (dower) is – in *al-Mut'ah* (advantageous marriage), he (the Imam) said, 'It is whatever they agree on, up to the time they want.'"

H 9903, Ch. 100, h 2

Muhammad ibn Yahya has narrated from Ahmad ibn Muhammad from al-Husayn ibn Sa'id Ahmad ibn Muhammad from Muhammad ibn Khalid al-Barqiy from al-Qasim ibn Muhammad al-Jawhariy from abu Sa'id from al-Ahwal who has said the following:

"This is concerning my question before abu 'Abd Allah, *'Alayhi al-Salam*, about the minimum amount of *mahr* (dower) in *al-Mut'ah* (advantageous marriage). He (the Imam) said, 'It can be a handful of wheat.'"

H 9904, Ch. 100, h 3

Ahmad ibn Muhammad has narrated from al-Husayn ibn Sa'id from Hammad ibn 'Isa from Shu'ayb ibn Ya'qub from abu Basir who has said the following:

"I once asked abu Ja'far, *'Alayhi al-Salam*, about *al-Mut'ah* (advantageous marriage) of women. He (the Imam) said, 'It is lawful and one dirham or more is enough (as *mahr* (dower)).'"

H 9905, Ch. 100, h 4

Muhammad ibn Yahya has narrated from Ahmad ibn Muhammad from Ali ibn al-Hakam from Ali ibn abu Hamzah from abu Basir who has said the following:

"This is concerning my question before abu 'Abd Allah, *'Alayhi al-Salam*, about *mahr* (dower) in *al-Mut'ah* (advantageous marriage) and that what it is? He (the Imam) said, 'It can be a handful of food items, wheat flour, or fine flour or dates.'"

H 9906, Ch. 100, h 5

Ali ibn Ibrahim has narrated from Muhammad ibn 'Isa from Yunus from certain persons of our people who have said the following:

"Abu 'Abd Allah, *'Alayhi al-Salam*, has said, 'The minimum amount of *mahr* (dower) in *al-Mut'ah* (advantageous marriage) can be even a handful of food.' Certain ones of them have narrated that even a *Miswak* (toothbrush) is acceptable."

Chapter 101 - Waiting Period in *al-Mut'ah* (advantageous marriage)

H 9907, Ch. 101, h 1

Ali ibn Ibrahim has narrated from his father from ibn abu 'Umayr from 'Umar ibn 'Udhaynah from Zurarah who has said the following:

"Abu 'Abd Allah, *'Alayhi al-Salam*, has said, 'Waiting period in *al-Mut'ah* (advantageous marriage) is one cycle of Hayd (menses) if she experiences Hayd (menses); and if she does not experience Hayd (menses) then it is one and a half month.'"

H 9908, Ch. 101, h 2

A number of our people have narrated from Sahl ibn Ziyad from Ahmad ibn Muhammad from ibn abu Nasr who has said the following:

"Abu al-Hassan al-Rida' has said that abu Ja'far, *'Alayhi al-Salam*, has said, 'Waiting period for *al-Mut'ah* (advantageous marriage) is forty five days and because of precaution it is forty five nights.'"

H 9909, Ch. 101, h 3

Muhammad ibn Yahya has narrated from Ahmad ibn Muhammad from ibn Faddal from ibn Bukayr from Zurarah who has said the following:

"He (the Imam), *'Alayhi al-Salam*, has said, 'Waiting period of *al-Mut'ah* (advantageous marriage) is forty five days. It is as if I see my father count it on his fingers as forty-five and when this time passes separation between them takes place without divorce.'"

Chapter 102 - Addition in Time

H 9910, Ch. 102, h 1

A number of our people have narrated from Sahl ibn Ziyad and Ali ibn Ibrahim has narrated from his father all from 'Abd al-Rahman ibn abu Najran and Ahmad ibn abu Nasr from abu Basir who has said the following:

"He (the Imam), *'Alayhi al-Salam*, has said, 'It is permissible if she extends for you and you extend for her when the time for both of you expires, by saying, 'I have made you lawful to myself up to another period of time with your agreement' and this is not lawful for anyone other than you until it expires.'"

H 9911, Ch. 102, h 2

Ali ibn Ibrahim has narrated from his father from ibn abu 'Umayr from 'Amr ibn 'Uthman from Ibrahim ibn al-Fadl and A number of our people have narrated from Sahl ibn Ziyad from 'Isma'il ibn Mehran from Muhammad ibn Aslam and Ahmad ibn Muhammad ibn Khalid from Muhammad ibn Ali from Muhammad ibn Aslam from Ibrahim ibn al-Fadl al-Hashimiy from Aban ibn Taghlib who has said the following:

"This is concerning my question before abu 'Abd Allah, *'Alayhi al-Salam*, about the case of a man who marries a woman in the manner of *al-Mut'ah* (advantageous marriage) for the duration of one month. Then it comes to his heart and he likes to have a condition for more than a month; if it is permissible to increase in her *mahr* (dower) to extend the number of days before it (the time already set) expires. He (the Imam) said, 'No, two conditions in one and the same condition are not permissible.' I then asked, 'What must he do about it?' He (the Imam) said, 'She can give up the remaining of the time in his favor as charity and then initiate a new condition of extension of time.'"

H 9912, Ch. 102, h 3

Ali ibn Ibrahim has narrated from his father from ibn abu 'Umayr from those who narrated to him who has said the following:

"He (the Imam), *'Alayhi al-Salam*, has said, 'If a woman marries a man in the manner of *al-Mut'ah* (advantageous marriage) she must complete waiting period for others. However, if the same man wants to marry her again because of him she does not need to complete a waiting period, so she can marry him in the manner of *al-Mut'ah* (advantageous marriage) whenever she wants.'"

Chapter 103 - Permissible Time Length

H 9913, Ch. 103, h 1
A number of our people have narrated from Sahl ibn Ziyad from ibn Mahbub from ibn Ri'ab from 'Umar ibn Hanzalah who has said the following:
"Abu 'Abd Allah, *'Alayhi al-Salam*, has said, 'He can arrange for a mutual agreement with her for any number of days they want.'"

H 9914, Ch. 103, h 2
Muhammad ibn Yahya has narrated from Ahmad ibn Muhammad from Muhammad ibn 'Isma'il who has said the following:
"In response to my question before al-Rida', *'Alayhi al-Salam*, about the case of a man who marries in the manner of *al-Mut'ah* (advantageous marriage) for one year or less or more, he (the Imam) said, 'It is permissible if it is a known matter for a known number of days.' I then asked if it terminates without divorce. He (the Imam) said, 'Yes, it terminates without divorce.'"

H 9915, Ch. 103, h 3
Muhammad ibn Yahya has narrated from Ahmad ibn Muhammad from ibn Faddal from ibn Bukayr from Zurarah who has said the following:
"Concerning my question before abu 'Abd Allah, *'Alayhi al-Salam*, about the case of a man who marries a woman in the manner of *al-Mut'ah* (advantageous marriage) for *Sa'ah* or *Sa'ahtayn* (one or two hours in the sense of the word before the invention of time clock). He (the Imam) said, '*Sa'ah* or *Sa'ahtayn* are not definite, however, they can set it as once or twice going to bed or one or two days and nights or similar things.'"

H 9916, Ch. 103, h 4
Muhammad has narrated from Ahmad ibn Muhammad from Muhammad ibn Khalid from Khalaf ibn Hammad who has said the following:
"I once sent (a message) to abu al-Hassan, *'Alayhi al-Salam*, and asked, 'How much is the minimum duration of time in *al-Mut'ah* (advantageous marriage) and if it is permissible to set the time for only one time going to bed. He (the Imam) said, 'Yes, it is permissible.'"

H 9917, Ch. 103, h 5
A number of our people have narrated from Sahl ibn Ziyad from ibn Faddal from al-Qasim ibn Muhammad from a man whom he mentioned who has said the following:
"I once asked abu 'Abd Allah, *'Alayhi al-Salam*, about the case of a man who married a woman (in the manner of *al-Mut'ah* (advantageous marriage)) for only once going to bed. He (the Imam) said, 'It is permissible, however, when the specified time ends he must turn his face away and must not look.'"

Chapter 104 - *Al-Mut'ah* (advantageous marriage) Several Times with one Woman

H 9918, Ch. 104, h 1
Ali ibn Ibrahim has narrated from his father from ibn abu 'Umayr from certain persons of our people from Zurarah who has said the following:

"I once asked abu Ja'far, *'Alayhi al-Salam*, saying, 'I pray to Allah to keep my soul in service for your cause, a man marries a woman in the manner of *al-Mut'ah* (advantageous marriage) and its appointed time expires, then another man marries her and she becomes strangers to him then the first man marries her and she becomes stranger to him and this takes place three times and she marries three husbands; if it is permissible for the first man to marry her again. He (the Imam) said, 'Yes, it is permissible, as many times as he wants; it is not like a free woman. She is hired and her case is similar to slave-girls.'"

H 9919, Ch. 104, h 2
Muhammad ibn Yahya has narrated from 'Abd Allah ibn Muhammad from Ali ibn al-Hakam from Aban from certain persons of his people who has said the following:

"About the case of a man who marries a woman in the manner of *al-Mut'ah* (advantageous marriage) many times, abu 'Abd Allah, *'Alayhi al-Salam*, has said, 'It is not unlawful, he can marry her in the manner of *al-Mut'ah* (advantageous marriage) as many times as he wants.'"

Chapter 105 - Withholding *Mahr* in the Case of Her Violation

H 9920, Ch. 105, h 1
Muhammad ibn Yahya has narrated from Ahmad ibn Muhammad from al-Husayn ibn Sa'id from Fadalah abu Ayyub from 'Umar ibn Aban from 'Umar ibn Hanzalah who has said the following:

"This is concerning my question before abu 'Abd Allah, *'Alayhi al-Salam*, about if I marry a woman for one month and she wants all of the *mahr* (dower) from me, but I am afraid of her acting against me. He (the Imam) said, 'You cannot withhold the *mahr* (dower) that is set but when she acts against the terms of marriage then you can take from her what is equal to what she has violated of the mutually agreed conditions.'"

H 9921, Ch. 105, h 2
Ali ibn Ibrahim has narrated from his father from ibn abu 'Umayr from Hafs ibn al-Bakhtariy who has said the following:

"Abu 'Abd Allah, *'Alayhi al-Salam*, has said, 'If something of *mahr* (dower) remains due on him and he learns that she has a husband, then what she has received belongs to her because of its making his going to bed with her lawful and he can withhold the remaining of *mahr* (dower).'"

H 9922, Ch. 105, h 3
Ali ibn Ibrahim has narrated from Salih ibn al-Sindiy from Ja'far ibn Bashir from 'Umar ibn Aban from 'Umar ibn Hanzalah who has said the following:

"I once said to abu 'Abd Allah, *'Alayhi al-Salam*, 'I marry a woman for one month and withhold a certain amount from her *mahr* (dower). He (the Imam) said, 'Yes, you can do so for what is equal to her violation of the condition. If the violation is half of the month you can withhold one-half, if it is one-third then withhold one-third.'

Muhammad ibn Yahya has narrated from Ahmad ibn Muhammad ibn 'Isa from Ali ibn al-Hakam from 'Umar ibn Hanzalah from abu 'Abd Allah, *'Alayhi al-Salam*, has narrated a similar Hadith."

H 9923, Ch. 105, h 4

Ali ibn Ibrahim has narrated from his father from ibn abu 'Umayr from Ishaq ibn 'Ammar who has said the following:

"About the case of a man who marries a woman in the manner of *al-Mut'ah* (advantageous marriage) with the condition that she must come to him every day to comply with the condition, or sets a condition to come to him in certain days; but she asks to be excused and does not come to comply with the condition; if it is proper for him to deduct for the days that she did not come and withhold from her *mahr* (dower) accordingly. To this question from me abu al-Hassan, *'Alayhi al-Salam*, said, 'Yes, he can consider how much she has violated, then withhold proportionate to what she has not complied, except the days of her Hayd (menses); they are for her and he cannot have what is not lawful for him in matters of going to bed with her.'"

H 9924, Ch. 105, h 5

Muhammad ibn Yahya has narrated from Ahmad ibn Muhammad from Ali ibn Ahmad ibn 'Ushaym who has said the following:

"Al-Rayyan ibn Shabib wrote to abu al-Hassan , *'Alayhi al-Salam*, asking about a man who marries in the manner of *al-Mut'ah* (advantageous marriage) for a certain amount of *mahr* (dower) for a certain number of days, pays her a part of her *mahr* (dower) and withholds the rest, then he goes to bed with her and before paying her the rest, learns that she has a husband who lives with her, if it is permissible for him to withhold the remaining of her *mahr* (dower) or it is not permissible. He (the Imam) wrote, 'He must not give her anything because of her disobedience to Allah, most Majestic, most Glorious.'"

Chapter 106 - Her Statement about Her is Considered True

H 9925, Ch. 106, h 1

A number of our people have narrated from Ahmad ibn Muhammad from ibn Khalid from Muhammad ibn Ali from Muhammad ibn Aslam from Ibrahim ibn al-Fadl from Aban ibn Taghlib who has said the following:

"I once said to abu 'Abd Allah, *'Alayhi al-Salam*, 'I may find on my way a beautiful woman but I am not certain if she is married or is a prostitute.' He (the Imam) said, 'It is not your responsibility; you can accept her words.'"

H 9926, Ch. 106, h 2

A number of our people have narrated from Ahmad ibn Muhammad ibn 'Isa from al-Husayn ibn Sa'id from Fadalah from Muyassir who has said the following:

"I once said to abu 'Abd Allah, *'Alayhi al-Salam*, 'I may find a woman in the wilderness where she has no one and I ask her if she has a husband. She says that she does not have a husband; if I can marry her. He (the Imam) said, 'Yes, you can do so; her words are accepted.'"

Chapter 107 - Virgins

H 9927, Ch. 107, h 1

Ali ibn Ibrahim has narrated from his father from ibn abu 'Umayr from Hafs ibn al-Bakhtariy who has said the following:

"About the case of a man who marries a virgin in the manner of *al-Mut'ah* (advantageous marriage), abu 'Abd Allah, *'Alayhi al-Salam*, has said, 'It is detestable because of disgrace to her family.'"

H 9928, Ch. 107, h 2

Muhammad ibn Yahya has narrated from Ahmad and 'Abd Allah sons of Muhammad ibn 'Isa from Ali ibn al-Hakam from Ziyad ibn abu al-Hallal who has said the following:

"I once heard abu 'Abd Allah, *'Alayhi al-Salam*, saying, 'Marriage with a virgin in the manner of *al-Mut'ah* (advantageous marriage) is permissible only if fear of disgrace to her family will not affect her.'"

H 9929, Ch. 107, h 3

Ali ibn Ibrahim has narrated from his father from ibn abu 'Umayr from Muhammad ibn abu Hamzah from certain persons of his people who have said the following:

"This is concerning my question before abu 'Abd Allah, *'Alayhi al-Salam*, about the case of a man who marries a virgin in the manner of *al-Mut'ah* (advantageous marriage). He (the Imam) said, 'It is permissible if he does not destroy her virginity.'"

H 9930, Ch. 107, h 4

Ali has narrated from his father from ibn abu 'Umayr from Jamil ibn Darraj who has said the following:

"This is concerning my question before abu 'Abd Allah, *'Alayhi al-Salam*, about the case of a man who marries a virgin girl in the manner of *al-Mut'ah* (advantageous marriage). He (the Imam) said, 'It is not unlawful as long as she is not under age (or it does cause her humiliation).'"

H 9931, Ch. 107, h 5

Ali has narrated from his father from ibn abu 'Umayr from a man who has said the following:

"I once asked abu 'Abd Allah, *'Alayhi al-Salam*, 'When is a girl not considered a child? Is it a girl who is six or seven years old?' He (the Imam) said, 'No, a nine-year-old girl is not considered a child and all of them are unanimous that a girl who is nine years old is not considered a child unless there is weakness in her reason, otherwise, when she becomes nine years old she becomes mature.'"

Chapter 108 - Marriage with Slave Girls

H 9932, Ch. 108, h 1

Ali ibn Ibrahim has narrated from his father from ibn abu Nasr who has said the following:

"Abu al-Hassan al-Rida', *'Alayhi al-Salam*, has said, 'Marriage in the manner of *al-Mut'ah* (advantageous marriage) is not permissible with a slave-girl without the permission of her people.'"

H 9933, Ch. 108, h 2

Muhammad ibn Yahya has narrated from 'Abd Allah ibn Muhammad from Ali ibn al-Hakam from Aban ibn 'Uthman from 'Isa ibn abu Mansur who has said the following:

"Abu 'Abd Allah, *'Alayhi al-Salam*, has said, 'It is not unlawful to marry a slave-girl in the manner of *al-Mut'ah* (advantageous marriage) by the permission of her master.'"

H 9934, Ch. 108, h 3

Muhammad ibn Yahya has narrated from Ahmad ibn Muhammad ibn 'Isa from Muhammad ibn 'Isma'il who has said the following:

"I once asked abu al-Hassan, *'Alayhi al-Salam*, 'A man has a free wife; if he can marry a slave-girl in the manner of *al-Mut'ah* (advantageous marriage) by the permission of her master.' He (the Imam) said, 'Yes, he can do so.' It also is narrated that marriage of a slave-girl in the manner of *al-Mut'ah* (advantageous marriage) when one has a free wife is not permissible.'"

H 9935, Ch. 108, h 4

Muhammad ibn Yahya has narrated from Ahmad ibn Muhammad from Ali ibn al-Hakam from Sayf ibn 'Amirah who has said the following:

"Abu 'Abd Allah, *'Alayhi al-Salam*, has said, 'It is not unlawful for one to marry in the manner of *al-Mut'ah* (advantageous marriage) the slave-girl of a woman but if the master is a man then *al-Mut'ah* (advantageous marriage) with her is not permissible without the permission of her master.'"

Chapter 109 - Child Conceived

H 9936, Ch. 109, h 1

Ali ibn Ibrahim has narrated from his father and A number of our people have narrated from Sahl ibn Ziyad from ibn abu Najran and Ahmad ibn Muhammad from ibn abu Nasr from 'Asem ibn Hamid from Muhammad ibn Muslim who has said the following:

"I once asked abu 'Abd Allah, *'Alayhi al-Salam*, 'A woman gives birth because of marriage in the form of *al-Mut'ah* (advantageous marriage).' He (the Imam) said, 'The child is his child.'"

H 9937, Ch. 109, h 2

Ali ibn Ibrahim has narrated from his father from ibn abu 'Umayr from and others who has said the following:

"He (the Imam), *'Alayhi al-Salam*, has said, 'The water (seed) belongs to man, he can place it (lawfully) wherever he wants, except that when the child comes he cannot deny him,' and he (the Imam) placed great stress against denying the child."

H 9938, Ch. 109, h 3

Ali ibn Ibrahim has narrated from al-Mukhtar ibn Muhammad al-Mukhtar Ahmad ibn Muhammad from Muhammad ibn al-Hassan from 'Abd Allah ibn al-Hassan all from al-Fath ibn Yazid who has said the following:

"I once asked abu al-Hassan, al-Rida', *'Alayhi al-Salam*, about the conditions of *al-Mut'ah* (advantageous marriage). He (the Imam) said, 'Of the conditions in it is setting up an appointed time and the amount of *mahr* (dower), if she agreed it then is lawful. You must not say as it is reported to me that people of Iraq say, "Water is mine and land is your land and I do not water your land except that if anything grows there it belongs to the owner of the land." In such case, where there are two conditions (responsibility for the child and denying the child) in one condition, it is invalid. If she is granted a child he must accept him and the issue is clear. If anyone wants to commit fraud against his soul he does it.'"

Chapter 110 - Inheritance

H 9939, Ch. 110, h 1

Muhammad ibn Yahya has narrated from Ahmad ibn Muhammad from ibn Faddal from ibn Bukayr from Muhammad ibn Muslim who has said the following:

"About the case of a man who marries a woman in the manner of *al-Mut'ah* (advantageous marriage), I once heard abu Ja'far, *'Alayhi al-Salam*, saying, 'They inherit from each other as long as they do not set a condition and the condition can only be set after marriage.'" (It perhaps is a reference to the case of ignoring the condition of the time limit in which case the marriage becomes permanent)

H 9940, Ch. 110, h 2

Ali ibn Ibrahim has narrated from his father from Ahmad ibn Muhammad from ibn abu Nasr who has said the following:

"Abu al-Hassan al-Rida', *'Alayhi al-Salam*, has said, 'Marriage in the manner of *al-Mut'ah* (advantageous marriage) can be with or without inheritance. There is inheritance if it is stipulated; and there is not any inheritance if it is not stipulated.' It also is narrated that there is not any inheritance no matter a condition is set or is not set.'"

Chapter 110 - Rare Ahadith

H 9941, Ch. 111, h 1

Muhammad ibn Yahya has narrated from Ahmad ibn Muhammad from Ali ibn al-Hakam from Bashir ibn Hamzah from a man from Quraysh who has said the following:

"Once a daughter of my uncle, who was quite wealthy, sent me a message saying, 'As you know, many men propose marriage to me, but I do not give myself in marriage to anyone and my message to you is not because of my desire for men except it has come to my notice that Allah, most Majestic, most Glorious, has made it lawful in His book and the Messenger of Allah, *O Allah, grant compensation to Muhammad and his family worthy of their services to Your cause*, explained it in his Sunnah but Zafar prohibited and I like to obey Allah, most Majestic, most Glorious, on His throne and obey the Messenger of Allah while Zafar has disobeyed. So marry me in the manner of *al-Mut'ah* (advantageous marriage).' I replied, 'Allow me to visit abu Ja'far, *'Alayhi al-Salam*, and ask him for his advice.' I visited him (the Imam) and informed him (the Imam) about it and he (the Imam) said, 'You can accept her proposal, may Allah grant you blessings as husband and wife.'"

H 9942, Ch. 111, h 2

Muhammad ibn Yahya has narrated from Ahmad ibn Muhammad from Muhammad ibn 'Isa from Yunus from certain persons of his people who has said the following:

"This is concerning my question before abu 'Abd Allah, *'Alayhi al-Salam*, about the case of a man who marries a woman in the form of *al-Mut'ah* (advantageous marriage) for an appointed time and one day she comes to him and says that she has committed fornication just before an hour or day; if he can go to bed with her when she has confessed her committing fornication. He (the Imam) said, 'It is not proper for him to go to bed with her.'"

H 9943, Ch. 111, h 3

A number of our people have narrated from Ahmad ibn Muhammad from certain persons of his people from Zur'ah ibn Muhammad from Sama'ah who has said the following:

"I once asked him (the Imam), *'Alayhi al-Salam*, 'A man goes to bed with a girl (slave-girl) in the manner of *al-Mut'ah* (advantageous marriage) and forgets to mention the conditions until he has gone to bed with her; if he must be punished as a fornicator. He (the Imam) said, 'No, but he can take advantage after forming marriage and ask Allah to forgive him because of what he has done.'"

H 9944, Ch. 111, h 4

Ahmad ibn Muhammad has narrated from certain persons of our people from 'Umar ibn 'Abd al-'Aziz ibn 'Isa ibn Sulayman from Bakkar ibn Kardam who has said the following:

"This is concerning my question before abu 'Abd Allah, *'Alayhi al-Salam*, about the case of a man who meets a woman, then asks her to give herself in marriage in the manner of *al-Mut'ah* (advantageous marriage) to him for a month; but does not identify the month. Times pass and he meets her after several years. He (the Imam) said, 'Had he specified the month he deserved it, if the month was not specified he could not claim anything from her.'"

H 9945, Ch. 111, h 5

Ali ibn Ibrahim has narrated from his father from ibn abu 'Umayr from certain persons of our people who have said the following:

"Abu 'Abd Allah, *'Alayhi al-Salam*, has said, 'It is not unlawful for a man to marry a woman in the manner of *al-Mut'ah* (advantageous marriage) because of leaving herself at his disposal, but it is necessary to give her something; if anything happens to him she will not inherit his legacy.'"

H 9946, Ch. 111, h 6

Ali has narrated from his father from certain persons of his people from Ishaq ibn 'Ammar who has said the following:

"I once asked abu al-Hassan, Musa, *'Alayhi al-Salam*, about the case of a man who marries a woman in the manner of *al-Mut'ah* (advantageous marriage), then people of her family leap in her case and give her in marriage publicly without her permission. She is a truthful person; if there is a solution to her case. He (the Imam) said, 'She must not allow her husband to approach her until the condition (of *al-Mut'ah* (advantageous marriage)) and her waiting period is over.' I then said, 'Her condition is for one year and her husband and her family do not wait for her.' He (the Imam) said, 'Her first husband must feel fear of Allah and give up to her as charity the remaining of the time when she is being troubled. It is peace time and believing people live with *Taqiyah* (conceal their belief).' I then said, 'He has given such charity and her waiting period is also complete; now what she must do?' He (the Imam) said, 'She, in private, can say to him that her family had lept in her case and had given her in marriage to him without her permission, command and instructions and that now she agrees, so he must allow to solemnize the marriage all over again in a correct manner between the two of them.'"

H 9947, Ch. 111, h 7
Muhammad ibn Yahya has narrated from Ahmad ibn Muhammad from Mu'ammar ibn Khallad who has said the following:
"I once asked abu al-Hassan al-Rida', *'Alayhi al-Salam*, about the case of a man who marries a woman in the manner of *al-Mut'ah* (advantageous marriage) and then takes her from one town to another town. He (the Imam) said, 'Another marriage is permissible but this is not permissible.'"

H 9948, Ch. 111, h 8
Ali ibn Ibrahim has narrated from his father from Nuh ibn Shu'ayb from Ali ibn Hassan from 'Abd al-Rahman ibn al-Kathir who has said the following:
"Abu 'Abd Allah, *'Alayhi al-Salam*, has said that once a woman came to 'Umar and said, 'I have committed fornication, so cleanse me.' He commanded to stone her to death 'Amir al-Mu'minin, *'Alayhi al-Salam*, was asked about it and he asked, 'How did you commit fornication?' She replied, 'I was passing through wilderness and I became thirsty severely. I ask an Arab man for water but he refused unless I made myself available for him. When thirst increased and I feared for my life he gave me water and I availed myself for him.' 'Amir al-Mu'minin said, 'This is marriage by the Lord of al-Ka'bah.'" (She must have been unmarried so *al-Mut'ah* (advantageous marriage) was possible).

H 9949, Ch. 111, h 9
Ali ibn Ibrahim has narrated from his father from ibn abu 'Umayr from 'Ammar ibn Marwan who has said the following:
"This is concerning my question before abu 'Abd Allah, *'Alayhi al-Salam*, about the case of a man who comes to a woman and asks her to marry in the manner of *al-Mut'ah* (advantageous marriage) and she agrees with the condition that he can do whatever a wife and a husband do like looking, touching each other and so on, except inserting his private organ into her private organ. Apart from this he can enjoy in whatever way he likes because she is afraid of being disgraced.' He (the Imam) said, 'He cannot have anything more than what is stipulated.'"

H 9950, Ch. 111, h 10
A number of our people have narrated from Sahl ibn Ziyad from Ali ibn Asbat and Muhammad ibn al-Husayn all from Hakam ibn Miskin from 'Ammar who has said the following:
"Abu 'Abd Allah, *'Alayhi al-Salam*, once said to Sulayman ibn Khalid and I, 'I have made *al-Mut'ah* (advantageous marriage) unlawful for you from my side as long as you are in al-Madinah because you come very often to me and I am afraid you will be caught and it will be said, "These are companions of Ja'far."'"

Chapters 112 to 137

Chapters one hundred twelve to one hundred and thirty seven deal with issues of slaves and slave-girls which are not of any practical benefit today and its translation may not be of any benefit as well, thus only chapter titles are preserved.

Chapter 112 - Legalizing one's slave-girl for His Brother in Belief or Husband

Chapter 113 - Conjugal Relation with the Slave-girl of one's Son

Chapter 114 - Quarantine of a Slave-girl

Chapter 115 - The Captives

Chapter 116 - The Case of one's Buying a Pregnant Slave-girl

Chapter 117 - A Man's Freeing His Slave-girl Then Designate Her Freedom as her *mahr* (dower)

Chapter 118 - Woman Lawful for Slaves in Marriage

Chapter 119 - Slave's Marriage without the Permission of the Master

Chapter 120 - Slave-girl's Marriage without the Permission of the Master

Chapter 121- Marriage of Slave-girl and Slave Man

Chapter 122 - A man's Giving his Slave-girl in Marriage to his Slave then Expresses His own Desire for Her

Chapter 123 - Marriage of Half Slave Half Free Person

Chapter 124 - Buying a Slave Girl Married to a Free Husband or a Slave

Chapter 125 - The Case of a Woman Whose Husband is a Slave Whom She inherits or Buys Him then Her husband becomes Her Slave

Chapter 126 - A Woman Whose Husband is a Slave then She Inherits him then Frees him then agrees to Marry Him

Chapter 127 - The Case of a Slave-girl Married to a Slave Who is then Freed or Both are freed

Chapter 128 - A Slave with a Free Wife and Is Set Free

Chapter 129 - The Case of Buying a Pregnant Slave-girl . . .

Chapter 130 - One' Conjugal Relation and then another's Conjugal Relation with a Slave Girl in the Same Menses Period . . .

Chapter 131 - Impregnating a Slave-girl and Accusations . . .

Chapter 132 - Rare Ahadith

Chapter 133 - Another Chapter about the previous Subject

Chapter 134 - A Slave Girl's Conjugal Relation with Several Men in the Same Menses Period

Chapter 135 - A Man Goes to Bed with His Slave-girl then Sells Her then She Gives Birth Before Six Months and the Case of a Man Who Sells a Slave-girl Without Quarantine then Her pregnancy Appears after being Touched by the other Man

Chapter 136 - The Child of Whose one Parent is a Slave and one is Free

Chapter 137 - A Woman's Marriage with Her Slave

Chapter 138 - Women Are Similar

H 9951, Ch. 138, h 1
Al-Husayn from Muhammad from Mu'alla' ibn Muhammad from al-Hassan ibn Ali from Hammad ibn 'Uthaman who has said the following:
"Abu 'Abd Allah, *'Alayhi al-Salam*, has said that the Messenger of Allah, *O Allah, grant compensation to Muhammad and his family worthy of their services to Your cause*, once saw a woman and he (the Messenger of Allah) liked her. He (the Messenger of Allah) then went to the house of 'Umm Salamah because it was her day, and he (the Messenger of Allah) went to bed with her, then he (the Messenger of Allah) came out to people and water was dropping down from his head and he said, 'O people, looking (to women) is from Satan; if one may experience such things he must go to his wife.'"

H 9952, Ch. 138, h 2
A number of our people have narrated from Sahl ibn Ziyad from Muhammad ibn al-Hassan al-Shammun from 'Abd Allah ibn 'Abd al-Rahman from Misma' who has said the following:
"Abu 'Abd Allah, *'Alayhi al-Salam*, has said that the Messenger of Allah, *O Allah, grant compensation to Muhammad and his family worthy of their services to Your cause*, has said, 'If anyone of you looks to a beautiful woman he must go to his wife because what she has is just like what she has.' A man then stood up and asked, 'O Messenger of Allah, what about those who do not have any wives?' He (the Messenger of Allah) said, 'He must raise his head to the sky, have fear of Him and ask Him through His generosity.'"

Chapter 139 - Detestability of Celibacy

H 9953, Ch. 139, h 1
A number of our people have narrated from Sahl ibn Ziyad from Ja'far ibn Muhammad al-Ash'ariy from ibn al-Qaddah who has said the following:
"Abu 'Abd Allah, *'Alayhi al-Salam*, has said that once wife of 'Uthman ibn Maz'un came to the Holy Prophet, *O Allah, grant compensation to Muhammad and his family worthy of their services to Your cause*, and said, 'O Messenger of Allah, 'Uthman, fasts during the day and stands up for *Salat* (prayer) during the night.' The Messenger of Allah, *O Allah, grant compensation to Muhammad and his family worthy of their services to Your cause*, came out with anger

carrying his shoes until he reached 'Uthman and found him performing *Salat* (prayer). When 'Uthman completed, he saw the Messenger of Allah, *O Allah, grant compensation to Muhammad and his family worthy of their services to Your cause*, who said to him, "O 'Uthman, why did Allah not sent me to behave like a monk, however, He has sent me to be right-minded, planner and magnanimous. I fast, perform *Salat* (prayer) and touch my wife. Whoever likes my nature (culture) must adopt my Sunnah (manners) and of my Sunnah is marriage.'"

H 9954, Ch. 139, h 2
Ja'far ibn Muhammad has narrated from 'Abd Allah ibn al-Qaddah who has said the following:

"Abu 'Abd Allah, *'Alayhi al-Salam*, has said that the Messenger of Allah, *O Allah, grant compensation to Muhammad and his family worthy of their services to Your cause*, once asked a man, 'Are you fasting this morning?' The man replied, 'No, I am not fasting.' He (the Messenger of Allah) asked, 'Have you fed a destitute person?' He replied, 'No, I have not done so.' He (the Messenger of Allah) then said, 'Go to your family, it will be a charity from you to them.'"

H 9955, Ch. 139, h 3
Ali ibn Ibrahim has narrated from his father and Abu Ali al-Ash'ariy has narrated from Muhammad ibn 'Abd al-Jabbar from Safwan from Ishaq ibn 'Ammar who has said the following:

"This is concerning my question before abu 'Abd Allah, *'Alayhi al-Salam*, about the case of a man who is on a journey with his wife and they cannot find water; if he can go to bed with his wife. He (the Imam) said, 'I do not like it unless he is afraid for himself.' I then asked, 'Is it about the case of seeking to satisfy one's lust or is about the case of pressing desire for women?' He (the Imam) said, 'Pressing desire for women of one's fear for one's self.' I then asked, 'Can one seek thereby pleasure?' He (the Imam) said, 'It is lawful.' I then asked, 'It is narrated from the Holy Prophet, *O Allah, grant compensation to Muhammad and his family worthy of their services to Your cause*, that once abu Dharr, may Allah grant him mercy, asked him about it and he (the Messenger of Allah) said, "You can go to your wife; you will be rewarded." He asked, "O Messenger of Allah, I go to my wife and receive reward?" The Messenger of Allah, *O Allah, grant compensation to Muhammad and his family worthy of their services to Your cause*, said, "It is like when you commit an unlawful act; you have sinned, so also is the case of your doing a lawful act; you receive rewards."' Abu 'Abd Allah, *'Alayhi al-Salam*, has said, 'Consider when one fears his soul, then performs a lawful act; he then is rewarded.'"

H 9956, Ch. 139, h 4
A number of our people have narrated from Ahmad ibn abu 'Abd Allah from his father from al-Qasim ibn Muhammad al-Jawhariy from Ishaq ibn Ibrahim al-Al-Ju'fiy who has said the following:

"I once heard abu 'Abd Allah, *'Alayhi al-Salam*, saying that the Messenger of Allah, *O Allah, grant compensation to Muhammad and his family worthy of their services to Your cause*, once went to the house of 'Umm Salamah, smelled a fine fragrance and asked, 'Had al-Hawla' come to you?' She replied, 'She is here, complaining against her husband.' Al-Hawla then came out and said, 'I pray to Allah to keep my soul in service for your cause, my husband turns away from me.' He (the Messenger of Allah) said, 'Use more perfume, O Hawla'. She said, 'I have not left any perfume without being tried to make him happy but he turns away from me.' He (the Messenger of Allah) then said, 'I wish he learns what he receives by coming forward to you.' She asked, 'What can he receive by being forthcoming to me?' He (the Messenger of Allah) said, 'If he comes to you he will be circled by two angels and he will be like one who has pulled his sword from its sheath in the way of Allah; and when he goes to bed with his wife, sins fall off of him like the falling of leaves from the tree and when he takes Ghusl (bath), he comes clean out of sins.'"

H 9957, Ch. 139, h 5
Al-Husayn from Muhammad has narrated from Mu'alla' ibn Muhammad from abu Dawud al-Mustariq from certain persons of his people who have said the following:

"Abu 'Abd Allah, *'Alayhi al-Salam,* has said, 'Three women came to the Messenger of Allah, *O Allah, grant compensation to Muhammad and his family worthy of their services to Your cause,* and one of them said, "My husband does not eat meat." The other one said, "My husband does not smell perfume." The other one said, "My husband does not go near the woman." The Messenger of Allah came out while his gown dragged behind him until he climbed on the pulpit, praised Allah and glorified Him; then said, "What has happened to certain people of my companions who do not eat meat, smell perfume and do not go near women. I however, eat meat, smell perfumes and go to women, thus, those who disregard my Sunnah are not of my people."'"

H 9958, Ch. 139, h 6
A number of our people have narrated from Sahl ibn Ziyad from Muhammad ibn al-Hassan al-Shammun from 'Abd Allah ibn 'Abd al-Rahman from Misma' abu Sayyar who has said the following:

"Abu 'Abd Allah, *'Alayhi al-Salam,* has said that the Messenger of Allah, *O Allah, grant compensation to Muhammad and his family worthy of their services to Your cause,* has said, 'Whoever loves to follow my nature (culture), he must follow my Sunnah; and of my Sunnah is marriage.'"

Chapter 140 - Rare Ahadith

H 9959, Ch. 140, h 1
A number of our people have narrated from Ahmad ibn Muhammad from ibn Khalid from Muhammad ibn Ali from Hakam ibn Miskin from 'Ubayd ibn Zurarah who has said the following:

"In our neighborhood there lived an old man who had a beautiful slave-girl for whom he had paid thirty thousand dirham; but he was not able to reach the satisfaction from her what he wanted and she would say, 'Place your hand between my two flanges, I feel the pleasure', but he did not like to do so. He asked Zurarah to ask abu 'Abd Allah, *'Alayhi al-Salam,* about it. Abu 'Abd Allah, *'Alayhi al-Salam,* said, 'It is not unlawful, if he receives help from any part of his body to help her, but he must not seek help from what is other than his body to help her receive satisfaction.'"

H 9960, Ch. 140, h 2

A number of our people have narrated from Sahl ibn Ziyad from Ja'far ibn Muhammad al-Ash'ariy from ibn al-Qaddah who has said the following:

"Abu 'Abd Allah, *'Alayhi al-Salam*, has said that the Messenger of Allah, *O Allah, grant compensation to Muhammad and his family worthy of their services to Your cause*, has said, 'When anyone of you goes to bed (for sexual intercourse) with his wife, he must not go like birds do. He must stay in and persist.' Certain ones have said that one must linger."

H 9961, Ch. 140, h 3

Al-Husayn from Muhammad has narrated from Mu'alla' ibn Muhammad from al-Washsha' from Ibrahim ibn abu Bakr al-Nahhas from Musa ibn Bakr who has said the following:

"About the case of a man whose clothes during going to bed with his wife fall off, abu al-Hassan, *'Alayhi al-Salam*, has said, 'It is not unlawful.'"

H 9962, Ch. 140, h 4

Muhammad ibn Yahya has narrated from Ahmad ibn Muhammad from 'Isma'il ibn Hammam from Ali ibn Ja'far who has said the following:

"I once asked abu al-Hassan, *'Alayhi al-Salam*, about the case of a man who kisses the vagina of a woman. He (the Imam) said, 'It is not unlawful.'"

H 9963, Ch. 140, h 5

Ali ibn Muhammad ibn Bandar has narrated from Ahmad ibn abu 'Abd Allah from his father from Ahmad ibn al-Nadr from Muhammad ibn Miskin al-Hannat from abu Hamzah who has said the following:

"This is concerning my question before abu 'Abd Allah, *'Alayhi al-Salam*, if a man can look at the vagina of his wife during sexual intercourse. He (the Imam) said, 'It is not unlawful.'"

H 9964, Ch. 140, h 6

Ali ibn Ibrahim has narrated from his father from ibn abu 'Umayr from a man from Ishaq ibn 'Ammar who has said the following:

"About the case of a man who looks at his wife when she is nude, abu 'Abd Allah, *'Alayhi al-Salam*, has said, 'It is not unlawful. Pleasure is but in such things.'"

H 9965, Ch. 140, h 7

Ali ibn Muhammad ibn Bandar has narrated from Ahmad ibn abu 'Abd Allah from his father from 'Abd Allah ibn al-Qasim from 'Abd Allah ibn Sinan who has said the following:

"Abu 'Abd Allah, *'Alayhi al-Salam*, has said, 'Beware of speaking when two sexual organs meet; it may cause dumbness and muteness.'"

H 9966, Ch. 140, h 8

Ali ibn Ibrahim has narrated from his father from Muhsin ibn Ahmad from Aban from Misma' ibn 'Abd al-Malik who has said the following:

"I once heard abu 'Abd Allah, *'Alayhi al-Salam*, saying, 'One who has dyed (his hairs) does not go to bed with his wife.' I then asked, 'Why one who has dyed does not go to bed with his wife?' He (the Imam) said, 'Because he is confined.'"

433

Chapter 141 - Detestability of Conjugal Relation in Certain Times

H 9967, Ch. 141, h 1

Ali ibn Ibrahim has narrated from his father from ibn abu 'Umayr from 'Abd al-Rahman ibn Salim from his father who has said the following:

"I once asked abu Ja'far, *'Alayhi al-Salam*, about going to bed with one's wife; if it is detestable anytime even though it is lawful.' He (the Imam) said, 'Yes, it is detestable between dawn and sunrise, from sunset to the disappearance of brightness in the west, on the day of sun eclipse, in the night of moon eclipse, in the day and night of black, red, and yellow winds and in the day and night of an earthquake. The Messenger of Allah, *O Allah, grant compensation to Muhammad and his family worthy of their services to Your cause*, passed the night in which a moon eclipse took place with a certain one of his wives and he did not do in that night what he did in other nights until the morning and she asked, "Were you disappointed last night?" He (the Messenger of Allah) replied, "No, but this phenomenon took place last night and I did not like to seek pleasure or amuse myself when Allah, most Majestic, most Glorious, has reproached certain people in His book, 'When they see darkness in the sky falling they say, "It is a thick piece of cloud." Leave them alone until they face their day in which they will be thunderstruck.' (52:44)'" Abu Ja'far, *'Alayhi al-Salam*, then said, 'By Allah, whoever after reading this Hadith goes to bed with his wife in such times that the Messenger of Allah, *O Allah, grant compensation to Muhammad and his family worthy of their services to Your cause*, has prohibited and he then is granted a child, will find with the child what he does not like.'"

H 9968, Ch. 141, h 2

A number of our people have narrated from Ahmad ibn Muhammad ibn Khalid from Bakr ibn Salih from Sulayman ibn Ja'far al-Ja'fariy who has said the following:

"Abu al-Hassan, *'Alayhi al-Salam*, has said, 'One who goes to bed with his wife in the night of the end of a lunar month when the moon is not visible at all may not remain safe from (misfortune of) premature birth of the child.'"

H 9969, Ch. 141, h 3

It is narrated from the narrator of the previous Hadith from his father from those whom he has mentioned who has said the following:

"Abu al-Hassan, *'Alayhi al-Salam*, has narrated from his father from his grandfather who has said, 'Of the issues that the Messenger of Allah, *O Allah, grant compensation to Muhammad and his family worthy of their services to Your cause*, taught Ali, *'Alayhi al-Salam*, as advice were the following: O Ali, you must not go to bed with your wife in the first night of a lunar month, in the night of the middle of the month, and in the last night of the month, because it is feared for the child of insanity (being possessed by Jinn).' Ali, *'Alayhi al-Salam*, asked, 'Why is it, O Messenger of Allah?' He (the Messenger of Allah) replied, 'It is because Jinn frequent overwhelming their women in the first night of a lunar month, in the night of the middle of the month and in the last night of the month. Have you not seen that one possessed by Jinn becomes epileptic in beginning of the month, in the end and in the middle of the night?'"

H 9970, Ch. 141, h 4
A number of our people have narrated from Sahl ibn Ziyad from Safwan from 'Abd Allah ibn Sinan who has said the following:
"Abu 'Abd Allah, *'Alayhi al-Salam*, has said, 'It is detestable for a man to go to bed with his wife in the night of his arrival from a journey until the morning.'"

H 9971, Ch. 141, h 5
Sahl ibn Ziyad has narrated from Muhammad ibn al-Hassan from Shammun from 'Abd Allah ibn 'Abd al-Rahman from Misma' abu Sayyar who has said the following:
"Abu 'Abd Allah, *'Alayhi al-Salam*, has said that the Messenger of Allah, *O Allah, grant compensation to Muhammad and his family worthy of their services to Your cause*, has said, 'I dislike for my followers that one of them goes to bed with his wife in the middle of the month or when it is new moon because the rebels of satans and Jinn overwhelm children of Adam; they become possessed by Jinn are and insane. You can see that those possessed become epileptic in the middle and in the beginning of the month'"

Chapter 142 - Detestability of Conjugal Relation in a Room with a Child

H 9972, Ch. 142, h 1
Ali ibn Ibrahim has narrated from his father from al-Qasim ibn Muhammad al-Jawhariy from Ishaq ibn Ibrahim from ibn Rashid from his father who has said the following:
"Abu 'Abd Allah, *'Alayhi al-Salam*, has said, 'A man with his wife must not go to bed in a house where a child exits because it leads to fornication.'"

H 9973, Ch. 142, h 2
Ali ibn Ibrahim has narrated from his father from 'Abd Allah ibn al-Husayn ibn Zayd from his father who has said the following:
"Abu 'Abd Allah, *'Alayhi al-Salam*, has said that the Messenger of Allah, *O Allah, grant compensation to Muhammad and his family worthy of their services to Your cause*, has said, 'By the One in whose Hand is my soul, if a man overwhelms his wife (engages in sexual intercourse) when there is a child in the house who is awake, sees and hears them speaking and their breathing, the child will not escape, a boy or girl, their involvement in fornication.' Ali ibn al-Husayn, *'Alayhi al-Salam*, whenever, he intended to overwhelm his wife, would close the door, pull down the curtains and send the servants out.'"

Chapter 143 - Words to Say during Conjugal Relation

H 9974, Ch. 143, h 1
Muhammad ibn Yahya has narrated from Ahmad ibn Muhammad ibn 'Isa and A number of our people have narrated from Ahmad ibn abu 'Abd Allah from ibn Mahbub from Jamil ibn Salih from abu Basir who has said the following:
"I heard a man saying to abu Ja'far, *'Alayhi al-Salam*, 'I pray to Allah to keep my soul in service for your cause, I am an aged man. I have married a virgin

young woman. I have not gone to bed with her as yet. I am afraid in bed on finding me of such age and the dye on my beard she may dislike me.' Abu Ja'far, *'Alayhi al-Salam*, 'When you are there ask her before approaching you to take Wudu'. You also should not approach her before taking Wudu' and performing two Rak'at *Salat* (prayer). Thereafter, speak of the glory of Allah and say, "*Allahumma Salli 'Ala Muhammad wa 'Ali Muhammad* (O Allah grant Muhammad and his family a compensation worthy of their serving Your cause)." Thereafter ask her and others present with her to say *A'min* (O Allah grant his wishes). Thereafter say, 'O Lord, provide her enough reasons to be kind to me, love me, be happy with me, grant me enough reason to be happy with her, bring us together in the best form of gathering, and the happiest kindness; You love what is lawful and dislike unlawful matters.' The Imam then said, 'You must bear in mind that kindness comes from Allah and hate comes from Satan so that people clash and dislike what Allah has made lawful.'"

H 9975, Ch. 143, h 2

Ali ibn Ibrahim has narrated from his father from ibn abu 'Umayr from abu Ayyub al-Khazzaz from abu Basir who has said the following:

"Abu 'Abd Allah, *'Alayhi al-Salam*, has said, 'When you meet your wife hold to her forehead and face al-Qiblah (al-Ka'bah) and say, 'O Lord, in Your trust I have taken her (in marriage) and with Your words I have made her lawful. If You have destined for me from her a child, then make the child a blessed one, pious, of the Shi'ah (followers) of the family of Muhammad and you must not make for Satan any share or portion in it (child).'"

H 9976, Ch. 143, h 3

Muhammad ibn Yahya has narrated from Ahmad ibn Muhammad ibn 'Isa and A number of our people have narrated from Ahmad ibn abu 'Abd Allah from al-Qasim ibn Yahya from his grandfather, al-Hassan ibn Rashid from abu Basir who has said the following:

"Abu Ja'far, *'Alayhi al-Salam*, once asked me, 'When one of you marries, does he know what to do?' I replied, 'I do not know.' He (the Imam) said, 'When he decides for it (marriage) he must perform two Rak'at *Salat* (prayer) then say, "O Lord, I want to marry so choose for me of women who is most chaste in matters of her private organs, most protective for me of herself and my assets, of most affluence in sustenance and of greatest blessing. Choose for me a fine child to be a virtuous successor in my lifetime and after my death."' He (the Imam) said, 'When you meet her place your hand over her forehead and say, "O Lord, according to Your book I have married her, in Your trust I have taken her (in marriage) and with Your words I have made her (private organs) lawful. If You have destined for me from her womb anything (child), then make the child a Muslim, upright and You must not make for Satan any share or portion in it (child).' I (the narrator) then asked, 'How can it be a share of Satan?' He (the Imam) said, 'Mention of the name of Allah keeps Satan away. If one goes to bed without mentioning the name of Allah, he sticks his penis, the act is from both of them but the seed is one.'"

436

H 9977, Ch. 143, h 4

It is narrated from the narrator of the previous Hadith from abu Yusuf from al-Mithamiy in a marfu' manner has said the following:

"Once, a man came to 'Amir al-Mu'minin, *'Alayhi al-Salam*, and said, 'I have just married, pray for me to Allah.' He (the Imam) said, 'Say, O Lord, with Your words I have made her marriage lawful and in Your trust I have taken her (in marriage); O Lord, make her child-bearing, loving and not clashing in dislike, use what is found and not ask what to bring home (this and that).'"

H 9978, Ch. 143, h 5

Ali ibn Ibrahim has narrated from his father from ibn abu 'Umayr from Aban from 'Abd al-Rahman ibn 'A'yan who has said the following:

"I once heard abu 'Abd Allah, *'Alayhi al-Salam*, saying, 'When a man wants to marry a woman he should say, "I authenticate my covenant with Allah which is: "maintain in a reasonable way or allow to go with kindness." (2:229)'"

Chapter 144 - Word to Say during Going to Bed with One's Wife

H 9979, Ch. 144, h 1

A number of our people have narrated from Sahl ibn Ziyad from al-Hassan ibn Mahbub from ibn Ri'ab from al-Halabiy who has said the following:

"About the case of a man who when going to bed with his wife is afraid of Satan's accompaniment, abu 'Abd Allah, *'Alayhi al-Salam*, has said that he should say, 'In the name of Allah' and seek protection with Allah against Satan.'"

H 9980, Ch. 144, h 2

Al-Husayn from Muhammad has narrated from Mu'alla' ibn Muhammad and A number of our people have narrated from Ahmad ibn Muhammad all from al-Washsha' from Musa ibn Bakr from abu Basir who has said the following:

"Abu 'Abd Allah, *'Alayhi al-Salam*, once said to me, 'O abu Muhammad, what does one of you say when his wife comes to him?' I replied, 'I pray to Allah to keep my soul in service for your cause, can a man say anything?' He (the Imam) said, 'Will you like if I teach you what to say?' I replied, 'Yes, please teach me.' He (the Imam) said, say, 'With the words of Allah I have made her private organs lawful and in trust of Allah I have taken her (in marriage). O Lord, if You have chosen for me in her womb anything, make it a virtuous, a pious and an upright Muslim and You must not make any share for Satan in him.' I then asked, 'By what means such share is found out?' He (the Imam) said, 'Have you not read the book of Allah, most Majestic, most Glorious, and he (the Imam) began to read, ". . . and make him share them in their wealth and children." (17:64) He (the Imam) then said, 'Satan comes and sits in relation to a woman like the man sits, speaks like a man does and goes to bed like a man does.' I then asked, 'By what means is it found out?' He (the Imam) said, 'This is found out by means of one's love for us and one's hatred toward us. Whoever loves us is from the seed of the servant (of Allah) and whoever hates us is from the seed of Satan.'"

H 9981, Ch. 144, h 3

A number of our people have narrated from Sahl ibn Ziyad from Ja'far ibn Muhammad al-Ash'ariy from ibn al-Qaddah who has said the following:

"Abu 'Abd Allah, *'Alayhi al-Salam*, has said that 'Amir al-Mu'minin, has said, 'When one of you goes to bed with his wife he should say, "In the name of Allah, by the help of Allah, O Lord, keep Satan away from me and from what You have granted me.' He (the Imam) said, 'If Allah decides to grant them a child Satan will never be able to harm the child.'"

H 9982, Ch. 144, h 4

A number of our people have narrated from Ahmad ibn Muhammad ibn Khalid from Ali ibn Hassan al-Wasitiy from 'Abd al-Rahman ibn al-Kathir who has said the following:

"I once was with abu 'Abd Allah, *'Alayhi al-Salam*. He (the Imam) mentioned Satan and called him greatly dangerous so much so that it frightened me and I said, 'I pray to Allah to keep my soul in service for your cause, what is the way out from it?' He (the Imam) said, 'When you decide to go to bed with your wife say, "In the name of Allah, most Beneficent, most Merciful, who is the only Lord, the one who deserves worship and has invented the skies and earth. O Lord, if You have decided for me a successor this night, do not allow a share in him for Satan, or a portion, or benefit. Make him a believer, a sincere one and clean of Satan and his filth, Glorious is Your praise.'"

H 9983, Ch. 144, h 5

It is narrated from the narrator of the previous Hadith from his father from Hamzah ibn 'Abd Allah from Jamil ibn Darraj from abu al-Walid from abu Basir who has said the following:

"Abu 'Abd Allah, *'Alayhi al-Salam*, once said to me, 'O abu Muhammad, what do you say when you go to bed with your wife?' I said, 'I pray to Allah to keep my soul in service for your cause, can I say anything?' He (the Imam) said, 'Yes, say, "O Lord, with Your words I have made her private organs lawful and in Your trust I have taken her (in marriage). If You have destined anything in her womb make it pious and clean and do not make any share in him for Satan."' I then asked, 'I pray to Allah to keep my soul in service for your cause, is there a share of Satan in it?' He (the Imam) said, 'Yes, have you not heard the words of Allah, most Majestic, most Glorious, in His book, ". . . he shares them in their assets and children." (17:64) Satan comes, sits as a man sits and comes down as a man does.' I asked, 'By what means is it found out?' He (the Imam) said, 'It is found out by means of love for us and hatred toward us.'"

H 9984, Ch. 144, h 6

Muhammad ibn Yahya has narrated from Ahmad ibn Muhammad from Ali ibn al-Hakam from Hisham ibn Salim who has said the following:

"About the case of the seeds which are from man and Satan when they share, abu 'Abd Allah, *'Alayhi al-Salam*, has said, 'Perhaps it is created from one of them or perhaps from both of them together.'"

Chapter 145 - Contraception

H 9985, Ch. 145, h 1

Muhammad ibn Yahya has narrated from Ahmad ibn Muhammad from ibn Faddal from ibn Bukayr from 'Abd al-Rahman ibn abu 'Abd Allah who has said the following:

"This is concerning my question before abu 'Abd Allah, *'Alayhi al-Salam*, about withdrawing before semen discharge. He (the Imam) said, 'It is up to the man's choice.'"

H 9986, Ch. 145, h 2

Ahmad ibn Muhammad al-'Asemiy has narrated from Ali ibn al-Hassan ibn Faddal from Ali ibn Asbat from his uncle Ya'qub from Muhammad ibn Muslim who has said the following:

"Abu Ja'far, *'Alayhi al-Salam*, has said, 'It is not unlawful to withdraw before semen discharge from the woman who is free, if he likes even if she may not like. She does not have any say in it.'"

H 9987, Ch. 145, h 3

Muhammad ibn Yahya has narrated from Ahmad ibn Muhammad from ibn Mahbub from al-'Ala' from Muhammad ibn Muslim who has said the following:

"I once asked abu 'Abd Allah, *'Alayhi al-Salam*, about withdrawing before semen discharge. He (the Imam) said, 'It is up to the man. He deals with it as he chooses.'"

H 9988, Ch. 145, h 4

Abu Ali al-Ash'ariy has narrated from Muhammad ibn 'Abd al-Jabbar from Safwan from ibn abu 'Umayr from 'Abd al-Rahman al-Haddhdha' who has said the following:

"Abu 'Abd Allah, *'Alayhi al-Salam*, has said that Ali ibn al-Husayn, *'Alayhi al-Salam*, did not consider withdrawing before semen discharge as unlawful and he (the Imam) read this verse, 'When your Lord took of children of Adam from their backs their offspring and made them to bear witness for their souls about the question, "Am I not your Lord?" They replied, "Yes, You are our Lord."' (7:171) Therefore, everything from which Allah has taken a covenant comes out even if it is on a blind (solid) rock.'"

Chapter 146 - Egocentricity, Pride or Jealousy of Women

H 9989, Ch. 146, h 1

A number of our people have narrated from Ahmad ibn Muhammad from ibn Khalid from 'Uthman ibn 'Isa from certain persons of his people who has said the following:

"Abu 'Abd Allah, *'Alayhi al-Salam*, has said, 'Pride is with men only and with women it is jealousy. Vanity is with men and for this reason Allah has prohibited women except to have one husband and for men He has made up to four (wives) lawful. Allah is most gracious. He does not place vanity and pride in them (women) then make three more with her lawful for him.'"

H 9990, Ch. 146, h 2

It is narrated from the narrator of the previous Hadith from Muhammad ibn Ali from Muhammad ibn al-Fudayl from Sa'd al-Jallab who has said the following:

"Abu 'Abd Allah, *'Alayhi al-Salam*, has said, 'Allah, most Majestic, most Glorious, has not placed pride in women. Such feeling comes from detested ones among them; however, the believing ones of them are free of pride. Allah has placed pride in men; He has made lawful for men up to four and those whom they own (slaves). For women He has made only their husband so if she wants more besides him she is a fornicator before Allah.' He (the narrator) has said that al-Qasim ibn Yahya has narrated from his grandfather al-Hassan ibn Rashid from abu Bakr al-Hadramiy from abu 'Abd Allah, *'Alayhi al-Salam*, except that he has said, *'Baghat'* (sought) instead of *'Aradat'* (wanted)."

H 9991, Ch. 146, h 3

Ali ibn Ibrahim has narrated from his father Muhammad ibn 'Isma'il has narrated from al-Fadl ibn Shadhan from all from ibn abu 'Umayr from 'Abd al-Rahman ibn al-Hajjaj in a marfu' manner has said the following:

"Once the Messenger of Allah, *O Allah, grant compensation to Muhammad and his family worthy of their services to Your cause*, was sitting that a nude woman came until she stood right in front of him and said, 'O Messenger of Allah, I have sinned, so cleanse me.' He (the narrator) has said that after her a man came running and threw a cloth on her. He (the Messenger of Allah) asked about the relation between the two of them.' He replied, 'She is my companion (wife), O Messenger of Allah. I went to bed with my slave-girl, and then she did what you have seen.' He (the Messenger of Allah) then said, 'The egotistic, or jealous cannot distinguish between the top and the bottom of the valley.'"

H 9992, Ch. 146, h 4

A number of our people have narrated from Ahmad ibn abu 'Abd Allah from Muhammad ibn al-Hassan from Yusuf ibn Hammad from those whom he has mentioned from Jabir who has said the following:

"Abu Ja'far, *'Alayhi al-Salam*, has said, 'Pride of women is jealousy and jealousy is the root of disbelief. When women become jealous they become angry and when they become angry they disbelieve except the Muslim ones among them.'"

H 9993, Ch. 146, h 5

It is narrated from the narrator of the previous Hadith from Muhammad ibn Sinan from Khalid al-Qalanisiy who has said the following:

"Once a man mentioned his wife before abu 'Abd Allah, *'Alayhi al-Salam*, and he praised her quite well. Abu 'Abd Allah, *'Alayhi al-Salam*, asked, 'Have you made her jealous?' He replied, 'No, I have not done so.' He (the Imam) said, 'Make her feel jealous.' He did so and he found the proof; then said to abu 'Abd Allah, *'Alayhi al-Salam*, that he has found the proof and she is as he (the Imam) has said.'"

H 9994, Ch. 146, h 6

Abu Ali al-Ash'ariy has narrated from Muhammad ibn 'Abd al-Jabbar from Safwan from Ishaq ibn 'Ammar who has said the following:

"I once said to abu 'Abd Allah, *'Alayhi al-Salam*, 'When a woman feels jealous against man, she causes disappointment for him.' He (the Imam) said, 'It is because of (her) love.'"

Chapter 147 - Love of Women for their Husbands

H 9995, Ch. 147, h 1

Muhammad ibn Yahya has narrated from Ahmad ibn Muhammad from Ali ibn al-Hakam from Mu'awiyah ibn Wahab who has said the following:

"I once heard abu 'Abd Allah, *'Alayhi al-Salam,* saying that the Messenger of Allah, *O Allah, grant compensation to Muhammad and his family worthy of their services to Your cause,* once returned from an armed expedition during which a large number of Muslims were killed. Women came to him (the Messenger of Allah) asking about their people who were killed. One woman came to him (the Messenger of Allah) and asked, 'O Messenger of Allah, what did so and so do?' He (the Messenger of Allah) asked, 'What is your relation with him?' She replied, 'He is my father.' He (the Messenger of Allah) said, 'You should thank Allah and ask for your happy return to Allah; he became a martyr.' She then did as he (the Messenger of Allah) had told her to do. Then she asked, 'What did so and so do, O Messenger of Allah?' He (the Messenger of Allah) asked, 'What is your relation with him?' She replied, 'He is my brother.' He (the Messenger of Allah) said, 'You should thank Allah and ask for your happy return to Allah; he became a martyr.' She then did as he (the Messenger of Allah) had told her to do. She then asked, 'What did so and so do, O Messenger of Allah?' He (the Messenger of Allah) asked, 'What is your relation with him?' She replied, 'He is my husband.' He (the Messenger of Allah) said, 'You should thank Allah and ask for your happy return to Allah, he became a martyr.' She then said, 'Woe and wretchedness is upon me!' The Messenger of Allah, *O Allah, grant compensation to Muhammad and his family worthy of their services to Your cause,* said, 'I did not think women have this much (loving feeling) for their husbands until I saw this woman.'"

H 9996, Ch. 147, h 2

Ahmad ibn Muhammad has narrated from Mu'ammar ibn Khallad who has said the following:

"I once heard abu al-Hassan, *'Alayhi al-Salam,* saying that the Messenger of Allah, *O Allah, grant compensation to Muhammad and his family worthy of their services to Your cause,* once said to daughter of Jahash, 'Your maternal uncle, Hamzah is killed.' She asked for a happy return to Allah and said, 'I expect good reward from Allah.' He (the Messenger of Allah) then told her, 'Your brother is also killed.' She asked for a happy return to Allah and said, 'I expect good reward from Allah.' He (the Messenger of Allah) then said, 'Your husband is also killed.' She placed her hand on her head and cried and sobbed. The Messenger of Allah, *O Allah, grant compensation to Muhammad and his family worthy of their services to Your cause,* said, 'Nothing for a woman is equal to her husband.'"

Chapter 148 - The Rights of Husband on His Wife

H 9997, Ch. 148, h 1

A number of our people have narrated from Ahmad ibn Muhammad from ibn Mahbub from Malik ibn 'Atiyyah from Muhammad ibn Muslim who has said the following:

"Abu Ja'far, *'Alayhi al-Salam*, has said that once a woman came to the Holy Prophet, *O Allah, grant compensation to Muhammad and his family worthy of their services to Your cause*, and asked, 'What is the right of husband on a woman?' He (the Messenger of Allah) said to her, 'She must yield to and obey him and must not oppose and disobey him. She must not give charity from his house without his permission and must not fast optionally without his permission. If she goes out of his house without his permission, the angels of skies and earth condemn her as well the angels of wrath and angels of mercy until she returns to her home.' She then asked, 'O Messenger of Allah, who has the greatest right on a man?' He (the Messenger of Allah) replied, 'His father has the greatest right.' She then asked, 'O Messenger of Allah, who has the greatest right on a woman?' He (the Messenger of Allah) replied, 'Her husband has the greatest right on her.' She then asked, 'How is it that I do not have as much right on him as he has on me?' He (the Messenger of Allah) said, 'No, not even one out of one hundred.' She then said, 'I swear by the One who has sent you as a prophet in all truth; I will never allow any man to have a hold of my neck.'"

H 9998, Ch. 148, h 2
Muhammad ibn Yahya has narrated from Ahmad ibn Muhammad from Ali ibn al-Hakam from Muhammad ibn al-Fudayl from Sa'd ibn abu 'Amr al-Jallab who has said the following:

"Abu 'Abd Allah, *'Alayhi al-Salam*, has said, 'If a woman passes a night and her husband is angry with her because of a right to which she does not yield, her *Salat* (prayer) is not accepted until he becomes happy with her. If a woman wears perfume for other than her husband, her *Salat* (prayer) is not accepted until she washes them clean just as she takes a Ghusl (bath) because of going to bed.'"

H 9999, Ch. 148, h 3
Ali ibn al-Hakam from has narrated from Musa ibn Bakr who has said the following:

"Abu 'Abd Allah, *'Alayhi al-Salam*, has said, 'The good deeds of three kinds of people cannot rise up. One is a runaway slave, a woman whose husband is not happy with her and one who drags his gown on the ground out of pride.'"

H 10000, Ch. 148, h 4
A number of our people have narrated from Sahl ibn Ziyad from Ali ibn Hassan from Musa ibn Bakr who has said the following:

"Abu Ibrahim, *'Alayhi al-Salam*, has said, 'Jihad (struggle for the cause of Allah) of a woman is her living a proper spousal life.'"

H 10001, Ch. 148, h 5
Muhammad ibn Yahya has narrated from 'Abd Allah ibn Muhammad from Ali ibn al-Hakam from Aban ibn 'Uthman from al-Hassan ibn al-Mundhir who has said the following:

"Abu 'Abd Allah, *'Alayhi al-Salam*, has said, '*Salat* (prayer) of three kinds of people is not accepted. One is a runaway slave from his masters until he places his hand in their hands, a woman who passes the night when her husband is angry with her and a man who leads a people in *Salat* (prayer) and they dislike him.'"

H 10002, Ch. 148, h 6

Muhammad ibn Yahya has narrated from Ahmad ibn Muhammad from ibn Mahbub from Malik ibn 'Atiyyah from Sulayman ibn Khalid who has said the following:

"Abu 'Abd Allah, *'Alayhi al-Salam*, has said that once a people came to the Messenger of Allah, *O Allah, grant compensation to Muhammad and his family worthy of their services to Your cause*, and said, 'O Messenger of Allah, we saw a people who prostrate for each other.' The Messenger of Allah, *O Allah, grant compensation to Muhammad and his family worthy of their services to Your cause*, said, 'If I were to command anyone to prostrate for others I would command the woman to prostrate for her husband.'"

H 10003, Ch. 148, h 7

A number of our people have narrated from Ahmad ibn Muhammad from ibn Khalid from al-Jamuraniy from ibn abu Hamzah from "'Amr ibn Jubayr al-'Arzamiy who has said the following:

"Abu 'Abd Allah, *'Alayhi al-Salam*, has said that once a woman came to the Messenger of Allah, *O Allah, grant compensation to Muhammad and his family worthy of their services to Your cause*, and asked, 'O Messenger of Allah, what is the right of husband on the wife?' He (the Messenger of Allah) said, 'Should I tell you a great deal about it?' She said, 'Tell me something about it.' He (the Messenger of Allah) said, 'She must not fast an optional fast without his permission, must not go out of her house without his permission, must wear the best of perfumes for him and the best of her dresses, wear the best of make up for him, make herself available for him in the mornings and evenings; and his rights on her are more than this.'"

H 10004, Ch. 148, h 8

It is narrated from the narrator of the previous Hadith from al-Jamuraniy from ibn abu Hamzah from abu al-Mighra' from abu Basir who has said the following:

"Abu 'Abd Allah, *'Alayhi al-Salam*, has said that once a woman came to the Messenger of Allah, *O Allah, grant compensation to Muhammad and his family worthy of their services to Your cause*, and asked, 'What is the right of husband on the wife?' He (the Messenger of Allah) said, 'Of his rights is to make herself available for him even when on the back of a camel and must not give anything without his permission. If she does it, she carries the sin and the reward is for him. She must not pass a night with him angry on her.' She asked, 'Even if he acts unjustly, O Messenger of Allah?' He (the Messenger of Allah) replied, 'Yes, even if he is as such."

Chapter 148 - Detestability for Women to Stop their Husband

H 10005, Ch. 149, h 1

A number of our people have narrated from Ahmad ibn abu 'Abd Allah from his father from Fadalah ibn Ayyub from abu al-Mighra' from abu Basir who has said the following:

"Abu Ja'far, *'Alayhi al-Salam*, has said that the Messenger of Allah, *O Allah, grant compensation to Muhammad and his family worthy of their services to Your cause*, has said to women, 'You must not prolong your *Salat* (prayer) to prevent your husbands.'"

H 10006, Ch. 149, h 2
It is narrated from the narrator of the previous Hadith from Musa ibn al-Qasim from abu Jamilah from Durays al-Kunasiy who has said the following:
"Abu 'Abd Allah, *'Alayhi al-Salam*, has said that once a woman came to the Messenger of Allah, *O Allah, grant compensation to Muhammad and his family worthy of their services to Your cause*, for a certain need and he (the Messenger of Allah) said to her, 'Perhaps you are of the *Musawwafat*.' She asked, 'What it means, O Messenger of Allah?' He (the Messenger of Allah) said, 'It is a woman whose husband calls her for something that he needs but she procrastinates until her husband begins to slumber and goes to sleep. The angels continue condemning her until her husband wakes up.'"

Chapter 150 - Detestability for Woman Ignoring Makeup

H 10007, Ch. 150, h 1
Muhammad ibn Yahya has narrated from Ahmad ibn Muhammad from ibn Mahbub from ibn Ri'ab from ibn abu Ya'fur who has said the following:
"Abu Ja'far, *'Alayhi al-Salam*, has said that the Messenger of Allah, *O Allah, grant compensation to Muhammad and his family worthy of their services to Your cause*, prohibited women from ignoring themselves due to laziness and turning themselves of no benefit for their husbands.'"

H 10008, Ch. 150, h 2
Ibn Mahbub has narrated from al-'Ala' from Muhammad ibn Muslim who has said the following:
"Abu Ja'far, *'Alayhi al-Salam*, has said, 'It is not proper for women to neglect themselves even from hanging a necklace from their necks. It is not proper for women to leave their hands without dye even if they are old.'"

H 10009, Ch. 150, h 3
A number of our people have narrated from Ahmad ibn abu 'Abd Allah from 'Abd al-Samad ibn Bashir who has said the following:
"Once, a woman came to abu 'Abd Allah, *'Alayhi al-Salam*, and said, 'I pray to Allah to keep you well, I am a celibate woman.' He (the Imam) asked, 'What does that mean to you?' She replied, 'I do not marry.' He (the Imam) asked, 'Why do you not marry?' She replied, 'I seek thereby excellence.' He (the Imam) said, 'You must change your mind. Had that been anything of excellence, Fatimah, *'Alayha al-Salam*, would have been more deserving of it than you because no one could succeed against her to excel.'"

Chapter 151 - Treating One's Wife with Honor

H 10010, Ch. 151, h 1
Humayd ibn Ziyad has narrated from al-Hassan ibn Muhammad ibn Sama'ah from more than one person from Aban from abu Maryam who has said the following:
"Abu Ja'far, *'Alayhi al-Salam*, has said that the Messenger of Allah, *O Allah, grant compensation to Muhammad and his family worthy of their services to Your cause*, has said, 'How can one of you hurt the woman whom he continues to embrace?'"

H 10011, Ch. 151, h 2

Ali ibn Ibrahim has narrated from his father from al-Nawfaliy from al-Sakuniy who has said the following:

"Abu 'Abd Allah, *'Alayhi al-Salam*, has said that the Messenger of Allah, *O Allah, grant compensation to Muhammad and his family worthy of their services to Your cause*, has said, 'A woman is like a doll which one chooses but does not waste or destroy.'"

H 10012, Ch. 151, h 3

Abu Ali al-Ash'ariy has narrated from certain persons of our people from Ja'far ibn 'Anbasah from 'Abbad ibn Ziyad al-Asadiy from 'Amr ibn abu al-Miqdam from Abu Ja'far, *'Alayhi al-Salam*, and Ahmad ibn Muhammad from those who narrated to him from Mu'alla' ibn Muhammad al-Basriy from Ali ibn Hassan from 'Abd al-Rahman ibn al-Kathir who has said the following:

"Abu 'Abd Allah, *'Alayhi al-Salam*, has said that it is in the letter of 'Amir al-Mu'minin to al-Hassan, *'Alayhi al-Salam*, which says, 'You must not give control of things beyond her own affairs to a woman; it is easier for her condition, comfortable for her mind and helps her beauty to last longer, because women are like sweet basil and not a wrestling champion and she must not allow her soul to bypass her grace and honor. Help her to cast down her eyes by your covering, withhold her with your veil, and not to incite her to intercede for others before you so that the recommended incline toward her and go before yourself for the rest. Your restraining yourself from women when they see you dominant is better than their seeing you in a condition of breaking apart.'"

Ahmad ibn Muhammad ibn Sa'id has narrated from Ja'far ibn Muhammad al-Hassaniy from Ali ibn 'Abdaka from al-Hassan ibn Zarif ibn Nasih from al-Husayn ibn 'Ulwan from Sa'd ibn Tarif from al-Asbagh ibn Nubatah from 'Amir al-Mu'minin, *'Alayhi al-Salam*, has narrated a similar Hadith except that he has said that 'Amir al-Mu'minin, *'Alayhi al-Salam*, wrote the letter to his son Muhammad, may Allah be pleased with him.

Chapter 152 - The Right of Wife on Husband

H 10013, Ch. 152, h 1

Abu Ali al-Ash'ariy has narrated from Muhammad ibn 'Abd al-Jabbar from Safwan ibn Yahya from Ishaq ibn 'Ammar who has said the following:

"I once asked abu 'Abd Allah, *'Alayhi al-Salam*, about the right of woman on her husband for which when he yields is a man of good deeds. He (the Imam) said, 'He must provide her sufficient food, clothes and forgive her if she acted ignorantly.' Abu 'Abd Allah, *'Alayhi al-Salam*, has said, 'My father had a woman who would disappoint him (the Imam) but he would forgive her.'"

H 10014, Ch. 152, h 2

A number of our people have narrated from Ahmad ibn abu 'Abd Allah from al-Jamuraniy from al-Hassan ibn Ali ibn abu Hamzah from "Amr ibn Jubayr al-'Arzamiy who has said the following:

"Abu 'Abd Allah, *'Alayhi al-Salam*, has said that once a woman came to the Holy Prophet, *O Allah, grant compensation to Muhammad and his family worthy of their services to Your cause*, and asked about the rights of a husband on a woman. He (the Messenger of Allah) informed her and then she asked about her right on him and he (the Messenger of Allah) said, 'He must provide her sufficient clothes, sufficient food to protect her against hunger and if she committed a sin forgive her.' She then asked if she had other rights besides these on her husband.' He (the Messenger of Allah) replied, 'No, there is nothing else.' She then said, 'No, by Allah I will never marry.' She then left and the Holy Prophet, *O Allah, grant compensation to Muhammad and his family worthy of their services to Your cause*, said, 'Come back.' She went back and he (the Messenger of Allah) said that Allah, most Majestic, most Glorious, says, 'If they maintain chastity it will be better for them.' (24:60)"

H 10015, Ch. 152, h 3

It is narrated from the narrator of the previous Hadith from 'Uthman ibn 'Isa from Sama'ah ibn Mehran who has said the following:

"Abu 'Abd Allah, *'Alayhi al-Salam*, has said, 'You must maintain piety before Allah about two weak ones'- he thereby meant the orphans and women and that 'they (women) must be treated with great privacy.'"

H 10016, Ch. 152, h 4

It is narrated from the narrator of the previous Hadith from Muhammad ibn Ali from Dhubyan ibn Hakim from Buhlul ibn Muslim from Yunus ibn 'Ammar who has said the following:

"Abu 'Abd Allah, *'Alayhi al-Salam*, gave in marriage to me a slave-girl who belonged to 'Isma'il, his son and said, 'Be good to her.' I then asked, 'What is the meaning of 'be good to her'?' He (the Imam) said, 'Provide her with sufficient food, clothes and forgive her sins against you.' He (the Imam) then said to her, 'You must go (with him), may Allah keep you on the middle path in what is for him.'"

H 10017, Ch. 152, h 5

It is narrated from the narrator of the previous Hadith from Muhammad ibn 'Isa from those whom he has mentioned from Shihab ibn 'Abd Rabbihi who has said the following:

"I once asked abu 'Abd Allah, *'Alayhi al-Salam*, about the rights of women on their husbands. He (the Imam) said, 'He must provide for her sufficient food, sufficient clothes to maintain her dignity and must not make a repugnant face on her; and when he has followed these instructions he then by Allah has fulfilled her rights.' I then asked about oil. He (the Imam) said, 'That is every other day.' I then asked about meat. He (the Imam) said, 'That is once every three days which is ten times every month and not more.' I then asked about dyes. He (the Imam) said, 'Dye is once every six months and four sets (kinds) of clothes every year, two sets (kinds) for winter and two for summer and it is not proper to leave her home to suffer from the poverty of three things: oil for the head, vinegar and ghee and one mud (a certain measurement) of food for each meal, because that is how much I use for myself and my family and for every human being one time meal must be measured which he may consume or gift it or give as charity and one must feed his family of the seasons' fruits. On *'Id* days one must provide additional food which is not consumed on other days.'"

H 10018, Ch. 152, h 6

Muhammad ibn Yahya has narrated from Ahmad ibn Muhammad from ibn Mahbub from al-'Ala' from Muhammad ibn Muslim who has said the following:

"Abu 'Abd Allah, *'Alayhi al-Salam*, has said that the Messenger of Allah, *O Allah, grant compensation to Muhammad and his family worthy of their services to Your cause*, has said, 'Jibril advised me about women (so much) that I began to think of divorce as an improper act unless it is because of openly proven indecency.'"

H 10019, Ch. 152, h 7

Abu Ali al-Ash'ariy has narrated from Muhammad ibn 'Abd al-Jabbar or others from ibn Faddal from Ghalib ibn 'Uthman from Rawh ibn 'Abd al-Rahim who has said the following:

"This is concerning my question before abu 'Abd Allah, *'Alayhi al-Salam*, about the words of Allah, most Majestic, most Glorious, '. . . one who suffers from constraint in his sustenance must spend from whatever Allah has granted him.' (65:7) He (the Imam) said, 'He must provide her with basic necessities and clothes, otherwise, judgment for separation between them must be issued.'"

H 10020, Ch. 152, h 8

Ali ibn Ibrahim has narrated from his father from ibn abu 'Umayr from Jamil ibn Darraj who has said the following:

"He (the Imam), *'Alayhi al-Salam*, has said, 'A man is not compelled, but for providing the expenses of his parents and children.' He (the narrator) has said that ibn abu 'Umayr has said, 'I asked Jamil about the woman and he said that 'Anbasah has narrated from abu 'Abd Allah, *'Alayhi al-Salam*, who has said that if one provides clothes for her which is sufficient to maintain her dignity, sufficient food to survive, she then must stay with him, otherwise, she is divorced.'"

Chapter 153 - Cordiality with Wife

H 10021, Ch. 153, h 1

Abu Ali al-Ash'ariy has narrated from Muhammad ibn 'Abd al-Jabbar from Safwan from Ishaq ibn 'Ammar who has said the following:

"Abu 'Abd Allah, *'Alayhi al-Salam*, has said that the Messenger of Allah, *O Allah, grant compensation to Muhammad and his family worthy of their services to Your cause*, has said, 'Women are like crooked ribs from which you can benefit by leaving it alone (the way it is); but on trying to straighten one only causes it to snap and break a part.' In another Hadith is said, 'You can benefit thereby.'"

H 10022, Ch. 153, h 2

A number of our people have narrated from Ahmad ibn Muhammad from Ali ibn al-Hakam from Aban al-Ahmar from Muhammad al-Wasitiy who has said the following:

"Abu 'Abd Allah, *'Alayhi al-Salam*, has said, 'Ibrahim, *'Alayhi al-Salam* once complained before Allah, most Majestic, most Glorious, because of the wicked moral behavior of Sarah and Allah most High, sent him revelation that said, 'Women are like crooked ribs, on trying to straighten you only cause it to snap and break apart but you can benefit by leaving it alone (the way it is), so you must exercise patience.'"

Chapter 154 - Necessary Obedience to Husband

H 10023, Ch. 154, h 1

A number of our people have narrated from Ahmad ibn Muhammad from ibn Khalid from his father from 'Abd Allah ibn al-Qasim al-Hadramiy from 'Abd Allah ibn Sinan who has said the following:

"Abu 'Abd Allah, *'Alayhi al-Salam*, has said, 'In the time of the Messenger of Allah, *O Allah, grant compensation to Muhammad and his family worthy of their services to Your cause*, a man left for a journey and instructed his wife not to leave her house until he comes back. He (the Imam) said that her father became ill so the woman sent someone to the Holy Prophet saying, 'My husband has gone on a journey and has instructed me not to leave the house until he comes back but my father has become ill; if you command me to visit him and return home.' The Messenger of Allah, *O Allah, grant compensation to Muhammad and his family worthy of their services to Your cause*, said, 'No, you must stay home and obey your husband.' He (the Imam) has said that her father's illness became serious and she sent a messenger the second time asking, 'If you command me to visit him.' He (the Messenger of Allah) said, 'No, you must stay home and obey your husband.' He (the Imam) has said that her father died and she sent a messenger to him (the Messenger of Allah) if she can join in his funeral for *Salat* (prayer).' He (the Messenger of Allah) said, 'No, you must stay home and obey your husband.' He (the Imam) has said that her father was buried and the Messenger of Allah, *O Allah, grant compensation to Muhammad and his family worthy of their services to Your cause*, sent her a message that said, 'Allah has forgiven you and your father because of your obeying your husband.'"

H 10024, Ch. 154, h 2

Muhammad ibn Yahya has narrated from Ahmad ibn Muhammad from Ali ibn al-Hakam from Ali ibn abu Hamzah from abu Basir who has said the following:

"I once heard abu 'Abd Allah, *'Alayhi al-Salam*, saying that once the Messenger of Allah, *O Allah, grant compensation to Muhammad and his family worthy of their services to Your cause*, gave a speech for women and said, 'O the community of women, you must give charity even if it is from your jewelries, a date or a piece of a date because the majority of you will be the fuel for the fire of hell if you frequently abuse and curse your associate (husband).' A woman from banu Salim who had reason said, 'O Messenger of Allah, we are mothers, who carry in our wombs and breastfeed. From us are daughters who highly value (parents and relatives) and kind sisters.' The Messenger of Allah was moved emotionally and said, 'Childbearing, birth-giving, breastfeeding and kindhearted ones, only if they do not bring to their husband's (bed) something that will make them to feel the heat of fire (due to involving themselves in indecent acts).'"

H 10025, Ch. 154, h 3

Muhammad ibn Yahya has narrated from Ahmad ibn Muhammad from ibn Mahbub from 'Abd Allah ibn Ghalib from Jabir al-Juhfiy who has said the following:

"Abu Ja'far, *'Alayhi al-Salam*, has said that once on the tenth of the month of Dhul al-Hajj the Messenger of Allah, *O Allah, grant compensation to*

Muhammad and his family worthy of their services to Your cause, moved out of the city of al-Madinah toward the backside of it on a camel without a saddle and passed by women, stopped higher than them and said, 'O community of women, you must give charity and obey your husbands; the majority of you will be in the fire.' When they heard it they wept and one woman from them stood up and asked, 'O Messenger of Allah, will we be in the fire with the unbelievers? By Allah, we are not unbelievers to be punished and to become of the people of the fire.' The Messenger of Allah said, 'This will happen if you deny the rights of your husbands.'"

H 10026, Ch. 154, h 4

Ibn Mahbub from 'Abd Allah ibn Sinan who has said the following:

"Abu 'Abd Allah, *'Alayhi al-Salam*, has said, 'A woman does not have permission with the existence of her husband to set free a slave, give charity, contract with a slave, give gift or make a vow in her assets without the permission of her husband except payment of Zakat or doing good to parents or keeping good relations with her relatives.'"

H 10027, Ch. 154, h 5

Ali ibn Ibrahim has narrated from his father from al-Nawfaliy from al-Sakuniy who has said the following:

"Abu 'Abd Allah, *'Alayhi al-Salam*, has said that the Messenger of Allah, *O Allah, grant compensation to Muhammad and his family worthy of their services to Your cause*, has said, 'Any woman who goes out of her house without the permission of her husband loses her right of maintenance until she comes back.'"

Chapter 155 - Lack of Virtue in Woman

H 10028, Ch. 155, h 1

A number of our people have narrated from Ahmad ibn Muhammad from ibn Khalid from his father from Muhammad ibn Sinan from ''Amr ibn Muslim from al-Thumaliy who has said the following:

"Abu Ja'far, *'Alayhi al-Salam*, has said that the Messenger of Allah, *O Allah, grant compensation to Muhammad and his family worthy of their services to Your cause*, has said, 'Of men very few find salvation and from women that number is even less and less.' It was asked, 'Why is it so O Messenger of Allah, *O Allah, grant compensation to Muhammad and his family worthy of their services to Your cause?*' He (the Messenger of Allah) replied, because they are unbelievers in anger (in it they may act like unbelievers) and believers in consent.'"

H 10029, Ch. 155, h 2

It is narrated from the narrator of the previous Hadith from Muhammad ibn Ali from Muhammad ibn al-Fudayl from Sa'd ibn abu ''Amr al-Jallab who has said the following:

"Abu 'Abd Allah, *'Alayhi al-Salam*, once said to the wife of Sa'd, 'How fortunate it is for you O Khansa', if Allah will not give you anything else besides your daughter, mother of al-Husayn; still Allah has given you a great deal of good. The case of a virtuous woman among women is like an *al-`A`sam* crow among the crows. It is the one which has one white leg.'"

H 10030, Ch. 155, h 3
Ali ibn Ibrahim has narrated from his father from ibn abu 'Umayr from Hafs ibn al-Bakhtariy who has said the following:
"Abu 'Abd Allah, *'Alayhi al-Salam*, has said, 'The existence of a believing woman (in rarity) is like *shammah* (a bright mark) on the body of a black bull.'"

H 10031, Ch. 155, h 4
Ahmad ibn Muhammad al-'Asemiy has narrated from Ali ibn al-Hassan ibn Faddal from Ali ibn Asbat from his uncle, Ya'qub ibn Salim from Muhammad ibn Muslim who has said the following:
"Abu Ja'far, *'Alayhi al-Salam*, has said that the Messenger of Allah, *O Allah, grant compensation to Muhammad and his family worthy of their services to Your cause*, has said, 'The existence of a virtuous woman is like an *al-`A`sam* crow which is so rare to find.' It was asked, 'What is an *al-`A`sam* crow?' He (the Messenger of Allah) replied, 'It is that which is very rare to find.' He (the Messenger of Allah) said, 'It is the one which has one white leg.'"

H 10032, Ch. 155, h 5
Muhammad ibn Yahya has narrated from Ahmad ibn Muhammad ibn 'Isa from ibn Mahbub from ibn Sinan from certain persons of his people who have said the following:
"Abu Ja'far, *'Alayhi al-Salam*, has said that the Messenger of Allah, *O Allah, grant compensation to Muhammad and his family worthy of their services to Your cause*, has said, 'No other thing serves Satan as the greatest army as women and anger do.'"

H 10033, Ch. 155, h 6
A number of our people have narrated from Ahmad ibn Muhammad from al-Barqiy from abu Ali al-Wasitiy in a marfu' manner who has said the following:
"Abu Ja'far, *'Alayhi al-Salam*, has said, 'When woman becomes old both parts of her goodness vanish and both parts of wickedness remain. Her beauty goes and she becomes barren and her tongue becomes very sharp.'"

Chapter 156 - Disciplinants for Women

H 10034, Ch. 156, h 1
Ali ibn Ibrahim has narrated from his father from al-Nawfaliy from al-Sakuniy who has said the following:
"Abu 'Abd Allah, *'Alayhi al-Salam*, has said that the Messenger of Allah, *O Allah, grant compensation to Muhammad and his family worthy of their services to Your cause*, has said, 'You must not lodge women in a chamber, do not teach them writing (that would lead to unlawful behavior), but teach them the spinning wheel and Chapter 24 of the Quran.'"

H 10035, Ch. 156, h 2
A number of our people have narrated from Sahl ibn Ziyad from Ali ibn Asbat from his uncle Ya'qub ibn Salim in a marfu' manner who has said the following:
"'Amir al-Mu'minin, *'Alayhi al-Salam*, has said, 'You must not teach your women chapter twelve of the Quran and do not read it for them; in it there is

sedition, instead teach them Chapter twenty-four of the Quran because in it there are exhortations.'"

H 10036, Ch. 156, h 3

A number of our people have narrated from Sahl ibn Ziyad from Ja'far ibn Muhammad al-Ash'ariy from ibn al-Qaddah who has said the following:

"Abu 'Abd Allah, *'Alayhi al-Salam*, has said that the Messenger of Allah, *O Allah, grant compensation to Muhammad and his family worthy of their services to Your cause*, has prohibited riding of a female's genital organ on a saddle.'"

H 10037, Ch. 156, h 4

A number of our people have narrated from Ahmad ibn abu 'Abd Allah from Muhammad ibn Ali from abu Ishaq from al-Harith al-'A'war who has said the following:

"'Amir al-Mu'minin, *'Alayhi al-Salam*, has said, 'You must not allow female organs to ride on saddle to excite them for indecent and sinful acts.'"

Chapter 156 - Disobedience to Women

H 10038, Ch. 157, h 1

Abu Ali al-Ash'ariy has narrated from Muhammad ibn 'Abd al-Jabbar from Safwan from Ishaq ibn 'Ammar who has said the following:

"I once asked abu al-Hassan, *'Alayhi al-Salam*, about the case of an affluent woman who has performed Hajjatu al-Islam and she asks her husband to take her for al-Hajj from her own assets if he can deny her. He (the Imam) said, 'Yes, he can do so by saying, "My right on you is greater than your right on me in this issue."'"

H 10039, Ch. 157, h 2

A number of our people have narrated from Ahmad ibn Muhammad from ibn Mahbub from 'Abd Allah ibn Sinan who has said the following:

"Abu 'Abd Allah, *'Alayhi al-Salam*, has said that women were mentioned before the Messenger of Allah, *O Allah, grant compensation to Muhammad and his family worthy of their services to Your cause*, and he (the Messenger of Allah) said, 'Disobey women in lawful matters before they command you to do unlawful acts and you must seek refuge with Allah against the wicked women and remain on your guard with the good ones of them.'"

H 10040, Ch. 157, h 3

Ali ibn Ibrahim has narrated from his father from al-Nawfaliy from al-Sakuniy who has said the following:

"Abu 'Abd Allah, *'Alayhi al-Salam*, has said that the Messenger of Allah, *O Allah, grant compensation to Muhammad and his family worthy of their services to Your cause*, has said, 'Whoever obeys his woman Allah throws him on his face in the fire.' It was asked, 'What kind of obeying is it?' He (the Messenger of Allah) replied, 'It is when she asks him to take her to public baths (like beach areas), wedding ceremonies (with dancing and so on) and *'Id* parties, mourning programs (with unlawful activities) and to find see-through clothes.'"

H 10041, Ch. 157, h 4

Through the same chain of narrators as that of the previous Hadith the following is narrated:

"He (the Imam), *'Alayhi al-Salam*, has said that the Messenger of Allah, *O Allah, grant compensation to Muhammad and his family worthy of their services to Your cause*, has said, 'Obeying the woman brings regret.'"

H 10042, Ch. 157, h 5

A number of our people have narrated from Ahmad ibn abu 'Abd Allah from his father from those whom he has mentioned from al-Husayn ibn al-Mukhtar who has said the following:

"Abu 'Abd Allah, *'Alayhi al-Salam*, has said that 'Amir al-Mu'minin, *'Alayhi al-Salam*, has said in one of his speeches, 'You must stay away from wicked women and remain on your guard with the good ones. If they command you to do good things oppose them so that they will not expect you to listen to their unlawful demand.'"

H 10043, Ch. 157, h 6

It is narrated from the narrator of the previous Hadith from his father in a marfu' manner who has said the following:

"Once women were mentioned before abu Ja'far, *'Alayhi al-Salam*, and he (the Imam) said, 'You must not ask for their advice in private (secret) matters and you must not listen to them in the issues about the relatives.'"

H 10044, Ch. 157, h 7

Muhammad ibn Yahya has narrated from Muhammad ibn al-Husayn from ''Amr ibn 'Uthman from al-Muttalib ibn Ziyad in a marfu' manner who has said the following:

"Abu 'Abd Allah, *'Alayhi al-Salam*, has said, 'You must ask refuge with Allah against the wicked ones of your women and remain on your guard with the good ones of them. You must not listen to them in lawful matters so that they command you to do unlawful acts.'"

H 10045, Ch. 157, h 8

It is narrated from the narrator of the previous Hadith from abu 'Abd Allah al-Jamuraniy from al-Hassan ibn Ali ibn abu Hamzah from Sandal from ibn Muskan from Sulayman ibn Khalid who has said the following:

"I once heard abu 'Abd Allah, *'Alayhi al-Salam*, saying, 'You must not take advice from women because there is weakness, feebleness and incapacity in them.'"

H 10046, Ch. 157, h 9

It is narrated from the narrator of the previous Hadith from Ya'qub ibn Yazid from a man of our people called abu 'Abd Allah, in a marfu' manner who has said the following:

"Abu 'Abd Allah, *'Alayhi al-Salam*, has said that 'Amir al-Mu'minin has said, 'There is blessing in opposing (unlawful desires) of women.'"

H 10047, Ch. 157, h 10

Through the same chain of narrators as that of the previous Hadith the following is narrated:

"'Amir al-Mu'minin *'Alayhi al-Salam*, has said, 'A man who follows (unlawful) policies of woman is condemned.'"

H 10048, Ch. 157, h 11

Muhammad ibn Yahya has narrated from Ahmad ibn Muhammad from al-Husayn ibn Sayf from Ishaq ibn 'Ammar in a marfu' manner who has said the following:

"Whenever the Messenger of Allah, *O Allah, grant compensation to Muhammad and his family worthy of their services to Your cause,* was about to embark on an armed expedition, he would call his wives for advice and then oppose them.'" (Details of such advice are not mentioned)

H 10049, Ch. 157, h 12

Ali has narrated from his father from '"Amr ibn 'Uthman from certain persons of his people who has said the following:

"Abu 'Abd Allah, *'Alayhi al-Salam,* has said, 'You must ask for refuge with Allah against the wicked ones of your women and remain on your guard with the good ones of them. You must not obey them in lawful matters so that they will not call you to do unlawful things. He (the Imam) said, 'The Messenger of Allah, *O Allah, grant compensation to Muhammad and his family worthy of their services to Your cause,* has said, 'You must not take advice from women about private (secret) matters and you must not listen to them about the matters of relatives. When a woman becomes old both parts of her goodness vanish and both parts of wickedness remain; her womb becomes barren, her moral manners turn to wickedness and her tongue becomes sharp. When man becomes old both parts of his wickedness vanish and both parts of his goodness remain; his reason becomes pure, his opinion firm and his moral behavior good.'"

Chapter 158 - Keeping Secrets

H 10050, Ch. 158, h 1

Ali ibn Ibrahim has narrated from his father and Muhammad ibn 'Isma'il has narrated from al-Fadl ibn Shadhan from all ibn abu 'Umayr from Ibrahim ibn 'Abd al-Hamid from Walid ibn Sabih who has said the following:

""Abu 'Abd Allah, *'Alayhi al-Salam,* has said that the Messenger of Allah, *O Allah, grant compensation to Muhammad and his family worthy of their services to Your cause,* has said, 'A woman must not walk in the center of the road. She must walk next to the wall or side of the road.'"

H 10051, Ch. 158, h 2

Ibn abu 'Umayr has narrated from Ibrahim ibn 'Abd al-Hamid from al-Walid ibn Sabih who has said the following:

"Abu 'Abd Allah, *'Alayhi al-Salam,* has said that the Messenger of Allah, *O Allah, grant compensation to Muhammad and his family worthy of their services to Your cause,* has said, 'If a woman wears perfumes then goes out of her house, she is then cursed and condemned until she returns to her home whenever she does.'"

H 10052, Ch. 158, h 3

Ali ibn Ibrahim has narrated from Salih al-Sindiy from Ja'far ibn Bashir from ibn Bukayr from a man who has said the following:

"Abu 'Abd Allah, *'Alayhi al-Salam,* has said, 'It is not proper for a woman to wear perfumes when she goes out of her house.'"

H 10053, Ch. 158, h 4

Muhammad ibn Yahya has narrated from 'Abd Allah ibn Muhammad ibn abu 'Umayr from Hisham ibn Salim who has said the following:

"Abu 'Abd Allah, *'Alayhi al-Salam*, has said that the Messenger of Allah, *O Allah, grant compensation to Muhammad and his family worthy of their services to Your cause*, has said, 'Women must not walk in the Surat (center) of the road but they must walk on either side – it (surat) is the middle of it.'"

H 10054, Ch. 158, h 5

Ali ibn Ibrahim has narrated from his father from and Muhammad ibn 'Isma'il has narrated from al-Fadl ibn Shadhan from all from ibn abu 'Umayr from Hafs ibn al-Bakhtariy who has said the following:

"Abu 'Abd Allah, *'Alayhi al-Salam*, has said, 'It is not proper for a woman to remove her veil before a Jewish woman or a Christian woman because they can describe it to their husband.'"

H 10055, Ch. 158, h 6

A number of our people have narrated from Sahl ibn Ziyad from Muhammad ibn al-Hassan Shammun from 'Abd Allah ibn 'Abd al-Rahman from Misma' abu Sayyariy who has said the following:

"Abu 'Abd Allah, *'Alayhi al-Salam*, has said that of the matters for which the Messenger of Allah, *O Allah, grant compensation to Muhammad and his family worthy of their services to Your cause*, took pledges from the women was that they must not sit in *Ihtibah* position and must not sit with men privately." (*Ihtibah* is sitting with knees and thighs raised against one's belly when sitting on one's hips, using one's arms or a piece of cloth as a ring around the knees and waist)

Chapter 159 - Detestable Matters for Women

H 10056, Ch. 159, h 1

Ali ibn Ibrahim has narrated from his father from al-Nawfaliy from al-Sakuniy who has said the following:

"Abu 'Abd Allah, *'Alayhi al-Salam*, has said that 'Amir al-Mu'minin, *'Alayhi al-Salam*, prohibited women from forming their hairs in raised portion at different parts of the head and hanging a part of their hairs on the forehead, drawings of dyes on their palms, saying that Israelite women were destroyed because of hanging hairs on their forehead and drawings of dyes on their palms.'"

H 10057, Ch. 159, h 2

A number of our people have narrated from Sahl ibn Ziyad from Muhammad ibn al-Hassan Shammun from 'Abd Allah ibn 'Abd al-Rahman from Misma' who has said the following:

"Abu 'Abd Allah, *'Alayhi al-Salam*, has said that the Messenger of Allah, *O Allah, grant compensation to Muhammad and his family worthy of their services to Your cause*, has said, 'It is not lawful for a woman during her experiencing Hayd (menses) to form her hairs in a knot or allow a portion to hang down her forehead.'"

H 10058, Ch. 159, h 3

Muhammad ibn Yahya has narrated from Ahmad ibn Muhammad from Ali ibn al-Nu'man from Thabit ibn abu Sa'id who has said the following:

"Abu 'Abd Allah, *'Alayhi al-Salam*, was asked about women: if they can form their hair in loops and knots. He (the Imam) said, 'It can be done from wool or her own hairs and it is *Makruh* (undesirable) for a woman to form loops and knots on her head from the hairs of other women; but if she joins her own hair with wool it is not harmful.'"

H 10059, Ch. 159, h 4

Muhammad ibn Yahya has narrated from Muhammad ibn al-Husayn from 'Abd al-Rahman abu Hashim from Salim ibn Mukram from Sa'd al-Iskaf who has said the following:

"Abu Ja'far, *'Alayhi al-Salam*, was asked about loops and knots that women form out of their hairs on their head and join it with their hairs. He (the Imam) said, 'It is not unlawful if it is for beautification before her husband.' I then asked, 'We are told that the Messenger of Allah, *O Allah, grant compensation to Muhammad and his family worthy of their services to Your cause*, condemned the one who joins and the one joined with.' He (the Imam) said, 'It is not about this case. The Messenger of Allah, *O Allah, grant compensation to Muhammad and his family worthy of their services to Your cause*, condemned the women who commits fornication when she is young; and when old she leads women to men for unlawful acts; thus, such woman is called, one who joins and the one who is joined,with are condemned.'"

Chapter 160 - Lawful Instances of Looking at Women

H 10060, Ch. 160, h 1

A number of our people have narrated from Ahmad ibn Muhammad ibn 'Isa from ibn Mahbub from Jamil ibn Darraj from Fudayl ibn Yasar who has said the following:

"This is concerning my question before abu 'Abd Allah, *'Alayhi al-Salam*, about the arms of women if they are of beautification about which Allah, most Blessed, most High, has said, '. . . they must not expose their beauty except for their husband.' (24:32) He (the Imam) said, 'Yes, whatever must be covered with the scarf is of their beauty and whatever is above their bracelet is of their beauty.'"

H 10061, Ch. 160, h 2

Muhammad ibn Yahya has narrated from Ahmad ibn Muhammad ibn 'Isa from Marwak ibn 'Ubayd from certain persons of our people who has said the following:

"I once asked abu 'Abd Allah, *'Alayhi al-Salam*, about how much of the body of a woman who is not of one's relatives one can look at. He (the Imam) said, 'It is her face, both hands (from wrist down) and both feet (from the ankles down).'"

H 10062, Ch. 160, h 3

Ahmad ibn Muhammad ibn 'Isa has narrated from Muhammad ibn Khalid and al-Husayn ibn Sa'id from al-Qasim ibn-'Urwah from 'Abd Allah ibn Bukayr from Zurarah who has said the following:

"About the words of Allah, most Blessed, most High, '. . . except what is exposed,' abu 'Abd Allah, *'Alayhi al-Salam*, said, 'The exposed beauty is kohl and rings.'"

H 10063, Ch. 160, h 4

Al-Husayn from Muhammad has narrated from Ahmad ibn Ishaq from Sa'dan ibn Muslim from abu Basir who has said the following:

"I once asked abu 'Abd Allah, *'Alayhi al-Salam*, about the words of Allah, most High, '. . . they must not show off their beauty except for what is exposed.' (24:32) He (the Imam) said, 'It is the items like ring, anklet and bracelet.'"

H 10064, Ch. 160, h 5

Muhammad ibn Yahya has narrated from Ahmad ibn Muhammad from Ali ibn al-Hakam from Sayf ibn 'Amirah from Sa'd al-Iskaf who has said the following:

"Abu Ja'far, *'Alayhi al-Salam*, has said, 'Once a young man from al-Ansar (people of al-Madinah) came face to face with a woman in al-Madinah. Women would wear their scarf behind their ears. He looked at her when she was coming, and when she passed by he kept looking, and she entered in an alley that he called alley of so and so people. He kept looking behind her until his face hit a piece of bone or glass in the wall which caused a deep cut on his face. When the woman went away he found blood flowing on his chest and clothes and he said, 'By Allah, I will go and tell it to the Messenger of Allah, *O Allah, grant compensation to Muhammad and his family worthy of their services to Your cause.*' He (the Imam) said that he went to him (the Messenger of Allah) and when he (the Messenger of Allah) saw him, he (the Messenger of Allah) asked, 'What has happened to you?' He inform him (the Messenger of Allah) and Jibril came with this verse, 'Tell the believers to cast down their eyes and protect their genital organs (against indecent acts), it is more clean for them; Allah is well aware of what they do.'" (24:31)

Chapter 161 - Rules for Women

H 10065, Ch. 161, h 1

Ali ibn Ibrahim has narrated from his father from ibn abu 'Umayr from Hammad ibn 'Uthaman from al-Halabiy who has said the following:

"Abu 'Abd Allah, *'Alayhi al-Salam*, read the words of Allah, '. . . if they leave aside their garment,'(24:60) and said these words refer to veil and gown.' I then asked, 'In front of whom can they leave their garments aside?' He (the Imam) said, 'It is in front of those before whom it is not considered a show off with beauty (see (24:31)); but if she did not leave them aside is better and the beautification which is permissible to expose is mentioned in another verse (of the book of Allah).'" (24:31)

H 10066, Ch. 161, h 2

Ali ibn Ibrahim has narrated from his father from ibn abu 'Umayr from Muhammad ibn abu Hamzah who has said the following:

"Abu 'Abd Allah, *'Alayhi al-Salam*, has said, 'Of the rules about women one is that they can leave their garments aside and this refers to their gown only.'"

H 10067, Ch. 161, h 3

A number of our people have narrated from Ahmad ibn Muhammad from ibn Mahbub from al-'Ala' ibn Razin from Muhammad ibn Muslim who has said the following:

"I once asked abu Ja'far, *'Alayhi al-Salam*, about the words of Allah, most Majestic, most Glorious, 'Of the rules for women whose marriage age has expired,' and that what kind of their garments is proper to leave aside?' He (the Imam) said, 'It is just the gown.'"

H 10068, Ch. 161, h 4
Ali ibn Ibrahim has narrated from his father from Hammad ibn 'Isa from Hariz ibn 'Abd Allah who has said the following:
"Abu 'Abd Allah, *'Alayhi al-Salam*, once read the words of Allah, '. . . that they can leave their garments aside' (24:31) then said, 'It is the gown and veil, if she is old.'"

Chapter 162 - Man without Sense of Conjugal Relation

H 10069, Ch. 162, h 1
Muhammad ibn 'Isma'il has narrated from al-Fadl ibn Shadhan from and Abu Ali al-Ash'ariy has narrated from Muhammad ibn 'Abd al-Jabbar from Safwan ibn Yahya from ibn Muskan from Zurarah who has said the following:
"I once asked abu Ja'far, *'Alayhi al-Salam*, about the words of Allah, most Majestic, most Glorious, '. . . the dependents who are not of the condition of sensing carnal desires among men. . . .' (24:31) He (the Imam) said, 'It is a reference to those who because of dimwittedness do not go near women.'"

H 10070, Ch. 162, h 2
Humayd ibn Ziyad from al-Hassan ibn Muhammad from more than one person from Aban ibn 'Uthman from 'Abd al-Rahman ibn abu 'Abd Allah who has said the following:
"This is concerning my question before abu 'Abd Allah, *'Alayhi al-Salam*, about the case of those among men who do not have the sense of carnal desires. He (the Imam) said, 'They are the dimwitted ones who are owned and do not go near women.'"

H 10071, Ch. 162, h 3
Al-Husayn from Muhammad has narrated from Mu'alla' ibn Muhammad and Ali ibn Ibrahim has narrated from his father all from Ja'far ibn Muhammad al-Ash'ariy from 'Abd Allah ibn Maymun al-Qaddah who has said the following:
"Abu 'Abd Allah, *'Alayhi al-Salam*, has narrated from his ancestors that there were two men in al-Madinah, one was called Hayt and the other was called Mani'. They spoke to a man when the Messenger of Allah, *O Allah, grant compensation to Muhammad and his family worthy of their services to Your cause*, was hearing, 'When you enter Taef, by the will of Allah, do not miss daughter of Ghaylan al-Thaqafiy because she is a candle for the stingy, completely beautiful, slim and sweet. When she sits she places one part on the other, and when she speaks she sings. She comes forward with four (hands and legs) and goes back with eight (hands, legs, shoulder bones and hips), between her legs there is something like a bowl.' The Holy Prophet, *O Allah, grant compensation to Muhammad and his family worthy of their services to Your cause*, said, 'I do not think you are of those who do not have a sense of feeling carnal desires.' The Messenger of Allah commanded to send them in exile to a

place called al-'Araya'. They would procrastinate every Friday (in attending prayer).'"

Chapter 163 - Looking at Taxpayers' Women

H 10072, Ch. 163, h 1
Ali ibn Ibrahim has narrated from his father from al-Nawfaliy from al-Sakuniy who has said the following:
"The Messenger of Allah, *O Allah, grant compensation to Muhammad and his family worthy of their services to Your cause,* has said, 'It is not unlawful for one to look at the hairs and hands of the taxpayer women.'"

Chapter 164 - Looking at Nomads and Bedouins

H 10073, Ch. 164, h 1
A number of our people have narrated from Ahmad ibn Muhammad ibn 'Isa from ibn Mahbub from 'Abbad ibn Suhayb who has said the following:
"I once heard abu 'Abd Allah, *'Alayhi al-Salam,* saying, 'It is not unlawful to look at the heads of the people of al-Tihamah and Arabs who live in black (tents) and *al-'Aluj* (faithless uneducated people) because even if they are prohibited they do not listen.' He (the Imam) said, 'In the case of insane and those whose reason is defeated (very weak) it is not unlawful to look at their hairs and body as long as it is not an intentional look.'"

Chapter 165 - Head Scarf for Slaves 'Umm Awlad (mother of children)

H 10074, Ch. 165, h 1
A number of our people have narrated from Ahmad ibn Muhammad ibn 'Isa from Muhammad ibn 'Isma'il ibn Bazi' who has said the following:
"I once asked abu al-Hassan, al-Rida', *'Alayhi al-Salam,* about the mother of children (slave-girls kept to give birth): if they can remove the covering from their heads before men. He (the Imam) said, 'She must use the veil.'"

H 10075, Ch. 165, h 2
Muhammad ibn Yahya has narrated from Ahmad ibn Muhammad from ibn Mahbub from Hisham ibn Salim from Muhammad ibn Muslim who has said the following:
"I once heard abu Ja'far, *'Alayhi al-Salam,* saying, 'A slave-girl is not required to wear a veil for *Salat* (prayer) as well as one who has planned for her freedom; and the one who has already contracted even if wearing veil for *Salat* (prayer) is made a condition when she is owned until she pays off all that is contracted and all things applicable to slaves in penal law apply to her also.'"

Chapter 166 - Shaking Hands with Women

H 10076, Ch. 166, h 1
A number of our people have narrated from Ahmad ibn Muhammad from 'Uthman ibn 'Isa from Sama'ah ibn Mehran who has said the following:

"This is concerning my question before abu 'Abd Allah, *'Alayhi al-Salam*, about men's shaking hands with women. He (the Imam) said, 'It is lawful for men to shake hands with women with whom marriage is not lawful, like sister, daughter, paternal and maternal aunts, daughter of sister or so. However, a woman with whom marriage is lawful shaking hands is unlawful, except from behind the cloth but he must not squeeze her palm.'"

H 10077, Ch. 166, h 2

Ali ibn Ibrahim has narrated from his father from ibn abu 'Umayr from abu Ayyub al-Khazzaz from abu Basir who has said the following:

"This is concerning my question before abu 'Abd Allah, *'Alayhi al-Salam*, if one can shake hands with women who are lawful for marriage. He (the Imam) said, 'No, it is not permissible except from behind the cloth.'"

H 10078, Ch. 166, h 3

Ali ibn Ibrahim has narrated from Muhammad ibn Salim from certain persons of his people from al-Hakam ibn Miskin who has said that Sa'idah and Minnah sisters of Muhammad ibn abu 'Amid Bayya' al-Sabiriy narrated to me the following:

"Once, we visited abu 'Abd Allah, *'Alayhi al-Salam*, and asked if a woman can visit her brother. He (the Imam) said, 'Yes, she can do so.' We then asked if she can shake hands with him. He (the Imam) said, 'It must be from behind the cloth.' One of them said, 'My sister, this one, visits her brothers.' He (the Imam) said, 'When you visit your brothers do not wear dyes.'"

Chapter 167 - The Holy Prophet's Forming Allegiance with Women

H 10079, Ch. 167, h 1

A number of our people have narrated from Ahmad ibn Muhammad from Khalid from Muhammad ibn Ali from Muhammad ibn Aslam al-Jabaliy from 'Abd al-Rahman ibn Salim al-Ashal from al-Mufaddal ibn 'Umar who has said the following:

"I once asked abu 'Abd Allah, *'Alayhi al-Salam*, 'How did the Messenger of Allah touch the hands of women for their pledge of allegiance? He (the Imam) said, 'He (the Messenger of Allah) asked for a bucket in which he would make wudu. He (the Messenger of Allah) poured water in it, then immersed his right hand in water and as soon as one of them pledged allegiance he (the Messenger of Allah) asked her to immerse her hand in the water and she did so whenever he (the Messenger of Allah), *O Allah, grant compensation to Muhammad and his family worthy of their services to Your cause*, did and this is how he touched their hands.'"

Ali ibn Ibrahim has narrated from his father from certain persons of his people from abu 'Abd Allah, *'Alayhi al-Salam*, a similar Hadith.

H 10080, Ch. 167, h 2

Abu Ali al-Ash'ariy has narrated from Ahmad ibn Ishaq from Sa'dan ibn Muslim who has said the following:

"Abu 'Abd Allah, *'Alayhi al-Salam*, once asked me, 'Do you know how the Messenger of Allah, *O Allah, grant compensation to Muhammad and his family worthy of their services to Your cause*, pledged allegiance with women?' I replied, 'Allah knows best and the child of His Messenger knows best.' He (the Imam) said, 'He (the Messenger of Allah) called them to come together around him (the Messenger of Allah) and asked for a bowl. The place was *Baram* (near al-Baqi'). He (the Messenger of Allah) poured water in the bowl just to moisten it and immersed his hand in it, then said, 'Listen all of you. I pledge allegiance with you with the condition that you will not call anything as partners of Allah, you must not steal, you must not fornicate, you must not kill your children, you must not accuse falsely fabricating all by yourselves and you must not disobey your husbands in lawful matters. Do you confirm and acknowledge?' They replied, 'Yes, we confirm.' He (the Messenger of Allah) then moved his hand from the bowl then said to them, 'Immerse your hands in the bowl and they also did so. The purified and holy hand of the Messenger of Allah, *O Allah, grant compensation to Muhammad and his family worthy of their services to Your cause*, must not have touched female hands who were not of his relatives.'"

H 10081, Ch. 167, h 3
A number of our people have narrated from Ahmad ibn Muhammad from 'Uthman ibn 'Isa from abu Ayyub al-Khazzaz from a man who has said the following:

"About the words of Allah, most Majestic, most Glorious, '. . . that they must not disobey you in lawful matters' (60:13) Abu 'Abd Allah, *'Alayhi al-Salam*, has said, 'lawful matters means not to tear one's shirt, slap one's face, crying, 'woe is me', must not remain behind near the grave, must not blacken clothes and must not spread hairs.'"

H 10082, Ch. 167, h 4
Muhammad ibn Yahya has narrated from Salmah ibn al-Khattab from Sulayman ibn Sama'ah al-Khuza'iy from Ali ibn 'Isma'il from 'Amr ibn abu al-Miqdam who has said the following:

"I once heard abu Ja'far, *'Alayhi al-Salam*, saying, 'Do you know what is the meaning of the words of Allah, '. . . that they must not disobey you in lawful matters?' (60:13) I replied, 'No, I do not know.' He (the Imam) said, 'The Messenger of Allah, *O Allah, grant compensation to Muhammad and his family worthy of their services to Your cause*, once said to Fatimah, *'Alayha al-Salam*, 'When I die, you must not cause abrasion to any face, you must not spread for me any hairs, you must not cry 'woe is me' and you must not call any gathering to mourn for me.' He (the Imam) then said, 'This is the lawful matter about which Allah, most Majestic, most Glorious, has spoken.'"

H 10083, Ch. 167, h 5
Ali ibn Ibrahim has narrated from his father from Ahmad ibn Muhammad from ibn abu Nasr from Aban who has said the following:

"Abu 'Abd Allah, *'Alayhi al-Salam*, has said that when the Messenger of Allah, *O Allah, grant compensation to Muhammad and his family worthy of their services to Your cause*, liberated Makkah men pledged allegiance; then women came to pledge allegiance; and Allah, most Majestic, most Glorious, said, 'O Holy prophet, when believing women come to pledge allegiance with you not to call anything as partner of Allah, not to steal, not to commit fornication, not to kill their children, not to accuse falsely of their own making, must not disobey you in lawful matters, then pledge allegiance with them and ask forgiveness from Allah for them, Allah is forgiving and merciful.' (60:13) Hind then said, 'We brought up children from the time they were infants but you killed them when they grew up.' 'Umm Hakim daughter of al-Harith ibn Hisham, wife of 'Ikramah ibn abu Jahl asked, 'O Messenger of Allah, what is that 'lawful matters' that Allah has commanded us not to disobey you? He (the Messenger of Allah) replied, 'You must not slap any face, abrade it, pull out any hair, tear apart front part of a shirt, blacken clothes and you must not cry 'woe is me'.' The Messenger of Allah, *O Allah, grant compensation to Muhammad and his family worthy of their services to Your cause*, pledged allegiance with them on this and then she said, 'O Messenger of Allah, how can we pledge allegiance to you?' He (the Messenger of Allah) said, 'I do not place my hand in the hands of women.' He (the Messenger of Allah) then asked for a bowl of water and immersed his hand in it and then moved it and told them to immerse their hands in the bowl and that was pledging allegiance.'"

Chapter 168 - Entering in the Chambers of Women

H 10084, Ch. 168, h 1

A number of our people have narrated from Ahmad ibn abu 'Abd Allah from his father from Harun ibn al-Jahm from Ja'far ibn 'Umar who has said the following:

"The Messenger of Allah, *O Allah, grant compensation to Muhammad and his family worthy of their services to Your cause*, prohibited men from entering the place of women without their permission.'"

H 10085, Ch. 168, h 2

Through the same chain of narrators as that of the previous Hadith the following is narrated: "Men must not enter the place of women without the permission of their guardian."

H 10086, Ch. 168, h 3

A number of our people have narrated from Ahmad ibn Muhammad from ibn Mahbub from abu Ayyub al-Khazzaz who has said the following:

"Abu 'Abd Allah, *'Alayhi al-Salam*, has said, 'A man must ask permission when entering the place of his father but the father does not ask permission from his son. He (the Imam) said, 'A man must ask permission from his daughter or sister if they are married.'"

H 10087, Ch. 168, h 4

Ahmad ibn Muhammad has narrated from ibn Faddal from abu Jamilah from Muhammad ibn Ali al-Halabiy who has said the following:

"I once asked abu 'Abd Allah, *'Alayhi al-Salam*, if a man is required to ask permission from his father. He (the Imam) said, 'Yes, I would ask permission from my father and my mother was not with him. She was my father's wife. My mother had died when I was a boy. I did not like to disturb their privacy and they also did not like it. It is very correct and fine to say *Salam* (the phrase of offering greeting of peace).'"

H 10088, Ch. 168, h 5

A number of our people have narrated from Ahmad ibn abu 'Abd Allah from 'Isma'il ibn Mehran from 'Ubayd ibn Mu'awiyah ibn Shurayh from Sayf ibn 'Amirah from 'Amr ibn Shamir from Jabir from abu Ja'far, *'Alayhi al-Salam*, from Jabir ibn 'Abd Allah al-Ansariy who has said the following:

"One day the Messenger of Allah, *O Allah, grant compensation to Muhammad and his family worthy of their services to Your cause*, came out to visit Fatimah, *'Alayha al-Salam*, and I was with him (the Messenger of Allah). When I reached the door, he (the Messenger of Allah) placed his hand on it and pushed then said, *'Al-Salamu 'Alaykum.'* Fatimah, *'Alayha al-Salam*, responded saying, *''Alaykum al-Salam*, O Messenger of Allah.' He (the Messenger of Allah) asked, 'Can I come in?' She said, 'Please come in, O Messenger of Allah.' He (the Messenger of Allah) then asked, 'Can I come in with the person who is with me?' She said, 'O Messenger of Allah, I do not have a veil on me.' He (the Messenger of Allah) said,, 'O Fatimah, take the extra of your bed sheet and use it as veil to cover your head.' She did accordingly and he (the Messenger of Allah) then said, *'Al-Salamu Alaykum.'* Fatimah, responded saying, *''Alayka al-Salam*, O Messenger of Allah.' He (the Messenger of Allah) asked, 'Can I come in?' She replied, 'Yes, O Messenger of Allah.' He (the Messenger of Allah) then asked, 'Can I come in with the person with me?' She replied, 'Yes, you may come with the person with you.' Jabir has said that the Messenger of Allah entered and I also entered and I saw the face of Fatimah looked yellow like the belly of a locust. The Messenger of Allah, *O Allah, grant compensation to Muhammad and his family worthy of their services to Your cause*, asked, 'What has happened, O Fatimah that your face looks yellow?' She replied, 'O Messenger of Allah, it is hunger.' He (the Messenger of Allah) prayed saying, 'O Lord, who satisfies hunger, repels the cause of loss, satisfy Fatimah daughter of Muhammad.' Jabir has said, 'I then saw blood flow through its course and her face turned to its normal color and thereafter she did not experience any more hunger.'"

Chapter 169 - Another Chapter about the Previous Subject

H 10089, Ch. 169, h 1

A number of our people have narrated from Ahmad ibn abu 'Abd Allah from his father and Muhammad ibn Yahya has narrated from Ahmad ibn Muhammad ibn 'Isa from al-Husayn ibn Sa'id all from al-Nadr ibn Suwayd from al-Qasim ibn Sulayman from Jarrah al-Mada'iniy who has said the following:

"Abu 'Abd Allah, *'Alayhi al-Salam*, has said, 'Your slaves and those of you who have not yet gained feeling of carnal desires must ask for your permission three times as Allah, most Majestic, most Glorious, has commanded. Those who have gained feeling of carnal desire must not enter the place of his mother, sister and maternal aunt or others without permission and you must not give permission unless he offers you *Salam* (the phrase of offering greeting of peace) in obedience to Allah, most Majestic, most Glorious.' He (the narrator) has said that abu 'Abd Allah, *'Alayhi al-Salam*, then said, 'Your servants who have gained feeling of carnal desires must ask you for permission during three times of privacy if they come to you in such times even if their home is the same as your home.' He (the Imam) said, 'They must ask you for permission after *al-*

'Isha' called *al-'Atmah*, in the morning and at noontime when you undress. Allah, most Majestic, most Glorious, has commanded as such because of privacy and at these times one is unaware and in retreat.'"

H 10090, Ch. 169, h 2
A number of our people have narrated from Ahmad ibn Muhammad from ibn Faddal from abu Jamilah from Muhammad al-Halabiy from Zurarah who has said the following:
"This is about the words of Allah, most Majestic, most Glorious, '. . . those whom your right hands possess' (24:58) abu 'Abd Allah, *'Alayhi al-Salam*, has said, 'It is just for men and not for women.' I then asked, 'Is it then necessary for women to ask permission in such hours?' He (the Imam) said, 'No, they can come and go.' About, '. . . those who have not gained feeling of carnal desire,' (24:58) he (the Imam) said, 'It is a reference to yourselves (free people).' He (the Imam) said, 'You must ask for permission, like those who have become mature, during the three hours.'"

H 10091, Ch. 169, h 3
Muhammad ibn Yahya has narrated from Ahmad ibn Muhammad and A number of our people have narrated from Ahmad ibn abu 'Abd Allah all from Muhammad ibn 'Isa from Yusuf ibn 'Aqil from Muhammad ibn Qays who has said the following:
"Abu Ja'far, *'Alayhi al-Salam*, has said, 'Those whom your right hands possess and who have not gained feeling of carnal desires must ask permission from you three times: before the morning *Salat* (prayer), at noontime when you undress and after *Salat* (prayer) of *al-'Isha'* which are three times of privacy and thereafter it is not unlawful for you and for them to come and go and move around each other. Those of you who have gained feeling of carnal desire must not enter in the place of your mother, sister, daughter and others without permission and you must not give permission unless he offers you Salam (the phrase of offering greeting of peace) because it is obedience to the Beneficent.'"

H 10092, Ch. 169, h 4
A number of our people have narrated from Ahmad ibn abu 'Abd Allah from his father from Khalaf ibn Hammad from Rib'iy ibn 'Abd Allah from al-Fudayl ibn Yasar who has said the following:
"About the words of Allah, most Majestic, most Glorious, 'O believers, those whom your right hands possess and those who have not yet gained feeling of carnal desire must ask permission from you three times', (24:58) abu 'Abd Allah, *'Alayhi al-Salam*; and in answer to a question about who such people are has said, 'They are male and female slaves and the children who are not yet mature. They must ask permission from you during the three hours of privacy; after *Salat* (prayer) of *al-'Isha'* which is *al-'Atmah*, when you undress at noon time and before the morning *Salat* (prayer). After the three privacy times, your slaves and children can come and go without permission if they wanted.'"

Chapter 170 - Lawful Looks of Master and Slave

H 10093, Ch. 170, h 1
Muhammad ibn Yahya has narrated from 'Abd Allah and Ahmad sons of Muhammad from Ali ibn al-Hakam from Aban ibn 'Uthman from 'Abd al-Rahman ibn abu 'Abd Allah who has said the following:

"I once asked abu 'Abd Allah, *'Alayhi al-Salam*, about a slave's looking at the hairs of the mistress. He (the Imam) said, 'It is not unlawful.'"

H 10094, Ch. 170, h 2
A number of our people have narrated from Ahmad ibn Muhammad from Muhammad ibn 'Isma'il from Ibrahim ibn abu al-Balad and Yahya ibn Ibrahim from his father Ibrahim from Mu'awiyah ibn 'Ammar who has said the following:

"Once we, about thirty people, were with abu 'Abd Allah, *'Alayhi al-Salam*, when my father came and abu 'Abd Allah, *'Alayhi al-Salam*, welcomed him, gave him a place just next to himself and turned to him (for speaking) for a long time. Then abu 'Abd Allah, *'Alayhi al-Salam*, said, 'Abu Mu'awiyah needs privacy, if you please provide us relief.' We all got up and my father said to me, 'O Mu'awiyah, come back.' I turned back and abu 'Abd Allah, *'Alayhi al-Salam*, asked, 'Is this your son?' He replied, 'Yes, and he thinks that people of al-Madinah do something unlawful.' He (the Imam) asked, 'What is it?' I then said, 'The woman of Quraysh or of Banu Hashim when riding, places her hand on the head of the black (slave) and her arms on his neck.' Abu 'Abd Allah, *'Alayhi al-Salam*, said, 'Son, have you not read al-Quran?' I replied, 'Yes, I read it.' He (the Imam) said, 'Read this verse, '. . . it is not unlawful for them about their fathers, sons, and whomever their right hands possess.' (33:55) He (the Imam) then said, 'It is not unlawful if a slave looks at one's hairs and legs (below the knees).'"

H 10095, Ch. 170, h 3
Ali ibn Ibrahim has narrated from his father and Muhammad ibn 'Isma'il has narrated from al-Fadl ibn Shadhan from ibn abu 'Umayr from Mu'awiyah ibn 'Ammar who has said the following:

"I once asked abu 'Abd Allah, *'Alayhi al-Salam*, about a slave's looking at the hairs and leg of his mistress. He (the Imam) said, 'It is not unlawful.'"

H 10096, Ch. 170, h 4
Muhammad ibn Yahya has narrated from Ahmad ibn Muhammad from ibn Mahbub from Yunus ibn 'Ammar and Yunus ibn Ya'qub all of them have said the following:

"Abu 'Abd Allah, *'Alayhi al-Salam*, has said, 'It is not lawful for a slave to look at any part of the body of his mistress except her hairs unintentionally.'"

In another Hadith it is said that it is not unlawful to look at her hairs if it is safe (from sinful feelings).

Chapter 171 - Castrated People

H 10097, Ch. 171, h 1
Humayd ibn Ziyad has narrated from al-Hassan ibn Muhammad from 'Abd Allah ibn Jabalah from 'Abd al-Malik ibn 'Utbah from al-Nakha'iy who has said the following:

"I once asked abu 'Abd Allah, *'Alayhi al-Salam*, about the case of a castrated slave; if he can look at his mistress when she takes a bath. He (the Imam) said, 'No, it is not lawful.'"

H 10098, Ch. 171, h 2

Ali ibn Ibrahim has narrated from his father from ibn abu 'Umayr from Muhammad ibn Ishaq who has said the following:

"I once asked abu al-Hassan, *'Alayhi al-Salam*, about the case of a man who has a castrated slave; if he can go to his women and provide them water for wudu and look at their hairs. He (the Imam) said, 'No, he can do so.'"

H 10099, Ch. 171, h 3

A number of our people have narrated from Ahmad ibn Muhammad from Muhammad ibn 'Isma'il ibn Bazi' who has said the following:

"I once asked abu al-Hassan, al-Rida', *'Alayhi al-Salam*, about the veil of the free women before castrated ones. He (the Imam) said, 'They would go in the presence of the daughters of abu al-Hassan, *'Alayhi al-Salam*, and they would not use veils.' I then asked if they were free. He (the Imam) said, 'No, they were not free.' I then asked, 'Is veil necessary the free ones before them (castrated) ones?' He (the Imam) said, 'No, it is not so.'"

Chapter 172 - The Time for Compulsory Head Scarf

H 10100, Ch. 172, h 1

A number of our people have narrated from Sahl ibn Ziyad and Ali ibn Ibrahim has narrated from his father from all from ibn abu Najran from 'Asem ibn Hamid from Muhammad ibn Muslim who has said the following:

"Abu Ja'far, *'Alayhi al-Salam*, has said, 'It is not proper for a girl who experiences Hayd (menses) not to use a veil except if she does not experience it.'"

H 10101, Ch. 172, h 2

Muhammad ibn 'Isma'il has narrated from al-Fadl ibn Shadhan from and abu Ali al-Ash'ariy has narrated from Muhammad ibn 'Abd al-Jabbar from Safwan ibn Yahya from 'Abd al-Rahman ibn al-Hajjaj who has said the following:

"I once asked abu Ibrahim, *'Alayhi al-Salam*, about the case of a girl who has not gained feeling of carnal desire, when must she use a veil to cover her head from non-relatives and when is it necessary to cover her head for *Salat* (prayer)? He (the Imam) said, 'It is not necessary for her to cover her head until *Salat* (prayer) becomes obligatory on her.'"

Chapter 173 - The Age When It Is Lawful to Kiss a Girl

H 10102, Ch. 173, h 1

Muhammad ibn Yahya has narrated from Ahmad ibn Muhammad from Ali ibn al-Hakam from 'Abd Allah ibn Yahya al-Kahiliy from abu Ahmad al-Kahiliy –I think I met him who has said the following:

"I once asked him (the Imam), *'Alayhi al-Salam*, about a girl who is not a relative to me who holds me and I carry her and kiss her. He (the Imam) said, 'When she becomes six years old then you must not place her in your lap.'"

H 10103, Ch. 173, h 2

Humayd ibn Ziyad has narrated from al-Hassan ibn Muhammad ibn Sama'ah from more than one person from Aban ibn 'Uthman from 'Abd al-Rahman ibn Yahya from Zurarah who has said the following:

"Abu 'Abd Allah, *'Alayhi al-Salam*, has said, 'When a free girl becomes six years old then it is not proper for you to kiss her.'"

H 10104, Ch. 173, h 3

A number of our people have narrated from Sahl ibn Ziyad from Harun ibn Muslim from certain persons of his narrators who have said the following:

"A certain person of banu Hashim once invited abu al-Hassan, al-Rida', *'Alayhi al-Salam*, along with a group of his people and a girl was brought in the gathering. People called her one by one and when she was brought near him (the Imam) he asked, 'How old is she?' It was said that she was five years old. He (the Imam) then asked her to stand back."

Chapter 174 - Another Chapter About the Previous Subject

H 10105, Ch. 174, h 1

Ali ibn Ibrahim has narrated from his father from al-Nawfaliy from al-Sakuniy who has said the following:

"Abu 'Abd Allah, *'Alayhi al-Salam*, has said that 'Amir al-Mu'minin was asked if a child can perform cupping on a woman. 'Amir al-Mu'minin, *'Alayhi al-Salam*, said, 'If he is good in cupping and describing then it is not unlawful.'"

H 10106, Ch. 174, h 2

A number of our people have narrated from Ahmad ibn abu 'Abd Allah who has said the following:

"Once ibn 'Umm Maktum asked permission from the Holy Prophet, *O Allah, grant compensation to Muhammad and his family worthy of their services to Your cause*, when 'Ai'shah and Hafsah were with him. He (the Messenger of Allah) asked them to go to the room and they said, 'He is blind.' He (the Messenger of Allah) said, 'If he cannot see you, you two can see him.'"

Chapter 175 - Treating a Female Patient

H 10107, Ch. 175, h 1

Muhammad ibn Yahya has narrated from Ahmad ibn Muhammad ibn 'Isa from Ali ibn al-Hakam from abu Hamzah al-Thumaliy who has said the following:

"I once asked him (the Imam), *'Alayhi al-Salam*, about the case of a Muslim woman who is afflicted with a misfortune in her body, like a broken part or wound in a place to which looking is not proper and men are more gentle to treat it than women: if he can look at it. He (the Imam) said, 'In an emergency he can treat her if she wants.'"

Chapter 175 - Offering Greeting of Peace to Women

H 10108, Ch. 176, h 1

Ali ibn Ibrahim has narrated from his father from Harun ibn Muslim from Mas'adah ibn Sadaqah who has said the following:

"Abu 'Abd Allah, *'Alayhi al-Salam*, has said that 'Amir al-Mu'minin has said, 'You must not initiate *Salam* (the phrase of offering greeting of peace) to women and you must not invite them for food; the Holy Prophet, *O Allah, grant compensation to Muhammad and his family worthy of their services to Your cause*, has said, "Women are tiredness (weakness in communication) and a matter of private nature thus, you must cover their tiredness with quietness and the privacy of their nature with homes.""""

H 10109, Ch. 176, h 2

Muhammad ibn Yahya has narrated from Ahmad ibn Muhammad from Muhammad ibn Yahya from Ghiyath ibn Ibrahim who has said the following:

"Abu 'Abd Allah, *'Alayhi al-Salam*, has said, 'You (men) must not offer *Salam* (the phrase of offering greeting of peace) to a woman.'"

H 10110, Ch. 176, h 3

Ali ibn Ibrahim has narrated from his father from Hammad ibn 'Isa from Rib'iy ibn 'Abd Allah who has said the following:

"Abu 'Abd Allah, *'Alayhi al-Salam*, has said that the Messenger of Allah, *O Allah, grant compensation to Muhammad and his family worthy of their services to Your cause*, would offer *Salam* (the phrase of offering greeting of peace) to women and they would respond in return and 'Amir al-Mu'minin would offer *Salam* (the phrase of offering greeting of peace) to women but disliked to offer *Salam* (the phrase of offering greeting of peace) to the young ones, saying, 'I am afraid their voice may attract me and make me feel negatively more than the reward I am seeking.'"

H 10111, Ch. 176, h 4

Ali ibn Ibrahim has narrated from his father from ibn abu 'Umayr from Hisham ibn Salim who has said the following:

"Abu 'Abd Allah, *'Alayhi al-Salam*, has said that the Messenger of Allah has said, 'Women are tiredness (weakness in communication) and a matter of private nature thus, you must cover the privacy of their nature with homes and their tiredness with quietness.'"

Chapter 177 - Vigilant Protectionism

H 10112, Ch. 177, h 1

A number of our people have narrated from Ahmad ibn Muhammad from ibn Khalid from 'Uthman ibn 'Isa from those whom he has mentioned who has said the following:

"Abu 'Abd Allah, *'Alayhi al-Salam*, has said, 'Allah, most High, is Vigilant (protective of His cause) and He loves every vigilant one and due to His vigilance He has made both apparent and hidden indecency unlawful.'"

H 10113, Ch. 177, h 2

It is narrated from the narrator of the previous Hadith from his father from al-Qasim ibn Muhammad al-Jawhariy from Habib al-Khath'amiy from 'Abd Allah ibn abu Ya'fur who has said the following:

"I once heard abu 'Abd Allah, *'Alayhi al-Salam*, saying, 'One who is not vigilant and protective, his heart is upside down.'"

H 10114, Ch. 177, h 3
It is narrated from the narrator of the previous Hadith Ahmad ibn Muhammad from Muhammad ibn Yahya has narrated from Ahmad ibn Muhammad ibn 'Isa all from ibn Mahbub from Ishaq ibn Jarir who has said the following:

"Abu 'Abd Allah, *'Alayhi al-Salam*, has said, 'When a man's vigilance is shaken in matters of protection for his family and wife or those married to him, like his slave-girl, but does not act vigilantly, Allah, most Majestic, most Glorious, sends a bird called al-Qafandar which sits on the upper portion of his door and gives him forty days and calls him saying, 'Allah is vigilant and loves vigilant people.' If he then acts vigilantly, changes and dislikes what has shaken his sense of protectionism, otherwise, the bird flies, sits on his head and hangs its wings on his eyes; then Allah, most Majestic, most Glorious, removes the spirit of belief and faith from him and the angels call him a pimp.'"

H 10115, Ch. 177, h 4
Ibn Mahbub has narrated from more than one person who has said the following:

"Abu 'Abd Allah, *'Alayhi al-Salam*, has said that the Messenger of Allah, *O Allah, grant compensation to Muhammad and his family worthy of their services to Your cause*, has said, 'Ibrahim, *'Alayhi al-Salam* was vigilant and protective and I am more vigilant and protective than he was. Allah cuts-off the noses of those who do not exercise vigilance in favor of the believing and Muslims.'"

H 10116, Ch. 177, h 5
Ali ibn Ibrahim has narrated from his father from Hammad ibn 'Isa from Ishaq ibn Jarir who has said the following:

"I once heard abu 'Abd Allah, *'Alayhi al-Salam*, saying, 'When a Satan called al-Qafandar, plays the lute in a man's home and men come in his house, that Satan places every part of his body on the similar one of that man, owner of the house, then he blows in him a blow and thereafter that man does not exercise any vigilance or protective measures even if people go to his women.'"

H 10117, Ch. 177, h 6
Muhammad ibn Yahya has narrated from Ahmad ibn Muhammad ibn 'Isa from Muhammad ibn Yahya from Ghiyath ibn Ibrahim who has said the following:

"Abu 'Abd Allah, *'Alayhi al-Salam*, has said that 'Amir al-Mu'minin once said, 'O people of Iraq I am informed that your women push men on the road, are you not ashamed?' In another Hadith it is said that 'Amir al-Mu'minin, *'Alayhi al-Salam*, said, 'Are you not ashamed of not exercising vigilance when your women go out in the market and become crowded with *al-'Aluj* (uneducated faithless ones)!'"

H 10118, Ch. 177, h 7
A number of our people have narrated from Ahmad ibn Muhammad from 'Uthman ibn 'Isa from ibn Muskan from Muhammad ibn Muslim who has said the following:

"Abu 'Abd Allah, *'Alayhi al-Salam*, has said, 'On the Day of Judgment Allah will not speak to three kinds of people and will not cleanse them and they suffer a painful suffering. One is an old fornicating man, a pimp and a woman who allows men to go in the bed of her husband with her.'"

H 10119, Ch. 177, h 8

Ahmad ibn Muhammad has narrated from ibn Faddal from 'Abd Allah ibn Maymun who has said the following:

"Abu 'Abd Allah, *'Alayhi al-Salam*, has said, 'Paradise is made unlawful for a pimp.'"

H 10120, Ch. 177, h 9

Abu Ali al-Ash'ariy has narrated from certain persons of his people from Ja'far ibn 'Anbasah from 'Ubadah ibn Ziyad al-Asadiy from 'Amr ibn abu al-Miqdam from Abu Ja'far, *'Alayhi al-Salam*, and Ahmad ibn Muhammad from al-'Asemiy from those who narrated to him from Mu'alla' ibn Muhammad from Ali ibn Hassan from 'Abd al-Rahman ibn Kathir who has said the following:

"Abu 'Abd Allah, *'Alayhi al-Salam*, has said that 'Amir al-Mu'minin in a letter to al-Hassan, *'Alayhi al-Salam*, has said, 'You must be on your guard against vigilance and protectionism in an improper instance because it can lead the ones (of women) with perfect manners into one of ill-behaving one, however, you must fortify their (women's) condition and if you find a defect then hasten to disapprove it regardless it is small or large. If you find their behavior doubtful, then the sin becomes great and deviation becomes easy.'"

Chapter 178 - No Vigilance and Protectionism against Lawful Matters

H 10121, Ch. 178, h 1

Ali ibn Ibrahim has narrated from his father from ibn abu 'Umayr from Jamil ibn Darraj who has said the following:

"Abu 'Abd Allah, *'Alayhi al-Salam*, has said, 'Vigilance and protectionism is not needed against lawful matters, in the light of the words of the Messenger of Allah, *O Allah, grant compensation to Muhammad and his family worthy of their services to Your cause*, "The two of you (Ali and Fatimah, *'Alayhim al-Salam*,) you must not do anything until I come back to you" and when he (the Messenger of Allah) came back he stretched his legs between them in the furnishing.'"

Chapter 179 - Women's' Attending *'Id*

H 10122, Ch. 179, h 1

Muhammad ibn Yahya has narrated from Ahmad ibn Muhammad from ibn Faddal from Marwan ibn Muslim from Muhammad ibn Shurayh who has said the following:

"This is concerning my question before abu 'Abd Allah, *'Alayhi al-Salam*, about women's going out for the two *'Id*. He (the Imam) said, 'No, except old women wearing their pairs of shoes.'" (Consult Fatwah about this hadith)

H 10123, Ch. 179, h 2

A number of our people have narrated from Ahmad ibn abu 'Abd Allah from Muhammad ibn Ali from Yunus ibn Ya'qub who has said the following:

"I once asked abu 'Abd Allah, *'Alayhi al-Salam*, about women going out for *'Id* and Friday *Salat* (prayer). He (the Imam) said, 'No, except old women.'" (Consult Fatwah about this hadith)

Chapter 180 - Lawful Matters for a Husband during His Wife's Menses

H 10124, Ch. 180, h 1

Muhammad ibn Yahya has narrated from Ahmad ibn Muhammad Ahmad ibn Muhammad from Muhammad ibn al-Husayn from Muhammad ibn 'Isma'il ibn Bazi' from Mansur ibn Yunus from Ishaq ibn 'Ammar from 'Abd al-Malik ibn 'Amr who has said the following:

"I once asked abu 'Abd Allah, *'Alayhi al-Salam*, about the case of a man whose wife experiences Hayd (menses) and of what he can enjoy with her. He (the Imam) said, 'He can enjoy everything except her front organ exactly.'"

H 10125, Ch. 180, h 2

Humayd ibn Ziyad has narrated from al-Hassan ibn Muhammad from 'Abd Allah ibn Jabalah from Mu'awiyah ibn 'Ammar who has said the following:

"I once asked abu 'Abd Allah, *'Alayhi al-Salam*, about what is permissible for a man to enjoy with his wife during her experiencing Hayd (menses). He (the Imam) said, 'Everything except her vulva.'"

H 10126, Ch. 180, h 3

Muhammad ibn Yahya has narrated from Salmah ibn al-Khattab from Ali ibn al-Husayn from Muhammad ibn abu Hamzah from Dawud al-Riqqiy from 'Abd Allah ibn Sinan who has said the following:

"This is concerning my question before abu 'Abd Allah, *'Alayhi al-Salam*, about what is permissible for a man to enjoy with his wife during her experiencing Hayd (menses). He (the Imam) said, 'Everything except her vulva.'"

H 10127, Ch. 180, h 4

Muhammad ibn Yahya has narrated from Salmah ibn a-Khattab from Ali ibn al-Husayn from Muhammad ibn Ziyad from Aban ibn 'Uthman and al-Husayn ibn Yusuf from 'Abd al-Malik ibn 'Amr who has said the following:

"I once asked abu 'Abd Allah, *'Alayhi al-Salam*, about what is permissible for a man to enjoy with his wife during her experiencing Hayd (menses). He (the Imam) said, 'Everything except her vulva.' He (the Imam) then said, 'A Woman is just like a doll for man.'"

H 10128, Ch. 180, h 5

Ali ibn Ibrahim has narrated from his father from ibn abu 'Umayr from al-Hassan ibn 'Atiyyah from 'Adhafir al-Sayrafiy who has said the following:

"Abu 'Abd Allah, *'Alayhi al-Salam*, asked, 'Do you see those who are born with deformities?' I replied, 'Yes, I see them.' He (the Imam) said, 'It is because their fathers go to bed with their wives during their experiencing Hayd (menses).'"

Chapter 181 - Conjugal Relations During Her Menses Before Ghusl

H 10129, Ch. 181, h 1

Muhammad ibn Yahya has narrated from Ahmad ibn Muhammad from ibn Mahbub from al-'Ala' ibn Razin from Muhammad ibn Muslim who has said the following:

"About the case of a woman whose blood discharge stops in the end of Hayd (menses), he (the Imam) said, 'If her husband has an intense desire he must instruct her to wash her vulva, then he can touch it before Ghusl (bath) if he wants.'"

H 10130, Ch. 181, h 2
Muhammad ibn Yahya has narrated from Salmah ibn al-Khattab from Ali ibn al-Hassan al-Tatariy from Muhammad ibn abu Hamzah from Ali ibn Yaqtin who has said the following:
"I once asked abu 'Abd Allah, *'Alayhi al-Salam*, about the case of a woman experiencing Hayd (menses) who finds herself clean and her husband goes to bed with her. He (the Imam) said, 'It is not unlawful but taking Ghusl (bath) is more likeable to me.'"

Chapter 182 - Anal of Women

H 10131, Ch. 182, h 1
Al-Husayn from Muhammad has narrated from Mu'alla' ibn Muhammad from al-Hassan ibn Ali from Aban from certain persons of his people who has said the following:
"This is concerning my question before abu 'Abd Allah, *'Alayhi al-Salam*, about coming to women from their rear. He (the Imam) said, 'She is a doll; you must not disappoint her.'"

H 10132, Ch. 182, h 2
Muhammad ibn Yahya has narrated from Ahmad ibn Muhammad from Ali ibn al-Hakam from who has said, 'I heard Safwan ibn Yahya who has said the following:
"I once said to al-Rida', *'Alayhi al-Salam*, that one of his followers has asked me to ask you a question in which he feels shy and intimidated. He (the Imam) asked, 'What is the question?' I asked, 'Can a man come to his wife in her anus?' He (the Imam) said, 'It is up to him.' I then asked, 'Do you do so?' He (the Imam) said, 'No, we do not do so.'"

Chapter 183 - Masturbation and Conjugal Relation with Animals

H 10133, Ch. 183, h 1
A number of our people have narrated from Ahmad ibn Muhammad from ibn Khalid from al-'Ala' ibn Razin from a man who has said the following:
"I once asked abu 'Abd Allah, *'Alayhi al-Salam*, about masturbation. He (the Imam) said, 'It is of the sinful acts. Going to bed with a slave-girl is better than this.'"

H 10134, Ch. 183, h 2
Ahmad ibn Muhammad from has narrated from abu Yahya al-Wasitiy from 'Isma'il al-Basriy from Zurarah ibn 'A'yun who has said the following:
"I once asked abu 'Abd Allah, *'Alayhi al-Salam*, about one's playing to cause his semen to discharge. He (the Imam) said, 'He is like going to bed with himself and there is no punishment on him (but it is like fornication as regards to sinfulness).'"

H 10135, Ch. 183, h 3

Muhammad ibn Yahya has narrated from Ahmad ibn Muhammad from Ahmad ibn al-Hassan from 'Amr ibn Sa'id Musaddiq ibn Sadaqah from 'Ammar ibn Musa who has said the following:

"About the case of a man who engages in sexual intercourse with animals or causes his semen to discharge, abu 'Abd Allah, *'Alayhi al-Salam*, has said, 'Whenever a man causes his semen to discharge in this or that way it is fornication.'"

H 10136, Ch. 183, h 4

A number of our people have narrated from Sahl ibn Ziyad from Ali ibn al-Rayyan who has said the following:

"A man once wrote to abu al-Hassan, *'Alayhi al-Salam*, and asked about a man who is with a woman and touches her from behind her clothes and his clothes and moves until he discharges semen; if it is like masturbation. He (the Imam) signed the answer that said, 'In it he has reached his goal (of a sinful act).'"

H 10137, Ch. 183, h 5

Ali ibn Muhammad al-Kulayniy has narrated from Salih ibn abu Hammad from Muhammad ibn Ibrahim al-Nawfaliy from al-Husayn ibn al-Mukhtar from certain persons of his people who has said the following:

"Abu 'Abd Allah, *'Alayhi al-Salam*, has said that the Messenger of Allah, *O Allah, grant compensation to Muhammad and his family worthy of their services to Your cause*, has said, 'Condemned is one who engages in sexual intercourse with animals.'"

Chapter 184 - Fornication

H 10138, Ch. 184, h 1

Ali ibn Ibrahim has narrated from his father from 'Uthman ibn 'Isa from Ali ibn Salim who has said the following:

"Abu 'Abd Allah, *'Alayhi al-Salam*, has said, 'On the Day of Judgment of the people the one who suffers the most intense suffering is one who places his seed in the womb of one who with whom going to bed is unlawful.'"

H 10139, Ch. 184, h 2

Ali ibn Ibrahim has narrated from his father from ibn abu 'Umayr from and 'Uthman ibn 'Isa from Ali ibn Salim who has said the following:

"Abu Ibrahim, *'Alayhi al-Salam*, has said, 'Stay away from fornication, it destroys one's sustenance and invalidates one's religion.'"

H 10140, Ch. 184, h 3

A number of our people have narrated from Sahl ibn Ziyad from Ja'far ibn Muhammad al-Ash'ariy fm 'Abd Allah ibn Maymun al-Qaddah who has said the following:

"Abu 'Abd Allah, *'Alayhi al-Salam*, has narrated from his father who has said that one who commits fornication faces six troubling issues, of which three are in this world and three in the next life. In this world it takes away light and beauty from his face, brings poverty and quicker death. In the next life, it is the anger of Allah, worse account and living in the fire forever.'"

H 10141, Ch. 184, h 4

Muhammad ibn Yahya has narrated from Ahmad ibn Muhammad from ibn Mahbub from Malik ibn 'Atiyyah from abu 'Ubaydah who said the following:

"Abu Ja'far, *'Alayhi al-Salam*, has said, 'It is in the book of Ali, *'Alayhi al-Salam*, that the Messenger of Allah, *O Allah, grant compensation to Muhammad and his family worthy of their services to Your cause*, has said, "When people after me will commit fornication in increasing numbers the number of deaths suddenly will also increase."'"

H 10142, Ch. 184, h 5

Muhammad ibn Yahya has narrated from Ahmad ibn Muhammad from Ali ibn al-Hakam from abu Hamzah who has said the following:

"Once I was with Ali ibn al-Husayn, *'Alayhi al-Salam*, when a man came and said, 'O abu Muhammad, I am addicted to women. One day I commit fornication and the other day I fast; if this can become expiation for the sin.' Ali ibn al-Husayn, *'Alayhi al-Salam*, said, 'There is not anything more beloved to Allah, most Majestic, most Glorious, than obedience to Him and not to disobey Him. So you must not fornicate and you must not fast.' Abu Ja'far, *'Alayhi al-Salam*, pulled him to himself holding his hand and said, 'O fornicator, you do the deeds of the people of hell and hope to enter paradise?'"

H 10143, Ch. 184, h 6

Muhammad ibn Yahya has narrated from Ahmad ibn Muhammad fm Ali ibn al-Hakam from Ali ibn Suwayd who has said the following:

"I once said to abu al-Hassan, *'Alayhi al-Salam*, 'I am addicted to looking at beautiful women and I like looking at them. He (the Imam) said, 'O Ali, it is not unlawful if Allah finds that your intention is truthful, but you must remain on your guard against fornication because it destroys bounties and invalidates religion.'"

H 10144, Ch. 184, h 7

Ali ibn Ibrahim has narrated from his father and a number of our people have narrated from Ahmad ibn Muhammad from abu al-'Abbas al-Kufiy all from 'Amr ibn 'Uthman from 'Abd Allah ibn Sinan who has said the following:

"Abu 'Abd Allah, *'Alayhi al-Salam*, has said, 'Once the disciples of Jesus gathered around him and said, "O teacher of goodness teach us guidance." Jesus said to them, "Moses has commanded you not to falsely swear by Allah and I command you not to swear even in a truthful manner." They said, "O Spirit of Allah, please give us more guidance." He then said, "Moses, the Holy Prophet of Allah, has commanded you not to commit fornication and I command you not to even speak to your souls about fornication, not to speak of committing fornication, because one who speaks to his soul about fornication is like one who decorates a house and smoke destroys the house even though it does not burn down the whole house.'"

H 10145, Ch. 184, h 8

Muhammad ibn Yahya has narrated from Ahmad ibn Muhammad from ibn Faddal from 'Abd Allah ibn Maymun al-Qaddah who has said the following:

"Abu 'Abd Allah, *'Alayhi al-Salam*, has said that Ya'qub said to his son, 'O son, do not commit fornication; even if a bird commits fornication it loses its feathers.'"

H 10146, Ch. 184, h 9

Ali ibn Ibrahim has narrated from his father from Hammad ibn 'Isa from Hariz ibn 'Abd Allah from al-Fudayl ibn Yasar who has said the following:

"Abu Ja'far, *'Alayhi al-Salam*, has said that the Messenger of Allah, *O Allah, grant compensation to Muhammad and his family worthy of their services to Your cause*, has said, "In fornication there are five disturbing issues: It destroys the beauty of the face, causes poverty, shortens one's life, makes the Beneficent angry, and sends one to the hellfire to suffer therein forever.'"

Chapter 185 - Female fornicator

H 10147, Ch. 185, h 1

A number of our people have narrated from Ahmad ibn Muhammad from 'Uthman ibn 'Isa from ibn Muskan from Muhammad ibn Muslim who has said the following:

"Abu 'Abd Allah, *'Alayhi al-Salam*, has said, 'Allah, does not speak to three kinds of people and they will suffer a painful suffering: One kind of such people is a woman who allows someone other than her husband to go to bed with her.'"

H 10148, Ch. 185, h 2

Ali ibn Ibrahim has narrated from his father from ibn abu 'Umayr from Ishaq ibn abu Hilal who has said the following:

"Abu 'Abd Allah, *'Alayhi al-Salam*, has said that 'Amir al-Mu'minin once said, 'Can I tell you about how great the sin of fornication is?' They replied, 'Yes, please tell us about it.' He (the Imam) said, 'It is a woman who allows someone other than her husband to go to bed with her; then gives birth thereby to a child and makes her husband responsible for the child. This is the woman to whom Allah does not speak and will not look to her on the Day of Judgment, will not purify her and she will suffer a painful suffering.'"

H 10149, Ch. 185, h 3

Ali has narrated from his father from al-Nawfaliy from al-Sakuniy who has said the following:

"Abu 'Abd Allah, *'Alayhi al-Salam*, has said, 'Allah's anger intensifies upon a woman who brings in her family a stranger who consumes their bounties and looks at their privacies.'"

Chapter 186 - Male Homosexuality

H 10150, Ch. 186, h 1

Ali ibn Ibrahim has narrated from his father from 'Isma'il ibn Marrar from Yunus from certain persons of his people who has said the following:

"I once heard abu 'Abd Allah, *'Alayhi al-Salam*, saying, 'The unlawfulness of homosexual unlawful sexual intercourse is more serious than unlawful heterosexual sexual intercourse; Allah destroyed a whole nation because of homosexual sexual intercourse but He has not destroyed as such because of heterosexual unlawful sexual intercourse.'"

H 10151, Ch. 186, h 2

Ali ibn Ibrahim has narrated from his father from ibn abu 'Umayr from abu Bakr al-Hadramiy who has said the following:

Abu 'Abd Allah, *'Alayhi al-Salam*, has said that the Messenger of Allah, *O Allah, grant compensation to Muhammad and his family worthy of their services to Your cause*, has said, 'One who engages in sexual intercourse with a boy, on the Day of Judgment will rise with the filth of such act and water of the world does not clean him, Allah becomes angry with him and condemns him, prepares hell for him and it is an evil destination.' He (the Imam) said, 'If a male engages in sexual intercourse with another male, Allah's throne trembles because of it. A man who allows anal sexual intercourse will be held by Allah on the bridge over the hell until He will complete the accounts of the creatures: then He will command to send him to hell in the levels of which he will suffer one after the other until he arrives in the lowest level from which he cannot come out.'"

H 10152, Ch. 186, h 3

Ali ibn Ibrahim has narrated from his father from al-Nawfaliy from al-Sakuniy who has said the following:

"Abu 'Abd Allah, *'Alayhi al-Salam*, has said that 'Amir al-Mu'minin has said, 'Homosexuality is other than anal sex, anal sex is disbelief.'"

H 10153, Ch. 186, h 4

Ali ibn Ibrahim has narrated from his father from Ahmad ibn Muhammad from ibn abu Nasr from Aban bin 'Uthman from abu Basir who has said the following:

"One of the two Imam, (abu Ja'far or abu 'Abd Allah), *'Alayhim al-Salam*, has said, 'In the case of the people of Lot mentioned in the Quran: "You engage in such indecent acts in which no one of the people of the world before had ever engaged,"' He (the Imam) said, 'Iblis (Satan) came to them in the form of a good looking person with femininity, with good looking clothes and he came to their young ones and asked them to have sex in his anus. Had he asked them to allow him have sex in their anus they would refuse but he did the opposite and when they did as he wanted them to do they enjoyed it. He went away and left them to engage in such indecent act with each other.'"

H 10154, Ch. 186, h 5

A number of our people have narrated from Ahmad ibn Muhammad ibn Khalid from Muhammad ibn Sa'id who has said, that informed me Zakariya ibn Muhammad from his father from 'Amr who has said the following:

"Abu Ja'far, *'Alayhi al-Salam*, has said, 'People of Lot were of the excellent people Allah had created. Iblis persuaded them very intensely. Due to their excellent manners, they would go to work together in groups and leave women behind at home. Iblis (Satan) would come to them every day and in their absence Iblis (Satan) would destroy their work accomplished in a day. One of them suggested keeping watch and seeing who destroys their work accomplished. They remained on their guard and found him out to be a very good looking boy. They said, 'So it is you who destroys our work every time.' They decided to kill him. They left him with a man for the night. During the night he cried and the man asked, 'What is the matter?' He replied, 'My father would allow me to sleep on his belly.' The man said, 'Fine, come and sleep on my belly.' He (the boy) began to rub the man until he taught him how to engage in anal sexual intercourse with him. The first to teach the indecent act was Iblis (Satan) and the second was this man. He then ran away and in the morning the man told everyone about what he had experienced with the boy and they liked it. They did not know it (the indecent act) before. They learned it and man began to practice the indecent act with another man. Thereafter, they even ambushed by-passers and engaged with them in the indecent act until their city failed the people. They neglected their women and turned to young boys. When he, Iblis (Satan), found out that his plan has worked and it has become strong among men he then turned to women in the form of a woman and said, 'Your men engage in sexual intercourse with each other.' They replied, 'Yes, we know it.' Lot all the time preached to them against it and Iblis (Satan) deceived them until women totally turned to women and men turned to men for sexual satisfaction. When Allah's point was established against them He sent Jibril, Michael and Israfil (three angels) in the form of young boys wearing gowns. They passed by Lot who was tilling the land. He asked, 'Where do you want to go? I have never seen any boys more beautiful than you.' They replied, 'Our master has sent us to the chief of this city.' He then asked, 'Is your master not informed that the people of this city commit indecent acts? O my sons, they by Allah take men and engage in anal sexual intercourse with them until they make them bleed.' They said, 'Our master has commanded us to pass through their middle.' He then said, 'I have one wish before you.' They asked, 'What is your wish?' He replied, 'You wait here until it is dark.' He (the Imam) said, 'They waited.' He (the Imam) said, 'He sent his daughter to bring them bread, water in a water-sack, and a gown for cover against cold. When his daughter went rain came in the valley and Lot said that now flood washes away the children thus, (you must) get up so we can move away to seek shelter of the wall. So Jibril, Michael and Israfil began to walk in the middle of the road. He said, 'Children, walk here.' They replied, 'Our master has commanded us to walk in their middle.' Lot was trying to benefit from the darkness. Iblis (Satan) took a child from the arms of a woman and threw him in a well and all people of the city came at the door of Lot for help. When they saw the young boys in his home they said, 'O Lot, this proves that you also do what we do' He said, 'They are my guests so you must not disgrace me about my guests.' They said, 'There are three of them. Take one and give two of them to us.' He (the Imam) said, 'He took them inside a room and said, 'I wish I had a family to defend me against you.' He (the Imam) said, 'The crowd began to press at the door, broke through the door of Lot and flattened Lot on the ground. Jibril said, 'We are the messengers of your Lord and they cannot reach you.' He took a handful of soil from Batha' and threw it against their faces and said, 'Ugly faces.' All people of the city became blind.' Lot said, 'O messengers of my Lord, what has my Lord commanded you to do about them?' They replied, 'He has commanded us to seize them in the morning.' He said, 'I have one wish before you.' They asked, 'What is your wish?' He replied, 'I request you to seize them now because I am afraid bada' (change of plan) may take place with my Lord.' They said, 'O Lot, the appointed time for them is the morning, is not the morning very near, for one who wants to seize them? Take your daughters and move away but depart your wife.'"

"Abu Ja'far, *'Alayhi al-Salam*, has said, 'May Allah grant mercy to Lot! If he knew who were with him in the room he would become certain of his victory when he said, 'I wish I had power against you or a strong support', what kind of support is stronger than Jibril who was in the room with him? Allah, most Majestic, most Glorious, said, to Muhammad, *O Allah, grant compensation to Muhammad and his family worthy of their services to Your cause*, " . . . from the unjust it is not far away," from the unjust ones in your followers if they do what people of Lot did.' He (the Imam) said that the Messenger of Allah has said, 'One who insists in engaging for anal sexual intercourse with men will not die before calling men to engage in anal sexual intercourse with him.'"

H 10155, Ch. 186, h 6

Ali ibn Ibrahim has narrated from his father from ibn abu 'Umayr from ibn Faddal from Dawud ibn Farqad from Abu Yazid al-Hammar who has said the following:

"Abu 'Abd Allah, *'Alayhi al-Salam*, has said, 'Allah, most Majestic, most Glorious, sent four angels for the destruction of the people of Lot: Jibril, Michael, Israfil and Karubil. They visited Ibrahim *'Alayhi al-Salam* wearing turbans on them. They offered him *Salam* (the phrase of offering greeting of peace) but he could not recognize them, and he found them in a very good appearance and said, 'No one will serve them other than myself.' Ibrahim liked serving guests very much; so he prepared for them and roasted a very meaty calf. When it was ready, he served them and brought it for them, 'He saw that their hands do not reach the food: he could not recognize them and he began to feel afraid of them' but when Jibril noticed he removed the turban from his face and he (Ibrahim) recognized him and asked, 'Are you he (jibril)?' He replied, 'Yes, I am he.' His wife Sarah, passed by and he gave her the good news of the birth of Ishaq (Isaac) who will be succeeded by Ya'qub. She asked, 'What has Allah, most Majestic, most Glorious, said?' They answered her by what the Quran has said. Ibrahim then asked, 'What for have you come?' They replied, 'We have come for the destruction of the people of Lot.' Ibrahim then asked, 'Will you destroy them even if there are one hundred believing people among them?' Jibril replied, 'No, we will not do so.' Ibrahim asked, 'Will you destroy them if there are fifty believing people among them?' Jibril replied, 'No, we will not do so.' He then asked, 'Will you destroy them if there are thirty believing people among them?' Jibril replied, 'No, we will not do so.' Ibrahim then asked, 'Will you destroy them if there are twenty believing people among them?' He replied, 'No, we will not do so.' He then asked, 'Will you destroy them if there are ten believing people among them?' He replied, 'No, we will not do so.' He then asked, 'Will you destroy them if there are five people among them?' He replied, 'No, we will not do so.' He then asked, 'Will you destroy if there is one believing person among them?' he replied, 'No, we will not do so.' Ibrahim then said, 'But Lot is there among them.' They replied, 'We know more about who is there. We will save him and his family, except his wife, who will be of those who remain behind.'

"Al-Hassan ibn Ali has said, 'What I know of the story is that Ibrahim tried to save them as it is mentioned in the words of Allah, most Majestic, most Glorious, 'He argued with us about the people of Lot.' They (angels) came to Lot when he was in a farm near the town. They offered him *Salam* (the phrase of offering greeting of peace) and they were wearing turbans. When he saw their good appearance in white dresses and white turbans he asked, 'Do you want the house?' They replied, 'Yes, we want the house.' He led them and they walked behind him. He then regretted to offer them the house and said, 'What is it that I have done? I am bringing them to a people whom I know how they are.' He turned back to them and said, 'You are coming to the wicked creatures of Allah.' Jibril said, 'We are not in a hurry about them until he testifies against them three times' and he said, 'This is one.' He then walked for an hour then turned back to them and said, 'You are coming to the wicked creatures of Allah.' Jibril said, 'These are two testimonies.' He then walked and when he arrived in the city he turned to them and said, 'You are coming to the wicked creatures of Allah.' Jibril said, 'This is the third testimony.' He entered and they entered with him until they entered his house. When his wife saw them in good appearance she climbed on the roof and clapped which they did not hear. She then started a fire and when they saw the smoke they came to the door running until they reached at the door and she came down to them and said, 'There are people with him the like of whom I have never seen in beauty and good appearance.' They came to the door to enter. When Lot saw them he stood up in front of them and said to them, 'O my people, have fear of Allah and do not humiliate me before my guests. Is there no man of reason among you?' He then said, 'These are my daughters and they are more clean for you'; he called them to the lawful matter.' They said, 'We have no right on your daughters and you know what we want.' He said to them, 'I wish I had enough power against you or a strong support'. Jibril then said, 'I wish he knew what kind of power he had with him?' He (the Imam) said, 'They overwhelmed him and entered the house. Jibril called them aloud to halt and he said, 'O Lot, allow them to come in. When they came in Jibril pointed his finger to them and they all turned blind as it is mentioned in the words of Allah, most Majestic, most Glorious, 'We turned their eyes blind.' Jibril called him and told him, 'I am the messenger of your Lord. Their hands will not reach you. Move with your family during a part of the night.' Jibril then said, 'We are sent to destroy them.' He said, 'O Jibril, do it quickly.' Jibril said, 'Their appointed time is in the morning, is the morning not near enough?' He commanded him and those with him to move away except his wife. He then picked it–the city- with his wing with ten layers of the land, then raised it until those in the heaven above the earth could hear the barking of their dogs, and crowing of their rosters. He then turned it upside down and made it to rain down on it (city) and those around the city with stones of *sijjil* (baked clay).'"

H 10156, Ch. 186, h 7

Ali ibn Ibrahim has narrated from his father from ibn abu 'Umayr from Muhammad ibn abu Hamzah from Ya'qub bin Shu'ayb who has said the following:

"About the words of Lot, 'These are my daughters and they are cleaner and pure,' (11:78) abu 'Abd Allah, *'Alayhi al-Salam*, has said, 'He offered them for marriage.'"

H 10157, Ch. 186, h 8

Ali ibn Ibrahim has narrated from his father from al-Nawfaliy from al-Sakuniy who has said the following:

"Abu 'Abd Allah, *'Alayhi al-Salam*, has said that the Messenger of Allah, *O Allah, grant compensation to Muhammad and his family worthy of their services to Your cause*, has said, 'You must remain on your guard against the children of the affluent people and the tyrant kings because their mischief is more intense than the mischief of the virgins in their private chambers.'"

H 10158, Ch. 186, h 9

Ali ibn Ibrahim has narrated from his father from 'Uthman bin Sa'id from Muhammad bin Sulayman from Maymun al-Ban who has said the following:

"Once I was with abu 'Abd Allah, *'Alayhi al-Salam*, when certain verses of Chapter 11 of the Quran were read, '. . . We rained down upon them piles of stones which were marked before your Lord and it is not far away from the unjust,' (11:78) he (the Imam) said, 'Whoever dies insisting on engaging in anal sexual intercourse will not die until Allah shoots him with one of those stones by which his death takes place but no one sees it.'"

H 10159, Ch. 186, h 10

Muhammad ibn Yahya has narrated from Ahmad ibn Muhammad from Muhammad ibn Yahya from Talhah bin Zayd who has said the following:

"Abu 'Abd Allah, *'Alayhi al-Salam*, has said that the Messenger of Allah, *O Allah, grant compensation to Muhammad and his family worthy of their services to Your cause*, has said, 'One who kisses a boy with lust, Allah on the Day of Judgment will harness him with a harness of fire.'"

Chapter 187 - One Who Allows Sexual Intercourse in His Anus

H 10160, Ch. 187, h 1

Muhammad ibn Yahya has narrated from Ahmad ibn Muhammad from Muhammad ibn Yahya from Talhah bin Zayd who has said the following:

"Abu 'Abd Allah, *'Alayhi al-Salam*, has said that the Messenger of Allah, *O Allah, grant compensation to Muhammad and his family worthy of their services to Your cause*, has said, 'One who allows sexual intercourse in his anus voluntarily and playfully, Allah throws lust of woman on him.'"

H 10161, Ch. 187, h 2

Ali ibn Ibrahim has narrated from his father from Ali ibn Ma'bad from 'Abd Allah ibn al-Dihqan from Durust ibn abu Mansur from 'Atiyyah brother of abu al-'Aram who has said the following:

"Once I mentioned before abu 'Abd Allah, *'Alayhi al-Salam*, one who allows sexual intercourse in his anus. He (the Imam) said, 'If Allah finds someone of any use at all He does not allow him to become involved in allowing sexual intercourse in his anus. In behind such people there is something like a womb of women upside down. Their timidity in gayness is like women. A son of Satan

479

called Zawal has shared with them. With whomever of men this Satan shares, he becomes a homosexual man and whomever of women this Satan shares she becomes of those to whom people come (for prostitution). A homosexual man who becomes forty years old and still does not stay away from his habit, he then is of the remaining individuals of Sadum. I do not mean thereby biological remaining; they however are of the same culture and clay.' He (the narrator) has said, that I then asked 'Is it the Sadum which was turned upside down?' He (the Imam) said, 'There were four cities: Sadum, Sarim, Ladma' and 'Amira.' He (the Imam) said, 'Jibril came when they were cut out from the core of the seventh earth. He placed his wing underneath the lowest of them and raised all of them until the inhabitants of the heaven above the world could hear the barking of their dogs and then he turned them upside down.'"

H 10162, Ch. 187, h 3

Muhammad has narrated from Ahmad ibn Muhammad from Ali ibn al-Hakam from 'Abd al-Rahman al-'Arzamiy who has said the following:

"Abu 'Abd Allah, *'Alayhi al-Salam*, has said that 'Amir al-Mu'minin has said, 'Of Allah's creatures there are those who have wombs in their backs like the wombs of women.' He (the Imam) said that 'Amir al-Mu'minin was asked, 'Why do not they then become pregnant?' He (the Imam) said, 'Because it is upside down. In their behind there is a gland like that of camel and when it is excited they become excited and when it is calm they are calm.'"

H 10163, Ch. 187, h 4

A number of our people have narrated from Ahmad ibn Muhammad from ibn Khalid from Muhammad ibn Ali from Ali ibn 'Abd Allah and 'Abd al-Rahman ibn Muhammad from abu Khadijah who has said the following:

"Abu 'Abd Allah, *'Alayhi al-Salam*, has said that the Messenger of Allah, *O Allah, grant compensation to Muhammad and his family worthy of their services to Your cause*, has condemned transvestites (those of men who pretend to be like women and women who pretend to be like men).' He (the Imam) said, 'They are hermaphrodites who engage in sexual intercourse with each other.'"

H 10164, Ch. 187, h 5

Ahmad has narrated from Ja'far ibn Muhammad al-Ash'ariy from ibn al-Qaddah who has said the following:

"Abu 'Abd Allah, *'Alayhi al-Salam*, has said, 'Once a man came to my father and said, 'O child of the Messenger of Allah, *O Allah, grant compensation to Muhammad and his family worthy of their services to Your cause*, I am in an unfortunate condition; please pray for me to Allah.' He was told that he allows sexual intercourse in his anus.' He (the Imam) said, 'Whoever Allah finds to be of any benefit at all He does not permit him to allow sexual intercourse in his anus.' He (the Imam) then said, 'Allah, most Majestic, most Glorious, has said, "I swear by my glory and majesty that whoever allows sexual intercourse in his anus will not sit on the *Istabraq* and silk of paradise.'"

H 10165, Ch. 187, h 6

A number of our people have narrated from Ahmad ibn Muhammad from al-Husayn ibn Sa'id and Muhammad ibn Yahya from Musa ibn al-Hassan from 'Umar ibn Ali ibn 'Amr ibn Yazid from

Muhammad ibn 'Umar from his brother al-Husayn from his father 'Umar ibn Yazid who has said the following:

"Once, when, I was with abu 'Abd Allah, *'Alayhi al-Salam*, a man also was there. He said, 'I pray to Allah to keep my soul in service for your cause, I love children.' He (the Imam) asked, 'Why is it?' He said, 'I carry them on my back.' Abu 'Abd Allah, *'Alayhi al-Salam*, placed his hand on his forehead and turned his face away from him. The man cried and abu 'Abd Allah, *'Alayhi al-Salam*, looked to him as if he sympathized and said, 'When you go to your town buy a healthy camel and tie it down firmly then take a sword and slash its hump to take away its skin and sit on it as it is naturally hot.' 'Umar has said that the man said, 'When I returned to my town I bought a healthy camel, tied it down firmly, took the sword and took away its skin and sat on it as it was naturally warm and on the back of the camel from me fell something like a small frog (lizard) and my problem calmed down.'"

H 10166, Ch. 187, h 7
Muhammad ibn Yahya has narrated from Musa ibn al-Hassan from al-Haytham al-Nahdiy in a marfu' manner who has said the following:

"A man once complained before abu 'Abd Allah, *'Alayhi al-Salam*, against an anal problem and abu 'Abd Allah, *'Alayhi al-Salam*, rubbed his back. A red worm fell off of him and he was cured.'"

H 10167, Ch. 187, h 8
A number of our people have narrated from Ahmad ibn abu 'Abd Allah from Muhammad ibn Sa'id from Zakariya ibn Muhammad from his father from 'Amr who has said the following:

"Abu Ja'far, *'Alayhi al-Salam*, has said, 'I swear upon myself that one who allows sexual intercourse in his anus will not be allowed to sit on the fine furnishings of paradise.' I then said to abu 'Abd Allah, *'Alayhi al-Salam*, that so and so is a man of reason and deep understanding, calls people to himself and Allah has made him to suffer from this sickness. He (the Imam) asked, 'Does he do it in the central Masjid?' I replied, 'No, he does not do it in the central Masjid.' He (the Imam) asked, 'Does he do it at the door of his house?' I replied, 'No, he does not do it there.' He (the Imam) asked, 'Where does he do it.' I replied, 'When he is in private.' He (the Imam) said, 'Allah then has not caused him to suffer from the sickness, he enjoys it and he will not be allowed to sit on the fine furnishings of paradise.'"

H 10168, Ch. 187, h 9
Ahmad has narrated from Ali ibn Asbat from certain persons of our people who have said the following:

"Abu 'Abd Allah, *'Alayhi al-Salam*, has said, 'Things may exist in our Shi'ah, but three things will not be in them, one who stretches his hand for begging, there is no blue or green among them and one who allows sexual intercourse in his anus.'"

H 10169, Ch. 187, h 10
Al-Husayn from Muhammad has narrated from Muhammad ibn 'Imran from 'Abd Allah ibn Jabalah from Ishaq ibn 'Ammar who has said the following:

"This is concerning my question before abu 'Abd Allah, *'Alayhi al-Salam*, about the hermaphrodites who suffer because of this misfortune (sexual intercourse in their anus). Will a believing person suffer from this sickness and people think Allah does not allow one whom He finds of any benefit at all to suffer from this sickness. He (the Imam) said, 'Yes, one may suffer from such sickness and you must not speak to such person because when you speak they find comfort.' I then asked, 'I pray to Allah to keep my soul in service for your cause, can they not bear patience?' He (the Imam) said, 'They are able to exercise patience but they want to enjoy. If Allah, most High causes one to suffer from such sickness he would be compelled and cannot bear patience or to control himself even in the presence of people. When he feels ashamed before people and does not do it in the presence of people but does it in private then it is not Allah who has caused him to suffer; in fact he enjoys it.'"

Chapter 188 - Lesbianism

H 10170, Ch. 188, h 1

Abu Ali al-Ash'ariy has narrated from al-Hassan ibn Ali al-Kufiy from 'Ubays ibn Hisham from Husayn ibn Ahmad al-Minqariy from Hisham al-Saydananiy who has said the following:

"Once a man asked 'Abd Allah, *'Alayhi al-Salam*, about this verse of the holy Quran, 'Before them people of Noah and the dwellers of al-Rass rejected (the truth). . . .' (50: 12) He (the Imam) made a gesture with his hand and rubbed one hand against the other saying, 'They were women with women (engaged in lesbianism).'"

H 10171, Ch. 188, h 2

Muhammad ibn Yahya has narrated from Ahmad ibn Muhammad from Ali ibn al-Hakam from Ishaq ibn Jarir who has said the following:

"A woman asked me to ask abu 'Abd Allah, *'Alayhi al-Salam*, for permission to visit him (the Imam). Permission was given and she came with her slave-girl and asked, 'O abu 'Abd Allah, what is the meaning of the word of Allah, most Majestic, most Glorious, ". . . the olive tree which is not eastern or western."' (24:35) He (the Imam) said, 'Allah does not give parables of the tree. He only gives parables about the children of Adam. Ask what you want.' She asked, 'Tell me about women with women and what the penalty is for it?' He (the Imam) said, 'Its penalty is like that for fornication and on the Day of Judgment they will be brought with dresses of fire which cause laceration, veiled with veils of fire, and loin cloths of fire. Posts of fire will be inserted inside them up to their heads and they will be thrown in the fire. You must take notice that the first ones who engage in such act were people of Lot. Men became satisfied with men and women were left without men, so they did as their men did.'"

H 10172, Ch. 188, h 3

Ali ibn Ibrahim has narrated from his father from 'Amr ibn 'Uthman from Yazid al-Nakha'iy from Bashir al-Nabbal who has said the following:

"I saw a man with abu 'Abd Allah, *'Alayhi al-Salam*, who said, 'I pray to Allah to keep my soul in service for your cause, what do you say about women with women (lesbianism)?' He (the Imam) said, 'I will not tell you anything about it until you take an oath to narrate, what I tell you, to women.' He (the narrator) has said that he took an oath and he (the Imam) said, 'They both will be in the fire and on them there will be seventy thousand dresses of fire and on every dress there will be a thick dry skin of fire. On them there will be two belts of fire and two crowns of fire over the dresses and two pairs of shoes of fire and they will be in the fire.'"

H 10173, Ch. 188, h 4

It is narrated from the narrator of the previous Hadith from his father from Ali ibn al-Qasim from Ja'far ibn Muhammad from al-Husayn ibn Ziyad from Ya'qub ibn Ja'far who has said the following:

"Once, a man asked abu 'Abd Allah, or abu Ibrahim, *'Alayhim al-Salam*, about women who practice women homosexuality (lesbianism). He (the Imam) was leaning, he sat straight and said, 'They are condemned, the one on her as well underneath her until she moves out of her clothes, the rider as well as the one being rode. Allah, most Blessed, most High, the angels and those who possess divine authority condemned them, as well as I and all remaining in the backs of men and wombs of women condemned them. It by Allah is greater fornication. No, by Allah there is no repentance for them. May Allah destroy Laqis, daughter of Satan who brought it.' The man said that it has come from people of Iraq. He (the Imam) said, 'No, by Allah, it was in the time of the Messenger of Allah, *O Allah, grant compensation to Muhammad and his family worthy of their services to Your cause*, before Iraq was there and about them the Messenger of Allah has said, 'Allah has condemned transvestites (men who pretend to be like women and women who pretend to be like men).'"

Chapter 189 - Protecting Others' Privacy Is One's Own Protection of Privacy

H 10174, Ch. 189, h 1

A number of our people have narrated from Ahmad ibn Muhammad from ibn Khalid from Sharif ibn Sabiq or a man from Sharif from al-Fadl ibn abu Qurrah who has said the following:

"When the scholar built the wall Allah, most Blessed, most High, sent revelation to Moses that said, 'I recompense sons for the hard works of the fathers, good recompense for good deeds and evil recompense for evil deeds. You must not commit fornication because fornication will be committed with your women. If one goes in the bed of a Muslim, someone will go in his bed as well. You will be recompensed as you provide recompense (as you sow so shall you reap).'"

H 10175, Ch. 189, h 2

Ali ibn Ibrahim has narrated from his father from ibn abu 'Umayr from Hisham ibn Salim who has said the following:

"Abu 'Abd Allah, *'Alayhi al-Salam*, has said, 'Do you not fear, when looking at women's behind, for your women being looked in the same way.'"

H 10176, Ch. 189, h 3

A number of our people have narrated from Ahmad ibn Muhammad from ibn Khalid from his father from those whom he has mentioned from Mufaddal al-Ju'fiy who has said the following:

"Abu 'Abd Allah, *'Alayhi al-Salam*, has said, 'How ugly of a man it is being seen in an imperfect (sinful) place, then impose it on us or the righteous ones of our people. O Mufaddal, do you know why it is said, 'If one commits fornication one day it will be committed against him.' I replied, 'No, I pray to Allah to keep my soul in service for your cause.' He (the Imam) said, 'In banu Israel, there was a female fornicator and a male fornicator who would go to her very often. The last time he went Allah made a certain expression to come through her tongue, "When you return to your wife you will find a man with her." He came out with his soul turned filthy because of what she had said and entered his home in a different condition, without asking for permission as he would do before and found a man in his bed with his wife. They took their case to Moses and Jibril came to Moses saying, "O Moses, whoever commits fornication one day fornication is committed against him." He looked at them and said, "Forgive, thus your wives will become chaste.""'

H 10177, Ch. 189, h 4

A number of our people have narrated from Ahmad ibn Muhammad from abu al-'Abbas al-Kufiy and Ali ibn Ibrahim has narrated from his father from 'Amr ibn 'Uthman from 'Abd Allah al-Dihqan from Durust from 'Abd al-Hamid who has said the following:

"The Messenger of Allah, *O Allah, grant compensation to Muhammad and his family worthy of their services to Your cause*, has said, 'Marry of the family of so and so because they have maintained chastity and so also their women have done and you must not marry of the family of so and so because they have transgressed and so also have their women done.' He (the Messenger of Allah) has said, 'It is written in the Torah, 'I am Allah and I kill the killers and turn the fornicators poor. O people, you must not commit fornication because fornication will be committed with your women. As you recompense likewise you will receive recompense.'"

H 10178, Ch. 189, h 5

Muhammad ibn Yahya has narrated from Ahmad ibn Muhammad from Muhammad ibn Sinan from Ali ibn Ribat from 'Ubayd ibn Zurarah who has said the following:

"Abu 'Abd Allah, *'Alayhi al-Salam*, has said, 'Be kind to your parents, your children will be kind to you, maintain chastity toward people's women; your women will maintain chastity.'"

H 10179, Ch. 189, h 6

A number of our people have narrated from Ahmad ibn Muhammad from ibn Khalid from certain persons of his people in a marfu' manner who has said the following:

"Abu 'Abd Allah, *'Alayhi al-Salam*, has said that the Messenger of Allah, *O Allah, grant compensation to Muhammad and his family worthy of their services to Your cause*, has said, 'You must maintain chastity and you must stay away from sinful deeds.'"

H 10180, Ch. 189, h 7

Muhammad ibn Yahya has narrated from Ahmad ibn Muhammad from Ali ibn al-Hakam from Mu'awiyah ibn Wahab from Maymun al-Qaddah who has said the following:

"I once heard abu Ja'far, *'Alayhi al-Salam*, saying, 'No worship is better than maintaining chastity in matters of one's stomach and genitals organs.'"

Chapter 190 - Rare Ahadith

H 10181, Ch. 190, h 1
Abu Ali al-Ash'ariy has narrated from Ahmad ibn Ishaq from Sa'dan ibn Muslim from abu Basir who has said the following:

"Abu 'Abd Allah, *'Alayhi al-Salam*, has said, 'No other thing is attended by the angels as horse racing is and a man's playing with his wife.'"

H 10182, Ch. 190, h 2
Ali ibn Ibrahim has narrated from his father from ibn abu 'Umayr from Aban ibn 'Uthman from Hariz from Walid who has said the following:

"Once a woman came to the Messenger of Allah, *O Allah, grant compensation to Muhammad and his family worthy of their services to Your cause*, to ask a question and the Messenger of Allah said, 'Child bearing, compassionate and kind to their children, had they not brought anyone (in the bed of their husband), it would have been said to them, 'Enter in paradise without any questions being asked.'"

H 10183, Ch. 190, h 3
It is narrated from the narrator of the previous Hadith from ibn abu 'Umayr from Sayf ibn 'Amirah from abu al-Sabbah al-Kinaniy who has said the following:

"Abu 'Abd Allah, *'Alayhi al-Salam*, has said, 'If a woman performs *Salat* (prayer) five times a day, fasts a month, obeys her husband and recognizes the right of Ali, *'Alayhi al-Salam*, she then can enter paradise from whichever door of the garden (paradise) she wants.'"

H 10184, Ch. 190, h 4
A number of our people have narrated from Ahmad ibn Muhammad from ibn Faddal from Yunus ibn Ya'qub from Sa'idah who has said the following:

"Abu al-Hassan, *'Alayhi al-Salam*, sent me to a woman of the Zubayr family to see her because he wanted to marry her. When I went to her she spoke to me softly and then said, 'Bring the lamp closer to me.' I took it close to her. Sa'idah has said, 'I looked at her - there was someone else with Sa'idah also – and asked if she agreed.' He (the narrator) has said that abu al-Hassan, *'Alayhi al-Salam*, married her and she lived with him (the Imam) until he (the Imam) died. When his slave-girls learned about it (this marriage) they began to hold his sleeves and clothes and he remained quiet, smiled and did not say anything to them. It is mentioned that he (the Imam) said, 'No other thing is like free women.'"

H 10185, Ch. 190, h 5
Ali ibn Ibrahim has narrated from his father from ibn abu 'Umayr from Hammad ibn 'Uthman from al-Halabiy who has said the following:

"This is concerning my question before abu 'Abd Allah, *'Alayhi al-Salam*, about the words of Allah, most Majestic, most Glorious, '. . . or that you touch women.' (5:6) He (the Imam) said, 'It means going to bed with woman but Allah covers and He loves covering private matters so He has not mentioned it by its name as you do.'"

H 10186, Ch. 190, h 6

Muhammad ibn Yahya has narrated from Ahmad ibn Muhammad from ibn Faddal from ibn Bukayr from Zurarah who has said the following:

"Abu Ja'far, *'Alayhi al-Salam*, has said that Fatimah, *'Alayha al-Salam*, in her will had asked 'Amir al-Mu'minin, Ali, *'Alayhi al-Salam*, to marry her sister's daughter after her death and he followed her instruction.'"

H 10187, Ch. 190, h 7

Ibn Faddal has narrated from ibn Bukayr from 'Ubayd ibn Zurarah who has said the following:

"I once asked abu 'Abd Allah, *'Alayhi al-Salam*, about the case of a man who marries his slave-girl; if it is proper for him to allow her to look at his private parts. He (the Imam) said, 'No, it is not proper and I do not allow my slave-girl to do so when I marry her.'"

H 10188, Ch. 190, h 8

Muhammad ibn Yahya has narrated from Ahmad ibn Muhammad from al-Hajjal from Tha'labah from Mu'ammar ibn Yahya who has said the following:

"I once asked abu Ja'far, *'Alayhi al-Salam*, about the narration of people from Ali, *'Alayhi al-Salam*, in the matters of reproductive issues of human beings about which he did not command or prohibit others except that he prohibited for himself and his children. I asked, 'How can this happen?' He (the Imam) said, 'It is because one verse has made it lawful and the other verse has made it unlawful.' I then said, 'This can happen only when one verse cancels the other, or that both are clear and that it is proper to follow both verses. He (the Imam) said, 'He has already explained it by prohibiting it for himself and his children.' I then asked, 'What prevented him to explain it to people? He (the Imam) replied, 'Because he was afraid of people's not listening to him. Had Ali, *'Alayhi al-Salam*, been able to establish a strong foothold he would execute all the rules of the book of Allah and all of the truth.'"

H 10189, Ch. 190, h 9

Muhammad ibn Yahya has narrated from Ahmad ibn Muhammad from Ali ibn Hadid from Jamil from certain persons of his people who have said the following:

"One of the two Imam, (abu Ja'far or abu 'Abd Allah), *'Alayhim al-Salam*, about the case of a man who confessed his raping the slave-girl of another man who gives birth from the rapist, has said that the slave-girl and the child is returned to the owner of the slave-girl if the rapist has made a confession.'"

H 10190, Ch. 190, h 10

A number of our people have narrated from Ahmad ibn Muhammad from ibn Faddal from al-Hakam ibn Miskin from Ishaq ibn 'Ammar who has said the following:

"Abu 'Abd Allah, *'Alayhi al-Salam*, has said, 'In banu Israel there was a king who had a judge who had a brother who was truthful and had a wife who had given birth to prophets. The king decided to send a person for a certain task so he asked his judge to find for him a reliable person. The judge said, 'I do not know anyone more truthful than my brother.' He called him to go for the task but he did not like it and said to his brother, 'I am afraid I may lose my wife.' He insisted and the man could not do anything but to go for the task. He told his brother, 'Brother, of the things that I leave behind no other thing is more important to me than my wife. Please take good care of her in whatever matters she may need.' His brother agreed and the man left for the task of the king but the woman did not like his leaving. The judge would come and ask her if she needed anything and would provide whatever she needed. He liked her and asked her to yield to his demand but she refused. He swore that if she did not agree he can inform the king that she has committed fornication. She said, 'I cannot yield to your demand and you can do whatever you like.' He went to the king and said, 'The wife of my brother has committed fornication and it is proved before me.' The king said, 'Cleanse her.' He went to her and said, 'The king has commanded me to stone you to death. What do you say now? I can stone you to death if you do not agree with what I ask you to do.' She said, 'I cannot agree with what you wish, so you can do whatever you like.' He took her out and placed her in a ditch and stoned, while people were with him. When he thought she was dead he left her and returned. When it became dark in the night and she was still alive she moved out of the ditch and dragged herself on her face out of the city to a monastery where a monk lived. She waited at the door until the morning when the monk opened the door, saw her and asked her about her story. She informed him about it, he felt sympathy for her, took her inside. He had a small son who was his only son in good condition. He treated her injuries until she was cured and gave his son to her to provide him care. The monk had an agent who worked for him. He liked the woman and asked her to yield to his demand but she refused. He tried hard but she did not yield to his demand and he said, 'If you do not agree I will try to kill you.' She said, 'I cannot agree with what you want, so you can do whatever you wish.' He attacked the child and cut his neck. He went to the monk and said, 'You entrusted a fornicator who committed fornication. You left your son with her and she has killed him.' The monk came to her and when he saw him he asked her, 'What is this? You know I helped you.' She informed him of her story and he said, 'I cannot feel good for you any more if you stay with me; so leave my place.' He made her to move away in the night, gave her twenty dirham, told her to spend it and that Allah will sufficiently support her. During the night she left and in the morning she arrived in a town where a man was being crucified, but he was still alive. She asked about his case and they said that he owed twenty dirham which he could not pay. Whoever cannot pay his debts is crucified according to the rules of the town unless he pays it off to his creditor. She took out the twenty dirham, paid to his creditor and asked them to release him. They brought him down from the hanging pole and he said to her, 'No one has ever done a favor to me greater than what you have done to me. You have saved me from being crucified and from death, thus I must serve you wherever you go.' He followed her until they came to the shore and saw a group of people and a ship. He asked her, 'Stay here so I go work for them to get food for you.' He went to them and asked, 'What does your ship carry?' They replied, 'It carries goods for business, like pearls, Ambergris and so on and we use this one for our own ride.' He then asked, 'How much is the value of the goods in your ship?' They replied, 'It is a great deal; we cannot count.' He then said, 'I have something with me who is better than what is in your ship.' They asked, 'What is with you?' he replied, 'There is a girl with me the like of whom you have never seen.' They asked, 'Do you sell her?' He replied, 'Yes, I want to sell her with the condition that one of you come with me to see her, then you can buy her from me and pay without telling her about it until I go away.' They said; 'It is up to you.' They sent one of them to look at her and that person said, 'I have never seen anyone like her in beauty.' They bought her from him for ten thousand dirham and paid him. He moved away and when he was far away they came to her and told her to move in the ship. She asked, 'Why must I move in the ship?' They replied, 'We have bought you from your master.' She said, 'He is not my master.' They said, 'Will you move on your own or we carry you in the ship?' She then walked with them and when they arrived at the shore, they could not trust each other about her, so they kept her in the ship with goods for trading and they themselves stayed in the other ship and set it to sail. Allah, most Majestic, most Glorious, sent winds that made all of them drown as well as their ship but she remained safe with the ship loaded with goods for trading until she arrived in an island of the islands of the sea. She tied down the ship and walked on the island, found water, trees and fruits. She said, 'From this water I will drink and from these fruits I will eat and worship Allah in this place.' Allah, most Majestic, most Glorious, then sent revelation to a prophet of the prophets of banu Israel to go to that king and tell him, 'On such and such island there is one of My servants. You and the people in your domain must go to my servant who is there and confess your sins before My servant there then ask that creature to forgive you; if that creature forgives you I will also forgive you.' The king along with the people in his dominion went to that island and saw a woman. The king came to her and said, 'My judge told me that his brother's wife has committed fornication and I commanded to stone her to death but no testimony was presented before me and I am afraid that I may have done something unlawful and I like that you ask forgiveness for me.' She said, 'Allah has forgiven you. Please sit down.' Then her husband came. He could not recognize her and said, 'I had a very excellent and virtuous wife but I left her when she did not like and I left her in the care of my brother. When I came back and asked about her, my brother told me that she had committed fornication and he stoned her to death and I am afraid that I may have lost her so ask forgiveness for me.' She said, 'Allah has forgiven you', and she made him to sit next to the king. Then the judge came and said, 'My brother had a wife who attracted me and I asked her to commit fornication but she refused and I informed the king that she has committed fornication and he commanded me to stone her to death. I stoned her to death and I had lied against her, so please ask forgiveness for me.' She said, 'Allah has forgiven you.' She then turned to her husband and asked him to listen. Then the monk came and told his story and said, 'I sent her away in the night and I am afraid that wild beasts may have killed her.' She said, 'Allah has forgiven, you please sit down.' Then the agent of the monk came and told his story and she asked the monk to listen, may Allah forgive you. Then the man, who was to be crucified came and told his story but she said, 'May Allah not forgive you.' He (the Imam) said that she then turned to her husband and said, 'I am your wife and whatever you heard is my story. I do not need any men anymore and I love that you take this ship with its contents and leave me by myself so I can worship Allah, most Majestic, most Glorious, on this island. As you have learned how much I have suffered at the hands of men.' He agreed, took the ship with its contents and allowed her to do what she wanted. The king and people in his dominion returned.'"

H 10191, Ch. 190, h 11
Ahmad ibn Muhammad has narrated from ibn abu Najran from those whom he has mentioned from abu 'Abd Allah, *'Alayhi al-Salam*, and Yazid ibn Hammad and others from abu Jamilah who has said the following:

"Abu Ja'far, and abu 'Abd Allah, *'Alayhim al-Salam*, have said, 'There is no one without a share in fornication. Fornication of the eyes is looking, of the mouth is kissing, of hands is touching, regardless if the genital organs materialize it or not.'"

H 10192, Ch. 190, h 12
Muhammad ibn Yahya has narrated from Ahmad ibn Muhammad from ibn Faddal from Ali ibn 'Uqbah from his father who has said the following:

"I once heard abu 'Abd Allah, *'Alayhi al-Salam*, saying, 'Looking is an arrow of the poisoned arrows of Satan, and there are many such arrows that cause regret for a long time.'"

H 10193, Ch. 190, h 13
A number of our people have narrated from Ahmad ibn abu 'Abd Allah from his father from Muhammad ibn Sinan from 'Abd Allah ibn Sinan who has said the following:

"Abu 'Abd Allah, *'Alayhi al-Salam*, has said that the Messenger of Allah, *O Allah, grant compensation to Muhammad and his family worthy of their services to Your cause*, has condemned tattooing persons and those who are tattooed, those who raise the price of a piece of goods for sale without the intention to buy and those who agree to such act.'"

H 10194, Ch. 190, h 14
It is narrated from the narrator of the previous Hadith from certain persons of Iraq from Muhammad ibn al-Muthanna' from his father from 'Uthman ibn Yazid from Jabir who has said the following:

"Abu Ja'far, *'Alayhi al-Salam*, has said that the Messenger of Allah, *O Allah, grant compensation to Muhammad and his family worthy of their services to Your cause*, has condemned a man who looks to the genitals of a woman who is not lawful for him, a man who has betrayed his brother about his wife and a man whom people need for his benefits but he asks for a bribe.'"

H 10195, Ch. 190, h 15
A number of our people have narrated from Ahmad ibn Muhammad ibn 'Isa from Ali ibn al-Hakam from Zur'ah ibn Muhammad who has said the following:

"There was a man in al-Madinah and he had a very beautiful slave-girl who attracted a man who liked her and he complained before abu 'Abd Allah, *'Alayhi al-Salam*, who told him to avoid looking to her and on seeing her say, 'I ask Allah from His extra bounties.' He followed the instruction. In a short time her master decided to leave for a journey and he came to the man and said, 'O so and so, you are my neighbor and the most trustworthy of all people to me. I must leave for a journey and I like to leave so and so my slave-girl in your care.' He replied, 'I do not have a wife and there is no woman in the house with me; then how can I keep your slave-girl with me?' He said, 'I will find her price for you and you take responsibility of that assets (her price) for me and when I will come back, sell her to me and I will buy her from you. If you like to benefit from her it is lawful for you.' He then did as he had said and made him responsible for the price of the slave-girl and left. She stayed with him as long as Allah wanted and he satisfied himself in what he wished. Thereafter a messenger of the Khalifah of Amawide came to buy slave-girls for him. She was one of those mentioned to be bought for him. The governor sent a person to him asking about the slave-girl of so and so. He said that so and so is not present. He was forced to sell and paid him with profits for him. When they took the slave-girl and left al-Madinah her master came back and the first thing he asked was about his slave-girl as to how she was doing. He informed him about what had happened and brought to him all that was paid for her; the price he had set and the extra profit and said, 'This is the price and this is the profit, so accept it.' He refused to accept more than the price he had set saying, 'The extra is for you in good health. Allah did it for him because of his good intentions.'"

H 10196, Ch. 190, h 16

Muhammad ibn Yahya has narrated from Ahmad ibn Muhammad from Muhammad ibn Yahya from Ghiyath ibn Ibrahim who has said the following:

"Abu 'Abd Allah, *'Alayhi al-Salam*, has said, 'It is not unlawful to sleep between the two of your slave-girls or free wives; your women are like dolls.'"

H 10197, Ch. 190, h 17

Through the same chain of narrators as that of the previous Hadith the following is narrated:

"It is *Makruh* (undesirable) to go to bed with one's wife facing al-Qiblah (al-Ka'bah)."

H 10198, Ch. 190, h 18

Muhammad ibn Yahya has narrated from Ahmad ibn Muhammad from Ja'far ibn Yahya al-Khuza'iy from certain persons of our people who has said the following:

"I once asked one of the two Imam, (abu Ja'far or abu 'Abd Allah), *'Alayhim al-Salam*, about the case of my buying a slave-girl who was born out of wedlock and she was involved with me in everything. He (the Imam) said, 'Ask her mother who her father is; then ask the one involved with her mother to make it lawful for you so that the child will be born fine.'" (According to the footnote it may not work properly).'"

H 10199, Ch. 190, h 19

Muhammad ibn Yahya has narrated from Ahmad ibn Muhammad from ibn Mahbub from abu Ayyub from Burayd al-'Ijliy who has said the following:

"I once asked abu Ja'far, *'Alayhi al-Salam*, about the words of Allah, most Majestic, most Glorious, '. . . We took from you a *ghaliz* (thick) pledge and oath from you.' He (the Imam) said, 'The pledge or oath refers to the term by which marriage is declared and '*ghaliz*' (thick) refers to the liquid that flows from man to woman.'"

H 10200, Ch. 190, h 20

Ibn Mahbub has narrated from Hisham ibn Salim from abu Basir who has said the following:

"I once asked abu Ja'far, *'Alayhi al-Salam,* about the case of a man who marries a woman and who says that she is pregnant and that she is his sister because of breastfeeding and that she has not completed her waiting period. He (the Imam) said, 'If he has gone to bed (engaged in sexual intercourse) with her, he must not accept her words but if he has not done so, he must investigate if he did not know before.'"

H 10201, Ch. 190, h 21

Abu Ali al-Ash'ariy has narrated from Muhammad ibn 'Abd al-Jabbar from Muhammad ibn 'Isma'il from Ali al-Nu'man from Suwayd al-Qala' from Sama'ah from abu Basir who has said the following:

"This is concerning my question before abu 'Abd Allah, *'Alayhi al-Salam,* about the case of a man who is found in a house with a woman who confirms that she is his wife and she confirms that he is her husband. He (the Imam) said, 'In the case of a certain man I can consider it permissible and in the case of a certain man if I find him as such I strike him (dead).'"

H 10202, Ch. 190, h 22

Muhammad ibn Yahya has narrated from Ahmad ibn Muhammad from certain persons of his people from al-Hassan ibn al-Husayn al-Darir from Hammad ibn 'Isa who has said the following:

"Abu 'Abd Allah, *'Alayhi al-Salam,* has narrated from his father who has said, that a man proposed marriage in a family and they asked, 'What is your business?' He replied, 'I sell animals.' They accepted his proposal and found out that he sells cats, so they took their dispute before 'Amir al-Mu'minin, *'Alayhi al-Salam,* who validated the marriage saying that cats are animals.'"

H 10203, Ch. 190, h 23

Ali ibn Ibrahim has narrated from his father from Nuh ibn Shu'ayb in a marfu' manner from 'Abd Allah ibn Sinan from certain persons of his people who has said the following:

"Once a man from al-Ansar (people of al-Madinah) came to the Messenger of Allah, *O Allah, grant compensation to Muhammad and his family worthy of their services to Your cause,* and said, 'This is my wife and daughter of my uncle. I do not know anything about her except good but she has given birth to a very dark skin child, with wide nostrils, curly hairs and pointed nose. I do not find anyone like him among my maternal uncles or ancestors. He (the Messenger of Allah) asked the woman, 'What do you say?' She said, 'No, by the One who has sent you in all truth as a prophet that I have never allowed anyone other than him to sit with me as he does.' He (the Imam) said that the Messenger of Allah, *O Allah, grant compensation to Muhammad and his family worthy of their services to Your cause,* bent down his head for a while and raised his head to the sky; then turned to the man and said, 'O you, take notice that between everyone and Adam there are ninety-nine veins all of which strike in lineage. When the seed falls in the womb those veins surge and ask Allah for resemblance to it. So this is from those veins which your ancestors did not get. Take your child with you.' The woman said, 'Thank you, O Messenger of Allah for providing me such a great relief.'"

H 10204, Ch. 190, h 24

Abu Ali al-Ash'ariy has narrated from 'Imran ibn Musa from Muhammad ibn 'Abd al-Hamid from Muhammad ibn Shu'ayb who has said the following:

"I once wrote to him (the Imam), *'Alayhi al-Salam*, about the case of a man who proposed marriage to the daughter of his uncle who instructed a certain one of his brothers to give his daughter in marriage to him and she is the one for whom he has proposed. The man by mistake gives her a different name and no one of that name exists in the family. Her name was Fatimah but he gives her a different name. He (the Imam) signed the answer which said, 'It is not harmful.'"

H 10205, Ch. 190, h 25

A number of our people have narrated from Ahmad ibn Muhammad from 'Abd Allah ibn al-Khazraj who has said the following:

"A man once wrote to him (the Imam), *'Alayhi al-Salam*, and asked him (the Imam) about his marriage proposal which had taken place many years, months and days ago and he is not certain if he asked to declare the terms of marriage or it was already declared. He (the Imam) answered him on the issue, 'It is not obligatory for him to do anything other than what his heart is tied down with and about which his decision is established.'"

H 10206, Ch. 190, h 26

Ali ibn Ibrahim has narrated from his father from and Muhammad ibn Ali from Muhammad al-Qasaniy from al-Qasim ibn Muhammad from Sulayman ibn Dawud, 'Isa ibn Yunus from al-Awza'iy from al-Zuhriy who has said the following:

"About the case of a man who claims to have married a woman in the presence of witnesses and her guardian but she denies it and the sister of this woman presents testimony that the man has married her in the presence of witnesses and her guardian but she does not prove the time of marriage. Ali ibn al-Husayn, *'Alayhi al-Salam*, issued a judgment in this case that said, 'The testimony of the man is admitted and accepted and the testimony of the woman is not accepted because the husband is entitled to claim his conjugal right and her sister wants to destroy such right so she must not be taken as truthful and her testimony is unacceptable without specifying the time before her time or proof of consummation of marriage (the couple's going to bed).'"

H 10207, Ch. 190, h 27

Ali ibn Ibrahim has narrated from his father from 'Abd al-'Aziz ibn al-Muhtadiy who has said the following:

"I once asked al-Rida', *'Alayhi al-Salam*, saying, 'I pray to Allah to keep my soul in service for your cause, my brother died and I married his widow and a man came saying that he had married her secretly. I asked her about it but she denied it vehemently saying, 'There has never been such a thing between us.' He (the Imam) said, 'Her confirming makes it obligatory on you to accept her words and her denial makes it obligatory on him to accept her denial.'"

H 10208, Ch. 190, h 28

Ali has narrated from his father from ibn abu Nasr from al-Mashriqiy who has said the following:

"I once asked al-Rida', *'Alayhi al-Salam*, about the case of a man who proposes marriage to a woman who is playful and joking about it. He asks the woman about it and she says, 'Yes.' He (the Imam) *'Alayhi al-Salam*, said, 'It does not mean anything valid.' I then asked, 'Can one marry her?' He (the Imam) said, 'Yes, he can do so.'"

H 10209, Ch. 190, h 29
Ali ibn Ibrahim has narrated from Harun ibn Muslim from Mas'adah ibn Sadaqah who has said the following:
"I once heard abu 'Abd Allah, *'Alayhi al-Salam*, saying, when he was asked about marriage in the month of Shawwal, 'The Holy Prophet, *O Allah, grant compensation to Muhammad and his family worthy of their services to Your cause*, married 'A'ishah in the month of Shawwal.' He (the Imam) then said, 'People of the earlier times considered marriage in the month of Shawwal as undesirable because plague occurred in virgins and slave-girls thus they disliked for this reason and not the other reasons.'"

H 10210, Ch. 190, h 30
Muhammad ibn Yahya has narrated from Ahmad ibn Muhammad from Ya'qub ibn Yazid from al-Husayn ibn Bashshar al-Wasitiy who has said the following:
"I once wrote to abu al-Hassan al-Rida', *'Alayhi al-Salam*, and asked, 'One of my relatives has proposed for marriage but there is something in his moral manners. He (the Imam) said, 'You must not give in marriage if his moral manners are bad.'"

H 10211, Ch. 190, h 31
Muhammad ibn Yahya has narrated from 'Abd Allah ibn Ja'far from Muhammad ibn Ahmad ibn Mutahhar who has said the following:
"I once wrote to abu al-Hassan Sahib al-'Askar saying, 'I have married four women and have not asked for their names. I want to divorce one of them and marry another woman. He (the Imam) wrote to me, 'Look for a mark on any one of them and then say, 'Bear witness that so and so who has such and such mark is divorced; then marry the other woman when waiting period is complete.'"

H 10212, Ch. 190, h 32
Muhammad ibn Yahya in a marfu' manner has narrated the following:
Abu 'Abd Allah, *'Alayhi al-Salam*, has said that 'Amir al-Mu'minin has said, 'A woman does not give birth before six months.'"

H 10213, Ch. 190, h 33
Muhammad ibn Yahya has narrated from Ahmad ibn Muhammad from ibn Mahbub from ibn Sinan who has said the following:
"Abu 'Abd Allah, *'Alayhi al-Salam*, has said, 'When two believing people come together by means of lawful marriage a caller from the sky announces, 'Allah, most Majestic, most Glorious, has given so and so in marriage to so and so, and when a wife and husband separate (divorce) in a lawful manner, a caller from the sky announces, 'Allah has given permission to so and so wife and husband to separate (divorce) from each other.'"

H 10214, Ch. 190, h 34
Ibn Mahbub has narrated from Ibrahim al-Karkhiy who has said the following:
"This is concerning my question before abu 'Abd Allah, *'Alayhi al-Salam*, about the case of a man who has four wives and spends the night with three of them in their assigned time and touches them but during the night for the fourth one he does not touch her; if it is sinful for him. He (the Imam) said, 'He must stay with her in her assigned night until the morning and it is not a sin if he did not touch her if he did not want it.'"

H 10215, Ch. 190, h 35
A number of our people have narrated from Ahmad ibn Muhammad from ibn Khalid from 'Uthman ibn 'Isa from ibn Muskan in a marfu' manner who has said the following:
"Abu 'Abd Allah, *'Alayhi al-Salam*, has said, 'Allah, most Majestic, most Glorious, has taken away lust from the women of banu Hashim and has placed it in their men and so also He has done with their followers. On the other hand Allah, most Majestic, most Glorious, has taken away lust from the men of banu 'Umayyah and has placed it in their women and so also He has done to their followers.'"

H 10216, Ch. 190, h 36
Muhammad ibn Yahya has narrated from in a marfu' manner the following:
"Once a man came to the Messenger of Allah, *O Allah, grant compensation to Muhammad and his family worthy of their services to Your cause*, and said, 'O Messenger of Allah, I do not have the means to get married and I complain before you against living unmarried.' He (the Messenger of Allah), said, 'Allow the hairs of your body to grow long and continue fasting.' He did as was told to do and the urge to satisfy his sexual desire vanished.'"

H 10217, Ch. 190, h 37
A number of our people have narrated from Ahmad ibn Muhammad from ibn Faddal from ibn Bukayr from Muhammad ibn Muslim who has said the following:
"Of the blessing of a woman is her being of light expenses and her giving birth with ease. Of the evil with her is intensified expenses and her giving birth with hardships and difficulties.'"

H 10218, Ch. 190, h 38
Ali ibn Ibrahim has narrated from his father from al-Nawfaliy from al-Sakuniy who has said the following:
"Abu 'Abd Allah, *'Alayhi al-Salam*, has said that the Messenger of Allah, *O Allah, grant compensation to Muhammad and his family worthy of their services to Your cause*, has said, 'A man must not sit in the seat of a woman who has just left it and it still has the warmth of her body.' The Holy Prophet was asked about the beautification of a woman for a blind person. He (the Messenger of Allah) said, 'It is perfumes and Henna because of the fineness of its whiff.'"

H 10219, Ch. 190, h 39
Ali ibn Ibrahim has narrated from his father from ibn abu 'Umayr from Hisham ibn Salim who has said the following:

"About the case of a man who marries a virgin woman, abu 'Abd Allah, *'Alayhi al-Salam*, has said, 'He must stay with her for seven days.'"

H 10220, Ch. 190, h 40

Al-Husayn from Muhammad has narrated from Mu'alla' ibn Muhammad from al-Hassan ibn Ali from Aban from Ibrahim ibn abu 'Abd Allah who has said the following:

"About the case of a man who marries a second wife and the amount of time for the new wife, abu 'Abd Allah, *'Alayhi al-Salam*, has said, 'It (the time) is three days; thereafter he divides it between the two.'"

H 10221, Ch. 190, h 41

Muhammad ibn Yahya has narrated from Ahmad ibn Muhammad from Ali ibn al-Hakam from Hisham ibn Salim who has said the following:

"Abu 'Abd Allah, *'Alayhi al-Salam*, has said that once abu Bakr and 'Umar went to 'Umm Salamah and asked her, 'O 'Umm Salamah, you lived with another man before the Messenger of Allah, *O Allah, grant compensation to Muhammad and his family worthy of their services to Your cause*. How is the Messenger of Allah compared to that man in matters of going to bed with his wife?' She said, 'He is no more than the other man.' They left and the Holy Prophet came. She stood up frightened of the coming of something from the heaven and informed him of what had happened. The Messenger of Allah, *O Allah, grant compensation to Muhammad and his family worthy of their services to Your cause*, became angry, his face turned overcast and perspiration due to anger emerged between his eyes. He (the Messenger of Allah) came out with his gown dragging behind him until he climbed on the pulpit. Al-Ansar (people of al-Madinah) hastened to pick up arms and commanded to ready their horses. He (the Messenger of Allah) climbed on the pulpit, praised Allah and spoke of His glory, then said, 'O people, what is the matter with certain people! They spy on me to find my faults and ask about my private matters in my absence and behind my back. By Allah, I am the most honorable among you in matters of ancestry, of more clean birth, a provider of more sincere advice for the sake of Allah in one's absence. Whoever of you may like to ask me about who his father is I can inform him about it.' A man then stood up and asked, 'Who is my father?' He (the Messenger of Allah) replied, 'He is so and so shepherd.' Another man stood up and asked, 'Who is my father?' He (the Messenger of Allah) said, 'He is your black slave.' A third man stood up and asked, 'Who is my father?' He (the Messenger of Allah) said, 'He is the one to whom you are ascribed.' Al-Ansar then pleaded saying, 'O Messenger of Allah, forgive us, Allah forgives you. Allah has sent you as mercy so forgive us, Allah will forgive you.' The Holy Prophet when spoken to would seem shy and perspire and would cast down his eyes before people due to shyness when they spoke to him. He (the Messenger of Allah) then climbed down the pulpit. At dawn Jibril descended with a dish of mashed meat and wheat from paradise and said, 'O Muhammad, this is made for you by *al-Hur al-'In*. You can eat it with Ali and his children; it is not proper that people other than you eat it.' The Messenger of Allah, *O Allah, grant compensation to Muhammad and his family worthy of their services to Your cause*, Ali, Fatimah, al-Hassan and al-Husayn ate it (the food that Jibril had brought from paradise) and it gave the Messenger of Allah the ability in matters of going to bed with his wives which was equal to that of forty men, thus he (the Messenger of Allah) could go to bed with all of his wives in one night if he so wanted.'"

H 10222, Ch. 190, h 42

A number of our people have narrated from Ahmad ibn Muhammad from abu al-'Abbas al-Kufiy from Muhammad ibn Ja'far from certain persons of his people who has said the following:

"Abu 'Abd Allah, *'Alayhi al-Salam*, has said, 'If one accumulates women without going to bed with them then if certain ones among them commit fornication, the sin will rest on such a man.'"

H 10223, Ch. 190, h 43

Ali ibn Ibrahim has narrated from his father from 'Uthman ibn 'Isa in a marfu' manner who has narrated the following:

"Once abu 'Abd Allah, *'Alayhi al-Salam*, was asked about the case of a man whose father had given him a slave-girl as a gift with whom he lived for a long time, then he recalled that his father had gone to bed with her and thus he stayed away from her. He (the Imam) said, 'You must not consider it to be true.'"

H 10224, Ch. 190, h 44

Abu Ali al-Ash'ariy has narrated from al-Hassan ibn Ali al-Kufiy from 'Uthman ibn 'Isa who has said the following:

"I once wrote to abu al-Hassan, al-Awwal, *'Alayhi al-Salam*, about the following case and I recognized his handwriting. It was about the mother of child of a man who was given to him as a gift by his father and she gave birth to several children; then she said, 'Your father had gone to bed with me before giving me to you as a gift,' He (the Imam) said, 'You must not consider her words as truthful ones; she is only trying to move away because of his bad moral behaviors.'"

H 10225, Ch. 190, h 45

Ali ibn Ibrahim has narrated from his father from al-Nawfaliy from al-Sakuniy who has said the following:

"Abu 'Abd Allah, *'Alayhi al-Salam*, has said that about the case of a woman who had committed fornication with a man before he went to bed 'Amir al-Mu'minin, *'Alayhi al-Salam*, said, 'They must be separated from each other and she did not deserve any *mahr* (dower) because the incident was from her side.'"

H 10226, Ch. 190, h 46

Muhammad ibn Yahya has narrated from Muhammad ibn al-Husayn from al-Hassan ibn Ali from Zakariya al-Mu'min' from ibn Muskan from certain persons of our people who have said the following:

"Abu 'Abd Allah, *'Alayhi al-Salam*, has said that once a man with his wife came to 'Umar and said, 'My wife, this one, is black and I am more black. She has given birth to a white boy.' 'Umar asked those who were present with him about their opinion. They said, 'We say that you must stone her to death because she is black and her husband is blacker and her child is white.' He (the Imam) said that 'Amir al-Mu'minin came when she was sentenced to be stoned to death. He (the Imam) asked, 'What is the case of the two of you?' They informed him (the

Imam) of their story.' He asked the black man, 'Do you accuse your wife?' He replied, 'No, I do not do so.' He (the Imam) then asked, 'Did you go to bed with her during her Hayd (menses)?' He said, 'One night she did say that she was experiencing Hayd (menses) but I thought she was avoiding cold weather, then I went to bed with her.' He (the Imam) then asked the woman, 'Did he go to bed with you when you were experiencing Hayd (menses)?' She replied, 'Yes, he did. You can ask him. I tried to avoid and refused.' He (the Imam) said, 'You both can go. Only blood has overwhelmed the seed and it turned white. Had it (blood) moved, he would become black but on becoming an adolescent he will become black.'"

H 10227, Ch. 190, h 47
Muhammad ibn Yahya has narrated from Ahmad ibn Muhammad from al-Husayn ibn Sa'id from al-Nadr ibn Suwayd from Yahya al-Halabiy from 'Amr ibn abu al-Miqdam from his father who has said the following:

"Ali ibn al-Husayn, *'Alayhi al-Salam*, has said, that he was asked about, '. . . the apparent and unapparent acts of indecency' (6:151, 7:33) He (the Imam) said, 'the apparent one is marriage with the wife of one's father and the unapparent one is fornication.'"

H 10228, Ch. 190, h 48
A number of our people have narrated from Sahl ibn Ziyad from Muhammad ibn al-Hassan ibn Shammun from 'Abd Allah ibn 'Abd al-Rahman from Misma' abu Sayyar who has said the following:

"Abu 'Abd Allah, *'Alayhi al-Salam*, has said that the Messenger of Allah, *O Allah, grant compensation to Muhammad and his family worthy of their services to Your cause*, has said, 'When one of you decides to go to bed with his wife he must not place her in a big rush.'"

H 10229, Ch. 190, h 49
Muhammad ibn Yahya has narrated from Ahmad ibn Muhammad from Ali ibn al-Hakam from Sayf ibn 'Amirah from Ibrahim ibn Maymun from Muhammad ibn Muslim who has said the following:

"This is concerning my question before abu 'Abd Allah, *'Alayhi al-Salam*, about the words of Allah, most Majestic, most Glorious, '. . . He gave everything its creation and then gave it guidance.' (20:52) He (the Imam) said, 'There is no creature of Allah but that He knows its shape and that it is a male or a female.' I then asked, 'What is the meaning of, 'then He gave it guidance'?' He (the Imam) said, 'He guided it to marriage or out of wedlock according to its shape and form.'"

H 10230, Ch. 190, h 50
A number of our people have narrated from Ahmad ibn Muhammad from ibn Khalid from his father or others from Sa'd ibn s; from al-Hassan ibn Jahm who has said the following:

"I once saw abu al-Hassan, *'Alayhi al-Salam*, had used dye. I said, 'I pray to Allah to keep my soul in service for your cause, I can see you have used dyes.' He (the Imam) said, 'Yes, readiness is of the matters that increases chastity of women and women neglect chastity because of their husband's neglect of readiness.' He (the Imam) then said, 'Will you be happy to see her without readiness?' I replied, 'No, it does not make me happy.' He (the Imam) said, 'In the same way it will not make her happy to see you without readiness.' He (the Imam) then said, 'It is of the moral behavior of the prophets to maintain cleanliness, use perfumes, shave the hairs and going to bed with one's wife very often.' He (the Imam) then said, 'Sulayman ibn Dawud, *'Alayhima al-Salam*, had one thousand women in one palace of whom three hundred were publicly known and seven hundred of them were secretly married. The Messenger of Allah, *O Allah, grant compensation to Muhammad and his family worthy of their services to Your cause*, had the ability equal to forty men of going to bed with his wives, he (the Messenger of Allah) had nine wives and moved among them every night and day.'"

H 10231, Ch. 190, h 51
It is narrated from the narrator of the previous Hadith from 'Uthman ibn 'Isa from Khalid ibn Najih who has said the following:

"People mentioned misfortune before abu 'Abd Allah, *'Alayhi al-Salam*, and he (the Imam) said, 'Misfortune is in three things: They are woman, a stumper and a house. Misfortune in woman is the large amount of her *mahr* (dower) and barren womb.'"

H 10232, Ch. 190, h 52
Ali ibn Ibrahim has narrated from his father from abu 'Abd Allah, al-Barqiy in a marfu' manner has said the following:

"When the Messenger of Allah, *O Allah, grant compensation to Muhammad and his family worthy of their services to Your cause*, gave Fatimah, *'Alayha al-Salam*, in marriage and people said, 'We wish her prosperity and sons, but he (the Messenger of Allah) said, 'No, we wish for her goodness and blessings.'"

H 10233, Ch. 190, h 53
Ali ibn Ibrahim has narrated from his father from ibn Mahbub from ibn Ri'ab from Muhammad ibn Qays who has said the following:

"Abu Ja'far, *'Alayhi al-Salam*, has said that once a woman of al-Ansar (people of al-Madinah) came to the Messenger of Allah, *O Allah, grant compensation to Muhammad and his family worthy of their services to Your cause*. She came in the house of Hafsah and she was well dressed and groomed. She came to the Messenger of Allah and said, 'O Messenger of Allah, *O Allah, grant compensation to Muhammad and his family worthy of their services to Your cause*, women do not propose for marriage to men. I am unmarried since a long time and I have no children. Are you interested in me? If you are interested I give myself to you as gift if you accept me.' The Messenger of Allah prayed for her and admired. He (the Messenger of Allah) then said, 'O sister (in belief) from al-Ansar (people of al-Madinah), may Allah on behalf of His Messenger grant you good recompense. Your men supported me and your women showed interest in me.' Hafsah then said, 'How shameless of you and being audacious, and craving for men.' The Messenger of Allah, *O Allah, grant compensation to Muhammad and his family worthy of their services to Your cause*, said to her, 'Leave her alone, O Hafsah, she is better than you. She has shown interest in the Messenger of Allah and you blame her and consider it a fault.' He (the Imam) said that he (the Messenger of Allah) said to the woman, 'You may leave, Allah has granted you kindness and has made paradise obligatory for you because of your showing interest in me and that you love me and want to make me happy. My command will soon come by the will of Allah. Allah, most Majestic, most Glorious, then revealed this, '. . . if a believing woman gifts herself to the prophet and if the prophet wants to marry her then she is for him only and not for the believing men.' (33:49) He (the Imam) said, 'Allah, most Majestic, most Glorious, made gifting of a woman herself to the Messenger of Allah, *O Allah, grant compensation to Muhammad and his family worthy of their services to Your cause*, lawful and it is not lawful for people other than him (the Messenger of Allah).'"

H 10234, Ch. 190, h 54
Muhammad ibn Yahya has narrated from Ahmad ibn Muhammad from al-'Abbas ibn Ma'ruf from Ali ibn Mahziyar from al-Mukhallad ibn Musa from Ibrahim ibn Ali from Ali ibn Yahya al-Yarbu'iy from Aban ibn Taghlib who has said the following:

"Abu Ja'far, *'Alayhi al-Salam*, has said that the Messenger of Allah, *O Allah, grant compensation to Muhammad and his family worthy of their services to Your cause*, has said, 'I am a human being like you. I marry from you and give in marriage to you except Fatimah, *'Alayha al-Salam*, because her marriage came from the heaven.'"

H 10235, Ch. 190, h 55
Muhammad ibn Yahya has narrated from Ahmad ibn Muhammad from Ali ibn al-Hakam from 'Umar ibn Hanzalah who has said the following:

"I once said to abu 'Abd Allah, *'Alayhi al-Salam*, 'I married a woman and asked about her and things were said about her.' He (the Imam) said, 'Why did you ask about her also? It is not obligatory on you to ask and investigate.'"

H 10236, Ch. 190, h 56
Ahmad ibn Muhammad has narrated from Ali ibn al-Hakam from his father from Sadir who has said the following:

"Abu Ja'far, *'Alayhi al-Salam*, once said to me, 'O Sadir, I have heard about the beauty and good manners of the women of al-Kufah with their husbands. Can you find for me a woman with beauty in a place?' I replied, 'I pray to Allah to keep my soul in service for your cause, I know one. She is daughter of so and so ibn Muhammad ibn al-Ash'ath ibn Qays.' He (the Imam) said, 'O Sadir, the Messenger of Allah, *O Allah, grant compensation to Muhammad and his family worthy of their services to Your cause*, has condemned a people and it remains in their descendents until the Day of Judgment and I dislike that my body touch the body of any of the people of fire.'"

H 10237, Ch. 190, h 57
A number of our people have narrated from Sahl ibn Ziyad from al-Hassan ibn Ali ibn al-Nu'man from Artat ibn Habib from abu Maryam al-Ansariy who has said the following:

"I once heard Ja'far ibn Muhammad, *'Alayhi al-Salam*, saying that the Messenger of Allah, *O Allah, grant compensation to Muhammad and his family worthy of their services to Your cause*, said, 'O Ali, instruct your women not to perform *Salat* (prayer) without having dressed well and not to use a necklace which is made of skin.'"

H 10238, Ch. 190, h 58

Muhammad ibn Yahya has narrated from Ahmad ibn Muhammad from al-Husayn ibn Sa'id from Safwan ibn Yahya from Khalid ibn 'Isma'il from a man of our people of the mountains who has said the following:

"I once mentioned to abu Ja'far, *'Alayhi al-Salam*, Zoroastrians and that they say, 'A marriage like the marriage of the sons of Adam and that they argue with us about it. He (the Imam) said, 'They cannot argue against you because of what Hibbahtu Allah found. Adam said, 'O Lord, find marriage for Hibbahtu Allah.' Allah, most Majestic, most Glorious, sent for him a Hawra' who gave birth to four boys, and then Allah raised her. When sons of Hibbahtu Allah grew up he said, 'O Allah find marriage for the sons of Hibbahtu Allah.' Allah, most Majestic, most Glorious, sent him revelation to propose marriage to a man (head of the family) of Jinn who was a Muslim and had four daughters, for the sons of Hibbahtu Allah. He gave them in marriage to them. Whatever is of beauty and forbearance, it is from al-Hawra' and whatever is of dimwittedness and temperament, is because of al-Jinn.'"

H 10239, Ch. 190, h 59

A number of our people have narrated from Ahmad ibn Muhammad from ibn Khalid from 'Uthman ibn 'Isa from 'Amr ibn Jami' who has said the following:

"Abu 'Abd Allah, *'Alayhi al-Salam*, has said that the Messenger of Allah, *O Allah, grant compensation to Muhammad and his family worthy of their services to Your cause*, has said, 'The words of a man to a woman, 'I love you' never goes away from her heart.'"

Chapter 191 - Explanation of Lawful and Unlawful Matters in Marriage, Indecency and Fornication

(It is of words of Yunus) Ali ibn Ibrahim has narrated from his father from 'Isma'il ibn Marrar and others from Yunus who has said the following:

(This passage is of the words of Yunus, not a Hadith from 'A'immah *'Alayhim al-Salam*, thus, it is not translated.)

Chapter 192 - Another Chapter About the Previous Subject

H 10240, Ch. 192, h 1

Ali ibn Ibrahim has narrated from his father from ibn abu 'Umayr from 'Abd Allah ibn Sinan who has said the following:

"A man once accused a Zoroastrian man before abu 'Abd Allah, *'Alayhi al-Salam*, he (the Imam) said, 'Hold it.' The man said, 'He marries his mother or sister.' He (the Imam) said, 'It is marriage among them in their religion.'"

End of the book of marriage of the book al-Kafi followed by the book al-'Aqiqah, by the will of Allah who is free of all defects.

All praise belongs to Allah, Lord of the worlds, *O Allah, grant compensation to Muhammad and his family worthy of their services to Your cause*, as well as all of his descendents with the greeting of peace a great deal.

Printed in Great Britain
by Amazon

33176425R00293

Select Ahadith from this Book

H 8185, Ch. 7, h 2

Muhammad ibn Yahya has narrated from Muhammad ibn al-Husayn, from Ali ibn al-Nu'man from Suwayd al-Qalanisiy from Bashir who has said the following:

"I once said to [the Sixth Imam], *'Alayhi al-Salam*, 'I saw a dream in which I said to you, "Fighting alongside an Imam to whom obedience is not obligatory is unlawful like consuming dead animals, blood and pork for food", and you said to me, "Yes, that is how it is."' [The Sixth Imam], *'Alayhi al-Salam*, then said, 'That is how it is. That is how it is.'"

H 8388, Ch. 12, h 3

A number of our people have narrated from Ahmad ibn Muhammad from ibn Faddal from Tha'labah and others from a man who has said the following:

"[The Sixth Imam], *'Alayhi al-Salam*, has said, 'Keeping one's wealth in a proper shape is part of belief.'"

H 8391, Ch. 12, h 6

It is narrated from him (narrator of previous Hadith) from certain persons of our people from Salih ibn Hamzah from certain persons of our people Hamzah who have said the following:

"[The Sixth Imam], *'Alayhi al-Salam*, has said, 'You must manage your wealth properly; it increases respect for you and freedom of want from envious ones.'"

H 8397, Ch. 15, h 1

Muhammad ibn Yahya has narrated from Ahmad ibn Muhammad from ibn Faddal from al-Hassan ibn al-Jahm who has said the following:

"I heard [the Eighth Imam], *'Alayhi al-Salam*, saying, 'If one saves food for one year, his burden becomes light and he feels comfortable. [The Fifth and Sixth Imam], *'Alayhim al-Salam*, would not buy anything before reserving their food for one year."

H 9411, Ch. 10, h 2

Muhammad ibn Yahya has narrated from Ahmad and 'Abd Allah sons of Muhammad ibn 'Isa from Ali ibn al-Hakam from Hisham ibn Salim who has said the following:

"[The Sixth Imam], *'Alayhi al-Salam*, has said, 'Once a man came to the Holy Prophet, *'Alayhi al-Salam*, and complained about his financial condition. He (the Holy Prophet) told him to become married and he did so after which he became affluent.'"

ISBN 978-0-9914308-7
9 00

9 780991 430871

TEACHING KIDS
GOOD MONEY
HABIT$

DISCOVER 7 WAYS to Raise
Financially Smart Children
Today for a Richer
Tomorrow

MARIO A. VASQUEZ